VW Transporter Owners Workshop Manual

John S Mead

Models covered
VW Transporter (air-cooled) with 1584 cc and 1970 cc engines

Does not cover water-cooled or Diesel-engined models
Does not cover alternative body or camper conversions produced by specialist manufacturers

ISBN 0 85696 638 X

ABCDE
FGHI

Printed in England   *(638–9N1)*

THE
BOOK

Haynes Publishing Group
Sparkford Nr Yeovil
Somerset BA22 7JJ England

Haynes Publications, Inc
861 Lawrence Drive
Newbury Park
California 91320 USA

British Library Cataloguing in Publication Data

Mead, John. S.
    VW Transporter 1979–1982 owners workshop manual.–
(Owners Workshop Manual)
    1. Volkswagen Transporter
    I. Title   II. Series
629.28'73   TL230.5.V6
ISBN 0–85696–638–X

Acknowledgements

Thanks are due to V.A.G.(UK) Ltd for the supply of technical information. The Champion Sparking Plug Company supplied the illustrations showing the various spark plug conditions. Castrol Limited supplied the lubrication data and Sykes-Pickavant Ltd provided some of the workshop tools. Special thanks are due to all those people at Sparkford who helped in the production of this manual

About this manual

Its aim

The aim of this manual is to help you get the best value from your vehicle. It can do so in several ways. It can help you decide what work must be done (even should you choose to get it done by a garage), provide information on routine maintenance and servicing, and give a logical course of action and diagnosis when random faults occur. However, it is hoped that you will use the manual by tackling the work yourself. On simpler jobs it may even be quicker than booking the car into a garage and going there twice, to leave and collect it. Perhaps most important, a lot of money can be saved by avoiding the costs a garage must charge to cover its labour and overheads.

The manual has drawings and descriptions to show the function of the various components so that their layout can be understood. Then the tasks are described and photographed in a step-by-step sequence so that even a novice can do the work.

Its arrangement

The manual is divided into eleven Chapters, each covering a logical sub-division of the vehicle. The Chapters are each divided into Sections, numbered with single figures, eg 5; and the Sections into paragraphs (or sub-sections), with decimal numbers following on from the Section they are in, eg 5.1, 5.2, 5.3 etc.

It is freely illustrated, especially in those parts where there is a detailed sequence of operations to be carried out. There are two forms of illustration: figures and photographs. The figures are numbered in sequence with decimal numbers, according to their position in the Chapter – eg Fig. 6.4 is the fourth drawing/illustration in Chapter 6. Photographs carry the same number (either individually or in related groups) as the Section or sub-section to which they relate.

There is an alphabetical index at the back of the manual as well as a contents list at the front. Each Chapter is also preceded by its own individual contents list.

References to the 'left' or 'right' of the vehicle are in the sense of a person in the driver's seat facing forwards.

Unless otherwise stated, nuts and bolts are removed by turning anti-clockwise, and tightened by turning clockwise.

Vehicle manufacturers continually make changes to specifications and recommendations, and these, when notified, are incorporated into our manuals at the earliest opportunity.

Whilst every care is taken to ensure that the information in this manual is correct, no liability can be accepted by the authors or publishers for loss, damage or injury caused by any errors in, or omissions from, the information given.

Introduction to the VW Transporter and Vanagon

Introduced in 1979 as a replacement for the previous Transporter, the new vehicle is entirely new in design, construction and layout, but retaining the traditional air-cooled flat four engine although now suitably revised.

In the UK the Transporter is available in 1.6 litre or 2.0 litre versions both with carburettor induction. The vehicle is available in a variety of versions from Pick-up truck to nine-seater bus, plus the various caravan conversions supplied by specialist firms using the Transporter as a basis.

In the USA the Transporter is known as the Vanagon and is supplied in two versions; the standard Vanagon which is a cross between a van and a station wagon, hence the name Vanagon, and the Vanagon Camper which is a fully equipped caravanette. All USA vehicles are powered by a fuel injected version of the 2.0 litre air-cooled flat four engine.

Contents

Volkswagen Transporter

General dimensions, weights and capacities

Dimensions
Turning circle .... 10 700 mm (421.5 in) (between walls)
Wheelbase .... 2460 mm (97 in)
Track .... 1570 mm (61.8 in)
Ground clearance (fully laden) .... 190 mm (7.5 in)
Length .... 4570 mm (180 in)
Width:
    All models except Pick-up .... 1845 mm (72.7 in)
    Pick-up .... 1870 mm (73.6 in)

Weights Consult your drivers handbook for the vehicle concerned according to specification, model and options fitted

Capacities
Engine oil (refill with filter change):
    1.6 litre engine .... 3.0 litre (5.3 Imp pt, 6.3 US pt)
    2.0 litre engine .... 3.5 litre (6.2 Imp pt, 7.4 US pt)
Manual transmission (including final drive) .... 3.5 litre (6.2 Imp pt, 7.4 US pt)
Automatic transmission .... 3.0 litre (5.3 Imp pt, 6.3 US pt)
Final drive (automatic transmission only) .... 1.2 litre (2.2 Imp pt, 2.6 US pt)
Fuel tank .... 60 litre (13.2 Imp gal, 15.6 US gal)

Use of English

As this book has been written in England, it uses the appropriate English component names, phrases, and spelling. Some of these differ from those used in America. Normally, these cause no difficulty, but to make sure, a glossary is printed below. In ordering spare parts remember the parts list may use some of these words:

English	American	English	American
Accelerator	Gas pedal	Locks	Latches
Aerial	Antenna	Methylated spirit	Denatured alcohol
Anti-roll bar	Stabiliser or sway bar	Motorway	Freeway, turnpike etc
Big-end bearing	Rod bearing	Number plate	License plate
Bonnet (engine cover)	Hood	Paraffin	Kerosene
Boot (luggage compartment)	Trunk	Petrol	Gasoline (gas)
Bulkhead	Firewall	Petrol tank	Gas tank
Bush	Bushing	'Pinking'	'Pinging'
Cam follower or tappet	Valve lifter or tappet	Prise (force apart)	Pry
Carburettor	Carburetor	Propeller shaft	Driveshaft
Catch	Latch	Quarterlight	Quarter window
Choke/venturi	Barrel	Retread	Recap
Circlip	Snap-ring	Reverse	Back-up
Clearance	Lash	Rocker cover	Valve cover
Crownwheel	Ring gear (of differential)	Saloon	Sedan
Damper	Shock absorber, shock	Seized	Frozen
Disc (brake)	Rotor/disk	Sidelight	Parking light
Distance piece	Spacer	Silencer	Muffler
Drop arm	Pitman arm	Sill panel (beneath doors)	Rocker panel
Drop head coupe	Convertible	Small end, little end	Piston pin or wrist pin
Dynamo	Generator (DC)	Spanner	Wrench
Earth (electrical)	Ground	Split cotter (for valve spring cap)	Lock (for valve spring retainer)
Engineer's blue	Prussian blue	Split pin	Cotter pin
Estate car	Station wagon	Steering arm	Spindle arm
Exhaust manifold	Header	Sump	Oil pan
Fault finding/diagnosis	Troubleshooting	Swarf	Metal chips or debris
Float chamber	Float bowl	Tab washer	Tang or lock
Free-play	Lash	Tappet	Valve lifter
Freewheel	Coast	Thrust bearing	Throw-out bearing
Gearbox	Transmission	Top gear	High
Gearchange	Shift	Torch	Flashlight
Grub screw	Setscrew, Allen screw	Trackrod (of steering)	Tie-rod (or connecting rod)
Gudgeon pin	Piston pin or wrist pin	Trailing shoe (of brake)	Secondary shoe
Halfshaft	Axleshaft	Transmission	Whole drive line
Handbrake	Parking brake	Tyre	Tire
Hood	Soft top	Van	Panel wagon/van
Hot spot	Heat riser	Vice	Vise
Indicator	Turn signal	Wheel nut	Lug nut
Interior light	Dome lamp	Windscreen	Windshield
Layshaft (of gearbox)	Countershaft	Wing/mudguard	Fender
Leading shoe (of brake)	Primary shoe		

Buying spare parts and vehicle identification numbers

Buying spare parts

Spare parts are available from many sources, for example: VW garages, other garages and accessory shops, and motor factors. Our advice regarding spare parts sources is as follows:

Officially appointed VW garages – This is the best source for parts which are peculiar to your car and are not generally available (eg complete cylinder heads, internal gearbox components, badges, interior trim etc). It is also the only place at which you should buy parts if your vehicle is still under warranty – non-VW components may invalidate the warranty. To be sure of obtaining the correct parts, it will always be necessary to give the storeman your vehicle identification number, and if possible, to take the 'old' part along for positive identification. Many parts are available under a factory exchange scheme – any parts returned should always be clean. It obviously makes good sense to go straight to the specialists on your car for this type of part as they are best equipped to supply you.

Other garages and accessory shops – These are ofen very good places to buy materials and components needed for the maintenance of your car (eg oil filters, spark plugs. bulbs, drivebelts, oils and greases, touch-up paint, filler paste, etc). They also sell general accessories, usually have convenient opening hours, charge lower prices and can often be found not far from home.

Motor factors – Good factors will stock all of the more important components which wear out relatively quickly (eg clutch components, pistons, valves, exhaust systems, brake pipes/seals and pads etc). Motor factors will often provide new or reconditioned components on a part exchange basis – this can save a considerable amount of money

Vehicle identification numbers

Modifications are a continuing and unpublicised process in vehicle manufacture quite apart from major model changes. Spare parts manuals and lists are compiled upon a numerical basis, the individual vehicle numbers being essential to correct identification of the component required.

When ordering spare parts, always give as much information as possible. Quote the model, year of manufacture, body and engine numbers as appropriate.

The vehicle identification number is located on a plate attached to the right-hand door pillar on UK models and on the facia, viewed through the windscreen on USA vehicles.

On all engines the engine number is stamped on top of the crankcase.

Vehicle identification plate location – UK vehicles

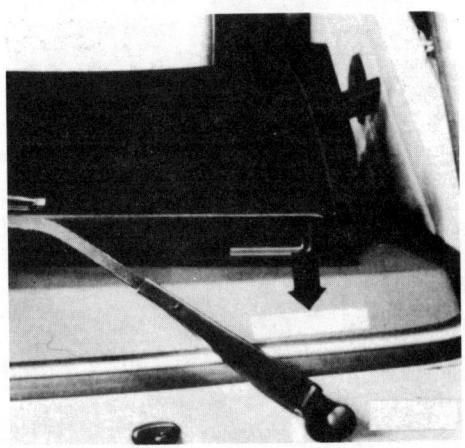

Vehicle identification plate location – USA vehicles

Engine number location – 1.6 litre

Engine number location – 2.0 litre

Spare wheel tray, retaining bolt and catch

Spare wheel removal

Tools and working facilities

Introduction

A selection of good tools is a fundamental requirement for anyone contemplating the maintenance and repair of a motor vehicle. For the owner who does not possess any, their purchase will prove a considerable expense, offsetting some of the savings made by doing-it-yourself. However, provided that the tools purchased meet the relevant national safety standards and are of good quality, they will last for many years and prove an extremely worthwhile investment.

To help the average owner to decide which tools are needed to carry out the various tasks detailed in this manual, we have compiled three lists of tools under the following headings: *Maintenance and minor repair, Repair and overhaul,* and *Special.* The newcomer to practical mechanics should start off with the *Maintenance and minor repair* tool kit and confine himself to the simpler jobs around the vehicle. Then, as his confidence and experience grow, he can undertake more difficult tasks, buying extra tools as, and when, they are needed. In this way, a *Maintenance and minor repair* tool kit can be built-up into a *Repair and overhaul* tool kit over a considerable period of time without any major cash outlays. The experienced do-it-yourselfer will have a tool kit good enough for most repair and overhaul procedures and will add tools from the *Special* category when he feels the expense is justified by the amount of use to which these tools will be put.

It is obviously not possible to cover the subject of tools fully here. For those who wish to learn more about tools and their use there is a book entitled *How to Choose and Use Car Tools* available from the publishers of this manual.

Maintenance and minor repair tool kit

The tools given in this list should be considered as a minimum requirement if routine maintenance, servicing and minor repair operations are to be undertaken. We recommend the purchase of combination spanners (ring one end, open-ended the other); although more expensive than open-ended ones, they do give the advantages of both types of spanner.

Combination spanners - 10, 11, 12, 13, 14 & 17 mm
Adjustable spanner - 9 inch
Spark plug spanner (with rubber insert)
Spark plug gap adjustment tool
Set of feeler gauges
Brake bleed nipple spanner
Screwdriver - 4 in long x $\frac{1}{4}$ in dia (flat blade)
Screwdriver - 4 in long x $\frac{1}{4}$ in dia (cross blade)
Combination pliers - 6 inch
Hacksaw (junior)
Tyre pump
Tyre pressure gauge
Oil can
Fine emery cloth (1 sheet)
Wire brush (small)
Funnel (medium size)

Repair and overhaul tool kit

These tools are virtually essential for anyone undertaking any major repairs to a motor vehicle, and are additional to those given in the *Maintenance and minor repair* list. Included in this list is a comprehensive set of sockets. Although these are expensive they will be found invaluable as they are so versatile - particularly if various drives are included in the set. We recommend the $\frac{1}{2}$ in square-drive type, as this can be used with most proprietary torque wrenches. If you cannot afford a socket set, even bought piecemeal, then inexpensive tubular box spanners are a useful alternative.

The tools in this list will occasionally need to be supplemented by tools from the *Special* list.

Sockets (or box spanners) to cover range in previous list
Reversible ratchet drive (for use with sockets)
Extension piece, 10 inch (for use with sockets)
Universal joint (for use with sockets)
Torque wrench (for use with sockets)
'Mole' wrench - 8 inch
Ball pein hammer
Soft-faced hammer, plastic or rubber
Screwdriver - 6 in long x $\frac{5}{16}$ in dia (flat blade)
Screwdriver - 2 in long x $\frac{5}{16}$ in square (flat blade)
Screwdriver - 1$\frac{1}{2}$ in long x $\frac{1}{4}$ in dia (cross blade)
Screwdriver - 3 in long x $\frac{1}{8}$ in dia (electricians)
Pliers - electricians side cutters
Pliers - needle nosed
Pliers - circlip (internal and external)
Cold chisel - $\frac{1}{2}$ inch
Scriber
Scraper
Centre punch
Pin punch
Hacksaw
Valve grinding tool
Steel rule/straight-edge
Allen keys
Selection of files
Wire brush (large)
Axle-stands
Jack (strong scissor or hydraulic type)

Special tools

The tools in this list are those which are not used regularly, are expensive to buy, or which need to be used in accordance with their manufacturers' instructions. Unless relatively difficult mechanical jobs are undertaken frequently, it will not be economic to buy many of these tools. Where this is the case, you could consider clubbing together with friends (or joining a motorists' club) to make a joint purchase, or borrowing the tools against a deposit from a local garage or tool hire specialist.

The following list contains only those tools and instruments freely available to the public, and not those special tools produced by the vehicle manufacturer specifically for its dealer network. You will find occasional references to these manufacturers' special tools in the text of this manual. Generally, an alternative method of doing the job without the vehicle manufacturers' special tool is given. However, sometimes, there is no alternative to using them. Where this is the case and the relevant tool cannot be bought or borrowed, you will have to entrust the work to a franchised garage.

Valve spring compressor
Piston ring compressor
Balljoint separator
Universal hub/bearing puller
Impact screwdriver
Micrometer and/or vernier gauge
Dial gauge
Stroboscopic timing light
Dwell angle meter/tachometer
Universal electrical multi-meter
Cylinder compression gauge

Lifting tackle
Trolley jack
Light with extension lead

Buying tools

For practically all tools, a tool factor is the best source since he will have a very comprehensive range compared with the average garage or accessory shop. Having said that, accessory shops often offer excellent quality tools at discount prices, so it pays to shop around.

There are plenty of good tools around at reasonable prices, but always aim to purchase items which meet the relevant national safety standards. If in doubt, ask the proprietor or manager of the shop for advice before making a purchase.

Care and maintenance of tools

Having purchased a reasonable tool kit, it is necessary to keep the tools in a clean serviceable condition. After use, always wipe off any dirt, grease and metal particles using a clean, dry cloth, before putting the tools away. Never leave them lying around after they have been used. A simple tool rack on the garage or workshop wall, for items such as screwdrivers and pliers is a good idea. Store all normal wrenches and sockets in a metal box. Any measuring instruments, gauges, meters, etc, must be carefully stored where they cannot be damaged or become rusty.

Take a little care when tools are used. Hammer heads inevitably become marked and screwdrivers lose the keen edge on their blades from time to time. A little timely attention with emery cloth or a file will soon restore items like this to a good serviceable finish.

Working facilities

Not to be forgotten when discussing tools, is the workshop itself. If anything more than routine maintenance is to be carried out, some form of suitable working area becomes essential.

It is appreciated that many an owner mechanic is forced by circumstances to remove an engine or similar item, without the benefit of a garage or workshop. Having done this, any repairs should always be done under the cover of a roof.

Wherever possible, any dismantling should be done on a clean, flat workbench or table at a suitable working height.

Any workbench needs a vice: one with a jaw opening of 4 in (100 mm) is suitable for most jobs. As mentioned previously, some clean dry storage space is also required for tools, as well as for lubricants, cleaning fluids, touch-up paints and so on, which become necessary.

Another item which may be required, and which has a much more general usage, is an electric drill with a chuck capacity of at least $\frac{5}{16}$ in (8 mm). This, together with a good range of twist drills, is virtually essential for fitting accessories such as mirrors and reversing lights.

Last, but not least, always keep a supply of old newspapers and clean, lint-free rags available, and try to keep any working area as clean as possible.

Spanner jaw gap comparison table

Jaw gap (in)	Spanner size
0.250	$\frac{1}{4}$ in AF
0.276	7 mm
0.313	$\frac{5}{16}$ in AF
0.315	8 mm
0.344	$\frac{11}{32}$ in AF; $\frac{1}{8}$ in Whitworth

Jaw gap (in)	Spanner size
0.354	9 mm
0.375	$\frac{3}{8}$ in AF
0.394	10 mm
0.433	11 mm
0.438	$\frac{7}{16}$ in AF
0.445	$\frac{3}{16}$ in Whitworth; $\frac{1}{4}$ in BSF
0.472	12 mm
0.500	$\frac{1}{2}$ in AF
0.512	13 mm
0.525	$\frac{1}{4}$ in Whitworth; $\frac{5}{16}$ in BSF
0.551	14 mm
0.563	$\frac{9}{16}$ in AF
0.591	15 mm
0.600	$\frac{5}{16}$ in Whitworth; $\frac{3}{8}$ in BSF
0.625	$\frac{5}{8}$ in AF
0.630	16 mm
0.669	17 mm
0.686	$\frac{11}{16}$ in AF
0.709	18 mm
0.710	$\frac{3}{8}$ in Whitworth; $\frac{7}{16}$ in BSF
0.748	19 mm
0.750	$\frac{3}{4}$ in AF
0.813	$\frac{13}{16}$ in AF
0.820	$\frac{7}{16}$ in Whitworth; $\frac{1}{2}$ in BSF
0.866	22 mm
0.875	$\frac{7}{8}$ in AF
0.920	$\frac{1}{2}$ in Whitworth; $\frac{9}{16}$ in BSF
0.938	$\frac{15}{16}$ in AF
0.945	24 mm
1.000	1 in AF
1.010	$\frac{9}{16}$ in Whitworth; $\frac{5}{8}$ in BSF
1.024	26 mm
1.063	$1\frac{1}{16}$ in AF; 27 mm
1.100	$\frac{5}{8}$ in Whitworth; $\frac{11}{16}$ in BSF
1.125	$1\frac{1}{8}$ in AF
1.181	30 mm
1.200	$\frac{11}{16}$ in Whitworth; $\frac{3}{4}$ in BSF
1.250	$1\frac{1}{4}$ in AF
1.260	32 mm
1.300	$\frac{3}{4}$ in Whitworth; $\frac{7}{8}$ in BSF
1.313	$1\frac{5}{16}$ in AF
1.390	$\frac{13}{16}$ in Whitworth; $\frac{15}{16}$ in BSF
1.417	36 mm
1.438	$1\frac{7}{16}$ in AF
1.480	$\frac{7}{8}$ in Whitworth; 1 in BSF
1.500	$1\frac{1}{2}$ in AF
1.575	40 mm; $\frac{15}{16}$ in Whitworth
1.614	41 mm
1.625	$1\frac{5}{8}$ in AF
1.670	1 in Whitworth; $1\frac{1}{8}$ in BSF
1.688	$1\frac{11}{16}$ in AF
1.811	46 mm
1.813	$1\frac{13}{16}$ in AF
1.860	$1\frac{1}{8}$ in Whitworth; $1\frac{1}{4}$ in BSF
1.875	$1\frac{7}{8}$ in AF
1.969	50 mm
2.000	2 in AF
2.050	$1\frac{1}{4}$ in Whitworth; $1\frac{3}{8}$ in BSF
2.165	55 mm
2.362	60 mm

General repair procedures

Whenever servicing, repair or overhaul work is carried out on the car or its components, it is necessary to observe the following procedures and instructions. This will assist in carrying out the operation efficiently and to a professional standard of workmanship.

Joint mating faces and gaskets

Where a gasket is used between the mating faces of two components, ensure that it is renewed on reassembly, and fit it dry unless otherwise stated in the repair procedure. Make sure that the mating faces are clean and dry with all traces of old gasket removed. When cleaning a joint face, use a tool which is not likely to score or damage the face, and remove any burrs or nicks with an oilstone or fine file.

Make sure that tapped holes are cleaned with a pipe cleaner, and keep them free of jointing compound if this is being used unless specifically instructed otherwise.

Ensure that all orifices, channels or pipes are clear and blow through them, preferably using compressed air.

Oil seals

Whenever an oil seal is removed from its working location, either individually or as part of an assembly, it should be renewed.

The very fine sealing lip of the seal is easily damaged and will not seal if the surface it contacts is not completely clean and free from scratches, nicks or grooves. If the original sealing surface of the component cannot be restored, the component should be renewed.

Protect the lips of the seal from any surface which may damage them in the course of fitting. Use tape or a conical sleeve where possible. Lubricate the seal lips with oil before fitting and, on dual lipped seals, fill the space between the lips with grease.

Unless otherwise stated, oil seals must be fitted with their sealing lips toward the lubricant to be sealed.

Use a tubular drift or block of wood of the appropriate size to install the seal and, if the seal housing is shouldered, drive the seal down to the shoulder. If the seal housing is unshouldered, the seal should be fitted with its face flush with the housing top face.

Screw threads and fastenings

Always ensure that a blind tapped hole is completely free from oil, grease, water or other fluid before installing the bolt or stud. Failure to do this could cause the housing to crack due to the hydraulic action of the bolt or stud as it is screwed in.

When tightening a castellated nut to accept a split pin, tighten the nut to the specified torque, where applicable, and then tighten further to the next split pin hole. Never slacken the nut to align a split pin hole unless stated in the repair procedure.

When checking or retightening a nut or bolt to a specified torque setting, slacken the nut or bolt by a quarter of a turn, and then retighten to the specified setting.

Locknuts, locktabs and washers

Any fastening which will rotate against a component or housing in the course of tightening should always have a washer between it and the relevant component or housing.

Spring or split washers should always be renewed when they are used to lock a critical component such as a big-end bearing retaining nut or bolt.

Locktabs which are folded over to retain a nut or bolt should always be renewed.

Self-locking nuts can be reused in non-critical areas, providing resistance can be felt when the locking portion passes over the bolt or stud thread.

Split pins must always be replaced with new ones of the correct size for the hole.

Special tools

Some repair procedures in this manual entail the use of special tools such as a press, two or three-legged pullers, spring compressors etc. Wherever possible, suitable readily available alternatives to the manufacturer's special tools are described, and are shown in use. In some instances, where no alternative is possible, it has been necessary to resort to the use of a manufacturer's tool and this has been done for reasons of safety as well as the efficient completion of the repair operation. Unless you are highly skilled and have a thorough understanding of the procedure described, never attempt to bypass the use of any special tool when the procedure described specifies its use. Not only is there a very great risk of personal injury, but expensive damage could be caused to the components involved.

Jacking and towing

To change a roadwheel first remove the spare wheel from its location under the front of the vehicle. To do this undo the retaining bolt securing the spare wheel tray, using the wheel nut spanner. Pull the catch to release the tray at the front and lift out the spare wheel. Apply the handbrake and chock the wheel diagonally opposite the one to be changed. Lever off the wheel trim and slightly loosen the wheel nuts/bolts using the spanner provided. Engage the jack in the jacking point nearest the wheel to be changed and raise the jack until the wheel is free of the ground. Unscrew the wheel nuts/bolts, remove the wheel and fit the spare. Tighten the wheel nuts/bolts, lower the jack then tighten them again. Refit the wheel trim, remove the jack and chocks and store the wheel in the spare wheel tray. Lift the tray until the catch engages and secure with the retaining bolt. Do not drive the vehicle without bolting the spare wheel tray in place.

To raise the car for maintenance or repair work use a sturdy scissor type or hydraulic jack positioned under the vehicle jacking points (photo). Once the vehicle is raised supplement the jack with axle stands or other sturdy supports and do not venture underneath until these are in place. To raise the front or rear completely, jack up one side, support it on stands then jack up the other side and support it also. Only use the jacking points, never parts of the suspension or vehicle floor.

Hooks and eyes are provided at the front and rear of the vehicle for towing or when being towed. If automatic transmission is fitted do not allow the vehicle to be towed faster than 30 mph and for a maximum of 30 miles. If the vehicle must be towed for a long distance, it should be suspended wheel free at the rear, or the driveshafts should be removed.

Jacking point locations

Vehicle jack engaged in front jacking point

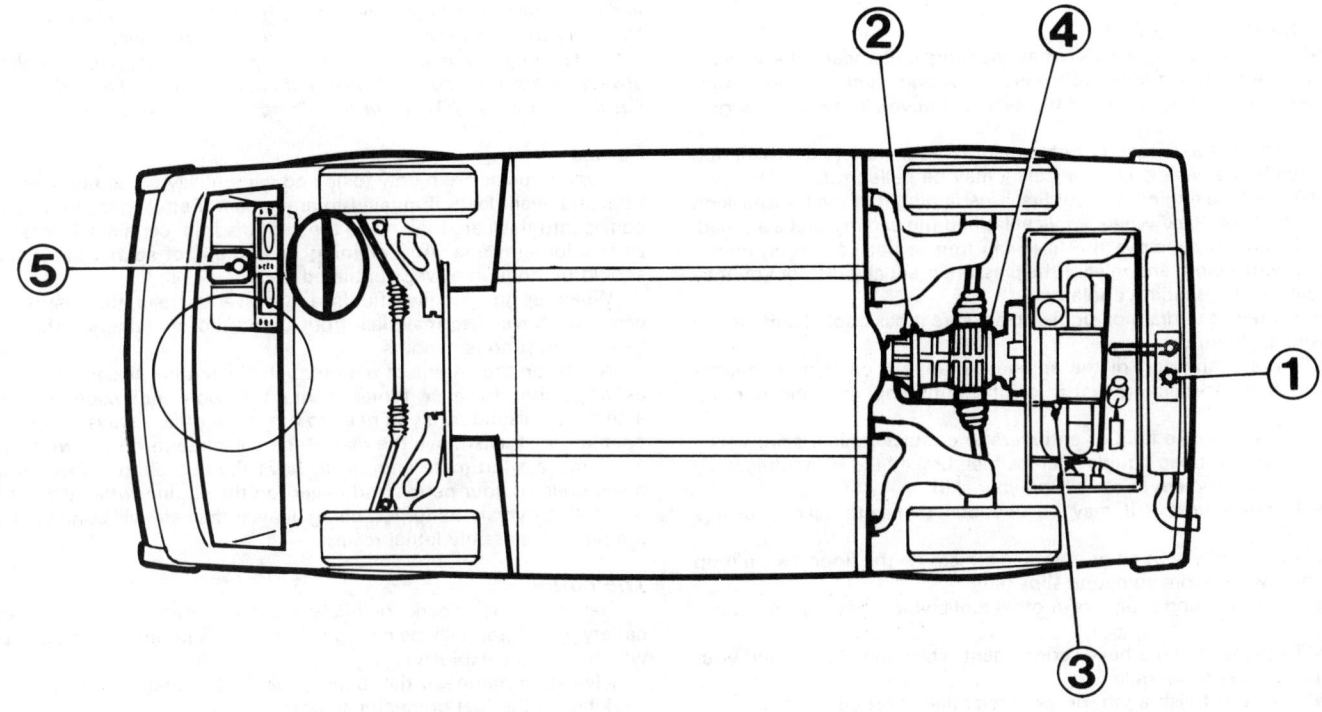

Recommended lubricants and fluids

Component or system	Lubricant type or specification
Engine (1)	SAE 15W/50 multigrade engine oil or equivalent
Manual transmission (including final drive) (2)	SAE 80 or 80W/90 gear oil
Automatic transmission (3)	Dexron automatic transmission fluid
Final drive (4)	SAE 90 gear oil
Brake fluid reservoir (5)	Hydraulic fluid to SAE J1703C or FMVSS 116 DOT 3
General greasing	Multi-purpose lithium based grease

Safety first!

Professional motor mechanics are trained in safe working procedures. However enthusiastic you may be about getting on with the job in hand, do take the time to ensure that your safety is not put at risk. A moment's lack of attention can result in an accident, as can failure to observe certain elementary precautions.

There will always be new ways of having accidents, and the following points do not pretend to be a comprehensive list of all dangers; they are intended rather to make you aware of the risks and to encourage a safety-conscious approach to all work you carry out on your vehicle.

Essential DOs and DON'Ts

DON'T rely on a single jack when working underneath the vehicle. Always use reliable additional means of support, such as axle stands, securely placed under a part of the vehicle that you know will not give way.

DON'T attempt to loosen or tighten high-torque nuts (e.g. wheel hub nuts) while the vehicle is on a jack; it may be pulled off.

DON'T start the engine without first ascertaining that the transmission is in neutral (or 'Park' where applicable) and the parking brake applied.

DON'T suddenly remove the filler cap from a hot cooling system – cover it with a cloth and release the pressure gradually first, or you may get scalded by escaping coolant.

DON'T attempt to drain oil until you are sure it has cooled sufficiently to avoid scalding you.

DON'T grasp any part of the engine, exhaust or catalytic converter without first ascertaining that it is sufficiently cool to avoid burning you.

DON'T allow brake fluid or antifreeze to contact vehicle paintwork.

DON'T syphon toxic liquids such as fuel, brake fluid or antifreeze by mouth, or allow them to remain on your skin.

DON'T inhale dust – it may be injurious to health (see *Asbestos* below).

DON'T allow any spilt oil or grease to remain on the floor – wipe it up straight away, before someone slips on it.

DON'T use ill-fitting spanners or other tools which may slip and cause injury.

DON'T attempt to lift a heavy component which may be beyond your capability – get assistance.

DON'T rush to finish a job, or take unverified short cuts.

DON'T allow children or animals in or around an unattended vehicle.

DO wear eye protection when using power tools such as drill, sander, bench grinder etc, and when working under the vehicle.

DO use a barrier cream on your hands prior to undertaking dirty jobs – it will protect your skin from infection as well as making the dirt easier to remove afterwards; but make sure your hands aren't left slippery. Note that long-term contact with used engine oil can be a health hazard.

DO keep loose clothing (cuffs, tie etc) and long hair well out of the way of moving mechanical parts.

DO remove rings, wristwatch etc, before working on the vehicle – especially the electrical system.

DO ensure that any lifting tackle used has a safe working load rating adequate for the job.

DO keep your work area tidy – it is only too easy to fall over articles left lying around.

DO get someone to check periodically that all is well, when working alone on the vehicle.

DO carry out work in a logical sequence and check that everything is correctly assembled and tightened afterwards.

DO remember that your vehicle's safety affects that of yourself and others. If in doubt on any point, get specialist advice.

IF, in spite of following these precautions, you are unfortunate enough to injure yourself, seek medical attention as soon as possible.

Asbestos

Certain friction, insulating, sealing, and other products – such as brake linings, brake bands, clutch linings, torque converters, gaskets, etc – contain asbestos. *Extreme care must be taken to avoid inhalation of dust from such products since it is hazardous to health.* If in doubt, assume that they *do* contain asbestos.

Fire

Remember at all times that petrol (gasoline) is highly flammable. Never smoke, or have any kind of naked flame around, when working on the vehicle. But the risk does not end there – a spark caused by an electrical short-circuit, by two metal surfaces contacting each other, by careless use of tools, or even by static electricity built up in your body under certain conditions, can ignite petrol vapour, which in a confined space is highly explosive.

Always disconnect the battery earth (ground) terminal before working on any part of the fuel or electrical system, and never risk spilling fuel on to a hot engine or exhaust.

It is recommended that a fire extinguisher of a type suitable for fuel and electrical fires is kept handy in the garage or workplace at all times. Never try to extinguish a fuel or electrical fire with water.

Note: *Any reference to a 'torch' appearing in this manual should always be taken to mean a hand-held battery-operated electric lamp or flashlight. It does NOT mean a welding/gas torch or blowlamp.*

Fumes

Certain fumes are highly toxic and can quickly cause unconsciousness and even death if inhaled to any extent. Petrol (gasoline) vapour comes into this category, as do the vapours from certain solvents such as trichloroethylene. Any draining or pouring of such volatile fluids should be done in a well ventilated area.

When using cleaning fluids and solvents, read the instructions carefully. Never use materials from unmarked containers – they may give off poisonous vapours.

Never run the engine of a motor vehicle in an enclosed space such as a garage. Exhaust fumes contain carbon monoxide which is extremely poisonous; if you need to run the engine, always do so in the open air or at least have the rear of the vehicle outside the workplace.

If you are fortunate enough to have the use of an inspection pit, never drain or pour petrol, and never run the engine, while the vehicle is standing over it; the fumes, being heavier than air, will concentrate in the pit with possibly lethal results.

The battery

Never cause a spark, or allow a naked light, near the vehicle's battery. It will normally be giving off a certain amount of hydrogen gas, which is highly explosive.

Always disconnect the battery earth (ground) terminal before working on the fuel or electrical systems.

If possible, loosen the filler plugs or cover when charging the battery from an external source. Do not charge at an excessive rate or the battery may burst.

Take care when topping up and when carrying the battery. The acid electrolyte, even when diluted, is very corrosive and should not be allowed to contact the eyes or skin.

If you ever need to prepare electrolyte yourself, always add the acid slowly to the water, and never the other way round. Protect against splashes by wearing rubber gloves and goggles.

When jump starting a car using a booster battery, for negative earth (ground) vehicles, connect the jump leads in the following sequence: First connect one jump lead between the positive (+) terminals of the two batteries. Then connect the other jump lead first to the negative (–) terminal of the booster battery, and then to a good earthing (ground) point on the vehicle to be started, at least 18 in (45 cm) from the battery if possible. Ensure that hands and jump leads are clear of any moving parts, and that the two vehicles do not touch. Disconnect the leads in the reverse order.

Mains electricity

When using an electric power tool, inspection light etc, which works from the mains, always ensure that the appliance is correctly connected to its plug and that, where necessary, it is properly earthed (grounded). Do not use such appliances in damp conditions and, again, beware of creating a spark or applying excessive heat in the vicinity of fuel or fuel vapour.

Ignition HT voltage

A severe electric shock can result from touching certain parts of the ignition system, such as the HT leads, when the engine is running or being cranked, particularly if components are damp or the insulation is defective. Where an electronic ignition system is fitted, the HT voltage is much higher and could prove fatal.

Routine maintenance

Maintenance is essential for ensuring safety and desirable for the purpose of getting the best in terms of performance and economy from your van. Over the years the need for periodic lubrication has been greatly reduced if not totally eliminated. This has unfortunately tended to lead some owners to think that, because no such action is required, the items either no longer exist, or will last forever. This is certainly not the case, it is essential to carry out regular visual examination as comprehensively as possible in order to spot any possible defects at an early stage before they develop into major expensive repairs.

The following service schedules are a list of the maintenance requirements and the intervals at which they should be carried out, as recommended by the manufacturers. Where applicable these procedures are covered in greater detail throughout this manual, near the beginning of each Chapter.

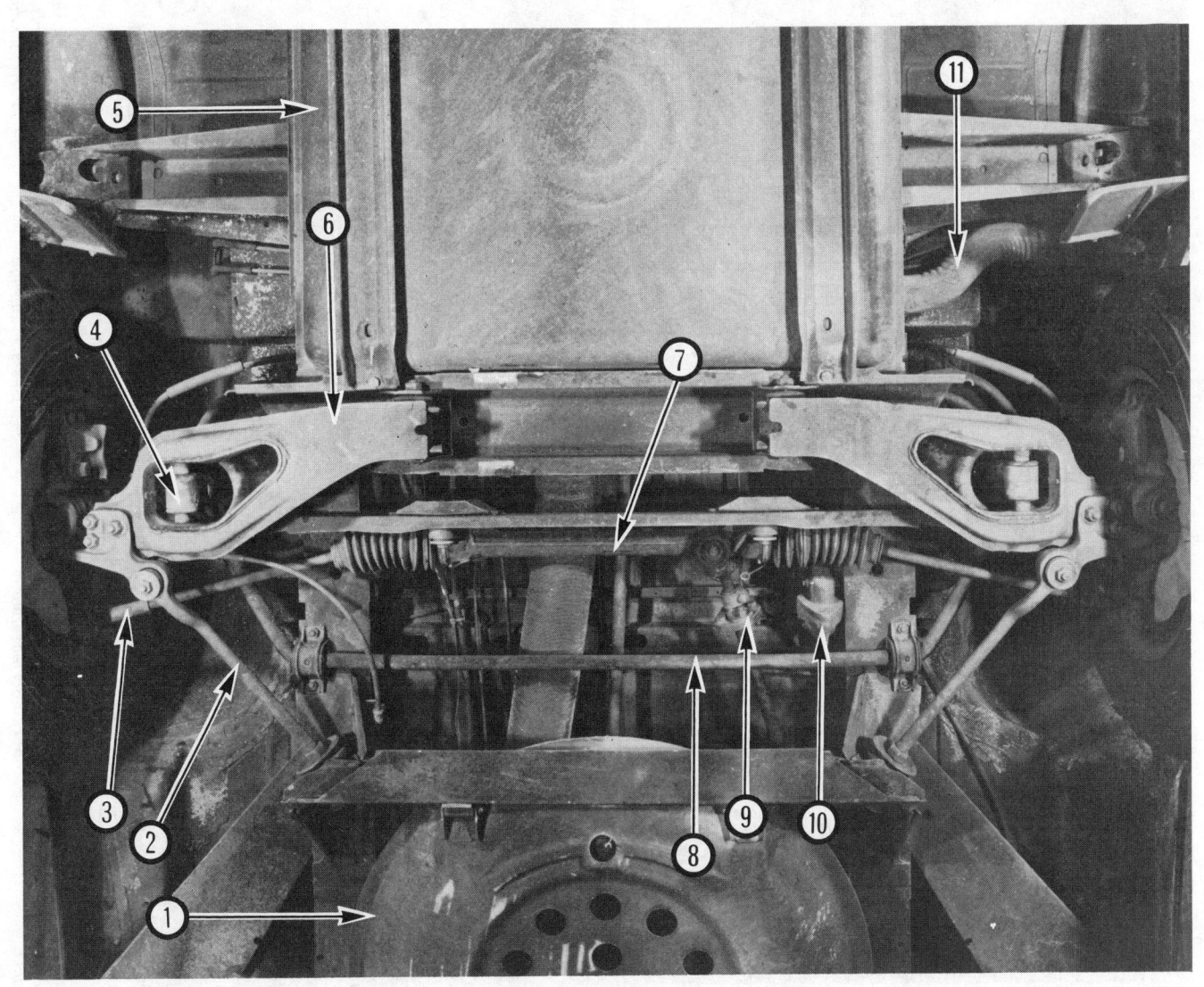

Front underbody view

1	Spare wheel carrier tray	4	Shock absorber lower mounting	7	Steering gear	10 Brake pressure regulator
2	Radius arm	5	Fuel tank	8	Anti-roll bar	11 Fuel filler pipe
3	Steering tie-rod	6	Track control arm	9	Universal coupling	

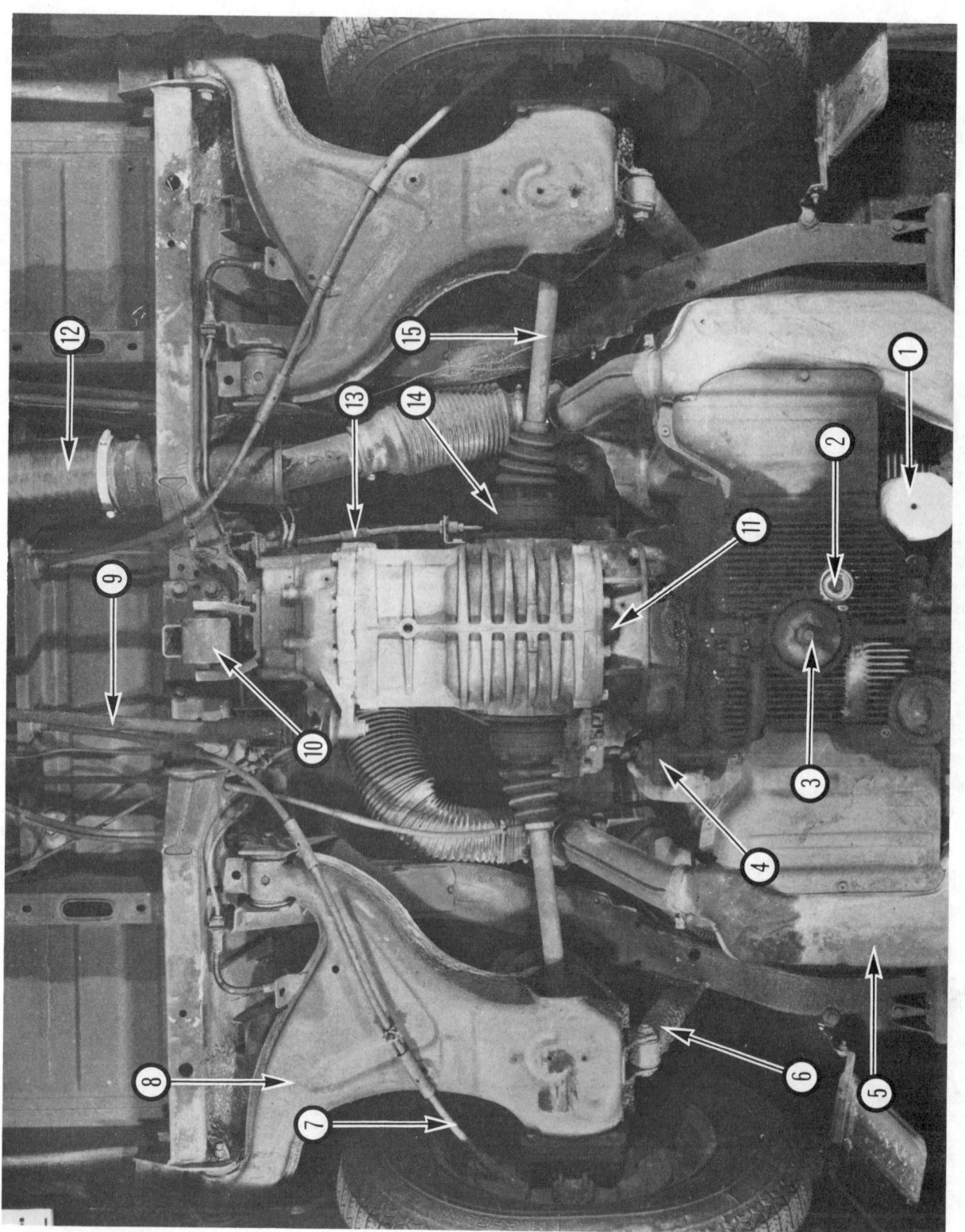

Rear underbody view (2.0 litre) model

1 Oil filter
2 Oil drain plug
3 Oil strainer
4 Fuel pump
5 Heat exchanger
6 Shock absorber
7 Handbrake cable
8 Rear suspension arm
9 Gearshift linkage
10 Transmission front mounting
11 Transmission drain plug
12 Heater duct
13 Clutch hydraulic fluid pipe
14 Driveshaft inner joint
15 Driveshaft

Engine component location (2.0 litre model)

1 Fan housing	7 Brake servo vacuum hose
2 Distributor vacuum unit	8 Left-hand carburettor
3 Distributor	9 Throttle damper
4 Ignition coil	10 Air cleaner element
5 Idle stabilizing unit	11 Vacuum unit
6 Ignition control unit	12 Right-hand carburettor
	13 Throttle linkage

Weekly or before a long journey

Check and if necessary top up the engine oil (photos)
Check operation of all lights, indicators, horn and wipers
Check and if necessary top up the windscreen washer reservoir (photo)
Check tyre pressures (cold) (photo)

Every 5000 miles (7500 km) or six months, whichever comes first

Renew the engine oil
Check and if necessary top up the battery (where applicable) (photo)
Check and if necessary adjust the clutch cable (where applicable)
Check the front brake pad thickness
Check the brake hydraulic fluid lever (photo)

Every 10 000 miles (15 000 km) or twelve months, whichever comes first

In addition to, or instead of, the work specified in the previous schedule
Renew the engine oil
Renew the engine oil filter
Check the engine for oil leaks or other fluid leaks
Check the carburettor or fuel injection idle speed and mixture settings
Check for fuel leaks, security of pipes, hoses, and cables
Check the exhaust system condition and security
Renew the contact breaker points and adjust the gap or dwell angle (where applicable)
Lubricate the distributor
Check the distributor cap for cracks and tracking, clean the HT leads
Check and if necessary adjust the ignition timing

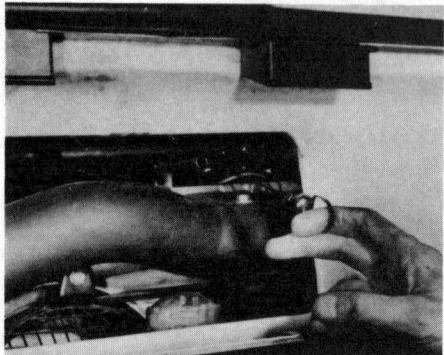
Check the engine oil level on the dipstick

Pull the oil filler tube out to fill

Top-up the windscreen washer reservoir

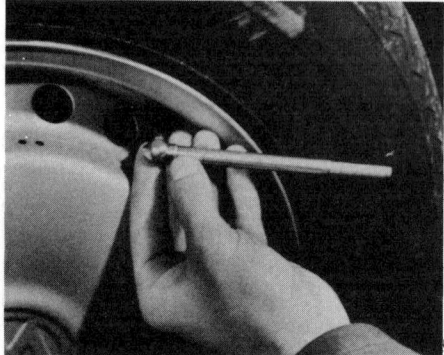
Check the tyre pressures

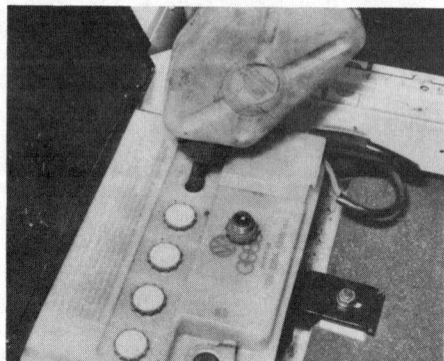
Top-up the battery

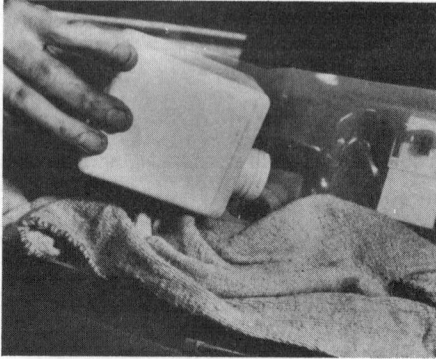
Top-up the brake fluid at the reservoir under the instrument panel cover

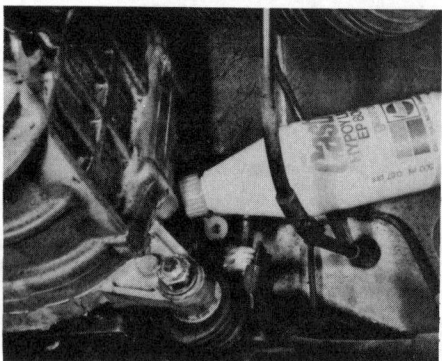
Top-up the manual transmission oil

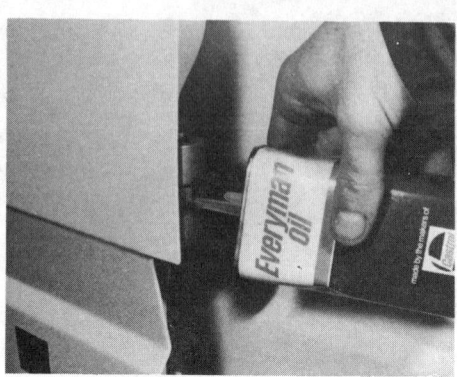
Lubricate the locks and hinges

Check the operation of the clutch and adjust if necessary (where applicable)
Check all clutch hoses, pipes and unions (where applicable)
Check for leaks around the transmission housings
Check the level of gear oil in the manual transmission and fluid in the automatic transmission (photo)
Check the operation of the gear linkage or selector mechanism
Check the condition of all suspension driveshaft and steering joints and linkages and check for excess free play
Check for damaged balljoint boots or rubber bellows
Check the tyres for condition, tread depth and pressure
Check the front brake pad linings and rear brake shoe linings for condition and thickness
Check the operation of the hand and foot brakes and adjust if necessary
Check and if necessary top up the brake fluid
Check the condition and security of all brake hydraulic pipes and hoses
Check the alternator drivebelt condition and tension, renew if necessary
Check the operation of all electrical equipment, instruments and accessories
Check the wiper blades and windscreen washers and top up the washer reservoir

Check the battery terminals and clean if necessary
Top up the battery with distilled water (where applicable)
Check the bodywork for operation of all doors, windows and locks and lubricate as necessary (photo)

Every 20 000 miles (30 000 km) or two years, whichever comes first

---

In addition to the work specified in the previous schedule
Renew the air cleaner filter element
Renew the fuel filter
Renew the brake hydraulic fluid

Every 30 000 miles (45 000 km) or three years, whichever comes first

---

In addition to the work specified in the previous schedules
Renew the automatic transmission fluid, clean the oil pan and oil strainer

Fault diagnosis

Introduction

The vehicle owner who does his or her own maintenance according to the recommended schedules should not have to use this section of the manual very often. Modern component reliability is such that, provided those items subject to wear or deterioration are inspected or renewed at the specified intervals, sudden failure is comparatively rare. Faults do not usually just happen as a result of sudden failure, but develop over a period of time. Major mechanical failures in particular are usually preceded by characteristic symptoms over hundreds or even thousands of miles. Those components which do occasionally fail without warning are often small and easily carried in the vehicle.

With any fault finding, the first step is to decide where to begin investigations. Sometimes this is obvious, but on other occasions a little detective work will be necessary. The owner who makes half a dozen haphazard adjustments or replacements may be successful in curing a fault (or its symptoms), but he will be none the wiser if the fault recurs and he may well have spent more time and money than was necessary. A calm and logical approach will be found to be more satisfactory in the long run. Always take into account any warning signs or abnormalities that may have been noticed in the period preceding the fault — power loss, high or low gauge readings, unusual noises or smells, etc — and remember that failure of components such as fuses or spark plugs may only be pointers to some underlying fault.

The pages which follow here are intended to help in cases of failure to start or breakdown on the road. There is also a Fault Diagnosis Section at the end of each Chapter which should be consulted if the preliminary checks prove unfruitful. Whatever the fault, certain basic principles apply. These are as follows:

Verify the fault. This is simply a matter of being sure that you know what the symptoms are before starting work. This is particularly important if you are investigating a fault for someone else who may not have described it very accurately.

Don't overlook the obvious. For example, if the vehicle won't start, is there petrol in the tank? (Don't take anyone else's word on this particular point, and don't trust the fuel gauge either!) If an electrical fault is indicated, look for loose or broken wires before digging out the test gear.

Cure the disease, not the symptom. Substituting a flat battery with a fully charged one will get you off the hard shoulder, but if the underlying cause is not attended to, the new battery will go the same way. Similarly; changing oil-fouled spark plugs for a new set will get you moving again, but remember that the reason for the fouling (if it wasn't simply an incorrect grade of plug) will have to be established and corrected.

Don't take anything for granted. Particularly, don't forget that a 'new' component may itself be defective (especially if it's been rattling round in the boot for months), and don't leave components out of a fault diagnosis sequence just because they are new or recently fitted. When you do finally diagnose a difficult fault, you'll probably realise that all the evidence was there from the start.

Electrical faults

Electrical faults can be more puzzling than straightforward mechanical failures, but they are no less susceptible to logical analysis if the basic principles of operation are understood. Vehicle electrical wiring exists in extremely unfavourable conditions — heat, vibration and chemical attack — and the first things to look for are loose or corroded connections and broken or chafed wires, especially where the wires pass through holes in the bodywork or are subject to vibration.

All metal-bodied vehicles in current production have one pole of the battery 'earthed', ie connected to the vehicle bodywork, and in nearly all modern vehicles it is the negative (–) terminal. The various electrical components — motors, bulb holders etc — are also connected to earth, either by means of a lead or directly by their mountings. Electric current flows through the component and then back to the battery via the bodywork. If the component mounting is loose or corroded, or if a good path back to the battery is not available, the

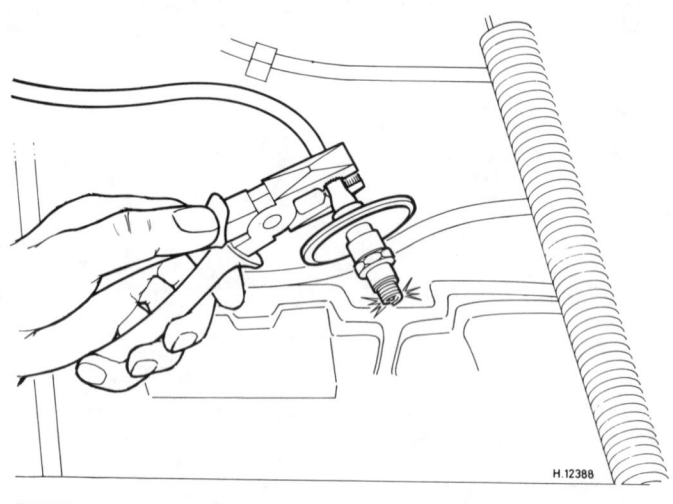

Crank engine and check for a spark. Note use of insulated tool

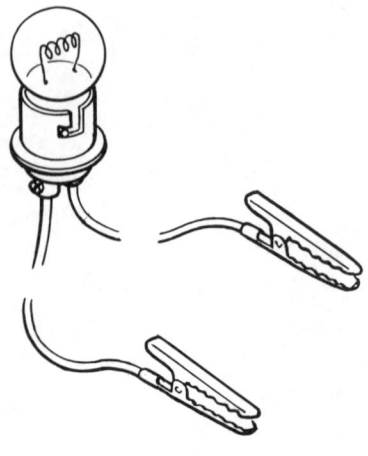

Simple test lamp is useful for tracing electrical faults

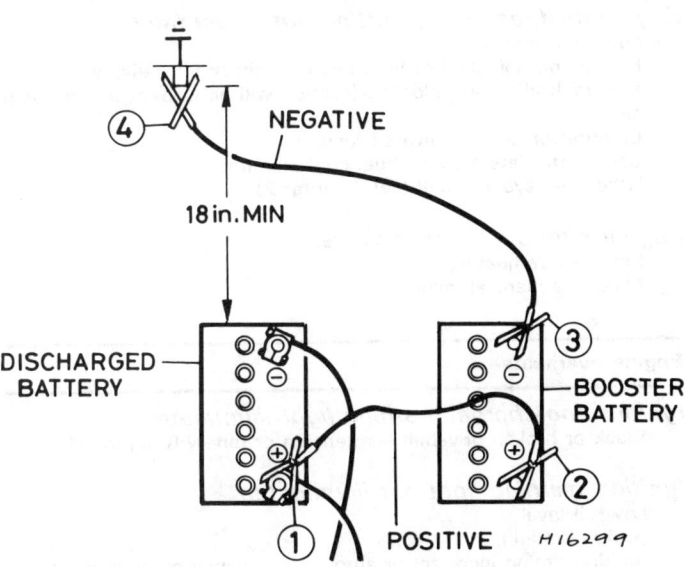

Jump start lead connections for negative earth vehicles – connect leads in order shown

circuit will be incomplete and malfunction will result. The engine and/or gearbox are also earthed by means of flexible metal straps to the body or subframe; if these straps are loose or missing, starter motor, generator and ignition trouble may result.

Assuming the earth return to be satisfactory, electrical faults will be due either to component malfunction or to defects in the current supply. Individual components are dealt with in Chapter 10. If supply wires are broken or cracked internally this results in an open-circuit, and the easiest way to check for this is to bypass the suspect wire temporarily with a length of wire having a crocodile clip or suitable connector at each end. Alternatively, a 12V test lamp can be used to verify the presence of supply voltage at various points along the wire and the break can be thus isolated.

If a bare portion of a live wire touches the bodywork or other earthed metal part, the electricity will take the low-resistance path thus formed back to the battery: this is known as a short-circuit. Hopefully a short-circuit will blow a fuse, but otherwise it may cause burning of the insulation (and possibly further short-circuits) or even a fire. This is why it is inadvisable to bypass persistently blowing fuses with silver foil or wire.

Spares and tool kit

Most vehicles are supplied only with sufficient tools for wheel changing; the *Maintenance and minor repair* tool kit detailed in *Tools and working facilities,* with the addition of a hammer, is probably sufficient for those repairs that most motorists would consider attempting at the roadside. In addition a few items which can be fitted without too much trouble in the event of a breakdown should be carried. Experience and available space will modify the list below, but the following may save having to call on professional assistance:

Spark plugs, clean and correctly gapped
HT lead and plug cap – long enough to reach the plug furthest from the distributor
Distributor rotor, condenser and contact breaker points
Drivebelt(s) – emergency type may suffice
Spare fuses
Set of principal light bulbs
Exhaust bandage
Roll of insulating tape
Length of soft iron wire
Length of electrical flex
Torch or inspection lamp (can double as test lamp)
Battery jump leads
Tow-rope
Ignition waterproofing aerosol
Litre of engine oil
Sealed can of hydraulic fluid
Emergency windscreen
'Jubilee' clips
Tube of filler paste

If spare fuel is carried, a can designed for the purpose should be used to minimise risks of leakage and collision damage. A first aid kit and a warning triangle, whilst not at present compulsory in the UK, are obviously sensible items to carry in addition to the above.

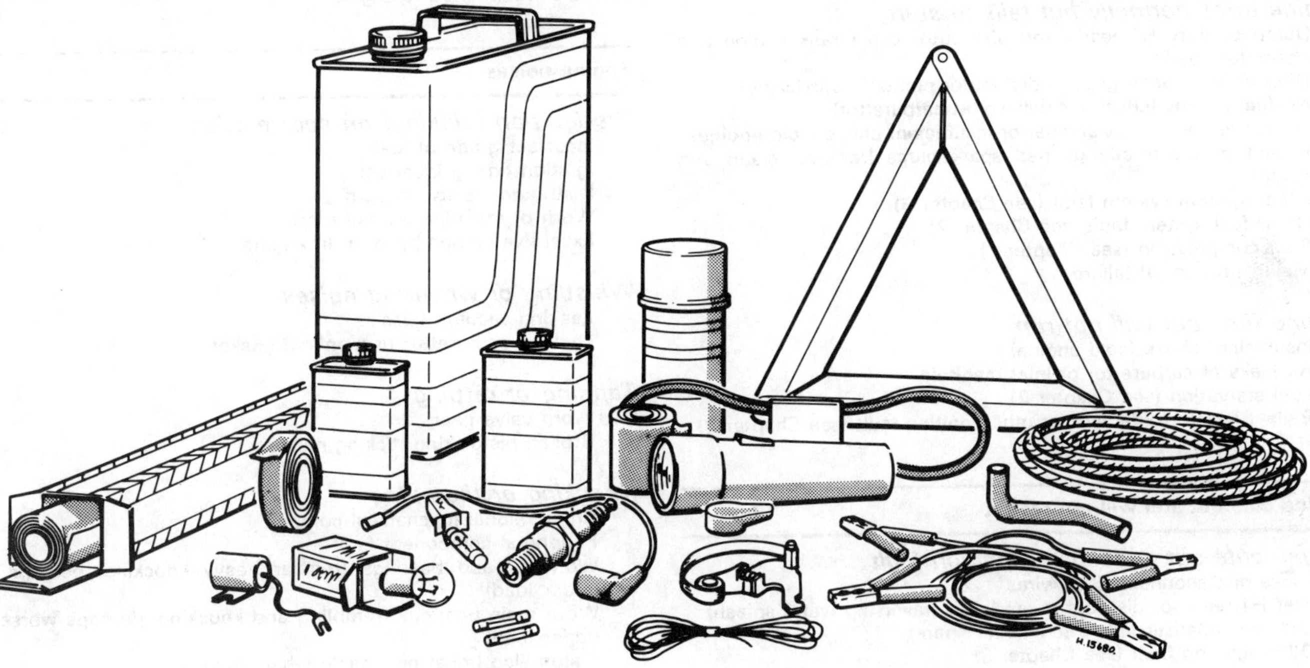

Carrying a few spares can save you a long walk!

When touring abroad it may be advisable to carry additional spares which, even if you cannot fit them yourself, could save having to wait while parts are obtained. The items below may be worth considering:

  Clutch and throttle cables
  Cylinder head gasket
  Alternator brushes
  Fuel pump repair kit
  Tyre valve core

One of the motoring organisations will be able to advise on availability of fuel etc in foreign countries.

Engine will not start

Engine fails to turn when starter operated
Flat battery (recharge, use jump leads, or push start)
Battery terminals loose or corroded
Battery earth to body defective
Engine earth strap loose or broken
Starter motor (or solenoid) wiring loose or broken
Automatic transmission selector in wrong position, or inhibitor switch faulty
Ignition/starter switch faulty
Major mechanical failure (seizure)
Starter or solenoid internal fault (see Chapter 10)

Starter motor turns engine slowly
Partially discharged battery (recharge, use jump leads, or push start)
Battery terminals loose or corroded
Battery earth to body defective
Engine earth strap loose
Starter motor (or solenoid) wiring loose
Starter motor internal fault (see Chapter 10)

Starter motor spins without turning engine
Flat battery
Starter motor pinion sticking on sleeve
Flywheel gear teeth damaged or worn
Starter motor mounting bolts loose

Engine turns normally but fails to start
Damp or dirty HT leads and distributor cap (crank engine and check for spark)
Dirty or incorrectly gapped distributor points (if applicable)
No fuel in tank (check for delivery at carburettor)
Excessive choke (hot engine) or insufficient choke (cold engine)
Fouled or incorrectly gapped spark plugs (remove, clean and regap)
Other ignition system fault (see Chapter 3)
Other fuel system fault (see Chapter 2)
Poor compression (see Chapter 1)
Major mechanical failure

Engine fires but will not run
Insufficient choke (cold engine)
Air leaks at carburettor or inlet manifold
Fuel starvation (see Chapter 2)
Ballast resistor defective, or other ignition fault (see Chapter 3)

Engine cuts out and will not restart

Engine cuts out suddenly — ignition fault
Loose or disconnected LT wires
Wet HT leads or distributor cap (after traversing water splash)
Coil or condenser failure (check for spark)
Other ignition fault (see Chapter 3)

Engine misfires before cutting out — fuel fault
Fuel tank empty
Fuel pump defective or filter blocked (check for delivery)
Fuel tank filler vent blocked (suction will be evident on releasing cap)
Carburettor needle valve sticking
Carburettor jets blocked (fuel contaminated)
Other fuel system fault (see Chapter 2)

Engine cuts out — other causes
Serious overheating
Major mechanical failure

Engine overheats

Ignition (no-charge) warning light illuminated
Slack or broken drivebelt — retension or renew (Chapter 10)

Ignition warning light not illuminated
Low oil level
Brakes binding
Ignition timing incorrect or automatic advance malfunctioning
Mixture too weak

Low engine oil pressure

Gauge reads low or warning light illuminated with engine running
Oil level low or incorrect grade
Defective gauge or sender unit
Wire to sender unit earthed
Engine overheating
Oil filter clogged or bypass valve defective
Oil pressure relief valve defective
Oil pick-up strainer clogged
Oil pump worn or mountings loose
Worn main or big-end bearings

Note: *Low oil pressure in a high-mileage engine at tickover is not necessarily a cause for concern. Sudden pressure loss at speed is far more significant. In any event, check the gauge or warning light sender before condemning the engine.*

Engine noises

Pre-ignition (pinking) on acceleration
Incorrect grade of fuel
Ignition timing incorrect
Distributor faulty or worn
Worn or maladjusted carburettor
Excessive carbon build-up in engine

Whistling or wheezing noises
Leaking vacuum hose
Leaking carburettor or manifold gasket

Tapping or rattling
Worn valve gear
Broken piston ring (ticking noise)

Knocking or thumping
Unintentional mechanical contact
Peripheral component fault
Worn big-end bearings (regular heavy knocking, perhaps less under load)
Worn main bearings (rumbling and knocking, perhaps worsening under load)
Piston slap (most noticeable when cold)

Chapter 1 Engine

Contents

Specifications

To avoid the risk of conversion inaccuracies, metric dimensions only are given

1.6 litre engine

General

Type	Four cylinder horizontally opposed overhead valve
Manufacturers code letters	CT
Bore	85.5 mm
Stroke	69.0 mm
Capacity	1584 cc
Compression ratio	7.4 : 1
Firing order	1–4–3–2

Crankshaft

Number of main bearings	4
Main bearing journal diameter:	
Nos 1, 2 and 3	54.97 to 54.99 mm
No 4	39.98 to 40.00 mm
Main journal minimum regrind diameter:	
Nos 1, 2 and 3	54.00 mm
No 4	39.00 mm
Main journal running clearance:	
Nos 1 and 3	0.04 to 0.10 mm
No 2	0.03 to 0.09 mm
No 4	0.05 to 0.10 mm
Crankpin journal diameter	54.98 to 55.00 mm
Crankpin journal running clearance	0.02 to 0.07 mm
Maximum ovality of journals	0.03 mm
Crankpin minimum regrind diameter	54.00 mm
Crankshaft endfloat	0.07 to 0.15 mm

Connecting rods

Type	Forged steel
Maximum endfloat on journal	0.7 mm
Crankpin maximum ovality	0.03 mm

Crankcase

Main bearing bore diameters:
Nos 1, 2 and 3	65.00 to 65.02 mm
No 4	50.00 to 50.03 mm
Camshaft bearing bore diameter	27.50 to 27.52 mm
Tappet bore diameters	19.00 to 19.03 mm

Camshaft and bearings

Bearing journal diameters	25.02 to 25.04 mm
Bearing journal running clearance	0.02 to 0.05 mm
Camshaft endfloat	0.16 mm maximum
Gear backlash	0 to 0.05 mm

Cylinders

Type	Single barrel finned cast iron
Oversizes	0.5 mm, 1.0 mm
Cylinder bore diameter:	
Standard:	
Blue	85.492 to 85.508 mm
Pink	85.502 to 85.518 mm
0.5 mm oversize:	
Blue	85.992 to 86.008 mm
Pink	86.002 to 86.018 mm
1.0 mm oversize:	
Blue	86.492 to 86.508 mm
Pink	86.502 to 86.518 mm

Pistons and rings

Maximum piston to cylinder bore clearance	0.2 mm
Maximum piston ring to groove clearance:	
Upper ring	0.12 mm
Lower ring	0.10 mm
Oil control ring	0.10 mm
Piston ring gaps:	
Upper ring	0.30 to 0.90 mm
Lower ring	0.30 to 0.90 mm
Oil control ring	0.25 to 0.95 mm
Piston oversizes	0.5 mm, 1.0 mm
Maximum weight variation between pistons	10g

Valves

Head diameter:	
Inlet	35.6 mm
Exhaust	30.1 mm
Stem diameter:	
Inlet	7.94 to 7.95 mm
Exhaust	8.91 to 8.92 mm
Maximum lateral rock in guide	1.2 mm
Valve seat angle	45°
Valve seat width	1.4 to 2.5 mm

Valve timing (at 1.0 mm valve lift)

Up to engine No CT 126491:	
Inlet opens	5° BTDC
Inlet closes	34° ABDC
Exhaust opens	38° BBDC
Exhaust closes	4° ATDC
From engine No CT 126492:	
Inlet opens	1° BTDC
Inlet closes	30° ABDC
Exhaust opens	36° BBDC
Exhaust closes	8° BTDC

Cooling system

Type	Ducted air
Thermostat length	46 mm at 85 to 90°C

Lubrication system

Oil pump type	Twin gear
Oil pump axial clearance	0.1 mm
Oil filter type	Full-flow renewable cartridge
Oil pressure at 80°C and 2000 rpm	2.0 bar minimum
Warning light switch operating pressure	0.15 to 0.45 bar
Oil capacity including filter	3.0 litre

2.0 litre engine
General
Type	Four cylinder horizontally opposed overhead valve
Manufacturers code letters	CU or CV
Bore	94.0 mm
Stroke	71.0 mm
Capacity	1970 cc
Compression ratio	7.4 : 1
Firing order	1–4–3–2

Crankshaft
Number of main bearings	4
Main bearing journal diameter:	
Nos 1, 2 and 3	59.97 to 59.99 mm
No 4	39.98 to 40.00 mm
Main journal running clearance:	
Nos 1 and 3	0.05 to 0.10 mm
No 2	0.03 to 0.09 mm
No 4	0.05 to 0.10 mm
Crankpin journal diameter	50.00 mm
Crankpin journal running clearance	0.02 to 0.07 mm
Maximum ovality of journals	0.03 mm
Crankshaft endfloat	0.07 to 0.15 mm

Connecting rods
Type	Forged steel
Maximum endfloat on journal	0.7 mm
Crankpin maximum ovality	0.03 mm

Crankcase
Main bearing bore diameters:	
Nos 1, 2 and 3	70.00 to 70.02 mm
No 4	50.00 to 50.03 mm
Camshaft bearing bore diameter	27.50 to 27.52 mm
Tappet bore diameter	23.96 to 23.98 mm

Camshaft and bearings
Bearing journal diameter	25.02 to 25.04 mm
Bearing journal running clearance	0.02 to 0.05 mm
Camshaft endfloat	0.16 mm maximum
Gear backlash	0 to 0.05 mm

Cylinders
Type	Single barrel finned cast iron
Oversizes	0.5 mm, 1.0 mm
Cylinder bore diameter:	
Standard:	
Blue	93.992 to 94.008 mm
Pink	94.002 to 94.018 mm
0.5 mm oversize:	
Blue	94.492 to 94.508 mm
Pink	94.502 to 94.518 mm
1.0 mm oversize:	
Blue	94.992 to 95.008 mm
Pink	95.002 to 95.018 mm

Pistons and rings
Maximum piston to cylinder bore clearance	0.2 mm
Maximum piston ring to groove clearance:	
Upper ring	0.12 mm
Lower and oil control rings	0.10 mm
Piston ring gaps:	
Upper and lower rings	0.40 to 0.90 mm
Oil control ring	0.25 to 0.95 mm
Piston oversizes	0.5 mm, 1.0 mm
Maximum weight variation between pistons	10g

Valves
Head diameter:	
Inlet	39.3 mm
Exhaust	33.0 mm
Stem diameter:	
Inlet	7.95 mm
Exhaust	8.92 mm
Maximum lateral rock in guide	1.2 mm

Valve seat angle:
  Inlet .... 29° 30'
  Exhaust .... 45°
Valve seat width .... 2.0 mm
Valve timing (at 1.0 mm lift):
  Inlet opens .... 2° BTDC
  Inlet closes .... 33° ABDC
  Exhaust opens .... 36° BBDC
  Exhaust closes .... 3° BTDC

Cooling system
  Type .... Ducted air
  Thermostat length .... 46 mm at 85 to 90°C

Lubrication system
  Oil pump type .... Twin gear
  Oil pump axial clearance .... 0.1 mm
  Oil filter type .... Full-flow renewable cartridge
  Oil pressure at 80°C and 2000 rpm .... 2.0 bar minimum
  Warning light switch operating pressure .... 0.15 to 0.45 bar
  Oil capacity including filter .... 3.5 litres

Torque wrench settings

	Nm	lbf ft
Engine to transmission	30	22
Engine bearer to chassis rails	25	18
Transmission mountings	30	22
Torque converter to driveplate	20	15
Fan housing to crankcase	20	15
Heat exchanger nuts	20	15
Intake manifolds to cylinder heads	20	15
Oil cooler nuts	8	6
Oil filter housing (2.0 litre engine)	25	18
Oil filler tube nuts	20	15
Engine bearer mounting bracket to crankcase	45	33
Engine bearer to rubber mountings	45	33
Rubber mountings to mounting bracket	20	15
Crankcase halves:		
M8 nuts	20	15
M10 nuts	30	22
M12 nuts	35	26
Fan hub to crankshaft:		
1.6 litre engine	350	258
2.0 litre engine	30	22
Flywheel to crankshaft:		
1.6 litre engine	350	258
2.0 litre engine	110	81
Torque converter driveplate to crankshaft	90	66
Cylinder head retaining nuts:		
1.6 litre engine	25	18
2.0 litre engine	30	22
Rocker shaft to cylinder head:		
1.6 litre engine	25	18
2.0 litre engine	15	11
Connecting rod big-end cap nuts	35	26
Oil pump housing to crankcase	25	18
Oil pressure relief valve to crankcase	20	15
Oil strainer to crankcase:		
1.6 litre engine	8	6
2.0 litre engine	13	10
Oil drain plug (2.0 litre engine)	25	18

1 General description

The 1.6 litre and 2.0 litre engines are of air cooled, four cylinder horizontally opposed configuration mounted behind the transmission at the rear of the vehicle. Both engines are of the same basic layout apart from the different positions of certain engine ancillaries and other minor variations.

The crankcase is of split configuration with detachable cylinder barrels. The crankshaft is supported at the crankcase join in four main bearings. Crankshaft endfloat is controlled by shims fitted between the flywheel and No 1 crankshaft main bearing.

The connecting rods are attached to the crankshaft by split shell type big-end bearings and to the pistons by fully floating gudgeon pins.

The aluminium alloy pistons are of the slipper type and are fitted with three piston rings, two compression rings and an oil control ring.

The camshaft is gear driven from the crankshaft and operates the rocker arms via pushrods and hydraulic tappets. The inlet and exhaust valves are each closed by a single valve spring and operate in guides pressed into the cylinder head.

Engine lubrication is by a gear type oil pump driven by the camshaft. An oil cooler, full flow filter, oil strainer and pressure relief valve are included in the lubrication system.

Engine cooling is by ducted air generated by a fan attached to the crankshaft. Sheet metal panels are used to direct the air around the various parts of the engine. A thermostat connected by a cable to twin air flaps diverts the air flow when the engine is cold to reduce warm up time.

2 Maintenance and inspection

1 At the intervals specified in Routine Maintenance at the beginning of this manual, carry out the following service operations on the engine.

2 Visually inspect the engine joint faces, gaskets and seals for any signs of oil leaks or deterioration. Pay particular attention to the areas around the rocker covers, cylinder heads, pushrod tubes and the crankcase joint. Rectify any leaks by referring to the appropriate Sections of this Chapter.

3 To drain the oil on 1.6 litre engines, place a suitable container beneath the crankcase and slacken the six oil strainer retaining bolts.

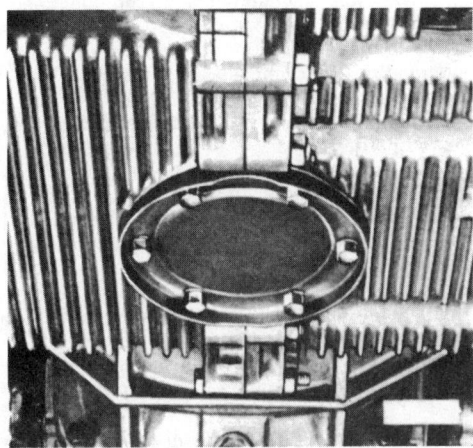

Fig. 1.1 Oil strainer retaining bolts – 1.6 litre engines (Sec 2)

Remove all but one bolt. Prise the strainer down on the side opposite the remaining bolt and allow the oil to drain. After draining remove the strainer plate and the strainer, and clean the strainer thoroughly. Clean the mating faces and refit using new gaskets.

4 To drain the oil on 2.0 litre engines, undo the drain plug on the crankcase and allow the oil to drain into a suitable container (photo). Renew the sealing washer on the drain plug if necessary and refit the plug after the oil has drained. At the intervals specified, undo the bolt in the centre of the strainer plate, remove the plate and take out the

2.4 Oil drain plug (A) and strainer retaining bolt (B) on 2.0 litre engines

strainer. Clean the strainer thoroughly and refit the assembly using new gaskets after cleaning all the mating faces.

5 On all engines the oil filter should be removed, using a strap or chain wrench, and discarded. Lubricate the rubber sealing ring of a new filter with clean engine oil and fit the filter, tightening it by hand only (photo). Do not use any tools.

2.5 Fitting a new oil filter

6 Refill the engine using the correct grade of oil through the extendible filler neck, accessible from behind the number plate. Fill until the level is nearly to the MAX mark on the dipstick then screw the cap on the filler neck securely. Start the engine, check for leaks then switch off. After allowing the oil to settle, recheck the level and top up if necessary. Maintain the level between the MIN and MAX marks on the dipstick at all times.

7 The cork rocker cover gaskets should be renewed at the specified intervals or sooner if they show any sign of leakage.

3 Major operations possible with the engine in the vehicle

The configuration of the engine and its location in the vehicle are such that very little major work can be done with the engine in place. It is possible however to remove all the various electrical, ignition and fuel system components as well as some parts of the exhaust system and these procedures are covered in the relevant Chapters of this manual. Apart from that it is recommended that the engine be removed for all other major operations. Fortunately this is not as difficult a task as on some vehicles and the power unit can be removed relatively easily.

4 Methods of engine removal

The engine is removed by lowering it out of the engine compartment and this may be done in unit with the transmission, or by leaving the transmission in the vehicle. A sturdy hydraulic trolley jack or an engine crane will be needed whichever method is adopted.

5 Engine (without manual or automatic transmission) – removal and refitting

1 Disconnect the battery negative terminal.

2 Refer to Chapter 2 and remove the air cleaner assembly.

3 Disconnect the wiring plug at the rear of the alternator and the additional wire at the in-line connector (where fitted) (photo).

5.3 Alternator wiring in-line connector

10 On engines with fuel injection, disconnect the control unit wiring plug, the right-hand wiring plug at the front bulkhead double relay, the resistor multi-plugs and the deceleration valve hose. On vehicles for California, disconnect the wire for the oxygen sensor.

11 On vehicles with automatic transmission remove the plug at the top of the crankcase, turn the engine as necessary until each torque converter retaining bolt is accessible and remove the three bolts.

12 Remove the transmission fluid dipstick and the dipstick tube grommet on vehicles with automatic transmission.

13 Jack up the rear of the vehicle and support it on axle stands.

14 Undo the two upper nuts securing the crankcase to the transmission bellhousing. Hold the bolts from below to stop them turning.

15 On engines with carburettor induction, disconnect the fuel inlet pipe from the pump and where applicable the return pipe from the carburettor. Plug the pipes after removal.

16 On engines with fuel injection, clamp the fuel feed hose and disconnect it from the fuel rail at the connection just in front of the engine bulkhead. Similarly disconnect the return hose from the pressure regulator. Both these hoses are accessible from below the vehicle.

17 Disconnect the wiring from the starter solenoid, release the cable ties and move the harness clear.

18 On 1.6 litre engines mark the position of the heater flap control cables in their cable connectors and disconnect them. Slacken the clips and detach the heater hoses. On 2.0 litre engines, slacken the heater flap housing clamp bolts and detach the housings (photo).

19 On vehicles with automatic transmission, disconnect the throttle rod at the gearbox lever.

4   Remove the engine oil dipstick.

5   Remove the throttle return spring then disconnect the accelerator cable from the throttle linkage (photo). Refer to Chapter 2 if necessary.

6   Remove the heater blower rubber bellows.

7   Detach the brake vacuum servo hose at the left-hand inlet manifold.

8   Disconnect the wiring at the ignition coil positive terminal and at the oil pressure switch.

9   Where applicable disconnect the wiring plugs at the ignition control unit and idle stabilizing unit.

20 Using a hydraulic trolley jack, a crane or other suitable equipment, support the engine and just take its weight.

21 Using a second jack, support the transmission centrally.

22 Undo the two nuts on the engine to transmission lower retaining studs (photo).

23 Undo the nut and remove the long bolt securing the transmission bracket to the rubber mounting.

24 Undo the two bolts each side securing the engine bearer to the chassis rails (photo).

5.5 Throttle return spring location

5.18 2.0 litre engine heater flap housing clamp bolt (arrowed)

5.22 Engine to transmission lower retaining nuts (arrowed)

5.24 Engine bearer retaining bolt

5.25 Withdrawing the engine from the transmission

5.26 Engine removed from under vehicle

25 Lower the engine and transmission assembly approximately 80 mm (3 in). Check that all cables, pipes and attachments in the engine compartment are clear and then carefully ease the engine rearward off the transmission (photo). On vehicles with automatic transmission, ensure that the torque converter remains on the transmission.

26 Continue lowering the engine and then withdraw it from under the rear of the vehicle (photo).

27 Refitting the engine is the reverse sequence to removal, but bear in mind the following points:

(a) On vehicles with manual transmission, lubricate the transmission input shaft sparingly with molybdenum disulphide grease

(b) On vehicles with automatic transmission check that the torque converter is properly seated as described in Chapter 6 before the engine is fitted

(c) Adjust the accelerator linkage as described in Chapter 2

(d) Tighten all nuts and bolts to the specified torque where applicable

Fig. 1.4 Engine wiring and component attachments – 1.6 litre engines (Sec 5)

4	Fuel inlet pipe	7	Ignition coil wiring
5	Fuel return pipe	8	Servo vacuum hose
6	Oil pressure switch		

Fig. 1.2 Engine wiring and component attachments – 2.0 litre engines with fuel injection (Sec 5)

| 4 | Heater blower bellows | 6 | Control unit wiring plug |
| 5 | Alternator wiring in-line connector | 7 | Dipstick |

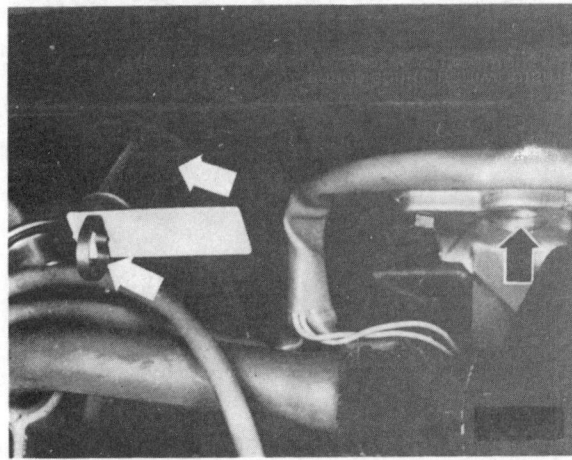

Fig. 1.5 Automatic transmission fluid dipstick and filler tube grommet (white arrows), and torque converter access plug (black arrow) (Sec 5)

Fig. 1.3 Engine electrical and related attachments – 2.0 litre engines with fuel injection (Sec 5)

| 11 | Double relay wiring plugs | A | Series resistance connector |
| | | B | Air valve |

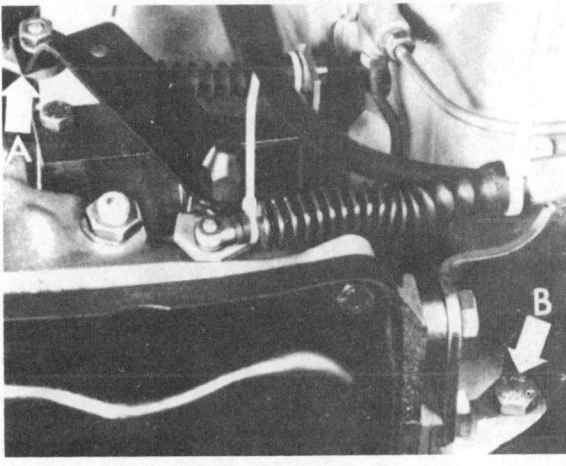

Fig. 1.6 Automatic transmission throttle rod attachment (A) and mounting bolt (B) (Sec 5)

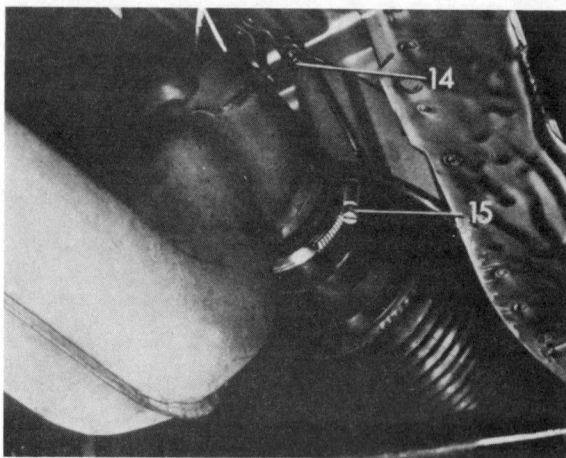

Fig. 1.7 Heater flap control cable (14) and hose connection (15) –
1.6 litre engines (Sec 5)

Fig. 1.8 Fuel feed hose connection (15) and starter solenoid wiring
(16) – 2.0 litre engines with fuel injection (Sec 5)

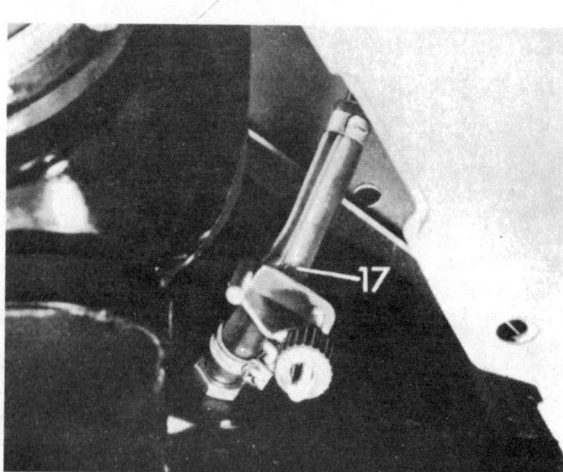

Fig. 1.9 Fuel return hose with clamp in place (17) – 2.0 litre
engines with fuel injection (Sec 5)

6   Engine (with manual or automatic transmission) – removal and refitting

1   Refer to Section 5 and carry out the operations described in paragraphs 1 to 18 with the exception of paragraphs 11 and 14.
2   Undo the socket-headed bolts securing the driveshaft inner constant velocity joints to the differential drive flanges. Move the driveshafts clear and tie them up so they do not hang unsupported.
3   On vehicles with cable operated clutches, undo the clutch cable wing nut and the two bolts securing the cable bracket to the transmission.
4   On vehicles with hydraulically operated clutches, detach the hydraulic pipe support bracket from the side of the transmission and

Fig. 1.10 Solenoid wiring (5) and driveshaft retaining bolts (6)
(Sec 6)

Fig. 1.11 Transmission attachments (Sec 6)

8	Reversing light wires	10	Earth strap
9	Gearshift guide pin retaining nut	11	Transmission mounting bolts

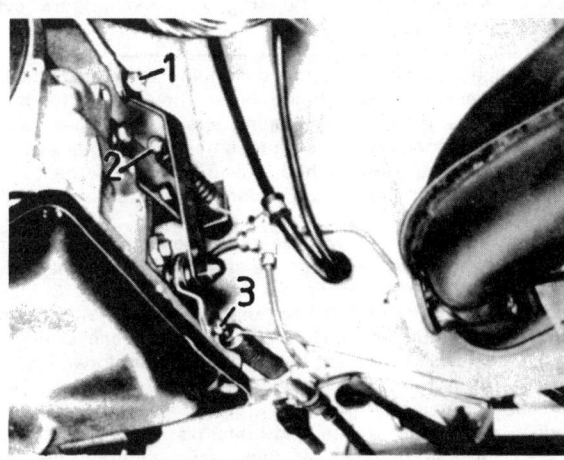

Fig. 1.12 Throttle rod (1) accelerator cable (2) and selector cable (3) at the automatic transmission (Sec 6)

undo the two clutch slave cylinder retaining nuts and bolts. Move the cylinder with hydraulic pipe and hose still attached, to one side.
5   On vehicles with automatic transmission remove the throttle rod, accelerator cable and selector cable from the gearbox lever. Also remove the selector lever from the side of the transmission. Remove the two bolts and move the selector cable and support bracket to one side.
6   On vehicles with manual transmission undo the retaining nut, move the guide pin forward and remove the gearshift rod from the transmission linkage.
7   On all vehicles, undo the bolt and remove the earth strap from the mounting bracket.
8   Where fitted disconnect the two reversing light wires from the switch (photo).

6.8 Reversing light wire locations (arrowed)

9   Using a hydraulic trolley jack in conjunction with a crane or other suitable equipment, take the weight of the engine and transmission assembly.
10 Undo the nut and remove the long bolt securing the transmission bracket to the rubber mounting.
11 Undo the two bolts each side securing the engine bearer to the chassis rails.

12 Check that all cables, pipes and attachments are well clear then slowly lower the engine and transmission assembly to the ground. Withdraw the unit from under the rear of the vehicle.
13 Refitting is the reverse sequence to removal bearing in mind the following points:

(a) Renew the engine bearer self-locking bolts
(b) Adjust the accelerator linkage and selector linkage if necessary, referring to Chapters 2 and 6 respectively
(c) Adjust the clutch cable, where applicable, as described in Chapter 4
(d) Tighten all retaining nuts and bolts to the specified torque where applicable

7   Engine and transmission assembly – separation and attachment

1   If the engine is to be separated from the transmission after removal as a complete assembly proceed as follows according to transmission type.

Manual transmission
2   This is simply a matter of undoing the two upper and two lower retaining nuts and withdrawing the transmission from the engine.
3   Before refitting lightly lubricate the input shaft splines with molybdenum disulphide grease.
4   Refit the two units and secure with the nuts tightened to the specified torque.

Automatic transmission
5   Remove the plug at the top of the crankcase, turn the engine as necessary until each torque converter retaining bolt is accessible through the plug hole then remove the three bolts.
6   Undo the four nuts securing the transmission to the engine and separate the two units. Make sure that the torque converter remains on the transmission.
7   Refitting is the reverse sequence to removal, but check that the torque converter is properly seated as described in Chapter 6 before fitting and tighten the nuts and bolts to the specified torque.

8   Engine dismantling and overhaul – general

1   If the engine has been removed for major overhaul or if individual components have been removed for repair or renewal, observe the following general hints on dismantling and reassembly.
2   Drain the oil into a suitable container and then thoroughly clean the exterior of the engine using a degreasing solvent or paraffin. Clean away as much of the external dirt and grease as possible before dismantling.
3   As parts are removed, clean them in a paraffin bath. However, do not immerse parts with internal oilways in paraffin as it is difficult to remove, usually requiring a high pressure hose. Clean oilways with nylon pipe cleaners.
4   Avoid working with the engine or any of the components directly on a concrete floor, as grit presents a real source of trouble.
5   Wherever possible work should be carried out with the engine or individual components on a strong bench. If the work must be done on the floor, cover it with a board or sheets of newspaper.
6   Have plenty of clean, lint-free rags available and also some containers or trays to hold small items. This will help during reassembly and also prevent possible losses.
7   Always obtain a complete set of new gaskets if the engine is being completely dismantled, or all those necessary for the individual component or assembly being worked on. Keep the old gaskets with a view to using them as a pattern to make a replacement if a new one is not available.
8   When possible refit nuts, bolts and washers in their locations after removal as this helps to protect the threads and avoids confusion or loss.
9   During reassembly thoroughly lubricate all the components, where this is applicable, with engine oil, but avoid contaminating the gaskets and joint mating faces.

10 When starting the engine after overhaul or repair to a major component, be prepared for some odd smells and smoke from parts getting hot and burning off oil deposits.

11 If new pistons, rings or crankshaft bearings have been fitted, the engine must be run-in for the first 500 miles (800 km). Do not exceed 45 mph (72 kph), operate the engine at full throttle or allow it to labour in any gear.

9 Engine ancillary components – removal

1 Before major dismantling begins the externally mounted ancillary components should be removed as follows.

2 Remove the clutch assembly, alternator, mechanical fuel pump and distributor by referring to the appropriate Chapters of this manual.

3 Note the location of the various wiring looms, tag each lead then disconnect and removal all the engine wiring.

4 On 1.6 litre engines undo the nuts securing the inlet manifold to the cylinder heads and remove the manifolds complete with carburettor.

5 On 2.0 litre engines with carburettor induction, detach the main vacuum pipe from the connections on the inlet manifold and crankcase (photo). Disconnect the throttle linkage at the carburettor ball sockets, move the connecting rod to one side and detach it from the carburettors. Recover the spring and spring seat (photos). Undo the retaining nuts and remove both inlet manifolds complete with carburettors (photo).

6 On 2.0 litre engines with fuel injection undo the retaining nuts and remove the manifold tubes and intake air distributor as a complete assembly.

7 The exhaust silencer should now be removed by referring to Chapter 2 for details of the various types. Depending on engine, greater access may be gained by removing some or all of the rear cover plates (photos).

10 Engine cooling ducts, fan housing, heat exchangers, cylinder heads and pistons – removal

1 The engine cooling ducts are something of a puzzle and vary considerably depending on engine type. They are not difficult to remove being retained with self-tapping screws and one or two bolts, but the actual positioning of the flanges needs to be carefully noted. Some overlap, some are attached individually and some cannot be removed even with all the screws undone until all the adjoining ducts are taken off.

2 The best approach is to remove all the screws, noting where any additional brackets, clips or fittings are attached and take each duct off in turn. Note how the ducts overlap as they are removed.

3 Remove the fan by undoing the three bolts and withdrawing the unit from the fan hub (photo). On 2.0 litre engines recover the spacer.

4 On 1.6 litre engines the fan hub should be withdrawn next before the fan housing is removed. To do this, undo the retaining bolt and draw off the hub using a puller.

5 Undo the fan housing retaining bolts, disconnect the thermostat cable from the fan housing air flaps and withdraw the housing (photos).

6 Undo the bolts securing the engine bearer mounting bracket to the crankcase and the bolts securing the bearer to the bracket. Remove the engine bearer followed by the mounting bracket (photos).

7 With the fan housing and engine bearer removed, more of the cooling ducts, cover plates and connecting elbows can be removed.

8 When access permits, the heat exchangers can be removed. Note their position and arrangement.

9 At a convenient stage in the dismantling, undo the bolts and remove the oil filler tube.

10 Undo the three nuts and lift off the oil cooler. Recover the sealing rings. On 1.6 litre engines also withdraw the spacer and gasket (photos).

11 On 2.0 litre engines undo the nuts and remove the oil filter housing (photo).

9.5A Disconnect the vacuum pipe connections (arrowed)

9.5B Move the throttle linkage connecting rod to one side ...

9.5C ... and recover the spring and seat from the ball stud

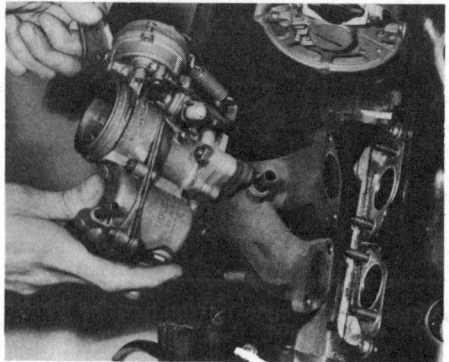

9.5D Remove the carburettors complete with manifolds

9.7A Remove the rear ...

9.7B ... and side cover plates

10.3 Removing the fan

10.5A Fan housing retaining bolts

10.5B Thermostat cable connection (arrowed) on fan housing

10.6A Remove the retaining bolts ...

10.6B ... and withdraw the engine bearer and mounting bracket

10.10A Undo the oil cooler retaining nuts ...

10.10B ... and slide the oil cooler off the studs

10.11 Removing the oil filter housing

10.14 Rocker shaft support retaining nuts (arrowed)

10.16 Removing the pushrod tubes

10.17 Cylinder head lower cover plate

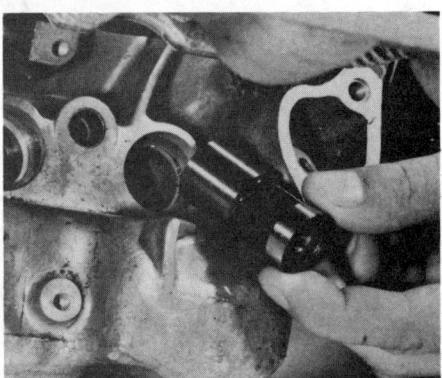

10.18 Keep the hydraulic tappets in order and upright after removal

12 Using a tapered dowel rod, withdraw the distributor driveshaft, noting that there is a small spring in its centre.
13 Spring back the retaining clamp and lift off the rocker covers.
14 Undo the rocker shaft support retaining nuts, lift away the pushrod tube retaining wire on 2.0 litre engines and remove the rocker shaft assemblies (photo).
15 Lift out the pushrods, keeping them in order.

16 The pushrod tubes can now be withdrawn upwards through the cylinder head openings (photo).
17 Remove the cover plate from the underside of the cylinder head and crankcase (photo).
18 Carefully withdraw the hydraulic tappets from their bores and store them in strict order in a vertical position, with their base downwards (photo).

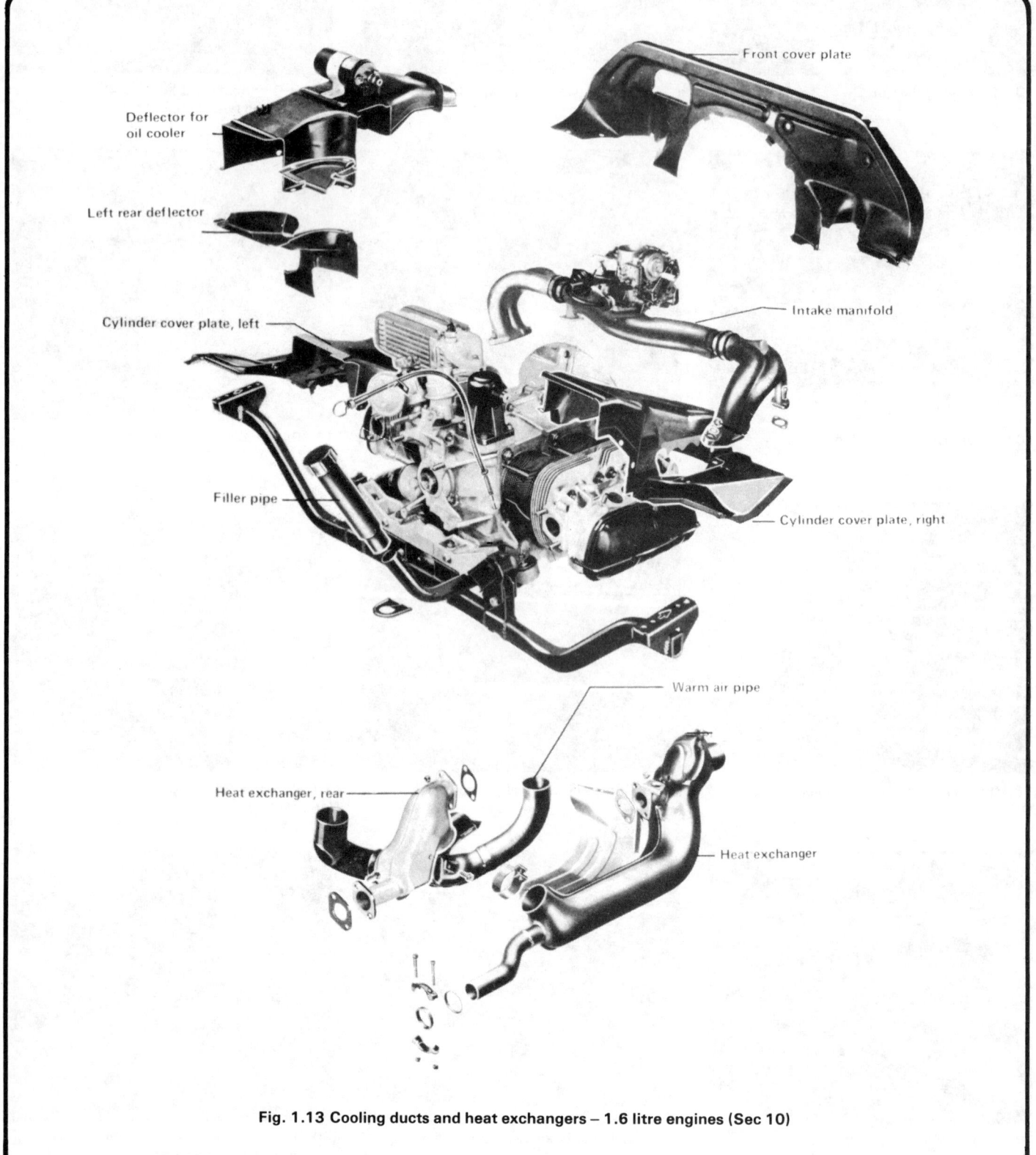

Fig. 1.13 Cooling ducts and heat exchangers – 1.6 litre engines (Sec 10)

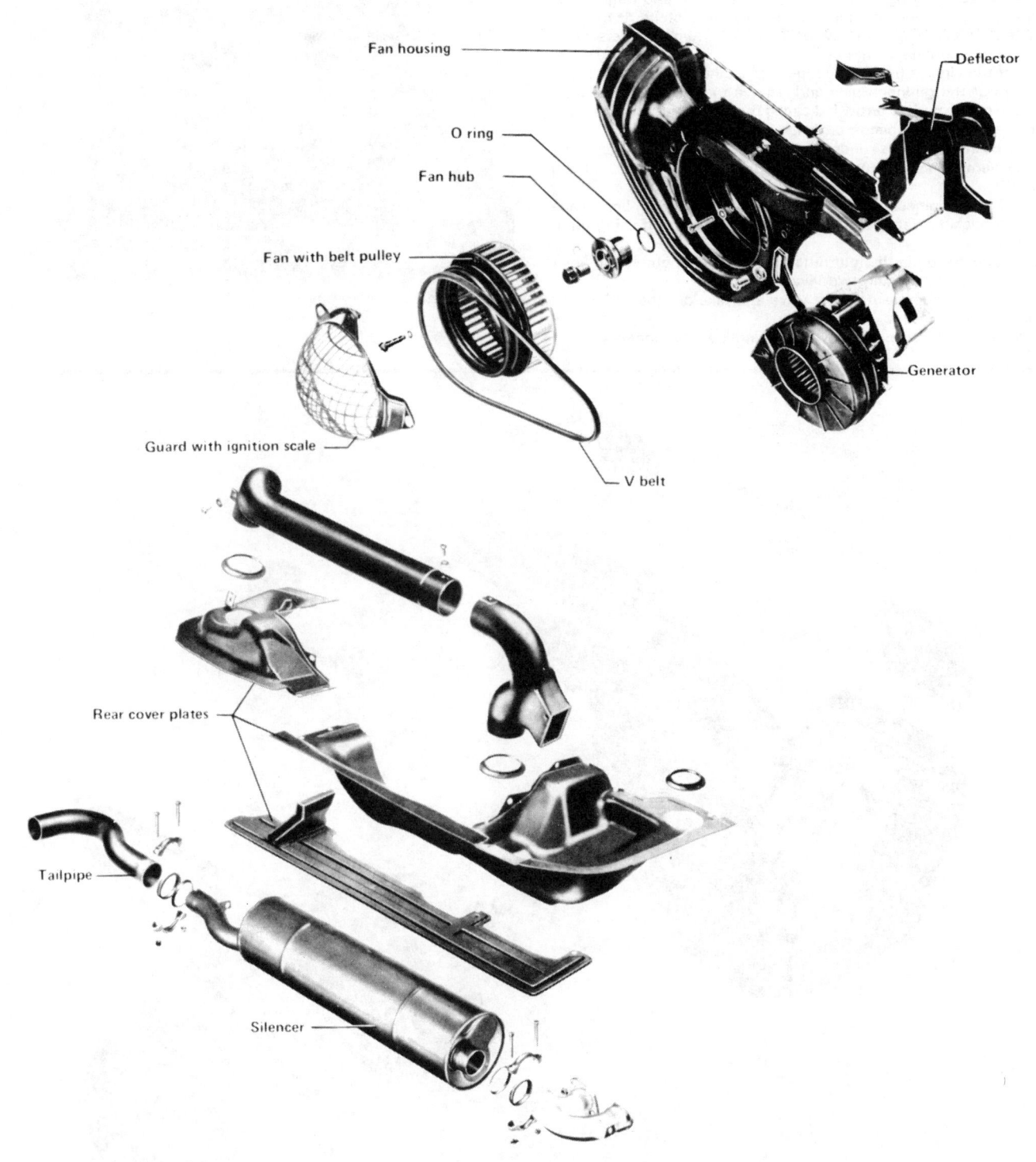

Fan housing

Deflector

O ring

Fan hub

Fan with belt pulley

Generator

Guard with ignition scale

V belt

Rear cover plates

Tailpipe

Silencer

Fig. 1.14 Fan housing and related components – 1.6 litre engines (Sec 10)

19 Slacken the cylinder head nuts in the reverse order to that shown in Fig. 1.35. Remove the nuts and withdraw the head from the studs and cylinder barrels (photo).

20 Repeat the removal procedure for the remaining cylinder head.

21 Remove the nuts or bolts and withdraw the thermostat and bracket from the crankcase, if still in position.

22 Note the sealing ring at the top of each cylinder and remove it.

23 Mark the cylinders and their corresponding pistons 1 to 4 as applicable then carefully withdraw each cylinder. Recover the second sealing ring at the base of the cylinder.

24 Extract the circlips from the gudgeon pins and holding the pistons firmly, tap out the gudgeon pins and remove the pistons. Make sure each piston has a mark or arrow indicating the side facing the flywheel, if not make one on the piston crown.

25 On 1.6 litre engines undo the four nuts and withdraw the crankcase ventilation housing with O-ring seal from the top of the crankcase.

26 On 2.0 litre engines undo the fan hub central retaining bolt, place three metal packing pieces behind the hub and draw it off using three bolts (photo).

27 On all engines undo the four nuts securing the oil pump and lever off the pump carefully using two levers (photo).

28 Unscrew the oil pressure relief valve and take out the spring and plunger.

29 Remove the oil strainer cover and oil strainer components.

10.19 Cylinder head removal

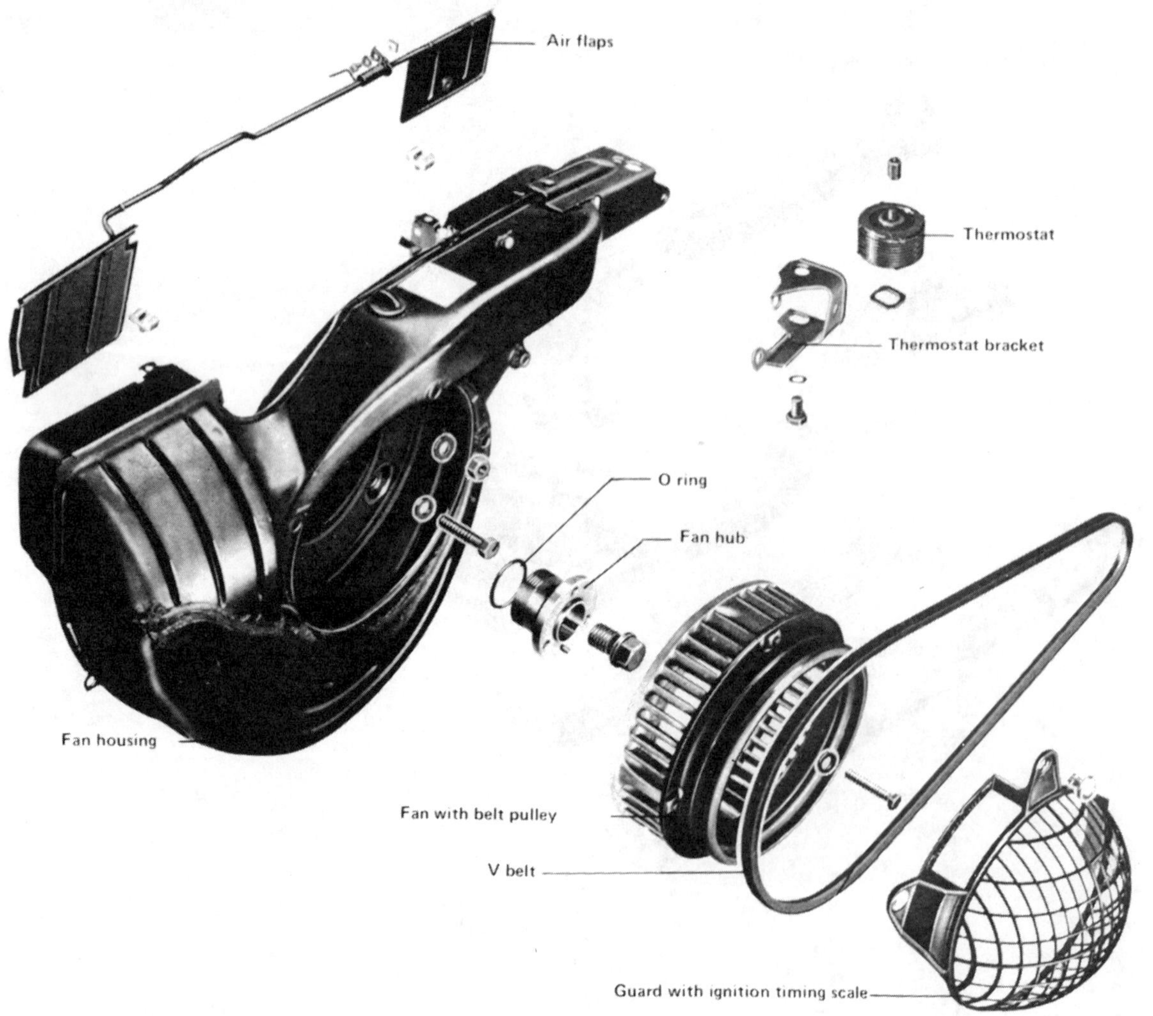

Air flaps

Thermostat

Thermostat bracket

O ring

Fan hub

Fan housing

Fan with belt pulley

V belt

Guard with ignition timing scale

Fig. 1.15 Cooling system components – 1.6 litre engines (Sec 10)

10.26 Using bolts and packing pieces to remove the fan hub

10.27 Use two levers carefully to remove the oil pump

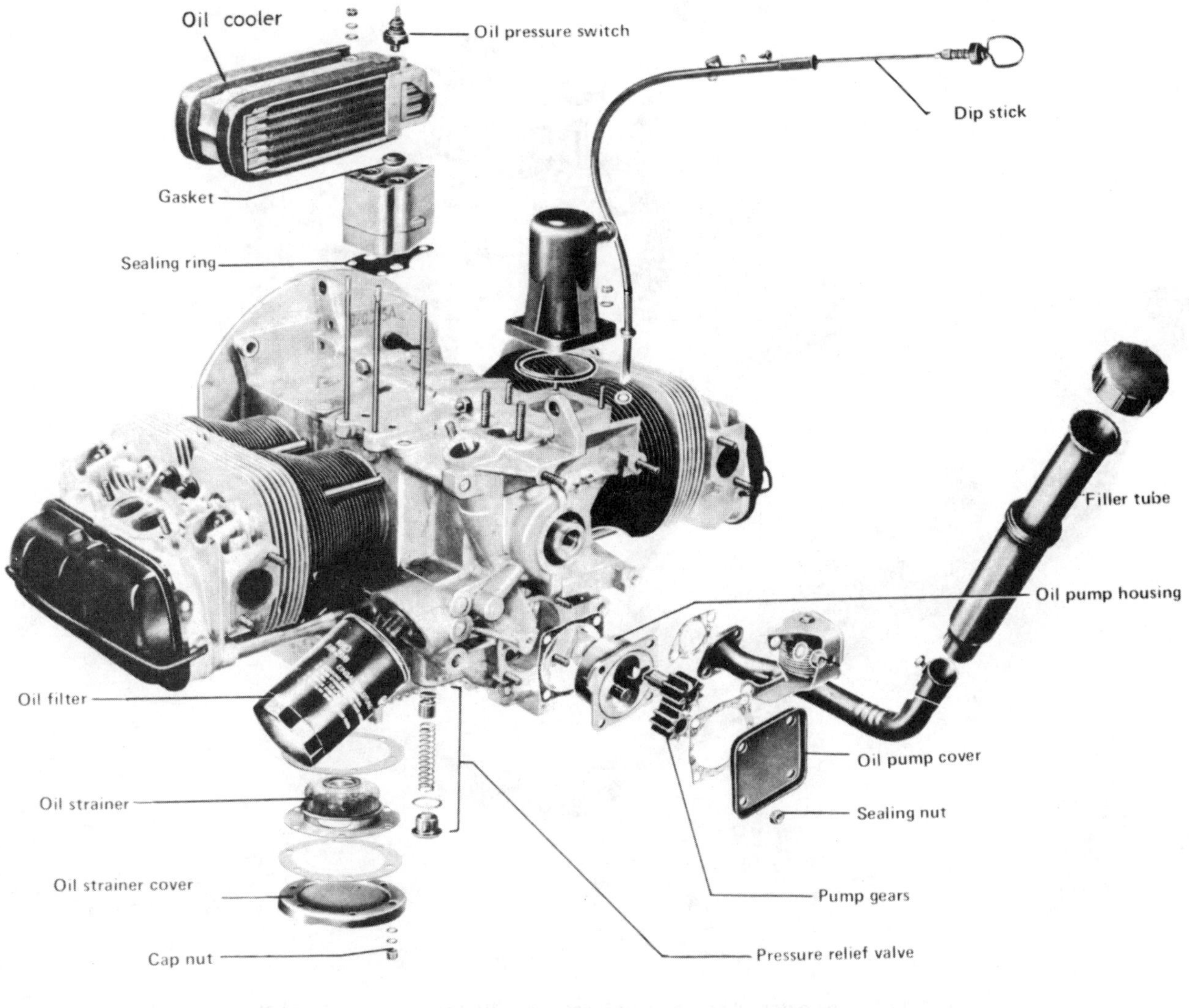

Oil cooler

Oil pressure switch

Dip stick

Gasket

Sealing ring

Filler tube

Oil pump housing

Oil filter

Oil strainer

Oil pump cover

Sealing nut

Oil strainer cover

Pump gears

Cap nut

Pressure relief valve

Fig. 1.16 Lubrication system components – 1.6 litre engines (Sec 10)

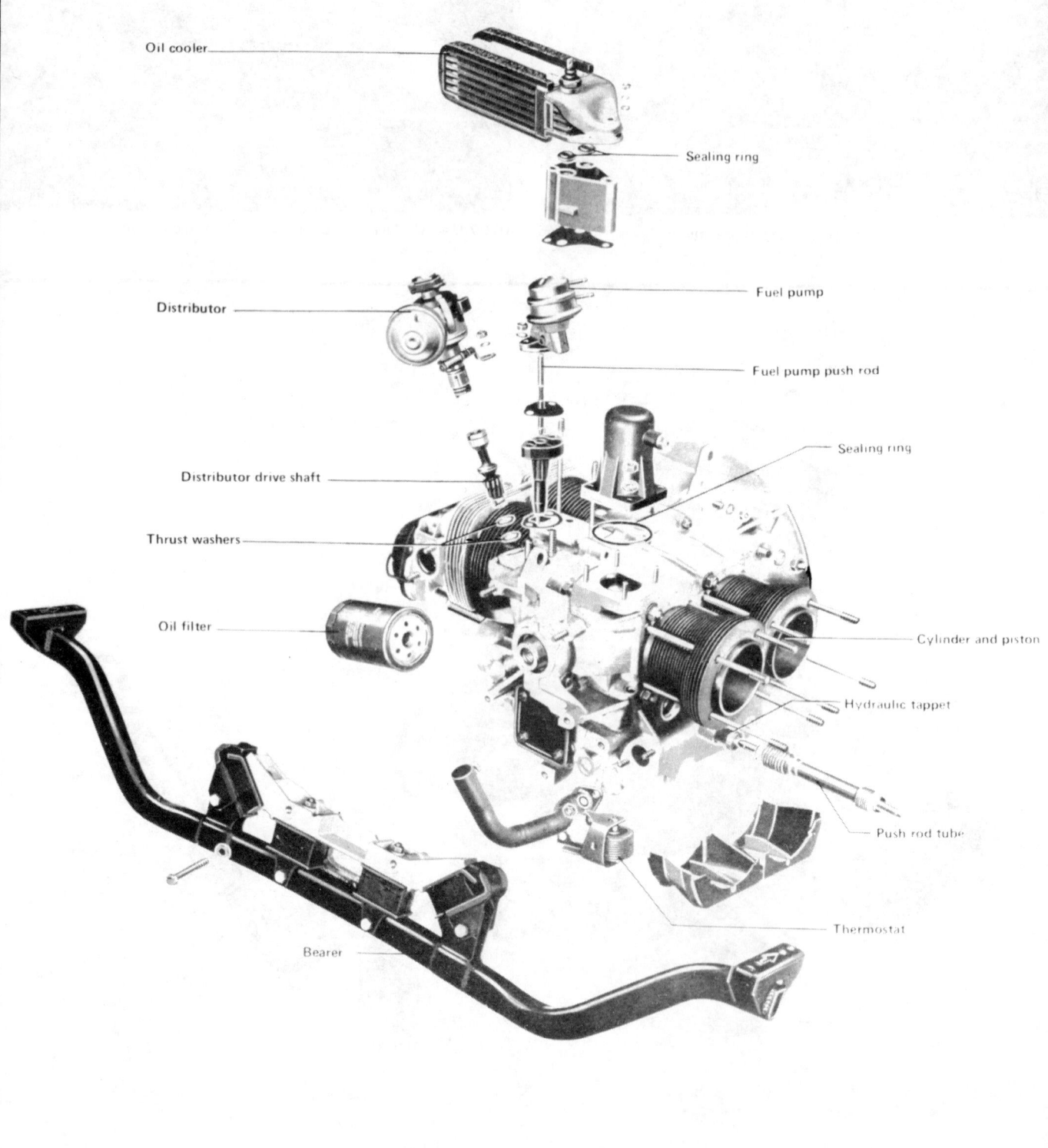

Oil cooler

Sealing ring

Distributor

Fuel pump

Fuel pump push rod

Distributor drive shaft

Sealing ring

Thrust washers

Oil filter

Cylinder and piston

Hydraulic tappet

Push rod tube

Thermostat

Bearer

Fig. 1.17 Engine external component locations – 1.6 litre engines (Sec 10)

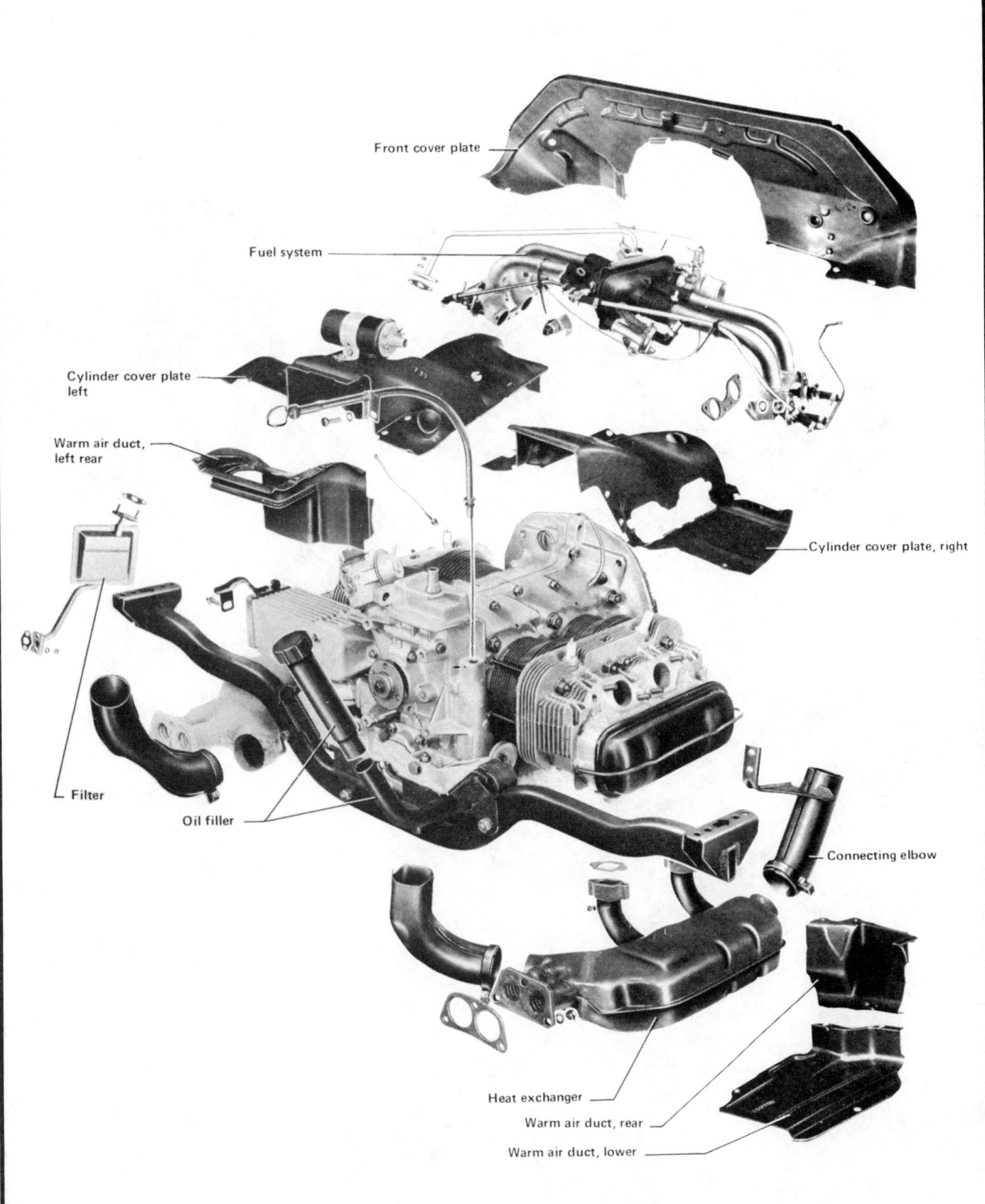

Front cover plate

Fuel system

Cylinder cover plate left

Warm air duct, left rear

Cylinder cover plate, right

Filter

Oil filler

Connecting elbow

Heat exchanger

Warm air duct, rear

Warm air duct, lower

Fig. 1.18 Cooling ducts and heat exchangers – 2.0 litre engines (Sec 10)

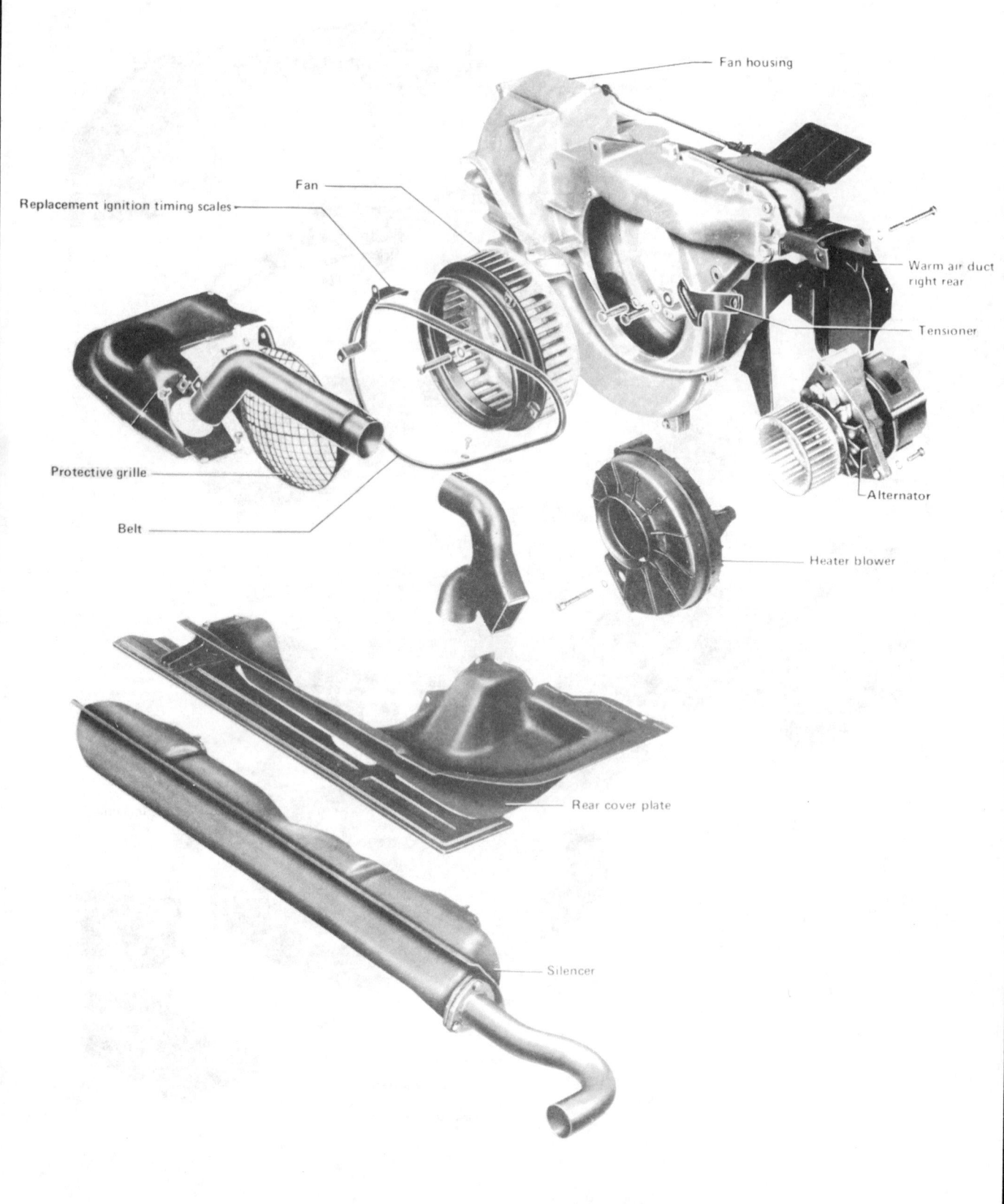

Fan housing

Replacement ignition timing scales

Fan

Warm air duct right rear

Tensioner

Protective grille

Alternator

Belt

Heater blower

Rear cover plate

Silencer

Fig. 1.19 Fan housing and related components – 2.0 litre engines (Sec 10)

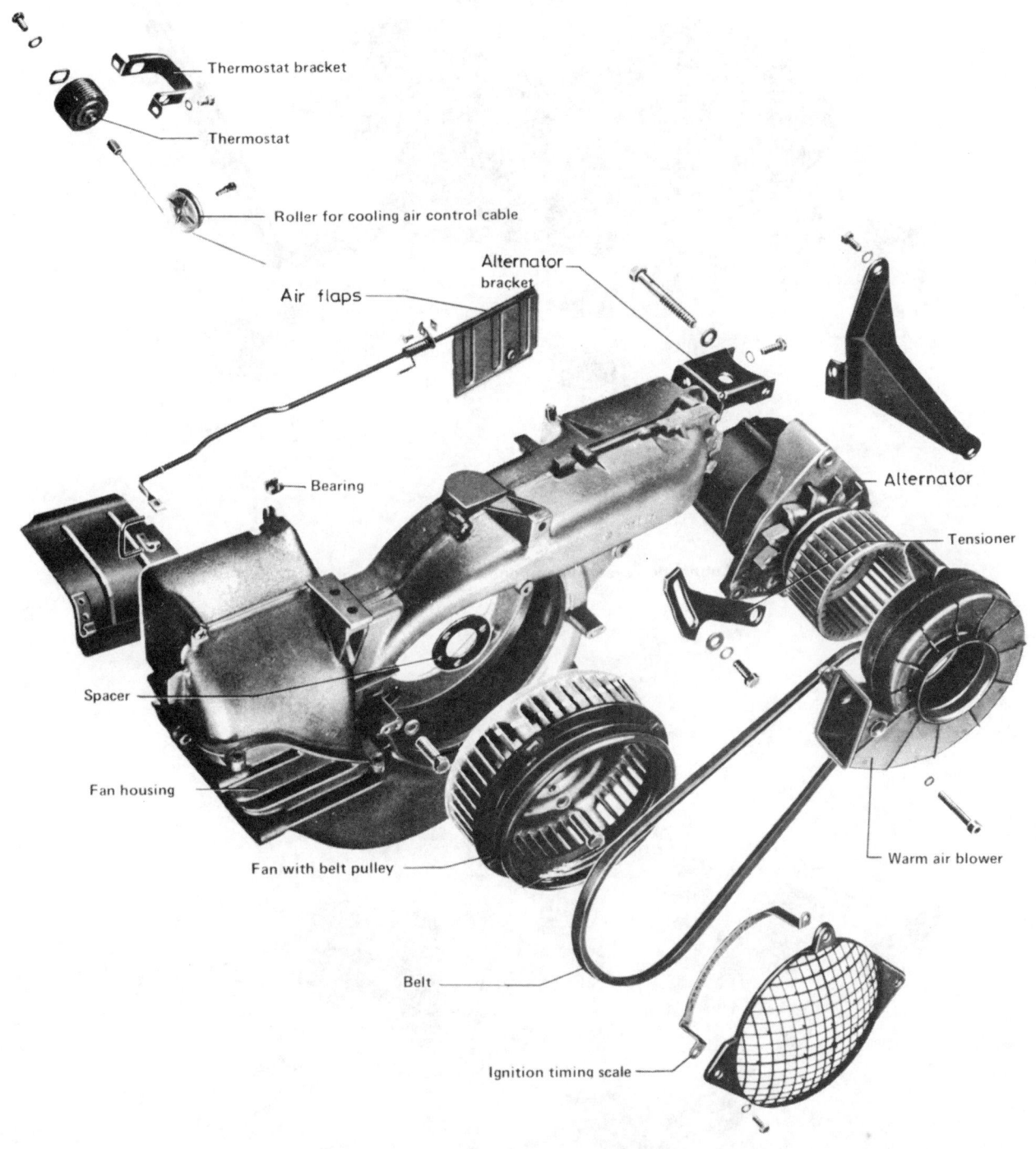

Thermostat bracket

Thermostat

Roller for cooling air control cable

Air flaps

Alternator bracket

Alternator

Bearing

Tensioner

Spacer

Fan housing

Fan with belt pulley

Warm air blower

Belt

Ignition timing scale

Fig. 1.20 Cooling system components – 2.0 litre engines (Sec 10)

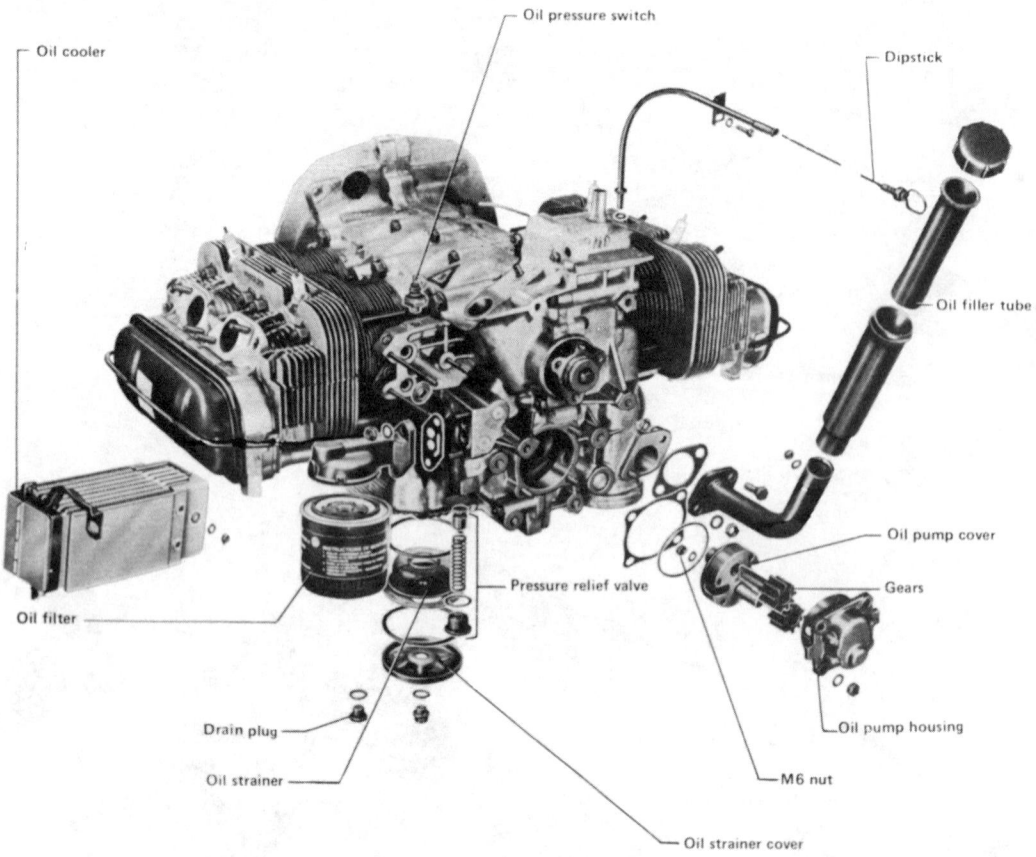

Oil cooler

Oil pressure switch

Dipstick

Oil filler tube

Oil pump cover

Gears

Pressure relief valve

Oil filter

Oil pump housing

Drain plug

Oil strainer

M6 nut

Oil strainer cover

Fig. 1.21 Lubrication system components – 2.0 litre engines (Sec 10)

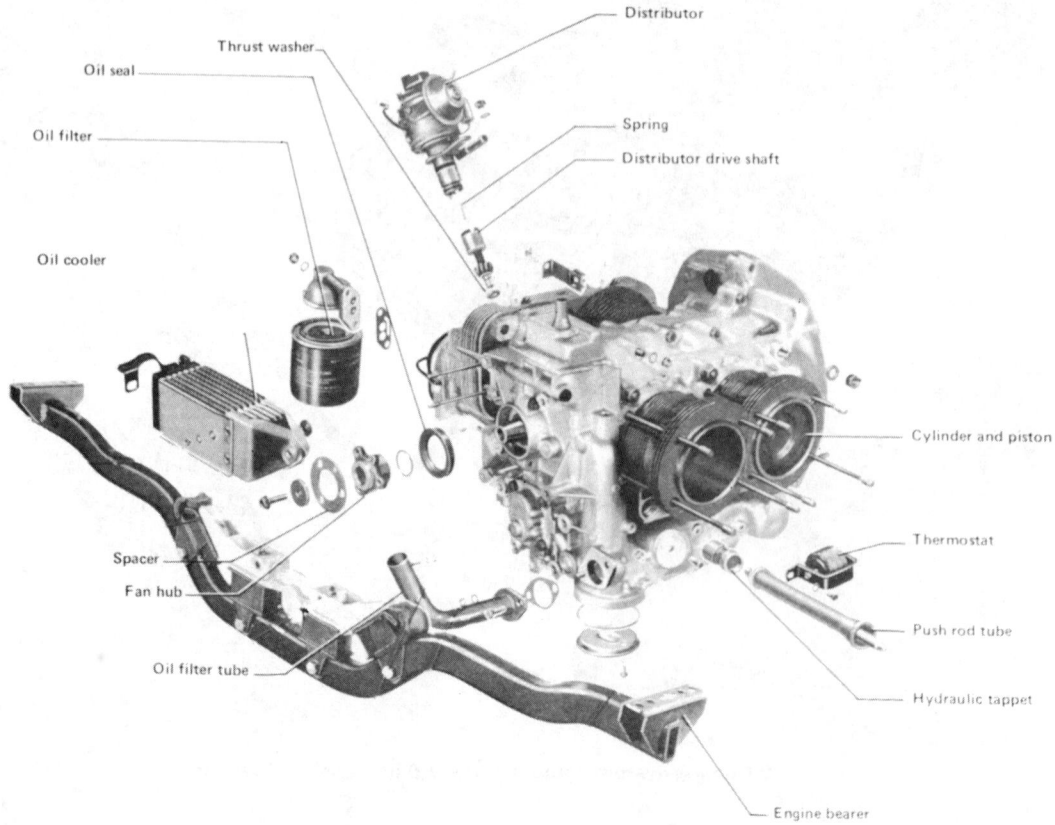

Distributor

Thrust washer

Oil seal

Spring

Oil filter

Distributor drive shaft

Oil cooler

Cylinder and piston

Spacer

Thermostat

Fan hub

Push rod tube

Oil filter tube

Hydraulic tappet

Engine bearer

Fig. 1.22 Engine external component locations (Sec 10)

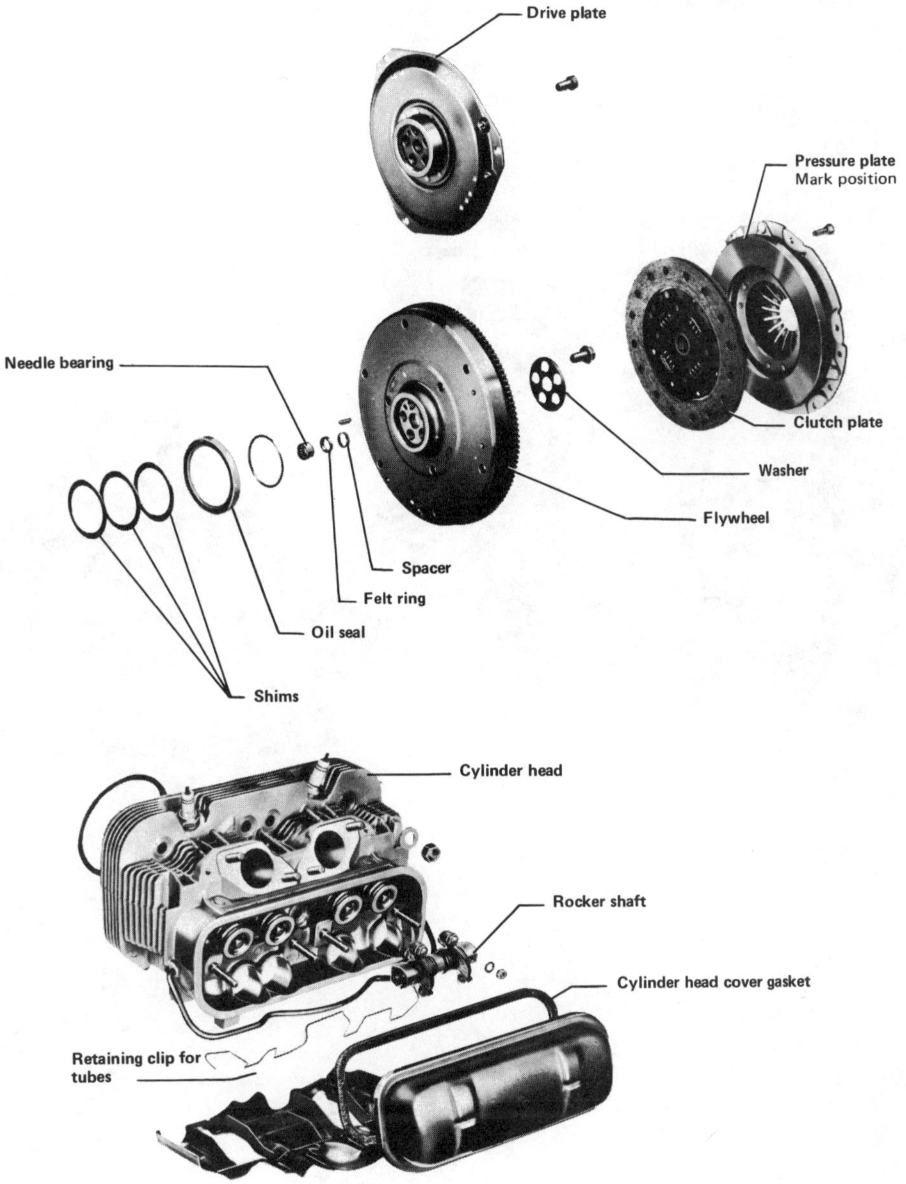
Drive plate
Pressure plate
Mark position
Needle bearing
Clutch plate
Washer
Flywheel
Spacer
Felt ring
Oil seal
Shims
Cylinder head
Rocker shaft
Cylinder head cover gasket
Retaining clip for
tubes

Fig. 1.23 Cylinder head and flywheel details (Sec 10)

2074
A

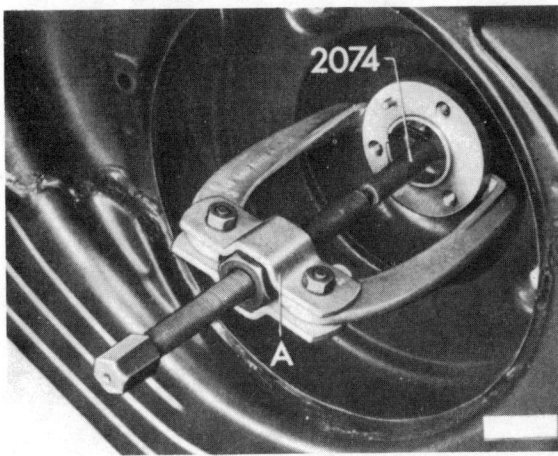

Fig. 1.24 Fan hub removal – 1.6 litre engines (Sec 10)

II
I

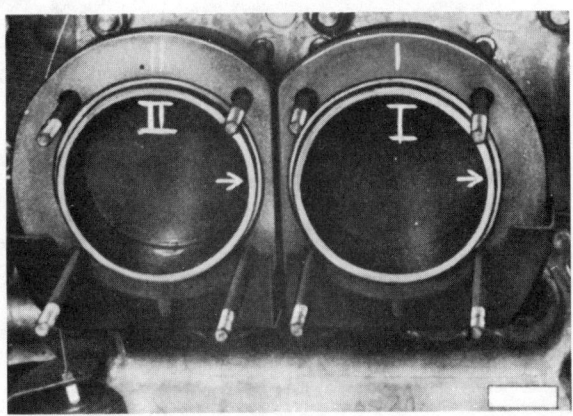

Fig. 1.25 Cylinders and pistons marked prior to removal (Sec 10)

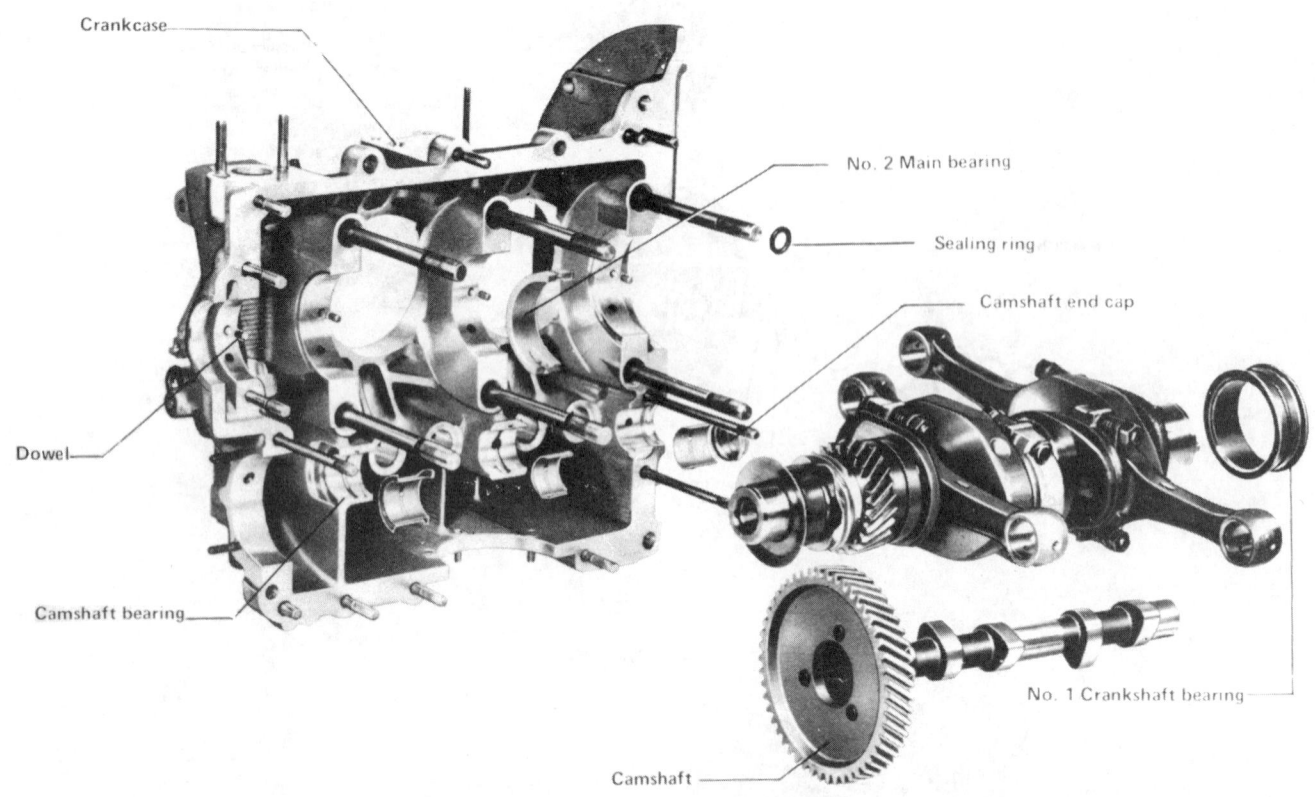

Crankcase

No. 2 Main bearing

Sealing ring

Camshaft end cap

Dowel

No. 1 Crankshaft bearing

Camshaft bearing

Camshaft

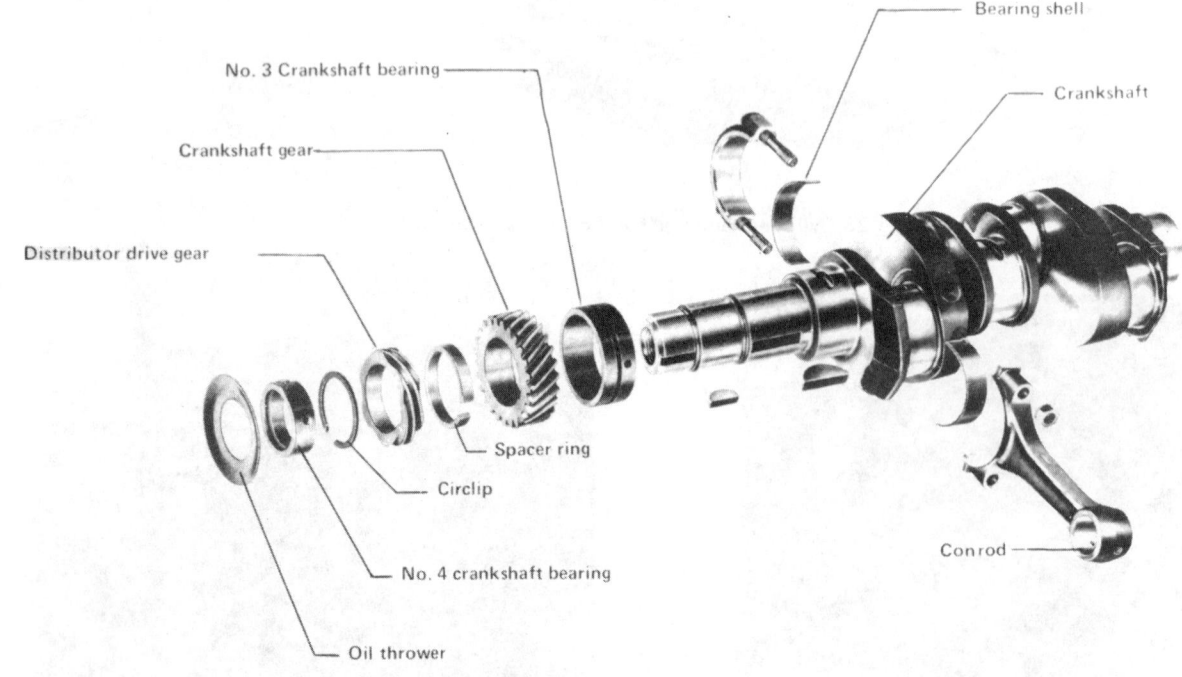

Bearing shell

No. 3 Crankshaft bearing

Crankshaft

Crankshaft gear

Distributor drive gear

Spacer ring

Circlip

No. 4 crankshaft bearing

Con rod

Oil thrower

Fig. 1.26 Crankcase, crankshaft and camshaft components (Sec 11)

11 Crankcase separation, crankshaft and camshaft removal

1 With the flywheel ring gear locked with a screwdriver against one of the crankcase studs, undo the retaining bolt(s) securing the flywheel or driveplate to the crankshaft.

2 Withdraw the flywheel or driveplate noting the O-ring seal and where applicable the felt seal on the inner face (photos). The shims controlling crankshaft endfloat are located behind the oil seal and can be taken out when the casings are separated.

3 Undo the nuts and remove the bolts holding the crankcase halves together. Work methodically using wooden blocks to support the crankcase whilst removing the bolts as there are studs sticking out in all directions.

4 Tap the halves apart, but do not tap too hard. If it will not come apart look for more studs or bolts. When all of these are out it does come easily. **Do not** push the faces apart with a wedge. Tap the right-hand half and lift it off the left-hand half leaving the crankshaft and camshaft in the lower half.

5 Put the right-hand half of the crankcase safely away and turn to the left-hand half. Lift out the camshaft and remove the white metal shell bearings from both halves of the crankcase noting which way they came out. Unless there are signs of wear there is no need to remove the bearings for more than a careful inspection, when they may be replaced right away.

6 With the camshaft removed, remove the shims from the end of the crankshaft, next remove the crankshaft (photo).

7 Lift off the oil thrower (where fitted) and slide off No 4 crankshaft bearing.

8 Extract the circlip then draw off the crankshaft gear and the distributor drive gear together using a puller (photos).

9 The circular main bearing (No 3) may now be removed for inspection. The Woodruff key from the camshaft drivegear should be stored safely.

10 No 1 main bearing, the circular one at the clutch end of the crankshaft, may be removed for inspection, and of course the shell bearings of No 2 main bearing.

11 All that remains is to remove the big-ends and inspect them and the crankshaft. Mark the bearing caps unless they are already marked (photo) so that they go back in the same place, the same way round. Remove the nuts from the connecting rod bolts and ease the cap from the rod. Remove the rod from the shaft and replace the cap on the connecting rod.

12 Finally, on the right-hand half take out the oil pick-up pipe (photo).

11.2A Removing the flywheel

11.6 Removing the crankshaft from the crankcase half

11.2B Note the O-ring and felt seal in the flywheel

11.8A Extract the circlip ...

11.8B ... then draw off the crankshaft gear and distributor drive gear together

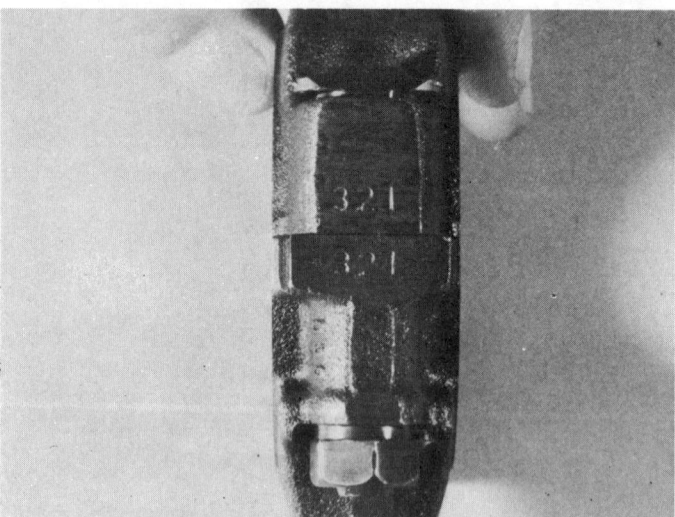

11.11 Identification markings on connecting rod and cap

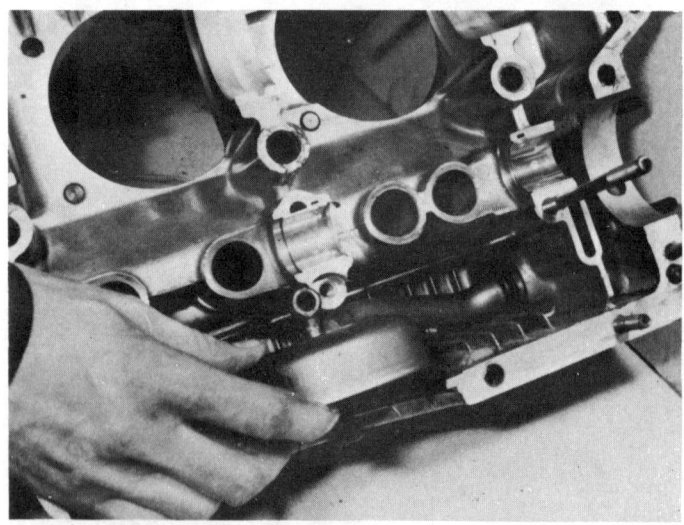

11.12 Removing the oil pick up pipe

12 Crankcase, crankshaft and camshaft – inspection

1   All the parts should now be cleaned again and oiled lightly.
2   Examine the two halves of the crankcase. Look for cracks, burrs, loose studs and any sign of rotating parts fouling the crankcase. If all is well set the two halves on one side.
3   Next examine the crankshaft. If it can be run between centres the main bearing surfaces must be checked to ensure the shaft is straight.
4   All bearing surfaces of the crankshaft must be checked for scoring or signs of overheating. Measure them accurately with a micrometer for ovality and diameter against the Specification or a replacement (photo).

12.4 Checking crankshaft journal diameters

5   The connecting rods should be examined for twist and bending. Unless special tools are available this is beyond the scope of the home mechanic and should be entrusted to an agent or machine shop. Unless something drastic has occurred the rods will not be distorted. If it has a seizure or sudden stop then take the rods along for checking. If rods are replaced they must be matched for weight. This again is a job for the agent.
6   Assuming the rods are in good order, and the shaft is satisfactory next examine the big-end shells. With the shells fitted correctly and the caps torqued to the right amount, the roundness or ovality of the bearing may be measured with an inside micrometer. Unless the bearings are nearly new, it is a false economy not to fit new big-ends right through.
7   If the shaft has to be reground then special shells must be fitted to both the big-ends and mains. Leave this job to the firm who do the grinding and make sure the shaft is assembled and runs freely when returned to you.
8   A reasonable test for a new big-end when assembled is that the rod should fall slowly under its own weight from just off top dead centre. If it doesn't it is too tight, but it must descend slowly or the clearances are too great.
9   The main bearings may only be examined and measured against Specification.
10 End play, both of mains and big-ends should be checked when the crankshaft is reassembled to the crankcase before the two halves of the crankcase are joined.
11 The camshaft must show no signs of wear or overheating on the cam surfaces. The gear must be firmly riveted to the shaft. If either of these do not seem right the shaft must be renewed.
12 The camshaft bearings must now be checked. They are all different so make sure the right partners go together. Check them against Specification and for superficial damage. Again, if there is the least doubt, renew the whole lot.

13 Cylinders, pistons and rings – inspection

1   Inspect the pistons, piston rings and cylinders for obvious signs of scoring, wear ridges or other damage.

2   The cylinder should be checked with a cylinder bore gauge or internal micrometer for taper and ovality. Measure at the top of the cylinder above the ridge worn by the top piston ring and then again halfway down the cylinder.

3   New pistons may be fitted to existing cylinders providing the cylinder is in a satisfactory condition. If the cylinder is worn a new piston and cylinder should be obtained. Pistons and cylinders are available in two oversizes and if one assembly is being replaced the new assembly must be of the same size group as the other three pistons and cylinders.

4   Pistons should be checked for ovality using a micrometer and the rings should be checked for excessive clearance in their grooves (photos).

5   Piston ring gaps may be checked by placing each ring squarely in the cylinder and measuring the gap with feeler gauges. If the gap is excessive the rings must be renewed. If the gaps are too small the edges may be ground until the gap is as specified.

Fig. 1.27 Measuring the cylinder bores for taper and ovality (Sec 13)

13.4A Checking the piston for ovality ...

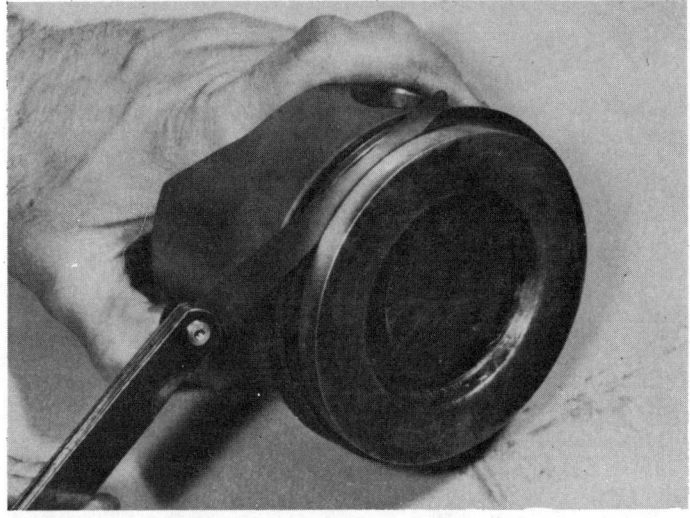

13.4B ... and excessive ring to groove clearance

Fig. 1.28 Checking piston ring gap (Sec 13)

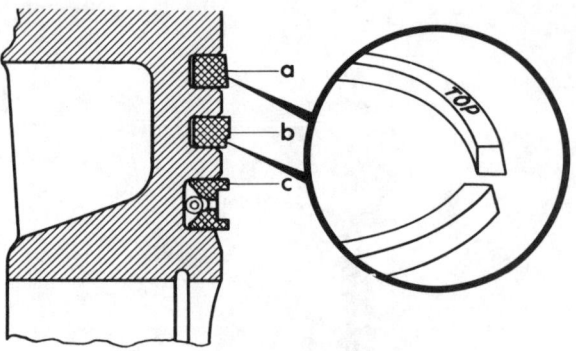

Fig. 1.29 Piston ring fitting details (Sec 13)

a *Upper ring (with the word*   c *Oil control ring assembly*
   TOP uppermost)
b *Lower ring (with the word*
   TOP uppermost)

6   If new rings are to be fitted to existing pistons, make sure that the groove in the piston is completely free of carbon then carefully fit the new rings by hand as shown in Fig. 1.29.

14 Valve gear and cylinder heads — inspection

1   Remove each valve from its location by compressing the spring caps and lifting out the collets (photos). Withdraw the spring and cap

then remove the valve from its guide. Remove all the valves in this way and keep them in order after removal.

2   Check the condition of the cylinder head visually after removing all traces of carbon from the combustion chambers and ports. The valve seat inserts should be free from severe pitting or any other sign of damage. The seats may be recut with special equipment, but if they are damaged beyond reclamation, a new head will be required.

3   The condition of the valve guides can be checked by 'rocking' the valve in the guide. If the movement is excessive, check the stem diameter of the valve with a micrometer. If this is not worn, new guides will be needed and this work must be left to a VW agent or machine shop.

4   If the valves appear satisfactory after removing all carbon, they may be lapped into their seats using coarse and fine grinding paste (photo). If the valve seats appear concave the inlet valves only may be refaced on valve grinding equipment. The exhaust valves must be renewed if worn.

5   Check the rockers and rocker shaft for signs of wear or excessive 'tip' of the rockers on the shafts. Check the valve springs for damaged or broken coils and check the pushrods for straightness.

6   Check the hydraulic tappets externally for signs of wear or excessive scuff marks. Unless the tappets were excessively noisy under all engine conditions they should not be dismantled. If however the plungers 'give', when pressed down firmly with the thumb, there is air in the pressure chamber and the tappet must be dismantled for bleeding. This will also be necessary if new tappets are being fitted.

7   To bleed the tappet, dismantle it by removing the circlip and lifting out the components in the order shown in Fig. 1.31.

8   Fill a small container with clean engine oil so that when the tappet is placed in, it is completely submerged (photo).

9   Insert the plunger spring followed by the plunger and valve assembly.

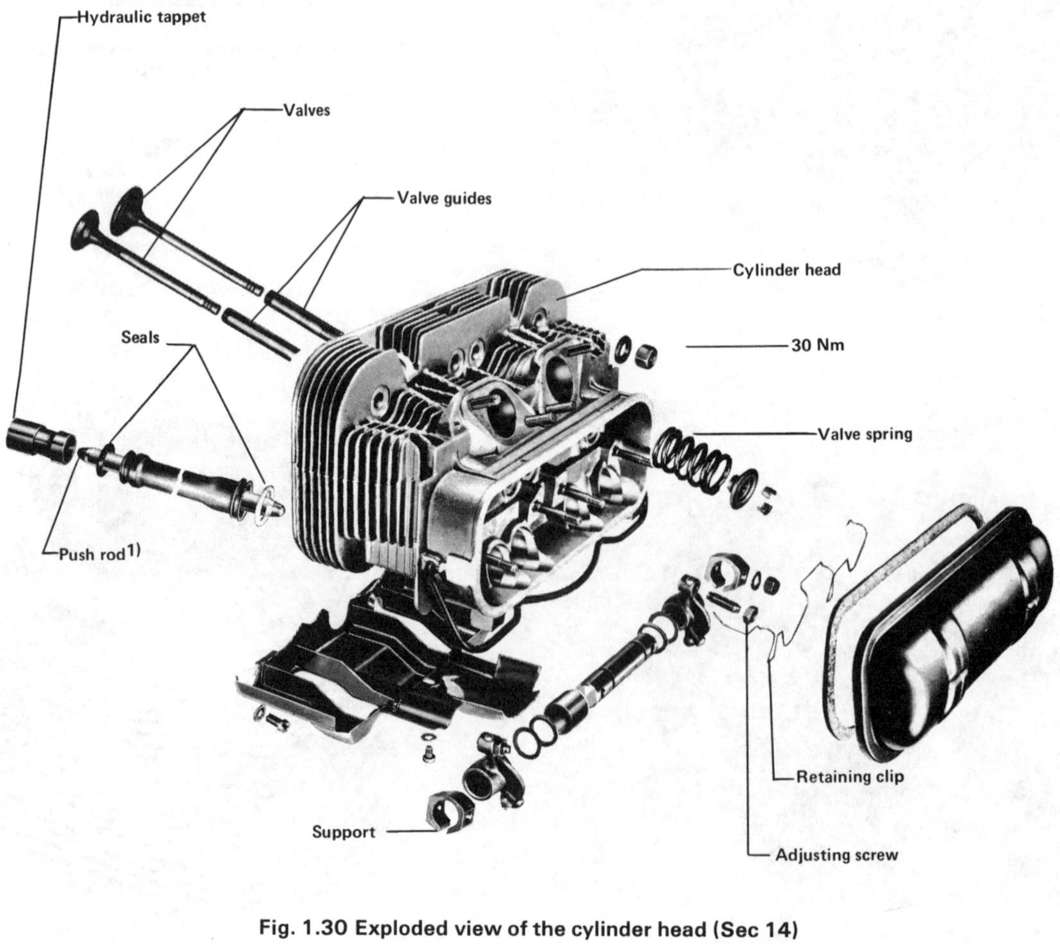

Fig. 1.30 Exploded view of the cylinder head (Sec 14)

14.1A Compress the valve springs ...

14.1B ... lift out the collets ...

14.1C ... and withdraw the valve

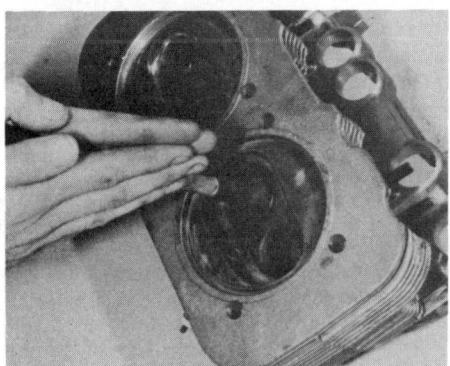
14.4 Lapping the valves into their seats

14.8 Immerse the tappet in oil to bleed all air

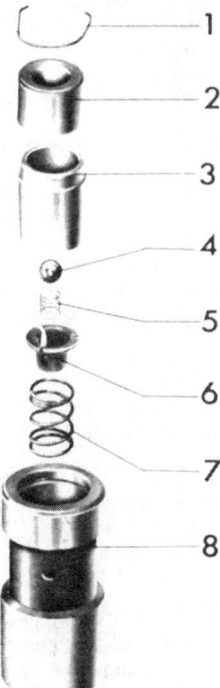

Fig. 1.31 Exploded view of a hydraulic tappet (Sec 14)

1	Circlip	5	Spring
2	Pushrod socket	6	Ball cap
3	Plunger	7	Spring
4	Ball	8	Tappet body

Fig. 1.32 Using a thin rod to depress the tappet ball for bleeding (Sec 14)

10 Using a thin rod inserted through the hole in the plunger, depress the spring loaded ball to allow the trapped air to escape.

11 Remove the rod and fit the pushrod socket. The socket must now be pushed down using a hollow blunt instrument (such as an old pushrod cut in half), with the tappet still in its oil, and with the whole assembly on a press. The force needed to push down the pushrod socket is quite high. Having done this the circlip can be fitted. If these facilities are not available compress the pushrod socket using a bolt and washers with the tappet on its side in a vice. This is not the approved method but as long as the tappet is kept liberally lubricated so that no air enters, it works.

12 After bleeding the tappets, store them vertically until they are needed for refitting.

15 Oil pump – inspection

1   Dismantle the oil pump by screwing a suitable bolt into the body and then withdrawing the body from the housing with a pair of grips (photos).

15.1A Screw a suitable bolt into the pump body ...

15.1B ... and pull the oil pump apart

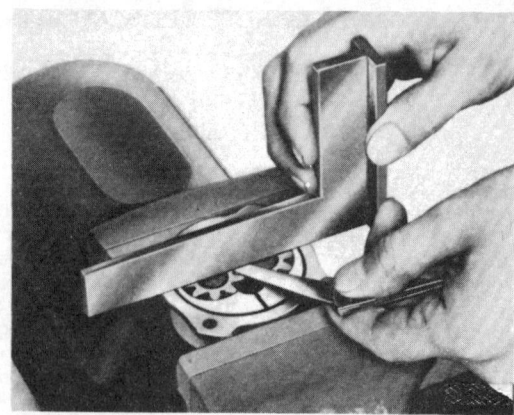

Fig. 1.33 Checking oil pump gear axial clearance (Sec 15)

2   Inspect the gears and body visually for scoring or wear ridges. If any are present, renew the pump.
3   If the pump appears satisfactory check the axial clearance of the gears using feeler gauges and a straight edge. If the clearances are greater than the specified amount, renew the pump.
4   Thoroughly lubricate the gears before reassembling them into the body and housing.

16 Cooling system – inspection

1   There is nothing to dismantle and measure in the cooling system other than to test the thermostat. This should be immersed in water at 70°C and the length should then be as given in the Specifications, measured across the bellows.
2   Check that the flaps work, the pulley goes round on its axis and that the cable is in good order.
3   Finally have a look at all the 'tin ware' to check for rust, bent flanges or other damage, and that it fits together properly.

17 Engine reassembly – general

1   To ensure maximum life with minimum trouble from a rebuilt engine, not only must everything be correctly assembled, but it must also be spotlessly clean. All oilways must be clear, and locking washers and spring washers must be fitted where indicated. Oil all bearings and other working surfaces thoroughly with engine oil during assembly.
2   Before assembly begins, renew any bolts or studs which have damaged threads.
3   Gather together a torque wrench, oil can, clean rags and a set of engine gaskets and oil seals, together with a new oil filter.

18 Crankcase, crankshaft and camshaft – reassembly

1   Lay the crankshaft on a clean surface and lubricate the bearing surfaces. Assemble the No 3 main bearing. The blind hole must be next to the crankshaft web (photo).
2   Heat the camshaft drive pinion in water to 80°C and slide it into position, the chamfer edge of the bore leading (photo) and then fit the spacer.
3   Now heat the distributor drive pinion to 80°C, slide it on (photo) and then fit the circlip.
4   Position the big-end shells in the connecting rods and caps and then position each rod and cap assembly adjacent to its big-end journal on the crankshaft (photo). The numbers on the ends of the cap and rod must be together and the same and the forged marks on the rods must be uppermost when in their normal running position.
5   Reassemble the caps and rods and progressively tighten the nuts to the specified torque (photo).
6   Measure the axial play of the connecting rods using feeler gauges and ensure that it is as specified (photo).
7   Place the locating dowels in place in the crankcase journals (photo), then assemble the centre main shell bearing to both halves of the crankcase (photo).
8   Slide No 1 main bearing onto the crankshaft with the dowel hole towards the flywheel followed by No 4 main bearing, oil groove away from the crankshaft (photos).
9   Fit the camshaft bearings to the crankcase, try the camshaft in position and remove it. Note that the flanged thrust bearing goes at the distributor end (photo).
10   Oil all the bearing surfaces of the mains and the crankshaft and camshaft, lift the crankshaft by the 2nd and 4th cylinder con rods and lower it into the crankcase, feeding No 1 and 3 con rods through the holes in the crankcase. Check that Nos 1, 3 and 4 mains have located properly with the dowels in place and that No 2 shell main is in place.
11   Rotate the crankshaft so that the two punch marks on the side of the camshaft drivegear are horizontal and install the camshaft so that the pip mark on the camshaft gear fits between the two marks on the drivegear (photos). Check all the bearing shells again.
12   Fit the sealing plug for the end of the camshaft into position (photo). This should be coated with jointing compound.
13   Insert the crankcase retaining bolts through from the underside of

18.1 Slide on No 3 main bearing ...

18.2 ... followed by the gear ...

18.3 ... then the spacer and distributor gear

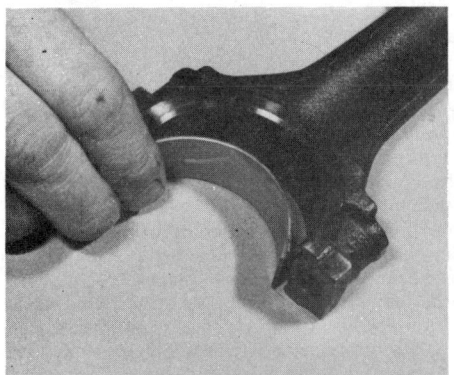

18.4 Fit the big-end shells to the rods and caps

18.5 Fitting the connecting rod to the crankshaft

18.6 Checking the connecting rod axial play

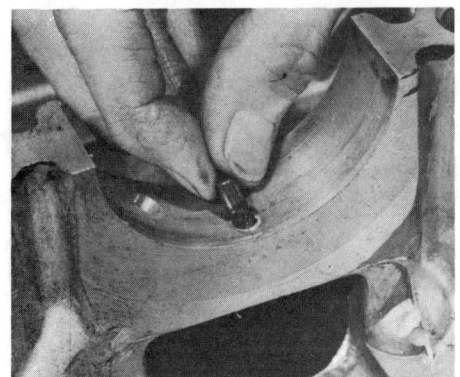

18.7A Place the locating dowels in the crankcase journals ...

18.7B ... then fit the centre main bearing shells

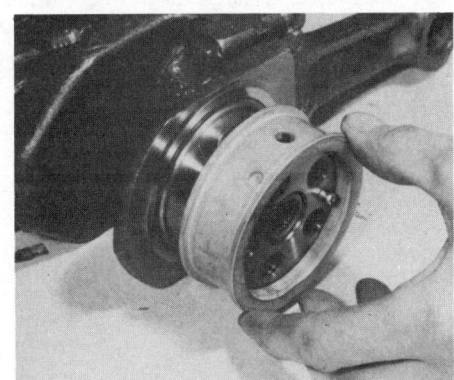

18.8A Fit No 1 main bearing ...

18.8B ... and No 4 main bearing to the crankshaft

18.9 Camshaft flanged thrust bearing

18.11A Fit the camshaft ...

18.11B ... with the timing marks on the two gears together

18.12 Fit the sealing plug with jointing compound

18.13 Plastic spacer on crankcase retaining bolt

the crankcase and slip on the plastic spacer washers, where fitted (photo).

14 Wipe carefully round the two mating surfaces of the crankcase and coat the one in which the crankshaft is installed with jointing compound. Use this sparingly.

15 Now turn to the other half of the casing. Install the oil suction pipe and the strainer. Use a new seal ring.

16 Check that the shell bearing for No 2 main bearing is in place correctly, and that the camshaft shells are safely in position; oil the bearing surfaces, and holding the crankcase by the cylinder bolts lower it carefully into position over the crankshaft and camshaft, feeding the connecting rods through the cylinder openings as the case is lowered (photo).

17 Install the bolts with the washer and sealing nuts, coating the heads of the bolts with sealing compound. The sealing rings of the nuts should be outwards. Install all the other nuts and bolts and tighten them slightly.

18 Turn the crankshaft through 360° to make sure that nothing is fouling and now tighten the nuts working diagonally as for a cylinder head. Check the rotation of the shaft again. If it is stiff in any way undo the nuts, split the case and search for the reason. It will probably be a bearing not seating properly. It is essential to find the reason before pressing on as damage will ensue if the casing is tightened further.

19 When all is correct tighten the large nuts and all the smaller ones working diagonally all the while. Check the rotation frequently (at the end of each round of tightening). Finally tighten to the specified torque.

20 Now fit the rest of the oil strainer (photos) and cover to the bottom of the sump. Refit the oil pressure relief valve and screw home the plug (photos). Check that the oil pressure switch is in place.

21 Prime the oil pump by filling it with oil then refit the pump using a new gasket (photos). Tighten the nuts to the specified torque.

22 Fit the sealing ring to the fan housing end of the crankshaft then tap a new oil seal into place. Fit the Woodruff key (if removed) followed by the fan hub. Tighten the hub retaining bolt to the specified torque (photos).

23 Going to the other end, install the flywheel with two shims behind it. Do not fit the seal yet.

24 Now measure the axial play of the crankshaft. If it is possible to

18.16 Fitting the two crankcase halves together

18.20A Fitting the oil strainer ...

18.20B ... and cover with a new gasket ...

18.20C ... then the side cover on 2.0 litre engines

18.20D Oil pressure relief valve plunger ...

18.20E ... spring and cap

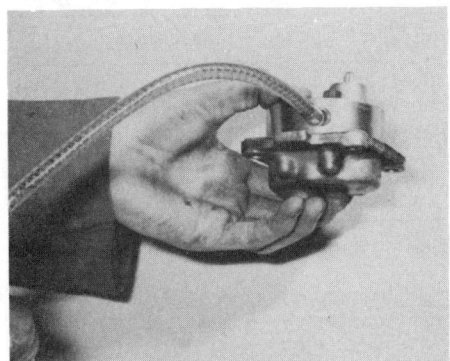

18.21A Prime the oil pump ...

18.21B ... then fit the pump with a new gasket

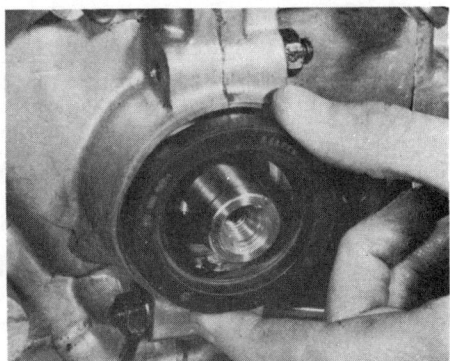

18.22A Fitting the fan housing end oil seal ...

18.22B ... and Woodruff key ...

18.22C ... followed by the fan hub

18.24A Crankshaft axial play adjustment shims

18.24B Ensure that the O-ring and felt seal are in place in the flywheel

18.24C Fitting the flywheel end oil seal

18.26 Tighten the bolts to the specified torque

obtain a dial gauge read the play on the dial gauge, otherwise you will have to rig up an arrangement to use feelers. The axial play should now have 0.10 mm subtracted from it and this will give the thickness of the third shim required. Shims of 6 thicknesses are available. Unless major repairs have been done the reinstallation of the old shims will usually meet the requirement. Having settled the shim problem remove the flywheel, install the shims (photo), the O-ring and felt seal in the flywheel, and the seal in the crankcase. Tap the seal fully into its location (photos).

25 On 1.6 litre engines turn the crankshaft so that No 1 connecting rod is at TDC then fit the flywheel so that the two trigger pins are adjacent to the TDC sensor on the right-hand crankcase half. Fit the retaining bolt and tighten it to the specified torque.

26 On 2.0 litre engines, fit the flywheel over the dowel peg, fit the locking plate and retaining bolts and tighten the bolts to the specified torque (photo).

Fig. 1.34 Flywheel positioning – 1.6 litre engines (Sec 18)

Trigger pins (arrowed) adjacent to TDC sensor

19 Cylinder head – reassembly

1   The clean cylinder head minus all carbon should now be assembled with the valves. The valves have been serviced, either machined or ground in and are ready for fitting.

2   Insert the valve into the guide, slip the spring over the stem, fit the spring cap, compress the spring with a valve lifter and fit the collets in place (photos).

3   If the collets are difficult hold them on the end of a screwdriver with a blob of grease and poke them into place that way.

4   When the valve is assembled compress the spring to open the valve and let it go sharply. This will indicate whether the collets are properly seated.

5   Clean off the flange of the cylinder head, and repeat for the second cylinder head.

20 Pistons, cylinders and cylinder heads – reassembly

1   Bleed the hydraulic tappets as described in Section 14, if this has not already been done, then insert each tappet into its original bore.

2   The gudgeon pin is a push fit in the piston. Heat the piston with an electric lamp and, fitting the piston over the small end bush, push the gudgeon pin through the bush (photo). Make sure that the right piston is being fitted to the particular connecting rod and that the arrow on the piston crown faces the flywheel. Secure the piston with the circlips then space the piston rings with their gaps at 120° to each other (photo).

3   A conventional piston ring compressor cannot be used effectively on this piston and cylinder arrangement, but two strips of metal formed as shown (photo) are useful alternatives.

4   Lubricate the cylinder, fit the seals to the bottom then slide them

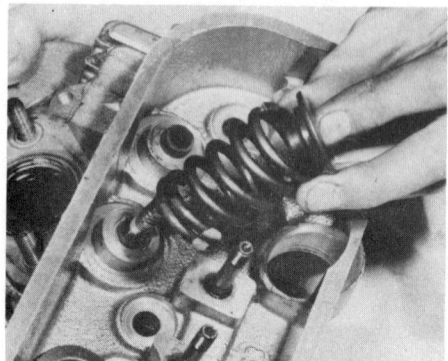
19.2A Fit the spring and cap over the valve ...

19.2B ...compress the spring and fit the split collets

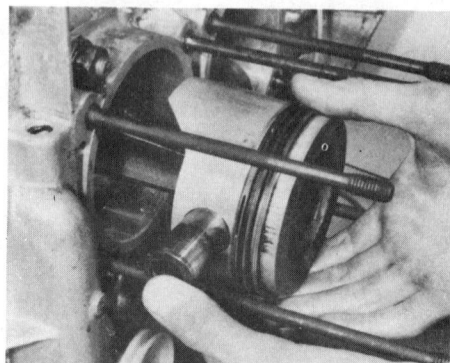
20.2A Fit the gudgeon pin to piston and connecting rod ...

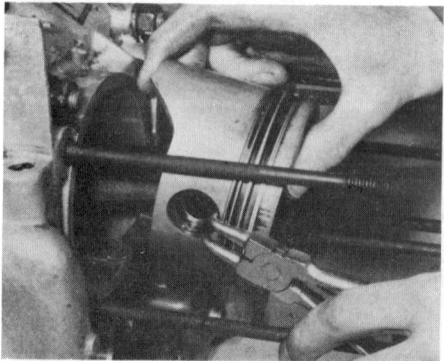
20.2B ... then secure with the circlips

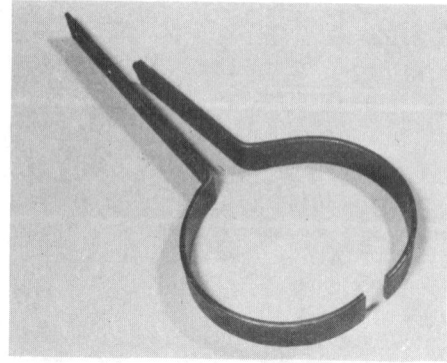
20.3 Home made piston ring compressor tool

20.4A Fit the seal to the cylinder ...

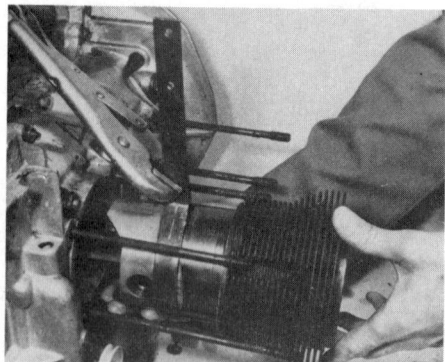
20.4B ... then fit the cylinder

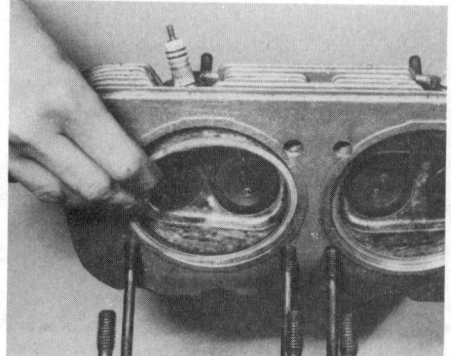
20.5 Fit the cylinder head with new sealing rings

20.6 Tighten the bolts in the correct sequence to the specified torque

over the pistons ensuring that the right cylinder is being fitted to the particular rod and piston. Clamp the metal strips around the piston rings and carefully tap the cylinder into place (photos).

5   When all four cylinders are in place install the sealing rings in over the cylinders and gently ease the heads over the studs (photo). Take care not to pinch the sealing rings.

6   Fit the nuts and washers to the studs and torque the head down using the sequence in Fig. 1.35. Tighten down progressively to the specified torque (photo).

7   Fit the deflector plates next. The right-hand one is the smaller of the two. There is one screw in the cylinder head and two in the crankcase.

21.2A Fit the pushrods in their original locations

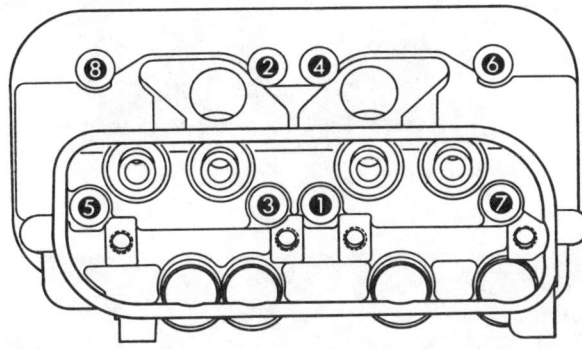

Fig. 1.35 Cylinder head tightening sequence (Sec 20)

21.2B Pushrod tubes retaining wire in place

21 Pushrods and rocker gear — reassembly

1   With new seals in place over the pushrod guide tubes, fit the tubes through the holes in the cylinder head (photo).

2   Now install the pushrods (photo) and assemble the rocker gear. The spring retainer for the tubes goes on first. This is a much bent piece of wire which fits round the studs and across the top of the pushrod tubes. Fit the rocker gear on the top of the retainer, engaging the tops of the pushrods in the cups while so doing (photo). Make sure that the pushrods are properly located in the hydraulic tappets then secure the rocker gear with the retaining nuts tightened to the specified torque (photo).

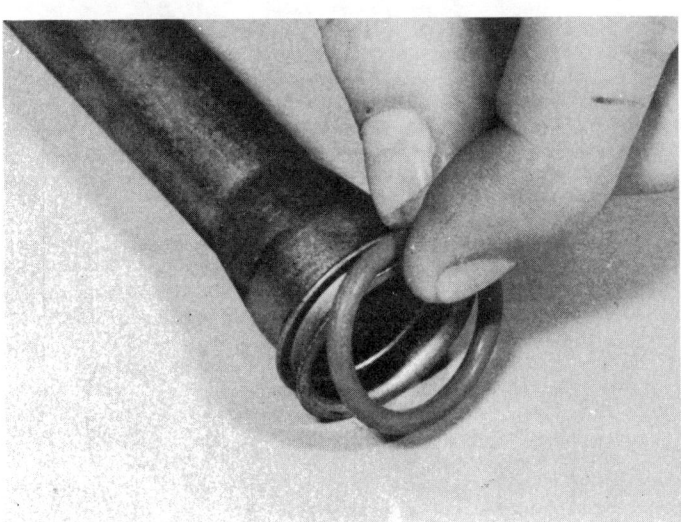
21.1 Fitting pushrod tube seals

21.2C Fitting the rocker gear

22 Oil cooler and filter – reassembly

1   Using a new O-ring seal refit the crankcase ventilation housing on 1.6 litre engines and secure the housing using the four nuts.
2   On 2.0 litre engines fit the oil filter housing using a new gasket and tighten the nuts securely. On all engines screw a new oil filter into position.
3   On 1.6 litre engines place the oil cooler spacer block over the studs using a new gasket then on all engines place new sealing rings in their locations (photo). Fit the oil cooler over the studs and secure with the retaining nuts.
4   Fit the oil filter tube using a new gasket.

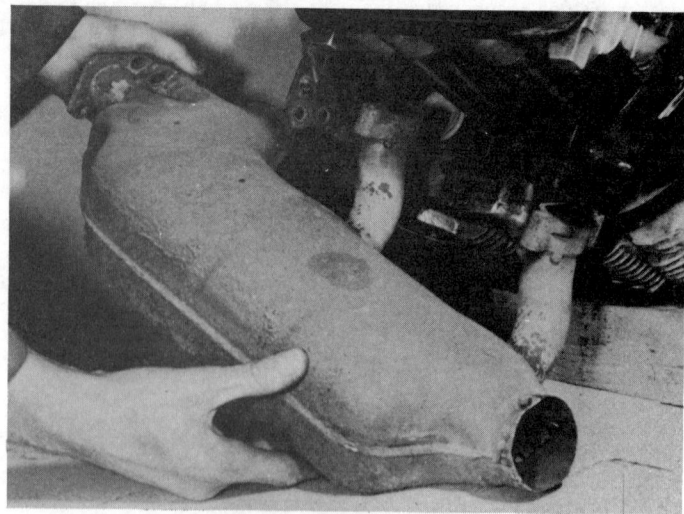
23.2A Fitting a heat exchanger ...

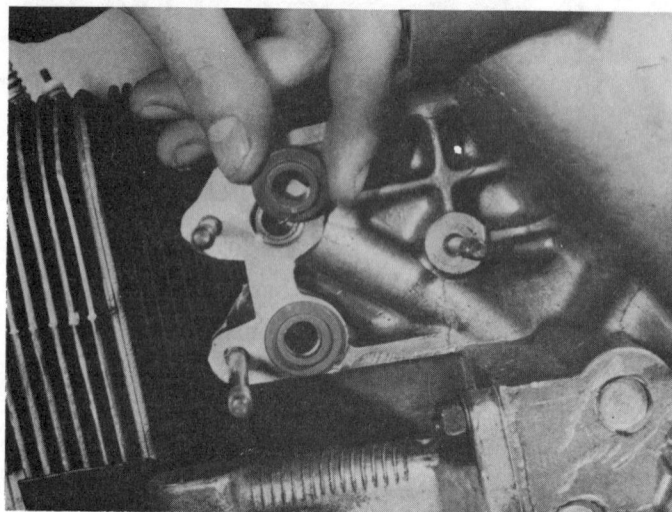
22.3 Use new sealing rings for the oil cooler

23 Heat exchangers, fan housing and cooling ducts – reassembly

1   Fit the thermostat at this stage and tie its control wire up so that it does not get lost inside the cooling ducts as these are fitted (photo).
2   Fit the right-hand heat exchanger using new gaskets then secure the deflector panel beneath it (photos).
3   The stage is now being reached where much of the duct 'tinware' can be refitted. The sequence will depend on the engine being worked on and the notes made during removal. Refer to the appropriate illustrations if in doubt.

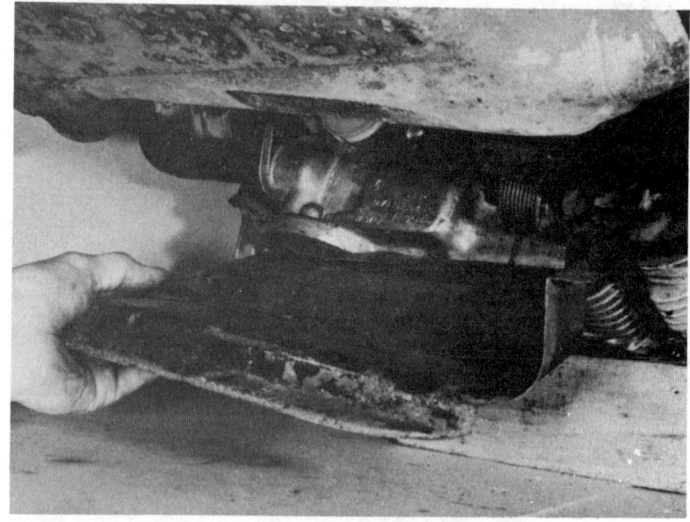
23.2B ... followed by the deflector plate

23.1 Thermostat in position on 2.0 litre engine

Fig. 1.36 Checking fan to housing clearance – 1.6 litre engines
(Sec 23)

23.4A Cylinder head front cover plate ...

23.4B ... and upper panel

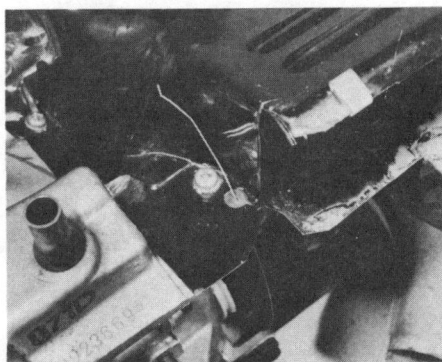

23.4C Thermostat wire routed through panel

23.5A Fitting the engine bearer

23.5B The arrow on the bearer faces the front of vehicle when installed

23.7 Fitting the spacer and fan

4   The front cylinder cover plates can be fitted as applicable (photo). When fitting the upper panels route the thermostat wire through the slots in the panel (photos).

5   Fit the left-hand heat exchanger followed by the engine bearer and mounting bracket. Note the arrow on the engine bearer which points to the front of the vehicle (photos).

6   Place the fan housing in position and fit the retaining nuts and bolts. Tighten the bolts fully on 2.0 litre engines, but finger tight only on 1.6 litre engines. On these engines place the fan in position on the hub and retain it with one bolt. Move the fan housing slightly so that a 9 mm feeler blade will pass all around the fan. Hold the housing in this position, remove the fan and tighten the housing bolts.

7   On all engines fit the fan and where applicable the spacer, then secure the fan to the hub (photo).

8   Secure the thermostat wire to the throttle flaps with the flaps in the closed position.

9   Refit the dipstick tube using a new O-ring seal.

24 Distributor driveshaft – refitting

1   Turn the engine over in the normal direction of rotation until No 1 piston approaches TDC on compression. Check this by viewing the inlet valve rocker arm for No 1 cylinder; it should be just closing as the notch on the fan hub approaches the TDC or O position on the timing scale. Now align the marks so that No1 pistion is at TDC.

2   Position the thrust washer(s) over the end of the driveshaft and retain them with a little grease. Insert the driveshaft into its location so that as it turns under the meshing action of the skew gears, it adopts the final fitted position shown in Fig. 1.37 for 1.6 litre engines and Fig. 1.38 for 2.0 litre engines. Note that on 1.6 litre engines the smaller segment, or offset, faces away from the fuel pump and on 2.0 litre engines the smaller segment, or offset, faces away from the distributor clamp stud (photos).

3   With the driveshaft in place, slide the preload spring into the centre of the driveshaft using a drill bit as a guide (photo).

24.2A Fit the distributor drivegear ...

24.2B ... so that it adopts the position shown on 2.0 litre engines

24.3 Fitting the preload spring

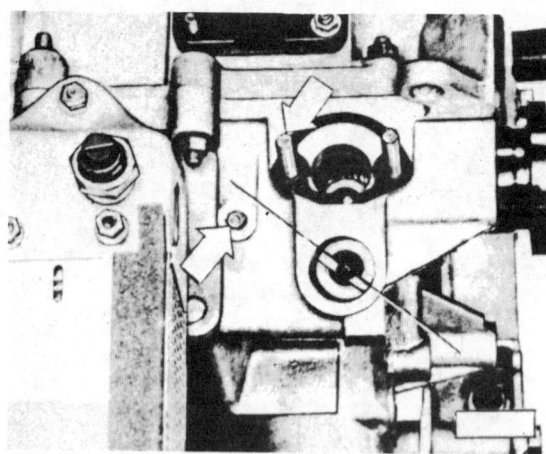

Fig. 1.37 Correct fitted position of distributor driveshaft – 1.6 litre engines (Sec 24)

Centreline through slot passes between studs (arrowed)

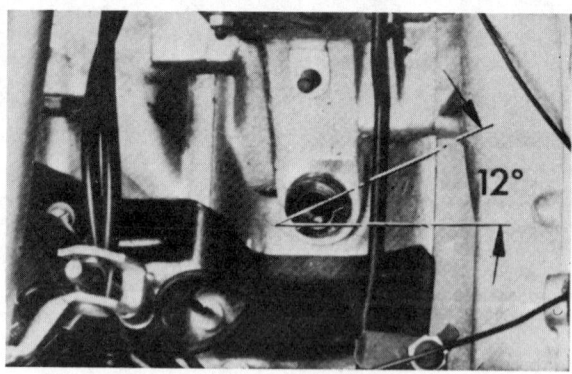

Fig. 1.38 Correct positioning of distributor driveshaft – 2.0 litre engines (Sec 24)

25 Engine ancillary components – refitting

The fitting of the engine ancillary components and the remainder of the reassembly now follows a reverse of the removal procedures contained in Section 9. Refer to the various Chapters concerned for details of the fitting and adjustment of the components where necessary.

26 Hydraulic tappets – initial setting

1   An initial basic setting for the hydraulic tappets must be carried out as follows whenever the rocker shaft assembly has been removed or a tappet renewed. After this initial setting has been carried out no further adjustment is required in service.

2   Position the engine so that No 1 piston is at TDC on compression with the distributor rotor arm pointing to the notch in the distributor body rim.

3   Slacken the rocker arm adjusting screws for No 1 cylinder until they are clear of the valve stems then turn them back until they make light contact with no clearance. From this position tighten the screws two further turns and tighten the lock nuts (photo).

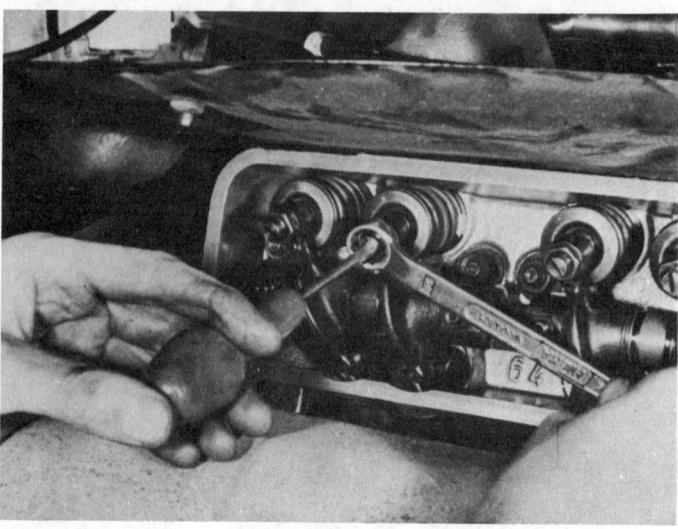

26.3 Hydraulic tappet initial setting

4   Repeat this procedure for cylinders 2, 3 and 4 respectively by turning the crankshaft anti-clockwise until the rotor arm moves 90° for each cylinder.

5   After carrying out this setting, refit the rocker covers using new gaskets (photo).

6   When the engine is started the tappets will be initially noisy and it may be some time after the engine has started before all the noise disappears completely. This is quite normal and is no cause for alarm.

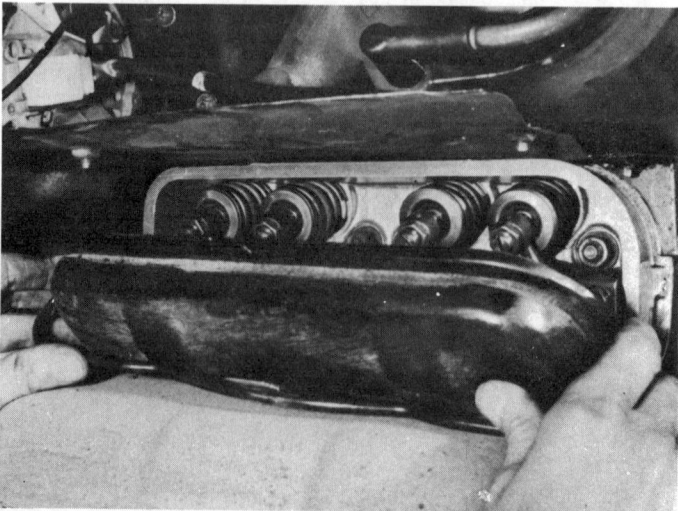

26.5 Fitting the rocker covers

27 Fault diagnosis – engine

Symptom	Reason(s)
Engine fails to start	Discharged battery
	Loose battery connection
	Loose or broken ignition leads or connectors
	Moisture on spark plugs, distributor cap, or HT leads
	Incorrect spark plug gaps
	Cracked distributor cap or rotor
	Other ignition system fault
	Empty fuel tank
	Faulty fuel pump
	Other fuel system fault
	Faulty starter motor
	Low cylinder compressions
Engine idles erratically	Inlet manifold air leak
	Fuel system adjustments incorrect
	Worn rocker arms
	Worn camshaft lobes
	Faulty fuel pump
	Faulty hydraulic tappet
	Loose crankcase ventilation hoses
	Emission control system fault
	Uneven cylinder compressions
	Ignition system fault
Engine misfires	Spark plugs worn or incorrectly gapped
	Dirt or water in fuel system
	Fuel system adjustments incorrect
	Burnt out valve
	Distributor cap cracked
	Uneven cylinder compressions
	Other fuel or ignition system fault
Engine stalls	Fuel system adjustments incorrect
	Inlet manifold air leak
	Ignition timing incorrect
Excessive oil consumption	Worn pistons, cylinder bores or piston rings
	Valve guides worn
	Oil leaking from rocker cover, pushrod tubes, crankcase seals or oil seals
Engine backfires	Fuel system adjustments incorrect
	Ignition timing incorrect
	Emission control system fault
	Inlet manifold air leak
	Sticking valve

Chapter 2
Fuel, exhaust and emission control systems

Contents

Specifications

System type

1.6 litre engine	Front mounted fuel tank, mechanical fuel pump, single downdraught carburettor
2.0 litre engine (UK vehicle)	Front mounted fuel tank, mechanical fuel pump, twin downdraught carburettors
2.0 litre engine (USA vehicles)	Front mounted fuel tank, electric fuel pump, fuel injection

Fuel pump
Type:

Engines with carburettor induction	Mechanical, driven by camshaft
Engines with fuel injection	Electric
Delivery pressure (mechanical pump)	0.2 to 0.3 bar (2.9 to 4.3 lbf/in^2)
Delivery rate (electric pump)	1 litre (1.76 Imp pt, 2.1 US pt)/minute

Carburettor
Type:

1.6 litre engine	Solex 34 PICT-4
2.0 litre engine	Solex 34 PDSIT-2 (left-hand), Solex 34 PDSIT-3 (right-hand)

Carburettor specification
Solex 34 PICT-4
Venturi diameter	26 mm (1.02 in)
Main jet	X132.5
Air correction jet	80Z
Pilot jet	60
Pilot air jet	120
Auxiliary fuel jet	42.5
Auxiliary air jet	90

Accelerator pump injection quantity:
With control valve system	0.95 to 1.25 cc/stroke
Without control valve system	1.15 to 1.45 cc/stroke
Float needle valve	1.5 mm (0.06 in)
Float weight	10.5 to 11.5 g (0.36 to 0.40 oz)
Float needle valve washer thickness	0.5 mm (0.02 in)
Choke flap gap	3.3 to 3.7 mm (0.13 to 0.15 in)

Throttle valve gap:
Carburettor removed	0.70 to 0.80 mm (0.027 to 0.031 in)
Carburettor installed (fast idle speed)	2100 to 2300 rev/min

Idle speed:
Setting value	800 to 900 rev/min
Test value	850 to 950 rev/min
Exhaust gas CO content	0.3 to 0.9%

Solex 34 PDSIT
Venturi diameter	26 mm (1.02 in)
Main jet	135 (132.5)*
Air correction jet	140
Pilot jet	50 (55)*
Pilot air jet	140
Auxiliary fuel jet	45
Auxiliary air jet	0.7
Accelerator pump injection quantity	0.55 to 0.85 cc/stroke
Float needle valve	1.2 mm (0.05 in)
Float needle valve washer thickness	1.0 mm (0.04 in)
Throttle valve gap	0.65 mm (0.03 in)

Idle speed:
Setting value	800 to 900 rev/min
Test valve	850 to 950 rev/min
Exhaust gas CO content	0.3 to 0.9%

From engine No. CU 002 632 (manual transmission); CU 003 083 (automatic transmission)

Fuel injection system specification
Temperature sensor resistance	Approximately 2500 ohms at 20°C

Intake air sensor terminal resistance:
Between terminals 6 and 9	200 to 400 ohms
Between terminals 7 and 8	100 to 500 ohms

Pressure regulator delivery pressure:
Vacuum hose disconnected	2.3 to 2.5 bar (33 to 35 lbf/in^2)
Vacuum hose connected	1.8 to 2.1 bar (28 to 30 lbf/in^2)
Fuel injector connecting plug terminal resistance	2 to 3 ohms
Auxiliary air regulator terminal resistance	30 ohms

Idle speed (fuel injection system)
USA except California:
Manual transmission	800 to 900 rev/min
Automatic transmission	850 to 1000 rev/min
California only (all models)	850 to 950 rev/min

Exhaust gas CO content (fuel injection system)
USA except California	0.5 to 1.5%
California only	0.3 to 1.1%

Fuel tank capacity
	60 litres (13.2 Imp gal, 16 US gal)

Fuel octane rating
UK vehicles	91 RON (two-star) minimum
USA vehicles	91 RON unleaded only

Torque wrench settings
	Nm	lbf ft
Fuel tank retaining bolts	25	18
Fuel injection manifold tubes to cylinder head	15	11
Intake air sensor to air cleaner	5	4
Exhaust system components M8 retaining bolts	20	15
CO test point cap on exhaust crossover pipe	15	11

1 General description

The fuel system on 1.6 litre and 2.0 litre engines for UK markets consists of a front mounted fuel tank, mechanical fuel pump and single or twin downdraught Solex carburettor(s). On 2.0 litre engine vehicles for the USA the carburettors are replaced by Bosch L-Jetronic AFC fuel injection. The air cleaner on all versions is of the disposable paper element type with automatic air temperature control on engines with carburettor induction.

A number of different types of exhaust systems are used according to engine size, year of manufacture and operating territory, and a description of these, the emission control systems and other major components are contained in the relevant Sections of this Chapter.

Warning: *Many of the procedures in this Chapter entail the removal of fuel pipes and connections which may result in some fuel spillage. Before carrying out any operation on the fuel system refer to the precautions given in Safety First! at the beginning of this manual and follow them implicitly. Petrol is a highly dangerous and volatile liquid and the precautions necessary when handling it cannot be overstressed.*

2 Maintenance and inspection

1   At the intervals given in Routine Maintenance carry out the following service operations to the fuel, exhaust and emission control components.
2   From underneath the vehicle carefully inspect the fuel pipes, vent pipes, hoses and unions for signs of chafing, leaks and corrosion. Renew any pipes that are severely pitted with corrosion or in any way damaged. Renew any hoses that show signs of cracking or other deterioration.
3   Examine the fuel tank for leaks or signs of corrosion or damage.
4   Renew the fuel filter in the fuel line between tank and pump (photo), ensuring that the new filter is fitted with the arrow on its body facing the direction of fuel flow, ie towards the pump.

2.4 Fuel filter location between fuel tank and pump

5   Check the various components of the exhaust system for corrosion, damage and security. Renew any components that show signs of deterioration or leaks.
6   Renew the air cleaner element and check the operation of the air temperature control (where applicable) as described in Sections 3 and 4.
7   From within the engine compartment check the security of all fuel pipes and check the fuel and vacuum pipes and hoses for kinks, chafing or deterioration.
8   Check and if necessary adjust the engine idle settings as described in Sections 12, 17 and 22 as applicable.

9   Check the operation of the accelerator cable and linkage and lubricate the pivots with a few drops of engine oil.
10 Check the various emission control systems by referring to the relevant Sections of this Chapter. Actual maintenance of the system should ideally be left to a VW agent who will have details of current maintenance schedules with regard to emission regulations pertaining to the vehicle operating territory.

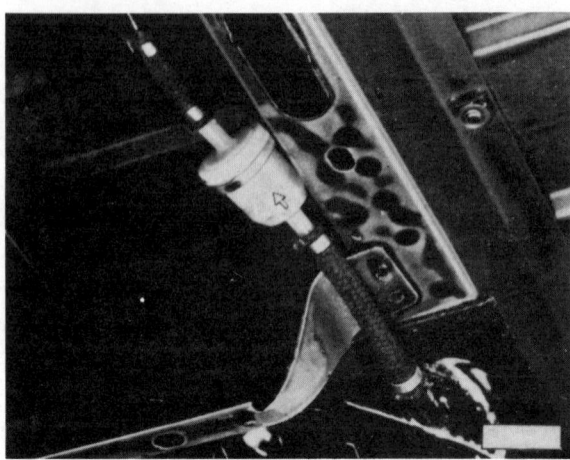

Fig. 2.1 Fuel filter positioned with arrow facing fuel flow direction (Sec 2)

3 Air cleaner and element (1.6 litre engine) – removal and refitting

1   To remove the air cleaner element detach the vacuum pipe at the intake spout vacuum unit.
2   Release the retaining clip on the upper housing and detach the air cleaner from its mountings.
3   Spring back the four clips, separate the housings and lift out the element.
4   To remove the complete assembly, identify the location of each vacuum pipe then disconnect the pipes from the upper housing.
5   Detach the breather hose and the carburettor intake hose, withdraw the unit from the fresh air intake and remove it from the engine.
6   Refitting the air cleaner assembly and element is the reverse sequence to removal.
7   The operation of the air temperature control system may be tested as follows.
8   With the air cleaner installed, and the engine idling at normal operating temperature, detach the brown vacuum pipe from the temperature regulator on the air cleaner. If the system is operating correctly, the flap valve in the vacuum unit will be heard to close as the pipe is detached. If this is not the case the temperature regulator may be at fault or there may be a loss of vacuum due to a leaking or damaged vacuum pipe.

4 Air cleaner and element (2.0 litre engine) – removal and refitting

Engines with carburettor induction

1   Identify the location of each vacuum pipe then disconnect the pipes from the air cleaner upper housing.
2   Detach the engine breather hose.
3   Slacken the retaining clip screws securing the air cleaner side arms to each carburettor.
4   Spring back the retaining clips, lift off the upper housing and take out the element (photos).
5   To remove the complete assembly, release the fresh air intake duct from the air cleaner vacuum unit, spring back the clips securing

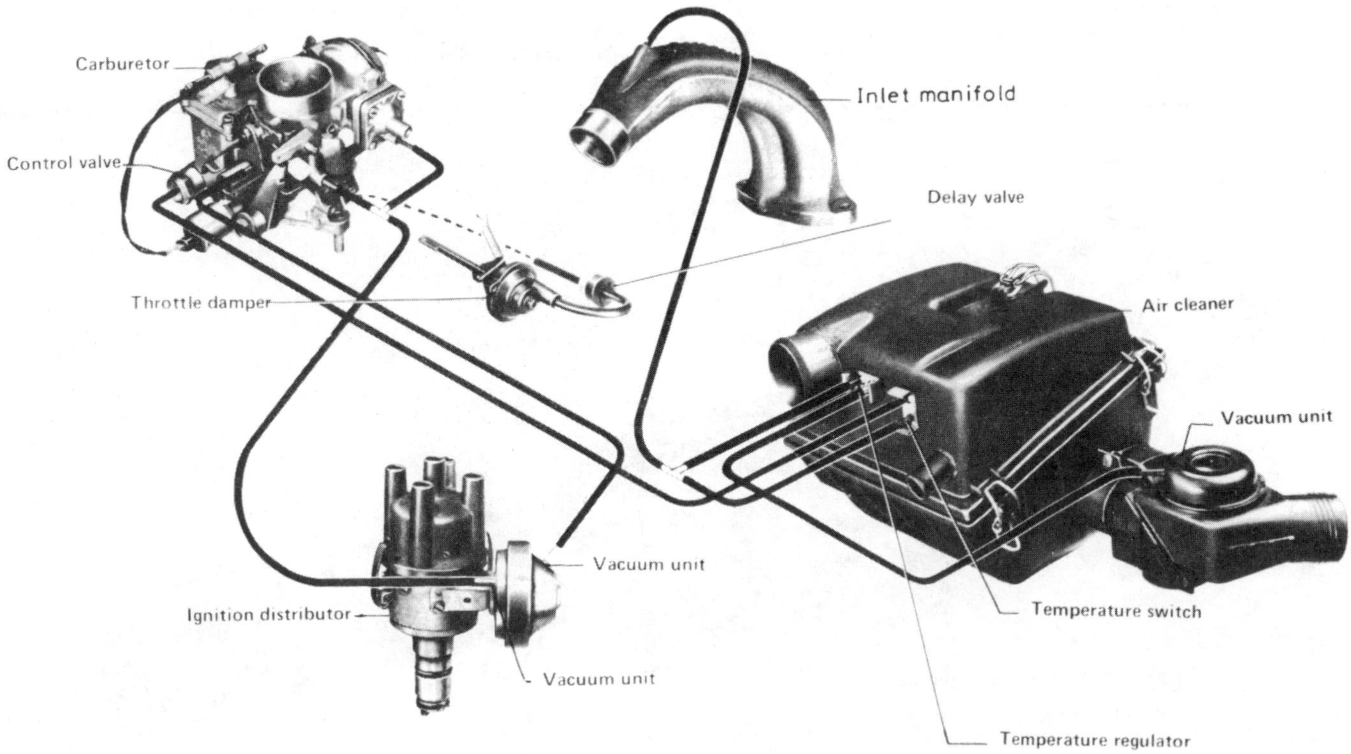

Carburetor

Control valve

Throttle damper

Inlet manifold

Delay valve

Air cleaner

Vacuum unit

Vacuum unit

Ignition distributor

Vacuum unit

Temperature switch

Temperature regulator

Fig. 2.2 Air cleaner assembly and vacuum hose layout – 1.6 litre engines (Sec 3)

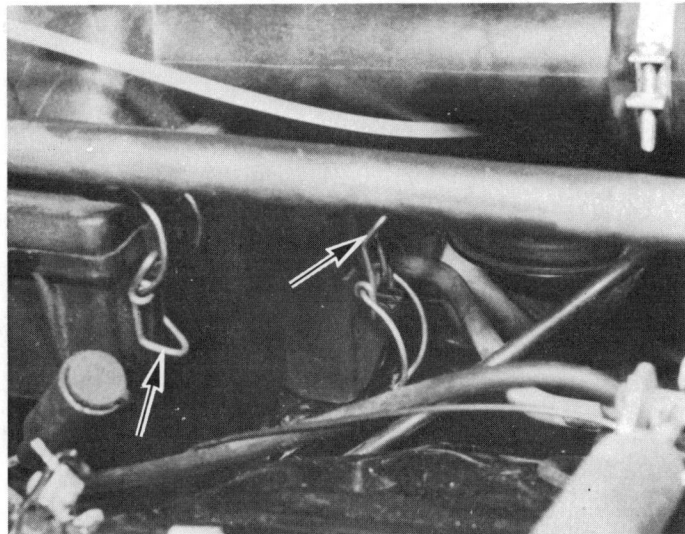

4.4A Air cleaner housing retaining clips (arrowed)

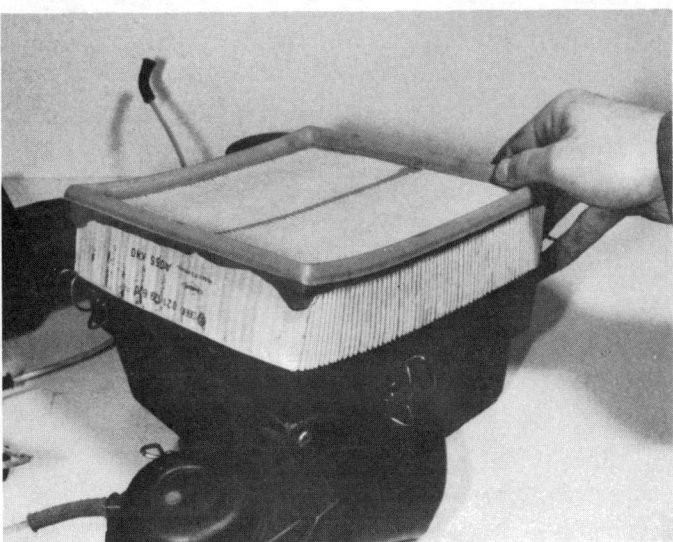

4.4B Removing the air cleaner element

the lower housing to the engine and remove the air cleaner from its location.

6   Refitting the air cleaner assembly and element is the reverse sequence to removal.

7   The operation of the air temperature control system may be checked using the procedure described in Section 3, paragraph 8.

Engines with fuel injection

8   To remove the element spring back the five retaining clips and lift up the upper part of the air cleaner housing just sufficiently to lift out the element.

9   Fit a new element ensuring that it is seated correctly, position the upper part of the housing over it and secure with the five clips.

10   To remove the complete assembly first disconnect the battery negative terminal.

11   Detach the crankcase breather hose from the housing upper part.

12   Disconnect the electrical wiring multi-plug from the air flow meter.

13   Slacken the retaining clip and detach the intake hose from the air flow meter.

14   The air cleaner assembly complete with air flow meter can now be removed from the engine.

15   Refitting is the reverse sequence to removal.

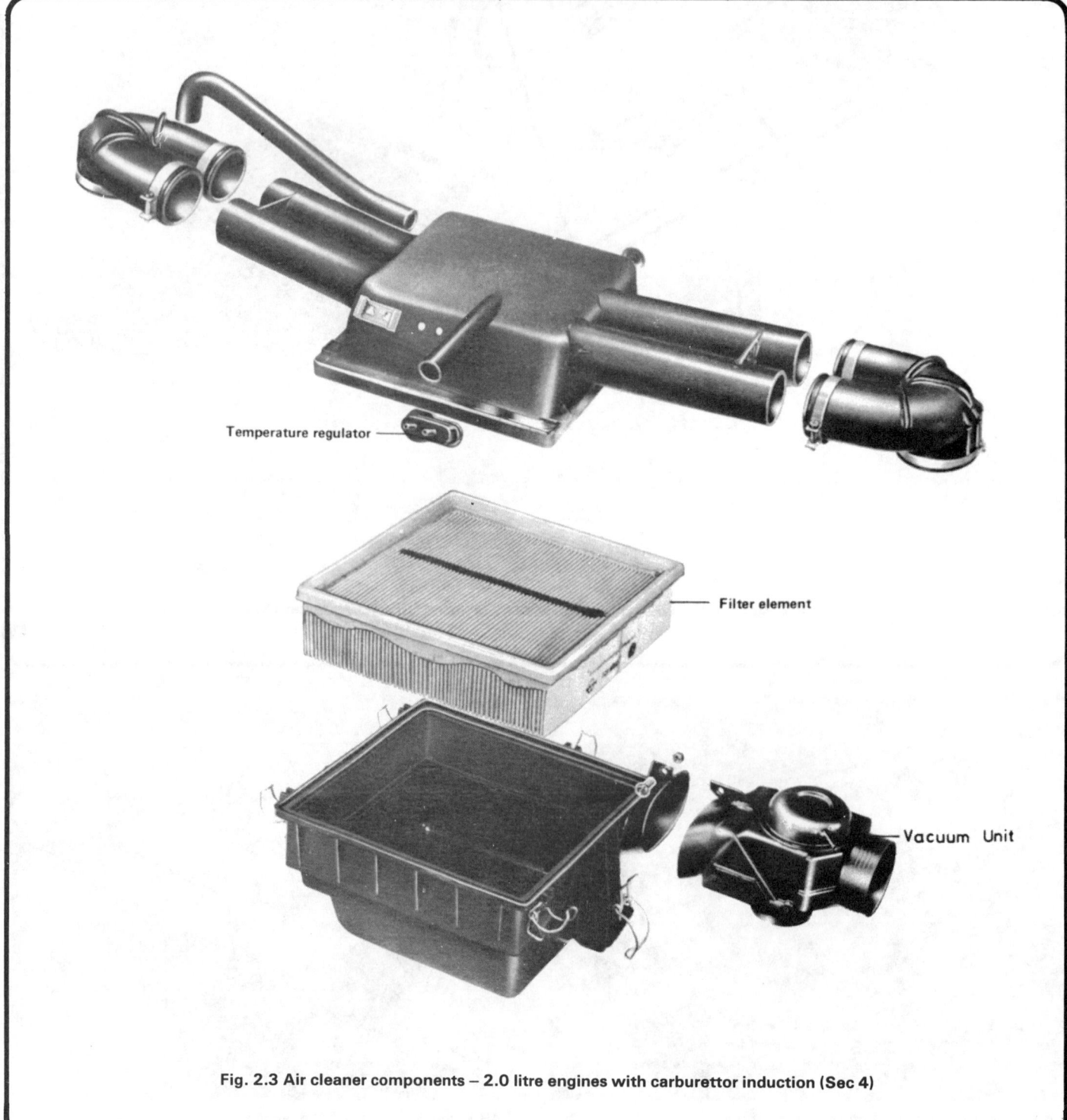

Temperature regulator

Filter element

Vacuum Unit

Fig. 2.3 Air cleaner components – 2.0 litre engines with carburettor induction (Sec 4)

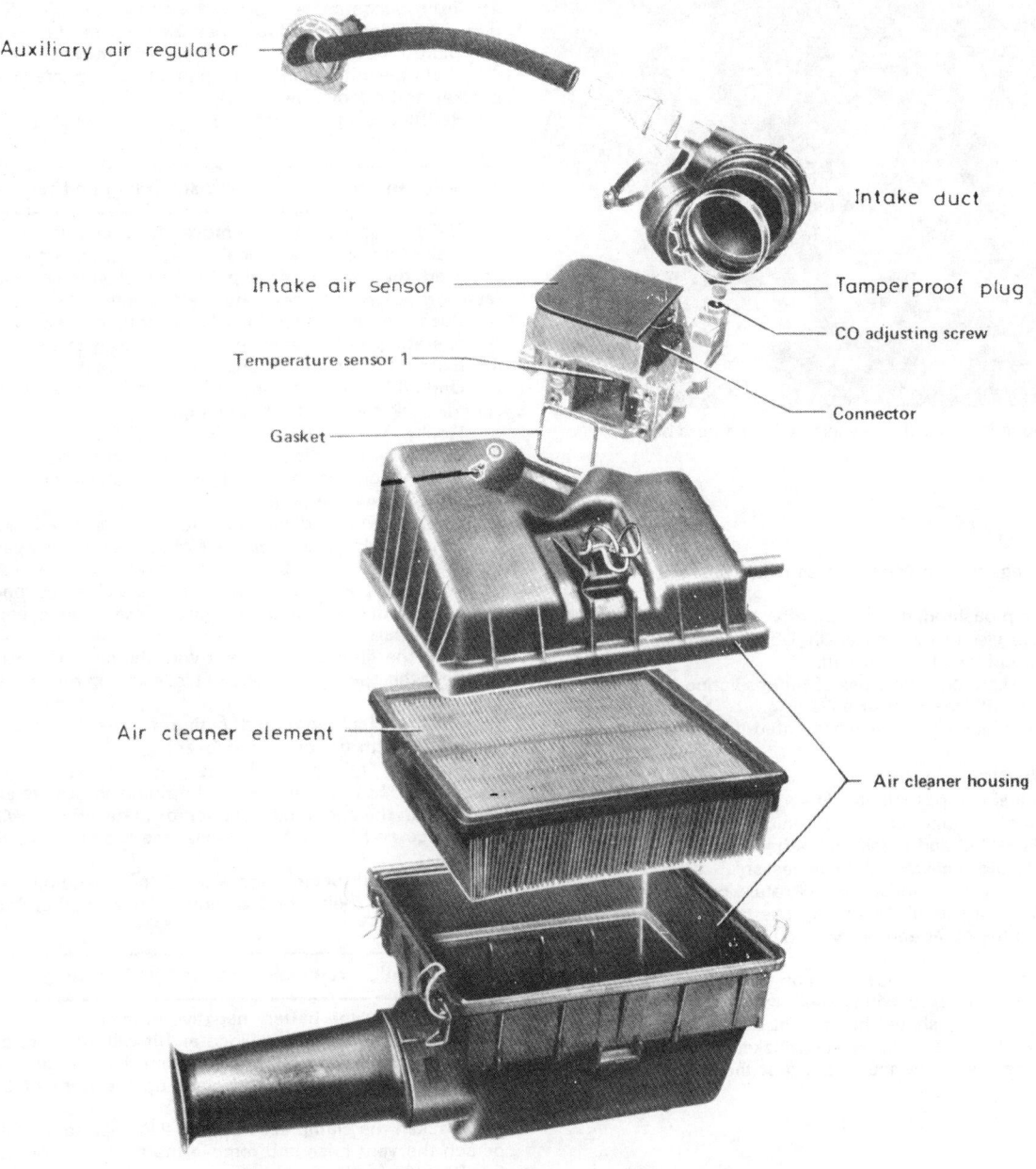

Auxiliary air regulator

Intake duct

Intake air sensor

Tamperproof plug

CO adjusting screw

Temperature sensor 1

Connector

Gasket

Air cleaner element

Air cleaner housing

Fig. 2.4 Air cleaner and intake air sensor components – 2.0 litre engines with fuel injection (Sec 4)

5 Fuel pump – removal, testing and refitting

Vehicles with carburettor induction

1   The mechanical fuel pump is situated on top of the crankcase adjacent to the distributor on 1.6 litre engines, and at the lower right-hand side of the crankcase adjacent to the flywheel on 2.0 litre engines (photo). Two different types of pump are used; the unit fitted to 1.6 litre engines is of sealed construction and cannot be dismantled, whilst the unit fitted to 2.0 litre engines may be overhauled and certain parts are available for repair.

2   To remove the pump first disconnect the battery negative terminal and, if working on a 2.0 litre engine, raise the vehicle at the rear and support it on axle stands.

3   Note the location of the fuel pipes and mark them to avoid confusion. Now disconnect the pipes from the pump and plug their ends to prevent fuel spillage.

4   Undo the two nuts on 1.6 litre engines or the two TORX type bolts using a suitable key or socket bit, on 2.0 litre engines. Withdraw the pump from its location and recover the insulating block and gaskets. The pump pushrod may be withdrawn if necessary at this stage.

5   To test the pump operation refit the fuel inlet pipe to the pump inlet and hold a wad of rag near the outlet. Depress the pump lever using a rod or small bolt and if the pump is satisfactory a strong jet of fuel should be ejected from the outlet when the lever is released. If this is not the case make sure that fuel will flow from the tank when the pipe is held below tank level. If so the pump is faulty and should be overhauled or renewed depending on type.

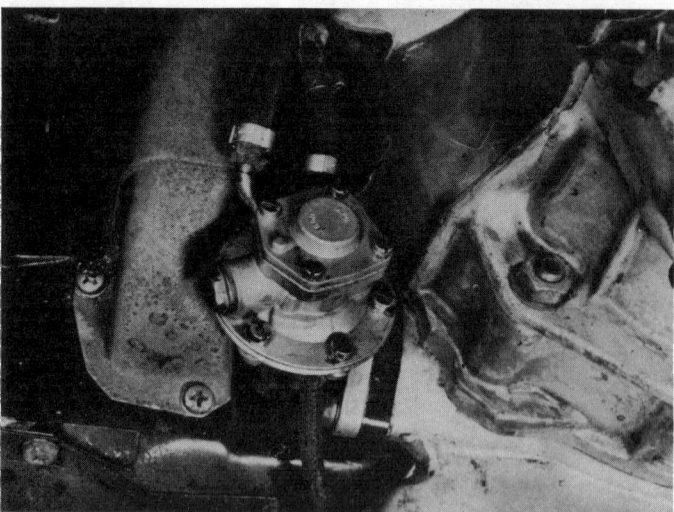

5.1 Fuel pump location on 2.0 litre engine (viewed from below)

6   Before refitting, clean away all traces of old gasket on all mating faces.

7   Refit the pump pushrod, if removed, after lubricating it thoroughly with molybdenum disulphide grease. On 1.6 litre engines the conical end of the pushrod faces the camshaft.

8   With new gaskets on both sides of the insulating block, refit the pump and secure with the nuts or bolts.

9   Refit the fuel pipes to the locations noted during removal.

Vehicles with fuel injection

10   The electric fuel pump is situated in series with the main fuel pipe from the tank to the engine, under the vehicle.

11   The pump is sealed and repair or overhaul is not possible. In the event of pump failure renewal will be necessary.

12   To test the pump disconnect the fuel return pipe at the pressure regulator and attach a suitable length of hose to the regulator nozzle, in its place. Place the other end of this hose in a jar of at least 500cc capacity.

13   Hold the intake air sensor open, turn on the ignition and allow the pump to run for exactly 30 seconds, then switch off.

14   The delivery quantity should be at least 500cc. If this is not the case make sure that the filter is not blocked, that the electrical connections at the pump are sound and that there is a minimum of

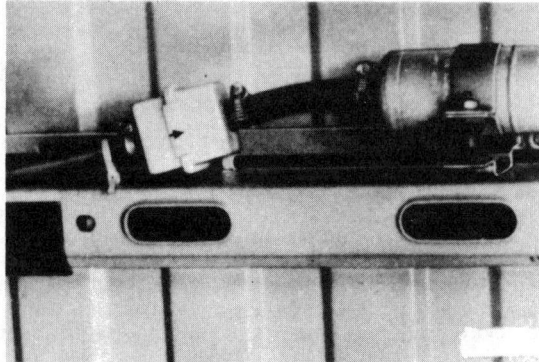

Fig. 2.5 Electric fuel pump and filter installation – 2.0 litre engines with fuel injection (Sec 5)

11.5 volts available at the pump terminals. If all these conditions are satisfactory the pump must be renewed.

15   To remove the pump first disconnect the battery negative terminal.

16   From beneath the vehicle, disconnect the electrical leads at the pump then detach the fuel pipes. Be prepared for some fuel spillage and plug the pipes as soon as they are removed.

17   Undo the nuts securing the pump retaining straps to the mounting bracket and remove the pump.

18   Refitting is the reverse sequence to removal.

6   Mechanical fuel pump – dismantling and reassembly

1   Refer to Section 5 and remove the fuel pump. Thoroughly clean it externally then prepare a clean uncluttered working area.

2   Mark the top part of the pump in relation to the housing, undo the retaining screws and separate the two parts.

3   Push the diaphragm down under thumb pressure, release it from the operating lever and lift it out together with the spring.

4   Extract the circlip, tap out the pin and remove the operating lever.

5   Undo the cover retaining screws, lift off the cover and take out the spring, gasket and cut-off diaphragm.

6   Finally unscrew the side plug and withdraw the filter.

7   Check the condition of the delivery and suction valves by blowing and sucking on the inlet port. If either of the valves is not sealing perfectly, renew the pump.

8   Inspect the two diaphragms for splits or deterioration and renew if necessary. Also check for wear of the operating lever and pivot pin.

9   Clean the filter by blowing it out with compressed air.

10   With new parts including new gaskets obtained, begin reassembly by refitting the cut-off diaphragm, gasket, spring and cover to the pump top part.

11   Refit the filter and secure it with the plug and washer.

12   Refit the operating lever and pin, securing the operating lever with the circlips.

13   Fit the diaphragm and spring to the housing, engaging the diaphragm with the operating lever.

14   Refit the two pump halves, aligning the marks made during dismantling, but do not tighten the retaining screws at this stage.

15   Push in the operating lever approximately 5 mm (0.2 in) below the pump face and hold it there whilst the top part retaining screws are tightened.

16   Fill the area behind and around the operating lever with multi-pupose grease then refit the pump as described in Section 5.

7   Fuel tank – removal, servicing and refitting

1   Disconnect the battery negative terminal.

2   A drain plug is not provided and it will therefore be necessary to syphon or hand pump all the fuel from the tank before removal.

3   Having emptied the tank, jack up the front of the vehicle and support it securely on stands.

4   Slacken the clamp securing the filler pipe to the filler neck elbow, detach the vent hose and remove the filler pipe (photo).

5   Disconnect the fuel feed and return pipes from the tank and plug their ends and the tank outlets after removal.

6   Support the tank on a jack with interposed block of wood.

7   Undo the bolts securing the tank support brackets to the underbody at one end and slip the other ends out of the locating channels.

8   Accurately mark the location of all accessible breather pipes and disconnect them. The number and location of the pipes varies according to model and export territory.

9   Slowly lower the tank and disconnect the remaining breather pipes and the fuel gauge sender unit wires.

10   With everything disconnected, carefully lower the tank and remove it from under the vehicle.

11   The expansion tanks can be removed if necessary by undoing the retaining nuts and removing them from under the wheel arches.

12   If the tank is contaminated with sediment or water, remove the sender unit, as described in Section 8, and swill the tank out with clean fuel. If the tank is damaged, or leaks, it should be repaired by a specialist or, alternatively, renewed. **Do not** *under any circumstances solder or weld the tank.*

13   Refitting the tank is the reverse sequence to removal.

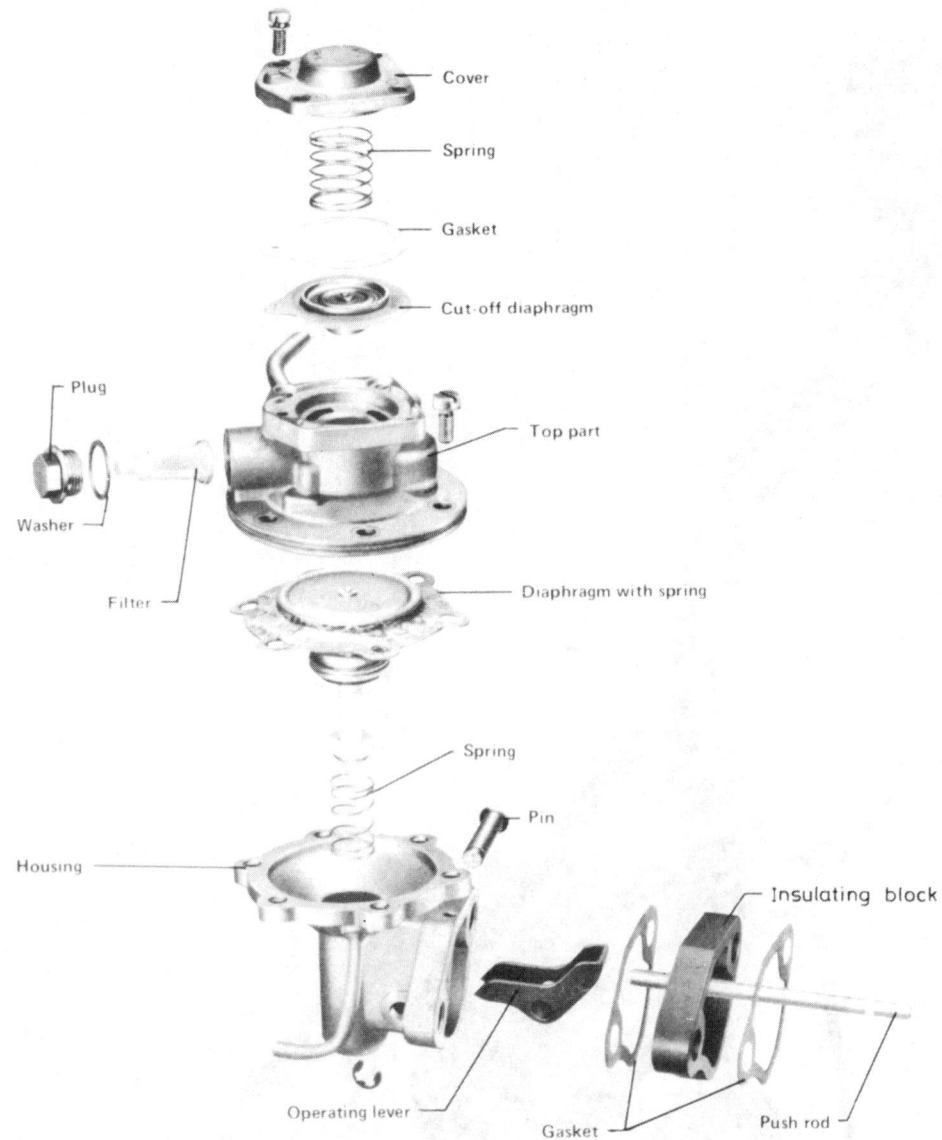

Cover

Spring

Gasket

Cut-off diaphragm

Plug

Top part

Washer

Filter

Diaphragm with spring

Spring

Pin

Housing

Insulating block

Operating lever

Gasket

Push rod

Fig. 2.6 Exploded view of the mechanical fuel pump – 2.0 litre engines with carburettor induction (Sec 6)

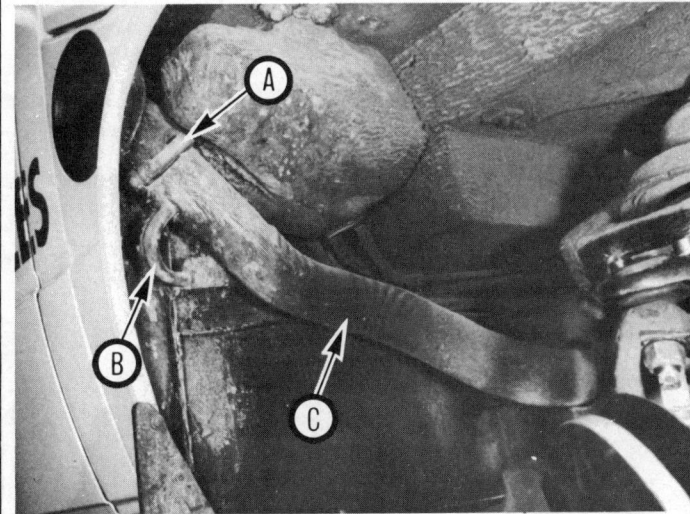

7.4 Retaining clamp (A) and vent hose ((B) on the fuel filler pipe (C)

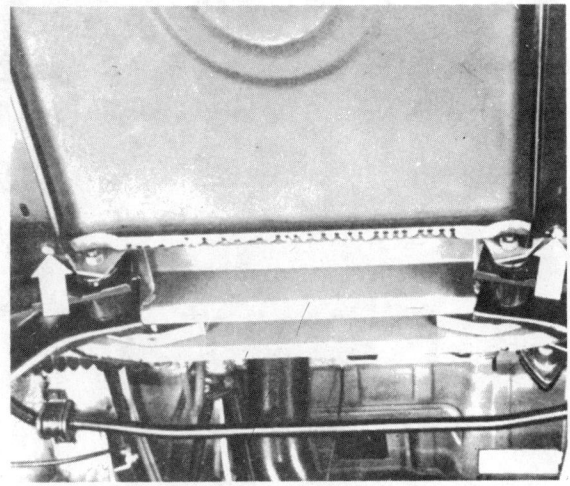

Fig. 2.7 Fuel tank support bracket retaining bolts (Sec 7)

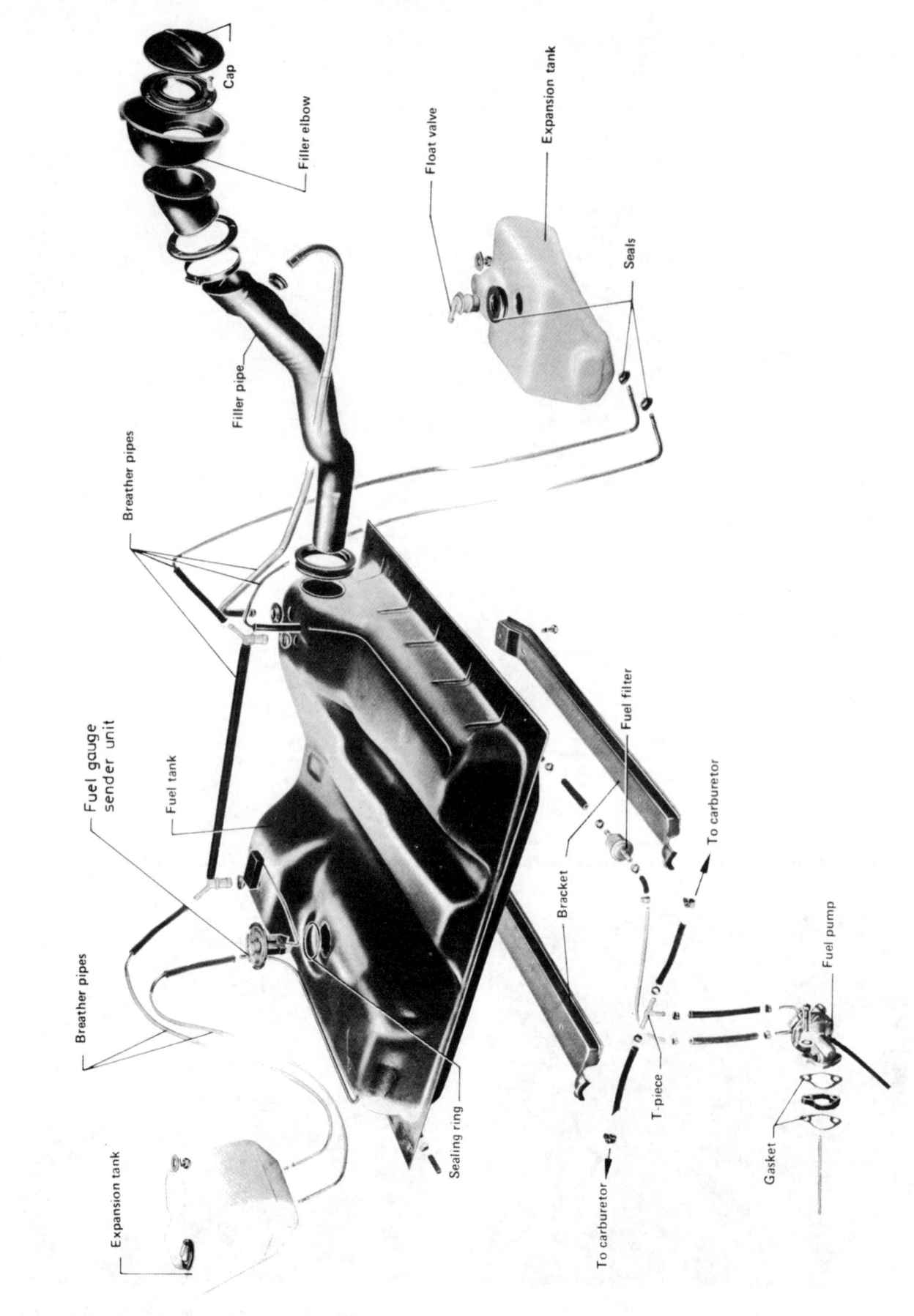

Cap

Filler elbow

Float valve

Expansion tank

Seals

Filler pipe

Breather pipes

Fuel gauge sender unit

Fuel tank

Breather pipes

Expansion tank

Sealing ring

Fuel filter

To carburetor

Bracket

To carburetor

T-piece

Fuel pump

Gasket

Fig. 2.8 Fuel tank and related component layout – typical (Sec 7)

8 Fuel gauge sender unit – removal and refitting

1   Refer to Section 7 and remove the fuel tank.
2   Note the angle at which the electrical connection on the sender unit adopts with relation to the tank, and mark the tank accordingly (Fig. 2.9).
3   Engage a screwdriver, flat bar or other suitable tool with the lugs of the locking ring and turn the ring anti-clockwise to release it.
4   Withdraw the locking ring, seal and sender unit.
5   Refitting is the reverse sequence to removal, but always use a new seal and position the sender unit as noted during removal.

9 Accelerator cable (manual transmission vehicles) – adjustment

1   Before adjusting the cable, check the condition of accelerator pedal pushrod, lever and the cable and ensure that there is no wear in the bushes and linkage. If necessary renew any worn parts with reference to the accompanying illustrations and lubricate the pedal linkage with multi-purpose grease.

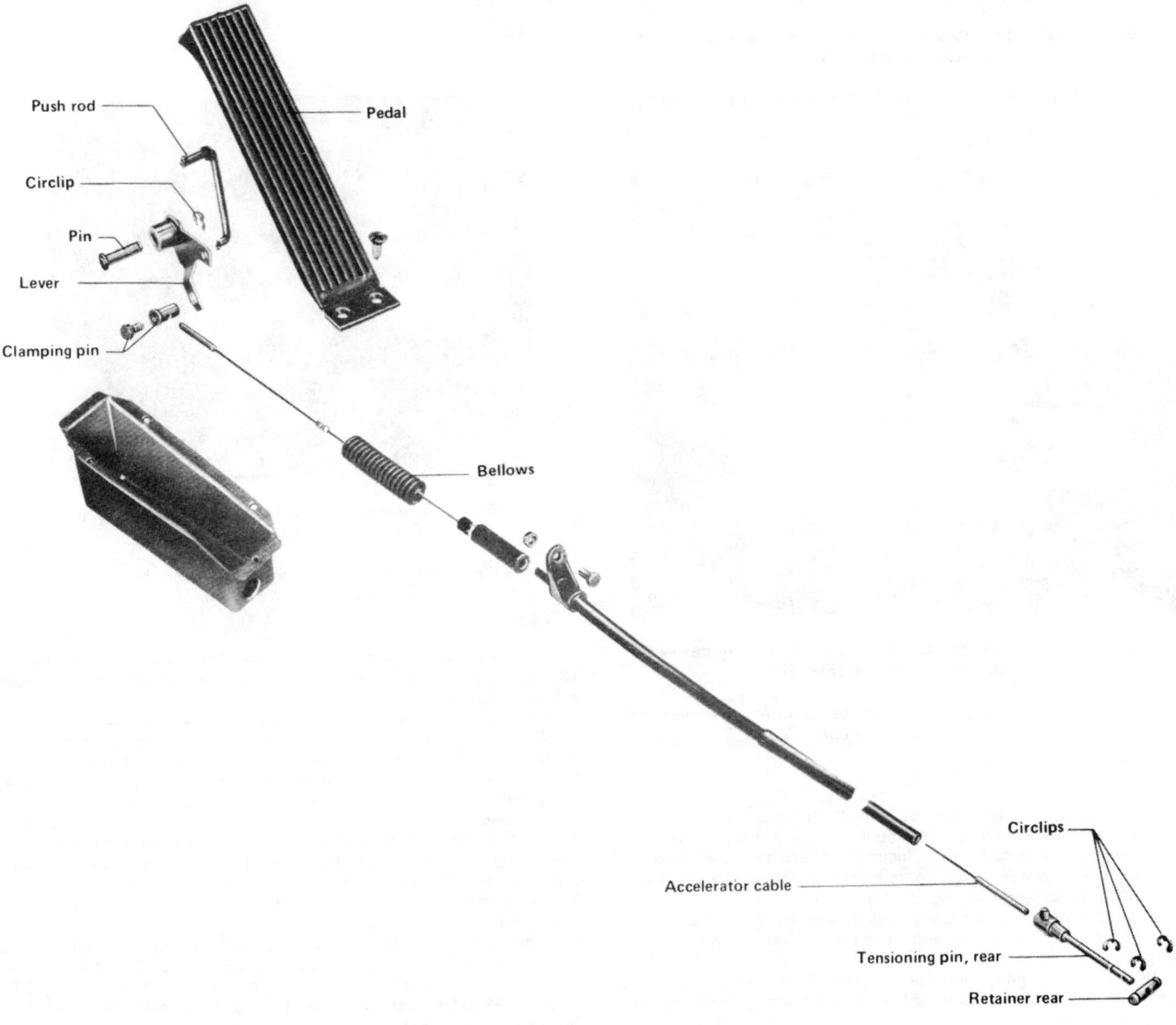

Fig. 2.9 Fuel gauge sender unit orientation (Sec 8)

Arrow indicates front of vehicle

Push rod

Pedal

Circlip

Pin

Lever

Clamping pin

Bellows

Circlips

Accelerator cable

Tensioning pin, rear

Retainer rear

Fig. 2.10 Accelerator pedal and cable arrangement – manual transmission vehicles (Sec 9)

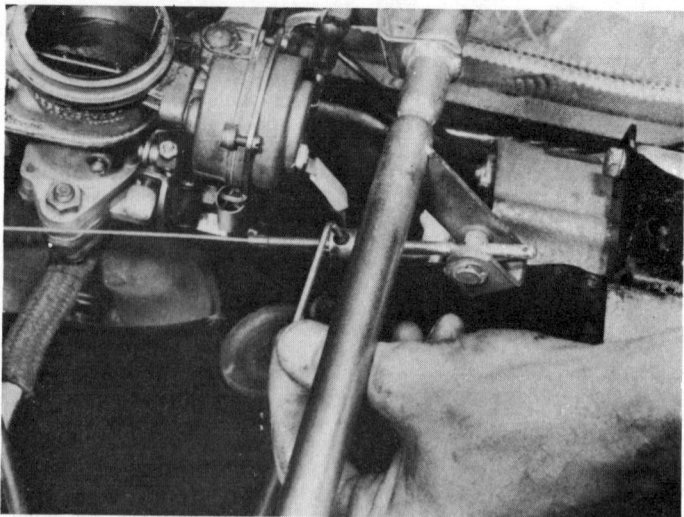

9.4 Using an Allen key to slacken the accelerator cable at the tensioning pin

Fig. 2.11 Accelerator cable adjustment – 1.6 litre engines with carburettor induction (Sec 9)

A = 1.0 mm (0.04 in) between throttle valve lever and stop – throttle fully open

Fig. 2.13 Accelerator cable adjustment – 2.0 litre engines with fuel injection (Sec 9)

A = 1.0 to 1.5 mm (0.04 to 0.06 in) between throttle lever and stop – throttle fully open

Fig. 2.12 Accelerator cable adjustment – 2.0 litre engines with carburettor induction (Sec 9)

A = 1.0 to 1.5 mm (0.04 to 0.06 in) between throttle valve lever and stop – throttle fully open

10 Accelerator linkage (automatic transmission vehicles) – checking and adjustment

2   Check the cable adjustment by depressing the accelerator pedal fully (engine switched off) and holding it in the full throttle position.
3   On engines with carburettor induction check that the specified clearance exists between the throttle lever or throttle valve lever and the stop on the carburettor (Fig. 2.11 and 2.12).
4   If the clearance is not as specified, slacken the cable at the clamping pin or tensioning pin and reposition the linkage as necessary (photo).
5   On engines equipped with fuel injection check that the specified clearance exists between the throttle lever and the stop of the throttle valve housing (Fig. 2.13).
6   If the clearance is not as specified, slacken the cable at the clamping pin and reposition the linkage as necessary.

1   Before carrying out any checks or adjustment visually inspect the accelerator linkage components for wear, excessive free play or deterioration of the protective rubber boots. If necessary renew any worn parts with reference to the accompanying illustrations.
2   To check the linkage adjustment depress the accelerator pedal to the full throttle position so that the the throttle lever or throttle valve lever is against its stop on the carburettor or throttle valve housing. Hold the pedal in this position.
3   Check that the gearbox lever on the side of the transmission is not in the kick-down position.
4   Now depress the accelerator pedal fully to the floor. Check that the override spring on the end of the adjusting rod is in tension and that the gearbox lever is in the kick-down position, approximately 1 to 2 mm (0.04 to 0.07 in) away from its stop. If this is not the case adjust the linkage as follows.
5   Slacken the adjusting rod locknut, extract the circlip and remove the override spring.

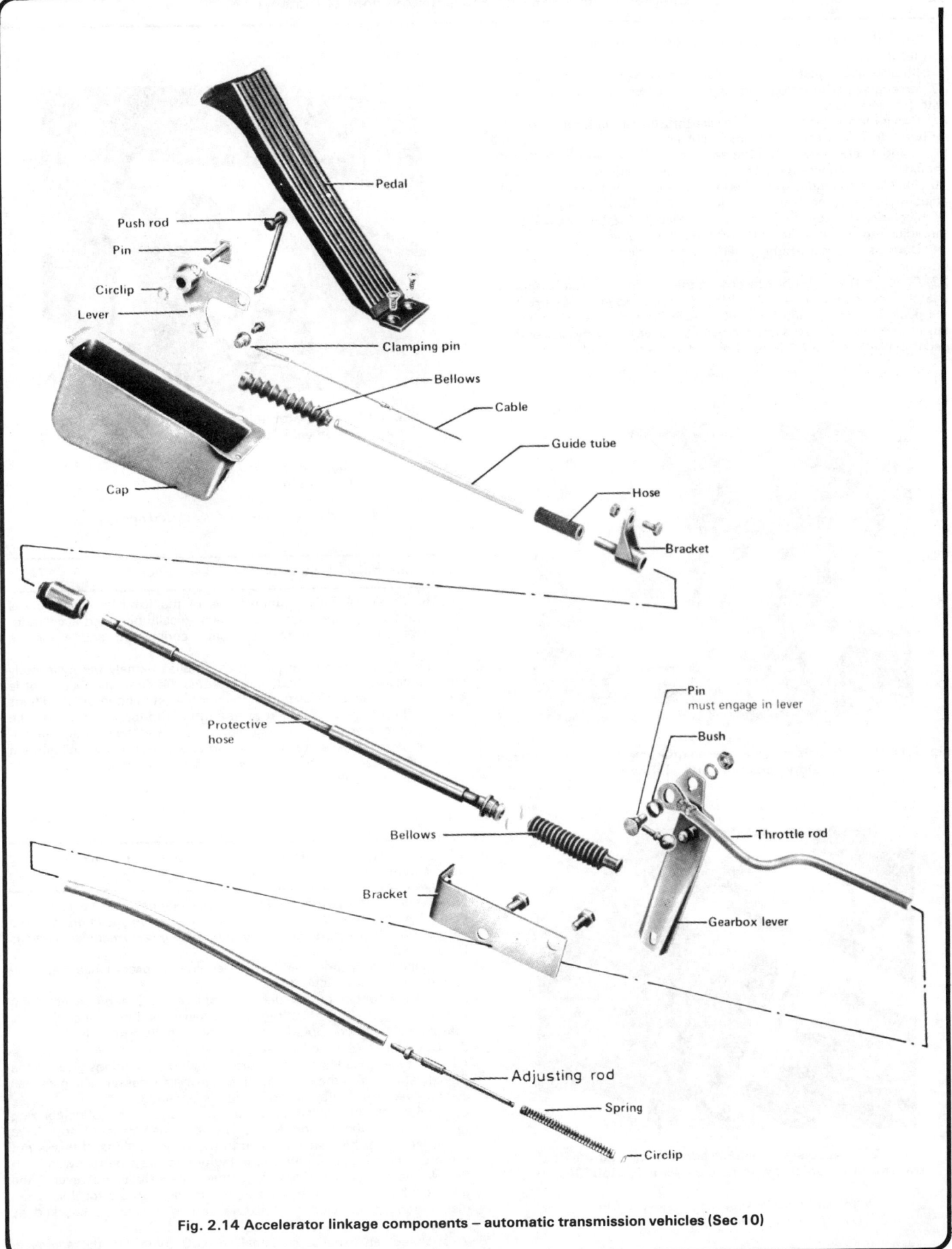

Fig. 2.14 Accelerator linkage components – automatic transmission vehicles (Sec 10)

6   Start the engine, allow it to reach normal operating temperature and let it idle.

7   If necessary adjust the engine idling speed as described in Section 17 for engines with carburettor induction or Section 22 for engines with fuel injection.

8   Switch the engine off and pull the throttle rod as far as it will go, by hand, to the throttle fully closed position.

9   Using a screwdriver, turn the adjusting rod as necessary so that its shoulder just contacts the pivot bush in the linkage or throttle lever.

10 Refit the override spring, start the engine and check that the adjustments have not altered the idling speed. Turn the adjusting rod as necessary to return the speed to the specified setting. Now tighten the adjusting rod locknut and switch off the engine.

11 Depress the accelerator pedal fully to the floor and hold it in this position.

12 Check that the gearbox lever is in the kickdown position, approximately 1 to 2 mm (0.04 to 0.07 in) away from its stop. Now release the pedal and check that the gearbox lever returns to the idle position out of kickdown. If necessary remove the cover below the accelerator pedal and adjust the cable position at the clamping bolt.

Fig. 2.17 Accelerator linkage adjustment – automatic transmission vehicles with fuel injection (Sec 10)

1   Adjusting rod locknut
2   Override spring
3   Circlip
Arrow indicates throttle fully closed position

Fig. 2.15 With throttle fully depressed gearbox lever (4) must be in kickdown position (arrow) (Sec 10)

11 Carburettor (1.6 litre engine) – description

The Solex 34 PICT carburettor is of the fixed jet, single barrel downdraught type incorporating a mechanically operated accelerator pump, automatic choke for cold start enrichment and a throttle damper.

The unit consists of two main assemblies namely the main body and top cover. The main body incorporates the float chamber, throttle barrel venturi, accelerator pump, the various jets and internal drillings and the throttle valve and linkage assembly. The top cover houses the fuel cut-off needle valve, the automatic choke and the throttle damper.

The carburettor is of simple design and layout and all adjustment and settings can be carried out using instruments readily available to the home mechanic.

12 Carburettor (1.6 litre engine) – idle speed and mixture adjustment

Note: *For the following adjustments the engine must be at normal operating temperature with the air cleaner in position on the carburettor. Also ensure that the ignition timing is correctly adjusted as described in Chapter 3.*

1   Connect a tachometer to the engine in accordance with the manufacturer's instructions.

2   Pull the connectors off the idle stabilizing unit and connect them together (Fig. 2.19). Detach the crankcase ventilation hose and ensure that all electrical equipment on the vehicle is switched off.

3   Start the engine and allow it to idle.

4   If the idle speed is not in accordance with the settings given in the Specifications, turn the idle adjusting screw as necessary using a small screwdriver until the specified setting is obtained.

5   Switch off the engine, reconnect the plugs to the idle stabilizing unit and start the engine again. The idle speed should now have increased to the test value shown in the Specifications. If this is not the case the idle stabilizing unit is faulty and must be renewed.

6   Normally this is the only adjustment necessary. However if the engine idle is uneven or erratic, or if the carburettor has been dismantled or renewed the mixture setting should be checked as follows.

7   Connect an exhaust gas analyser (CO meter) to the engine in accordance with the manufacturer's instructions.

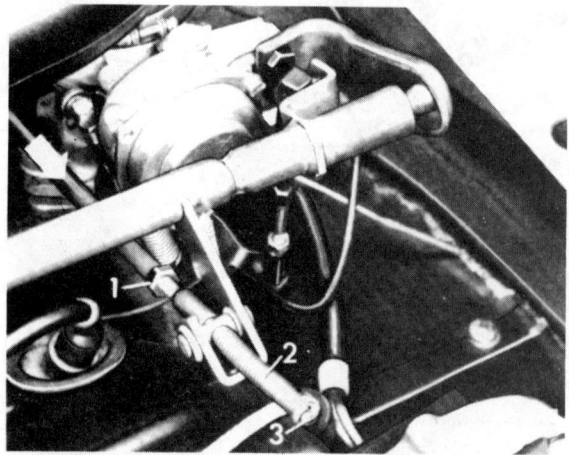

Fig. 2.16 Accelerator linkage adjustment – automatic transmission vehicles with carburettor induction (Sec 10)

1   Adjusting rod locknut   3   Circlip
2   Override spring

Arrow indicates throttle fully closed position

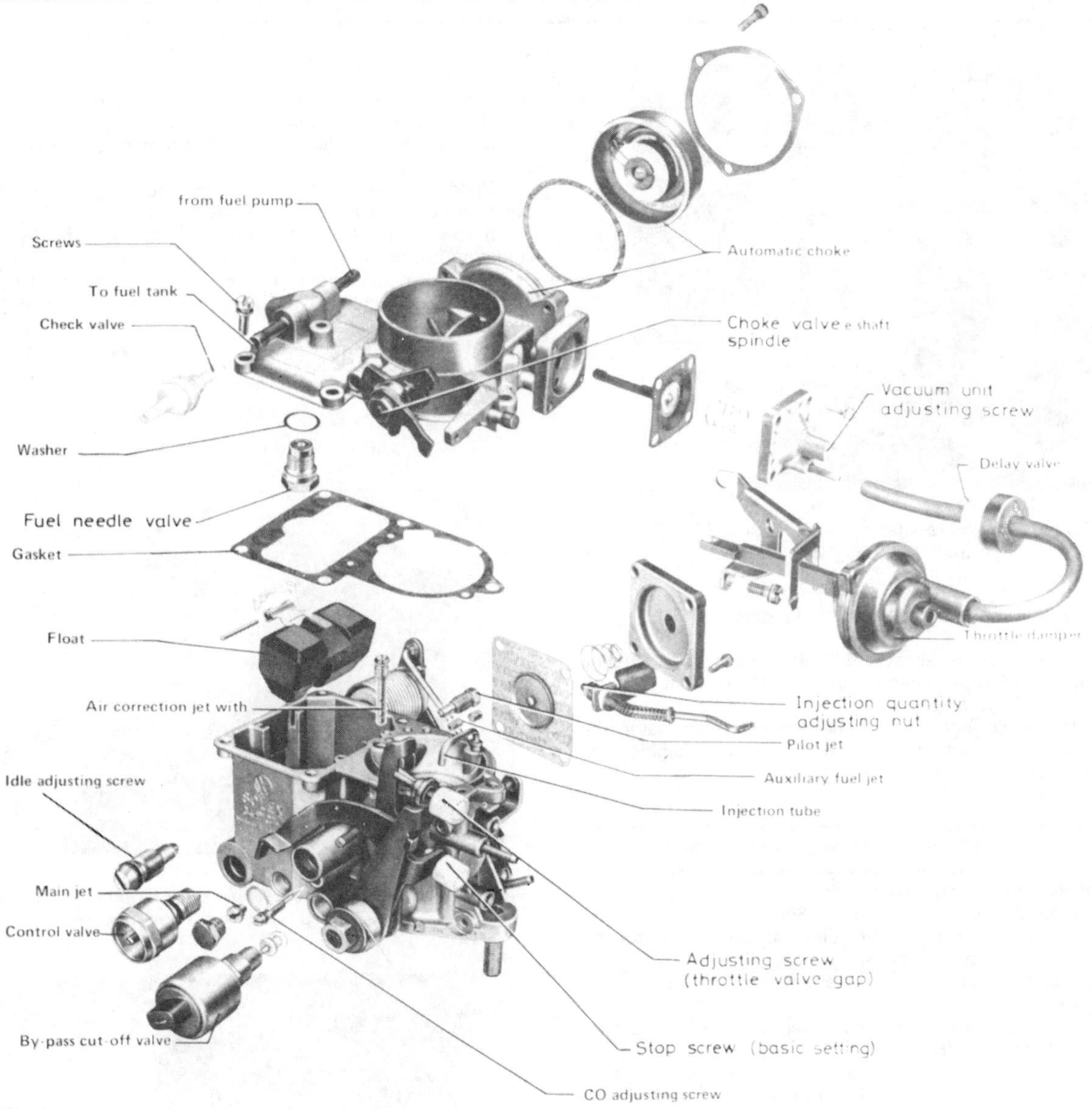

Screws

from fuel pump

To fuel tank

Check valve

Washer

Fuel needle valve

Gasket

Float

Air correction jet with

Idle adjusting screw

Main jet

Control valve

By-pass cut-off valve

Automatic choke

Choke valve shaft spindle

Vacuum unit adjusting screw

Delay valve

Throttle damper

Injection quantity adjusting nut

Pilot jet

Auxiliary fuel jet

Injection tube

Adjusting screw (throttle valve gap)

Stop screw (basic setting)

CO adjusting screw

Fig. 2.18 Exploded view of the Solex 34 PICT-4 carburettor (Sec 11)

Fig. 2.19 Connectors removed from idle stabilizing unit and joined together (arrow) (Sec 12)

Fig. 2.20 Idle adjusting screw (arrowed) on Solex 34 PICT-4 carburettor (Sec 12)

Fig. 2.21 CO adjusting screw (arrowed) on Solex 34 PICT-4 carburettor (Sec 12)

8   Carry out the operations described in paragraphs 1 to 5 if this has not already just been done.
9   Remove the tamperproof cap (where fitted) from the CO adjusting screw then turn the screw as necessary until the CO content as given in the Specifications is obtained.
10 After adjustment, correct the idle speed if necessary using the previously described procedure then switch off the engine and disconnect the instruments.

13 Carburettor (1.6 litre engine) – removal and refitting

1   Disconnect the battery negative terminal.
2   Remove the air cleaner as described in Section 3.
3   Disconnect the fuel inlet and return pipes at the carburettor top cover and plug the pipes after removal.
4   Disconnect the electrical lead at the automatic choke and at the bypass cut-off valve.
5   Note the position of the various vacuum pipes at their carburettor connections and disconnect them.
6   Disconnect the accelerator cable from the carburettor linkage.
7   Undo the nuts securing the carburettor to the manifold and withdraw the unit.
8   Refitting is the reverse sequence to removal bearing in mind the following points:

   (a) Use a new gasket between the carburettor and inlet manifold and ensure that the mating faces are clean
   (b) Adjust the accelerator cable as described in Section 9
   (c) Adjust the carburettor idle settings as described in Section 12

14 Carburettor (1.6 litre engine) – setting and adjustment of components

Note: *Under normal operating conditions only the carburettor idle adjustments described in Section 12 will need attention. Checking and adjustment of the following settings is not a routine operation and should only be necessary after carburettor overhaul or if the operation of the carburettor is suspect*

Accelerator pump injection quantity

1   On early versions of this carburettor the injection quantity was regulated by a control valve on the carburettor main body, and controlled by vacuum in conjuction with a temperature switch in the air cleaner. On later versions the system has been deleted and the air cleaner and vacuum pipes modified accordingly.
2   To check the injection quantity warm the engine up to normal operating temperature then switch it off.
3   Disconnect the battery negative terminal and remove the air cleaner as described in Section 3.

4   Place a suitable tube over the injection tube and have a graduated measuring glass available to collect the fuel.
5   Operate the throttle linkage by hand to fill the tube then direct the tube into the measuring glass.
6   Operate the throttle linkage through five full strokes then remove the measuring glass.
7   Divide the injected quantity in the measuring glass by five to give the quantity per stroke.
8   If this is not in accordance with the specified value turn the adjusting nut as necessary. Screw the nut in to increase the quantity, or screw it out to decrease it (Fig. 2.23). Check also that the injected fuel strikes the collar in the discharge arm and carefully bend the injection tube if necessary.
9   Refit the air cleaner and reconnect the battery.

Fig. 2.22 Measuring accelerator pump injection quantity – Solex 34 PICT-4 carburettor (Sec 14)

Fig. 2.23 Injection quantity adjusting nut – Solex 34 PICT-4 carburettor (Sec 14)

a   To increase   b   To decrease

Throttle valve basic setting

10 This setting is adjusted during manufacture and should not be altered. If the adjusting screw is accidently disturbed it may be reset as follows.
11 Warm the engine up to normal operating temperature then allow it to idle.
12 Disconnect the distributor vacuum advance pipe at its connection on the carburettor and connect a vacuum gauge in its place.

13 Remove the tamperproof cap from the throttle valve stop screw then turn the screw clockwise until vacuum is recorded on the gauge.
14 Turn the screw anti-clockwise until the vacuum just falls to zero then turn the screw anti-clockwise a further quarter of a turn.
15 The engine idling speed and CO content should now be adjusted as described in Section 12.

Fig. 2.24 Throttle valve stop screw (1) for throttle valve basic setting – Solex 34 PICT-4 carburettor (Sec 14)

Choke valve gap

16 This adjustment may be carried out with the carburettor in position on the engine or removed.
17 Mark the relationship of the automatic choke body to the housing on the carburettor top cover.
18 Undo the screws, lift off the retaining ring and remove the automatic choke body and gasket.
19 Push the vacuum diaphragm pullrod towards the vacuum unit as far as it will go using a screwdriver.
20 Hold the choke flap operating arm against the pullrod then turn the vacuum unit adjusting screw as necessary until a twist drill of diameter equal to the specified choke flap gap will just fit between the choke flap and the throttle barrel wall.
21 After adjustment refit the automatic choke ensuring that the peg on the choke flap operating arm engages with the loop in the choke body. Align the marks made during removal before tightening the retaining ring screws.

Throttle valve gap

22 This adjustment may be carried out with the carburettor in position on the engine or removed. If the carburettor is in place, proceed to paragraph 25.
23 With the carburettor removed, hold the choke flap closed by hand. In this position a twist drill of diameter equal to the specified throttle valve gap should just fit between the throttle valve and the venturi wall.
24 If adjustment is necessary remove the tamperproof cap over the throttle valve adjusting screw and turn the screw until the correct gap is obtained.
25 If the carburettor is in position on the engine, warm the engine up until normal operating temperature is obtained then switch off.
26 Position the throttle valve adjusting screw on the third step of the fast idle cam then start the engine again without touching the accelerator.
27 If necessary remove the tamperproof cap and turn the screw until the specified fast idle speed is obtained.

Fig. 2.26 Throttle valve gap adjustment with carburettor removed – Solex 34 PICT-4 carburettor (Sec 14)

1   Throttle valve adjusting screw
Drill bit of specified diameter arrowed

Fig. 2.25 Choke valve gap adjustment – Solex 34 PICT-4 carburettor (Sec 14)

Choke flap operating arm and vacuum unit adjusting screw arrowed

Fig. 2.27 Throttle valve gap adjustment with carburettor installed – Solex 34 PICT-4 carburettor (Sec 14)

Throttle valve adjusting screw on third step of fast idle cam (arrowed)

Throttle damper adjustment

28 Warm the engine up until normal operating temperature is obtained then allow the engine to idle.

29 Press the lever on the linkage against the adjusting screw on the top cover (Fig. 2.28) and check that the engine speed increases to approximately 1600 rev/min. If necessary turn the adjusting screw to achieve the specified speed after removing the tamperproof cap.

30 Increase the engine speed to approximately 3000 rev/min so that the throttle damper lever is pulled against the adjusting screw.

31 Release the throttle valve lever. The damper lever should slowly lift the adjusting screw and the throttle valve should close fully after approximately 3 seconds.

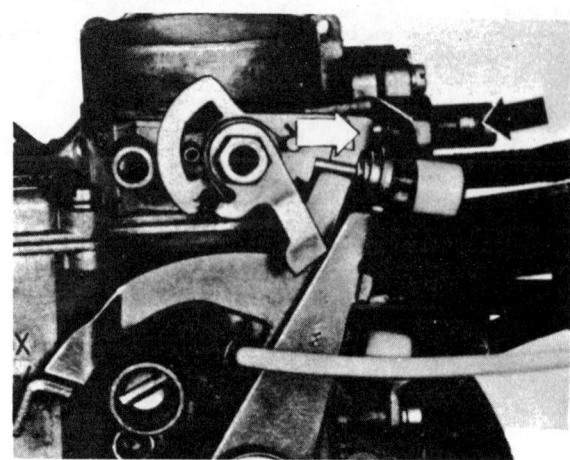

Fig. 2.28 Throttle damper adjustment – Solex 34 PICT-4 carburettor (Sec 14)

White arrow – lever on linkage   *Black arrow – adjusting screw*

15 Carburettor (1.6 litre engine) – overhaul

1 Major carburettor overhaul is not a routine operation and should only be carried out when components are obviously worn. Removing the top cover, cleaning out the sediment from the float chamber and clearing the jets with compressed air is usually sufficient to keep a carburettor operating efficiently. When a unit has covered a high mileage, it will probably be more economical to replace it with a new or exchange careburettor rather than to renew individual components.

2 With the carburettor removed from the engine and cleaned externally, begin dismantling as follows.

3 Undo the retaining screws and separate the top cover from the main body. Recover the gasket.

4 Remove the accelerator pump and choke vacuum unit housings and carefully inspect the diaphragm for signs of cracks or deterioration.

5 Place a finger over the fuel return outlet and blow through the fuel feed outlet. Check that as the fuel cut-off needle valve is raised it shuts off the flow and opens again as soon as it is released.

6 Unscrew the various jets. Blow through them and the carburettor drillings with compressed air.

7 It is recommended that the automatic choke, throttle linkage and the various tamperproofed adjusting screws be left undisturbed.

8 Thoroughly clean the float chamber removing all sediment then obtain a carburettor repair kit consisting of new diaphragms, gaskets and washers if these parts are required.

9 Reassemble the carburettor using the reverse sequence to removal, but carry out the checks and adjustments described in Section 14 as work proceeds.

16 Carburettor (2.0 litre engine) – description

The Solex 34 PDSIT carburettor is of the fixed jet, single barrel downdraught type incorporating a mechanically operated accelerator pump, automatic choke for cold start enrichment and a throttle damper. An unusual twin carburettor installation is used on the 2.0 litre engine whereby the two carburettors are not exactly the same. Engine idling is controlled by the carburettor on the left-hand bank which is equipped with a bypass idle system. The correctly metered idle mixture is supplied to both manifolds by distribution pipes from the left-hand carburettor which also houses the idle speed and mixture screws. Apart from this difference however the two carburettors are identical and operate in unison throughout the engine speed range.

Each carburettor consists of three main assemblies namely the upper and centre parts and the throttle valve part. The upper part houses the fuel cut-off needle valve, the automatic choke and the idle adjusting screws. The centre part contains the float chamber, venturi, accelerator pump and the various jets and internal drillings. The throttle valve part contains the throttle linkage and basic idle mixture screw.

The carburettor is straightforward in design and layout and all adjustments and settings can be carried out using instruments readily available to the home mechanic.

17 Carburettor (2.0 litre engine) – idle speed and mixture adjustment

Note: *For the following adjustments the engine must be at normal operating temperature with the air cleaner in position on the carburettor. Also ensure that the ignition timing is correctly adjusted as described in Chapter 3.*

1 Connect a tachometer to the engine in accordance with the manufacturer's instructions.

2 Pull the connectors off the idle stabilizing unit and connect them together (Fig. 2.19). Detach the crankcase ventilation hose at the air cleaner and ensure that all electrical equipment on the vehicle is switched off.

3 Start the engine and allow it to idle.

4 If the idle speed is not in accordance with the settings given in the Specifications, turn the idle adjusting screw as necessary until the specified setting is obtained.

5 Switch off the engine, reconnect the plugs to the idle stabilizing unit and start the engine again. The idle speed should now have increased to the test value shown in the Specifications. If this is not the case the idle stabilizing unit is faulty and must be renewed.

6 Normally this is the only adjustment necessary. However if the engine idle is uneven or erratic, or if the carburettor has been dismantled or renewed, the bypass idling mixture setting should be checked as follows.

7 Connect an exhaust gas analyser (CO meter) to the engine in accordance with the manufacturer's instructions.

8 Carry out the operations described in paragraphs 1 to 5 if this has not already just been done.

9 Remove the tamperproof cap, if fitted, from the bypass idling mixture screw then turn the screw as necessary until the CO content as given in the Specifications is obtained.

10 If it is not possible to obtain a CO content within the specified limits then the basic idle mixture should be set as follows before repeating the previous adjustments.

11 Ensure that the throttle valve basic setting is correct as described in Section 19.

12 Pull the connectors off the idle stabilizing unit and join them together.

13 Disconnect the operating rod ball socket from the throttle linkage on the right-hand carburettor.

14 Disconnect the electrical lead from the bypass idle cut-off valve.

15 Remove the tamperproof caps from the basic idle mixture screws on both carburettors, carefully screw both screws in fully then unscrew them two and a half turns.

16 Start the engine and turn both basic idle mixture screws uniformly until the engine speed is 500 to 700 rpm and the CO content is 3 to 5%.

17 Disconnect the electrical lead at the fuel cut-off valve of the left-hand carburettor and note the drop in engine speed. Reconnect the wire and repeat the process on the right-hand carburettor. If the engine speed differs greatly between the two carburettors repeat the operations described in paragraphs 15 and 16.

18 Reconnect the throttle linkage operating rod ball socket ensuring that the socket will fit over the ball without altering the position of the

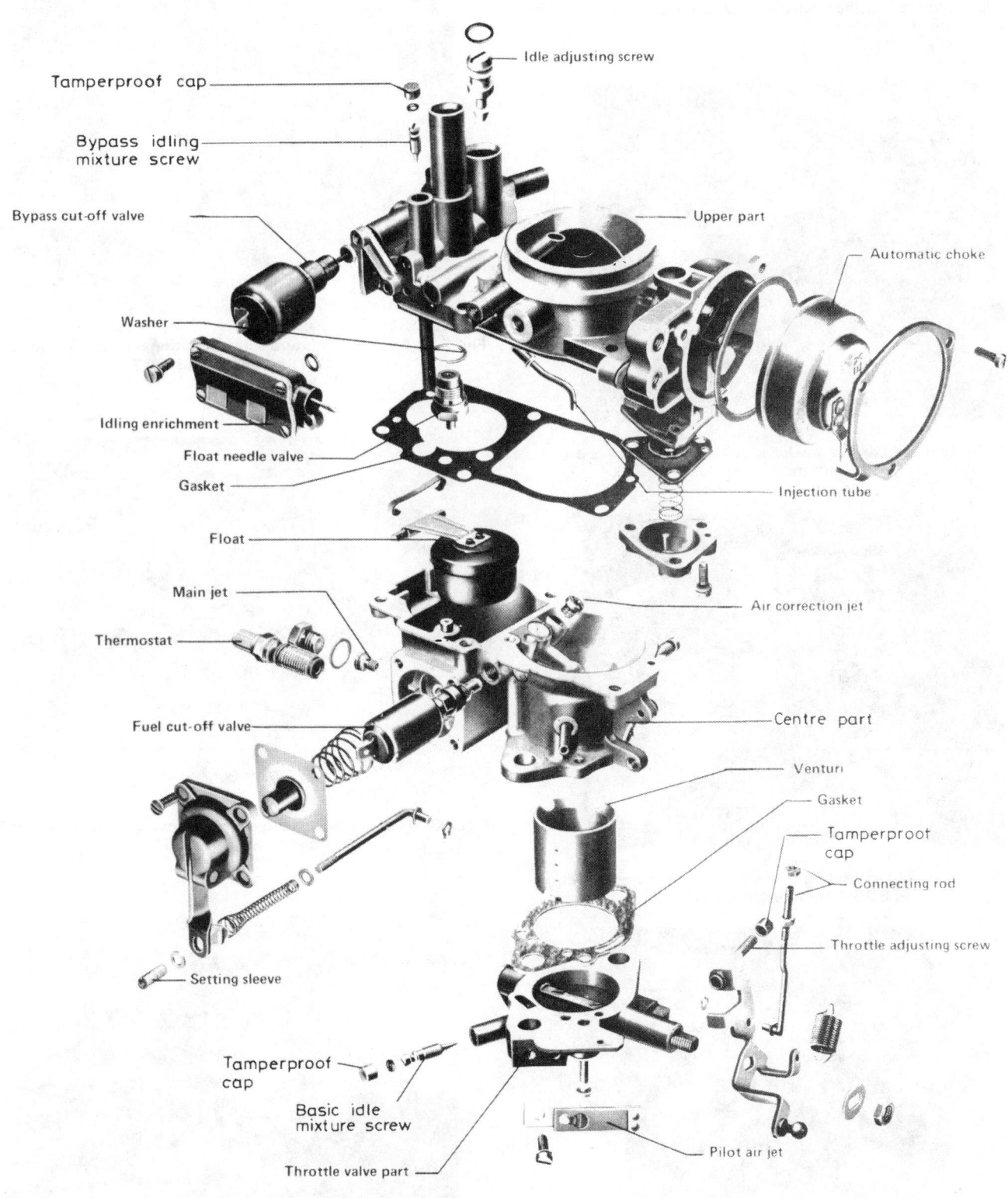

Fig. 2.29 Exploded view of the Solex 34 PDSIT carburettor (Sec 16)

Idle adjusting screw

Tamperproof cap

Bypass idling mixture screw

Bypass cut-off valve

Upper part

Automatic choke

Washer

Idling enrichment

Float needle valve

Gasket

Injection tube

Float

Main jet

Air correction jet

Thermostat

Fuel cut-off valve

Centre part

Venturi

Gasket

Tamperproof cap

Connecting rod

Throttle adjusting screw

Setting sleeve

Tamperproof cap

Basic idle mixture screw

Pilot air jet

Throttle valve part

throttle. If necessary slacken the locknuts and alter the length of the operating rod.

19 Reconnect the electrical lead to the bypass idle cut-off valve.

20 Increase the engine speed to a fast idle for 30 seconds to clear the manifolds of excess fuel then carry out the adjustments described in paragraphs 1 to 9.

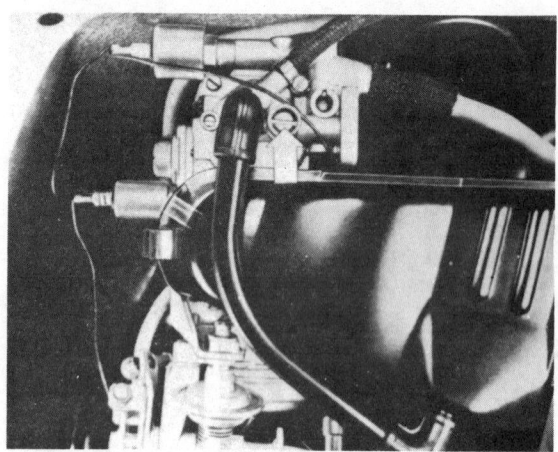

Fig. 2.30 Idle adjusting screw location (arrowed) – Solex 34 PDSIT carburettor (Sec 17)

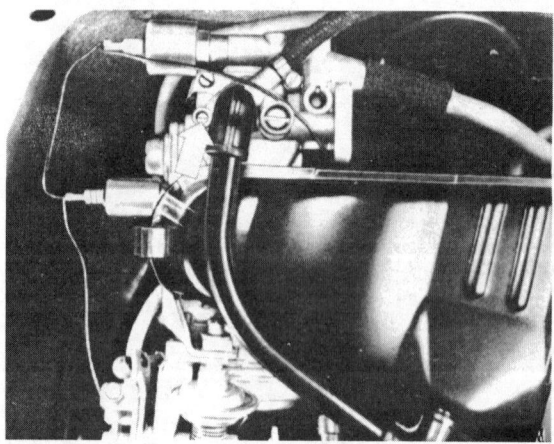

Fig. 2.31 Bypass idling mixture screw location (arrowed) – Solex 34 PDSIT carburettor (Sec 17)

Fig. 2.32 Bypass idle cut-off valve (arrowed) – Solex 34 PDSIT carburettor (Sec 17)

Fig. 2.33 Basic idle mixture screw location (arrowed) – Solex 34 PDSIT carburettor (Sec 17)

Fig. 2.34 Fuel cut-off valve location (arrowed) – Solex 34 PDSIT carburettor (Sec 17)

Fig. 2.35 Throttle linkage operating rod adjustment point (arrowed) – Solex 34 PDSIT carburettor (Sec 17)

18.4 Carburettor bypass cut-off valve (A), fuel cut-off valve (B) and idle enrichment device terminals (C)

18.6 Throttle linkage operating rod ball socket (arrowed)

18.7 Removing the linkage cross-shaft

18 Carburettor (2.0 litre engine) – removal and refitting

1　Disconnect the battery negative terminal.
2　Remove the air cleaner as described in Section 4.
3　Disconnect the fuel inlet pipe from the carburettor and plug its end after removal.
4　Disconnect the electrical leads at the automatic choke and at the bypass cut-off valve. Label the leads to avoid confusion when refitting. If the left-hand carburettor is being removed, disconnect the electrical leads at the fuel cut-off valve and idling enrichment device (photo).
5　Note the position of the various vacuum pipes at their carburettor connections and disconnect them.
6　Release the throttle linkage operating rod ball socket from the ball stud on the linkage lever (photo).
7　Move the linkage cross-shaft sideways and lift out the spring and ball seat (photo).
8　Undo the nuts securing the carburettor to the manifold and withdraw the unit from the engine.
9　Refitting is the reverse sequence to removal bearing in mind the following points:

 (a)　Use a new gasket between the carburettor and inlet manifold and ensure that the mating faces are clean
 (b)　Adjust the accelerator cable as described in Section 9 or 10 if necessary
 (c)　Adjust the carburettor idle settings as described in Section 17

19 Carburettor (2.0 litre engine) – refitting and adjustment of components

1　Refer to the introductory note at the beginning of Section 14 before proceeding.

Accelerator pump injection quantity
2　Warm the engine up to normal operating temperature then switch it off.
3　Disconnect the battery negative terminal then remove the air cleaner as described in Section 4.
4　Release the throttle linkage operating rod ball socket from the ball stud on the carburettor linkage lever.
5　Open the choke flap fully and retain it in the open position.
6　Place a suitable tube over the injection tube and have a graduated measuring glass available to collect the fuel.
7　Operate the throttle linkage by hand to fill the tube then direct the tube into the measuring glass.
8　Operate the throttle linkage through five full strokes then remove the measuring glass.
9　Divide the injected quantity in the measuring glass by five to give the injected quantity per stroke.
10　If this is not in accordance with the specified value, turn the setting sleeve as necessary. Screw the sleeve in to increase the quantity and screw it out to decrease it (Fig. 2.36). Check also that the injected fuel goes into the gap in the throttle valve and carefully bend the injection tube if necessary.
11　Refit the throttle linkage, air cleaner and battery negative terminal.

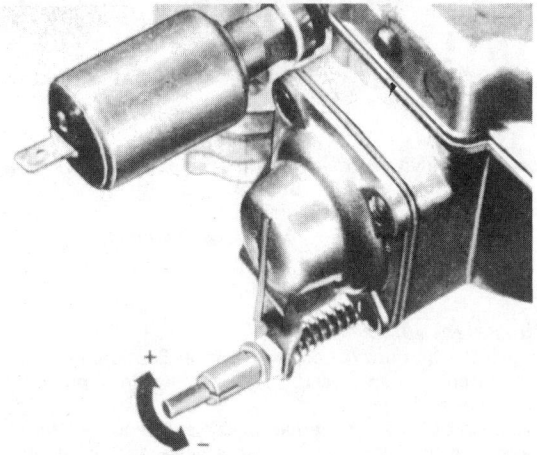

Fig. 2.36 Accelerator pump injection quantity adjustment – Solex 34 PDSIT carburettor (Sec 19)

Turn the setting sleeve as shown to increase or decrease the quantity

Throttle valve basic setting
12　This setting is adjusted during manufacture and should not be altered. If the adjusting screw is accidently disturbed it may be reset as follows.
13　Remove the carburettor as described in Section 18.
14　Remove the tamperproof cap from the throttle adjusting screw (Fig. 2.37).

Fig. 2.37 Throttle adjusting screw location (arrowed) – Solex 34 PDSIT carburettor (Sec 19)

15 Turn the screw so that the throttle is fully closed. Now turn the screw so that the throttle valve is open by not more than 0.1 mm (0.004 in) from the fully closed position (Fig. 2.38).
16 Refit the carburettor as described in Section 18.

Fig. 2.38 Throttle valve basic setting – Solex 34 PDSIT carburettor (Sec 19)

a = Specified throttle valve opening

Throttle valve gap

17 Remove the carburettor as described in Section 18.
18 Hold the choke flap closed, open the throttle approximately half way then release it again.
19 A twist drill of diameter equal to the specified throttle valve gap should now just fit between the throttle valve and the venturi wall.
20 If necessary alter the position of the adjusting nuts on the connecting rod to obtain the specified setting.
21 Refit the carburettor as described in Section 18.

Fig. 2.39 Throttle valve gap adjustment – Solex 34 PDSIT carburettor (Sec 19)

Connecting rod adjusting nuts arrowed

Throttle damper adjustment

22 With the throttle linkage closed, a gap of approximately 1.0 mm (0.04 in) should exist between the contact pad of the throttle linkage cross-shaft and the damper plunger when the plunger is pressed fully in.
23 If necessary slacken the locknut and screw the damper in or out to achieve the specified gap.
24 Tighten the locknut after adjustment.

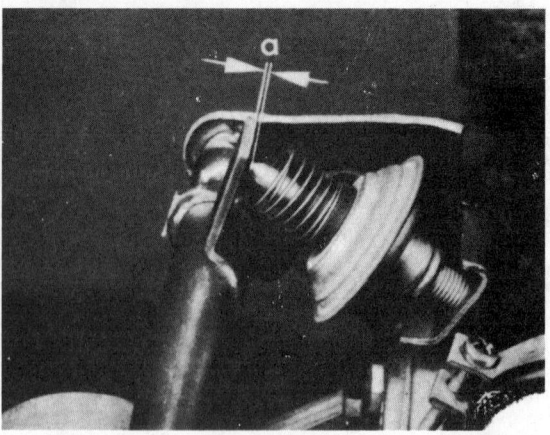

Fig. 2.40 Throttle damper adjustment – Solex 34 PDSIT carburettor (Sec 19)

a = Specified gap between pad and plunger

20 Carburettor (2.0 litre engine) – overhaul

1 Refer to paragraph 1 of Section 15 before proceeding.
2 With the carburettor removed from the engine and cleaned externally, begin dismantling as follows.
3 Extract the circlip securing the connecting rod to the linkage lever, undo the screws and lift off the carburettor upper part.
4 Undo the screws, lift off the cover and withdraw the vacuum diaphragm beneath the automatic choke. It is not recommended that the automatic choke be removed, but if it is, mark the body in relation to the carburettor housing first. Remove the choke unit, noting how the tag on the operating lever engages.
5 Lift the float out of the carburettor centre port.
6 Extract the circlip and withdraw the accelerator pump rod from the linkage lever. Undo the screws, lift off the accelerator pump cover and withdraw the diaphragm.
7 Undo the screws and remove the throttle valve port from the centre port.
8 Unscrew the various jets and blow through them and the carburettor drillings with compressed air.

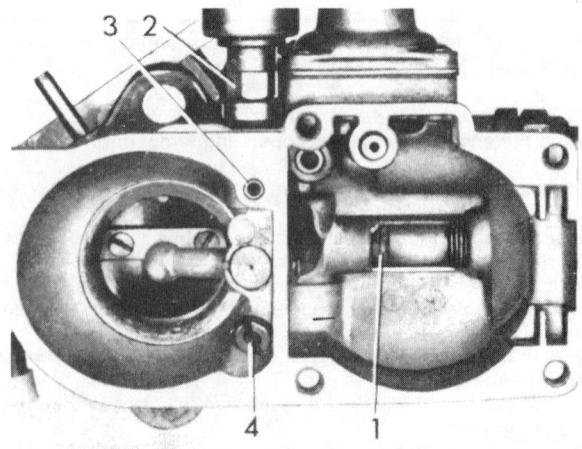

Fig. 2.41 Jet arrangement in the carburettor body centre part – Solex 34 PDSIT carburettor (Sec 20)

1	*Main jet*	*3*	*Pilot air jet*
2	*Pilot jet*	*4*	*Air correction jet and emulsion tube*

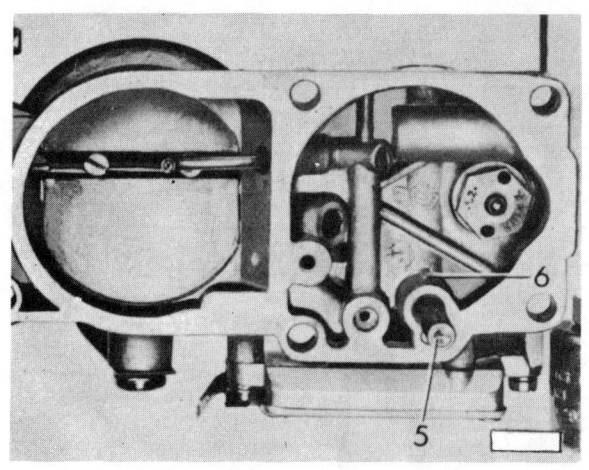

Fig. 2.42 Jet arrangement in the carburettor body upper part – Solex 34 PDSIT carburettor (Sec 20)

5   *Auxiliary fuel jet*   6   *Auxiliary air jet*

9 Carefully inspect the two diaphragms for signs of cracks or deterioration.

10 Blow through the fuel inlet and check that the flow is shut off as the fuel cut-off needle valve is raised and opened as soon as the needle valve is released.

11 It is recommended that the remainder of the carburettor components and the various tamperproofed adjusting screws be left undisturbed.

12 Thoroughly clean the float chamber removing all sediment then obtain a carburettor repair kit consisting of new diaphragms, gaskets and washers if these parts are required.

13 Reassemble the carburettor using the reverse sequence to removal, but carry out the checks and adjustments described in Section 19 as work proceeds.

---

21 Fuel injection system (2.0 litre engine) – description

A Bosch AFC (air flow controlled) fuel injection system is fitted to 2.0 litre engine vehicles for USA market territories.

The main components of the system are an electrically operated fuel pump, an electronically controlled (computer) unit and the necessary sensors, fuel injectors, fuel lines and induction manifolds.

Basically, the quantity of fuel delivered is dependent upon the volume of air being drawn into the engine. This in turn is affected by

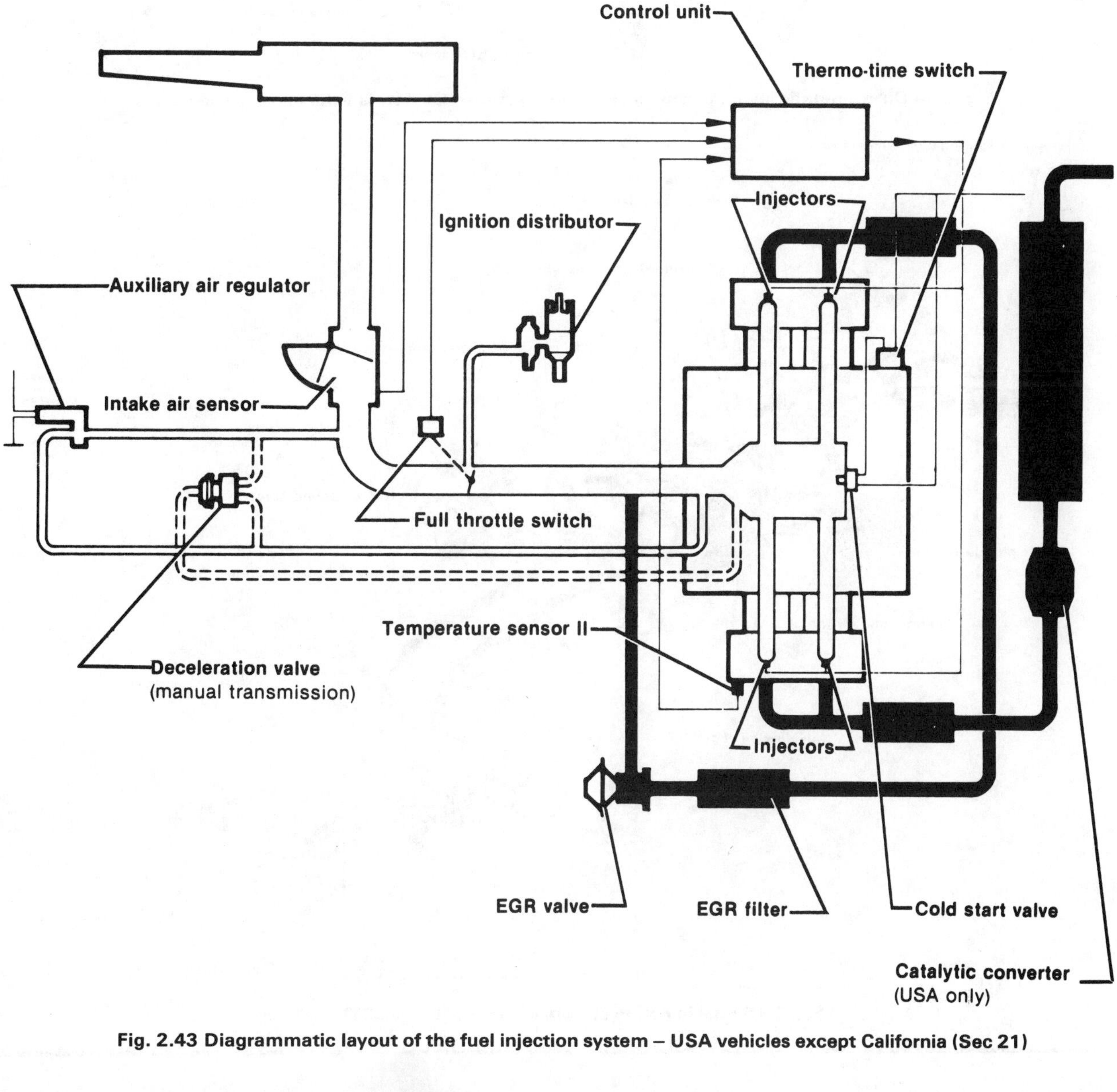

Fig. 2.43 Diagrammatic layout of the fuel injection system – USA vehicles except California (Sec 21)

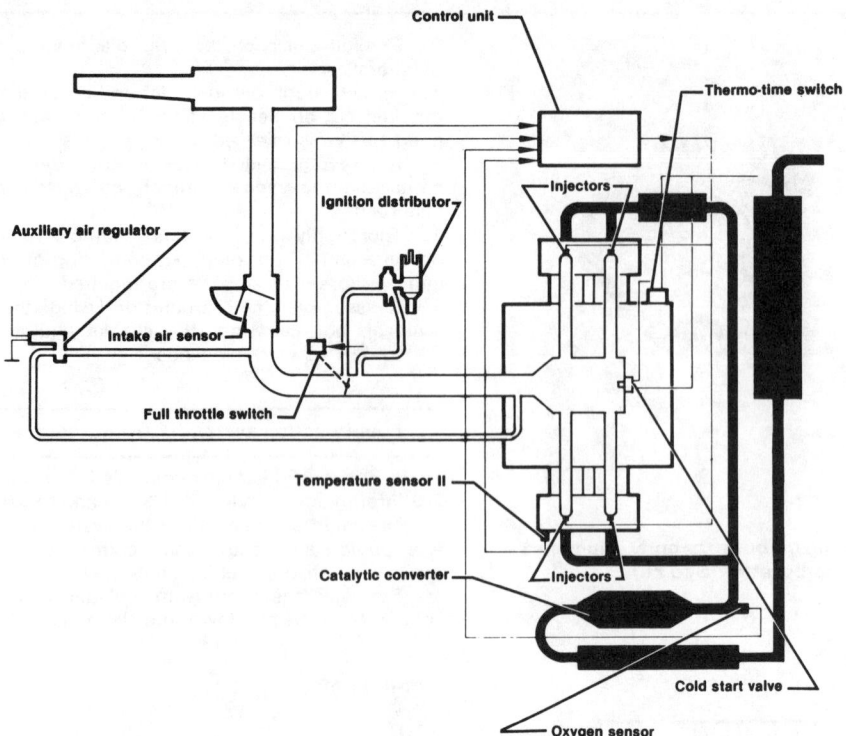

Fig. 2.44 Diagrammatic layout of the fuel injection system – California vehicles only (Sec 21)

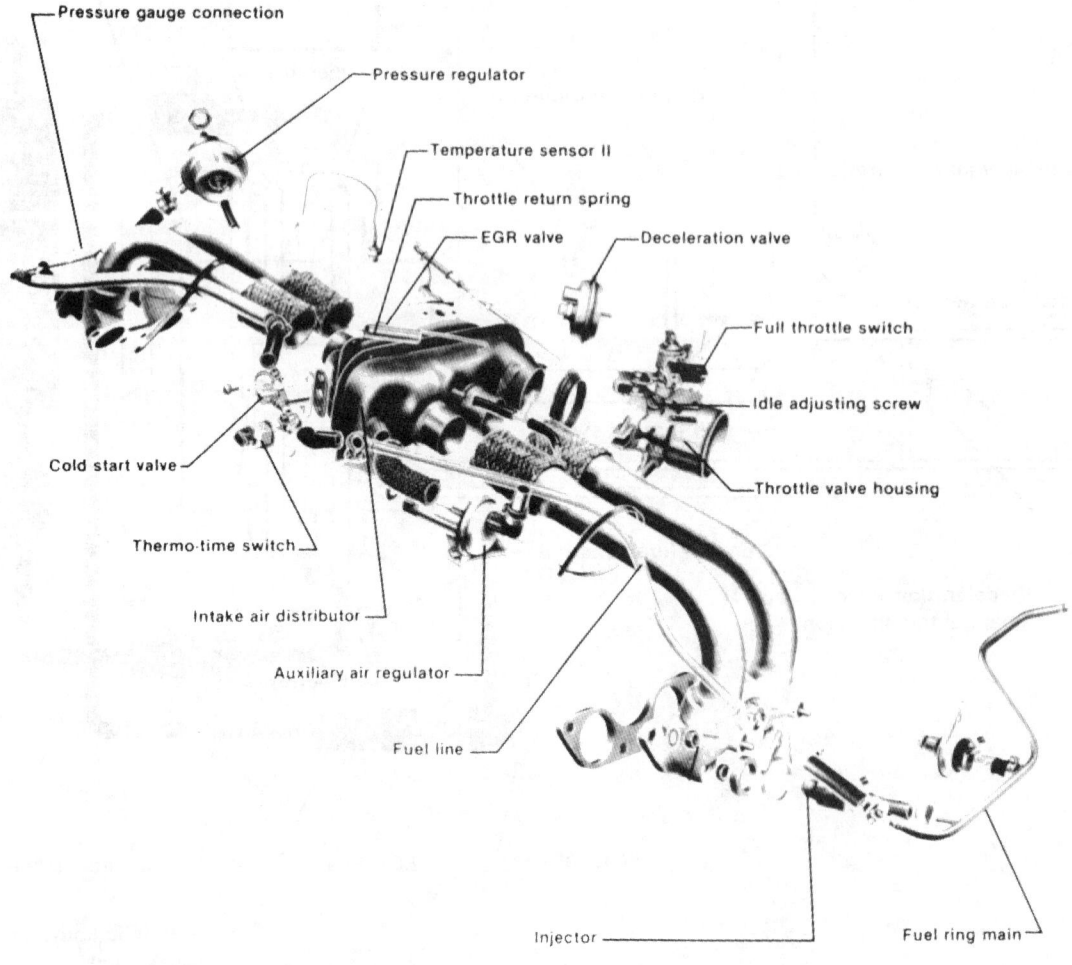

Fig. 2.45 Fuel injection system components (Sec 21)

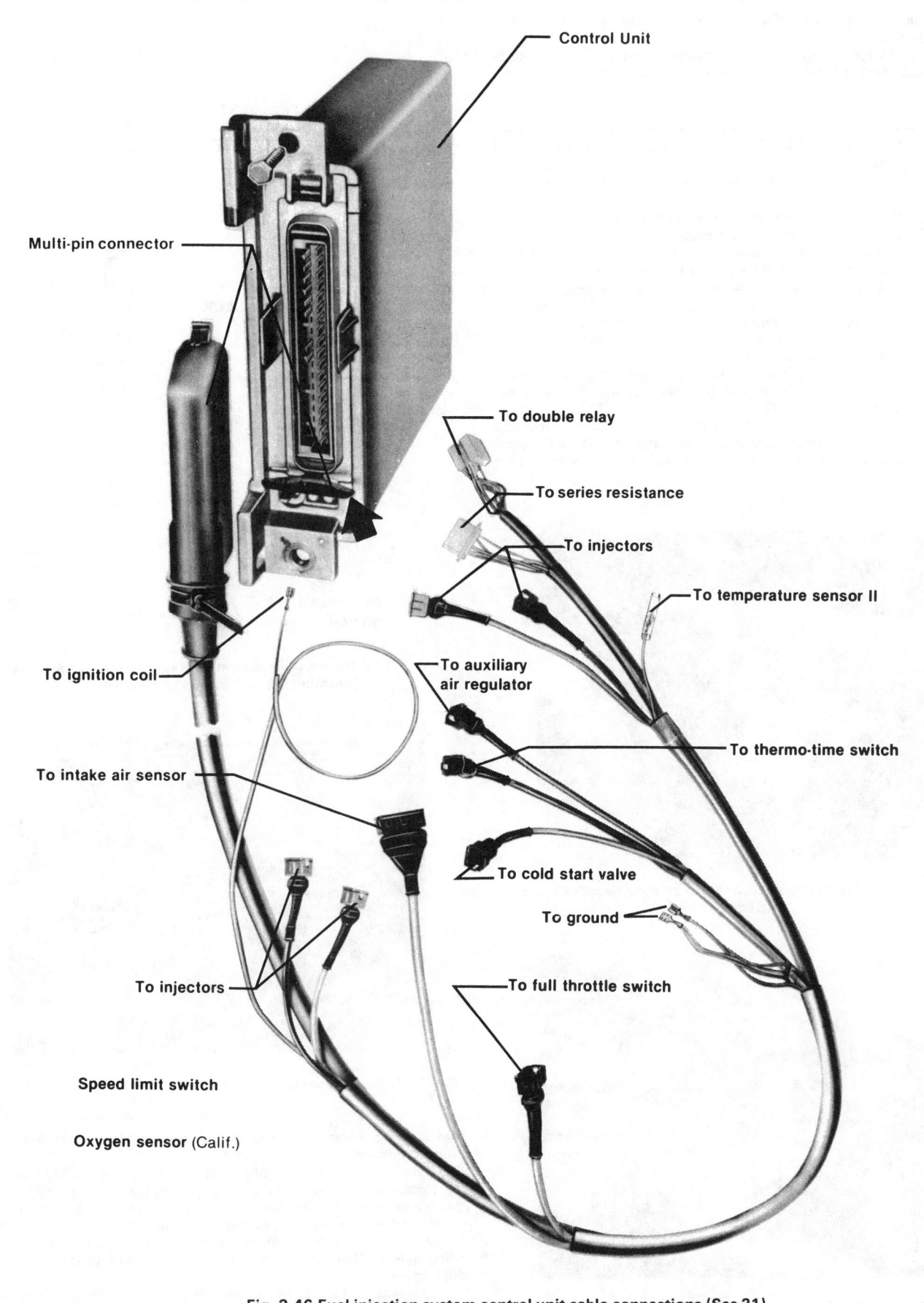

Control Unit

Multi-pin connector

To double relay

To series resistance

To injectors

To temperature sensor II

To ignition coil

To auxiliary
air regulator

To thermo-time switch

To intake air sensor

To cold start valve

To ground

To injectors

To full throttle switch

Speed limit switch

Oxygen sensor (Calif.)

Fig. 2.46 Fuel injection system control unit cable connections (Sec 21)

temperature, engine operating load and distributor advance and ignition timing.

A cold start valve automatically ensures that the fuel/air mixture delivered is correct for instant ignition at initial starting with a cold engine.

22 Fuel injection system (2.0 litre engine) – idle speed and mixture adjustment

USA except California

1   Allow the engine to reach normal operating temperature by running it for at least 15 minutes preferably longer.
2   Switch the engine off and ensure that the contact breaker points and ignition timing are correctly adjusted as described in Chapter 3.
3   Connect a tachometer to the engine in accordance with the manufacturer's instructions.
4   Disconnect and plug the charcoal filter hose at the air cleaner and ensure that all electrical equipment on the vehicle is switched off.
5   Start the engine and allow it to idle.
6   If the idle speed is not in accordance with the settings given in the Specifications, turn the idle adjusting screw on the throttle valve housing to achieve the specified speed.
7   Adjustment of the mixture should not be undertaken unless the intake air sensor has been renewed or the engine or fuel injection system have been the subject of major overhaul. Even then, make sure

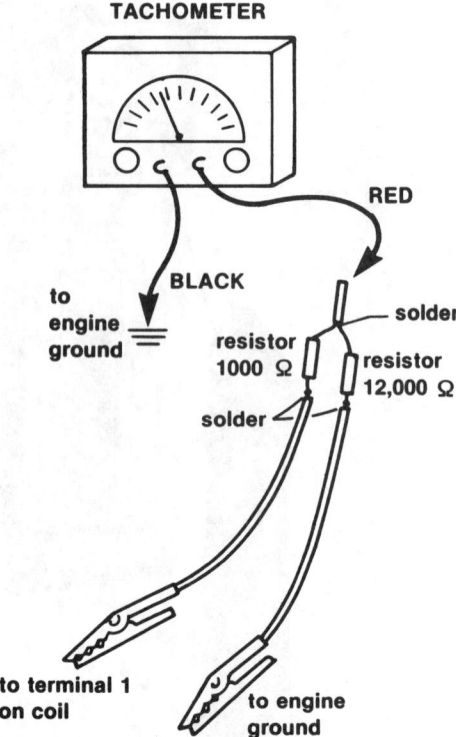

Fig. 2.49 Resistive lead connecting diagram – idle speed adjustment on California vehicles (Sec 22)

Fig. 2.47 Idle adjusting screw (arrowed) on throttle valve housing (Sec 22)

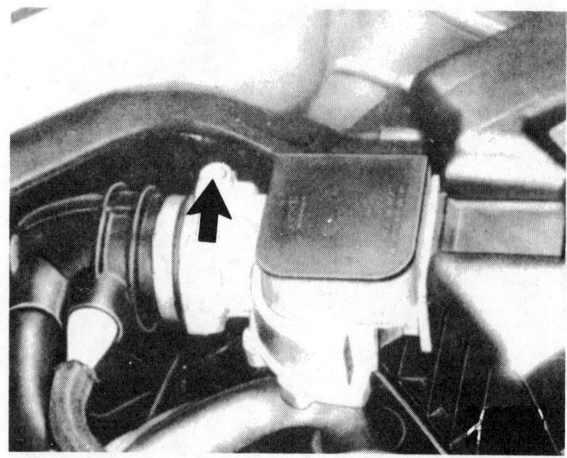

Fig. 2.48 CO adjusting screw (arrowed) on the intake air sensor (Sec 22)

Fig. 2.50 Oxygen sensor lead connecting plug (arrowed) (Sec 22)

that existing emission control legislation permits adjustment by the home mechanic.
8   Before carrying out any adjustments it will be necessary to remove the tamperproof plug over the CO adjusting screw. To do this remove the temperature sensor, drill a 2.5 mm (0.1 in) diameter hole in the centre of the tamperproof plug, approximately 3.5 mm (0.13 in) deep. Screw in a 3 mm (0.12 in) self-tapping screw and pull out the plug using pliers. Refit the temperature sensor and proceed with the adjustment.
9   Connect a CO meter in accordance with the manufacturer's instructions and with the probe inserted at the CO test point on the exhaust crossover pipe (Fig. 2.59).

10 With the engine idling at the specified idle speed, turn the CO adjusting screw as necessary to obtain the correct reading on the meter.

11 If the correct CO content cannot be obtained the injectors or spark plugs may need attention or there may be a leak at the gasket between manifold and cylinder head.

12 After completing the adjustments fit a new tamperproof plug to the adjusting screw, remove the instruments and reconnect the charcoal filter hose.

California only

13 Allow the engine to reach normal operating temperature by running it for at least 15 minutes preferably longer.

14 Connect a tachometer to the engine in accordance with the manufacturer's instructions and incorporating resistive leads as shown in Fig. 2.49.

15 Pull the connectors off the idle stabilizing unit and connect them together (Fig. 2.19).

16 Disconnect and plug the hose for the charcoal filter at the air cleaner and ensure that all electrical equipment on the vehicle is switched off.

17 Start the engine and allow it to idle.

18 If the idle speed is not in accordance with the settings given in the Specifications, turn the idle adjusting screw on the throttle valve housing to achieve the specified speed.

19 Switch off the engine, reconnect the plugs to the idle stabilizing unit and start the engine once again. Open the throttle by hand to raise the engine speed slightly and then release it. The idle speed should return to the specified value. If not make sure that the ignition timing is set correctly (Chapter 3) then repeat the adjustment.

20 Adjustment of the mixture follows the same procedure described in paragraphs 7 to 12, but adjustment should be carried out with the oxygen sensor lead disconnected at the plug connector.

---

23 Fuel injection system components (2.0 litre engines) — description, testing, removal and refitting

---

Control unit

1 The control unit is located on the right-hand side of the engine compartment. The sealed unit cannot be tested without special equipment and apart from checking the continuity of the connector and lead, no further work can be done.

Temperature sensor

2 The sensor is screwed into the cylinder head just above No 3 cylinder.

3 To test the temperature sensor, disconnect the lead from it and connect an ohmmeter between the sensor terminal and earth. The resistance should be as given in the Specifications. If it varies much from this figure renew the sensor making sure that the rubber seal fits snugly in the cylinder cover plate when the new sensor is fitted.

Intake air sensor

4 The intake air sensor can be tested in the following way after having pulled the multi-plug connector from it.

5 Connect an ohmmeter between terminals 6 and 9. The resistance should be as specified.

6 Now connect the ohmmeter between terminals 7 and 8. The resistance should be as specified.

Pressure regulator

7 This is essentially a spring loaded diaphragm which controls the pressure level of fuel supplied by the fuel pump and returns excess fuel to the fuel tank. Engine vacuum is also a contributing factor in operating the diaphragm.

8 The pressure regulator is located on the engine front cover plate just ahead of No 1 cylinder.

9 To test the regulator, make sure that the engine is warm and switched off.

10 Unscrew the plug from the pressure testing tap located on the fuel rail.

11 Connect a suitable pressure gauge to the tap and disconnect and plug the vacuum hose from the pressure regulator.

12 Start the engine when the pressure gauge should indicate a

Fig. 2.51 Intake air sensor terminals (Sec 23)

reading equal to the value shown in the Specifications. If the reading is outside the limits specified, renew the regulator.

13 Repeat the test with the vacuum hose reconnected when the pressure should also be as given in the Specifications. If the reading on the pressure gauge is outside the limits, renew the regulator.

14 Sometimes a faulty pressure regulator may be suspected when in fact it is one of the following components which is to blame.

Restriction in fuel line
Clogged fuel filter
Dirt or water in system
Low fuel pump pressure

15 Renewal of the pressure regulator is straightforward but first disconnect the battery and plug the fuel hoses as soon as they are disconnected from the regulator.

Fuel injector

16 The fuel injectors spray fuel into the induction housings and have fuel and electrical connections.

17 First remove the injector from the engine. To do this, unscrew the nut which holds the injector retainer to the stud on the intake manifold flange. As the injector is withdrawn, take care not to knock the injector nozzle against the cylinder cover plate. When refitting an injector, always use new seals (small one around the nozzle and large one around the barrel of the injector). For the purposes of this test, withdraw the fuel injector but do not disconnect its electrical lead or fuel pipe connection to the fuel rail.

18 Disconnect the distributor LT lead from the ignition coil and operate the starter for a few seconds.

19 Whilst the starter motor is turning, observe the fuel spray pattern from the injector nozzle. This should be of even cone shape.

20 If the test proves satisfactory, proceed with electrical checks, First

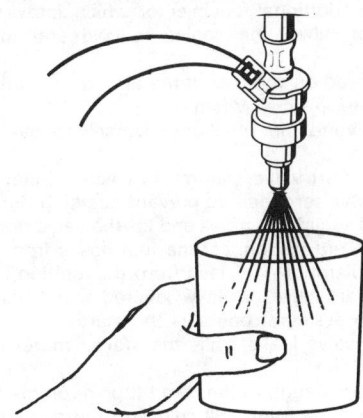

Fig. 2.52 Fuel injector spray pattern (Sec 23)

pull the lead from the injector and connect a test lamp to the plug on the end of the disconnected lead. Operate the starter motor when the test lamp should flicker.

21　If the test lamp does not flicker, suspect the double relay which is located within the engine compartment.

22　Check also the fuel injection system control unit is earthing satisfactorily.

23　Check the resistance between the injector connecting plug terminals. This should be as shown in the Specifications.

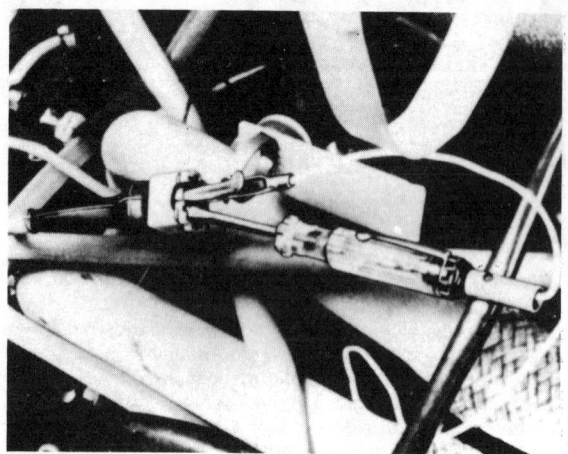

Fig. 2.53 Checking fuel injector connecting plug (Sec 23)

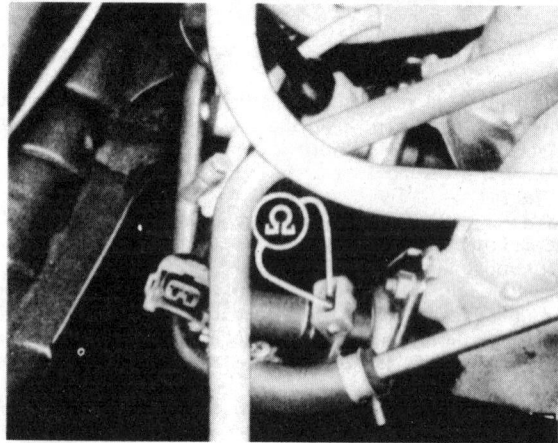

Fig. 2.54 Checking injector resistance (Sec 23)

Cold start valve

24　This is in fact an additional fuel injector which sprays fuel into the air intake distributor when the engine is cold and the starter is operated.

25　The valve is located on the rear of the air intake distributor and is controlled by the thermo-time switch.

26　Failure of the valve to inject fuel or conversely to leak, will prevent the engine starting.

27　To test the cold start valve, pull off its electrical connecting plug and tape over the valve terminals to prevent sparking during the test.

28　Remove the two securing screws and lift the valve from the intake air distributor but do not disconnect the fuel hoses from the valve.

29　Disconnect the distributor LT lead from the ignition coil terminal.

30　Hold the cold start valve partially covered with a cloth to catch ejected fuel while an assistant operates the starter.

31　If the cold start valve leaks while the starter motor is operating, renew the valve.

32　Connect a pressure gauge to the take off point on the fuel rail (see paragraph 10). With the engine still cold and the distributor LT lead disconnected from the ignition coil, operate the starter motor for a few seconds to generate pressure in the fuel system.

33　With the connecting plug disconnected from the valve, connect a jump lead between one of the valve terminals and a good earth.

34　Using a second jump lead, connect the remaining valve terminal to the switch (+) terminal of the ignition coil.

35　Switch on the ignition and the fuel pressure gauge should indicate a drop, slowly and evenly. Catch the ejected fuel in a container.

36　If these tests prove positive but the engine is still difficult to start when cold, check out the thermo-time switch.

37　Refitting the cold start valve is a reversal of removal but use a new gasket.

Thermo-time switch

38　This switch is located directly beneath the intake air distributor under the induction branch for No 4 cylinder. The switch controls the operation of the cold start valve.

39　Testing of the switch must only be carried out with the engine cold.

40　Pull the lead from the cold start valve and connect a test lamp between the valve terminals.

41　Disconnect the distributor LT lead from the ignition coil (−) terminal.

42　Have an assistant operate the starter when the test lamp should immediately light up brightly. After a few seconds (11 seconds maximum) the test lamp should dim or go out.

43　If the test shows the switch to be faulty, renew it after removing the intake air distributor. Use a socket to unscrew the switch from its bracket.

Auxiliary air regulator

44　This regulator is located on the engine crankcase between the engine box-shaped breather and No 2 cylinder induction manifold.

45　The purpose of the regulator is to admit extra air and fuel during the warming up period.

46　To test the operation of the regulator, disconnect the air hose from the flexible duct which runs between the intake air sensor and the throttle valve housing.

47　Start the engine which should be cold and feel for suction (vacuum) at the end of the disconnected hose. Seal the hose with the finger and the engine speed should decrease. As the engine warms up, the vacuum at the open pipe should disappear. If this does not happen, switch off the engine and disconnect the lead from the auxiliary air regulator. Using an ohmmeter, measure the resistance between the two terminals on the regulator. This should be as given in the Specifications. If it deviates from this, renew the regulator by extracting the two screws which hold it in position.

Deceleration valve

48　Disconnect, from the intake air sensor, the hose running to the deceleration valve.

49　Start the engine and run it at 3000 rpm for a few seconds and then release the throttle lever suddenly. Have the finger on the end of the disconnected hose when the throttle is released and suction (vacuum) should be felt. If not renew the valve.

Full throttle switch

50　To check the switch for correct adjustment, connect a test lamp between the non-insulated spade terminal on the throttle switch as indicated and a good earth. Switch on the ignition.

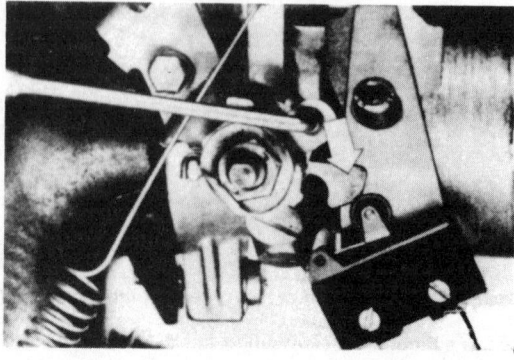

Fig. 2.55 Adjusting the full throttle switch (arrowed) (Sec 23)

51 Depress the accelerator pedal and just before full throttle position is reached, the test lamp should come on. If it does not, adjust the switch in the following way.

52 Depress the accelerator pedal fully with the test lamp connected and the ignition on, release the switch mounting screws and move the position of the switch until the test lamp comes on. Tighten the switch screws but making sure that the switch roller is in alignment with the point of the cam on the plate.

Throttle valve housing

53 The throttle valve housing incorporates the throttle valve which is cable operated from the accelerator pedal.

54 To remove the throttle valve housing, refer to Section 4 and remove the air cleaner and intake air sensor.

55 Release the flexible duct from the inlet end of the throttle valve housing also disconnect the throttle return spring from the lever on the throttle valve plate spindle.

56 Disconnect the accelerator cable as described in Section 9 or 10 and pull off the vacuum hoses from the throttle valve housing.

57 On vehicles equipped with automatic transmission, disconnect the vacuum hose from the idle speed regulator.

58 Extract the two screws which hold the throttle valve housing to the intake air distributor. On automatic transmission vehicles, remove the idle speed regulator.

59 Disconnect the electrical leads from the throttle valve switch and lift the throttle valve housing away.

60 Refitting is a reversal of removal.

Intake air distributor

61 Remove the intake air sensor and air cleaner and then disconnect the flexible duct from the inlet end of the throttle valve housing.

62 Disconnect the throttle return spring and the EGR adjuster rod and then repeat the operations described in para's 56 and 57.

63 Slide the four manifold hoses from the intake air distributor and onto the intake manifold tubes, (refer to Fig. 2.45).

64 Unscrew the nuts which hold the intake air distributor to the crankcase, lift the intake air distributor away and disconnect the electrical leads from the full throttle switch.

65 Refitting is a reversal of removal, use new gaskets and tighten the bolts, nuts and screws securely.

Manifold tubes

66 The manifold tubes can be removed without the prior need to remove the intake air distributor. By doing this, the cylinder heads and the cylinders can be removed without having to further dismantle the intake air system.

67 Remove the air cleaner and the fuel injectors as described in Section 4 and earlier in this Section.

68 Unscrew the nuts which hold the manifold tubes to the cylinder head and withdraw the tubes.

69 Refitting is a reversal of removal, use new gaskets and tighten the nuts to the specified torque.

24 Emission control systems – general

Three types of emission control systems may be used in part or in whole according to vehicle operating territory. These are a crankcase ventilation system, exhaust emission control system and a fuel evaporative loss system.

Crankcase ventilation system

1 A closed circuit is used whereby engine crankcase emissions are recirculated to the air cleaner. From an oil separator on the crankcase a breather hose directs fumes to the air cleaner where they are mixed with the intake air and later burned in the engine.

Exhaust emission control system

2 A system of exhaust gas recirculation (EGR) is used to lower the formation of nitrogen oxide during combustion. By diverting a quantity of exhaust gas back into the inlet manifold to be mixed with the incoming mixture, the combustion process is cleaner and the nitrogen oxide emissions are reduced. An EGR valve controls the delivery of exhaust gas, through a filter to the manifold.

3 A catalytic converter is incorporated in the exhaust system to convert carbon monoxide and hydrocarbons into carbon dioxide and water. The catalytic converter is located in the exhaust system between manifold and silencer and the exhaust gases pass through it before being released into the atmosphere.

4 An oxygen sensor mounted in the exhaust manifold monitors the oxygen content of the exhaust gas and relays this information to the fuel injection control unit. The control unit then alters the fuel injection time accordingly so that the engine always receives an accurately metered air/fuel mixture.

Fuel evaporative loss system

5 The fuel system, tank and fuel lines are effectively sealed from the atmosphere to prevent the escape of hydrocarbon vapours. Fuel tank venting is through expansion tanks which allow expansion and contraction of the fuel without allowing any escape of vapour.

6 A charcoal filter is used in the tank vent lines to remove hydrocarbons from the fuel vapors. Fresh air entering the filter cleans the charcoal and routes the hydrocarbons back to the engine where they are burned during normal combustion.

25 EGR valve – adjustment

1 This valve is mechanically actuated and is located on the intake air distributor.

2 Rough idle or a tendency to stall may indicate that the valve requires adjustment.

3 To adjust, have the engine at the normal operating temperature with the idle speed correctly set to the specified figure.

4 Release the locknuts on the threaded adjuster rod and shorten the effective length of the rod until the idle speed suddenly drops which indicates that the exhaust gases have started to recirculate. From this setting, increase the effective length of the rod by turning the adjuster as follows:

Manual transmission 1 1/6 turns
Automatic transmission 5/6 mm

5 Without disturbing the adjustment, tighten the locknuts.

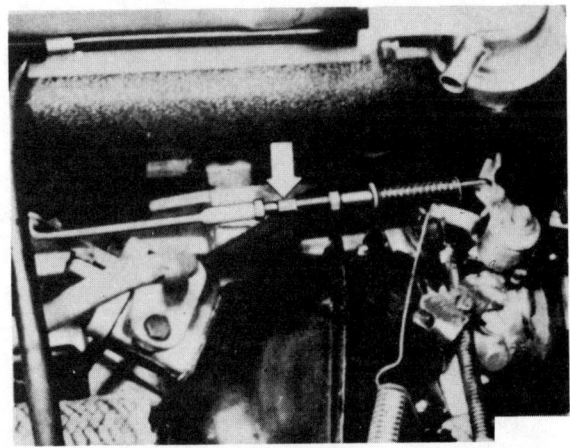

Fig. 2.56 EGR valve threaded adjuster rod (arrowed) (Sec 25)

26 Oxygen sensor – checking

1 Ensure that the engine is at normal operating temperature then connect a tachometer and CO meter to the engine in accordance with the manufacturer's instructions. Ensure that the probe for the CO meter is entered in the test point of the crossover tube and not in the tailpipe.

2 Start the engine and if necessary adjust the idle speed and mixture as described in Section 22.

3 Disconnect the oxygen sensor to control unit wiring plug.

4 With the engine idling disconnect the vacuum hose at the pressure regulator and plug the hose. Check that the CO reading has now increased to 2.5%.

5   Reconnect the oxygen sensor wiring plug and check that the CO reading returns to its normal specified value.

6   If this is not the case the oxygen sensor or the wiring between the sensor and control unit may be faulty or there may be a leak in the exhaust system between the cylinder head and the catalytic converter.

27 Exhaust system – removal and refitting

1   Numerous exhaust systems have been fitted according to engine size, operating territory, emission control equipment fitted and year of manufacture. The accompanying illustrations show a typical selection.

2   Removal and refitting of the system components is not always an easy task. Although the systems consist chiefly of bolt together sections, corrosion is always a problem and lack of accessibility often more of one.

3   A visible inspection and reference to the illustrations will show how the system comes apart and in what sequence. Before starting work, liberally soak all nuts and bolts in penetrating oil, leave it to stand for a while and then soak them again. Renew all gaskets when refitting the system and ensure that all mating faces are perfectly clean with all traces of old gasket removed.

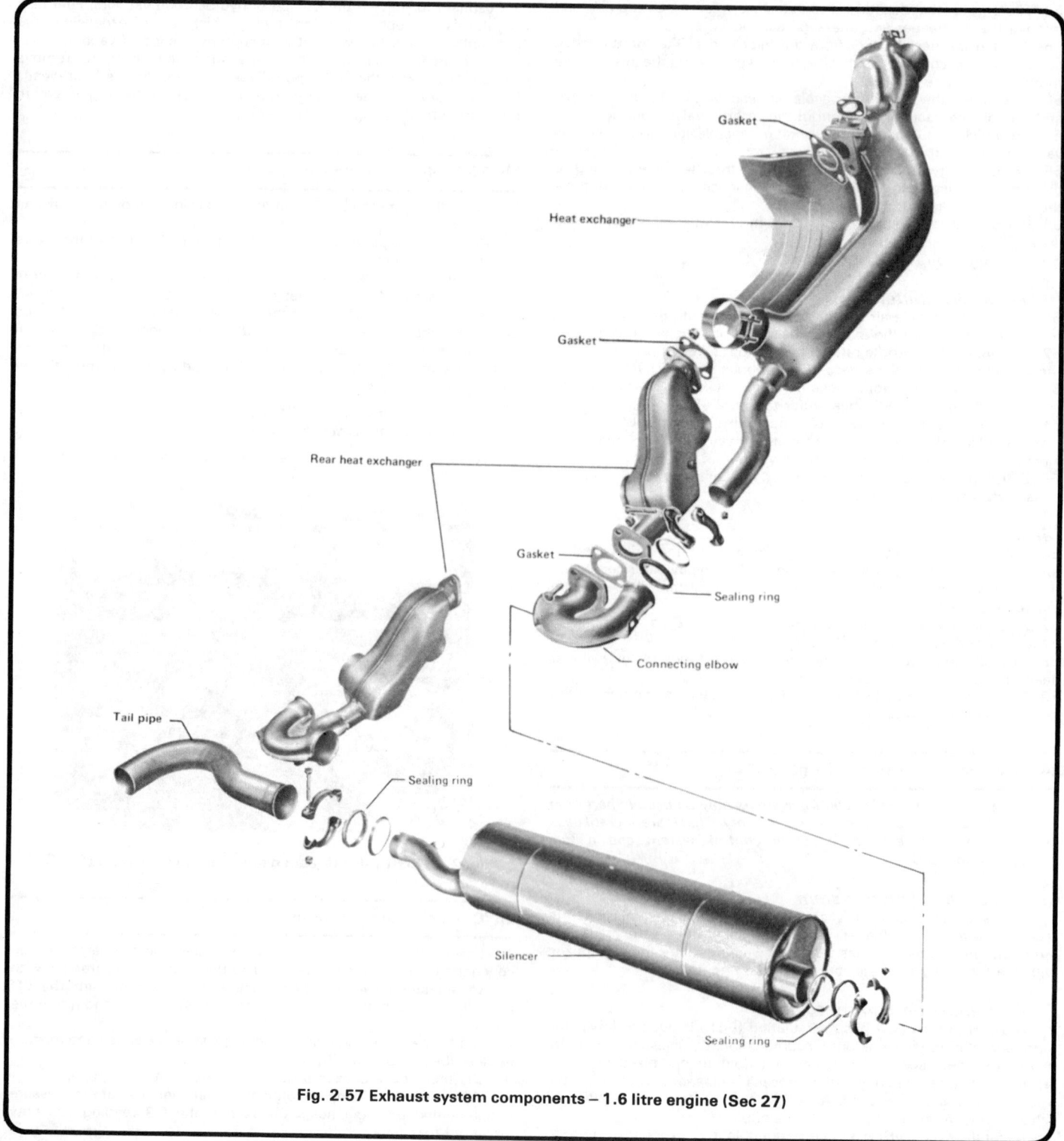

Fig. 2.57 Exhaust system components – 1.6 litre engine (Sec 27)

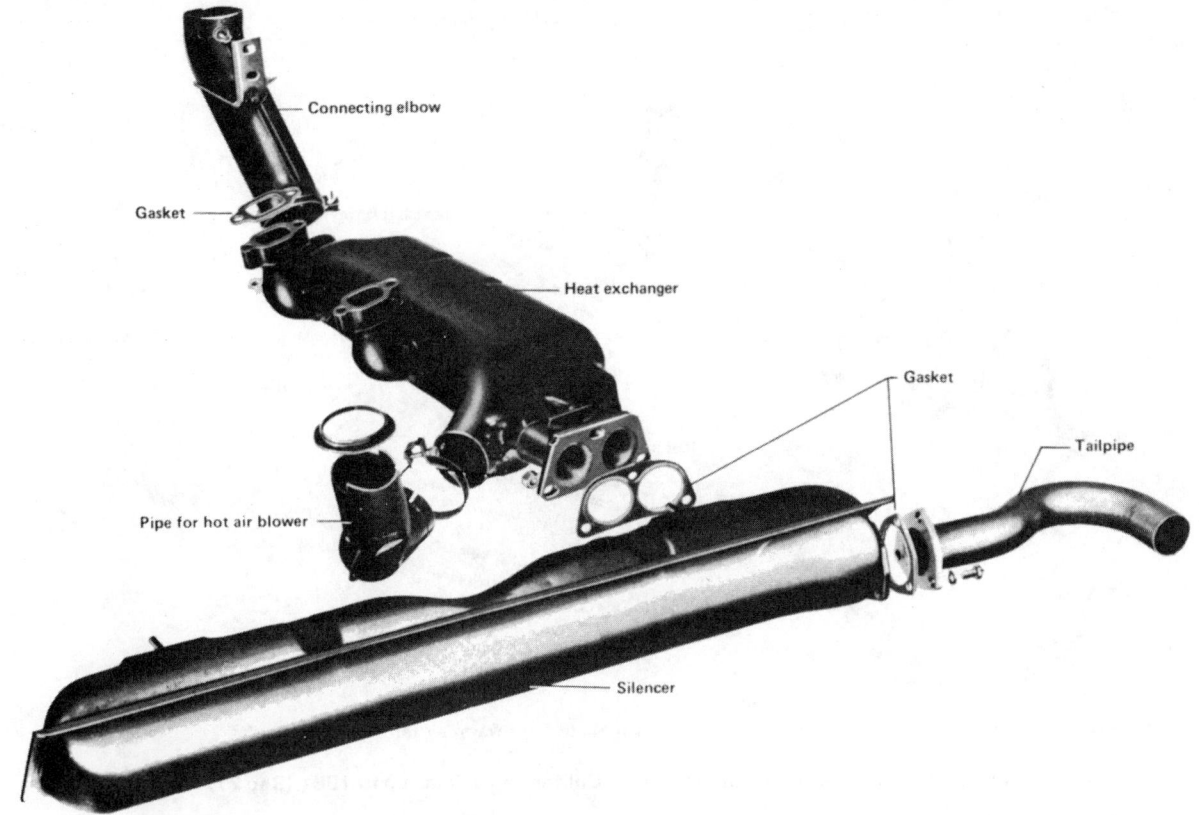

Fig. 2.58 Exhaust system components – 2.0 litre engine with carburettor induction (Sec 27)

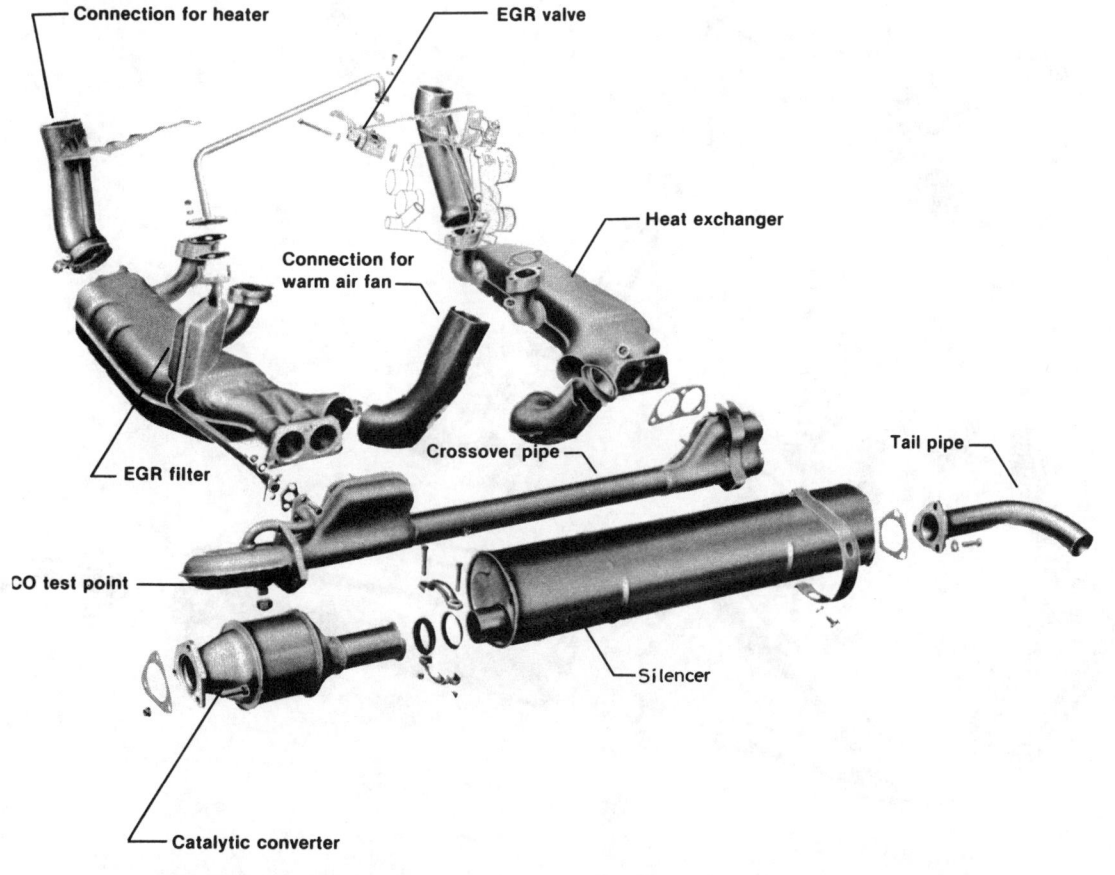

Fig. 2.59 Exhaust system components – USA vehicles except California (Sec 27)

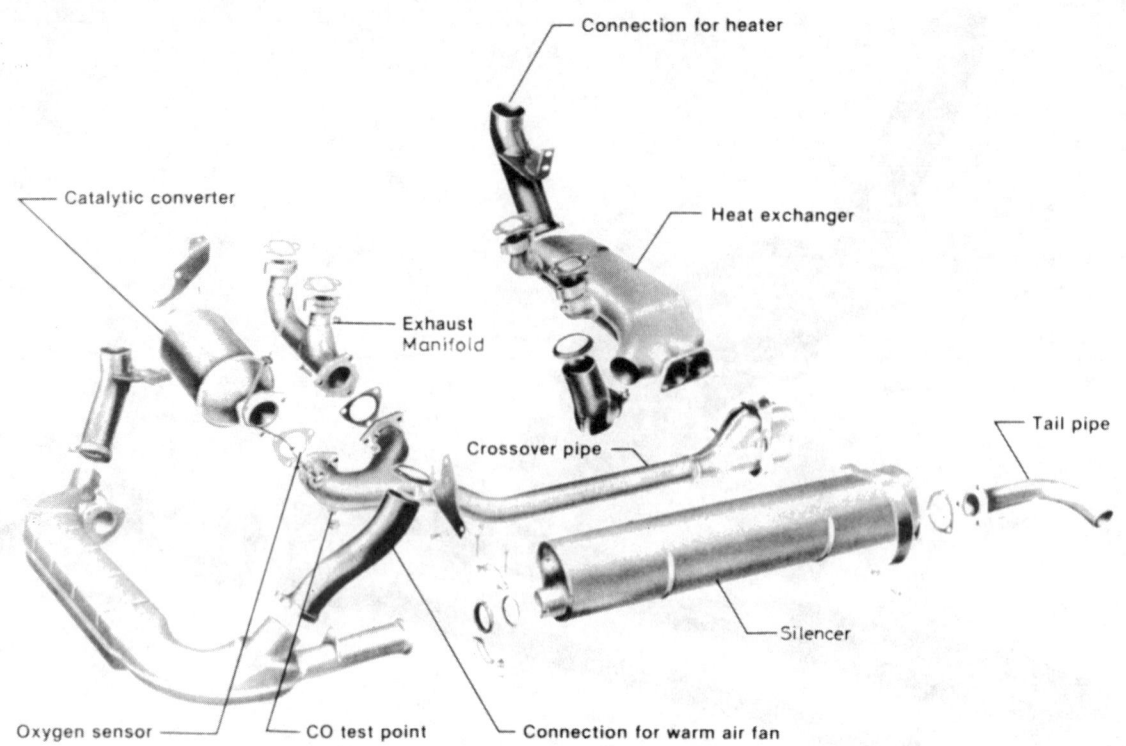

Connection for heater

Catalytic converter

Heat exchanger

Exhaust Manifold

Tail pipe

Crossover pipe

Silencer

Oxygen sensor

CO test point

Connection for warm air fan

Fig. 2.60 Exhaust system components – California vehicles up to 1981 (Sec 27)

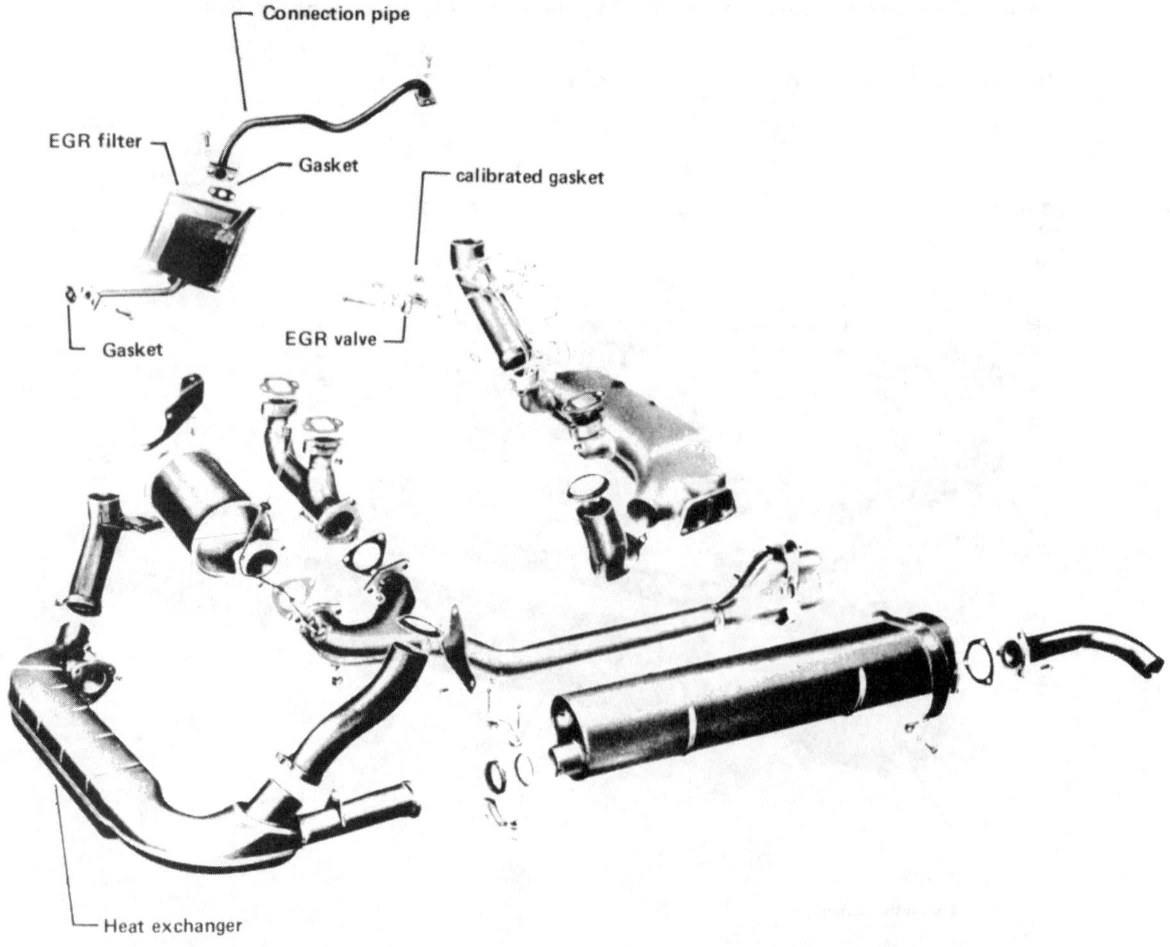

Connection pipe

EGR filter

Gasket

calibrated gasket

Gasket

EGR valve

Heat exchanger

Fig. 2.61 Exhaust system components – California vehicles from 1981 (Sec 27)

28 Fault diagnosis – fuel, exhaust and emission control systems

Unsatisfactory engine performance and excessive fuel consumption are not necessarily the fault of the fuel system or carburettor. In fact they more commonly occur as a result of ignition and timing faults. Before acting on the following it is necessary to check the ignition system first. Even though a fault may lie in the fuel system it will be difficult to trace unless the ignition is correct. The faults below, therefore, assume that this has been attended to first (where appropriate)

Accurate diagnosis of faults on fuel injection and emission control equipment entails the use of equipment not normally available to the home mechanic. Faults on these systems should therefore be referred to a VW agent.

System	Reason(s)
Difficult starting when cold	Faulty or sticking automatic choke or linkage
	Fuel tank empty or pump defective
	Float needle valve sticking
Difficult starting when hot	Faulty or sticking automatic choke or linkage
	Dirty or choked air cleaners
	Float chamber flooding
	Carburettor idle settings incorrect
	Fuel tank empty or pump defective
Excessive fuel consumption	Leakage from tank, pipes, pump or carburettor
	Air cleaner choked
	Carburettor idle settings incorrect
	Float chamber flooding
	Carburettor worn
	Excessive engine wear or other internal fault
Fuel starvation	Leak on suction side of pump, or pump faulty
	Fuel tank vents restricted
	Fuel pipes or hoses restricted
	Incorrect float level
	Blocked carburettor jets
	Blocked fuel pump or carburettor filter (where applicable)
Poor performance, hesitation or erratic running	Carburettor idle settings incorrect
	Carburettor component settings incorrect
	Faulty carburettor accelerator pump
	Air cleaner temperature control inoperative
	Leaking carburettor or manifold gasket
	Blocked carburettor jets
	Fuel starvation

Chapter 3 Ignition system

Contents

Specifications

Part A: Conventional ignition system

Type .... Mechanical contact breaker and coil ignition

Application .... 2.0 litre vehicles with L-Jetronic fuel injection

Firing order .... 1 – 4 – 3 – 2 (No 1 cylinder on right-hand side of engine nearest the flywheel)

Distributor
Type .... Bosch
Direction of rotation .... Clockwise (viewed from cap)
Contact breaker points gap .... 0.40 to 0.60 mm (0.016 to 0.020 in)
Dwell angle .... 44 to 50°

Ignition timing
Timing mark location .... Notch on crankshaft pulley, timing scale on fan housing
Setting (vacuum pipe disconnected)
   Manual transmission .... 7.5° BTDC at 800 to 950 rev/min
   Automatic transmission .... 7.5° BTDC at 850 to 1000 rev/min

Spark plugs
Type .... Champion N288 or equivalent
Electrode gap .... 0.6 to 0.7 mm (0.024 to 0.028 in)

Ignition coil
Type .... Bosch
Primary resistance .... 2.6 to 3.1 ohms
Secondary resistance .... 6 to 12 K ohms

Part B: Electronic ignition system

Type .... Bosch (Hall effect) breakerless with idle stabilization

Application .... 1.6 and 2.0 litre vehicles with carburettor induction

Firing order .... 1 – 4 – 3 – 2 (No 1 cylinder on right-hand side of engine nearest the flywheel)

Distributor
Type .... Bosch
Direction of rotation .... Clockwise (viewed from cap)

Ignition timing
Timing mark location .... Notch on crankshaft pulley, timing scale on fan housing
Setting (vacuum pipes connected) .... 4 to 6° ATDC at 800 to 900 rev/min

Spark plugs
Type:
    Standard application (temperatures mainly below
    25°C – 77°F) .... Champion N7 or equivalent
    Hot climates (temperatures mainly above 25°C – 77°F) .... Bosch W174T2 or equivalent
Electrode gap .... 0.6 to 0.7 mm (0.024 to 0.028 in)

Ignition coil
Type .... Bosch
Primary resistance .... 0.52 to 0.76 ohms
Secondary resistance .... 2.4 to 3.5 K ohms

Torque wrench settings

	Nm	lbf ft
Spark plugs	30	22

Part A: Conventional ignition system

1 General description

The ignition system is divided into two circuits, low tension and high tension. The low tension (LT), or primary circuit, consists of the battery, ignition switch, low tension or primary coil winding, and the contact breaker points and condenser, both located at the distributor. The high tension (HT) or secondary circuit, consists of the high tension or secondary coil windings, the heavy ignition lead from the centre of the coil to the distributor cap, and the rotor arm and the spark plug leads. The ignition system is based on feeding low tension voltage from the battery to the coil where it is converted to high tension voltage. The high tension voltage is powerful enough to jump the spark plug gap in the cylinders many times a second under high compression pressures, providing the system is in good condition and all adjustments are correct.

The ignition advance is controlled both mechanically and by vacuum, to ensure that the spark occurs at just the right instant for the particular engine load and speed. The mechanical governor consists of two lead weights, which move out from the distributor shafts as the engine speed rises, due to centrifugal force. The vacuum control consists of a diaphragm, one side of which is connected via a small bore tube to the carburettor, and the other side to the contact breaker plate. Depression in the inlet manifold and carburettor, which varies with engine speed and throttle opening, causes the diaphragm to move, so moving the contact breaker plate, and advancing or retarding the spark.

2 Maintenance and inspection

1 At the intervals specified in Routine Maintenance at the beginning of this manual, carry out the following service operations on the ignition system.
2 Remove the distributor cap and thoroughly clean it inside and out with a dry lint-free rag. Examine the four HT lead segments inside the cap. If the segments appear badly burned or pitted, renew the cap. Make sure that the carbon brush in the centre of the cap is free to move and that it protrudes by approximately 3.0 mm (0.125 in) from its holder.

3 With the distributor cap removed, lift off the rotor arm and the protective plastic cover. Carefully apply two drops of engine oil to the felt pad in the centre of the distributor shaft. Also lubricate the centrifugal advance weights by applying a few drops of oil through one of the holes in the baseplate. Avoid contaminating the contact breaker points with oil during this operation.
4 Renew the contact breaker points as described in Section 4, then after setting the gap adjust the ignition timing as described in Section 8.
5 Renew the spark plugs as described in Section 9. If the spark plugs have been renewed within the service interval, clean them and reset the electrode gap using the procedure also described in Section 9.
6 Check the security and condition of all leads and wiring associated with the ignition system. Make sure that no chafing is occurring on any of the wires and that all connections are secure, clean and free of corrosion. Pay particular attention to the HT leads which should be carefully inspected for any sign of corrosion on their end fittings which if evident should be carefully cleaned away. Wipe clean the HT leads over their entire length before refitting.

3 Contact breaker points – adjustment

1 Remove the engine compartment cover, spring back the two distributor cap retaining clips and lift up the cap.
2 Clean the inside and outside of the cap with a clean, dry cloth. Scrape away any small deposits from the four terminal studs inside the cap and examine it thoroughly for cracks or surface deterioration. Inspect the carbon brush contact in the centre of the cap to ensure it is not broken and moves freely in and out of its plastic holder. Ensure that the brush protrudes by approximately 3.0 mm (0.125 in) from its holder. Renew the cap if it is cracked or if the carbon brush or terminal studs are excessively corroded or worn away.
3 Lift off the rotor arm followed by the protective plastic cover over the contact breaker assembly.
4 Gently prise the contact breaker points open and examine the condition of their faces. If they are rough, pitted or dirty, it will be necessary to renew them as described in Section 4 before proceeding with the adjustment.
5 Assuming that the points are in a satisfactory condition, or have been renewed, the gap between their faces can be measured and if necessary adjusted as follows.

method described in paragraph 8, until the correct dwell angle is obtained.

16 On completion refit the protective plastic cover, rotor arm and distributor cap and, if removed, the spark plugs and leads.

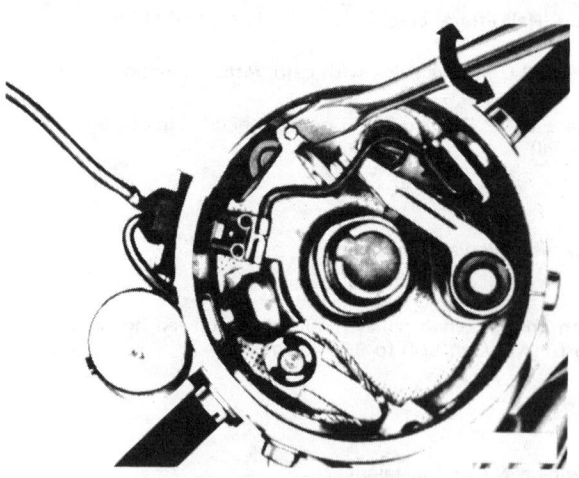

Fig. 3.1 Using a screwdriver engaged with the contact breaker points and the two pips on the baseplate to set the points gap or dwell angle (Sec 3)

6 Turn the engine over until the contact breaker arm is on the peak of one of the four distributor shaft cam lobes and the points are fully open. If manual transmission is fitted the engine can be turned quite easily by releasing the handbrake, engaging top gear and pushing the vehicle forward until the points are fully open. If automatic transmission is fitted it will be necessary to obtain VW tool 3052 or make up a similar tool which will engage with the boss and machined slot in the centre of the fan hub. To gain access to this boss, tip back the number plate and, working through the aperture, undo the three bolts securing the protective grille and timing scale in position. Lift off the grille and timing scale, engage the tool with the boss and turn the engine as necessary. Alternatively the points gap may be adjusted using a dwell meter as described from paragraph 10 onwards.

7 With the points fully open a feeler blade of thickness equal to the specified contact breaker points gap should just slide between the two contact faces.

8 If adjustment is necessary, slacken the screw securing the contact breaker assembly to the distributor baseplate. Engage a screwdriver between the slot in the breaker assembly and the two adjacent pips on the baseplate then move the assembly as necessary to obtain the correct setting. Tighten the retaining screw and then recheck the gap.

9 Refit the protective plastic cover, rotor arm and distributor cap. On automatic transmission models refit the grille and timing scale if these components were removed.

10 If a dwell meter is available, a far more acccurate method of setting the contact breaker points gap is by measuring and if necessary adjusting the dwell angle.

11 The dwell angle is the number of degrees of distibutor cam rotation during which the contact breaker points are closed, i.e. the period from when the points close after being opened by one cam lobe until they are opened again by the next cam lobe. The advantages of setting the points by this method are that any wear of the distributor shaft or cam lobes is taken into account, and also the inaccuracies of using a feeler blade are eliminated. In general a dwell meter should be used in accordance with the manufacturer's instructions. However, the use of one type of meter is outlined as follows.

12 To set the dwell angle, remove the distributor cap, rotor arm and protective plastic cover from the distributor. Connect one lead of the dwell meter to the '+' terminal (15) on the ignition coil and the other lead to the '-' terminal (1) on the coil.

13 Whilst an assistant turns on the ignition and operates the starter, observe the reading on the dwell meter scale. With the engine turning over on the starter the reading should be as stated in the Specifications. Note: *Fluctuation of the dwell meter needle indicates that the engine is not turning over fast enough to give a steady reading. If this is the case, remove the spark plugs and repeat the checks.*

14 If the dwell angle is too small, the contact breaker points gap is too wide, and if the dwell angle is excessive the gap is too small.

15 Adjust the points gap whilst the engine is cranking using the

4 Contact breaker points – removal and refitting

1 The contact breaker points should be renewed at the intervals given in Routine Maintenance at the beginning of this manual or sooner if they become burned, pitted or badly worn.

2 Remove the engine compartment cover, spring back the distributor cap retaining clips and place the distributor cap to one side. Lift off the rotor arm and the protective plastic cover.

3 Undo and remove the screw securing the contact breaker points assembly to the baseplate, disconnect the LT lead spade connector and remove the contact breaker points.

4 Apply a smear of multi-purpose grease to the distributor shaft cam lobes then place the new contact breaker points assembly in position. Reconnect the LT lead and refit the retaining screw. Tighten the screw finger tight only at this stage.

5 Refer to Section 3 and adjust the points gap or dwell angle then refit the protective cover, rotor arm and distributor cap.

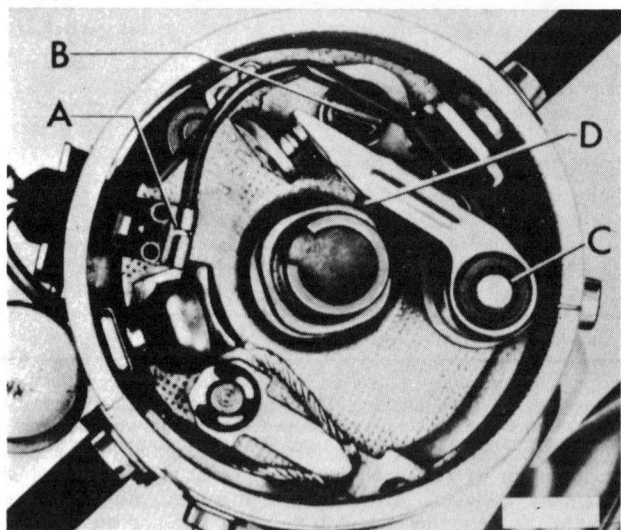

Fig. 3.2 Contact breaker points renewal (Sec 4)

A   LT lead spade connector
B   Points assembly securing screw
C   Pivot post – lubricate sparingly with engine oil
D   Distributor shaft cam – lubricate sparingly with a smear of multi-purpose grease

5 Condenser – removal, testing and refitting

1 The purpose of the condenser (sometimes known as a capacitor) is to ensure that when the contact breaker points open, there is no sparking across them, which would cause swift wear of their faces and prevent the rapid collapse of the magnetic field in the coil. This would cause a reduction in coil HT voltage and ultimately lead to engine misfire.

2 If the engine becomes very difficult to start, or begins to miss after several miles of running, and the contact breaker points show signs of excessive burning, the condition of the condenser must be suspect. A further test can be made by separating the points by hand with the ignition switched on. If this is accompanied by a strong bright flash, it is indicative that the condenser has failed.

3 Without special test equipment, the only sure way to diagnose condenser trouble is to substitute a suspect unit with a new one and note if there is any improvement.

4 To remove the condenser from the distributor, take off the distributor cap, rotor arm and plastic cover.

5 Withdraw the contact breaker points LT lead from the spade terminal, located inside the distributor casing.
6 Separate the LT lead connecting the coil to the distributor at the cable joining connector.
7 Undo and remove the screws securing the condenser and LT lead assembly to the distributor casing and lift off the complete assembly. Note that the condenser is supplied complete with LT lead and LT spade tag and mounting grommet.
8 Refitting the condenser is the reverse procedure to removal.

6 Distributor – removal and refitting

1 Remove the engine compartment cover then pull the HT leads off the spark plugs after marking them to ensure correct refitment. Refer to Fig. 3.3 for the cylinder numbering sequence.
2 Spring back the distributor cap retaining clips, lift off the cap and place it to one side.
3 Remove the spark plug from No 1 cylinder (on the right-hand side of the engine nearest the flywheel).
4 Place a finger over the plug hole and turn the engine over until compression can be felt building up in the cylinder. If manual transmission is fitted the engine can be turned quite easily by releasing the handbrake, engaging top gear and pushing the vehicle forward as necessary. If automatic transmission is fitted it will be necessary to obtain VW tool 3052 or make up a similar tool which will engage with the boss and machined slot in the centre of the fan hub. To gain access to this boss, tip back the number plate and, working through the aperture, undo the three bolts securing the protective grille and timing scale in position. Lift off the grille and then refit the timing scale as it will be necessary to have this in place for subsequent reference. The tool can now be engaged with the boss and the engine turned as necessary.
5 When compression can be felt in No 1 cylinder, continue turning the engine whilst at the same time viewing the timing scale above the crankshaft pulley, through the aperture behind the number plate. Turn the engine until the notch in the crankshaft pulley is aligned with the 'O' mark on the timing scale. This is the TDC position for No 1 cylinder.
6 With the engine in this position the distributor rotor arm should be pointing towards the No 1 cylinder HT lead segment in the cap and should also be pointing towards the notch in the rim of the distributor body.
7 Disconnect the distributor vacuum advance pipe from the vacuum unit and the LT lead at the wiring connector.
8 Undo the nut and remove the washer securing the distributor clamp to the stud on the crankcase then withdraw the distributor upwards and out of its location.
9 Before refitting the distributor, check that the engine has not been inadvertently turned whilst the distributor was removed; if it has, return it to the original position as described in paragraphs 4 and 5.
10 Position the rotor arm so that it is pointing to the notch in the rim of the distributor body and then insert the distributor into its location. Turn the rotor arm very slightly as necessary so that the boss at the base of the distributor engages with the driveshaft, position the clamp over the retaining stud and push the distributor fully home. Refit the washer and retaining nut and tighten the nut securely.
11 Reconnect the vacuum advance pipe to the vacuum unit and the LT lead at the connector.
12 Obtain an initial static setting for the ignition timing, to enable the engine to be started, as follows.
13 Turn the engine anti-clockwise approximately one quarter of a turn.
14 Refer to the Specifications for the ignition timing setting and then turn the engine clockwise until the notch in the crankshaft pulley is aligned with the appropriate mark on the timing scale.
15 With the engine in this position the contact breaker points should just be opening with the rotor arm approaching the notch in the rim of the distributor body. If this is not the case, slacken the long distributor clamp pinch-bolt, turn the distributor body clockwise initially, then slowly turn it back anti-clockwise until the points are just opening with the rotor arm approaching the notch. Now tighten the pinch-bolt.
16 Refit the spark plug, distributor cap and leads. On automatic transmission models, refit the protective grille over the crankshaft pulley and the timing scale.
17 The ignition timing should now be accurately adjusted using a stroboscopic timing light as described in Section 8.

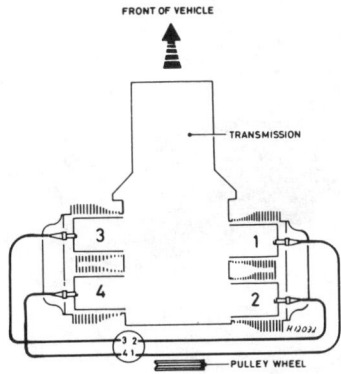

Fig. 3.3 Cylinder numbering sequence and HT lead arrangement (Sec 6)

Fig. 3.4 VW tool 3052 or a similar alternative can be used to turn the engine (Sec 6)

Fig. 3.5 Correct positioning of distributor rotor arm aligned with notch in distributor body rim with engine at TDC for No 1 cylinder, prior to distributor removal (Sec 6)

7 Distributor – dismantling, inspection and reassembly

1 Remove the distributor from the engine as described in Section 6.
2 Prepare a clean uncluttered working area and begin dismantling by removing the contact breaker points and condenser as described in Sections 4 and 5 respectively.

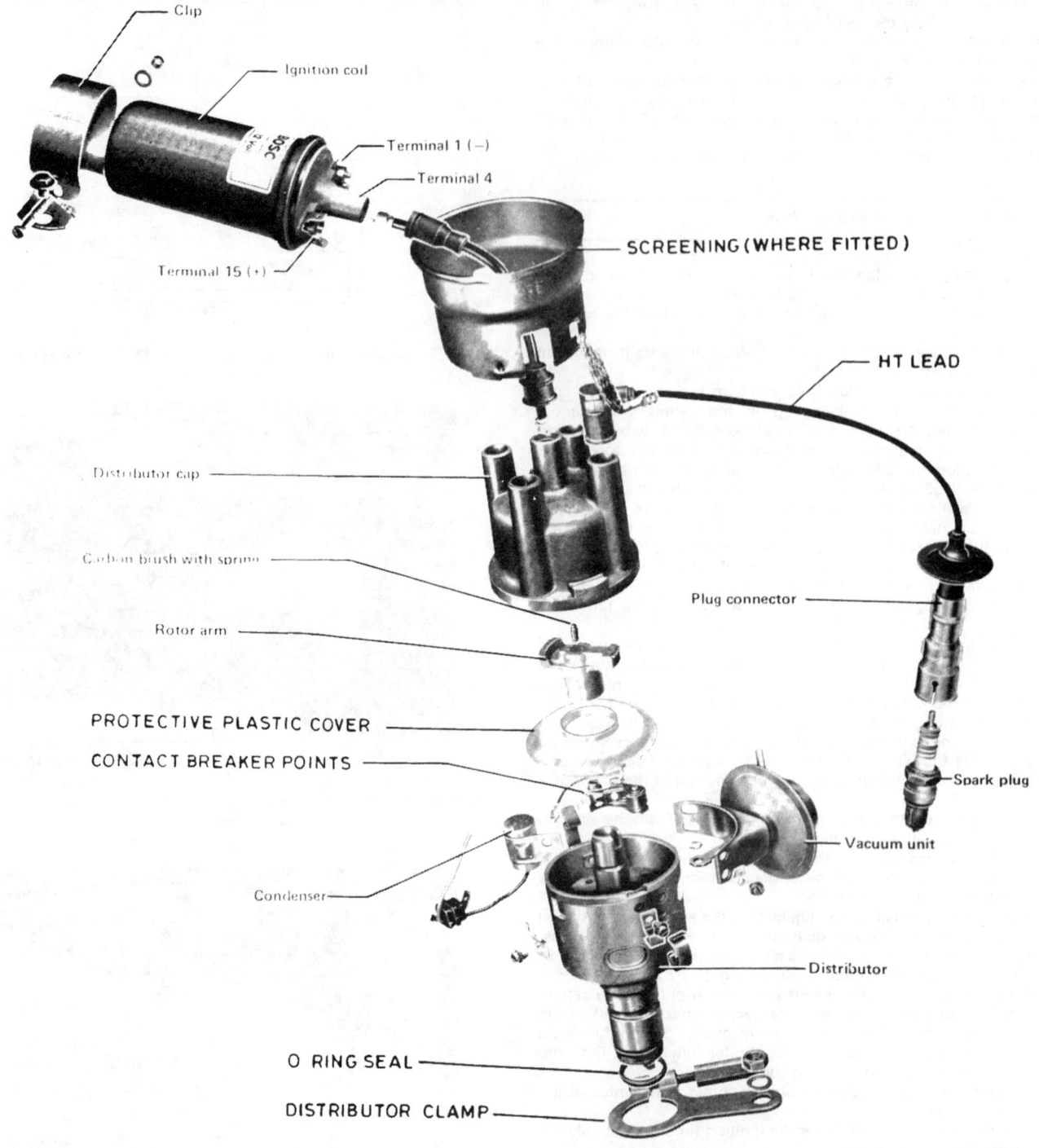

Clip

Ignition coil

Terminal 1 (–)

Terminal 4

Terminal 15 (+)

SCREENING (WHERE FITTED)

HT LEAD

Distributor cap

Carbon brush with spring

Rotor arm

Plug connector

PROTECTIVE PLASTIC COVER

CONTACT BREAKER POINTS

Spark plug

Vacuum unit

Condenser

Distributor

O RING SEAL

DISTRIBUTOR CLAMP

Fig. 3.6 Exploded view of the conventional ignition distributor (Sec 7)

3   Using a screwdriver carefully release the circlip securing the vacuum unit pullrod to the baseplate peg.
4   Undo the two vacuum unit retaining screws, slip the pullrod off the baseplate peg and withdraw the unit from the distributor body.
5   Undo the screws securing the distributor cap retaining clips to the body and lift off the clips.
6   Undo the remaining screw and tag then withdraw the baseplate.
Note: *This is the practical limit of dismantling which may be undertaken since none of the parts below the baseplate can be renewed separately.*
7   With the distributor dismantled, examine the contact breaker points and distributor cap as described in Section 3.

8   Examine the rotor arm for cracks and ensure that it is a snug fit on the distributor shaft. Any slight burning apparent on the end of the metal portion of the arm may be removed with a fine file. If the rotor arm is badly burned, cracked, or a loose fit on the shaft, it should be renewed.
9   Hold the drive boss at the base of the distributor with one hand and turn the upper part of the distributor shaft clockwise with the other. Firm spring resistance should be felt with no slackness or binding apparent. Check that the centrifugal advance weights move freely and return under the tension of the springs. Also check that there is no side play of the distributor shaft relative to the distributor body which would indicate wear in the distributor shaft bushes. Any

faults noticed during this inspection will necessitate renewal of the complete distributor as component parts are not available separately.

10 The vacuum unit may be checked for correct operation by sucking the vacuum pipe connection while observing the action of the pullrod. If no movement of the rod is apparent when suction is applied, it is likely that the diaphragm in the vacuum unit is punctured, necessitating renewal of this unit.

11 Begin reassembly by applying a few drops of engine oil to the centrifugal advance weight pivots and the felt pad in the centre of the distributor shaft.

12 Locate the baseplate in the distributor body and secure it in position with the retaining screw and tag. Now refit the distributor cap retaining clips and tighten all the screws securely.

13 Engage the vacuum unit pullrod with the baseplate peg then secure the unit with the retaining screws.

14 Refit the condenser and contact breaker points as described in Sections 5 and 4 respectively.

15 Fit a new O-ring seal to the base of the distributor body if necessary then refit the distributor as described in Section 6.

8 Ignition timing – adjustment

1 For prolonged engine life, efficient running, performance and economy it is essential for the fuel/air mixture in the combustion chambers to be ignited by the spark plugs at precisely the right moment in relation to engine speed and load. For this to occur the ignition timing must be set accurately and should be checked at the intervals given in Routine Maintenance or whenever the position of the distributor has been altered. To accurately check and adjust the ignition timing it is necessary to use a stroboscopic timing light, whereby the timing is checked with the engine running at idling speed.

2 The timing marks consists of a scale attached to the fan housing and marked in degrees before and after top dead centre (TDC), and a corresponding notch on the crankshaft pulley. Access to the timing marks is through the body aperture behind the rear number plate (photo).

8.2 The ignition timing scale (arrowed) is attached to the fan housing and is viewed through the body aperture behind the number plate

3 Before carrying out any checks or adjustments, ensure that the contact breaker points are in good condition and correctly set as described in Section 3.

4 Start the engine, allow it to reach normal operating temperature and then switch off.

5 Connect a stroboscopic timing light to the HT lead of No 1 cylinder (right-hand side of the engine nearest the flywheel) and make any other electrical connections according to timing light type by following the manufacturer's instructions. Connect a tachometer to the engine following the manufacturer's instructions for this instrument also.

6 Disconnect the vacuum advance pipe from the distributor vacuum unit, start the engine again and allow it to idle. Check that the engine is idling at the specified speed for ignition timing and, if necessary adjust the idling speed as described in Chapter 2.

7 Refer to the Specifications for the correct ignition timing setting and then point the timing light at the timing scale. The notch in the crankshaft pulley will appear stationary and if the timing is correct will be aligned with the specified mark on the scale.

8 If the marks are not aligned, slacken the distributor clamp pinch-bolt and then slowly turn the distributor body in whichever direction is necessary to align the marks. Hold the distributor in this position and tighten the pinch-bolt.

9 Open the throttle slightly and note the movement of the timing marks. If the centrifugal advance mechanism in the distributor is working correctly, the marks should appear to move away from each other as the engine speed increases. The same should happen if the vacuum advance pipe is reconnected with the engine running at a fast idling speed, indicating that the vacuum unit is satisfactory.

10 After checking the timing, readjust the engine idling speed if necessary then switch off the engine and disconnect the instruments.

9 Spark plugs and HT leads – general

1 The correct functioning of the spark plugs is vital for the proper running and efficiency of the engine. The spark plugs should be renewed at the intervals given in Routine Maintenance. If misfiring or bad starting is experienced within the service period, they must be removed, cleaned and regapped.

2 To remove the plugs, first mark the HT leads to ensure correct refitment, and then pull them off the plugs. Using a spark plug spanner, or suitable deep socket and extension bar, unscrew the plugs and remove them from the engine.

3 The condition of the spark plugs will also tell much about the overall condition of the engine.

4 If the insulator nose of the spark plug is clean and white, with no deposits, this is indicative of a weak mixture, or too hot a plug. (A hot plug transfers heat away from the electrode slowly – a cold plug transfers it away quickly).

5 If the tip and insulator nose are covered with hard black-looking deposits, then this is indicative that the mixture is too rich. Should the plug be black and oily, then it is likely that the engine is fairly worn, as well as the mixture being too rich.

6 If the insulator nose is covered with light tan to greyish brown deposits, then the mixture is correct and it is likely that the engine is in good condition.

7 If there are any traces of long brown tapering stains on the outside of the white portion of the plug, then the plug will have to be renewed, as this shows that there is a faulty joint between the plug body and the insulator, and compression is being lost.

8 Plugs should be cleaned by a sand blasting machine, which will free them from carbon more thoroughly than cleaning by hand. The machine will also test the condition of the plugs under compression. Any plug that fails to spark at the recommended pressure should be renewed.

9 The spark plug gap is of considerable importance as, if it is too large or too small, the size of the spark and its efficiency will be seriously impaired. The spark plug gap should be set to the figure given in the Specifications at the beginning of this Chapter.

10 To set it, measure the gap with a feeler gauge, and then bend open, or close, the *outer* plug electrode until the correct gap is achieved. The centre electrode should *never* be bent as this may crack the insulation and cause plug failure, if nothing worse.

11 To refit the plugs, screw them in by hand initially and then fully tighten to the specified torque. If a torque wrench is not available, tighten the plugs until initial resistance is felt as the sealing washer contacts its seat and then tighten by a further eighth of a turn. Refit the HT leads in the correct order, ensuring that they are a tight fit over the plug ends. Periodically wipe the leads clean to reduce the risk of HT leakage by arcing.

10 Ignition coil – description and testing

1 The ignition coil is located on top of the engine cowling, adjacent to the distributor. Periodically the electrical connections should be

checked for security and the coil wiped clean to prevent high tension (HT) voltage loss through arcing.

2 If the operation of the coil is suspect the resistance of the primary and secondary windings may be checked with an ohmmeter. To do this disconnect the leads at the coil terminals after first marking them to ensure correct refitment.

3 Using the ohmmeter, measure the coil primary resistance between the two LT terminals (1 and 15). Now measure the secondary resistance between the negative LT terminal (1) and the HT terminal in the centre of the coil (4). Compare the values obtained with those given in the Specifications. If the primary or secondary resistance is outside the specified tolerance, the coil must be renewed.

4 To renew the coil, disconnect the leads (if this has not already been done to test the unit), slacken the clamp bolt and slide the coil out of its bracket. Refitting is the reverse of the removal procedure.

11 TDC sensor – general

1 All models covered by this manual incorporate a TDC sensor which is used for ignition system checking purposes in conjunction with VW test equipment.

2 Without a suitable ignition tester it is unlikely that this device will be of use to the home mechanic, but it is useful to know its location and purpose.

3 The sensor is situated on the upper face of the crankcase and consists of a lead with a plug on one end. When connected to the tester, the sensor at the other end of the lead monitors the exact position of the crankshaft by detecting the position of two metal studs in the flywheel.

4 Removal and refitting of the sensor can only be carried out with the engine dismantled and is removed by pushing out of the crankcase towards the flywheel side. Refitting is the reverse of this procedure.

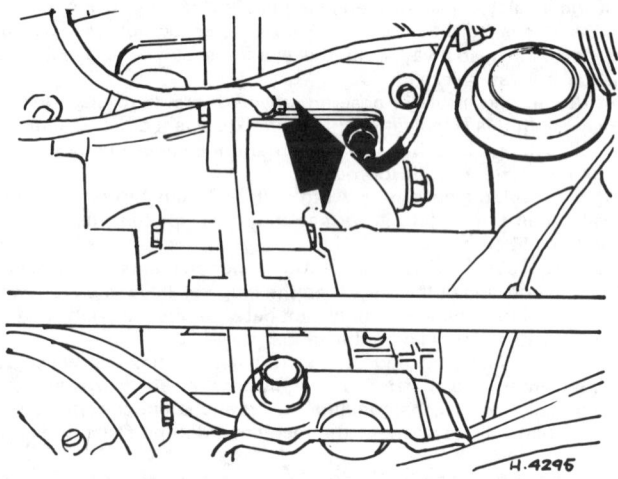

Fig. 3.7 TDC sensor location (arrowed) on crankcase upper face
(Sec 11)

12 Fault diagnosis – conventional ignition system

1 By far the majority of breakdown and running troubles are caused by faults in the ignition system either in the low tension or high tension circuits.

2 There are two main symptoms indicating faults. Either the engine will not start or fire, or the engine is difficult to start and misfires. If it is a regular misfire, (ie the engine is running on only two or three cylinders) the fault is almost sure to be in the secondary or high tension circuit. If the misfiring is intermittent the fault could be in either the high or low tension circuits. If the vehicle stops suddenly, or will not start at all, it is likely that the fault is in the low tension circuit. Loss of power and overheating, apart from faulty carburation settings, are normally due to faults in the distributor or to incorrect ignition timing.

Engine fails to start

3 If the engine fails to start and the vehicle was running normally when it was last used, first check that there is fuel in the petrol tank. If the engine turns over normally on the starter motor and the battery is evidently well charged, then the fault may be in either the high or low tension circuits. First check the HT circuit.

4 One of the commonest reasons for bad starting is wet or damp spark plug leads and distributor. Remove the distributor cap. If condensation is visible internally dry the cap with a rag and also wipe over the leads. Refit the cap.

5 If the engine still fails to start, check that voltage is reaching the plugs by disconnecting each plug lead in turn at the spark plug end, and holding the end of the cable with rubber or an insulated tool about 6 mm ($\frac{1}{4}$ in) away from the cylinder block. Spin the engine on the starter motor.

6 Sparking between the end of the cable and the block should be fairly strong with a regular blue spark. If voltage is reaching the plugs, then remove them and clean and regap them. The engine should now start.

7 If there is no spark at the plug leads, take off the HT lead from the centre of the distributor cap and hold it to the block as before. Spin the engine on the starter once more. A rapid succession of blue sparks between the end of the lead and the block indicates that the coil is in order and that the distributor cap is cracked, the rotor arm is faulty or the carbon brush in the top of the distributor cap is not making good contact with the spring on the rotor arm.

8 If there are no sparks from the end of the lead from the coil, check the connections at the coil end of the lead. If it is in order start checking the low tension circuit. Possibly, the points are in bad condition. Clean and reset them as described in this Chapter, Section 3.

9 Use a 12V voltmeter or a 12V bulb and two lengths of wire. With the ignition switched on and the points open, test between the low tension wire to the coil and earth. No reading indicates a break in the supply from the ignition switch. Check the connections at the switch to see if any are loose. Refit them and the engine should run. A reading shows a faulty coil or condenser, or broken lead between the coil and the distributor.

10 Take the condenser wire off the points assembly and with the points open test between the moving point and earth. If there is now a reading then the fault is in the condenser. Fit a new one and the fault is cleared.

11 With no reading from the moving point to earth, take a reading between earth and the distributor terminal of the coil. A reading here shows a broken wire which will need to be replaced between the coil and the distributor. No reading confirms that the coil has failed and must be renewed, after which the engine will run once more. Remember to refit the condenser wire to the points assembly. For these tests it is sufficient to separate the points with a piece of dry paper while testing with the points open.

Engine misfires

12 If the engine misfires regularly run it at a fast idling speed. Pull off each of the plug caps in turn and listen to the note of the engine. Hold the plug cap in a dry cloth or with a rubber glove as additional protection again a shock from the HT supply.

13 No difference in engine running will be noticed when the lead from the defective cylinder is removed. Removing the lead from one of the good cylinders will accentuate the misfire.

14 Remove the plug lead from the plug which is not firing and hold it about 6 mm ($\frac{1}{4}$ in) away from the block. Restart the engine. If the sparking is fairly strong and regular, the fault must lie in the spark plug.

15 The plug may be loose, the insulation may be cracked, or the points may have burnt away giving too wide a gap for the spark to jump. Worse still, one of the points may have broken off. Either renew the plug, or clean it, reset the gap, and then test it.

16 If there is no spark at the end of the plug lead, or if it is weak and intermittent, check the ignition lead from the distributor to the plug. If the insulation is cracked or perished, renew the lead. Check the connections at the distributor cap.

17 If there is still no spark, examine the distributor cap carefully for tracking. This can be recognised by a very thin black line running between two or more electrodes, or between an electrode and some other part of the distributor. These lines are paths which now conduct electricity across the cap thus letting it run to earth. The only answer is a new distributor cap.

18 Apart from the ignition timing being incorrect, other causes of

Are your plugs trying to tell you something?

Normal.
Grey-brown deposits, lightly coated core nose. Plugs ideally suited to engine, and engine in good condition.

Heavy Deposits.
A build up of crusty deposits, light-grey sandy colour in appearance.
Fault: Often caused by worn valve guides, excessive use of upper cylinder lubricant, or idling for long periods.

Lead Glazing.
Plug insulator firing tip appears yellow or green/yellow and shiny in appearance.
Fault: Often caused by incorrect carburation, excessive idling followed by sharp acceleration. Also check ignition timing.

Carbon fouling.
Dry, black, sooty deposits.
Fault: over-rich fuel mixture.
Check: carburettor mixture settings, float level, choke operation, air filter.

Oil fouling.
Wet, oily deposits. Fault: worn bores/piston rings or valve guides; sometimes occurs (temporarily) during running-in period.

Overheating.
Electrodes have glazed appearance, core nose very white – few deposits. Fault: plug overheating. Check: plug value, ignition timing, fuel octane rating (too low) and fuel mixture (too weak).

Electrode damage.
Electrodes burned away; core nose has burned, glazed appearance. Fault: pre-ignition. Check: for correct heat range and as for 'overheating'.

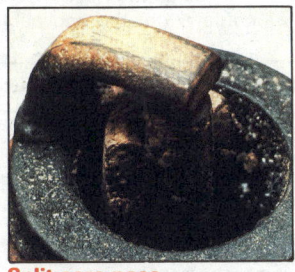

Split core nose.
(May appear initially as a crack). Fault: detonation or wrong gap-setting technique. Check: ignition timing, cooling system, fuel mixture (too weak).

WHY DOUBLE COPPER IS BETTER FOR YOUR ENGINE.

Unique Trapezoidal Copper Cored Earth Electrode

50% Larger Spark Area

Copper Cored Centre Electrode

Champion Double Copper plugs are the first in the world to have copper core in both centre <u>and</u> earth electrode. This innovative design means that they run cooler by up to 100°C – giving greater efficiency and longer life. These double copper cores transfer heat away from the tip of the plug faster and more efficiently. Therefore, Double Copper runs at cooler temperatures than conventional plugs giving improved acceleration response and high speed performance with no fear of pre-ignition.

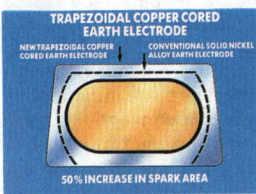

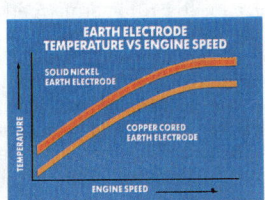

Champion Double Copper plugs also feature a unique trapezoidal earth electrode giving a 50% increase in spark area. This, together with the double copper cores, offers greatly reduced electrode wear, so the spark stays stronger for longer.

 FASTER COLD STARTING

 FOR UNLEADED OR LEADED FUEL

 ELECTRODES UP TO 100°C COOLER

 BETTER ACCELERATION RESPONSE

 LOWER EMISSIONS

 50% BIGGER SPARK AREA

 THE LONGER LIFE PLUG

Plug Tips/Hot and Cold.
Spark plugs must operate within well-defined temperature limits to avoid cold fouling at one extreme and overheating at the other.
Champion and the car manufacturers work out the best plugs for an engine to give optimum performance under all conditions, from freezing cold starts to sustained high speed motorway cruising.
Plugs are often referred to as hot or cold. With Champion, the higher the number on its body, the hotter the plug, and the lower the number the cooler the plug. For the correct plug for your car refer to the specifications at the beginning of this chapter.

Plug Cleaning
Modern plug design and materials mean that Champion no longer recommends periodic plug cleaning. Certainly don't clean your plugs with a wire brush as this can cause metal conductive paths across the nose of the insulator so impairing its performance and resulting in loss of acceleration and reduced m.p.g.
However, if plugs are removed, always carefully clean the area where the plug seats in the cylinder head as grit and dirt can sometimes cause gas leakage.
Also wipe any traces of oil or grease from plug leads as this may lead to arcing.

misfiring have already been dealt with under the Section dealing with the failure of the engine to start. To recap, these are that

    (a)   *The coil may be faulty giving an intermittent misfire*
    (b)   *There may be a damaged wire or loose connection in the low tension circuit*
    (c)   *The condenser may be faulty*
    (d)   *There may be a mechanical fault in the distributor (broken driving spindle or contact breaker spring)*

19 If the ignition timing is too far retarded, it should be noted that the engine will tend to overheat, and there will be a quite noticeable drop in power. If the engine is overheating and the power is down, and the ignition timing is correct, then the carburettor should be checked, as it is likely that this is where the fault lies.

Part B: Electronic ignition system

13 General description

The ignition system is divided into two circuits, low tension and high tension. The high tension (HT) circuit is similar to that of the conventional ignition system and consists of the high tension coil windings, the heavy ignition lead from the centre of the coil to the distributor cap, the rotor arm, spark plugs and spark plug leads. The low tension (LT) circuit consists of the battery, ignition switch, low tension or primary coil windings and a vane and pick-up unit operating in conjunction with a control unit. The vane and pick-up unit are located in the distributor and carry out the same function as the contact breaker points and condenser used on conventional systems.

The vane is a four-toothed wheel (one for each cylinder) that is fitted to the distributor shaft in place of the conventional contact breaker operating cam.

The pick-up unit is fitted to the distributor baseplate and consists of basically a coil and permanent magnet.

The control unit is located in the engine compartment and is an amplifier module that is used to boost the voltage induced by the pick-up coil (photo).

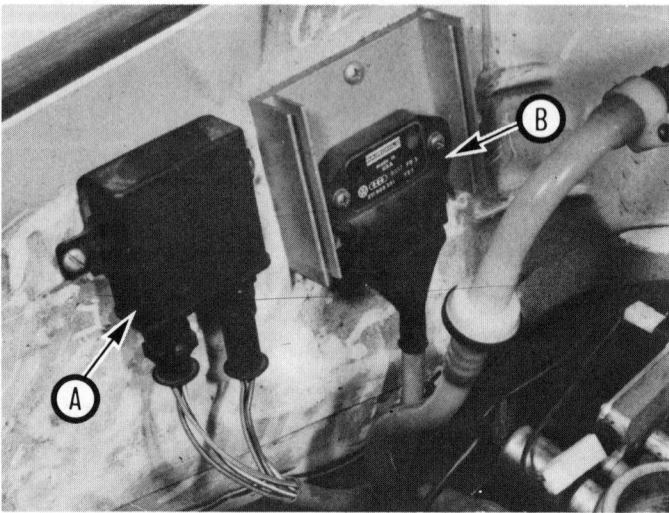

13.1 Idle stabilizing unit (A) and ignition control unit amplifier module (B) located on the left-hand side of the engine compartment

When the ignition switch is on, the ignition primary circuit is energised. When the distributor vane 'teeth' or 'spokes' approach the magnetic coil assembly, a voltage is induced which signals the amplifier to turn off the coil primary circuit. A timing circuit in the amplifier module turns on the coil current again after the coil magnetic field has collapsed.

When switched on, current flows from the battery through the ignition switch, through the coil primary winding, through the amplifier module and then to ground (earth). When the current is off, the magnetic field in the ignition coil collapses, inducing a high voltage in

the coil secondary windings. This is conducted to the distributor cap where the rotor arm directs it to the appropriate spark plug. This process is repeated for each power stroke of the engine.

The distributor is fitted with devices to control the actual point of ignition according to the engine speed and load. As the engine speed increases, two centrifugal weights within the distributor body, and connected to the vane armature, move outwards. This alters the position of the vane in relation to the distributor shaft and advances the spark accordingly. A vacuum advance and retard unit is attached externally to the distributor body and connected by a pullrod to the baseplate.

Variations in inlet manifold vacuum cause a diaphragm within the unit to deflect thus moving the pullrod. The baseplate and pick-up unit move under the action of the pullrod thus advancing or retarding the spark according to engine load. An idle stabilizing unit consisting of an additional electronic module and located in the engine compartment adjacent to the control unit, maintains a stable engine idling speed. The unit advances or retards the spark as necessary when the engine is idling so that a near constant idling speed is obtained under all conditions of engine load.

14 Electronic ignition system – precautions

When working on the electronic ignition system the following precautions must be strictly observed to prevent damage to the electronic components and to avoid the risk of personal injury.

1 The voltages produced are considerably higher than those produced by a conventional system. Extreme care must be taken if work is being done with the ignition switched on, particularly by persons fitted with a cardiac pacemaker.
2 The ignition must be switched off before any ignition wiring, including HT leads or test equipment wiring, is disconnected or connected.
3 If, for any reason, the engine is to be cranked on the starter without starting, remove the HT lead from the centre of the distributor cap and earth it.
4 A starting boost with a rapid charger is only permissible for one minute at a maximum of 16.5 volts.
5 If the engine is to be steam cleaned, de-greased, or washed in any way, the ignition must be switched off.
6 The battery must be completely disconnected (both leads removed) before any electric welding or spot welding on the vehicle takes place.
7 Where there is a known or suspected defect in the ignition system, the wiring plug at the control unit must be disconnected if the vehicle is to be towed.
8 Do not connect a condenser to the negative terminal (1) of the ignition coil.
9 Never substitute the standard fitting 1K ohm rotor arm (marked R1) with a different type.
10 For the purposes of radio suppression, only 1K ohm spark plug HT leads with 1K ohm to 5K ohm spark plug connectors may be used.

15 Maintenance and inspection

1 Maintenance and inspection operations on the electronic ignition system are the same as for conventional systems with the exception of renewal and adjustment of the contact breaker points. Refer to Section 2 and carry out the applicable operations as described.

16 Distributor – removal and refitting

1 Remove the engine compartment cover then pull the HT leads off the spark plugs after marking them to ensure correct refitment. Refer to Fig. 3.3 for the cylinder numbering sequence.
2 Spring back the distributor cap retaining clips, lift off the cap and place it to one side.
3 Remove the spark plug from No 1 cylinder (on the right-hand side of the engine nearest the flywheel).
4 Place a finger over the plug hole and turn the engine over until compression can be felt building up in the cylinder. If manual transmission is fitted the engine can be turned quite easily by releasing the handbrake, engaging top gear and pushing the vehicle forward as necessary. If automatic transmission is fitted it will be necessary to

obtain VW tool 3052 or make up a similar tool which will engage with the boss and machined slot in the centre of the fan hub (Fig. 3.4). To gain access to this boss, tip back the number plate and, working through the aperture, undo the three bolts securing the protective grille and timing scale in position. Lift off the grille and then refit the timing scale as it will be necessary to have this in place for subsequent reference. The tool can now be engaged with the boss and the engine turned as necessary.

5　When compression can be felt in No 1 cylinder, continue turning the engine whilst at the same time viewing the timing scale above the crankshaft pulley, through the aperture behind the number plate. Turn the engine until the notch in the crankshaft pulley is aligned with the 'O' mark on the timing scale. This is the TDC position for No 1 cylinder.

6　With the engine in this position the distributor rotor arm should be pointing towards the No 1 cylinder HT lead segment in the cap and should also be pointing towards the notch in the rim of the distributor body (Fig. 3.5).

7　Disconnect the distributor vacuum advance and retard pipes from the vacuum unit making a note of which side of the unit the respective pipes are fitted.

8　Disconnect the control unit wiring plug from the socket on the distributor body (photo).

9　Undo the nut and remove the washer securing the distributor clamp to the stud on the crankcase then withdraw the distributor upwards and out of its location (photo).

10　Before refitting the distributor, check that the engine has not been inadvertently turned whilst the distributor was removed. If it has, return it to the original position as described in paragraphs 4 and 5.

11　Position the rotor arm so that it is pointing to the notch in the rim of the distributor body and then insert the distributor into its location. Turn the rotor arm very slightly as necessary so that the boss at the base of the distributor engages with the driveshaft. Position the clamp over the retaining stud and push the distributor fully home. Refit the washer and retaining nut and tighten the nut securely.

12　Reconnect the vacuum and retard pipes to the vacuum unit and reconnect the control unit wiring plug to the distributor socket.

13　Check that the rotor arm is still pointing to the notch on the rim of the distributor body. If not, slacken the distributor clamp pinch-bolt and turn the distributor body as necessary. Now tighten the pinch-bolt.

14　Refit the spark plug, distributor cap and HT leads. If removed, refit the protective grille over the crankshaft pulley and the timing scale.

15　Refer to Section 18 and adjust the ignition timing.

17　Distributor – dismantling, inspection and reassembly

1　Remove the distributor from the engine as described in Section 16, then prepare a clean uncluttered working area.

2　Begin dismantling by lifting off the rotor arm followed by the protective plastic cover (photos).

16.9 Distributor removal

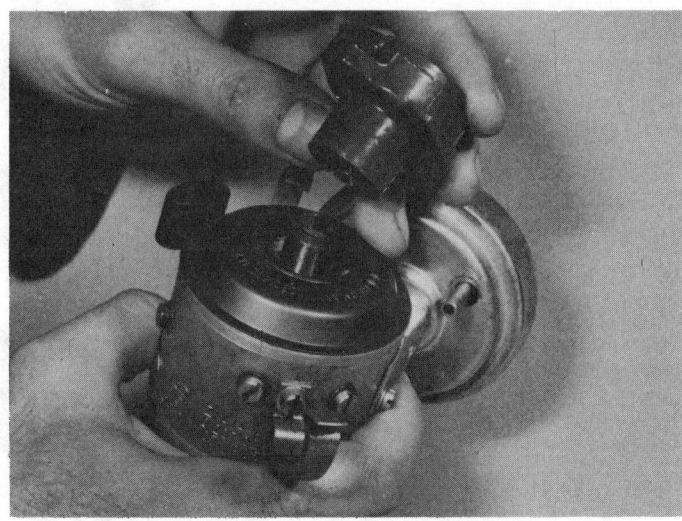

17.2A Begin dismantling the distributor by removing the rotor arm ...

16.8 Distributor control unit wiring plug (A) vacuum advance pipe connection (B) and clamp retaining nut with earth tag (C)

17.2B ... followed by the protective plastic cover

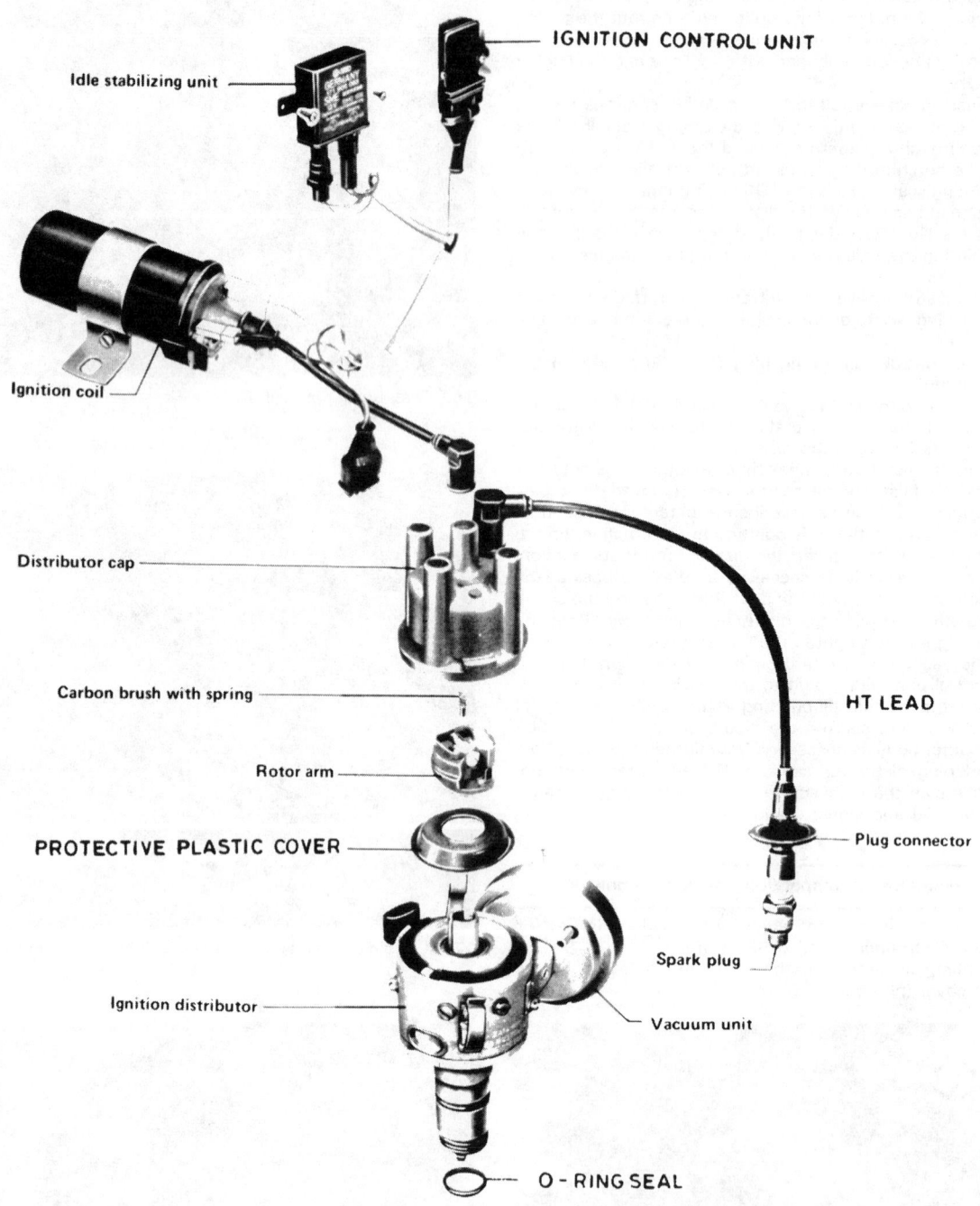

Fig. 3.8 Exploded view of the electronic ignition distributor (Sec 17)

3   Using circlip pliers, extract the vane retaining circlip (photo). Carefully prise the vane off the distributor shaft using two thin screwdrivers positioned opposite each other under the vane centre boss (photo).

4   Recover the small locating pin from the groove in the distributor shaft (photo).

5   Again using circlip pliers extract the second circlip on the distributor shaft (photo).

6   Undo the screws around the side of the distributor body which secure the vacuum unit, distributor cap clips and the baseplate. Note the different lengths of the screws and their locations (photo).

7   Disengage the vacuum unit pullrod from the baseplate peg and withdraw the unit.

8   Release the wiring socket from the side of the distributor body then lift out the baseplate (photo).

9   This is the practical limit of dismantling which may be undertaken

17.3A Extract the retaining circlip (arrowed) ...

17.3B ... then carefully withdraw the vane (arrowed) using two screwdrivers if necessary

17.4 Recover the small locating pin (arrowed) ...

17.5 ... then extract the second circlip

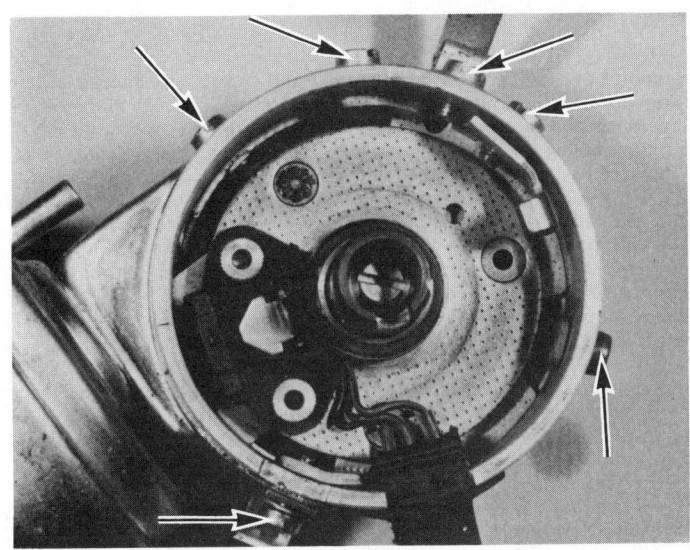

17.6 Undo and remove the screws around the side of the distributor body (arrowed) and withdraw the vacuum unit

17.8 Release the wiring socket and lift out the baseplate assembly

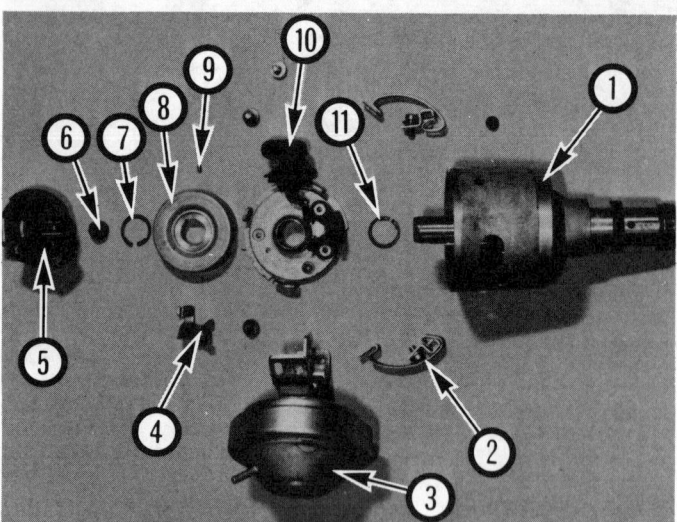

17.9 Distributor component parts

1	Distributor body	6	Felt pad
2	Distributor cap clip	7	Circlip
3	Vacuum unit	8	Vane
4	Baseplate support	9	Locating pin
5	Rotor arm	10	Baseplate and pick-up unit
		11	Circlip

17.13 Lubricate both centrifugal advance weight pivot and contact areas (A) and the distributor shaft (B) before reassembly

17.18 If necessary renew the O-ring at the base of the distributor

since none of the parts below the baseplate can be renewed separately. Lay out all the components in their order of removal and carry out a careful inspection as follows (photo).

10 Examine the rotor arm for cracks and ensure that it is a snug fit on the distributor shaft. Any slight burning on the end of the metal portion of the arm may be removed with a fine file. If the rotor arm is badly burned, cracked, or a loose fit on the shaft, it should be renewed.

11 Hold the drive boss at the base of the distributor with one hand and turn the upper part of the distributor shaft clockwise with the other. Firm spring resistance should be felt with no slackness or binding apparent. Check that the centrifugal advance weights move freely and return under the tension of the springs. Any faults noticed during this inspection will necessitate renewal of the complete distributor as component parts are not available separately.

12 The vacuum unit may be checked for correct operation by sucking the vacuum pipe connections whilst observing the action of the pullrod. If no movement of the rod is apparent when suction is applied, it is likely that the diaphragm in the vacuum unit is punctured necessitating renewal of this unit.

13 Begin reassembly by applying a few drops of engine oil to the centrifugal advance weight pivots and to the centre of the distributor shaft (photo).

14 Locate the baseplate in position and secure it to the distributor body with the retaining screws.

15 Engage the vacuum unit pullrod with the baseplate peg then refit the vacuum unit retaining screws and the distributor cap clips. Tighten all the screws securely.

16 Refit the lower circlip to the distributor shaft. Place the small locating pin in its groove then carefully push the vane down into contact with the circlip. Secure this assembly with the remaining circlip.

17 Refit the protective plastic cover, followed by the rotor arm.

18 Renew the O-ring seal at the base of the distributor if necessary (photo).

19 The distributor can now be refitted as described in Section 16.

18 Ignition timing – adjustment

1   For prolonged engine life, efficient running, performance and economy it is essential for the fuel/air mixture in the combustion chambers to be ignited by the spark plugs at precisely the right moment in relation to engine speed and load. For this to occur the

ignition timing must be set accurately and should be checked at the intervals given in Routine Maintenance or whenever the position of the distributor has been altered. To check accurately and adjust the ignition timing it is necessary to use a stroboscopic timing light, whereby the timing is checked with the engine running at idling speed.

2   The timing marks consist of a scale attached to the fan housing and marked in degrees before and after top dead centre (TDC) and a corresponding notch on the crankshaft pulley. Access to the timing marks is through the body aperture behind the rear number plate (photo 8.2).

3   Start the engine, allow it to reach normal operating temperature and then switch off.

4   Connect a stroboscopic timing light to the HT lead of No 1 cylinder (right-hand side of the engine nearest the flywheel) and make any other electrical connections necessary according to timing light type by following the manufacturer's instructions. Connect a tachometer to the engine following the manufacturer's instructions for this instrument also.

5   Disconnect the two electrical plugs at the idle stabilizing unit and join them together (photo).

6   Start the engine again and allow it to idle. Check that the engine is idling at the specified speed for ignition timing and, if necessary adjust the idling speed as described in Chapter 2.

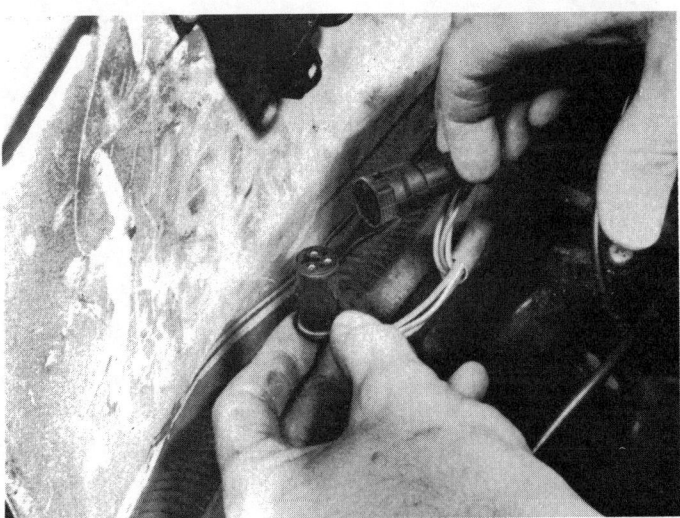

18.5 Before checking ignition timing, remove both wiring plugs from the idle stabilizing unit and join them together

7   Refer to the Specifications for the correct ignition timing setting and then point the timing light at the timing scale. The notch in the crankshaft pulley will appear stationary and if the timing is correct will be aligned with the specified mark on the scale.

8   If the marks are not aligned, slacken the distributor clamp pinch-bolt and then slowly turn the distributor body in whichever direction is necessary to align the marks. Hold the distributor in this position and tighten the pinch-bolt.

9   Open the throttle slightly and note the movement of the timing marks. If the centrifugal advance mechanism in the distributor is working correctly, the marks should appear to move away from each other as the engine speed increases. The same should happen if the vacuum pipe on the retard side of the vacuum unit is disconnected with the engine running at a fast idle. If the marks do not move after disconnecting the vacuum pipe then either the vacuum unit is faulty or the carburettor throttle valve basic setting or throttle linkage adjustments are incorrect (see Chapter 2).

10   After adjustment, reset the engine idling speed if necessary and then switch off the engine. Disconnect the instruments and reconnect the two wiring plugs to the idle stabilizing unit.

19 Spark plugs and HT leads – general

Refer to Part A: Section 9.

20 Ignition coil – description and testing

Refer to Part A: Section 10.

21 TDC sensor – general

Refer to Part A: Section 11.

22 Fault diagnosis – electronic ignition system

Fault diagnosis in the HT circuit of the electronic ignition system is the same as described in Part A: Section 12 for conventional systems. If a fault is suspected in the LT circuit, special test equipment is needed to diagnose the problem accurately and this work should be left to a VW dealer or suitably equipped auto electrician.

Chapter 4 Clutch

Contents

Specifications

Type .... Single dry plate, diaphragm spring, cable or hydraulically operated

Clutch disc diameter
Cable operated type .... 215 mm (8.46 in)
Hydraulically operated type .... 228 mm (8.97 in)

Clutch free play
Cable operated type .... 10 to 25 mm (0.39 to 0.98 in) at clutch pedal
Hydraulically operated type .... Approximately 0.5 mm (0.02 in) at clutch pedal

Clutch cable guide bend (see text) .... 35 to 45 mm (1.37 to 1.77 in)

Hydraulic fluid type .... Universal brake and clutch fluid conforming to US standard FMVSS
116 DOT 3 or 116 DOT 4

Torque wrench settings

	Nm	lbf ft
Cover assembly to flywheel	25	18
Master cylinder to bracket	25	18
Slave cylinder to bracket	25	18

1 General description

All manual transmission models are equipped with a single dry plate diaphragm spring clutch. The unit consists of a steel cover which is bolted to the flywheel and contains the pressure plate and diaphragm spring.

The clutch disc is free to slide along the splined gearbox input shaft and is held in position between the flywheel and the pressure plate by the pressure of the diaphragm spring. Friction lining material is riveted to the clutch disc, which has a spring cushioned hub to absorb transmission shocks and help ensure a smooth take-up of the drive.

Depending on vehicle specification the clutch may be operated either mechanically by a cable or hydraulically by a master and slave cylinder. The clutch release mechanism is similar for both types and consists of a release shaft and release bearing which are mounted in the clutch housing on the end of the gearbox.

Periodic maintenance is necessary on cable operated clutches and consists of checking and adjusting the free play of the cable. The hydraulically operated clutch assembly is self adjusting, and requires no maintenance other than periodically checking the hydraulic fluid level in the master cylinder reservoir. The clutch hydraulic fluid is supplied by the brake master cylinder reservoir and reference should be made to Chapter 9 for level checking procedures.

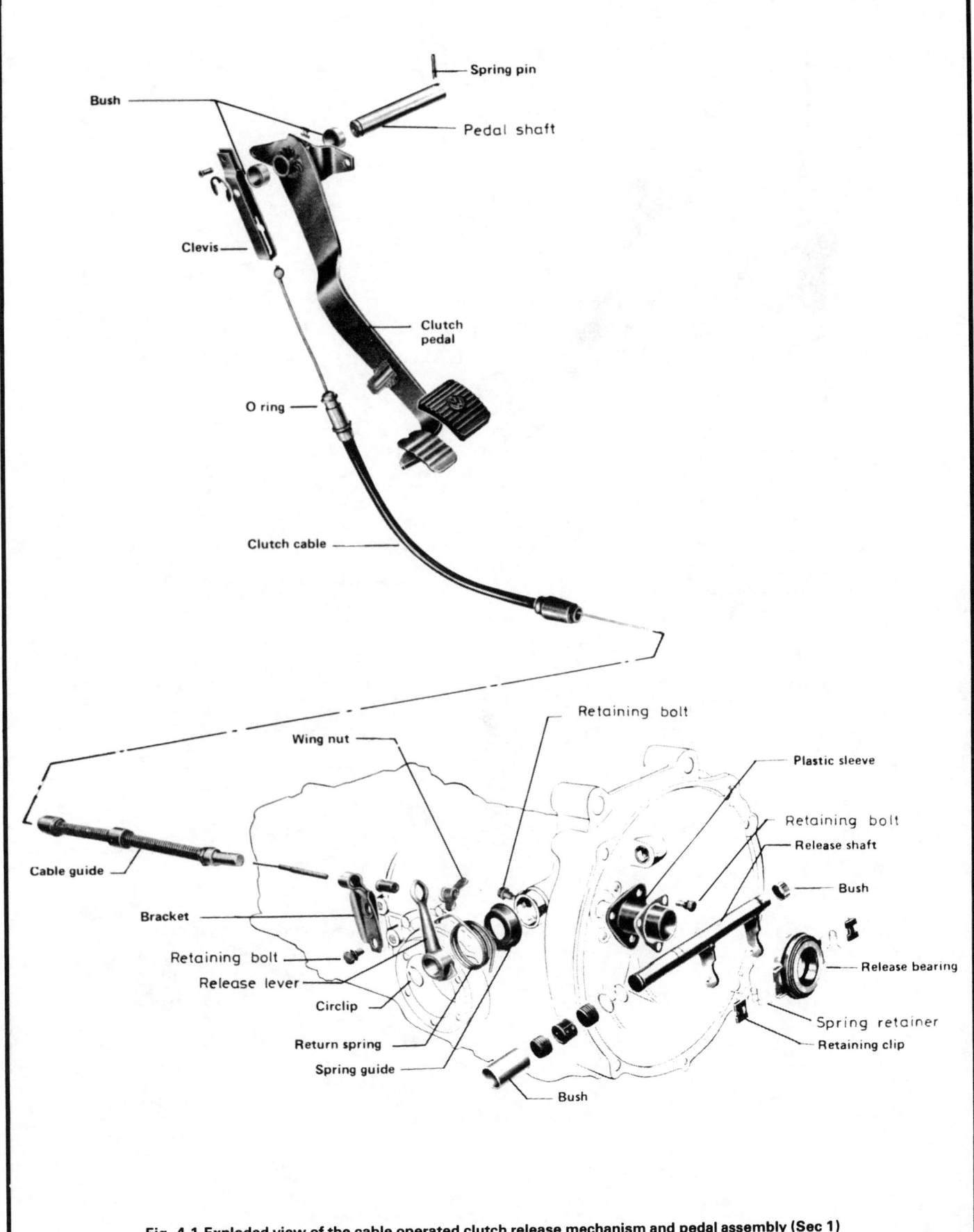

Fig. 4.1 Exploded view of the cable operated clutch release mechanism and pedal assembly (Sec 1)

108

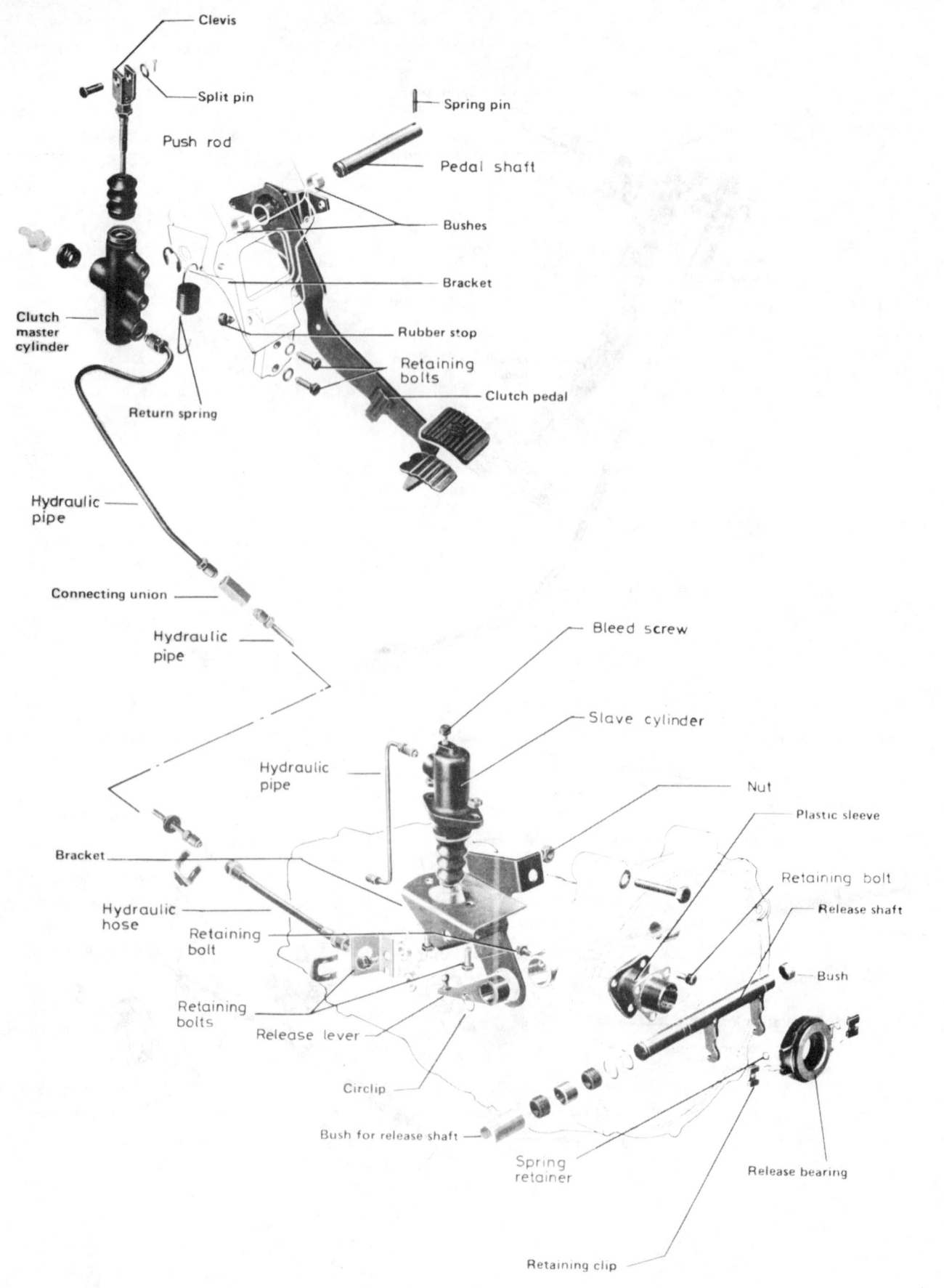

Fig. 4.2 Exploded view of the hydraulically operated clutch release mechanism and pedal assembly (Sec 1)

2 Clutch free play – adjustment

On all vehicles equipped with cable operated clutches a degree of free play must exist in the cable if the clutch is to operate efficiently. If the amount of free play is insufficient the clutch will start to slip as wear takes place on the clutch disc friction linings.

1 To check the amount of free play at the clutch pedal, press the pedal down by hand, and using a ruler, measure the distance the pedal moves until initial resistance is felt. The measurement should be within the tolerance shown in the Specifications.

2 If adjustment is necessary jack up the rear of the vehicle and support it on axle stands.

3 Turn the wing nut located at the gearbox end of the clutch cable to either increase or decrease the free play. As a guide, approximately 2 mm (0.07 in) of free play at the clutch lever should give the correct amount of free play at the clutch pedal.

4 After carrying out the initial adjustment, depress the clutch pedal hard several times and recheck the measurement. It may be necessary to adjust the wing nut again.

5 When the free play is correct, lower the vehicle to the ground.

6 On vehicles equipped with hydraulically operated clutches provision is made for adjustment of the free play between the master cylinder piston and pushrod. This adjustment is carried out during manufacture and should only require attention during service if the master cylinder or clutch pedal are removed for overhaul or renewal. Adjustment is carried out by slackening the locknut on the pushrod and then turning the pushrod in the desired direction to achieve the specified clearance. The locknut is then retightened.

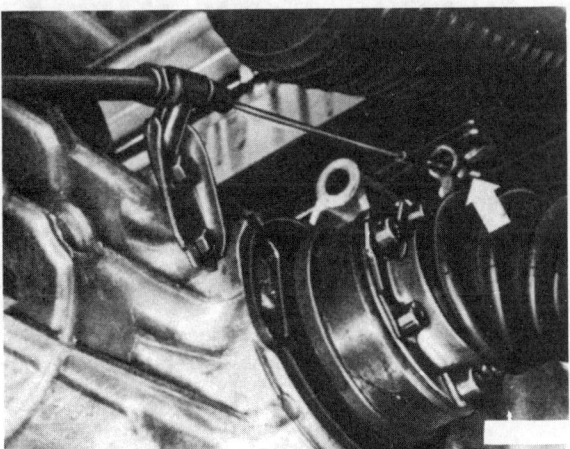

Fig. 4.3 Location of the clutch free play adjusting wing nut (arrowed) at the end of the cable (Sec 2)

3 Clutch hydraulic system – bleeding

On vehicles equipped with a hydraulically operated clutch, air will have been introduced into the system if any of the hydraulic components have been removed or disconnected. For the clutch to function correctly all air must be removed from the system. This process is known as bleeding.

1 To bleed the system, first gather together a clean glass jar, a suitable length of rubber or plastic tubing, which is a tight fit over the bleed screw on the clutch slave cylinder, and a tin of the specified hydraulic fluid. The help of an assistant will also be required. If a one-man do-it-yourself bleeding kit as used for bleeding the brake hydraulic system is available, this can be used quite satisfactorily for the clutch also. Full information on the use of these kits will be found in Chapter 9.

2 Jack up the rear of the vehicle and support it on axle stands.

3 From inside the car remove the instrument panel cover and if necessary top up the fluid level in the brake master cylinder reservoir until it is up to the MAX mark. (The clutch and brake hydraulic systems are both supplied from a common reservoir). Keep the reservoir topped up during subsequent operations.

4 From under the rear of the vehicle wipe clean the area around the bleed screw on the slave cylinder and remove the rubber dust cover.

5 Connect one end of the bleed tube to the bleed screw, and insert the other end of the tube in the jar containing sufficient clean hydraulic fluid to keep the end of the tube submerged.

6 Open the bleed screw half a turn and have your assistant depress the clutch pedal and then slowly release it. Continue this procedure until clean hydraulic fluid, free from air bubbles emerges from the tube. Now tighten the bleed screw at the end of a downstroke.

7 Check the operation of the clutch pedal. It may take a few further strokes for the pressure to build up and then it should feel normal. Any sponginess would indicate air still present in the system.

8 On completion remove the bleed tube and refit the dust cover. Top up the master cylinder reservoir if necessary and refit the cap and instrument panel cover. Fluid expelled from the hydraulic system should now be discarded as it will be contaminated with moisture, air and dirt, making it unsuitable for further use.

9 Finally lower the vehicle to the ground and check the operation of the clutch.

4 Clutch assembly – removal and refitting

1 To gain access to the clutch assembly it is first necessary to remove the gearbox as described in Chapter 5.

2 Before removing the clutch assembly from the flywheel, inspect the periphery of the clutch cover in the area of the retaining bolts for any aligning marks that may be visible. If no markings are present, scribe a line between the clutch cover and flywheel to ensure correct reassembly should the original components be refitted.

3 Remove the clutch assembly by unscrewing the six retaining bolts in a diagonal sequence half a turn at a time to prevent distortion of the cover flange.

4 With the bolts removed lift the clutch assembly off the flywheel locating dowels. Be prepared to catch the clutch disc which will fall out at this stage – it is not attached to the cover assembly or flywheel.

5 It is important that no oil or grease is allowed to come into contact with the clutch disc friction linings, or the pressure plate and flywheel faces. It is advisable to handle the parts with clean hands and to wipe off the pressure plate and flywheel faces with a clean dry rag before inspection or refitting commences.

6 To refit the clutch place the clutch disc against the flywheel with the extended boss in the centre of the hub facing away from the flywheel.

7 Place the cover assembly in position over the dowels and with the previously made alignment marks in line (photo). Secure the cover with the six retaining bolts and tighten them finger tight so that the clutch disc is gripped but can still be moved.

4.7 Refitting the clutch disc and cover assembly

8   The clutch disc must now be centralised so that when the engine and gearbox are mated, the gearbox input shaft splines will pass through the splines in the centre of the hub.

9   Centralisation can be carried out by inserting a round bar or long screwdriver through the hole in the centre of the hub, so that the end of the bar rests in the small hole in the crankshaft containing the input shaft spigot bearing. Moving the bar sideways or up and down will move the clutch disc in whichever way is necessary to achieve centralisation.

10 Centralisation is easily judged by removing the bar and viewing the clutch disc hub in relation to the crankshaft spigot bearing and the hole in the centre of the diaphragm spring. When the hub appears exactly in the centre all is correct. Alternatively if an old input shaft or universal clutch aligning tool (photo) can be obtained, this will eliminate all the guesswork, obviating the need for visual alignment.

4.10 Using a universal clutch aligning tool to centralise the clutch disc

11 Tighten the cover retaining bolts fully in a diagonal sequence to ensure the cover plate is pulled down evenly without distortion of the flange. Tighten the bolts to the torque setting given in the Specifications.

12 The gearbox can now be refitted to the vehicle as described in Chapter 5.

5 Clutch assembly – inspection

1   With the clutch disc and pressure plate removed from the flywheel, clean off all traces of asbestos dust using a dry cloth. This is best done outside or in a well ventilated area; *asbestos dust is harmful and must not be inhaled.*

2   Examine the clutch disc friction linings for wear and loose rivets, and the disc for rim distortion, cracks, broken hub springs and worn splines. The surface of the friction linings may be highly glazed, but as long as the clutch material pattern can be clearly seen, this is satisfactory. If the friction material is less than 1.00 mm (0.039 in) above the rivet heads, or if the linings are black in appearance (indicating oil contamination), the disc must be renewed. If oil contamination is evident, usually from a leaking crankshaft rear oil seal or gearbox input shaft seal, the leak must be rectified before refitting the clutch assembly.

3   Check the machined faces of the flywheel and pressure plate. If either is grooved or heavily scored, it should be machined until smooth, or preferably, renewed.

4   If the pressure plate is cracked or split, or if the diaphragm spring is damaged or its pressure suspect, a new unit must be fitted.

5   Also, check the release bearing for smoothness of operation. There should be no harshness or slackness in it. It should spin reasonably freely, bearing in mind it has been pre-packed with grease.

6   When considering renewing clutch components individually, bear in mind that new parts (or parts from different manufacturers) do not always bed into old ones satisfactorily. A clutch pressure plate or disc renewed separately may sometimes cause judder or snatch. Although expensive, the clutch pressure plate, disc and release bearing should be renewed together, as a complete assembly, wherever possible.

6 Clutch release mechanism – removal, overhaul and refitting

The clutch release mechanism is contained within the transmission clutch housing and it is necessary to remove the transmission as described in Chapter 5 to gain access to these components.

1   With the transmission on the bench check the release bearing for smoothness of operation. There should be no harshness or slackness in it and it should spin reasonably freely bearing in mind it has been pre-packed with grease. It a definite roughness can be felt the bearing should be renewed. It is not possible to dismantle the release bearing for cleaning or for packing with fresh grease.

2   To remove the bearing carefully prise off the spring retainers and the retaining clips then lift the bearing off the release shaft and guide sleeve (photo).

6.2 Clutch release bearing spring retainers (A) and retaining clips (B)

3   Check the release shaft for play in the support bushes. If play is evident it is likely to be at the end nearest to the release lever. If the bushes are worn the release shaft should be removed and the bushes renewed as follows.

4   If a cable operated clutch is fitted, remove the circlip and then withdraw the release lever and return spring off the release shaft. On models equipped with a hydraulically operated clutch, undo and remove the two slave cylinder retaining nuts and bolts and lift off the cylinder. Undo and remove the large nut and bolt securing the slave cylinder mounting bracket to the gearbox casing. Extract the circlip, slide off the release lever and then remove the mounting bracket (photo).

5   On all models undo and remove the bolt which locates the release shaft bushes in the casing (photo).

6   From inside the clutch housing withdraw the release shaft inner circlip from its groove (photo) and slide it together with the washer, towards the centre of the shaft.

7   Slide the release shaft to the left to release one end from its bush then withdraw the shaft from the clutch housing. The bushes and the two concertina type grease seals can now be removed also.

8   The release mechanism is now completely dismantled. All the parts should be cleaned and then carefully inspected for wear. Pay particular attention to the bushes and grease seals and renew any

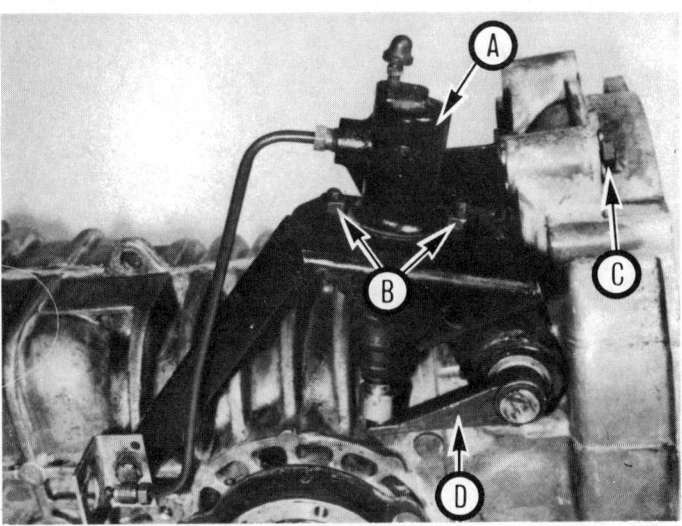

6.4 Clutch slave cylinder and mounting bracket assembly

A   Slave cylinder   C   Mounting bracket retaining bolt
B   Slave cylinder retaining nuts   D   Release lever

parts that are worn (photo). Note that the bush that supports the other end of the release shaft is still in position in the gearbox casing. Special tools are required to remove and refit this bush and the work should be left to a VW dealer. This bush however is not subject to the same loads and wear is uncommon.

9   Lubricate the components with multi-purpose grease and begin reassembly by placing the release shaft in position. Make sure that the inner circlip and washer are in place on the shaft before you do this (photo).

10 Now slide on the large bush (photo), followed by the inner grease seal, small bush and then the outer grease seal. Make sure that the holes in the bushes face towards the locating bolt hole and are correctly aligned to accept the bolt. Refit the bolt and tighten it fully.

11 Slide the release shaft inner circlip and washer towards the end of the shaft and locate the circlip into its groove.

12 Refitting the remainder of the release mechanism is the reverse sequence to removal. When refitting the release bearing smear a trace of molybdenum disulphide grease on the guide sleeve, contact fingers and the thrust face. Ensure also that the spring retainers and retaining clips are correctly located and secure.

13 Check that the mechanism operates smoothly and then refit the gearbox using the procedure described in Chapter 5.

7   Clutch cable – removal and refitting

1   Jack up the rear of the vehicle and support it on axle stands.

2   Working underneath undo and remove the cable adjusting wing nut and then slide the cable out of the clutch release lever and cable support bracket.

3   Release the cable from its support clips and/or brackets on the vehicle underbody.

4   From inside the cab release the inner cable end from the clevis attached to the clutch pedal and then withdraw the complete inner and outer cable from the cab.

5   The cable can now be removed from under the vehicle.

6   Refitting the cable is the reverse sequence to removal. Note however that when fitted, the cable guide must have a 35 to 45 mm (1.37 to 1.77 in) bend in it (Fig. 4.4). This bend is obtained by varying the number of packing washers between the cable guide end fitting and the bracket on the gearbox. If the cable guide is bent too much the clutch will be stiff to operate with creaking noises and possible breakage of the cable. If the guide is not bent enough the clutch may

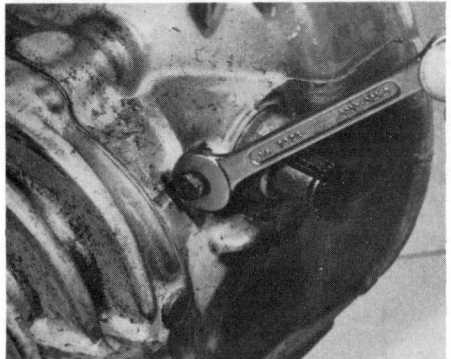

6.5 Removing the locating bolt for the release shaft bushes

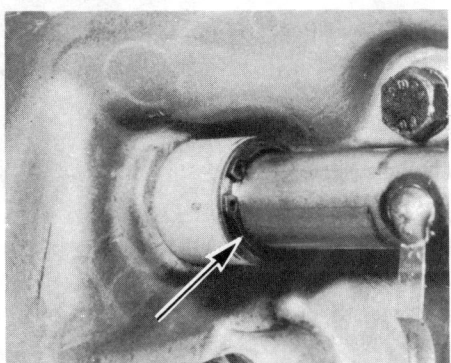

6.6 Release shaft inner retaining circlip (arrowed)

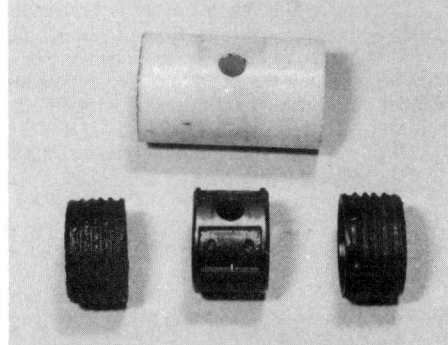

6.8 Release shaft support bushes and grease seals

6.9 Refitting the release shaft ...

6.10 ... and large support bush

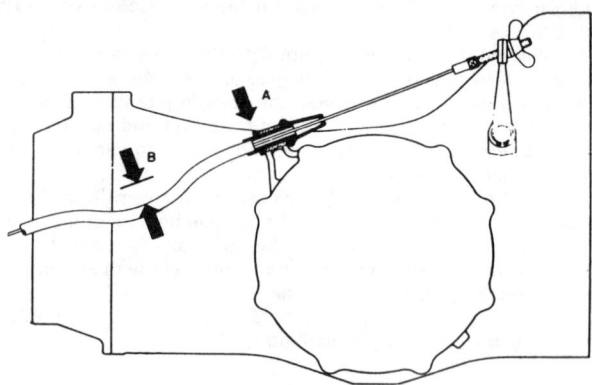

Fig. 4.4 Bend in clutch cable guide (B) is adjusted by varying the number of washers between cable end fitting (A) and bracket (Sec 7)

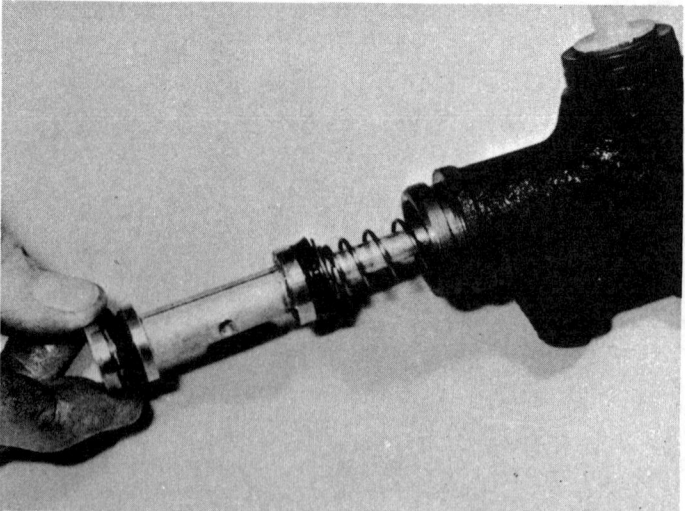

9.4 Withdrawing the clutch master cylinder piston and spring assembly

be jerky in operation. It is therefore important to get the bend just right if the clutch is to operate smoothly.

7   With the cable installed, all supports or brackets attached and the guide bend properly set, adjust the clutch free play as described in Section 2.

8   Clutch master cylinder – removal and refitting

On vehicles equipped with a hydraulically operated clutch, the master cylinder is located inside the cab at the base of the clutch and brake pedal mounting bracket. Hydraulic fluid for the unit is supplied from the brake master cylinder reservoir.

1   To remove the master cylinder first cover the floor beneath the pedals with some old rags. Some hydraulic fluid will be spilled during the removal sequence – this is unavoidable.

2   Carefully pull the hydraulic fluid supply hose off the outlet on the cylinder and quickly plug the hose with an old bolt or a rod of suitable diameter.

3   Unscrew the hydraulic pipe union at the base of the cylinder and carefully ease out the pipe.

4   Finally undo and remove the two master cylinder retaining bolts and lift out the cylinder. Note that as the cylinder is removed the pushrod and clevis will stay behind as they are still attached to the clutch pedal.

5   Refitting is the reverse sequence to removal. Bleed the clutch hydraulic system after refitting the master cylinder using the procedure described in Section 3.

6   Check the free play between the pushrod and master cylinder piston after refitting is completed and adjust the pushrod if the free play is more than 0.5 mm (0.02 in). Adjustment is carried out by slackening the locknut and turning the pushrod in the desired direction to increase or decrease the free play.

9   Clutch master cylinder – dismantling, inspection and re-assembly

1   Before dismantling the master cylinder, prepare a clean uncluttered working area on the bench.

2   Remove the dust cover from the master cylinder and then extract the piston retaining circlip and washer.

3   Tap the end of the cylinder on a block of wood until the piston emerges from the end of the cylinder bore.

4   Withdraw the piston from the cylinder together with the return spring (photo). Carefully remove the spring from the piston and recover the spring retainer.

5   Lay the parts in the order of removal (photo) and then carefully remove the main and secondary cup seals from the piston, noting which way round they are fitted.

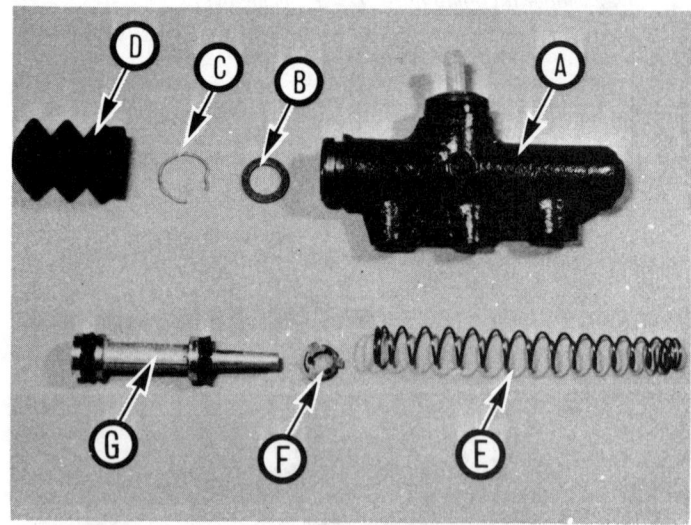

9.5 Component parts of the clutch master cylinder

A	Master cylinder body	E	Return spring
B	Washer	F	Spring retainer
C	Circlip	G	Piston assembly
D	Rubber dust cover		

6   Wash the components in clean hydraulic fluid and then wipe dry with a lint free cloth.

7   Examine the cylinder bore and piston carefully for signs of scoring or wear ridges. If these are apparent renew the complete master cylinder. If the condition of the components appears satisfactory a new set of rubber seals must be obtained. Never re-use old seals as they will have deteriorated with age even though this may not be evident during visual inspection.

8   Begin reassembly by thoroughly lubricating the internal components and the cylinder bore in clean hydraulic fluid.

9   Using fingers only place the main and secondary cup seals in position with the lip of the seals facing towards the spring.

10   Place the spring retainer and spring in position over the piston and carefully insert this assembly into the cylinder bore. Take care not to allow the lips of the seals to roll over as they are inserted.

11   Push the piston assembly fully into the cylinder bore and then refit the washer and retaining circlip. Smear the inside of the dust cover with rubber grease and place it in position over the end of the cylinder.

12   The assembled master cylinder can now be refitted to the car as described in Section 8.

10 Clutch slave cylinder – removal and refitting

1 Jack up the rear of the vehicle and support it on axle stands.
2 Using a brake hose clamp or a pair of self-locking grips with their jaws suitably protected, clamp the flexible hydraulic fluid hose located on the left-hand side of the gearbox. This will prevent loss of fluid when the hydraulic pipe union at the slave cylinder is disconnected.
3 Wipe the area around the hydraulic pipe union on the side of the slave cylinder and then unscrew the union nut. Carefully pull the pipe clear of the cylinder.
4 Undo and remove the two nuts and bolts securing the slave cylinder to the mounting bracket and lift away the cylinder.
5 Refitting is the reverse sequence to removal bearing in mind the followng points:

    (a) Lubricate the clutch release lever with multi-purpose grease
    (b) Place the slave cylinder retaining bolt nearest the engine in position in the bracket before fitting the cylinder
    (c) Bleed the clutch hydraulic system as described in Section 3 after fitting

11 Clutch slave cylinder – dismantling, inspection and reassembly

1 With the slave cylinder on the bench wipe off the exterior with a clean rag until it is free from dirt.
2 Release the small wire retaining ring securing the rubber dust cover to the pushrod and withdraw the pushrod.
3 Now release the large wire retaining ring securing the rubber dust cover to the cylinder and withdraw the dust cover.
4 Extract the circlip and then tap the cylinder on a block of wood until the piston emerges from the cylinder bore. Lift out the piston followed by the return spring.
5 Remove the dust cover from the bleed screw and then undo and remove the screw.
6 Thoroughly clean all the parts in clean hydraulic fluid and wipe dry with a lint free cloth.
7 Lay out all the components in the order of removal ready for inspection (photo).

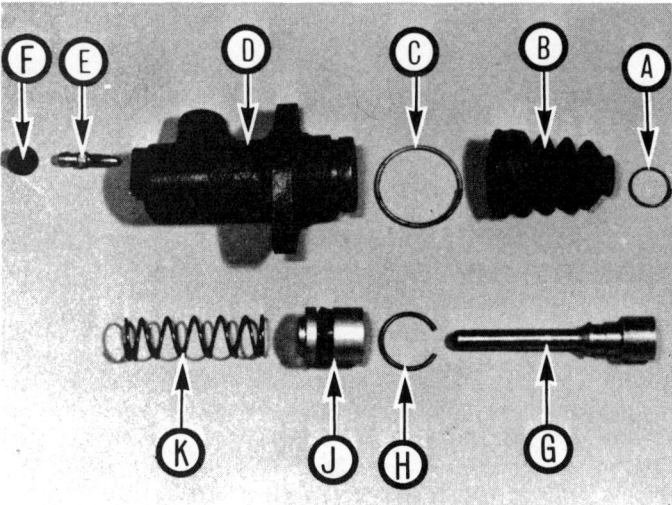

11.7 Component parts of the clutch slave cylinder

A	Wire retaining ring (small)	F	Dust cover
B	Rubber dust cover	G	Pushrod
C	Wire retaining ring (large)	H	Circlip
D	Slave cylinder body	J	Piston and seal
E	Bleed screw	K	Return spring

8 Carefully examine the piston and cylinder bore for signs of scoring, pitting or wear ridges and if apparent renew the complete cylinder assembly. If these parts are in a satisfactory condition a new set of rubber seals must be obtained. Never re-use old seals as they will have

deteriorated with age even though this may not be evident during visual inspection.
9 Begin reassembly by thoroughly lubricating the internal components and the cylinder bore in clean hydraulic fluid.
10 Using fingers only remove the old seal from the piston and carefully ease on the new one. The lip of the seal must be toward the spring end of the piston.
11 Insert the spring and then the piston into the cylinder bore taking care not to allow the lip of the seal to roll over as it is inserted.
12 Push the piston fully into the cylinder bore and then refit the retaining circlip.
13 Smear the inside of the rubber dust cover with rubber grease and then place it in position over the end of the cylinder. Secure with the large wire retaining ring.
14 Insert the pushrod into the dust cover and ease the end of the cover into the machined groove in the pushrod. Secure the dust cover to the pushrod with the small wire retaining ring.
15 Finally refit the bleed screw and dust cover.
16 The assembled slave cylinder can now be refitted as described in Section 10.

12 Clutch pedal – removal and refitting

The clutch pedal is removed in conjunction with the brake pedal and full information will be found in Chapter 9.

13 Fault diagnosis – clutch

1 There are four main faults to which the clutch is subject: judder, drag, slip and squeal. These are dealt with separately below. There are also faults which are due to maladjustment or defects in the operating mechanism. It is important to ascertain whether the clutch itself or its operating mechanism is at fault since some of the symptoms are similar.

Clutch judder

2 Clutch judder is a self-evident condition which occurs when the engine or gearbox mountings are worn or soft; when there is oil on the faces of the clutch plate; when the clutch pressure plate or diaphragm spring are worn, damaged or out of alignment, or when, in the case of cable operated clutches, the bend in the cable guide is either excessive or insufficient.
3 The reason for clutch judder is that due to one of the faults just listed the clutch disc is not smoothly taking up the drive and is snatching.
4 Clutch judder normally occurs when the clutch pedal is released in first or reverse gears and the whole vehicle shudders as it moves backwards or forwards.

Clutch drag

5 Clutch drag is a condition which occurs when there is a leak in the clutch hydraulic actuating mechanism or an incorrectly adjusted clutch cable, depending on type of system fitted; when there is oil on the friction linings of the clutch disc causing them to stick to the pressure plate or flywheel; or when the clutch disc is not sliding freely on the splines of the gearbox input shaft.
6 The reason for clutch drag is that due to any or a combination of the faults just listed, the clutch pressure plate is not completely freeing from the clutch disc even when the clutch pedal is fully depressed.
7 If clutch drag is suspected, the condition can be confirmed by difficulty in engaging first or reverse gears from rest, difficulty in changing gear and very sudden take up of the clutch drive at the fully depressed end of the clutch pedal travel as the pedal is released.
8 On cable operated clutches check the adjustment of the cable and the bend in the cable guide. On hydraulic clutches check the free play at the master cylinder pushrod and make sure that it is not excessive. Also check for leaks at the master and slave cylinders and the hydraulic fluid pipe. Fluid in one of the rubber dust covers fitted over the end of the master and slave cylinders is a sure sign of leaking rubber seals.
9 If these points are checked and found to be in order, then the fault lies internally in the clutch and it will be necessary to remove the clutch for examination.

Clutch slip

10 If the clutch is slipping, the engine speed will increase on acceleration without a corresponding increase in road speed. Slip is usually progressive, first being noticed on steep hills or when carrying heavy loads, eventually occurring under light acceleration on the flat.

11 On cable operated clutches check that the free play at the pedal is correct and that the bend in the cable guide is correct. On hydraulic clutches make sure that there is a small amount of free play between the master cylinder piston and the pushrod when the pedal is released.

12 If the fault persists after adjustment it may be due to wear or contamination of the clutch disc or insufficient pressure from the diaphragm spring on the pressure plate. In either case it will be necessary to remove the clutch for examination.

Clutch squeal

13 If a squealing or rumbling noise is heard when the clutch is depressed, this indicates a worn clutch release bearing which will have to be renewed.

Chapter 5 Manual transmission

Contents

Specifications

Type .... Four forward speeds (all synchromesh) and reverse. Final drive integral with main gearbox

Identification code 091

Gearbox ratios
1st .... 3.78 : 1
2nd .... 2.06 : 1
3rd .... 1.26 : 1
4th:
    1.6 litre models .... 0.823 : 1
    2.0 litre models .... 0.852 : 1
Reverse .... 3.28 : 1

Final drive ratios
1.6 litre models .... 5.43 : 1 or 5.86 : 1
2.0 litres .... 4.57 : 1

Transmission overhaul data
3rd gear axial play .... 0.05 to 0.20 mm (0.002 to 0.008 in)
Axial play adjustment .... Selective circlips
Minimum synchro ring to gear clearance .... 0.5 mm (0.02 in)
Gearshift linkage adjustment dimension:
    Up to Chassis No. 25 BH 137 156 .... 19 mm (0.75 in)
    From Chassis No. 25 BH 137 156 .... 22 mm (0.86 in)

Lubricant capacity
Gearbox and final drive combined .... 3.5 litres (6.16 Imp pints, 7.25 US pints)

Torque wrench settings

	Nm	lbf ft
Clutch housing to engine	30	22
Driveshaft to differential flange	45	33
Transmission front mounting bracket to body	25	18
Clutch housing to gearbox housing	20	15
Geartrain housing to gearbox housing	20	15
Gearshift housing to geartrain housing	20	15
Pinion shaft taper roller bearing retaining ring	225	166
Selector fork retaining bolts	25	18
Relay shaft bracket retaining bolts	25	18
Reversing light switch	30	22
Drain and filler plugs	20	15
Gearshift bracket to gearshift shaft	20	15
Guide pin retaining nut	45	33
Gearshift linkage clamp bolt	20	15
Gear lever to front shift rod	5	4
Gear lever plate to mounting plate	10	7

1   General description

The manual transmission fitted to vehicles covered by this manual has four forward and one reverse gear. All forward gears are engaged through synchromesh units to obtain smooth, silent gear changes.

The transmission consists of four main housings bolted together to from the complete assembly. The clutch housing contains the clutch release mechanism and, when the transmission is attached to the engine, houses the flywheel and clutch assembly. The gearbox housing contains the final drive (differential) and is located between the clutch and geartrain housings. The input shaft, pinion shaft, gears and selector mechanism are located within the geartrain housing which has the gearshift housing bolted to its front face in the form of an end cover. This last unit contains the gear selector shaft and attachment for the external gear selector linkage.

Gear selection is by a floor mounted lever connected by a remote control housing and a series of rods, to the mechanism at the gearshift housing.

2   Maintenance and inspection

1   At the intervals given in Routine Maintenance at the beginning of this manual, inspect the transmission joint faces and oil seals for any signs of damage, deterioration or oil leakage.

2   With the vehicle in a level plane either over a pit, raised on a hoist or supported on stands, check and if necessary top up the transmission oil. The filler plug is located on the right-hand side of the transmission above the gearshift rod (photo). Removal of the filler plug entails the use of a large Allen key. A suitable alternative, however, is to lock the two nuts together on the thread of a suitable bolt, insert the hexagonal

2.2 Transmission oil level/filler plug (arrowed)

head of the bolt into the filler plug and then unscrew the plug using a spanner on the innermost nut. The oil level should be maintained up to the level of the filler plug orifice.

3   Although not considered necessary by the manufacturers, the diligent home mechanic may wish to renew the oil in the interests of extended transmission life every 30 000 miles (45 000 km) or three years (photo).

4   It is also advisable to check for excess free play or wear in the gear linkage and check the gear lever adjustment as described in Section 19.

2.3 Transmission oil drain plug (arrowed)

3   Transmission – removal and refitting

1   As the majority of the work is carried out from below, drive the vehicle over a pit, raise it on ramps or a hoist, or securely support it at the rear on axle stands.

2   Disconnect the battery negative terminal.

3   On vehicles equipped with a cable operated clutch, undo and remove the cable adjusting wing nut then slip the cable end out of the clutch release lever. Undo the two bolts securing the cable support bracket to the gearbox housing and move the cable assembly to one side.

4   On vehicles with a hydraulically operated clutch, undo the two nuts and bolts securing the clutch slave cylinder to the support bracket on the clutch housing (photo). Now undo the bolt securing the flexible hose support bracket to the gearbox housing (photo). Lift the slave cylinder out of its location and tie it up out of the way with the hydraulic fluid pipe still connected.

5   Undo the nut securing the gearshift rod guide pin to the lug on the geartrain housing whilst holding the guide pin with a second spanner

3.4A Clutch slave cylinder retaining bolts (arrowed) ...

3.4B ... and hose support bracket retaining bolt (arrowed)

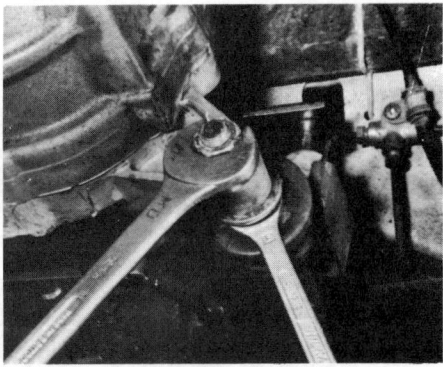

3.5 Removing the gearshift guide pin

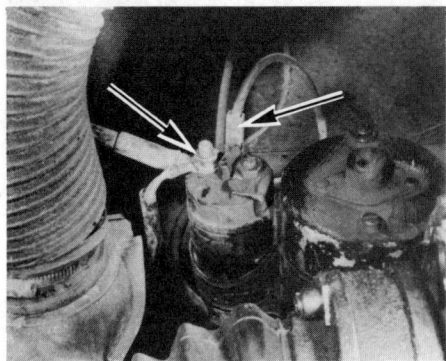

3.6 Remove the starter motor wiring at the terminals arrowed

3.8 Upper engine to transmission retaining nuts (arrowed)

3.9 Disconnect the reversing light switch wires

to stop it turning (photo). Withdraw the guide pin from the lug, lower the gearshift rod to disengage the transmission linkage, then move the rod to one side.

6   Make a note of the wiring connections at the rear of the starter motor solenoid and disconnect them (photo).

7   Using a suitable Allen key, undo and remove the socket headed bolts securing both driveshaft inner constant velocity joints to the differential drive flanges. Recover the washers from under the bolt heads and tie the driveshafts up using string or wire. Do not let the driveshafts hang unsupported.

8   Refer to Chapter 2 and remove the air cleaner to provide access to the two upper engine to transmission retaining nuts (photo). Undo the two nuts from within the engine compartment while the bolts are held from below.

9   Disconnect the two wires at the reversing light switch (photo).

10   Position a jack with interposed block of wood beneath the engine and raise the jack until the engine is just supported.

11   Position a second jack beneath the transmission in the same way.

12   Undo the two nuts at the base of the clutch housing securing the transmission to the engine studs.

13   Undo the nut and bolt securing the earth braid to the transmission mounting bracket (photo).

14   Undo the four bolts securing the transmission front mounting bracket to the vehicle underbody, lower the two jacks until the transmission is clear at the front, then withdraw the unit from the engine.

15   Refitting the transmission is the reverse sequence to removal, bearing in mind the following points:

(a)   *Apply a trace of molybdenum disulphide grease to the input shaft splines before refitting the transmission*

(b)   *Ensure that the transmission is fully secured to the engine, with the engine cover plates correctly located in relation to the body and the engine compartment seal aligned, before finally tightening the transmission mounting bracket bolts*

(c)   *On vehicles equipped with cable operated clutches, check the bend of the cable guide and then adjust the cable as described in Chapter 4, Sections 7 and 2 respectively*

(d)   *Refill the transmission with the specified lubricant to the level of the filler plug orifice*

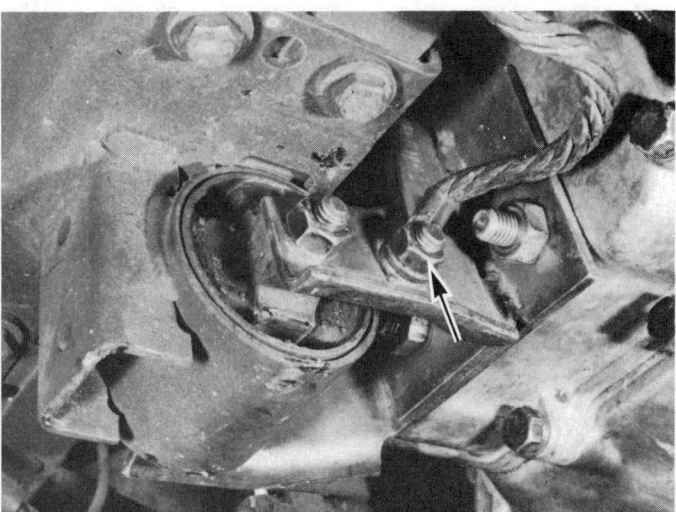

3.13 Disconnect the earth braid for the transmission mounting bracket (arrowed)

Fig. 5.1 Transmission removal (Sec 3)

1 *Clutch cable support bracket bolts (where applicable)*
2 *Clutch cable wing nut (where applicable)*
3 *Clutch housing to engine retaining nuts*
4 *Driveshaft inner joint retaining bolts*

4 Transmission overhaul – general

Repair and overhaul of the transmission is considerably involved and cannot be carried out successfully without extensive garage equipment and preferably access to certain VW special tools. Although the transmission can, with some improvisation, be dismantled into its major assemblies, problems arise if dismantling is carried further, particularly if new parts are required. Preloads, running clearances and adjustments are carried out during manufacture using special jigs. Although the parts can be marked during dismantling and refitted in their original positions when reassembling, this is only possible if the same parts are being used. If new parts are needed the special jigs will also be required to assemble the parts correctly and this can only be done by a VW agent suitably equipped to carry out the work. Also there is a cost consideration as the new parts plus the labour charges to carry out the setting up, may often exceed the price of an exchange or good secondhand transmission.

If the transmission develops a fault or is suspect in any way, an accurate diagnosis of the fault whilst the transmission is still in the vehicle is essential, even if it is necessary to seek professional help for this. The contents of this Chapter can then be thoroughly studied giving a good idea of the work involved and whether or not it is a practical proposition to undertake. If you do decide to proceed, allow plenty of time, ensure that any special tools or alternatives required are available and if possible engage the help of someone experienced in this type of work.

Before starting work, drain the oil and thoroughly clean the exterior of the housings using paraffin or a suitable solvent. Dry the unit with a lint free rag. Make sure that an uncluttered working area is available with some small containers and trays handy to store the various parts. Mark the position of all critical components before they are disturbed, label them if necessary and store them safely. When reassembling, have all new parts, gaskets and tools ready before starting. Ensure absolute cleanliness and lubricate each part with the recommended grade of gear oil as it is assembled.

5 Transmission – separating the housings

1 Refer to Chapter 4 and remove the clutch release bearing and shaft and where applicable the slave cylinder support bracket. Remove the transmission front mounting and bracket from the gearshift housing.
2 Using a screwdriver or punch, knock out the plastic cap in the centre of the right-hand drive flange (photo). Note that new plastic caps for the drive flanges will be required on reassembly.
3 Extract the drive flange retaining circlip and the dished washer located behind the circlip (photo).

5.2 Remove the plastic cap from the centre of the drive flange

5.3 Extract the circlip and dished washer

4 Screw a suitable bolt into the differential stud shaft then, using a puller, extract the drive flange (photo).
5 Undo the two retaining bolts and washers then lift off the right-hand locking plate (photo).
6 Using a punch or small file, accurately mark the right-hand differential adjusting ring in relation to the gearbox housing (photo). Use two marks on the right-hand ring and housing to avoid confusion with the left-hand ring which, when removed, should be identified with only one mark.

5.4 Using a puller and suitable bolt to remove the drive flange

5.5 Remove the locking plate

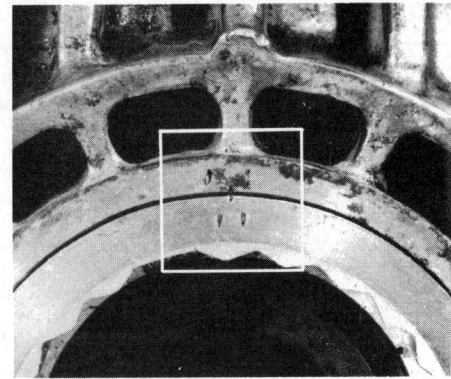

5.6 Left-hand differential adjusting ring identification and alignment marks made prior to removal

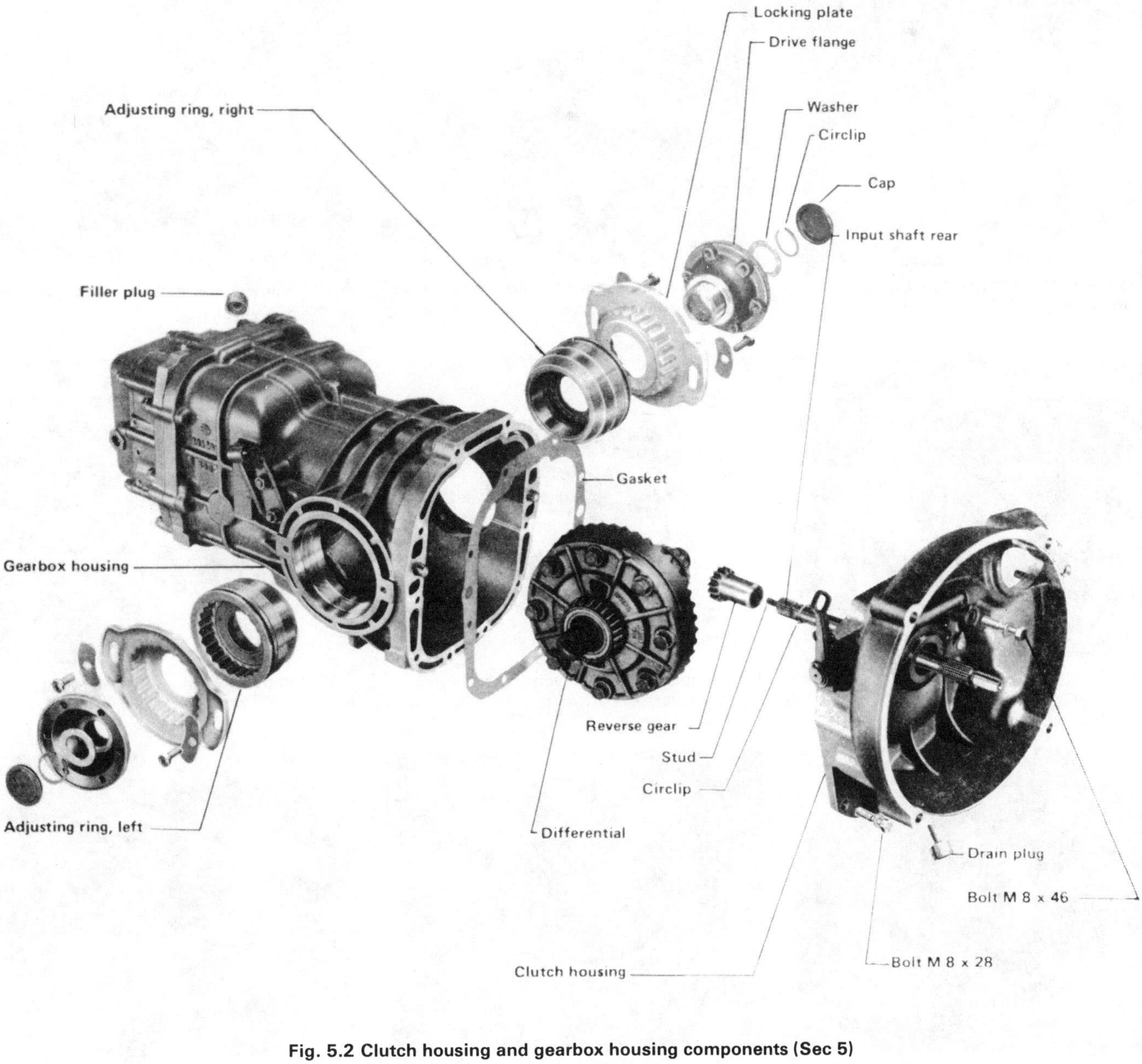

Adjusting ring, right

Locking plate

Drive flange

Washer

Circlip

Cap

Input shaft rear

Filler plug

Gearbox housing

Gasket

Reverse gear

Stud

Circlip

Adjusting ring, left

Differential

Clutch housing

Drain plug

Bolt M 8 x 46

Bolt M 8 x 28

Fig. 5.2 Clutch housing and gearbox housing components (Sec 5)

7   If a depth micrometer or vernier is available, accurately measure and record the depth of the adjusting ring upper face below the edge of the gearbox housing (photo). Alternatively, count and record the number of turns of the ring needed for removal.

8   Unscrew the retaining ring a turn only at this stage, using VW tool 381/15. Alternatively make up a suitable compromise using an exhaust clamp, bolt and washer (photo).

9   Repeat the operations described in paragraphs 2 to 8 on the left-hand drive flange and retaining ring.

10 Undo the bolts securing the clutch housing to the gearbox housing noting the different bolt lengths. Tap the housing off the locating dowels then withdraw it off the input shaft (photo).

11 Turn the crownwheel until the cut-out in the gear carrier is uppermost.

12 Extract the reverse gear retaining circlip from the input shaft (photo). Slide reverse gear towards the end of the shaft then unscrew

the rear part of the shaft. Withdraw the input shaft rear part, reverse gear and shaft retaining stud (photo).

13 Unscrew the two differential adjusting rings and remove them from the gearbox housing (photo).

14 Manipulate the differential as necessary and remove it from the gearbox housing (photo).

15 It is now necessary to remove the retaining ring which secures the pinion shaft bearing assembly to the gearbox housing. If possible VW tool 381/14 should be used to unscrew the retaining ring (Fig. 5.5). If this tool is not available, the ring may be split using a chisel providing care is taken to prevent damage to the threads of the bearing assembly. If this method is adopted a new retaining ring will obviously be required when reassembling.

16 With the retaining ring removed, lift out the thrust ring (photo).

17 At the other end of the transmission, undo the nut and remove the gearshift bracket from the gearshift shaft (photo). As the bracket is

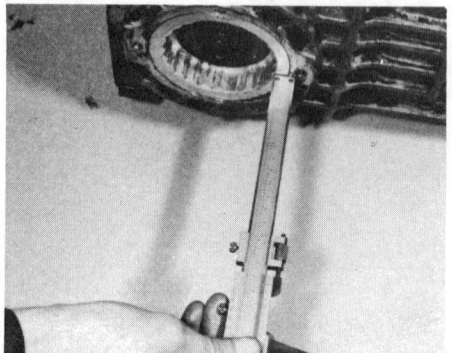

5.7 Using a vernier to measure the adjusting ring depth

5.8 Using a home made tool to unscrew the adjusting ring

5.10 Removing the clutch housing from the gearbox housing

5.12A Reverse gear retaining circlip (arrowed) on input shaft

5.12B Input shaft and reverse gear components

5.13 Remove the differential adjusting rings ...

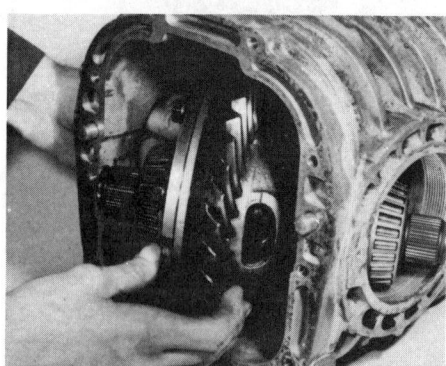

5.14 ... then withdraw the differential

5.16 Pinion shaft bearing thrust ring

5.17 Gearshift bracket retaining nut (arrowed)

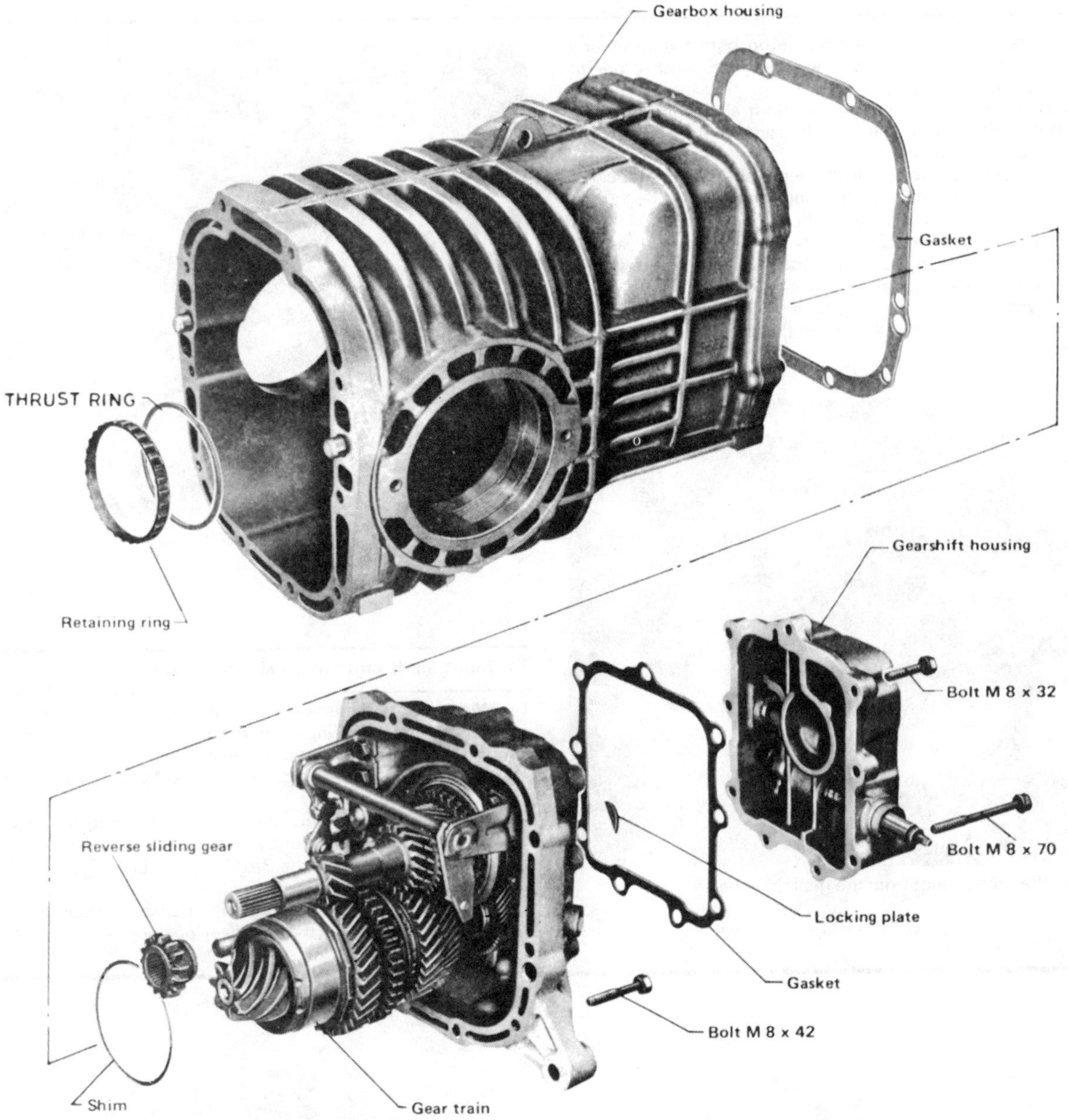

Gearbox housing

Gasket

THRUST RING

Retaining ring

Gearshift housing

Bolt M 8 x 32

Bolt M 8 x 70

Reverse sliding gear

Locking plate

Gasket

Bolt M 8 x 42

Shim

Gear train

Fig. 5.3 Geartrain housing and gearbox housing separation (Sec 5)

VW381/15

Fig. 5.4 VW special tool for differential adjusting ring removal (Sec 5)

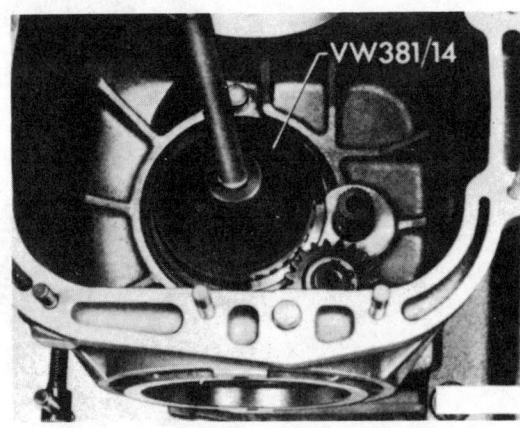

VW381/14

Fig. 5.5 VW special tool for pinion shaft retaining ring removal (Sec 5)

removed, check that there is a master spline on both the shaft and bracket, otherwise mark the two parts in relation to each other to ensure refitment in the same position.

18 Withdraw the rubber boot from the gearshift shaft (photo).

19 Undo the bolts securing the gearshift housing in place noting the position of the two longer bolts.

20 Withdraw the housing and recover the input shaft bearing locking plate from its recess in the geartrain housing (photo).

21 Undo the bolts securing the geartrain housing to the gearbox housing. Separate the two housings by tapping the pinion with a plastic mallet, or hammer and block of wood. As soon as the pinion bearing is free withdraw the geartrain housing complete with gears and shafts. Recover the reverse sliding gear which will be dislodged during this operation and also the shim from the shoulder of the pinion shaft taper roller bearing.

5.20 Input shaft bearing locking plate location (arrowed)

5.18 Removing the rubber boot from the gearshift shaft

6   Input shaft and pinion shaft – removal

1   With the transmission housings separated as described in the previous Section, the input shaft and pinion shaft assemblies can be removed from the geartrain housing as follows.

2   Accurately mark the position of the 1st/2nd selector fork on the 1st/2nd shift rod.

3   Undo and remove the selector fork retaining bolt, slide the shift rod out of the housing slightly then withdraw the fork (photos).

4   Mark the position of the 3rd/4th selector fork on the 3rd/4th shift rod (photo).

5   Return the 1st/2nd rod to the neutral position then move the 3rd/4th fork and rod to the 3rd gear position.

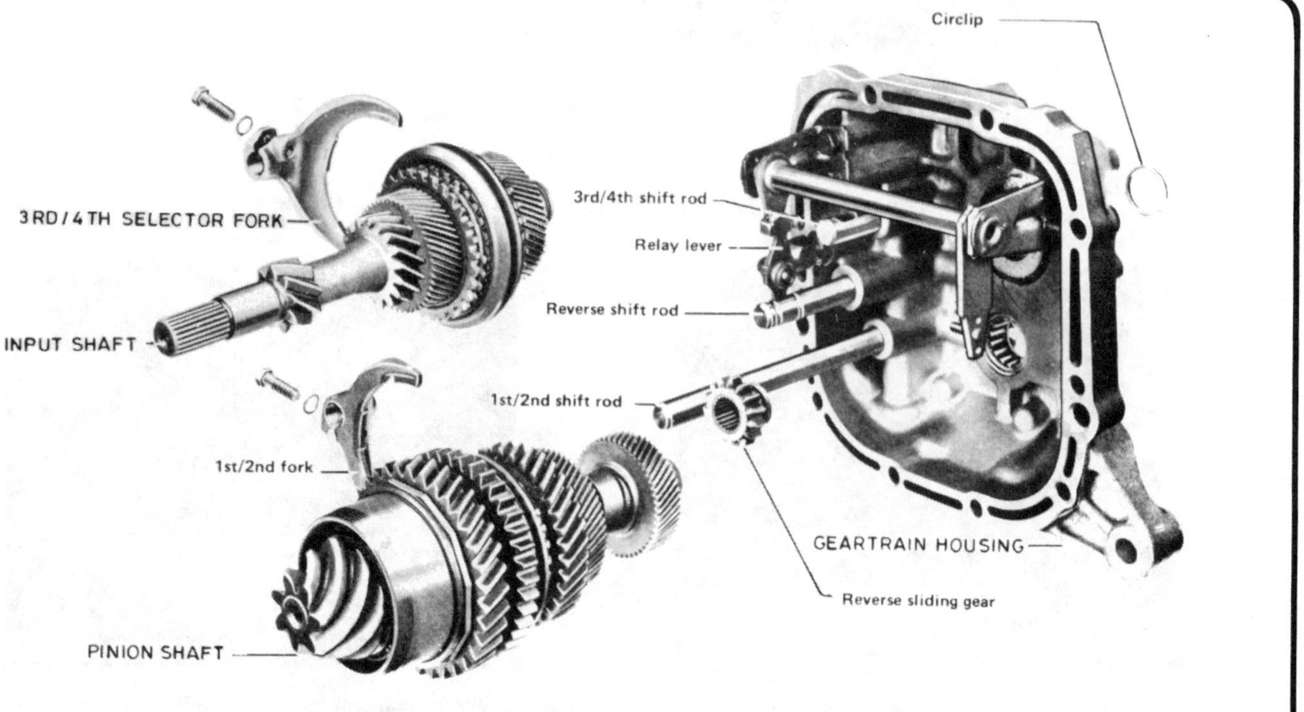

Circlip

3RD/4TH SELECTOR FORK

INPUT SHAFT

3rd/4th shift rod

Relay lever

Reverse shift rod

1st/2nd fork

1st/2nd shift rod

PINION SHAFT

GEARTRAIN HOUSING

Reverse sliding gear

Fig. 5.6 Input shaft, pinion shaft and geartrain housing components (Sec 6)

6.3A Undo the 1st/2nd selector fork retaining bolt (arrowed) ...

6.3B ... slide the rod out slightly and withdraw the fork

6.4 3rd/4th selector fork and retaining bolt location (arrowed)

6 Undo and remove the 3rd/4th selector fork retaining bolt, pull the rod back until the fork is free, but leave the fork in place on the synchro sleeve.

7 Accurately mark the position of the relay lever support in relation to the union nut. Slacken the union nut, turn the relay lever as necessary and remove it from the support. Note the fitted direction of the relay lever.

8 Extract the retaining circlip from the end of the input shaft (photo), then mount the geartrain housing on a press bed. Support the pinion shaft then press the input shaft down and out of its bearing in the housing. Ensure that both shafts hang free during this operation and do not jam.

9 As soon as the input shaft is free of its bearing, lift both shafts and associated gears together out of the housing.

6.8 Input shaft retaining circlip removal

7 Input shaft – dismantling

1 Slide 4th gear complete with its synchro ring off the shaft, followed by the needle roller bearing.

2 Extract the circlip securing the 3rd/4th synchro unit to the input shaft.

3 Using a press or suitable gear puller, remove 3rd gear and the 3rd/4th synchro unit together from the input shaft (photo).

4 Extract the remaining circlip and the 3rd gear needle roller bearing from the shaft.

7.3 Using a hydraulic gear puller to remove 3rd gear and the 3rd/4th synchro unit from the input shaft

DISMANTLING AND ASSEMBLING INPUT SHAFT

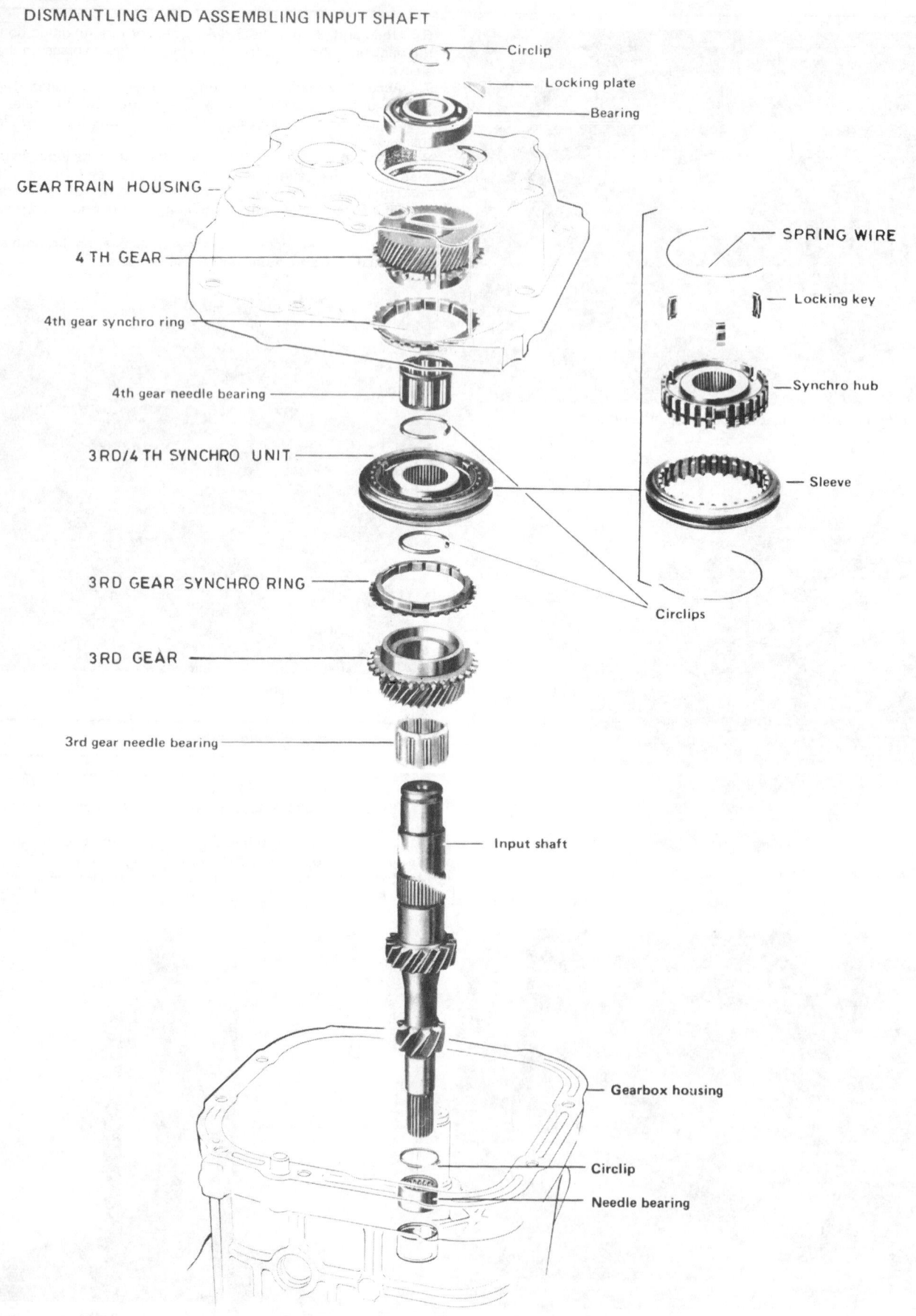

Circlip

Locking plate

Bearing

GEAR TRAIN HOUSING

4 TH GEAR

4th gear synchro ring

4th gear needle bearing

3RD/4TH SYNCHRO UNIT

3RD GEAR SYNCHRO RING

3RD GEAR

3rd gear needle bearing

SPRING WIRE

Locking key

Synchro hub

Sleeve

Circlips

Input shaft

Gearbox housing

Circlip

Needle bearing

Fig. 5.7 Exploded view of the transmission input shaft (Sec 7)

8 Pinion shaft – dismantling

1   Using a press or suitable arrangement of gear puller and spacers, hold 4th gear down to relieve the tension on the retaining circlip. Extract the circlip; release the tool and withdraw 4th gear. Take care during this operation as there is considerable tension on 4th gear due to the action of the spiral spacer spring. If the tool should slip there is a very great risk of personal injury.

2   Lift off the spacer spring then extract the 3rd gear retaining circlip.

3   Withdraw 3rd gear from the pinion shaft. If it is tight, support the gear and tap out the shaft using a plastic or copper mallet.

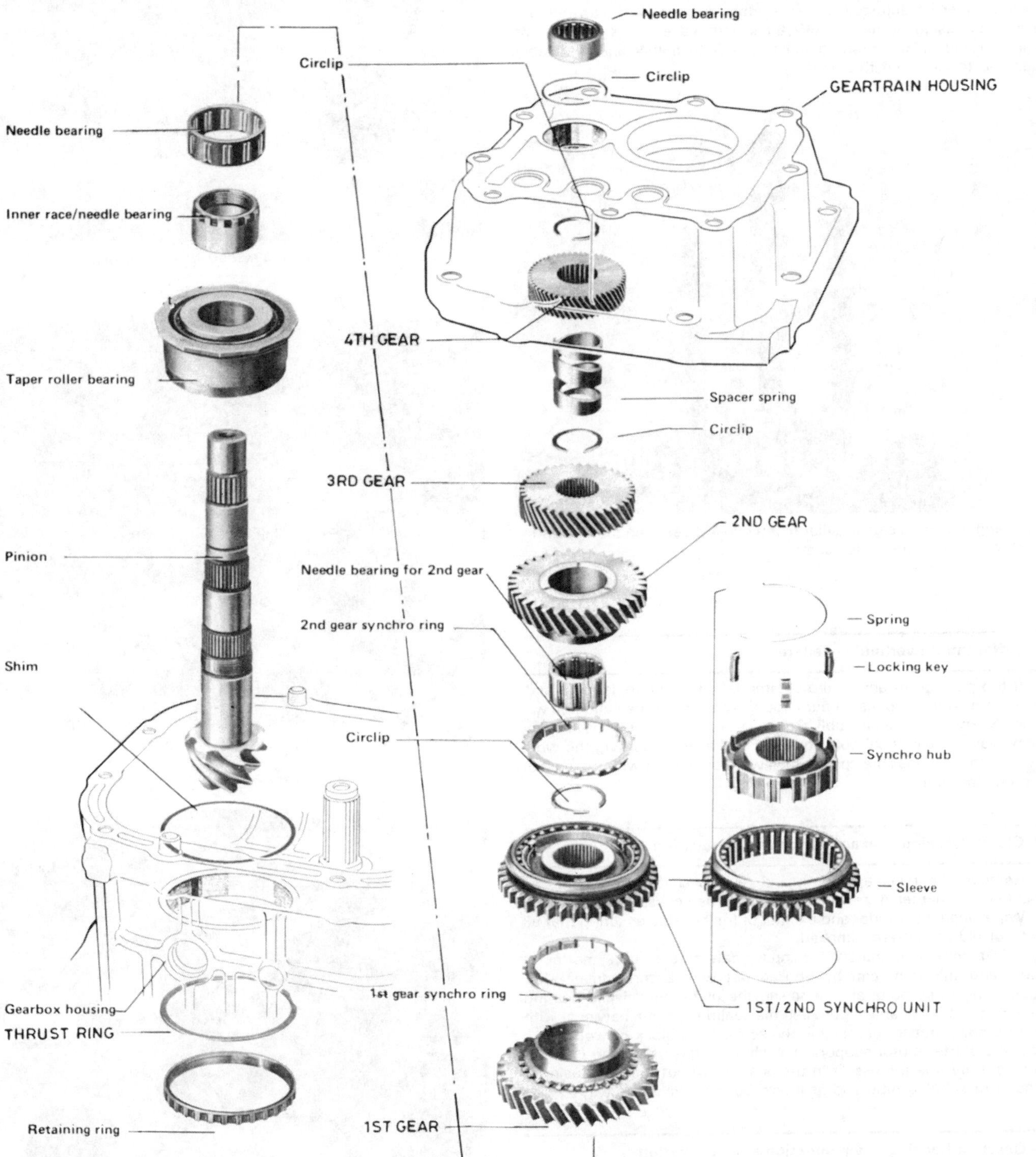

Fig. 5.8 Exploded view of the transmission pinion shaft (Sec 8)

4　Slide off 2nd gear followed by the needle roller bearing.
5　Extract the remaining circlip securing the 1st/2nd synchro unit to the pinion shaft.
6　Using a press or suitable gear puller, remove 1st gear and the 1st/2nd synchro unit together from the pinion shaft (photo).
7　Slide off the 1st gear needle roller bearing.
8　If it is necessary to remove the pinion shaft taper roller bearing for renewal or for any other reason, the pinion depth in relation to the differential crownwheel, and the turning torque of the shaft within the bearing, must be adjusted on reassembly. As this work can only be carried out using numerous VW tools, fixtures and jigs the task of bearing removal and refitting must be left to a VW agent suitably equipped to carry out this work.

11.1A Extract the circlip and dished washer (arrowed) ...

8.6 Using a hydraulic gear puller to remove 1st gear and the 1st/2nd synchro unit from the pinion shaft

9　Differential overhaul – general

1　If the position of any of the differential components is disturbed, very careful setting up, using numerous VW tools, fixtures and jigs will be necessary during reassembly. Therefore, if the differential is suspect in any way, consult a suitably equipped VW agent regarding the work involved and the possible cost of such work compared with the cost of an exchange unit.

10　Clutch housing – examination and renovation

1　Remove the release bearing and release shaft components as described in Chapter 4, renewing any parts as necessary.
2　Wipe clean the interior and exterior of the housing ensuring that all traces of old gasket are removed.
3　It is advisable to renew the input shaft oil seal as a matter of course and this item can be hooked out with a screwdriver after undoing the three bolts and removing the plate and release bearing guide sleeve. Fill the space between the sealing lips of a new seal with multi-purpose grease then install the seal with a block of wood.
4　If the starter motor support bush shows signs of scoring or if the motor armature is a loose fit in the bush, drive out the bush using a mandrel or suitable tube and fit a new bush in the same way.

11　Gearbox housing – examination and renovation

1　Extract the circlip, dished washer and reverse drivegear then withdraw the reverse shaft from the gearbox housing (photos).
2　Clean the housing thoroughly inside and out ensuring that all traces of old gasket are removed. Examine the housing for damage particularly around the mating faces.

11.1B ... then withdraw the reverse drivegear ...

11.1C ... and reverse shaft from the gearbox housing

Mechanical clutch control

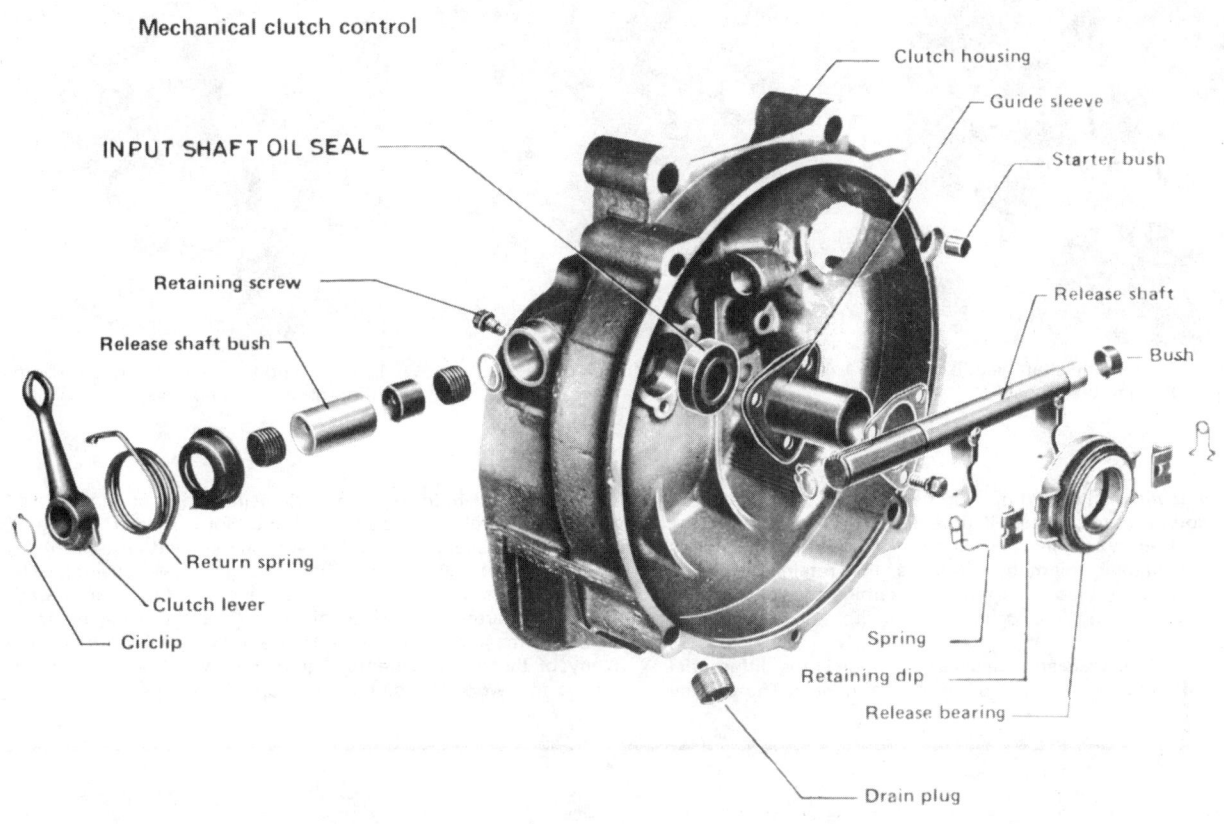

INPUT SHAFT OIL SEAL

Retaining screw

Release shaft bush

Return spring

Clutch lever

Circlip

Clutch housing

Guide sleeve

Starter bush

Release shaft

Bush

Spring

Retaining dip

Release bearing

Drain plug

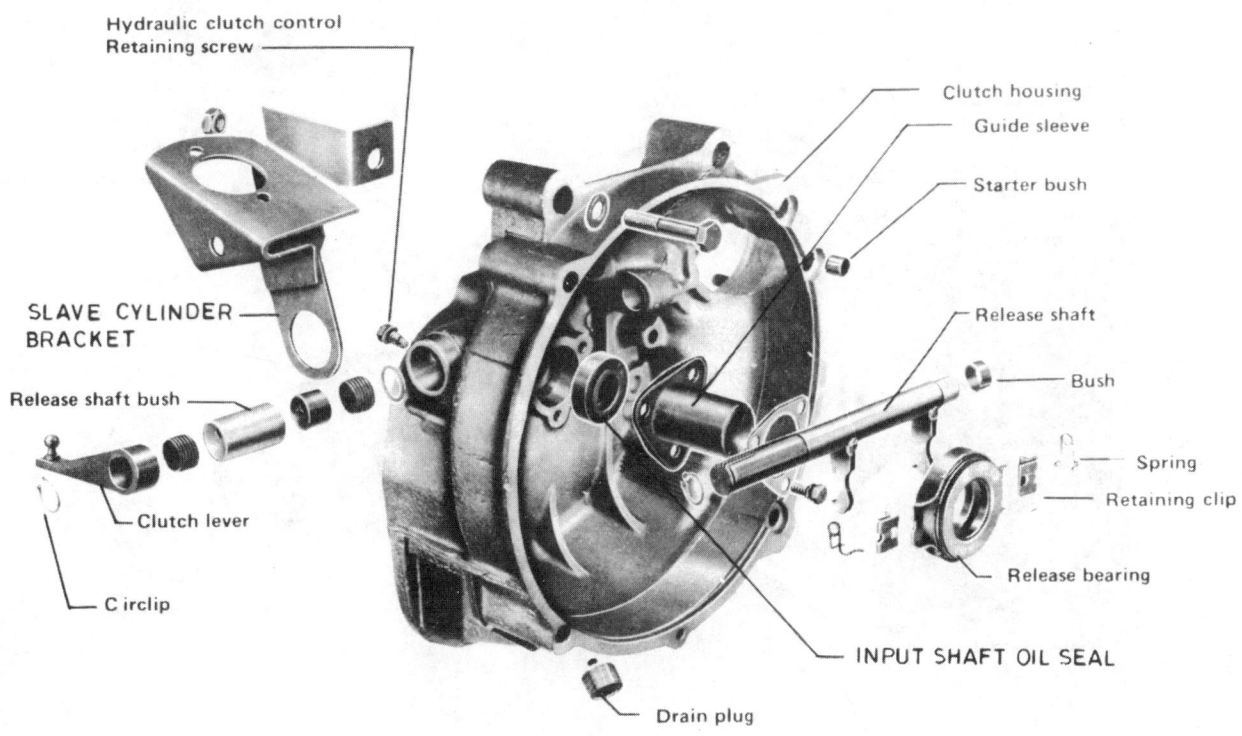

Hydraulic clutch control
Retaining screw

SLAVE CYLINDER BRACKET

Release shaft bush

Clutch lever

Circlip

Clutch housing

Guide sleeve

Starter bush

Release shaft

Bush

Spring

Retaining clip

Release bearing

INPUT SHAFT OIL SEAL

Drain plug

Fig. 5.9 Clutch housing and related components (Sec 10)

11.3 Input shaft and reverse shaft needle roller bearings in the gearbox housing

11.4A Renew the drive flange oil seal ...

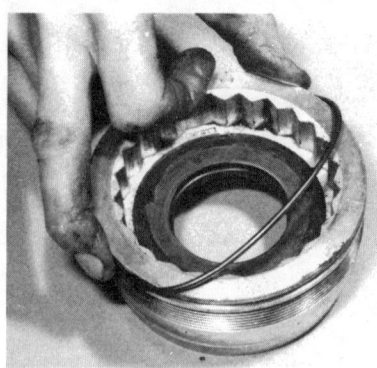

11.4B ... and the sealing O-ring on both differential adjusting rings

3   Inspect the reverse shaft and the two needle roller bearings in the housing for scoring or roughness. If necessary the bearings can be removed and refitted by tapping them out of the housing using tubes or mandrels of suitable diameter. Remove the retaining circlips securing the bearings in place first (photo). Examine the teeth of the reverse drivegear for pitting, scoring or chipping. Renew this component if necessary.

4   The drive flange oil seals and the sealing O-rings in the differential adjusting rings should be renewed as a matter of course. The oil seal is tapped out from inside to outside using a drift or suitable tube then a new seal carefully tapped in using a block of wood (photo). The O-ring is simply slipped off and a new one slipped on (photo).

5   If it is necessary to renew the gearbox housing, differential adjusting rings or the differential bearing outer races in the adjusting rings, very careful setting up of the differential using numerous VW tools, fixtures and jigs will be necessary during reassembly. Therefore, if any of these components require renewal it will be necessary to entrust this work to a suitably equipped VW agent.

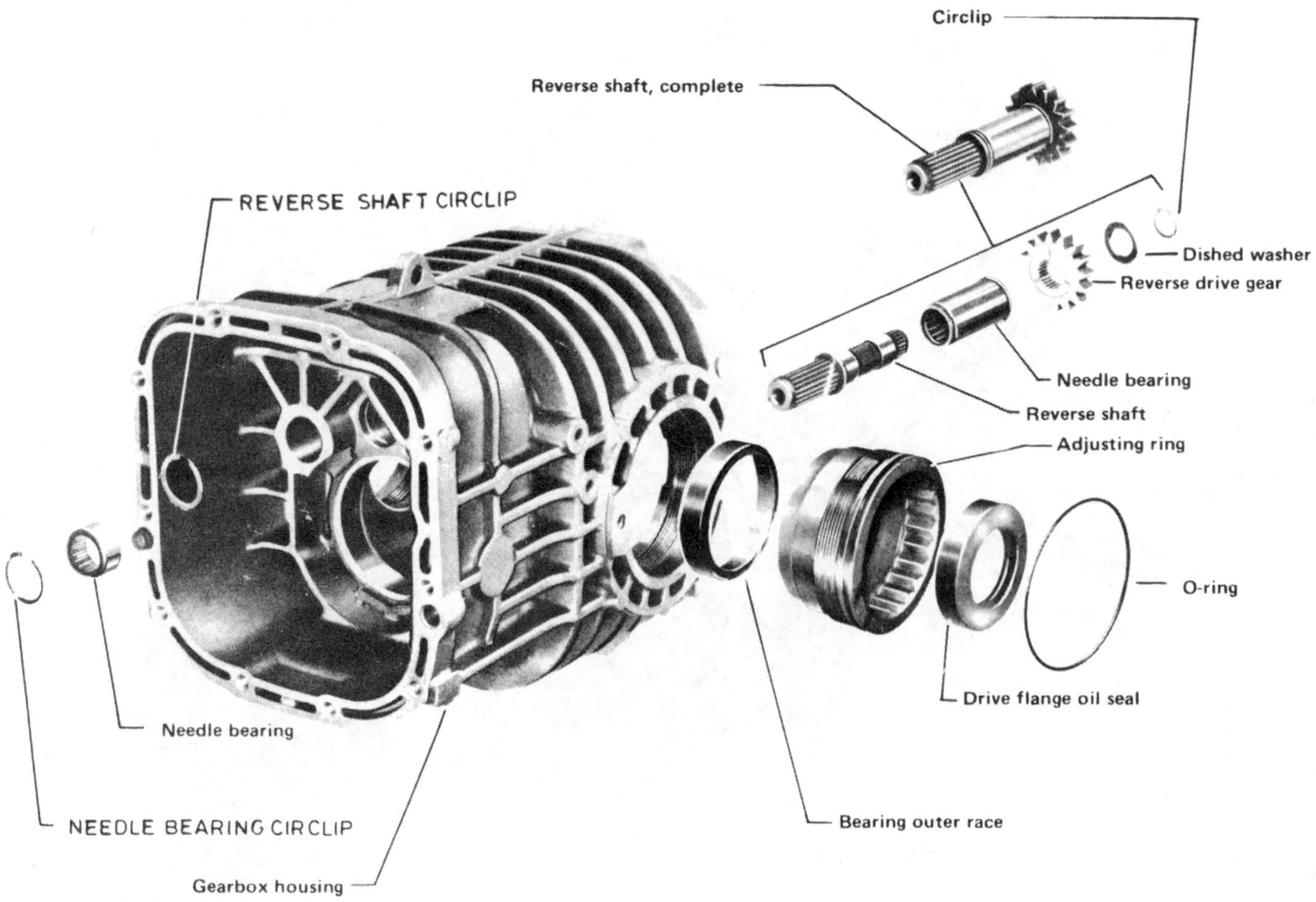

Fig. 5.10 Gearbox housing and related components (Sec 11)

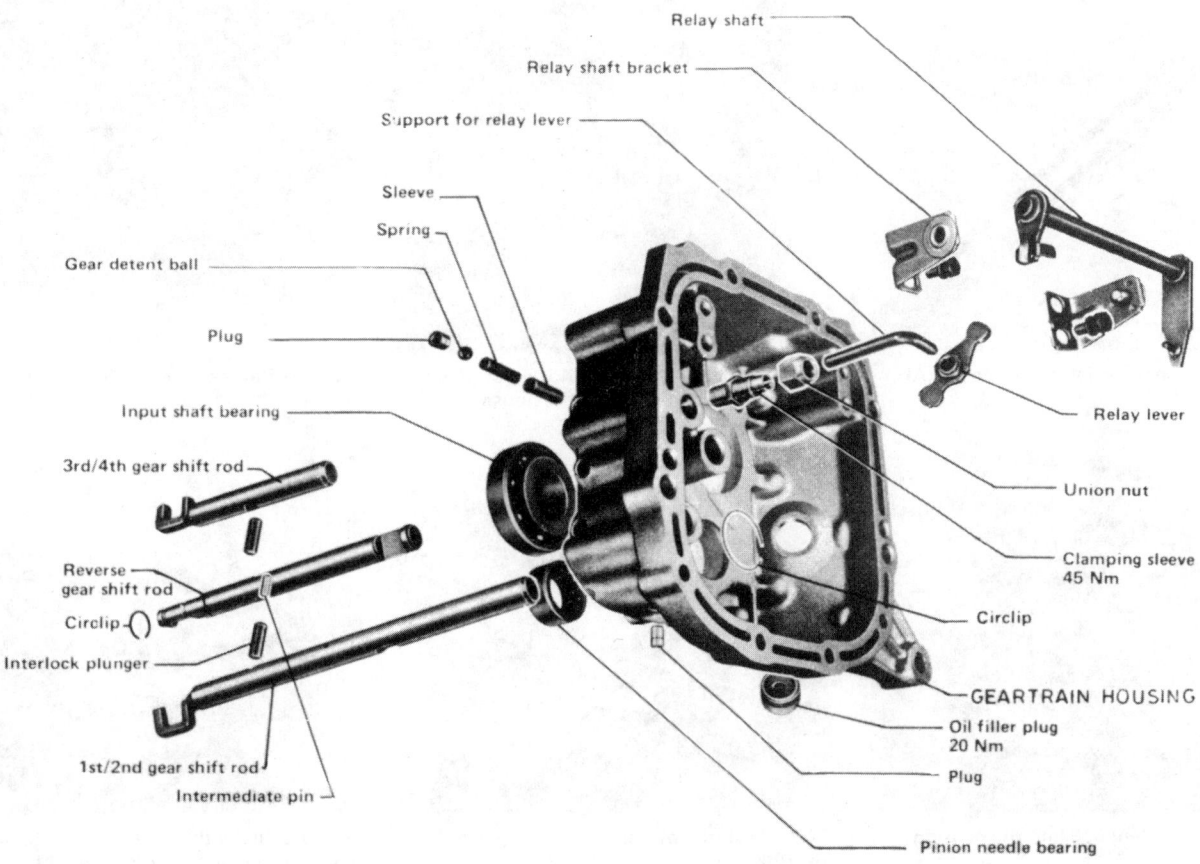

Fig. 5.11 Geartrain housing and shift mechanism (Sec 12)

12 Geartrain housing — examination and renovation

1 Wipe the housing clean inside and out ensuring that all traces of old gasket are removed.

2 Inspect the pinion shaft needle roller bearing and the input shaft ball bearing for signs of wear or scoring of the rollers or roughness of the balls when the bearing is spun. If renewal is necessary a press will be required. Both bearings are pressed out from inside to outside. When fitting a new pinion shaft bearing it must be pressed in until it contacts the circlip. The input shaft bearing must be pressed in until it contacts the shoulder in the housing. Ensure that the bearing is fitted with the milled edge on the outer race aligned with the cut-out in the housing (photo).

3 Unless the gear shift rods and selector mechanism are known to be worn or are suspect it is advisable not to disturb their position or dismantle these components. The position of these parts is critical and

if any of them are renewed, the whole assembly must be accurately adjusted on a VW jig. This will also be necessary if the set position of these parts is lost, so it is essential to mark everything before removal. If dismantling is to be carried out proceed as follows.

4 Mark the position of the relay shaft brackets on both sides of the pedestals to which they are attached, using quick drying paint on a fine file (photo). The relay lever support union nut should already have been marked during previous dismantling operations.

5 Undo the relay lever support union nut and withdraw the support and lever, if not already removed previously.

6 Undo the four bolts and lift off the relay shaft with its two support brackets.

7 Screw a 6 mm bolt into the centre of one of the detent plugs and extract the plug by pulling on the bolt with a self-locking wrench (photo). Remove all four detent plugs in this way. New plugs will be required when reassembling.

12.2 Ensure that milled edge on outer race and cut-out in geartrain housing (arrowed) are aligned when fitting bearing

12.4 Mark the position of the relay shaft brackets (A) and relay lever support (B) before removal

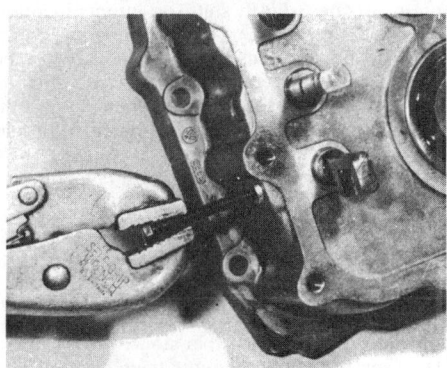

12.7 Detent plug removal

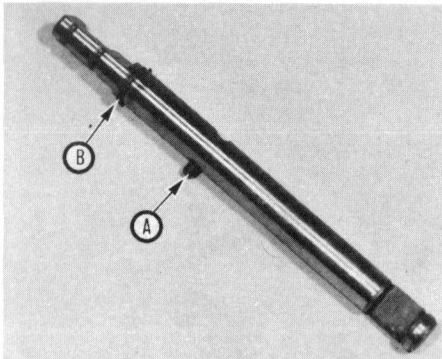

12.9 Reverse shift rod intermediate pin (A) and circlip (B)

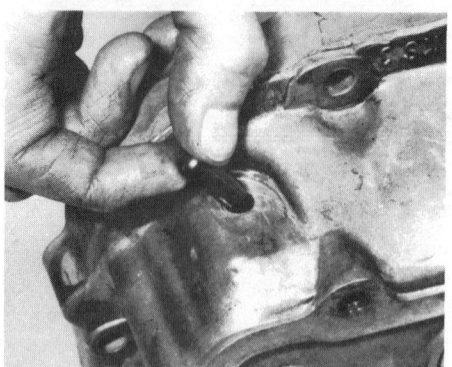

12.10 Recover the two interlock plungers from the hole in the side of the housing

12.12A Reassemble the 3rd/4th detent spring ...

12.12B ... and detent ball into the housing

12.13 Push the ball and spring down and insert the shift rod

12.17 With all the shift rods positioned correctly, tap in the new detent plugs

8 Ensure that all the shift rods are in neutral then withdraw the 1st/2nd rod from the housing. Be prepared to catch the detent ball and spring which will be ejected as the rod is removed.

9 Now remove the reverse and 3rd/4th shift rods in the same way. Recover the small intermediate pin located in the centre of the reverse rod (photo).

10 Tap the housing to release the two interlock plungers from the hole on the side of the housing (photo).

11 Examine all the components for signs of scoring or wear ridges particularly on the detent ball contact areas and on the ends of the shift rods and relay lever.

12 Obtain new parts as necessary and begin reassembly by inserting a spring and ball into the 3rd/4th shift rod detent location (photos). Use a little grease to retain the detent ball.

13 Push the ball and spring down using a screwdriver or round bar and insert the 3rd/4th shift rod into its location (photo). Push the rod in until it can be felt to locate in the neutral detent position.

14 Drop an interlock plunger through the hole in the side of the housing so that it contacts the 3rd/4th shift rod.

15 Make sure that the intermediate pin and the circlip are in position on the reverse shift rod, place a detent spring and ball in their location and insert the rod as before.

16 Refit the remaining interlock plunger then the spring, ball and 1st/2nd shift rod.

17 Ensure that the rods are all positioned as shown then tap in the new detent plugs (photo).

18 Refit the relay shaft and brackets, align the previously made marks (where applicable) and tighten the retaining bolts.

19 Place the relay lever and support in position and tighten the union nut finger tight only at this stage.

20 If any of the components have been renewed, it will be necessary to have the position of the selector forks and relay lever adjusted on a VW agent's alignment jig. This should be done after the geartrains have been refitted, but before the housings are reassembled.

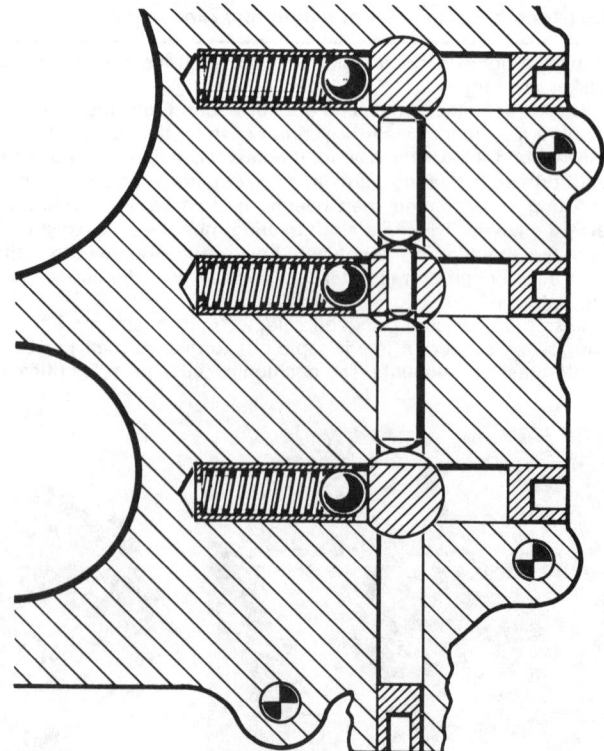

Fig. 5.12 Detent ball and interlock plunger position in geartrain housing (Sec 12)

13 Gearshift housing – examination and renovation

1 Wipe the housing clean on the inside and outside and ensure that all traces of old gasket are removed.

2 Examine the shafts for side play in their bushes and for signs of wear or scoring particularly on the rocker lever and shift finger. If any wear is apparent, dismantle the housing as follows and renew the parts as necessary.

3 Extract the circlip securing the shift finger to the gearshift shaft. Unscrew the reversing light switch, if fitted, and prise the finger off the shaft.

4 Extract the remaining circlip, withdraw the gearshift shaft and recover the spring and washer.

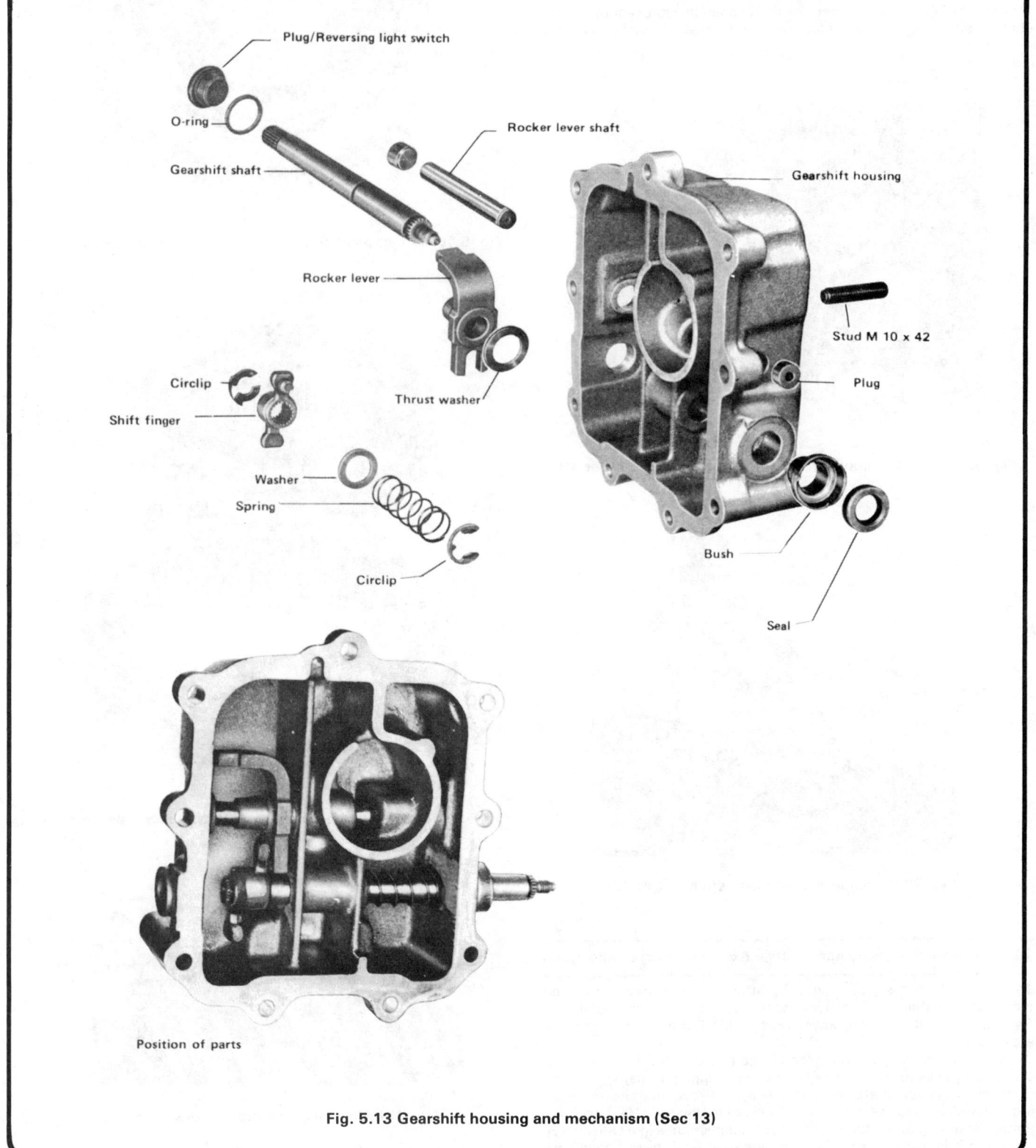

Fig. 5.13 Gearshift housing and mechanism (Sec 13)

5   Screw a 6 mm bolt into the centre of one of the end plugs and pull
the bolt and plug out of the housing using a self-locking wrench.
Remove the other plug in the same way.
6   Using a suitable punch tap out the rocker lever shaft and recover
the rocker lever and washer.
7   Renew the gearshift shaft oil seal by hooking it out with a
screwdriver then tapping a new seal squarely into place.
8   If necessary the gearshift shaft bush can be renewed by twisting
it out with a pair of grips. Tap a new bush into the housing using a tube
of suitable diameter.
9   Reassembly is the reverse of the dismantling procedure. Ensure
that all parts are thoroughly lubricated with gear oil during assembly.

Fig. 5.16 Correct positioning of synchro unit spring wires (Sec 14)

Fig. 5.14 Gearshift housing rocker lever shaft removal (Sec 13)

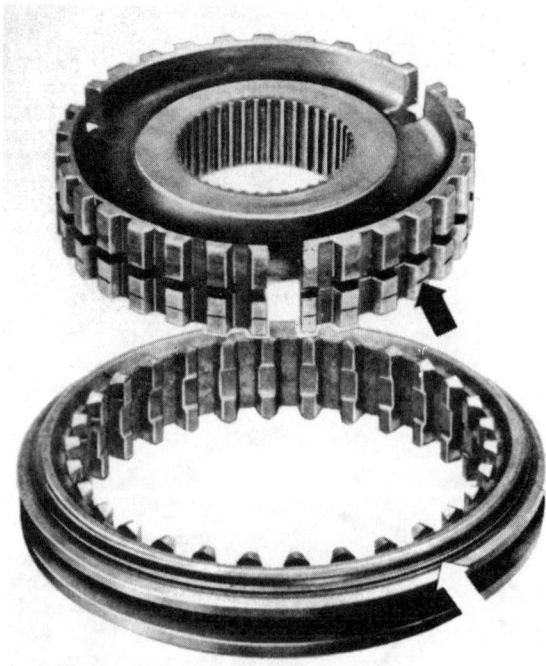

Fig. 5.17 Identification grooves on 3rd/4th synchro sleeve and hub
(Sec 14)

Fig. 5.15 Gearshift shaft bush removal (Sec 13)

14 Synchro units, gears and shafts – examination and renovation

1   Dismantle the synchro units by lifting out the spring wires on
either side of the hub and then separating the hub from the sleeve.
Recover the three locking keys which will fall out as the parts are
separated.
2   Examine the dog teeth on the sleeve and hub and the surface of
the locking keys for obvious signs of wear, chipping or damage. None
of these parts are matched and a hub or sleeve may be renewed
individually if wear is obvious. If, however, the vehicle has been
jumping out of gear and the rest of the transmission is in a satisfactory
condition it is likely that the synchro unit is at fault. In this case both

Fig. 5.18 Checking synchro ring wear (Sec 14)

a = Synchro ring to gear clearance

the hub and sleeve, locking keys and springs should be obtained for the gear concerned.

3   The hub and sleeve for the 1st/2nd synchro unit may be reassembled in any position in relation to each other. With the locking keys in place, fit the spring wires with their ends at 120° to each other and facing in opposite directions.

4   When reassembling the 3rd/4th synchro unit the identification grooves on the outer face of the sleeve and hub must be on opposite sides (Fig. 5.17). Also the hub and sleeve should be assembled in various positions until the position in which they slide smoothly with the minimum of backlash is found. The locking keys and spring wires can then be fitted with the spring wire ends at 120° to each other and facing in opposite directions.

5   Examine all the gears and the shafts for signs of obvious damage such as chipped teeth, or for wear, pitting or scoring. All the gears on the pinion shaft are matched to corresponding gears on the input shaft and must only be renewed in pairs. Similarly the pinion shaft itself is matched to the differential and both these components can only be renewed in pairs. Also, if renewal of the pinion shaft is necessary, accurate setting up of the pinion and differential will be required and this can only be successfully carried out by a VW agent.

6   Place each synchro ring onto the cone of its respective gear and measure the synchro ring to gear clearance as shown in Fig. 5.18. Refer to the Specifications for the appropriate clearances. Check also the condition of the synchro ring teeth. If the teeth are worn or the clearances are not as specified the synchro ring(s) should be renewed.

7   Pay close attention to the remainder of the shaft components and renew any that show signs of wear or damage. Ensure that the ends of the selector forks are a snug fit in the synchro sleeve grooves and if in doubt compare them with new parts.

15   Input shaft – reassembly

1   Slide the caged needle roller bearing onto the shaft, expand the retaining circlip and locate it securely in its groove (photo).

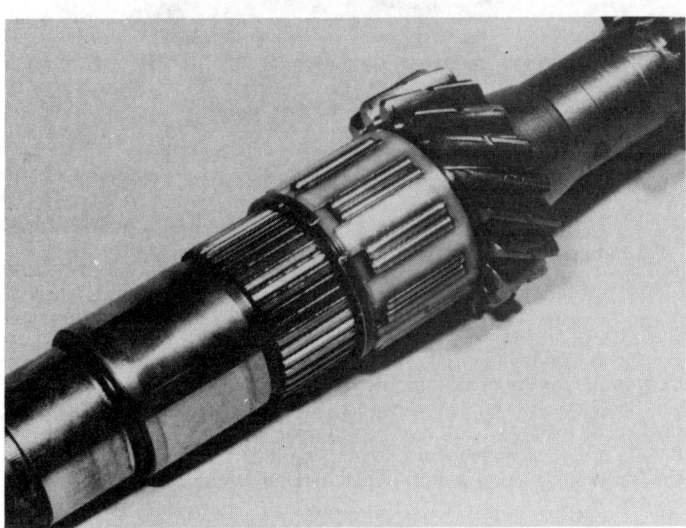

15.1 Fit the needle roller bearing and circlip to the input shaft

15.2 Place 3rd gear over the bearing

15.3 Fit the synchro ring ...

15.4 ... followed by the 3rd/4th synchro unit with the groove on the sleeve (arrowed) facing away from 3rd gear

2   Place 3rd gear over the needle roller bearing with the teeth of the gear towards the splined end of the input shaft (photo).

3   Fit the synchro ring to the cone face of 3rd gear (photo).

4   Position the 3rd/4th synchro unit on the shaft ensuring that the groove on the synchro sleeve faces away from the gears already on the shaft (photo).

5   Support the synchro unit over protected vice jaws and drive the input shaft fully into the hub (photo). Alternatively fit the shaft using a press. Whichever method is adopted, ensure that the notches in the synchro rings locate under the locking keys in the hub as the hub is fitted.

15.5 Drive the input shaft fully into the synchro unit hub ...

15.7B ... followed by the synchro ring then 4th gear

15.6 ... then fit the retaining circlip

15.8 Retain the gears in place using strong elastic bands

15.7A Slide on the needle roller bearing ...

6   Fit the retaining circlip to the input shaft ensuring that the circlip locates fully in its groove (photo).

7   Slide on the remaining needle roller bearing, locate the synchro ring in the synchro hub, then fit 4th gear (photos).

8   As an aid to subsequent assembly, retain the gears in position on the input shaft using a strong elastic band (photo).

16 Pinion shaft – reassembly

1   Place the 1st gear needle roller bearing over its inner race and then fit 1st gear over the bearing (photos).

2   Fit the synchro ring to the cone face of 1st gear (photo).

3   Position the 1st/2nd synchro unit on the shaft with the selector fork groove in the synchro sleeve facing away from 1st gear. Using a hammer and tube of suitable diameter, a press, or puller arrangement (photo), fit the synchro unit fully onto the shaft. Ensure that the notches in the synchro ring locate under the locking keys in the hub as the hub is fitted.

4   Fit the retaining circlip to the pinion shaft ensuring that the circlip locates fully in its groove (photo).

5   Place the 2nd gear synchro ring in position on the synchro unit, slide on the needle roller bearing and then 2nd gear (photos).

6   Locate 3rd gear on the pinion shaft with its shoulder towards 2nd

16.1A Fit the 1st gear needle roller bearing to the pinion shaft ...

16.1B ... then slide 1st gear over the bearing

16.2 Fit the synchro ring then the 1st/2nd synchro unit

16.3 Using a hydraulic gear puller to fit the synchro unit

16.4 Secure the synchro unit in place with the circlip

16.5A Place the synchro ring in position ...

16.5B ... slide on the needle roller bearing and 2nd gear

16.6 Fit 3rd gear with its shoulder towards 2nd gear

16.7 Fit the circlip then measure the 3rd gear axial play

16.8A Slide on the spacer spring ...

16.8B ... followed by 4th gear with its shoulder towards the spring

16.9 Compress the spring and fit the retaining circlip

gear (photo). Fit the gear fully using the same method as adopted for the synchro unit.

7   Make sure that the gear is fully home then fit the retaining circlip (photo). Using feeler gauges measure the clearance between the circlip and the gear face. This clearance is the 3rd gear axial play and must be within the tolerance given in the Specifications. Various thicknesses of circlips are available if the measured play is outside the specified limits.

8   Locate the spacer spring on the shaft followed by 4th gear with the shoulder of the gear towards the spring (photos).

9   Compress the spring using a press or puller arrangement (photo) and fit the final retaining circlip.

Fig. 5.19 Measuring 3rd gear axial play (Sec 16)

17 Input shaft and pinion shaft – refitting

1   Position the 3rd/4th selector fork in its groove in the synchro sleeve with the retaining bolt side of the fork boss towards the splined end of the input shaft.

2   Hold the pinion and input shafts together with the gears in mesh and carefully locate the shafts in their bearings in the geartrain housing. At the same time locate the selector fork over the 3rd/4th shift rod (photo).

3   Press the input shaft fully into its bearing then refit the retaining circlip.

4   Move the relay lever as necessary so that the previously made marks are aligned and tighten the union nut.

5   Move the 3rd/4th selector fork and shift rod as necessary to align the marks made during removal. Refit the fork retaining bolt and tighten it fully. Now return the fork and rod to neutral.

6   Pull the 1st/2nd shift rod out just sufficiently to allow the 1st/2nd

selector fork to be fitted. The open side of the fork faces the geartrain housing.

7   Return the rod to neutral, align the marks on the rod and fork then fit and fully tighten the retaining bolt.

17.2 Locate the two assembled shafts onto the geartrain housing

18 Transmission – reassembling the housings

1   Fit the reverse shaft to the gearbox housing followed by the reverse drive gear. Tap the gear fully onto the shaft then install the dished washer and circlip. Ensure that the circlip locates fully in its groove.

2   Position the shim over the pinion shaft taper roller bearing and retain it with a little grease (photo).

3   Place a new gasket in position on the front face of the gearbox housing.

4   Engage reverse gear by moving the shift rod and then position the geartrain housing and gears ready to enter the gearbox housing. With the help of an assistant, hold the reverse sliding pinion in mesh with the teeth of the 1st/2nd synchro unit and also engaged with the selector peg of the relay shaft. Lower the housing and gears into the gearbox housing and at the same time guide the reverse sliding pinion onto the reverse shaft (photo).

5   Tap the geartrain housing fully home, refit the retaining bolts and progressively tighten them to the specified torque (photo).

6   Place the thrust ring over the pinion shaft taper roller bearing and then screw on a new retaining ring.

7   The retaining ring should be tightened to the specified torque, slackened off, then retightened to the same torque again using VW tool 381/14. Alternatively, if facilities are available a suitable tool can

18.2 Fit the shim to the pinion shaft taper roller bearing

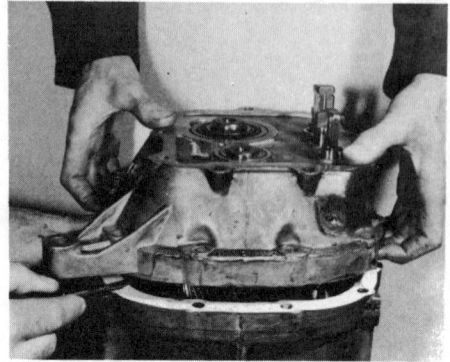

18.4 Have an assistant hold the reverse sliding pinion in mesh whilst the housings are reassembled

18.5 Tighten the retaining bolts to the specified torque

18.7A Home made tool for tightening the pinion shaft bearing retaining ring

18.7B Home made tool in use

18.8 Peen the retaining ring at the indents in the bearing outer race

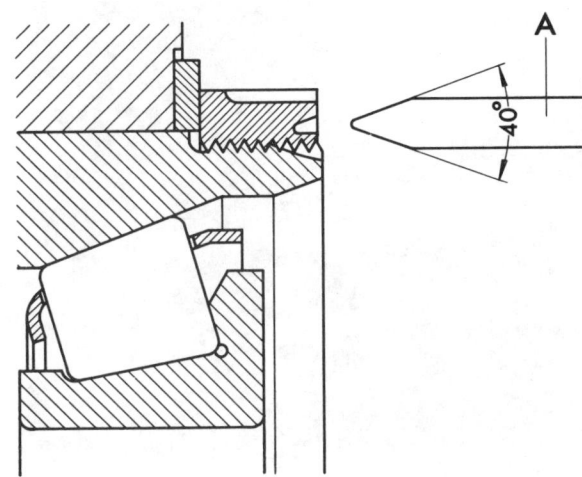

Fig. 5.20 Sectional view of pinion bearing and retaining ring (Sec 18)

A = Suitable peening tool

be made up from a large tube with mild steel 'legs' welded to one end to engage with the notches on the retaining ring (photos).

8   After tightening the ring it must be peened using a chisel or rod with a 40° pointed end, at the two indents in the bearing outer race (Fig. 5.20) (photo).

9   Locate the input shaft bearing locking plate in its recess in the geartrain housing then place a new gasket on the housing face.

10   Fit the gearshift housing ensuring that the relay lever engages with the hooked end of the 3rd/4th shift rod (photo).

11   Secure the housing with the retaining bolts tightened progressively to the specified torque.

12   Refit the rubber boot to the gearshift shaft, apply some locking compound to the splines of the gearshift bracket and refit the bracket to the shaft. Ensure that the marks made during removal are aligned if there is no master spline (photo). Secure the bracket with the retaining nut.

13   Lay the differential in its fitted position in the gearbox housing, but do not fit the adjusting rings at this stage. Turn the differential so that the cut-out on the gear carrier is uppermost.

14   Position the reverse gear retaining circlip approximately half way down the input shaft rear part then slide reverse gear on behind it. Screw the input shaft rear part onto the front part, back it off one spline then slide the reverse gear over the join in the two shafts. The retaining circlip can now be pushed down the shaft with a suitable tube until it locates in its groove.

15   Place a new gasket on the mating face of the gearbox housing and refit the clutch housing. Take care not to damage the oil seal as the housing slides over the input shaft.

16   Secure the clutch housing with the retaining bolts tightened to the specified torque.

17   Screw the two differential adjusting rings into their locations in the gearbox housing making sure that the previously marked left-hand ring goes on the left-hand side and vice versa.

18   Screw the rings down, counting the number of turns or until the pre-recorded depth is reached according to the method used during removal. Now align the previously made marks.

19   Refit the locking plates, washers and retaining screws.

20   Refit the two drive flanges using a long bolt and suitable tube or socket to press them fully onto their shafts (photos).

21   Secure the drive flanges with the dished washers and new circlips (photo). Tap the circlip with a hammer and tube to compress the washer and ensure proper location of the circlip in its groove.

22   Fit a new plastic cap to the centre of each drive flange and tap them squarely into place (photo).

18.10 Relay lever (A) must engage with shift rod (B) as gearshift housing is fitted

18.12 Use a thread locking compound to secure the gearshift bracket and align the master spline or the marks made during removal

18.20A Locate the drive flanges in position ...

18.20B ... and using a long bolt, nut and tube or socket fit them fully onto the shafts

18.21 Secure the drive flanges with the dished washer and a new circlip ...

18.22 ... then fit new plastic caps

23   Refit the transmission front mounting and bracket to the gearshift housing then refit the clutch release bearing components as described in Chapter 4.

19 Gearshift linkage – adjustment

1   Jack up the front of the vehicle and securely support it on axle stands. Remove the spare wheel.
2   Slide up the rubber boot around the gear lever then check that the two holes in the gear lever plate are aligned with the two holes directly below in the mounting plate (Fig. 5.21). If not slacken the two retaining bolts or screws, align the two plates then tighten the bolts or screws.
3   Move the gear lever to the neutral position.
4   From under the vehicle slacken the clamp pinch-bolt securing the centre and rear shift rods together.
5   Refer to the Specifications for the gearshift linkage adjustment dimension then make up a gauge using any suitable material equal in width to this dimension.
6   Position the metal tag or "stop finger" at the base of the gear lever centrally along the length of the stop plate in the housing. Place the gauge between the stop finger and stop plate then tighten the clamp pinch-bolt (Fig. 5.23). As the clamp is tightened ensure that the upper face of the bracket on the rear shift rod is just touching the upper nylon ball of the gearshift bracket on the transmission.
7   Refit the spare wheel, lower the vehicle to the ground and check that all gears can be engaged.

Fig. 5.22 Centre and rear shift rod clamp location (Sec 19)

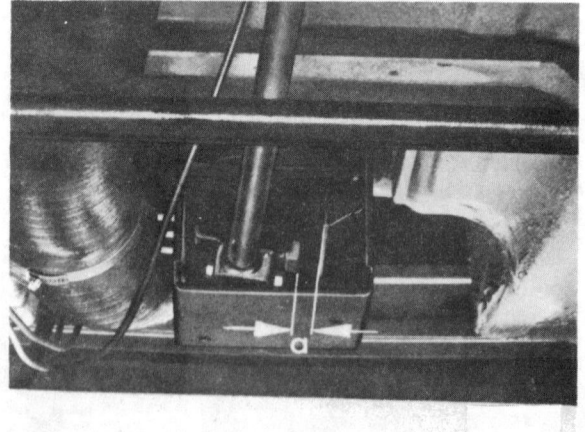

Fig. 5.23 Gearshift linkage adjustment (Sec 19)

a = Specified adjustment dimension

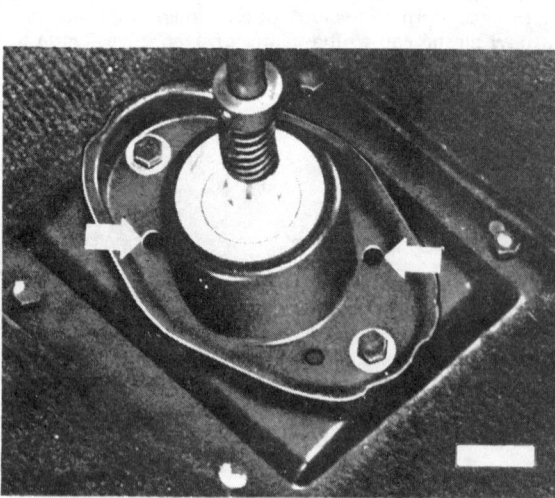

Fig. 5.21 Gear lever plate alignment holes (arrowed) (Sec 19)

20 Gearshift linkage – removal, overhaul and refitting

1   Position the vehicle over an inspection pit, raise it on a hoist or jack it up at the front and rear and securely support it on axle stands.
2   Remove the spare wheel.

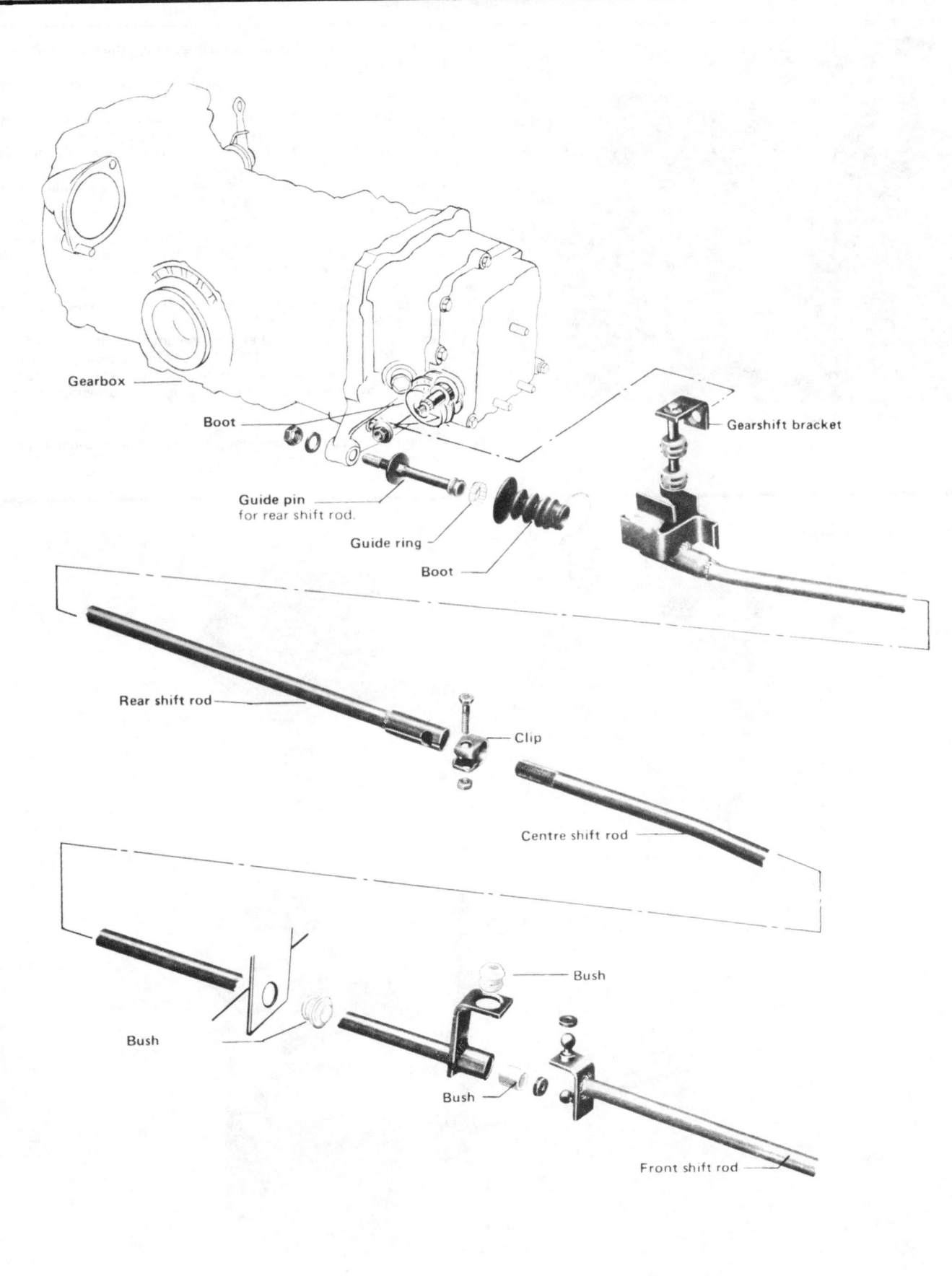

Gearbox

Boot

Guide pin
for rear shift rod.

Guide ring

Boot

Gearshift bracket

Rear shift rod

Clip

Centre shift rod

Bush

Bush

Bush

Bush

Front shift rod

Fig. 5.24 Gearshift linkage components (Sec 20)

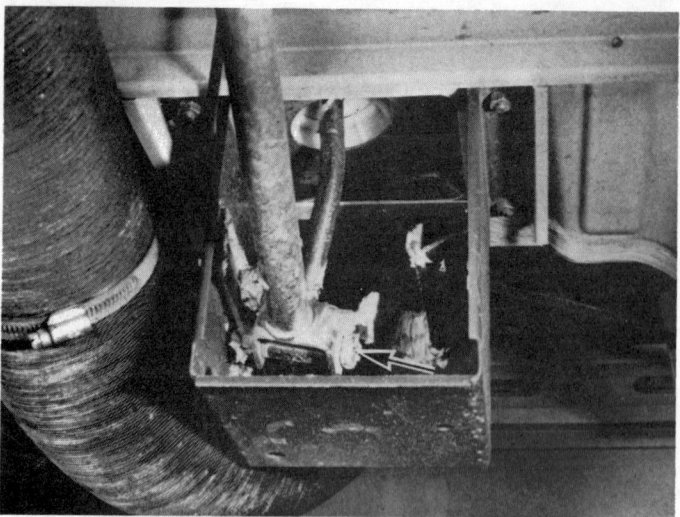

20.3 Gear lever to front shift rod retaining bolt (arrowed)

3   Undo the nut and withdraw the bolt securing the front shift rod to the gear lever (photo).
4   Slacken the clamp pinch-bolt securing the centre and rear shift rods together.
5   Lower the linkage at the front then withdraw the front and centre shift rods from the rear shift rod and centre support bush.
6   At the rear, hold the guide pin with a spanner then undo the guide pin retaining nut with a second spanner.
7   Push the guide pin out of the bracket on the transmission and withdraw the rear shift rod from under the vehicle.
8   Refer to Fig. 5.24 and examine the condition of the support bushes, rubber boot and the shift rods. Renew any parts that show signs of wear or damage. If the centre shift rod support bush requires renewal it will be necessary to remove the petrol tank to provide access as described in Chapter 2.
9   Lubricate all the bushes, joints and friction surfaces with the special VW lubricant.
10 Before refitting ensure that the transmission is in neutral by moving the transmission gearshift bracket as far as it will go rearwards then move it forward again one notch. In this position it should be possible to move the bracket in and out if the transmission is in neutral.
11 Refitting the linkage is the reverse sequence to removal. Carry out the adjustment procedure described in the previous Section before tightening the clamp pinch-bolt.

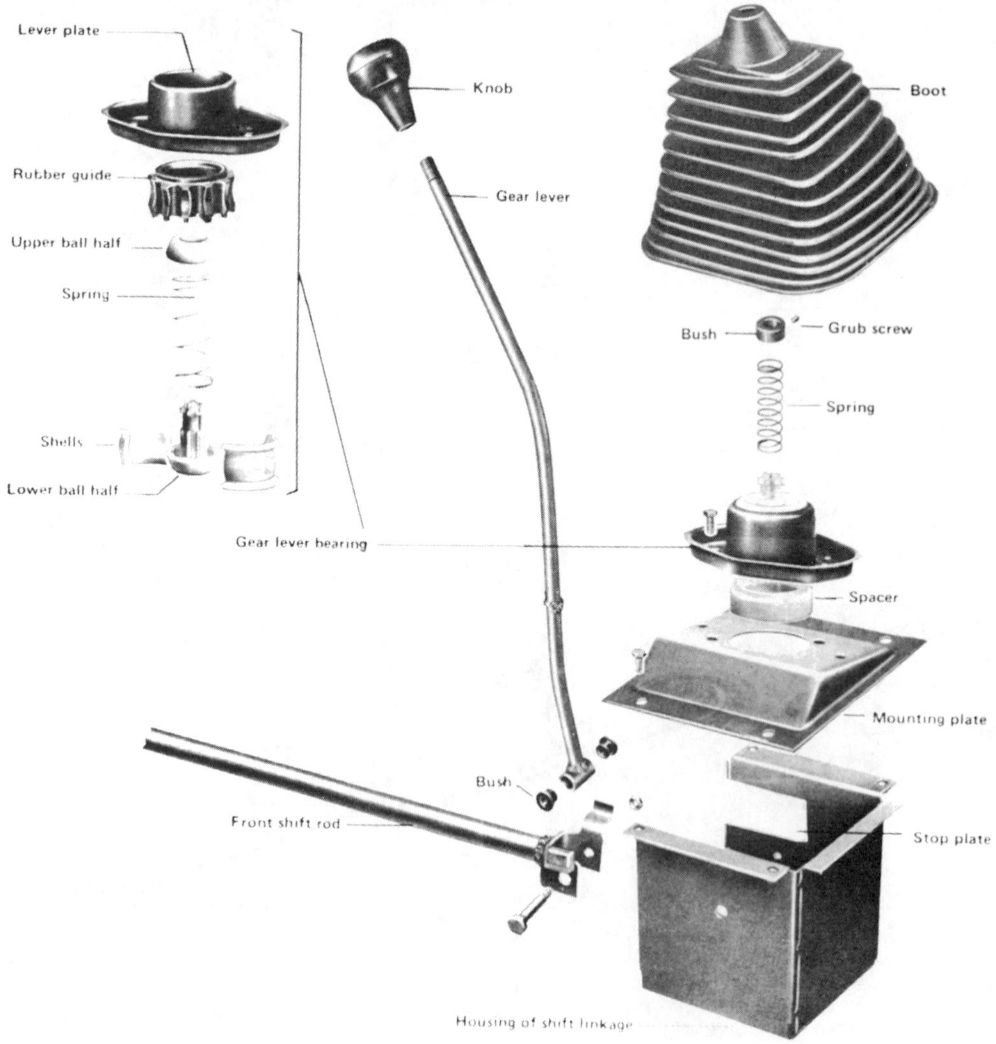

Fig. 5.25 Exploded view of the gear lever and housing (Sec 21)

21 Gear lever and housing – removal, overhaul and refitting

1   Jack up the front of the vehicle and securely support it on axle stands. Remove the spare wheel.

2   From below undo the nut and withdraw the bolt securing the front shift rod to the gear lever.

3   From above, unscrew the gear lever knob then slide the rubber boot up and off the gear lever.

4   Undo the two bolts or screws securing the lever plate to the mounting plate and lift out the gear lever assembly (photo).

5   Slacken the grub screw then withdraw the bush and spring upwards off the gear lever. The lever can now be slid down and out of the bearing assembly.

6   If further dismantling is necessary, push the rubber guide out of the lever plate, spread the two shells and withdraw the upper ball half, spring and lower ball half.

7   Inspect all the parts before assembly with VW special lubricant.

8   Locate the two shells in the rubber guide noting that the guide is installed in the lever plate with its shoulder upwards.

9   Spread the shells and insert the lower ball half followed by the spring and upper ball half. Now fit this assembly into the lever plate.

10 The remainder of the reassembly and refitting is the reverse of the dismantling and removal procedures.

21.4 Gear lever plate retaining screws (arrowed)

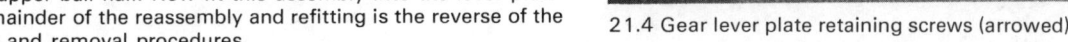

22 Fault diagnosis – manual transmission

Symptom	Reason(s)
Transmission noisy in neutral	Input shaft bearings worn
Transmission noisy only when moving (in all gears)	Pinion shaft bearings worn Differential bearings worn Wear, damage or incorrect adjustment of differential crownwheel and pinion teeth
Transmission noisy in only one gear	Worn, damaged or chipped gear teeth
Transmission jumps out of gear	Worn synchro units Worn shift rod detents or weak springs Worn selector forks Incorrect gearshift rod, fork or mechanism adjustment
Ineffective synchromesh	Worn synchro rings
Difficulty in engaging gears	Clutch fault Incorrect gearshift linkage adjustment Incorrect gearshift rod, fork or mechanism adjustment

Chapter 6 Automatic transmission

Contents

Specifications

Type .... Three element torque converter, hydraulically controlled epicycle geartrain and integral final drive assembly

Identification .... Manufacturers type 090

Gear ratios
Final drive 4.09:1
First gear 2.55:1
Second gear 1.45:1
Third gear 1.00:1
Reverse gear 2.46:1

Lubricant type
Automatic transmission .... ATF Dexron
Final drive .... SAE 90EP hypoid gear oil

Lubricant capacity
Automatic transmission:
   Refill after fluid change .... 3.0 litres (5.28 pints, 6.34 US pints)
     Total capacity – dry unit .... 6.0 litres (10.56 Imp pints, 12.68 US pints)
Final drive .... 1.25 litres (2.20 Imp pints, 2.62 US pints)

Torque wrench settings

	Nm	lbf ft
Oil pan to transmission	20	15
Driveshaft to drive flange	45	33
Drive flange to differential	25	18
Torque converter to driveplate	30	22
Transmission to final drive housing	30	22
Engine to transmission	30	22
Front mounting to transmission	45	33
Front mounting to body	25	18

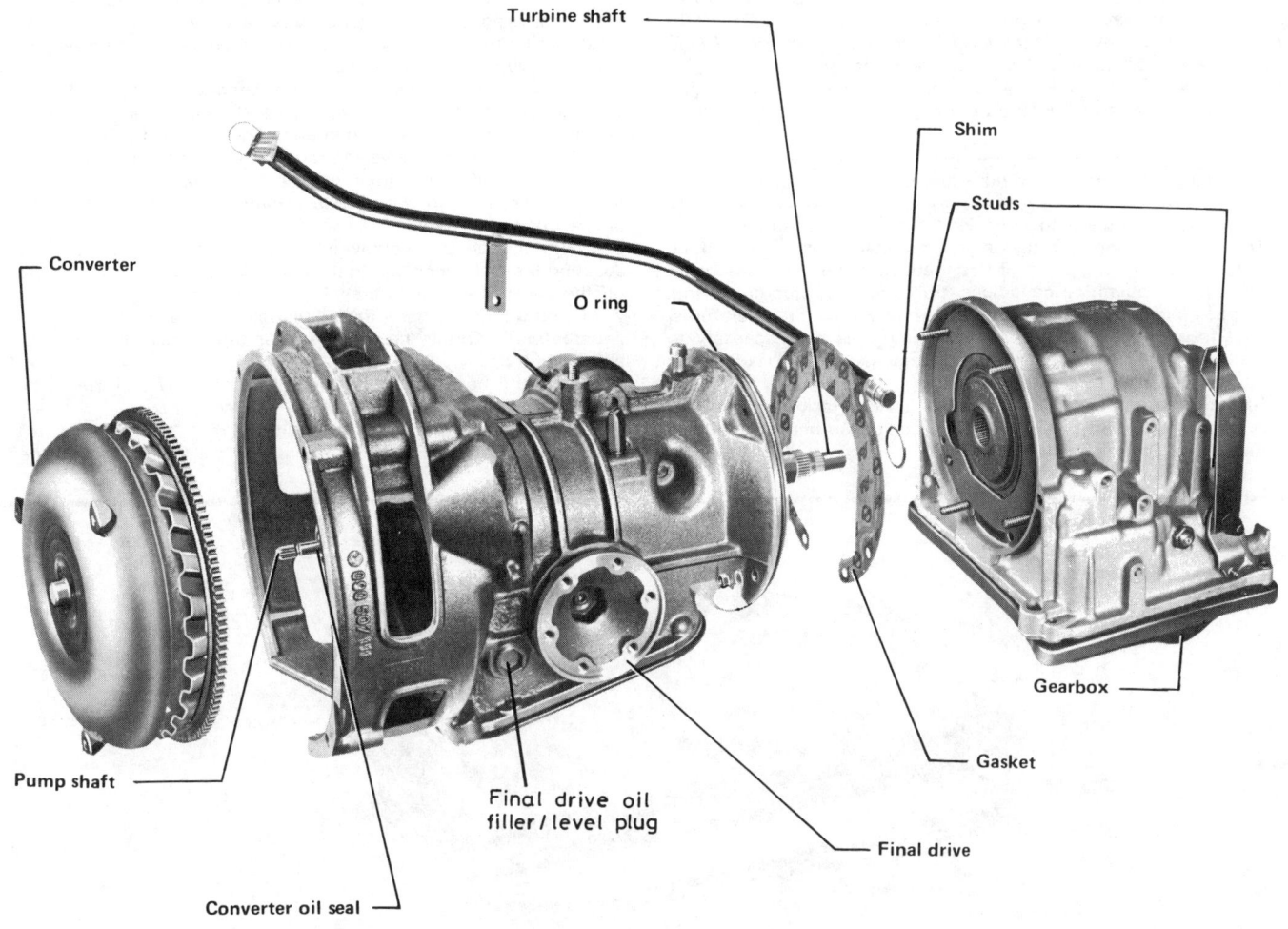

Fig. 6.1 The main components of the automatic transmission assembly (Sec 1)

Labels: Turbine shaft, Shim, Studs, Converter, O ring, Pump shaft, Final drive oil filler / level plug, Gearbox, Gasket, Final drive, Converter oil seal

1 General description

The automatic transmission fitted as an optional extra consists of three main assemblies, namely the torque converter, which takes the place of the conventional clutch, the epicyclic geartrain, and the final drive. These assemblies are housed within two castings which are bolted together and then attached to the engine casing at the rear.

In view of the complexity of the automatic transmission and the need for special tools and equipment when carrying out overhaul work or repairs, the following Sections are therefore confined to supplying general information and any service information or instruction that can be used by the owner. In the event of a fault developing on the transmission or a major adjustment being necessary, this work should be left to the local main agents who will have the necessary tools and equipment for diagnosis and rectification.

2 Maintenance and inspection

1   At the intervals specified in Routine Maintenance at the beginning of this manual, carry out the following service operations on the automatic transmission and final drive.
2   Inspect the transmission joint faces and oil seals for any signs of damage, deterioration or oil leakage.
3   Check the level of the automatic transmission fluid by strictly following the procedure described in Section 3.
4   At less frequent intervals drain the automatic transmission fluid, clean the oil pan and filter screen and then refill the transmission with fresh fluid. Details of this operation will be found in Section 4.

5   At the same service intervals check the level of gear oil in the final drive assembly and top up if necessary. The filler/level plug is located on the right-hand side of the final drive housing and the oil level must be maintained up to the filler plug orifice. Ensure that the vehicle is standing on level ground when checking the level or topping up. Note that there is no service requirement to drain the final drive oil and no provision for draining is made.

3 Automatic transmission fluid – level checking

1   The automatic transmission and torque converter are lubricated and operated by a special fluid which must be maintained at the correct level to ensure the efficient operation and reliability of these units. It is recommended that whenever the engine oil is checked the automatic transmission fluid level is checked also using the procedure described below. The final drive assembly is lubricated separately by a hypoid gear oil. It is only necessary to check the level in this unit at the recommended service intervals as described in Routine Maintenance at the beginning of this manual.
2   The fluid level must only be checked when the automatic transmission fluid is lukewarm (40° to 60°C, 104° to 140°F) ie after a short drive of about one to two miles.
3   To check the level first make sure that the vehicle is standing on level ground. Now move the selector lever to N, apply the handbrake, and leave the engine idling.
4   Remove the engine compartment cover and withdraw the transmission dipstick. Wipe the dipstick on a clean lint free cloth, reinsert it, withdraw it a second time and observe the fluid level.
5   The level must be between the two marks on the dipstick. If it is too low add a quantity of the specified fluid through the dipstick/filler

tube using a funnel and rubber hose or tube to avoid spillage. **Note:** *The difference between the two marks is approximately 0.5 litre (0.88 Imp pints, 1.16 US pints). If the level is too high a quantity of fluid must be drained off as described in the next Section.*

6   After checking the fluid level, refit the dipstick, secure the engine compartment cover and switch off the engine.

---

4   Automatic transmission fluid – draining and refilling

1   Under normal operating conditions the automatic transmission fluid must be changed at the intervals recommended in Routine Maintenance at the beginning of this manual. If the vehicle is being used in arduous operating conditions (trailer towing, stop/go driving, continuous mountain driving or in areas of high ambient temperatures) the fluid must be changed more frequently. It is not necessary to change the hypoid gear oil in the final drive housing as this is filled for life and no provision is made for draining.

2   To drain the automatic transmission fluid first jack up the rear of the vehicle and support it on axle stands positioned beneath the rear suspension crossmember.

3   Working underneath, thoroughly clean the area around the oil pan to transmission casing joint face and also the transmission dipstick/filler tube union on the side of the pan. *Absolute cleanliness is essential when draining the fluid.*

4   Place a suitable bowl or container beneath the dipstick/filler tube union and unscrew the retaining nut. Carefully ease the end of the tube out of its location in the oil pan and allow the fluid to drain.

5   Now undo and remove the four bolts securing the oil pan to the casing and lift off the pan and gasket. **Note:** *Do not run the engine or tow the vehicle with the oil pan removed or with the transmission drained of fluid.*

6   With the oil pan removed undo and remove the two screws securing the oil filter screen to the underside of the valve assembly. Lift off the cover plate, filter screen and the gasket.

7   Clean off all the parts in paraffin and dry them thoroughly with a lint free cloth. Obtain new gaskets for the oil pan and filter screen before refitting.

8   Place the new gasket on the valve assembly and refit the filter screen and cover plate. Secure with the two screws.

9   With the new gasket in position, refit the oil pan to the transmission casing. Secure the pan with the four bolts tightened to

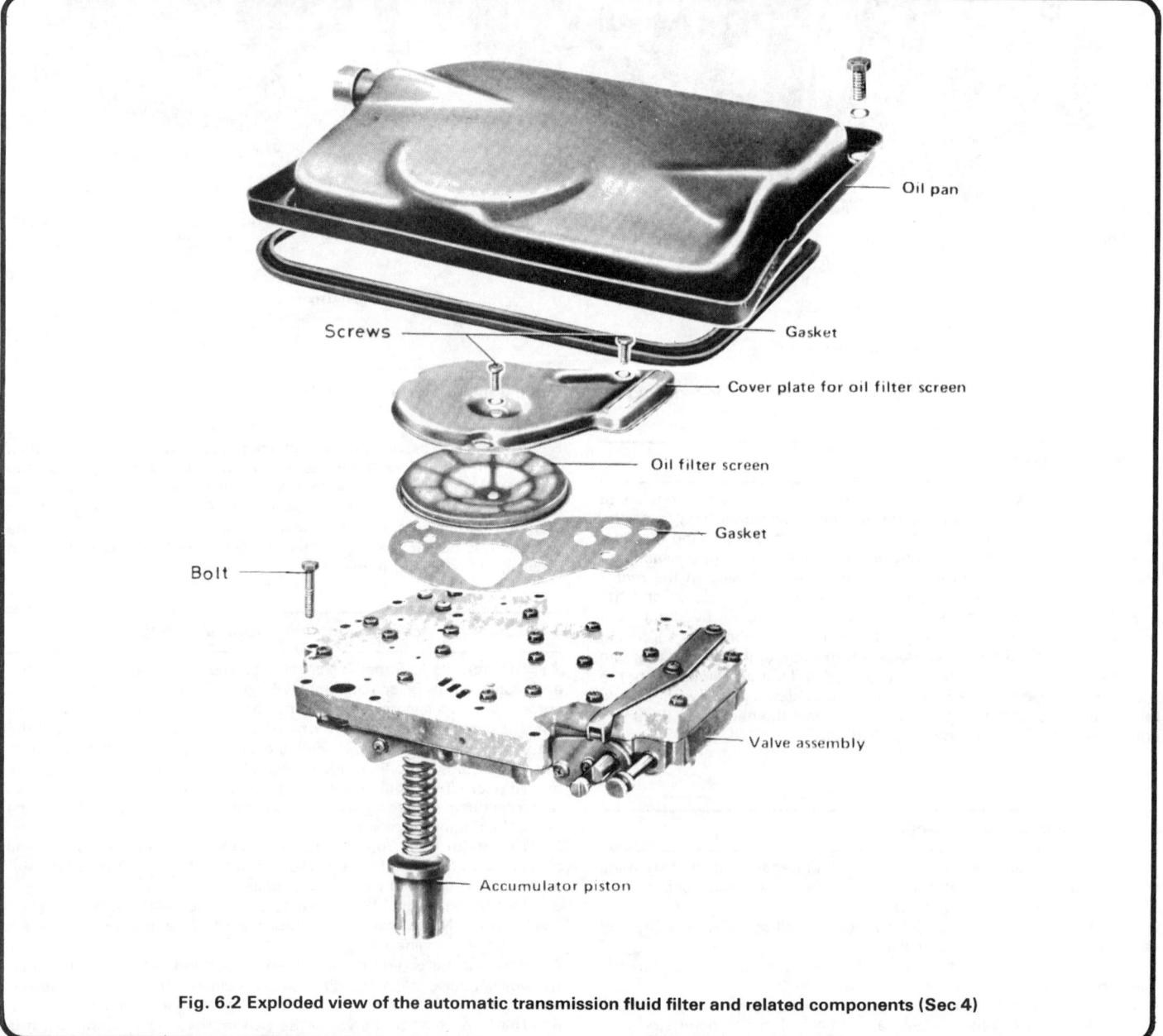

Fig. 6.2 Exploded view of the automatic transmission fluid filter and related components (Sec 4)

the specified torque. Attach the dipstick/filler tube and tighten the union nut securely.

10 Lower the vehicle to the ground and fill the transmission with 2.5 litres (4.4 Imp pints, 5.2 US pints) of the specified automatic transmission fluid.

11 Start the engine and move the selector lever through all the gear positions, returning to the N position.

12 With the engine idling check the fluid level in the transmission and if necessary top up to the lower mark on the dipstick.

13 Final topping up of the fluid level should be carried out as described in Section 3, paragraphs 2 to 6 inclusive.

5 Automatic transmission – removal and refitting

The automatic transmission may be removed together with the engine as described in Chapter 1, or separately, leaving the engine in the vehicle as described in this Section. If the transmission is being removed for repair or overhaul make sure that any suspected faults are referred to a VW main dealer before the unit is removed. With this type of transmission the fault must be confirmed using specialist test equipment and this can only be done with the transmission installed in the vehicle.

1 First disconnect the battery earth terminal and then remove the engine compartment cover.

2 Undo and remove the three bolts securing the protective grille to the fan housing and lift away the grille complete with ignition timing scale.

3 Refer to Chapter 2 and remove the air cleaner assembly.

4 Withdraw the grommet from the upper left-hand side of the crankcase to provide access to the torque converter retaining bolts.

5 Turn the engine until one of the three torque converter retaining bolts becomes accessible through the hole previously covered by the grommet. To turn the engine it will be necessary to obtain VW tool 3052 or make up a similar tool which will engage with the boss and machined slot in the centre of the fan hub. Undo and remove the bolt and then turn the engine and remove the remaining two converter bolts.

6 Undo and remove the two upper bolts securing the engine to the transmission casing.

7 Remove the transmission dipstick from the filler tube.

8 Jack up the rear of the vehicle and support it on axle stands positioned under the rear suspension crossmember.

9 Using a suitable key undo and remove the six socket headed bolts each side that secure the driveshaft inner joints to the transmission drive flanges. Move the joints away from the drive flanges and lower the inner ends of the shafts to the ground.

10 Refer to Chapter 10 and remove the starter motor.

11 Undo and remove the bolt securing the dipstick/filler tube support bracket to the transmission casing.

12 Undo and remove the nut and spring washer securing the throttle operating rod to the lever on the side of the transmission casing.

Fig. 6.4 VW tool 3052 used to turn engine. Tool locates in machined slot in fan hub (arrowed) (Sec 5)

Fig. 6.5 Location of the driveshaft inner joint retaining bolts (arrowed) (Sec 5)

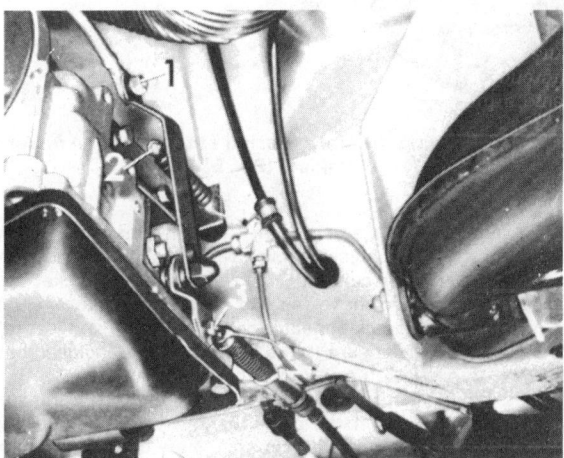

Fig. 6.6 Control connections on right-hand side of transmission casing (Sec 5)

1 Throttle operating rod retaining nut   3 Selector cable circlip
2 Accelerator cable ball socket

Fig. 6.3 Torque converter retaining bolt access hole in the crankcase (Sec 5)

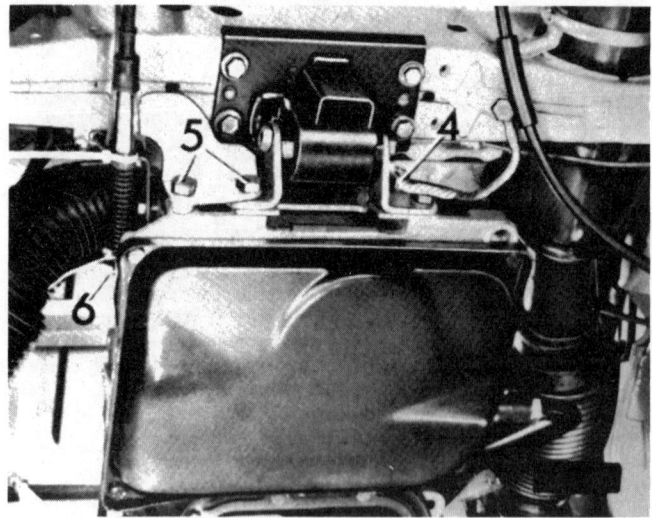

Fig. 6.7 Attachments at front of transmission casing (Sec 5)

4   Earth strap
5   Selector cable support bracket retaining bolts
6   Selector cable

Fig. 6.8 Removing the transmission assembly from under the vehicle (Sec 5)

13 Using a wide blade screwdriver carefully prise the accelerator cable socket off the transmission lever. Now undo and remove the two bolts securing the accelerator cable support bracket to the transmission casing and move the cable and bracket to one side.
14 Position a suitable jack beneath the transmission and just take the weight of the unit. Make sure that a block of wood is placed between the jack and transmission to protect the casing and spread the load.
15 Extract the circlip securing the selector cable to the transmission selector lever and slide off the cable. Recover the small sealing ring that will remain in place on the lever pin. Now undo and remove the two bolts and spacer securing the selector cable support bracket to the transmission casing. Place the cable and bracket to one side.
16 Undo and remove the bolt securing the earth strap to the transmission casing and lift away the strap.
17 Undo and remove the four bolts securing the transmission mounting bracket to the body crossmember.

18 Suitably support the engine using a second jack and interposed block of wood, then undo and remove the two lower transmission casing to engine retaining nuts.
19 The transmission can now be drawn away from the engine, and, as soon as it is clear of the two lower studs, lowered to the ground. Whilst doing this make sure that the torque converter stays in place on the transmission and does not fall out. As soon as is convenient, secure it in position using a length of wire inserted through the openings in the side of the casing. Note also that it may be necessary to lower the two jacks slightly to provide clearance between the transmission and crossmember. If so check that nothing is fouling or being strained in the engine compartment or under the vehicle as the jacks are lowered.
20 With the transmission lowered to the ground slide it out from under the vehicle.
21 Refitting the automatic transmission is the reverse sequence to removal bearing in mind the following points:

(a) Ensure that the torque converter is in position on the transmission and properly seated as described in Section 6 before refitting the transmission
(b) Observe the correct torque wrench settings on all retaining nuts and bolts where applicable
(c) After refitting, fill the transmission with the specified fluid using the procedure described in Section 4 if the unit is dry, or Section 3 if only topping up is required

6   Torque converter – removal and refitting

1   Begin by removing the transmission assembly from the vehicle as described in Section 5, and then drain the automatic transmission fluid using the procedure described in Section 4.
2   Release the retaining wire used to hold the converter in place during removal of the transmission and slide the unit off the pump driveshaft and one-way clutch splines. Have some rags handy to catch

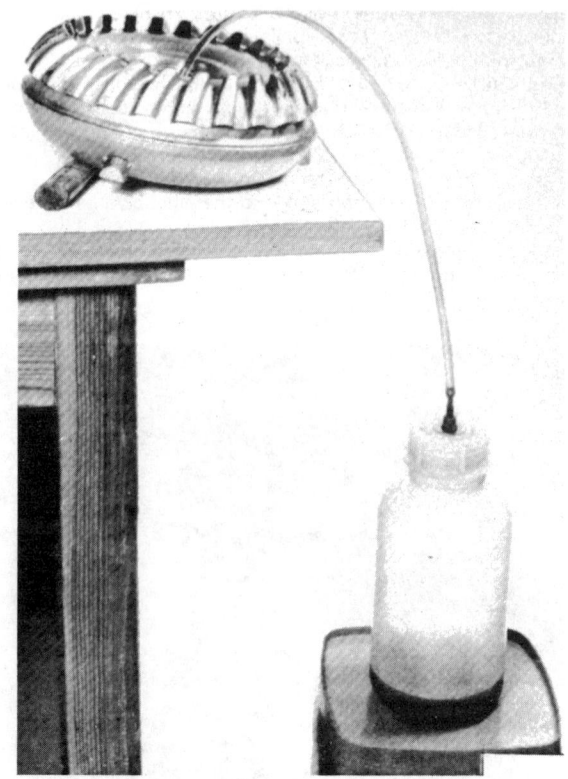

Fig. 6.9 Draining the torque converter by means of a syphon (Sec 6)

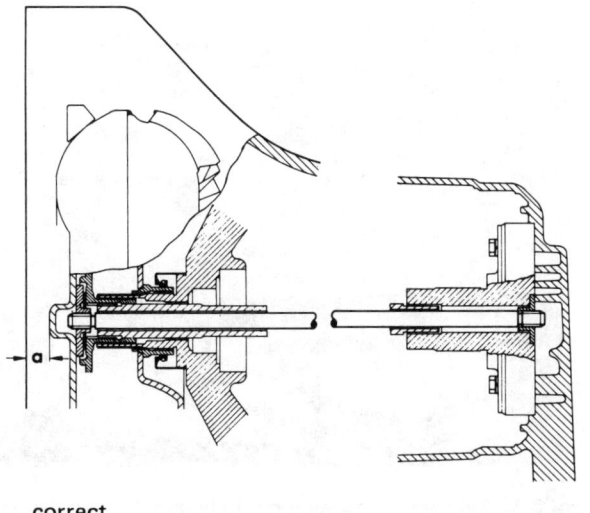

correct

Fig. 6.10 Correct seating of torque converter and pump driveshaft (Sec 6)

Dimension a = approximately 10 mm (2.5 in)

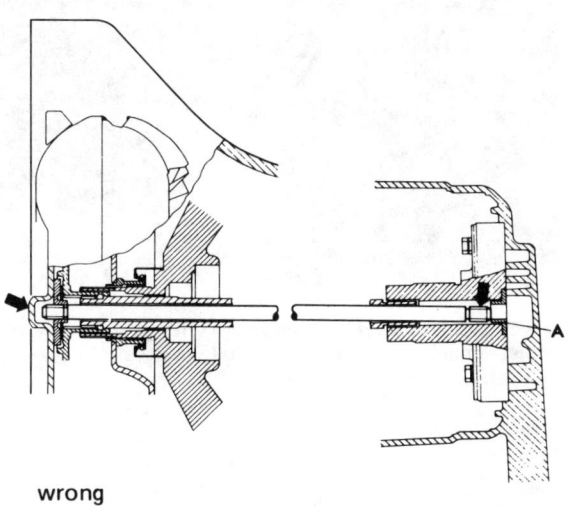

wrong

Fig. 6.11 Pump driveshaft dislodged from pump driveplate (A) resulting in insufficient clearance between torque converter boss and casing flange (Sec 6)

bottle are ideal). Affix one end of the tube to the bottle either by cutting a hole in the top, inserting the tube and then sealing the hole, or by attaching the tube to the union or valve in the bottle top if that type is being used. Place the other end of the tube in the torque converter hub so it touches the bottom. Squeeze the bottle then release it to start the syphon. As soon as the fluid starts to flow unscrew the top slightly to relieve pressure in the bottle. **Note:** *the fluid in the torque converter can only be completely drained by syphoning. There are obviously other ways of starting a syphon than the one described but do not under any circumstances start it by sucking on the tube, automatic transmission fluid is poisonous.*

6   To refit the torquer converter to the transmission, position it squarely over the pump driveshaft and one-way clutch support and turn it back and forth slightly to engage the splines. When the torque converter is properly seated the clearance between the transmission casing flange and the converter centering boss should be approximately 10mm (2.5in) (Fig. 6.10). If this is not the case it is likely that the pump driveshaft has slipped forward out of engagement with the pump driveplate splines (Fig. 6.11). To overcome this problem, remove the torque converter, manipulate the driveshaft until it can be pushed fully into engagement with the pump driveplate and then refit the converter a second time. It should now be possible to properly seat the torque converter and obtain the necessary clearance.

7   Retain the unit in position with a suitable length of wire until the transmission is refitted to the vehicle.

7   Final drive – removal and refitting

1   First remove the automatic transmission assembly from the vehicle as described in Section 5, and the torque converter as described in the previous Section.

2   It is now possible to remove the final drive housing from the main gearbox leaving the transmission separated into its three main assemblies. These can then be renewed individually or taken to a VW dealer for repair or overhaul.

3   Make sure that the casings are thoroughly cleaned off externally using paraffin or a suitable solvent and a plentiful supply of clean rags.

4   Undo and remove the four nuts and washers securing the final drive and main gearbox casings together and carefully separate the two units. Recover the gasket from the main gearbox and the axial play adjusting shim from the pinion shaft. Note that the thickness of this shim is critical and must be recalculated if any of the components in the main gearbox or final drive are dismantled or renewed. Calculation of the shim thickness is rather involved and it is advisable to take the two assemblies to a VW dealer and have him determine the thickness required.

5   Refitting the final drive is the reverse sequence to removal bearing in mind the following points:

(a)   *Ensure that the axial play adjusting shim is in position on the pinion shaft before fitting*

(b)   *Always use a new gasket between the final drive and main gearbox and a new O-ring on the final drive casing periphery*

(c)   *Tighten all retaining nuts and bolts to the specified torque where applicable*

(d)   *Ensure that the pump driveshaft is fully inserted in the pump driveplate before refitting the torque converter*

(e)   *After refitting the assembled transmission in the vehicle top up or refill the final drive with the specified type and quantity of hypoid gear oil*

8   Final drive flange oil seal – removal and refitting

The final drive flange oil seals can be renewed with the transmission in place in the vehicle using the following procedure.

1   Jack up the rear and place axle stands under the rear suspension crossmember.

2   Using a suitable key undo and remove the six socket headed bolts securing the driveshaft inner joint to the final drive flange.

3   Undo and remove the socket headed retaining bolt in the centre of the final drive flange. To prevent the flange from turning refit two of

any fluid that may be spilled as the converter is removed. After removal lay it flat on the bench with the starter ring gear uppermost.

3   It is not possible to overhaul the torque converter as it is welded together and cannot be separated. If tests have shown the unit to be faulty a factory exchange torque converter should be obtained. The one item which can be renewed is the bush in the centre of the hub. However special tools are required to do this and if the bush is worn the job of renewal should be left to a VW dealer.

4   If the automatic transmission fluid is dirty due to wear of the clutch linings or if the transmission is being overhauled or renewed, the fluid in the torque converter should be syphoned off as follows.

5   Obtain a suitable length of small bore plastic tube and a plastic bottle with a sealed top. (windscreen washer tube and an old washer

the driveshaft retaining bolts and lever against them with a screwdriver or suitable bar.

4   Place a tray or bowl beneath the drive flange to catch any oil that may spill out and then withdraw the drive flange. If it is tight, ease it out using two screwdrivers as levers.

5   The oil seal can now be removed using a suitable hooked tool or screwdriver to lever it out.

6   Fill the space between the lips of a new seal with multi-purpose grease and fit the seal to the housing. Tap the seal fully into position using a block of wood.

7   The remainder of the refitting is the reverse sequence to removal. Top up the final drive with the specified type of gear oil after refitting.

Fig. 6.13 Selector rod to lever retaining nut, bolt and washers (Sec 9)

Fig. 6.12 Removing the final drive flange retaining bolt (Sec 8)

9   Gear selector mechanism – adjustment

1   Adjustment of the gear selector mechanism is catered for by the provision of an elongated slot at the forward end of the selector rod. Adjustment is carried out as follows.

2   With the selector lever in the P position, start the engine and allow it to idle.

3   Make sure that the handbrake is fully applied and then slowly move the selector lever to the R position. As you do this note the change in engine speed and the point at which the transmission can be felt to take up the drive. Now move the lever to N again noting the change in engine speed and the point when the drive can be felt releasing.

4   If the adjustment of the mechanism is correct the drive take up should be just before the selector lever engages with the gate detent in the R position. The drive should release just after the lever is moved out of R towards N.

5   If this is not the case move the selector lever to P and switch off the engine.

6   From under the front of the vehicle undo and remove the nut, bolt and washers securing the selector rod to the gear selector lever.

7   Move the operating lever on the right-hand side of the transmission fully rearward into the P position.

8   Now push the selector rod towards the rear and whilst holding it in this position, refit the nut, bolt and washers securing the rod to the selector lever.

9   Carry out the checks described in paragraphs 2 and 3 again and if necessary make small adjustments to the position of the selector rod.

10   Finally check that the engine will only start when the selector lever is in the P or N position. This condition is achieved by the correct positioning of a contact plate located inside the gear lever console. If

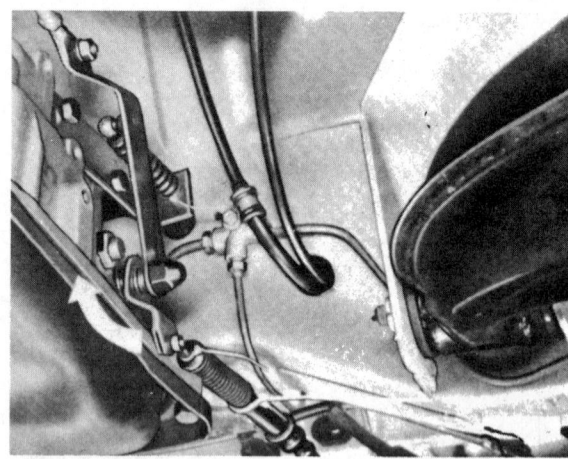

Fig. 6.14 Adjust selector mechanism with gear lever in P and transmission selector lever moved fully rearward in direction of arrow (Sec 9)

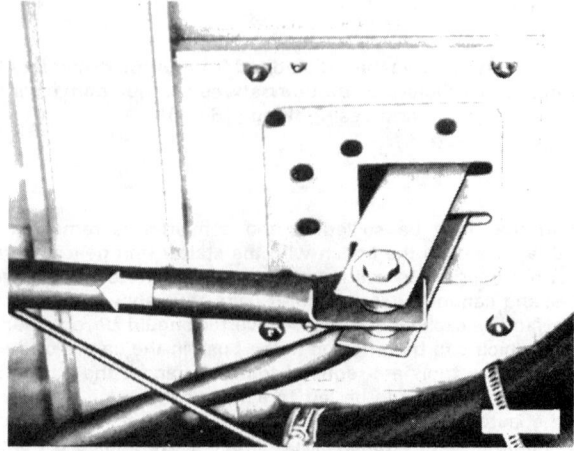

Fig. 6.15 Selector rod is moved fully rearwards with gear lever in P during adjustment sequence (Sec 9)

adjustment is required remove the console as described in Section 10, and then reposition the contact plate as necessary.

10 Gear selector mechanism – removal and refitting

Selector rod and cable

1   Jack up the rear of the vehicle and support it on axle stands placed under the rear suspension crossmember.
2   Using a small screwdriver carefully prise off the small circlip securing the selector cable to the transmission selector lever on the right-hand side of the transmission casing. Slide the cable off the lever pin and recover the sealing ring.
3   Undo and remove the two bolts securing the selector cable bracket to the transmission casing noting the position of the spacer on the outer bolt.
4   Undo and remove the two nuts and bolts securing the intermediate support bracket to the body crossmember.
5   At the front of the vehicle undo and remove the nut, bolt and washers securing the selector rod to the gear selector lever.
6   Withdraw the rod and cable assembly rearward through the body crossmember and remove it from under the vehicle.
7   If it is wished to separate the rod from the cable, slide back the rubber boot and using a parallel pin punch tap out the spring pin that retains the two parts together.
8   Reassembling the rod and cable and refitting the assembly to the vehicle is the reverse sequence to removal. Adjust the selector mechanism as described in Section 9 after refitting.

Gear selector lever and console

9   Undo and remove the small grub screw securing the handle to the gear lever and lift off the handle.
10 Using a small screwdriver carefully prise up the gear selector cover and remove it from the housing.
11 Undo and remove the four screws securing the console to the floor and lift it up over the gear lever. Disconnect the wiring for the illumination bulbs.
12 From under the front of the vehicle undo and remove the nut, bolt and washers securing the selector rod to the lever and the four nuts securing the lever bracket to the floor.
13 The lever and bracket assembly can now be removed from inside the vehicle after disconnecting the contact plate wiring.
14 Refitting is the reverse sequence to removal. Adjust the selector mechanism as described in Section 9 after refitting.

11 Fault diagnosis – automatic transmission

1   Before the automatic transmission is removed for repair of a suspected malfunction, it is imperative that the cause be traced and confirmed. To do this requires specialist experience and various gauges not normally found in the DIY mechanic's workshop.
2   If any fault arises that cannot be cured by attention to the fluid level or adjustment of the selector mechanism or accelerator linkage (see Chapter 2), take the vehicle to a VW main dealer for diagnosis and repair.

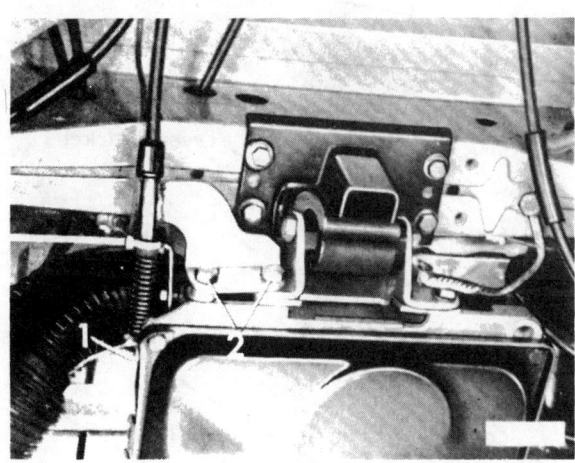

Fig. 6.16 Selector cable to transmission lever attachment (1) and support bracket retaining bolt (2) (Sec 10)

Fig. 6.17 Selector cable intermediate support bracket (Sec 10)
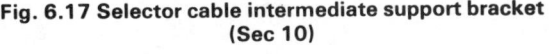

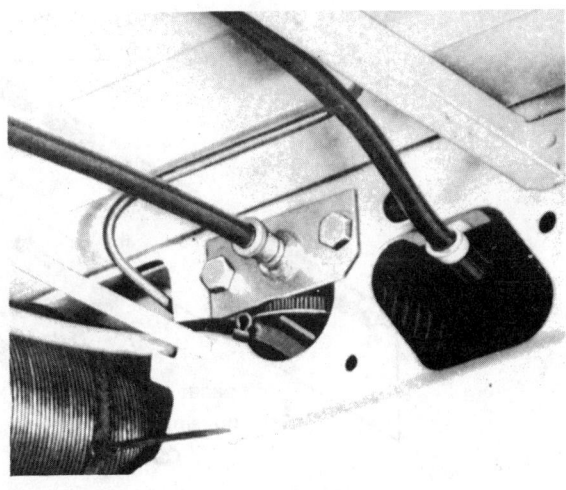

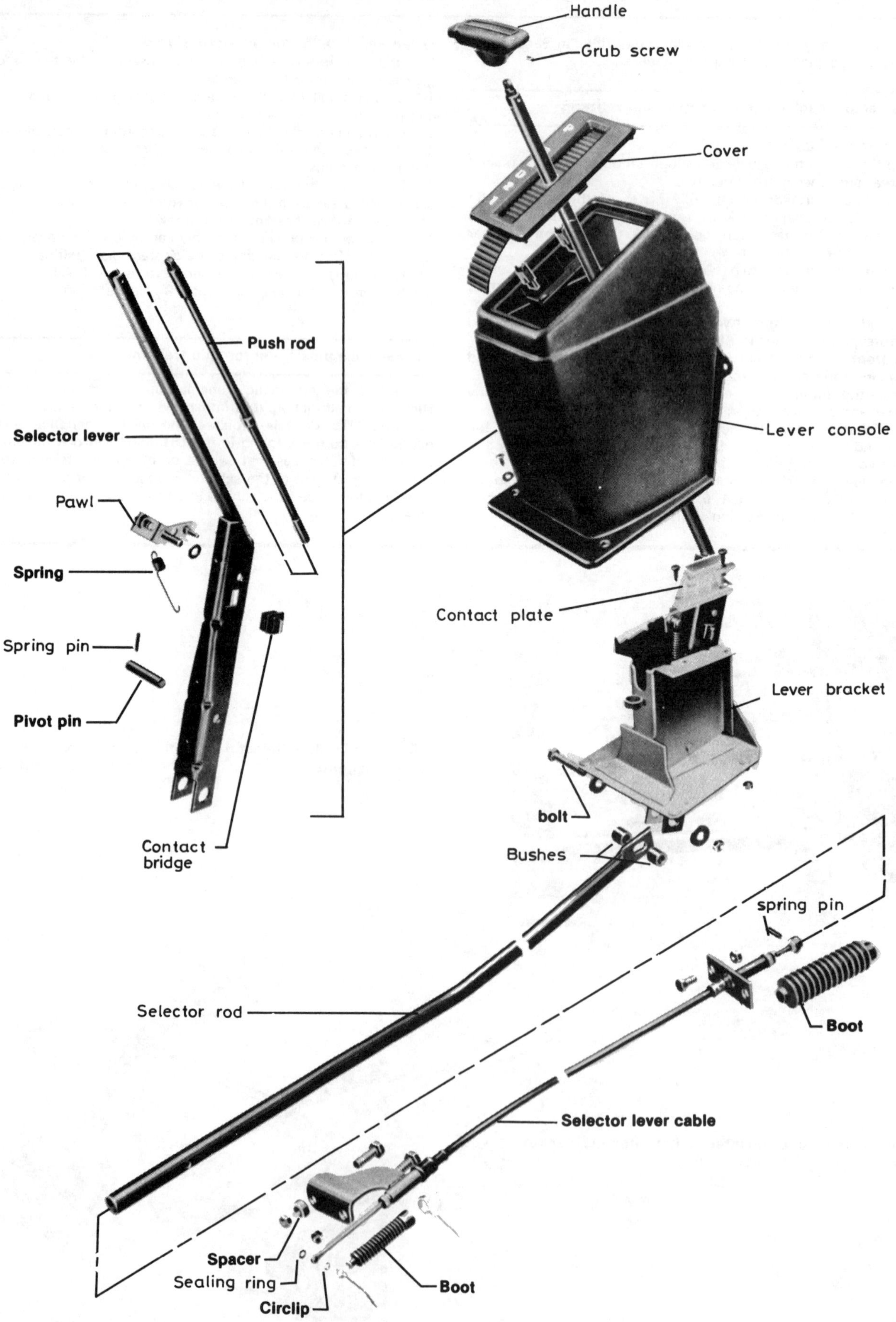

Handle

Grub screw

Cover

Push rod

Lever console

Selector lever

Pawl

Spring

Contact plate

Spring pin

Pivot pin

Lever bracket

Contact bridge

bolt

Bushes

spring pin

Selector rod

Boot

Selector lever cable

Spacer

Sealing ring

Circlip

Boot

Fig. 6.18 Exploded view of the gear selector mechanism (Sec 10)

Chapter 7 Rear suspension and driveshafts

Contents

Specifications

Rear suspension

Type	Independent by trailing arms, coil springs and telescopic shock absorbers
Camber angle	−50′ ± 30′
Maximum permissible difference between sides	30′
Toe setting (per wheel)	0° ± 10′

Driveshafts

Type	Solid shaft with inboard and outboard homokinetic constant velocity joints

Driveshaft length

Manual gearbox	547.8 mm (21.5 in)
Automatic transmission:	
Left-hand shaft	531.0 mm (20.9 in)
Right-hand shaft	579.3 mm (22.8 in)

Torque wrench settings

	Nm	lbf ft
Trailing arm to mounting bracket	105	78
Shock absorber to trailing arm and body	90	66
Wheel bearing housing to trailing arm	140	103
Driveshaft to differential and wheel shaft	45	33
Wheel hub to wheel shaft (castellated nut)	350	258
Brake shoe pivot assembly to wheel bearing housing	65	48
Brake wheel cylinder to wheel bearing housing	20	15
Roadwheel to hub	170	125

1 General description

The independent rear suspension is by trailing arms, coil springs and telescopic shock absorbers. Drive is taken from the differential to the rear wheels by two solid steel driveshafts incorporating a constant velocity joint at each end.

The trailing arms are secured to brackets on the vehicle underbody by bolts which pass through rubber bushes in the arm. The brackets incorporate elongated horizontal and vertical slots to provide for adjustment of rear wheel alignment and camber angle.

The driveshaft constant velocity joints are bolted to the differential drive flanges at their inner ends and to the wheel shaft flanges at their outer ends. The wheel shafts are supported in roller and ball bearings contained within a housing bolted to the trailing arm. The wheel shafts are splined to accept the rear hubs to which the brake drum and roadwheel are attached.

No maintenance is required on the rear suspension assembly other than a periodic visual inspection for damage or deterioration of the constant velocity joint rubber boots.

2 Maintenance and inspection

1   At the intervals given in Routine Maintenance at the beginning of this manual, the following service operations should be carried out to the rear suspension components and driveshaft assemblies.

Rear suspension
2   Jack up the rear of the vehicle and securely support it on axle stands. Release the handbrake.
3   Visually inspect the rear suspension components, attachments and linkages for any obvious signs of wear or damage.

4   Grasp the roadwheel at the '12 o'clock' and '6 o'clock' positions and try to rock it. Any excess movement here indicates wear in the rear wheel bearings or slackness in the wheel shaft retaining nut. Wear may also be accompanied by a rumbling sound or noticeable roughness when the wheel is turned. If this is the case further investigation is required and reference should be made to Sections 5 and 6.

Shock absorbers
5   Check for any sign of fluid leakage around the shock absorber body or for any damage or deformation of the unit.
6   The efficiency of the shock absorber may be checked by bouncing the vehicle at each corner. Generally speaking the body will return to its normal position and stop after being depressed. If it rises and returns on a rebound the shock absorber is probably suspect. Examine also the upper and lower mountings for any sign of wear or deterioration of the rubber bushes. Renewal procedures are contained in Section 6.

Driveshafts
7   Carefully inspect the rubber boots protecting the inner and outer constant velocity joints. If they are torn, split, or show signs of deterioration they should be renewed as soon as possible, as described in Section 4. Very rapid wear of the joint internal components due to water and grit entry will occur if a damaged rubber boot is not renewed quickly. Wear in the joints is detected by a knock or clunk when accelerating or decelerating often in conjunction with a vibration from the rear of the vehicle.
8   The constant velocity joints are lubricated and sealed during assembly and therefore, providing the rubber boots remain intact, require no further lubrication in service.

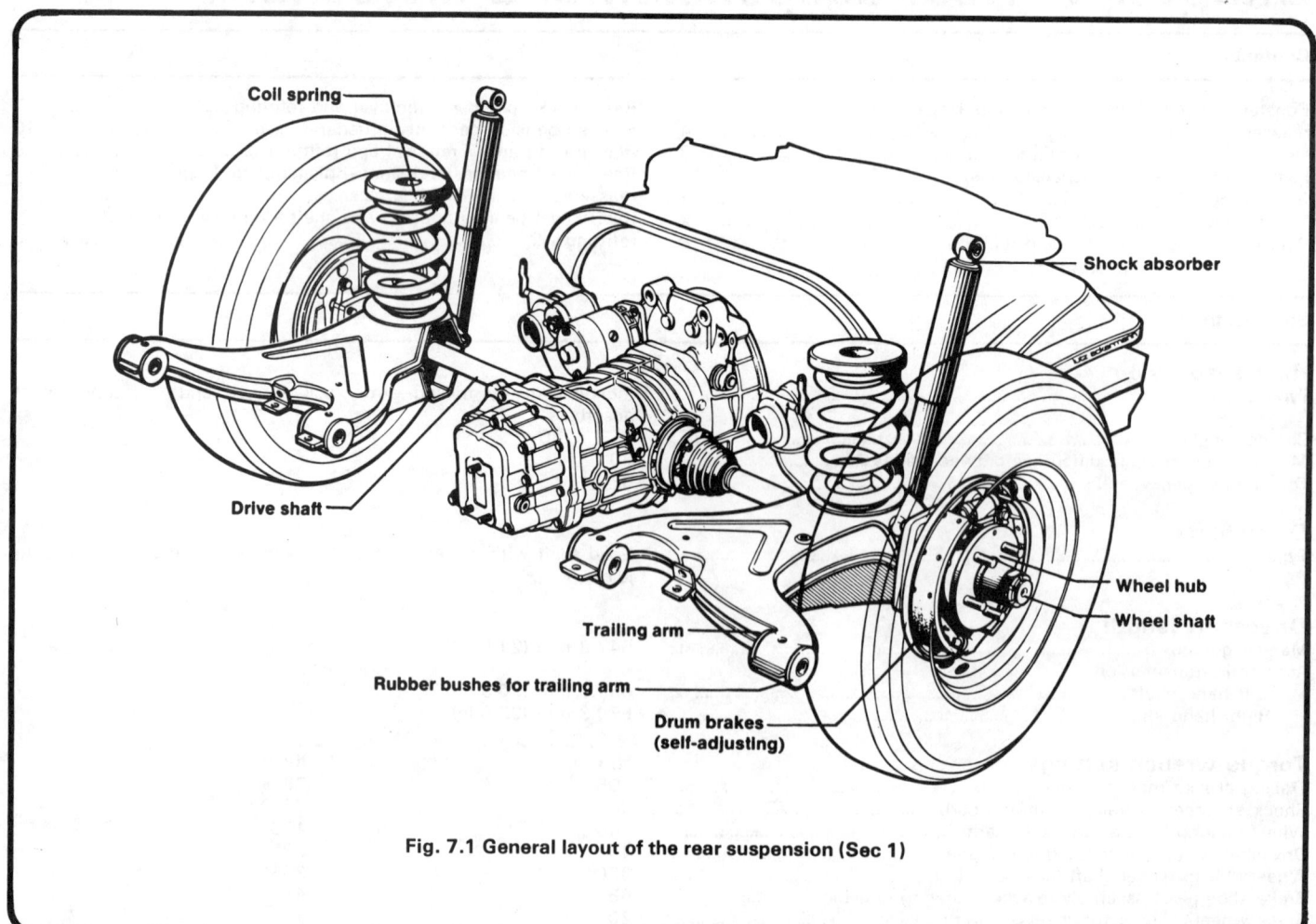

Fig. 7.1 General layout of the rear suspension (Sec 1)

3 Driveshaft – removal and refitting

1 Jack up the rear of the car and support it on axle stands.
2 Using an Allen key of the appropriate size, undo and remove the socket headed bolts securing the inner constant velocity joint to the differential drive flange (photo). Recover the tab washers fitted behind each pair of bolts.
3 The bolts securing the outer joint to the wheel shaft are rather inaccessible as the joint is housed within a recess in the trailing arm. If an ordinary key is cut in half a metric socket of the appropriate size can be placed over the key and the bolts removed using an extension bar and ratchet (photo). When all the retaining bolts have been removed together with the tab washers, lift the driveshaft away.
4 Refitting is a direct reversal of the removal procedure. Tighten the socket headed retaining bolts to the specified torque given in the Specifications.

4 Constant velocity joint – dismantling, inspection and reassembly

1 Remove the driveshaft from the car as described in the previous Section.
2 Secure the driveshaft in a vice and then extract the circlip from the end of the shaft.
3 Using a suitable drift tap the protective cap off the joint and then slide the cap and rubber boot towards the centre of the driveshaft.
4 Support the joint across the vice jaws with the driveshaft hanging down. Using a large drift, drive the shaft downwards and out of the joint. The rubber boot and protective cap can now be removed from the driveshaft.
5 With the joint removed from the driveshaft pivot the ball hub and ball cage assembly through approximately 90° and then push it out of the joint outer member.
6 Remove the six balls from the cage, tilt the ball hub and position it so that the two grooves in the ball track are aligned with the cage edge and then separate the two parts.
7 Wash all the components in paraffin and wipe dry with a lint free cloth.
8 Carefully examine the six steel balls, the ball hub, ball cage and the outer member for wear ridges, pitting or scoring. Make sure that the tracks in which the balls run are not grooved or damaged and that the slots in the ball cage are not appreciably wider than the balls. The balls themselves must be quite spherical with no sign of ridging or pitting. Also check the rubber boot, that protects the joint, for cracks, splits or deterioration. It is advisable to renew the rubber boot whenever a joint is dismantled, as a matter of course. If a rubber boot fails in service, water and grit will enter the joint causing rapid wear of the internal components.
9 If inspection shows any of the joint parts to be worn or damaged a complete new assembly must be obtained. The balls, ball hub, ball

3.2 Removing the inner constant velocity joint to differential drive flange retaining bolts

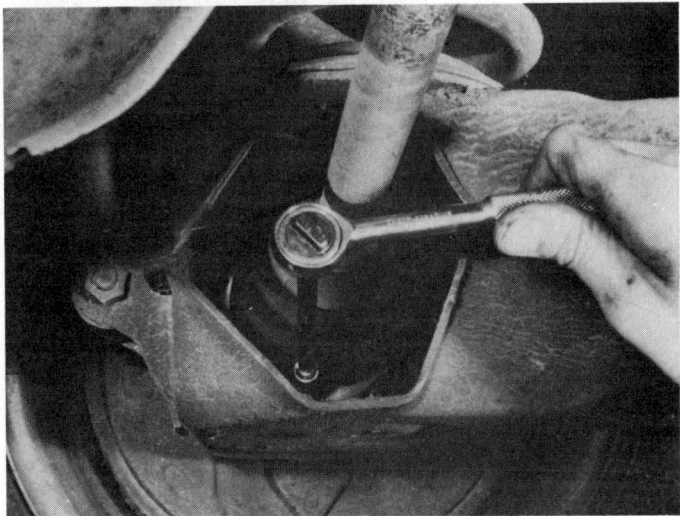

3.3 The outer constant velocity joint retaining bolts are inaccessible requiring the use of an extension bar and ratchet

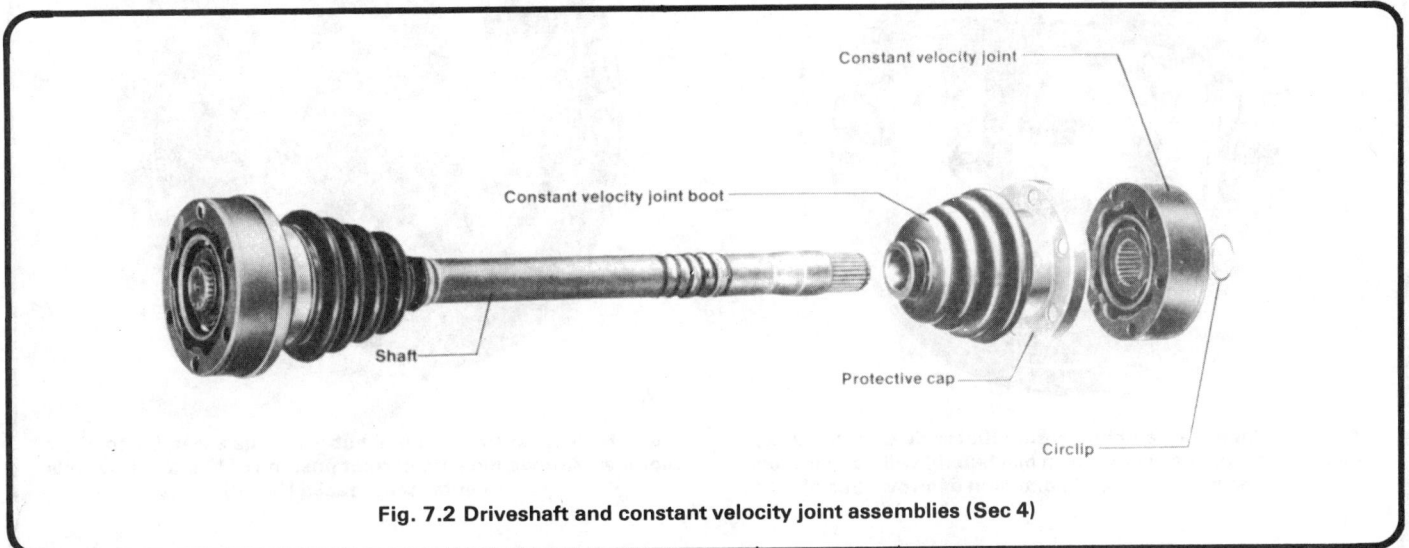

Fig. 7.2 Driveshaft and constant velocity joint assemblies (Sec 4)

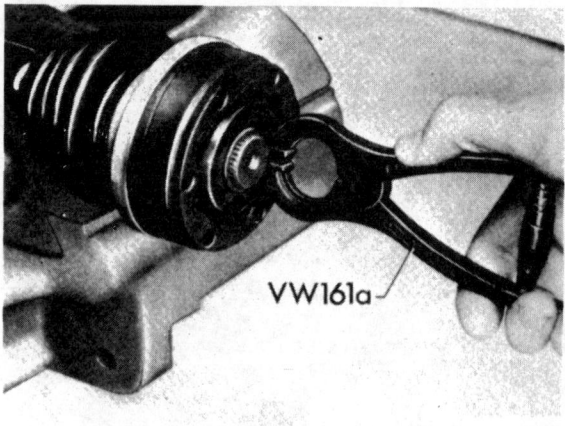

Fig. 7.3 Removing circlip from end of driveshaft (Sec 4)

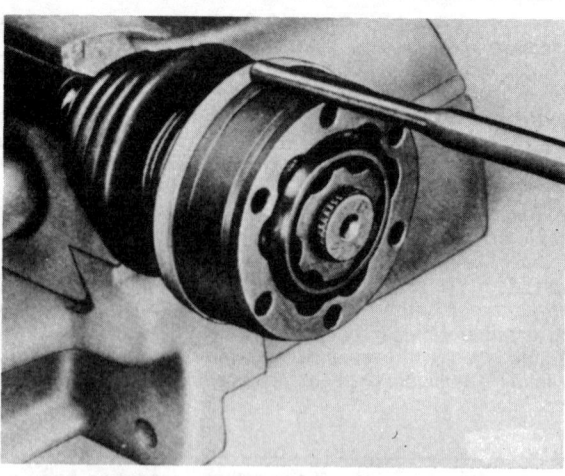

Fig. 7.4 Using a drift to tap off joint protective cap (Sec 4)

Fig. 7.5 Removing ball hub and ball cage assembly from constant velocity joint outer member (Sec 4)

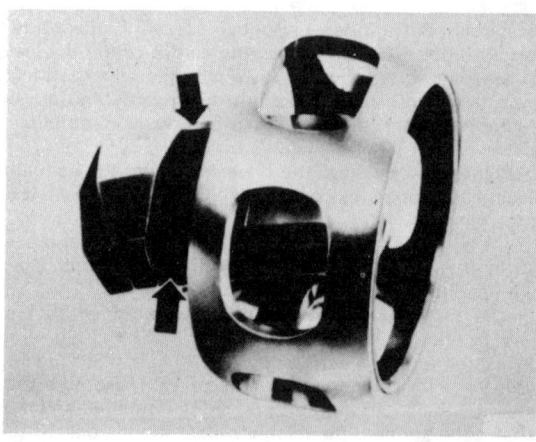

Fig. 7.6 With the two grooves in the ball hub (arrowed) aligned with the ball cage edge the two parts can be separated (Sec 4)

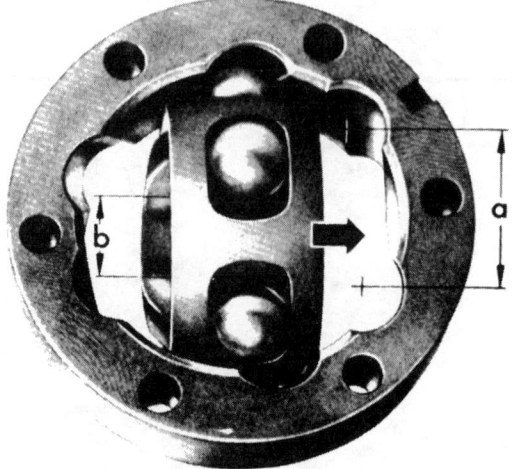

Fig. 7.7 When reassembling ensure that wide track in outer member (a) and narrow track in ball hub (b) will be together when the hub is moved in direction of arrow (Sec 4)

Fig. 7.8 Final assembly of ball hub and cage assembly to outer member. Arrows indicate correct position of hub to allow balls to enter their tracks (Sec 4)

cage and outer member all belong to a tolerance group which is selected during manufacture. For this reason new parts are not available separately, only as a completely assembled constant velocity joint. The exception to this is the rubber boots which may be obtained individually.

10 If the joint components are in a satisfactory condition the unit should be reassembled as follows.

11 First obtain a 90g (3.2 oz) tube of VW type G-6 grease from your VW dealer. Do not use any other type of grease in the joint.

12 Align the two grooves in the ball hub track with the edge of the ball cage and insert the hub into the cage. Now press the six balls into the cage slots and ball hub tracks.

13 When the joint is assembled the chamfer on the inside diameter of the ball hub splines must be towards the larger diameter side of the outer member. Bearing this in mind place the hub, cage and ball assembly into the outer member as shown in Fig. 7.7. Make sure that a wide ball track in the outer member and a narrow track in the ball hub will be on the same side when the hub is swung into its fitted position.

14 Pivot the ball hub and cage into the outer member ensuring that the balls all enter their tracks correctly. It may be necessary to pivot the ball hub out of the cage slightly to achieve this.

15 Firmly press the edge of the ball cage towards the outer member until the whole assembly swings fully into position.

16 Check that the ball hub can be moved in and out by hand over the full range of axial movement.

17 With the joint fully assembled press 90g (3.2 oz) of the special grease equally into both sides of the joint. (45g, 1.6 oz each side).

18 Position the new rubber boot on the driveshaft and then refit the joint. Press or drift the joint fully on to the driveshaft splines until it contacts the register. Now refit the circlip to its groove making sure that it is fully seated. Tap it home with a suitable tube if necessary.

19 Slide up the rubber boot and position the protective cap over the joint. Carefully tap the periphery of the cap until it is fully in place.

20 The driveshaft can now be refitted to the car as described in Section 3.

5 Rear wheel bearing housing and shaft assembly – removal and refitting

1 Remove the hub cap and extract the split pin from the wheel shaft castellated retaining nut.

2 With the handbrake firmly applied, slacken the wheel shaft nut using a socket and long bar. This nut will be extremely tight.

3 Jack up the rear of the vehicle and support it on axle stands. Remove the appropriate rear roadwheel.

4 Remove the driveshaft as described in Section 3.

5 Refer to Chapter 9 and remove the rear brake shoes.

6 Unscrew the wheel shaft castellated retaining nut and then using a universal puller, draw off the rear wheel hub.

7 Using a brake hose clamp or self-locking grips with their jaws suitably protected, clamp the flexible hydraulic brake hose located at the front of the suspension trailing arm. This will prevent loss of hydraulic fluid during subsequent operations.

8 Unscrew the brake hydraulic pipe union at the rear of the wheel cylinder. Carefully ease the pipe out of the cylinder and protect its end against dirt ingress.

9 Withdraw the handbrake cable from its location in the brake backplate.

10 From the front of the backplate undo and remove the two bolts securing the brake shoe pivot assembly and backplate to the wheel bearing housing. Lift off the pivot assembly. It may be necessary to ease it away using a screwdriver as it is located by a dowel pin which is often tight.

11 From the rear of the backplate undo and remove the single bolt securing the wheel cylinder and backplate to the wheel bearing housing. Undo and remove the wheel cylinder bleed screw and then lift off the cylinder.

12 The brake backplate can now be removed from the wheel bearing housing. Again note the dowel pin.

13 Finally undo and remove the four bolts and washers securing the wheel bearing housing to the trailing arm and lift away the assembly.

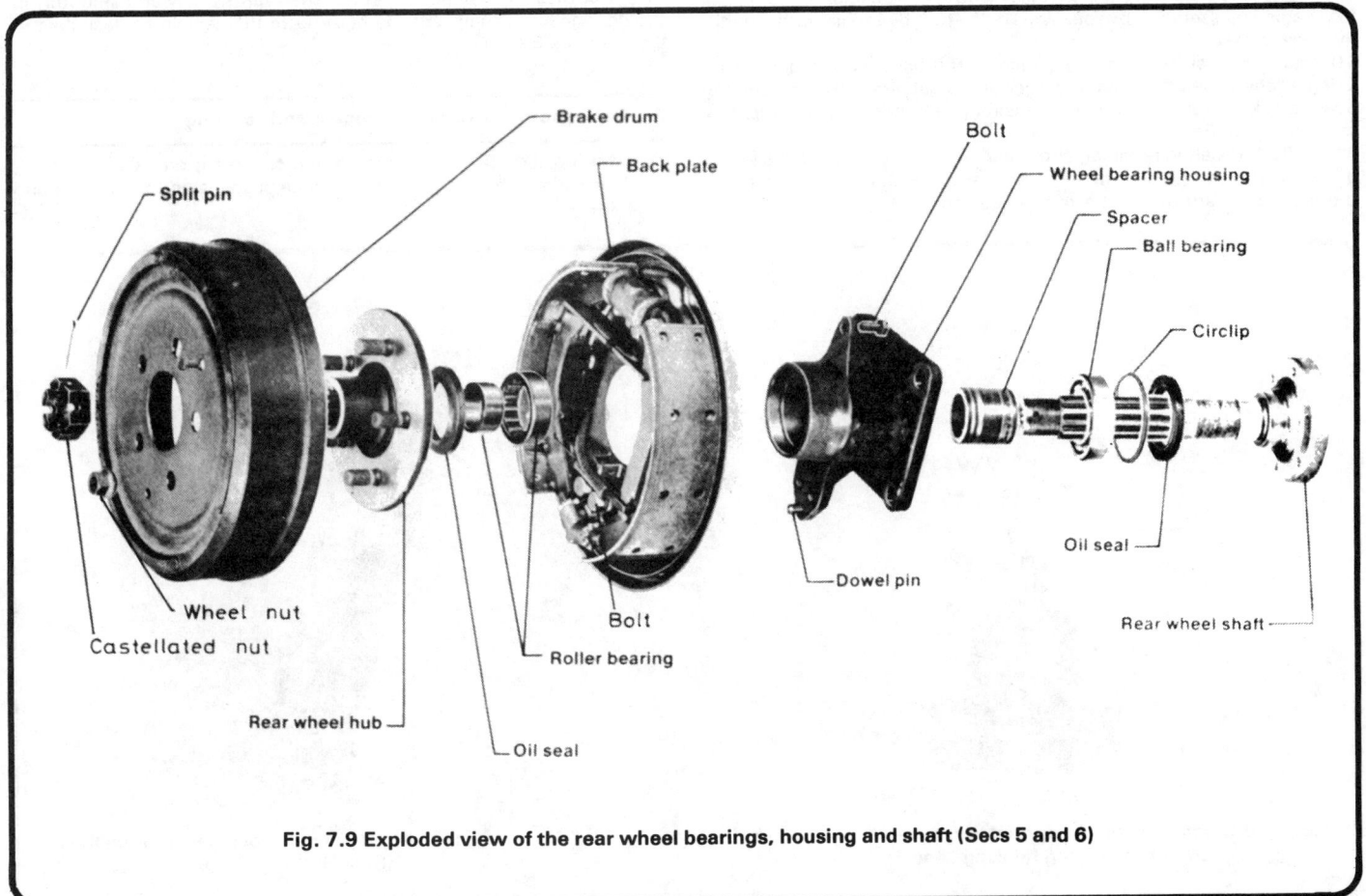

Fig. 7.9 Exploded view of the rear wheel bearings, housing and shaft (Secs 5 and 6)

14 Refitting is the reverse sequence to removal, bearing in mind the following points:

   (a) *Tighten all retaining nuts and bolts to the specified torque where applicable*

   (b) *It will be necessary to bleed the brake hydraulic system after refitting the brake shoes and drum. Full information will be found in Chapter 9*

   (c) *When refitting the wheel shaft retaining nut, tighten the nut to the specified torque and then continue until the split pin holes are aligned. Use a new split pin and make sure that the vehicle is standing on its wheels when tightening the nut*

6   Rear wheel bearings and shaft – dismantling, inspection and reassembly

1   Remove the rear wheel bearing housing and shaft assembly from the vehicle as described in the previous Section.

2   With the bearing housing supported in a vice, drive out the wheel shaft using a soft metal drift or preferably use a press.

3   Using a large screwdriver lever out the oil seals on both sides of the bearing housing. It will be necessary to obtain new oil seals before reassembling as the old ones will be damaged during removal.

4   From the wheel side of the housing lift out the roller bearing inner race and then slide out the spacer located between the bearings.

5   Now turn the housing over and knock out the roller bearing outer race with a soft metal drift.

6   Extract the circlip from behind the ball bearing and then remove this bearing in the same way.

7   Thoroughly wash all the parts in paraffin and dry them with a lint free cloth.

8   Examine the rollers and inner race of the roller bearing for signs of pitting, scoring or wear ridges. Spin both the bearings and check for roughness, remembering that they are dry. If in doubt repack them with fresh multi-purpose grease and spin them again. Renew the bearings if they are suspect, together with the oil seals.

9   Begin reassembly by packing both the bearings with multi-purpose grease.

10   Place the ball bearing in position in the housing and drive it in using a tube of suitable diameter against the outer race. Make sure the bearing is kept square during fitting and drive it in until it contacts the register in the housing.

11   Refit the bearing retaining circlip and the inner oil seal. Use a block of wood when tapping in the seal and make sure that the open side of the seal is toward the centre of the housing.

Fig. 7.11 Removal of the bearing housing oil seals with a screwdriver (Sec 6)

12   Pack the space between the bearings in the centre of the housing with grease and place the bearing spacer in position.

13   Drift in the roller bearing outer race using the same procedure as for the ball bearing. Insert the roller bearing inner race followed by the oil seal. Tap in the seal until it is flush with the housing.

14   Place the flange of the wheel shaft face down on the bench and lay the assembled bearing housing over the shaft. Make sure that the shaft enters the ball bearing inner race and bearing spacer squarely.

15   Using a tube of suitable diameter in contact with the roller bearing inner race, drive or press the bearing housing onto the wheel shaft as far as it will go. As you do this make sure that the bearing inner races do not tip slightly and jam on the shaft otherwise they may crack.

16   After reassembly check that the shaft turns freely and smoothly in the bearings and then refit the housing to the vehicle as described in the previous Section.

7   Rear shock absorber – removal and refitting

1   Jack up the rear of the vehicle and support it on axle stands.

2   Place a jack beneath the appropriate suspension trailing arm and raise the arm slightly.

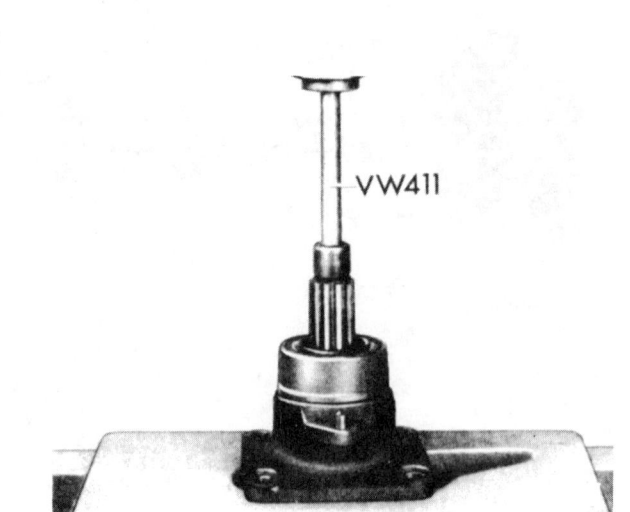

Fig. 7.10 Using a press and special tool to remove wheel shaft from bearing housing (Sec 6)

Fig. 7.12 Using a vice to press in new shock absorber bushes (Sec 7)

3   Undo and remove the nut and bolt securing the shock absorber to the trailing arm and the bolt securing it to the bracket on the vehicle underbody (photos). Ease the shock absorber out of its locations and lift it away.

4   With the unit removed hold it in an upright position and fully extend and compress it several times. The shock absorber should operate with a smooth even pressure, free from dead areas, over the whole stroke. If not the shock absorber must be renewed. It must also be renewed if there is any damage or deterioration of the chrome on the piston rod or if there is evidence of excessive fluid loss. Shock absorbers may be renewed individually if they become defective early in their service life. It is advisable to renew them in pairs if they have been in service for more than 30 000 miles (48 000 km). There are quite a number of different types of shock absorbers available for Transporter models and their derivatives and care must be taken to ensure that compatible types are fitted.

5   The shock absorber rubber bush and steel sleeve can be renewed separately. The bush and sleeve can be removed by pressing them out in a vice using tubes of suitable diameter. When refitting make sure that they are pressed fully into position and lubricate the rubber bush with a little liquid detergent to ease installation.

6   Refitting the shock absorber to the vehicle is the reverse sequence to removal.

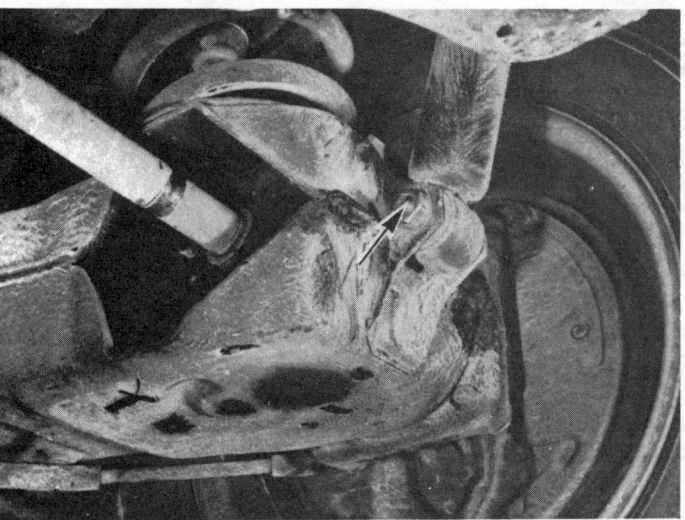

7.3A Shock absorber to trailing arm (arrowed) ...

7.3B ... and vehicle underbody mountings

8   Rear coil spring – removal and refitting

1   Jack up the rear of the vehicle and support it on axle stands positioned clear of the rear suspension trailing arms.

2   Place a jack beneath the trailing arm and raise the arm slightly.

3   Undo and remove the nut and bolt securing the shock absorber lower mounting to the trailing arm. Release the mounting and pivot the shock absorber clear of the arm.

4   Slowly lower the jack and trailing arm until all the tension is released from the spring. Now pull the trailing arm down and lift out the spring, lower packing and upper spring plate. On some models it may be necessary to remove the driveshaft inner joint from the differential as described in Section 3 to allow the trailing arm to be lowered sufficiently.

5   The springs are colour coded by means of paint marks to indicate their load group and vehicle application. The number of paint marks indicates the load group and the colour of the marks denotes the vehicle to which they are fitted. Only springs of the same load group may be fitted to one axle.

6   Refitting the rear coil spring is the reverse sequence to removal. Make sure that the locating contours, in the lower packing, seat correctly in the trailing arm and that the end of the spring engages in the contour. The upper spring plate should be turned so that the end of the spring locates in the depression.

9   Rear trailing arm – removal and refitting

1   Jack up the rear of the vehicle and support it on axle stands placed well clear of the trailing arms. Remove the rear roadwheel.

2   Refer to Section 3 and remove the driveshaft.

3   Using a brake hose clamp or self-locking grips with their jaws suitably protected, clamp the rear flexible brake hose located just in front of the trailing arm. This will prevent loss of hydraulic fluid during subsequent operations.

4   Clean off the area around the flexible brake hose to metal brake pipe union at the bracket on the trailing arm. Unscrew the brake pipe union, lift away the retaining clip and withdraw the hose. Plug the end of the hose to prevent dirt ingress.

5   Wipe the area around the metal brake pipe to wheel cylinder union at the rear of the brake backplate. Unscrew the union nut and withdraw the pipe from the cylinder. Release the pipe from the retaining clip on the trailing arm and lift off the metal pipe.

6   Undo and remove the four bolts securing the wheel bearing housing and brake assembly to the trailing arm. Release the handbrake cable from the support clip on the underside of the arm and lower the housing and brake assembly to the ground.

7   Refer to Section 8 and remove the rear coil spring.

8   Mark the locations of the trailing arm retaining bolts in the mounting brackets as a guide to refitting. The mounting brackets have elongated slots to provide for rear suspension adjustment and if the original positions are not marked the settings will be lost.

9   Undo and remove the trailing arm retaining nuts, bolts and washers and lever the arm out of its mountings. Note that the outer retaining bolt has a protective cap over the bolthead which must first be removed.

10 Now withdraw the arm from under the vehicle.

11 If necessary the rubber mounting bushes can be removed by drawing them out with a large diameter tube, suitable packing washers and a long bolt or stud and nut. New bushes are fitted in the same way making sure they are liberally lubricated with liquid detergent to ease installation.

12 Refitting the trailing arm is the reverse sequence to removal bearing in mind the following points:

(a)   Ensure that all nuts and bolts are tightened to the specified torque settings where applicable

(b)   Bleed the brake hydraulic system as described in Chapter 9 after refitting

(c)   It is advisable to have the rear suspension geometry checked by a VW dealer even if the location of the trailing arm retaining bolts was accurately marked before removal (see Section 10)

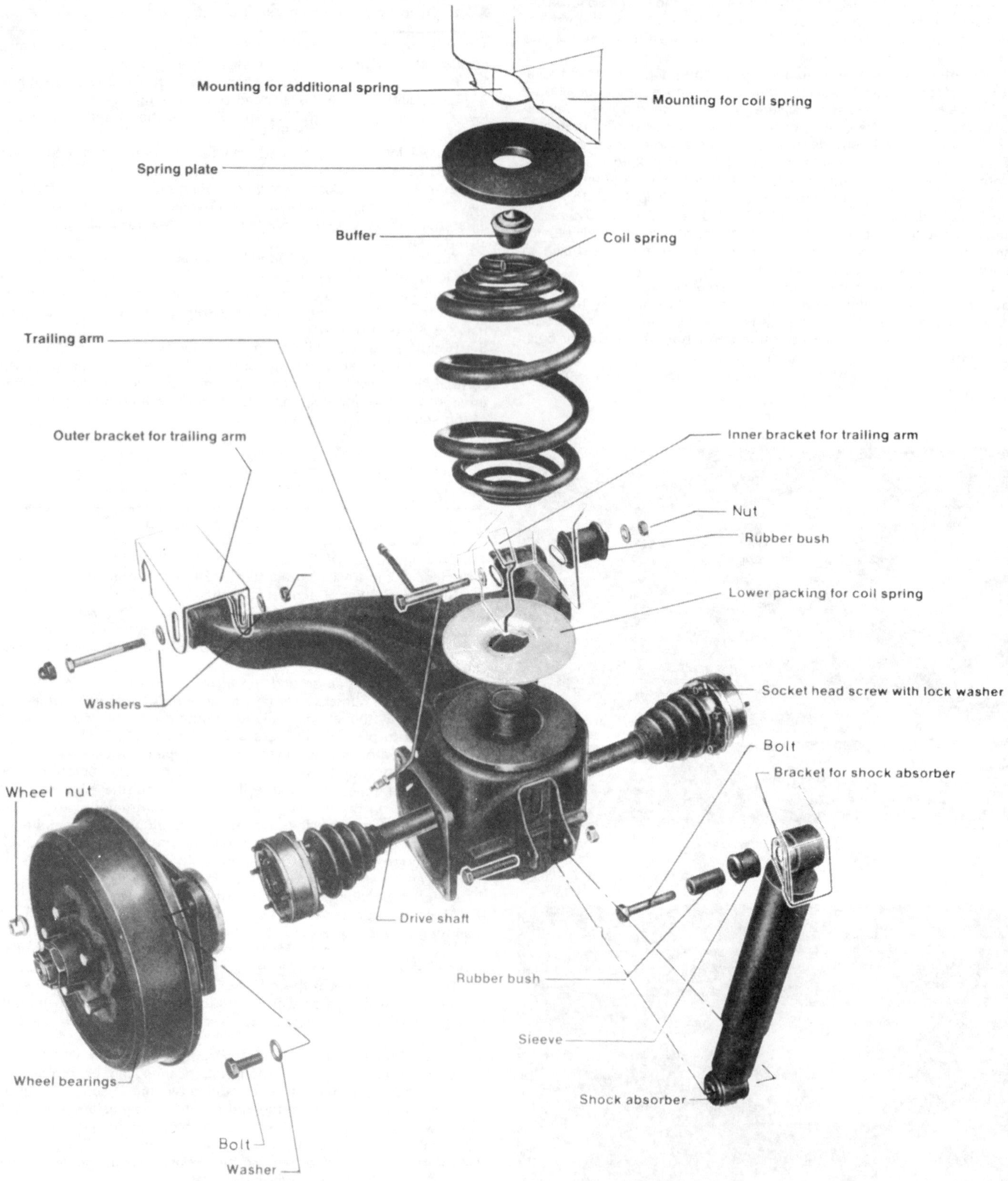

Mounting for additional spring

Mounting for coil spring

Spring plate

Buffer

Coil spring

Trailing arm

Outer bracket for trailing arm

Inner bracket for trailing arm

Nut

Rubber bush

Lower packing for coil spring

Washers

Socket head screw with lock washer

Bolt

Bracket for shock absorber

Wheel nut

Drive shaft

Rubber bush

Wheel bearings

Sleeve

Bolt

Washer

Shock absorber

Fig. 7.13 Exploded view of the trailing arm and spring components (Secs 8 and 9)

10 Rear suspension geometry – general

1   The rear suspension trailing arm mounting brackets are provided with elongated slots for the retaining bolts to allow for adjustment of the suspension angles.

2   The outer bracket incorporates a vertical slot for camber adjustment and the inner bracket a horizontal slot for adjustment of the rear wheel alignment (toe setting).

3   Adjustment is carried out by slackening the retaining bolts and moving the trailing arm in the desired direction to achieve the correct setting.

4   Due to the need for special gauges and equipment to carry out this adjustment it is recommended that the vehicle be taken to a VW dealer to have the work done. Adjustment should only be necessary if the trailing arm retaining bolts have been disturbed or if rear tyre wear appears to be excessive or uneven.

11 Fault diagnosis – rear suspension and driveshafts

Symptom	Reason(s)
Vibration	Wheels out of balance Defective tyre Bent or distorted driveshaft Worn constant velocity joints Worn rear wheel bearings
Noise	Worn rear wheel bearings Worn constant velocity joints
Knock or clunk on acceleration or deceleration	Worn constant velocity joints Constant velocity joint retaining bolts loose Worn wheel shaft or hub splines or retaining nut loose Worn trailing arm bushes Loose wheel nuts
Excessive bouncing or pitching on bumpy roads	Shock absorbers worn Shock absorber mounting bushes worn Rear springs weak
Excessive rear tyre wear	Rear suspension geometry incorrect Defective, out of balance or incorrectly inflated tyre

Chapter 8 Front suspension and steering

Contents

Specifications

Front suspension

Type .... Independent by upper and lower suspension arms, coil springs, telescopic shock absorbers, radius rods and anti-roll bar

Steering gear

Type .... Rack and pinion with relay gear and connecting shaft
Steering wheel turns (lock-to-lock) 3.75
Turning circle .... 9083 mm (357.6 in) between kerbs

Front suspension geometry (unladen)

Camber .... 0° ± 30′
Castor .... 7° 15′ ± 15′
Castor – maximum difference side to side .... 1°
Toe setting .... 2.0 mm ± 3.5 mm (0.078 in ± 0.13 in) toe-in

Torque wrench settings

Front suspension

	Nm	lbf ft
Upper wishbone to body	75	55
Lower track control arm to body	90	66
Shock absorber upper mounting	30	22
Shock absorber lower mounting	150	111
Upper balljoint to wishbone	55	40
Upper balljoint to steering knuckle	110	81
Lower balljoint to adaptor	110	81
Adaptor to track control arm	65	48
Radius rod to body bracket	100	74
Anti-roll bar link to radius rod	20	15
Anti-roll bar to body	20	15
Tie-rod balljoint to steering knuckle	30	22
Brake caliper to steering knuckle	160	118

Steering

	Nm	lbf ft
Steering box to body*	25	18
Relay gear to body	25	18
Two arm flange to flexible coupling disc*	20	15
Two arm flange to column, connecting shaft, or pinion*	20	15
Steering wheel to column	50	37
Steering column to body	25	18
Tie-rod inner joint to rack	70	52
Tie-rod balljoint to steering knuckle	30	22

* Always use new self-locking nuts

1 General description

The front suspension is of the independent type incorporating upper and lower suspension arms, coil springs, telescopic shock absorbers, radius rods and an anti-roll bar.

The upper suspension arm or wishbone is attached to the vehicle at its inner end by rubber bushes and a spindle which incorporates eccentric washers for camber adjustment. At its outer end the wishbone is attached to the steering knuckle by a balljoint.

The lower suspension arm or track control arm pivots at its inner end on a rubber bush and is attached at its outer end to the steering knuckle by an adaptor and balljoint. Fore and aft movement of the track control arm is controlled by a radius rod which is adjustable to provide for alterations of the castor angle. An anti-roll bar interconnects each track control arm to reduce excess body roll when cornering.

Attached to the steering knuckle is the disc brake caliper and the one piece hub and disc assembly incorporating the front wheel bearings.

The steering gear is of the rack and pinion type with adjustable tie-rods to cater for alterations to the front wheel toe setting. Movements of the steering wheel are transmitted to the steering gear via an upper and lower column, relay box and connecting shaft. Three flexible couplings and a safety coupling are used to connect the upper and lower columns and connecting shaft to the relay box and steering gear. In the event of a frontal impact the upper and lower steering columns are designed to separate at the safety coupling thus reducing the risk of injury to the driver.

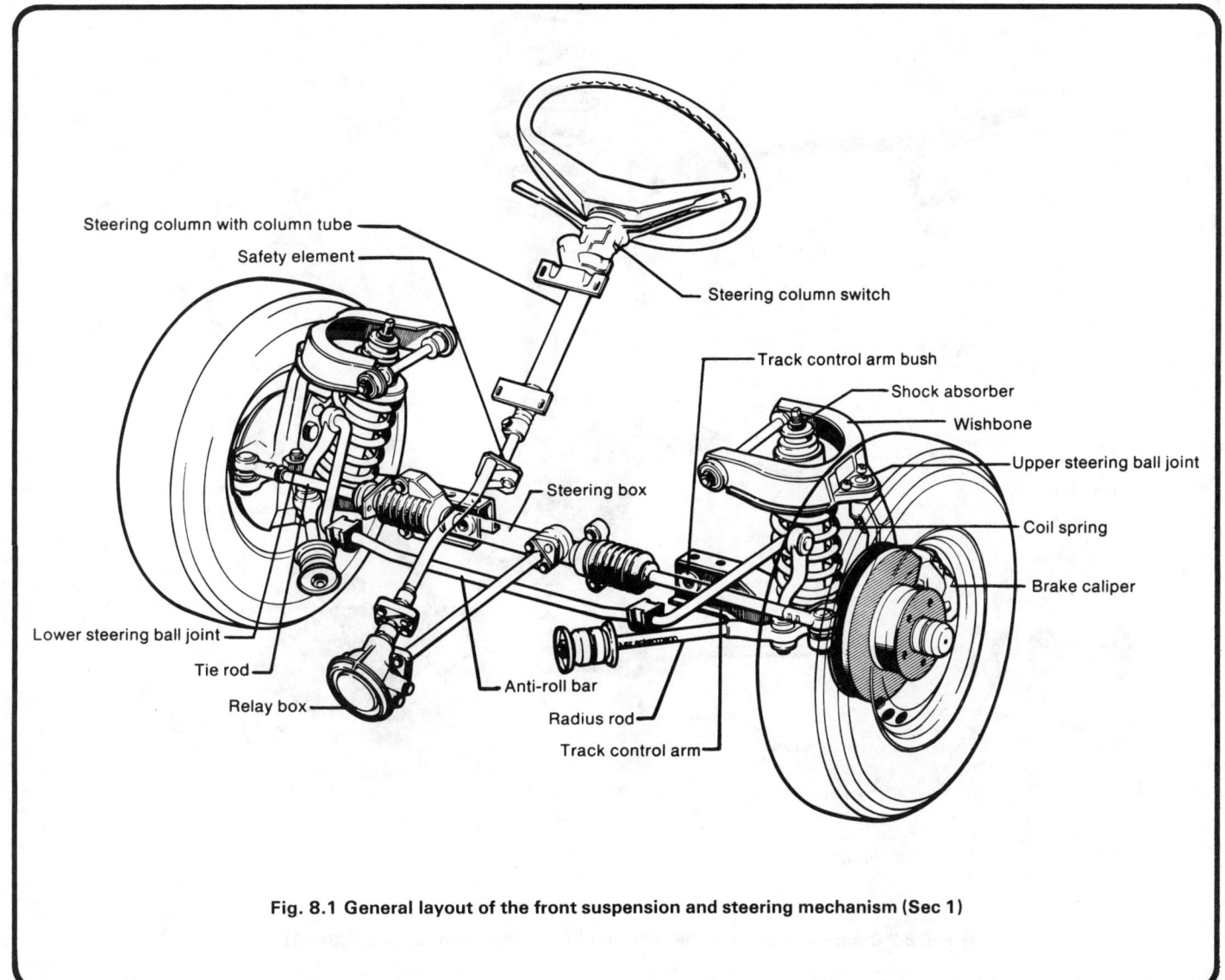

Fig. 8.1 General layout of the front suspension and steering mechanism (Sec 1)

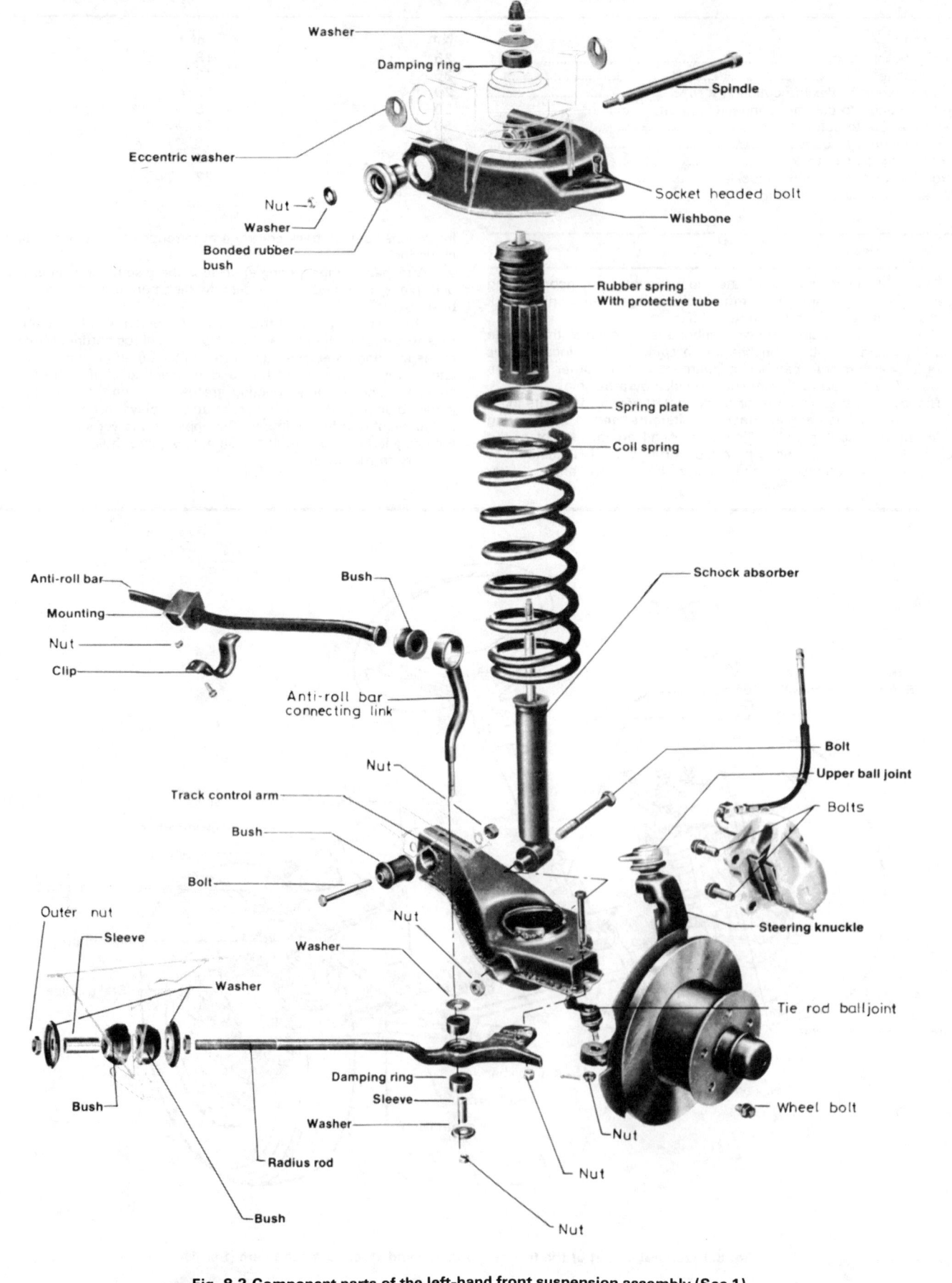

Washer

Damping ring

Spindle

Eccentric washer

Nut

Washer

Bonded rubber bush

Socket headed bolt

Wishbone

Rubber spring
With protective tube

Spring plate

Coil spring

Anti-roll bar

Bush

Schock absorber

Mounting

Nut

Clip

Anti-roll bar
connecting link

Nut

Bolt

Upper ball joint

Bolts

Track control arm

Bush

Bolt

Steering knuckle

Nut

Outer nut

Sleeve

Washer

Washer

Tie rod balljoint

Bush

Damping ring

Sleeve

Washer

Nut

Wheel bolt

Radius rod

Nut

Bush

Nut

Fig. 8.2·Component parts of the left-hand front suspension assembly (Sec 1)

2   Maintenance and inspection

1   At the intervals given in Routine Maintenance at the beginning of this manual, a thorough inspection of all steering and suspension components should be carried out using the following procedure as a guide.

2   Jack up the front of the vehicle and securely support it on axle stands.

3   Visually inspect the rubber boots on the steering knuckle balljoints and steering tie-rod balljoints for splits, chafing or deterioration. Renew the balljoint assemblies as described in Sections 6 or 13 if any damage is apparent. Carry out a similar inspection of the steering box rubber bellows and renew these as described in Section 16 if necessary.

4   Grasp the roadwheel at the '12 o'clock' and '6 o'clock' positions and try to rock it. Very slight free play should be felt, but if the movement is appreciable further investigation is necessary to determine the source. Continue rocking the wheel whilst an assistant depresses the footbrake. If the movement is now eliminated or significantly reduced, it is likely that the front hub bearings require adjustment as described in Section 3. If the free play is still evident with the footbrake depressed, then there is wear in the suspension joints or mountings. Pay close attention to the steering knuckle upper and lower balljoints and the track control arm and upper wishbone mounting bushes. Renew any worn components as described in the appropriate Sections of this Chapter.

5   Now grasp the roadwheel at the '9 o'clock' and '3 o'clock' positions and try to rock it as before. Any movement felt now may again be caused by excessive slackness in the hub bearings or by wear in the steering tie-rod outer balljoint or in the inner joint of the tie-rod itself. If the outer balljoint is worn, visual movement will be obvious. If the inner joint is suspect it can be felt by placing a hand over the steering box rubber bellows and gripping the tie-rod. If the roadwheel is now rocked again, movement will be felt at the inner joint if wear has taken place. Repair procedures are contained in Sections 13 and 15 respectively.

6   Using a large screwdriver as a lever, check for wear in the anti-roll bar and radius rod mountings by levering against these components. Some movement is to be expected as the mountings are made of rubber, but excessive wear should be obvious. Renew any bushes that are worn.

7   With the vehicle standing on its wheels, have an assistant turn the steering wheel back and forth about one eighth of a turn each way whilst the steering gear components are viewed from below. There should be no lost movement whatever between the steering wheel and the roadwheels. If this is not the case, closely observe the joints and mountings previously described, but in addition check the steering gear flexible couplings, the relay gear and connecting shafts and the steering box itself for any signs of wear or free play. Any wear should be visually apparent and must be rectified as described in the appropriate Sections of this Chapter.

8   Check for any signs of damage or fluid leakage around the shock absorber body and inspect the condition and security of the mountings. Should any fluid be noticed the shock absorber is defective internally and renewal is necessary.

9   The efficiency of the shock absorbers may be checked by bouncing the front of the vehicle at each corner. Generally speaking the body will return to its normal position and stop after being depressed. If it rises and returns on a rebound, the shock absorber is probably suspect. Further details will be found in Section 11.

3   Front hub bearings – adjustment

1   To check the adjustment of the hub bearings, jack up the front of the vehicle and support it on axle stands. Grasp the roadwheel at the '12 o'clock' and '6 o'clock' positions and try to rock it. Watch carefully for any movement in the suspension balljoints which can easily be mistaken for hub movement.

2   If the front wheel hub movement is excessive proceed as follows.

3   Remove the wheel trim and roadwheel, then by judicious tapping and levering withdraw the dust cap from the centre of the hub.

4   Using a small punch or screwdriver, tap up the peening that secures the hub retaining nut to the groove in the stub axle. **Note:** *If*

the hub nut has been peened more than twice, obtain and fit a new hub nut before proceeding with the adjustment.

5   Tighten the hub nut until it is just possible to move the thrust washer behind the nut using a screwdriver and finger pressure.

6   Spin the hub and check that it turns freely with just a trace of endfloat.

7   Peen the nut into the groove in the stub axle using a small punch and then refit the dust cap and roadwheel. Finally lower the vehicle to the ground.

4   Front hub bearings – removal and refitting

1   Jack up the front of the vehicle and support it on axle stands. Remove the wheel trim and the roadwheel.

2   Refer to Chapter 9 and remove the front disc brake pads.

3   Undo and remove the large nut securing the upper balljoint to the steering knuckle and then release the flexible brake hose support bracket from the ball-pin.

4   Undo and remove the two brake caliper retaining bolts, withdraw the caliper complete with brake hose and pipe from the steering knuckle and tie it up out of the way using string or wire. Avoid placing undue strain on the flexible hose and brake pipe.

5   By judicious tapping and levering withdraw the dust cap from the centre of the hub.

6   Using a small punch or screwdriver, tap up the peening that secures the hub retaining nut to the groove in the stub axle. Now undo and remove the hub nut. **Note:** *If the hub nut has been peened more than twice it will be necessary to obtain a new nut before refitting.*

7   Carefully slide the complete hub and disc assembly off the stub axle. Take care to hold the outer bearing and thrust washer in place as the hub is withdrawn otherwise they will fall out.

8   With the hub assembly on the bench, lift out the thrust washer and the outer bearing.

9   Turn the hub over and using a large screwdriver as a lever, extract the inner oil seal. Note that a new seal must be used when refitting.

10   Lift out the inner bearing and then support the hub assembly on blocks of wood. Using a tapered drift inserted through the centre of the hub, drive out the outer bearing outer race. Now turn the hub over again and remove the inner bearing outer race in the same way (photo).

4.10 Remove the hub inner bearing outer race with a drift inserted through the centre of the hub

11   Thoroughly wash all the parts in paraffin and wipe dry using a lint free cloth.

12   Inspect the bearing rollers and their outer races for signs of rusting, pitting, scoring or overheating and if evident obtain a new set of bearings.

13   Inspect the oil seal journal face of the stub axle for signs of damage or grooving. Any slight grooving may be polished out with fine

emery tape, but if the grooving is very bad a new steering knuckle assembly will be required. On later models the oil seal journal ring is manufactured as a separate component and pressed onto the stub axle. In this case it will only be necessary to renew the ring and not the complete steering knuckle in the event of damage or grooving to the journal face. Note that models with renewable oil seal journal rings are also equipped with modified oil seals. Bear this in mind when ordering new parts.

14 To reassemble the bearings carefully drift the new outer races into position using a tube or large socket of suitable diameter. Make sure that they are fitted with their larger diameters facing outward and driven fully home until they contact the register in the hub.

15 Pack the space between the bearings in the hub and also the bearings themselves with multi-purpose grease (photo).

16 Place the inner bearing in position in the hub. Fill the space between the two sealing lips of a new oil seal with grease and lay the seal on the hub with the open face toward the bearing. Using a block

of wood tap the seal into position until it is flush with the hub flange (photos).

17 Refit the hub assembly to the stub axle and push it on as far as it will go. Slide on the outer bearing followed by the thrust washer and hub nut (photos).

18 Tighten the hub nut whilst spinning the hub and continue tightening until the hub becomes stiff to turn.

19 Now back off the nut until the hub turns easily again. Slowly tighten the hub nut once more until the thrust washer can just be moved using a screwdriver and finger pressure.

20 Peen the flange of the hub nut into the groove in the stub axle and then refit the dust cap (photo).

21 Place the brake caliper over the disc and refit the two retaining bolts. Tighten the bolts to the specified torque.

22 Engage the brake flexible hose support bracket with the upper balljoint and refit the retaining nut. Tighten the nut to the specified torque.

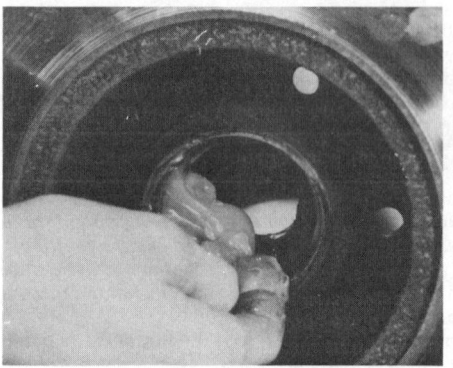

4.15 Pack the space between the bearings in the hub with multi-purpose grease

4.16A Place the inner bearing in position ...

4.16B ... lay the oil seal on the hub with the open side toward the bearing ...

4.16C ... and then tap the seal home using a block of wood

4.17A Refit the hub assembly to the stub axle ...

4.17B ... slide on the outer bearing ...

4.17C ... followed by the thrust washer and hub nut

4.20 The hub nut is retained by peening the flange into the groove in the stub axle

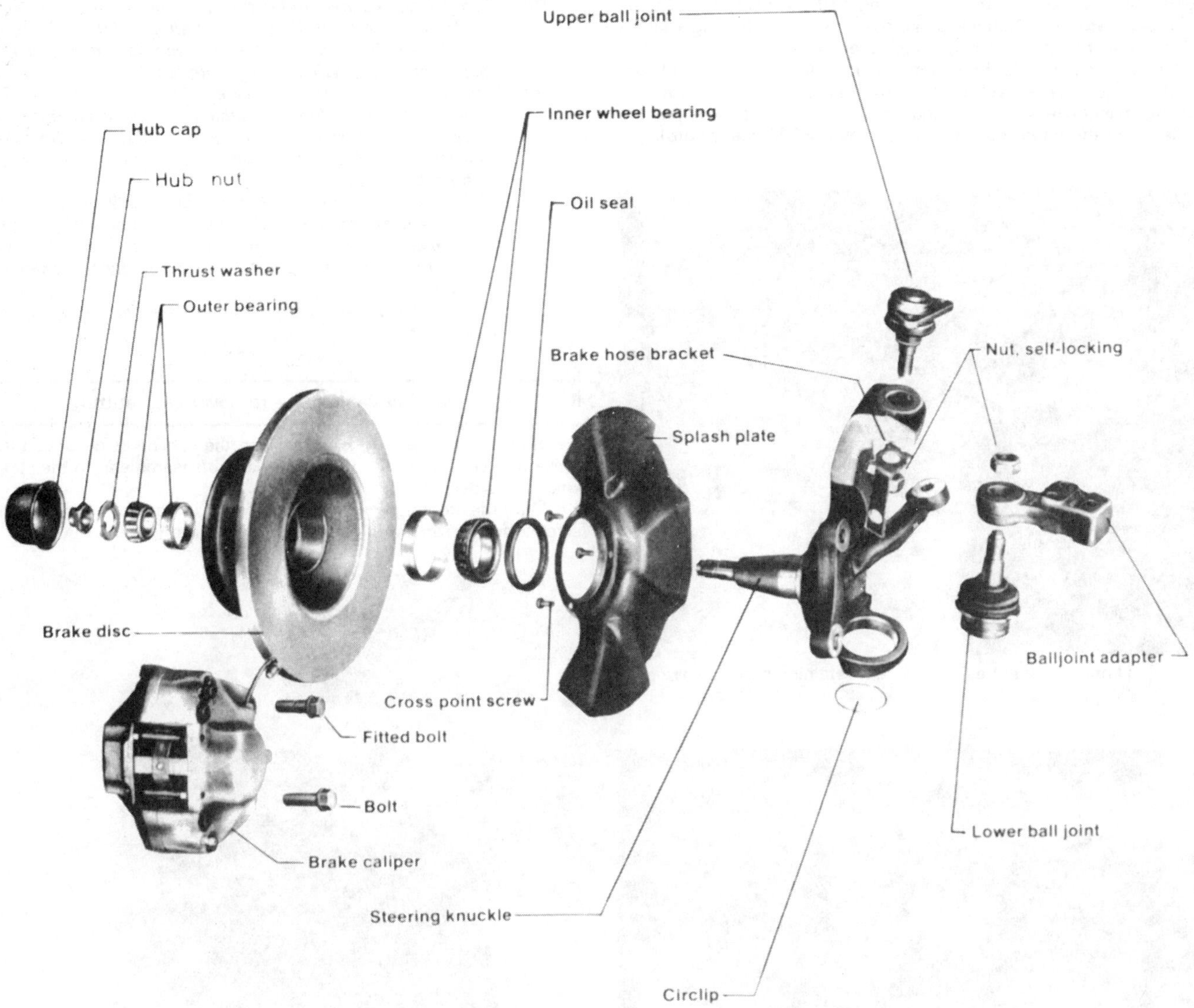

Upper ball joint

Inner wheel bearing

Hub cap

Hub nut

Oil seal

Thrust washer

Outer bearing

Brake hose bracket

Nut, self-locking

Splash plate

Balljoint adapter

Brake disc

Cross point screw

Fitted bolt

Bolt

Brake caliper

Lower ball joint

Steering knuckle

Circlip

Fig. 8.3 Exploded view of the front hub bearings and steering knuckle assembly (Sec 4)

Fig. 8.4 The front hub bearings are correctly adjusted when it is just possible to move the thrust washer using a screwdriver and finger pressure (Sec 4)

23 Refit the brake pads using the procedure described in Chapter 9 and then refit the roadwheel and wheel trim. Make sure that there is at least 25.4 mm (1.0 in) clearance between the roadwheel and the brake hose when the steering is turned to full right or left lock. If necessary bend the support bracket slightly to achieve this clearance.
24 Finally lower the vehicle to the ground.

5 Steering knuckle – removal and refitting

1 Jack up the front of the vehicle and support it on axle stands. Remove the wheel trim and the roadwheel.
2 Refer to Chapter 9 and remove the front disc brake pads.
3 Undo and remove the large nut securing the upper balljoint to the steering knuckle and then release the flexible brake hose support bracket from the ball-pin.
4 Undo and remove the two brake caliper retaining bolts, withdraw the caliper complete with brake hose and pipe from the steering knuckle and tie it up out of the way using string or wire. Avoid placing any excessive strain on the flexible hose or brake pipe.
5 Extract the split pin and then undo and remove the nut securing the steering tie-rod balljoint to the steering knuckle arm. Release the

balljoint tapered shank from the steering knuckle using a universal balljoint separator. Alternatively strike the side of the steering knuckle arm using two hammers to shock the taper free.

6   Undo and remove the three bolts and locknuts securing the lower balljoint adaptor to the track control arm and radius rod (photo).

7   Using a suitable key undo and remove the two socket headed bolts securing the upper balljoint to the upper wishbone (photo).

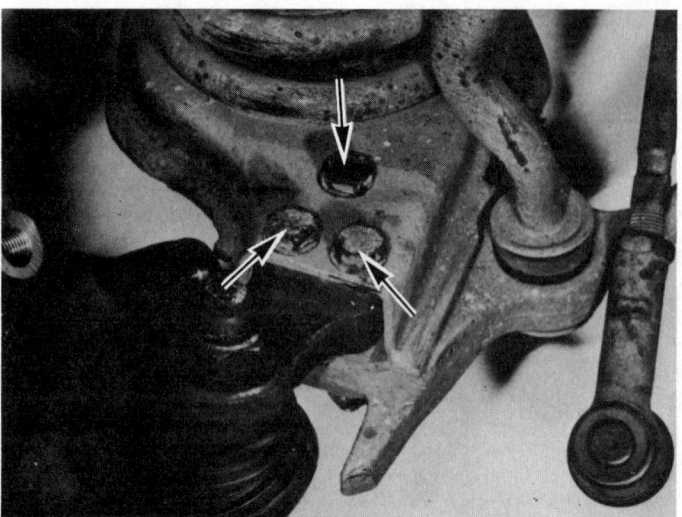

5.6 Steering knuckle lower balljoint adaptor retaining bolts (arrowed)

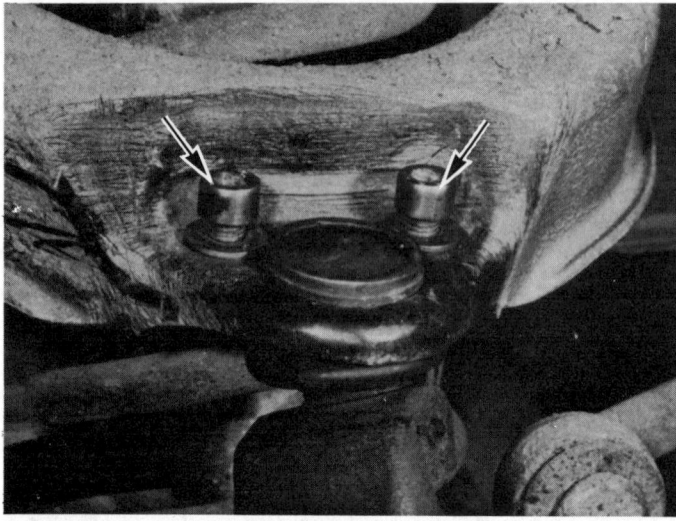

5.7 The steering knuckle upper balljoint is secured to the wishbone with two socket headed bolts (arrowed)

8   If working on the left-hand side knuckle, release the retaining ring and withdraw the speedometer cable from the rubber sleeve in the knuckle.

9   Lift up the upper wishbone slightly to release it from the balljoint and then withdraw the steering knuckle assembly complete with hub and balljoints from the front suspension.

10   If it is wished to completely dismantle the steering knuckle, the hub assembly and the balljoints may be removed using the procedures described in the appropriate Sections of this Chapter.

11   Refitting the steering knuckle is the reverse sequence to removal bearing in mind the following points:

(a)   Tighten all retaining nuts and bolts to the specified torque where applicable

(b)   Fit a spring washer under the head of each lower balljoint adaptor retaining bolt if one is not already fitted. If a washer is not used the bolt heads may become embedded in the track control arm when fully tightened.

(c)   If the left-hand steering knuckle was removed a new rubber sleeve for the speedometer cable must be fitted and pushed in as far as possible using a suitable tool. Smear the speedometer cable with jointing compound before inserting it in the rubber sleeve

(d)   After refitting ensure that there is at least 25.4 mm (1.0 in) clearance between the roadwheel and the brake flexible hose when the steering is turned to full right or left lock. If necessary bend the support bracket slightly to achieve this clearance

(e)   Always use a new split pin to secure the tie-rod balljoint retaining nut

6   Steering knuckle balljoints – removal and refitting

1   Remove the steering knuckle from the vehicle as described in the previous Section and then remove the hub assembly from the steering knuckle as described in Section 4.

2   With the steering knuckle on the bench undo and remove the three screws and lift off the brake disc splash plate (photo).

6.2 Removing the brake disc splash plate from the steering knuckle

3   To remove the upper balljoint, undo and remove the retaining nut and then release the balljoint tapered shank from the steering knuckle using VW tool No 267A. If this tool cannot be obtained it may be possible to shock the taper free by striking the steering knuckle flange with a medium hammer whilst resting the knuckle on a solid steel or iron block (photo). Once the taper is released the balljoint can be lifted away.

4   Removal of the lower balljoint is a little more difficult. A press will be required and also in this case VW tool 267A is essential. The procedure is as follows.

5   First undo and remove the nut securing the balljoint to the balljoint adaptor. Using tool 267A release the adaptor from the tapered shank of the balljoint.

6   Using a small screwdriver extract the circlip from its groove in the lower body of the balljoint.

7   Support the flange of the steering knuckle on the press bed using suitable tubing or the VW tools shown in Fig. 8.6. Now press the joint out of the knuckle.

8   With the balljoints removed inspect the rubber boots for damage or deterioration and check the joints for excessive free play. Individual parts are not available separately, therefore if the rubber boot is damaged or the joint is worn a complete balljoint must be obtained.

9   Refitting the balljoints is basically the reverse of the removal

6.3 Using a hammer and steel block to free the upper balljoint shank from the steering knuckle

sequence. In the case of the lower balljoint make sure that it is fitted with the flat side of the shoulder towards the stub axle. Press the joint fully home and ensure that the circlip seats fully into its groove. Do not tighten the adaptor retaining nut until the steering knuckle has been refitted otherwise the rubber boot may be damaged.

10 Refitting the hub assembly and steering knuckle is a straightforward reverse of the removal procedure described in Sections 4 and 5 respectively.

7 Radius rod – removal and refitting

1 Jack up the front of the vehicle and support it on axle stands.
2 Undo and remove the nut securing the anti-roll bar connecting link to the radius rod. Lift off the lower shouldered washer and rubber damping ring.
3 Undo and remove the outer nut securing the radius rod to the body mounted bracket (photo). Take care not to disturb the position of the inner nut otherwise the castor angle setting will be disturbed (photo). Lift off the large shouldered washer and the rubber bush.
4 Undo and remove the three nuts securing the radius rod to the track control arm. Pull the radius rod down to release it from the anti-roll bar connecting link and then withdraw it rearwards out of the front

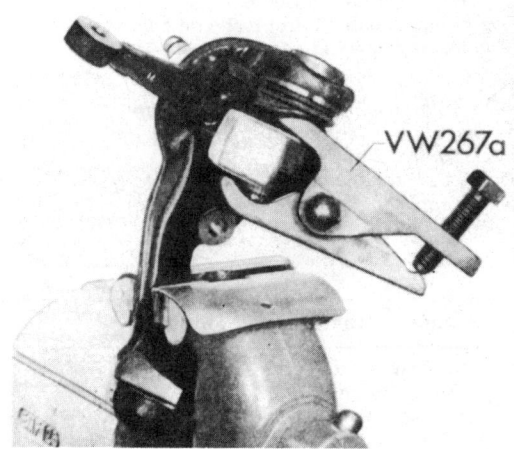

Fig. 8.5 Using VW special tool to remove adaptor from lower balljoint (Sec 6)

7.3A Radius rod outer retaining nut, shouldered washer and rubber bush

Fig. 8.6 Using a press and VW special tools to remove the lower balljoint from the steering knuckle (Sec 6)

7.3B The radius rod inner nut must not be disturbed otherwise the castor angle will be affected

mounting bracket. Recover the steel sleeves, washers and bushes from the front of the radius rod and the anti-roll bar link attachment. **Note:** *If the radius rod is to be renewed or if it is necessary to remove the remaining front mounting nut, mark its position on the radius rod before doing so. This can then be used as a guide to its approximate position when refitting.*

5   Refitting the radius rod is the reverse sequence to removal bearing in mind the following points:

(a) *Renew the front mounting rubber bushes and anti-roll bar connecting link damping rings if they show signs of deterioration or compression damage*
(b) *All shouldered washers must be fitted with their shoulders facing away from the appropriate rubber bush or damping ring*
(c) *Tighten all retaining nuts and bolts to the specified torque*
(d) *If a new radius rod has been fitted or if the position of the front mounting inner nut has been altered the front suspension geometry and wheel alignment should be checked by a VW dealer (see Section 22)*

8 Anti-roll bar – removal and refitting

1   Jack up the front of the vehicle and support it on axle stands. Remove the wheel trim and both front roadwheels.
2   Undo and remove the nuts securing the two anti-roll bar connecting links to the radius rods. Lift off the shouldered washers and the lower rubber damping rings (photo).
3   Swivel the anti-roll bar upwards to release the connecting links from the radius rods and recover the steel sleeve, upper damping ring and shouldered washer from each link.
4   Undo and remove the two nuts and bolts each side securing the anti-roll bar mounting clips to the chassis members (photo). Rotate the anti-roll bar to clear the steering tie-rod and withdraw the bar from under the front of the vehicle.
5   With the anti-roll bar removed slip off the two split mounting bushes from the centre of the bar and the two connecting links from each end.
6   Inspect the bushes and connecting link damping rings for deterioration of the rubber and renew as necessary.
7   Refitting the anti-roll bar is the reverse sequence to removal bearing in mind the following points:

(a) *The connecting link shouldered washers must be fitted with their shoulders facing away from the damping rings*
(b) *Tighten all retaining nuts and bolts to the specified torque*

9 Track control arm – removal and refitting

1   Begin by removing the radius rod using the procedure described in Section 7.
2   Extract the split pin and undo and remove the nut securing the steering tie-rod balljoint to the steering knuckle arm. Release the balljoint tapered shank from the steering knuckle using a universal

balljoint separator. Alternatively strike the side of the steering knuckle arm using two hammers to shock the taper free.
3   Place a jack beneath the track control arm and raise the arm slightly.
4   Undo and remove the long through bolt and nut securing the shock absorber lower mounting to the track control arm. Use a long tapered drift or suitable round bar to tap the bolt out of its location in the arm.
5   Using a suitable key undo and remove the two socket headed bolts securing the steering knuckle upper balljoint to the wishbone.
6   Support the steering knuckle and hub assembly to avoid straining the flexible brake hose or speedometer cable (where applicable). Now slowly lower the jack beneath the track control arm until all tension is released from the coil spring.
7   Undo and remove the nut, bolt and spring washer securing the track control arm inner mounting to the chassis member. Using a stout screwdriver lever the arm out of its mounting location (photo).
8   Lower the jack fully and then draw the track control arm towards the centre of the vehicle until it is clear of the lower balljoint adaptor which locates in the centre of the arm. Now lift away the track control arm and take out the coil spring complete with upper spring plate.
9   Temporarily refit the steering knuckle upper balljoint to the wishbone using the two socket headed bolts.
10   With the track control arm removed carefully inspect the inner mounting for signs of damage or deterioration of the rubber. If renewal is necessary the mounting may be removed using tubes of suitable diameter and a press or wide opening vice. Coat the new mounting with liquid detergent to aid refitting.
11   Refitting the track control arm is the reverse sequence to removal bearing in mind the following points:

(a) *When refitting the coil spring ensure that the upper spring plate is in position and that the straight end of the spring is at the bottom, correctly engaged in the depression in the track control arm*
(b) *Tighten all retaining nuts and bolts to the specified torque where applicable and use a new split pin to secure the tie-rod balljoint nut*

10 Upper wishbone – removal and refitting

1   Jack up the front of the vehicle and support it on axle stands. Remove the wheel trim and the front roadwheel.
2   Using a suitable key undo and remove the two socket headed bolts securing the steering knuckle upper balljoint to the wishbone (photo). Lift the wishbone slightly and carefully move the steering knuckle to one side.
3   Undo and remove the wishbone spindle retaining nut and washer and recover the eccentric washer. Now slide out the spindle and recover the second eccentric washer.
4   Ease the wishbone out of its mounting location and remove it from the vehicle.
5   Inspect the bonded rubber bushes in the wishbone and renew them if they show signs of damage or deterioration. If renewal of the

8.2 Anti-roll bar connecting link to radius rod mounting (arrowed)

8.4 Anti-roll bar to chassis member mounting

9.7 Track control arm inner mounting

10.2 Upper wishbone to balljoint retaining bolts (A) and spindle retaining nut (B)

11.3 Shock absorber upper domed retaining nut, locknut, washer and damping ring assembly (arrowed)

bushes is necessary this work must be carried out by a VW dealer. The bush casings are spot welded in position to prevent them turning in the wishbone. Before the bushes can be removed the spot welds must be carefully ground off allowing the bushes to be pressed out. After refitting, the new bushes must also be spot welded in place.

6   To refit the wishbone position it over its mounting location and then slide one of the eccentric washers onto the spindle. Install the spindle ensuring that the flat side is vertical and facing toward the centre of the vehicle. Position the eccentric washer with the larger space downwards.

7   Fit the second eccentric washer also with the larger space downward followed by the plain washer and retaining nut. Tighten the nut to the specified torque.

8   Position the steering knuckle upper balljoint in the hole in the wishbone and secure with the two socket headed bolts. Again observe the correct torque setting.

9   Finally refit the roadwheel and wheel trim then lower the vehicle to the ground.

10   It will be necessary to have the front suspension geometry and wheel alignment checked by a VW dealer (see Section 22). The two eccentric washers determine the suspension camber angle setting and this must always be reset if the position of the washers is disturbed.

11 Front shock absorber – removal and refitting

1   Jack up the front of the vehicle and support it on axle stands. Remove the wheel trim and the front roadwheel.

2   Place a jack beneath the track control arm, but clear of the shock absorber lower mounting, and then raise the arm slightly.

3   Undo and remove the shock absorber upper domed retaining nut followed by the locknut. Lift off the washer and rubber damping ring (photo).

4   Now undo and remove the long through bolt and nut securing the shock absorber to the track control arm (photo).

5   Withdraw the shock absorber and rubber spring down through the centre of the track control arm and remove it from the vehicle.

6   With the unit removed hold it in an upright position and fully extend and compress it several times. The shock absorber should operate with a smooth even pressure, free from dead areas, over the whole stroke. If this is not the case the shock absorber must be renewed. It must also be renewed if there is any damage or deterioration of the chrome on the piston rod or if there is evidence of excessive fluid loss. Shock absorbers may be renewed individually if they become defective early in their service life. It is advisable to renew them in pairs if they have been in service for more than 30 000 miles (48 000 km). There are quite a number of different types of shock absorbers available for Transporter models and their derivatives, and care must be taken to ensure that compatible types are fitted.

11.4 The shock absorber lower mounting bolt and nut is accessible from either side of the track control arm

7   Refitting the shock absorber to the vehicle is the reverse sequence to removal. Ensure that the mounting nuts and bolts are tightened to the specified torque.

12 Coil spring – removal and refitting

1   Removal of the front coil spring necessitates removal of the track control arm also, and details of both these operations will be found in Section 9.

13 Steering tie-rod balljoint – removal and refitting

1   Jack up the front of the vehicle and support it on axle stands. Remove the wheel trim and the front roadwheel.

2   Slacken the locknut that secures the steering tie-rod to the balljoint by an eighth of a turn only.

3   Extract the split pin and then undo and remove the nut securing the balljoint to the steering knuckle arm. Release the balljoint tapered shank from the steering knuckle using a universal balljoint separator (photos). Alternatively strike the side of the steering knuckle arm using two hammers to shock the taper free.

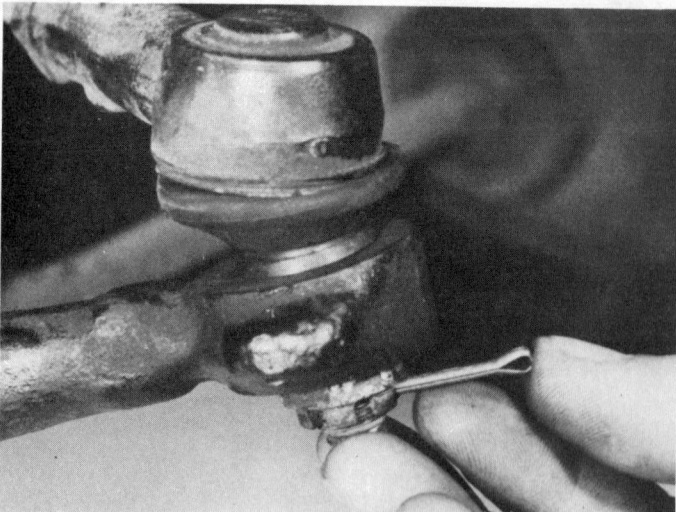

13.3A Remove the split pin and locknut ...

the right-hand steering tie-rod balljoint to the steering knuckle arm. Release the balljoint tapered shank from the steering knuckle using a universal balljoint separator. Alternatively strike the side of the steering knuckle arm using two hammers to shock the taper free. Now repeat this procedure for the left-hand tie-rod balljoint.

3   Undo and remove the two bolts and locknuts securing the flange of the pinion shaft to the steering box flexible coupling disc (photo).

4   Undo and remove the four nuts, bolts and washers securing the steering box to the chassis crossmember (photo). Lower the box to the ground and withdraw it from under the vehicle.

5   With the steering box removed inspect the four rubber mounting bushes for damage or deterioration and renew as necessary. The bushes may be removed using a press or wide opening vice and a suitable mandrel and tube. The new bushes are fitted in the same way ensuring that the flat sides of the bushes are vertical with the steering box held in its fitted position. Lubricate the bushes in liquid detergent to aid refitting.

6   The removal and refitting of the rubber bellows and tie-rods are described in the following Sections.

7   Refitting the steering box is the reverse sequence to removal. Ensure that all retaining nuts and bolts are tightened to the specified torque and use new split pins in the tie-rod balljoint nuts.

13.3B ... then release the tie-rod balljoint using a universal balljoint separator

14.3 Steering box pinion flange to coupling disc retaining bolts (arrowed)

4   The balljoint can now be unscrewed from the steering tie-rod.

5   Refitting is the reverse sequence to removal. If the position of the locknut on the tie-rod was only disturbed by an eighth of a turn as described, then after refitting, the front wheel alignment should still be approximately correct. It is advisable however to have the setting checked accurately as soon as possible (see Section 22).

6   Make sure that the balljoint locknut and retaining nut are tightened to the specified torque and in the case of the retaining nut, aligned to the next split pin hole. Always use a new split pin to secure the nut.

14 Steering box – removal and refitting

The rack and pinion steering box is non-adjustable and apart from the tie-rods and rubber bellows, cannot be dismantled for repair or overhaul. Should the steering box become damaged or excessively worn it will be necessary to obtain a factory exchange unit from a VW dealer. The removal and refitting procedures are as follows.

1   Jack up the front of the vehicle and support it on axle stands. Remove the wheel trim and both front roadwheels.

2   Extract the split pin and then undo and remove the nut securing

14.4 Steering box to crossmember retaining bolts (arrowed)

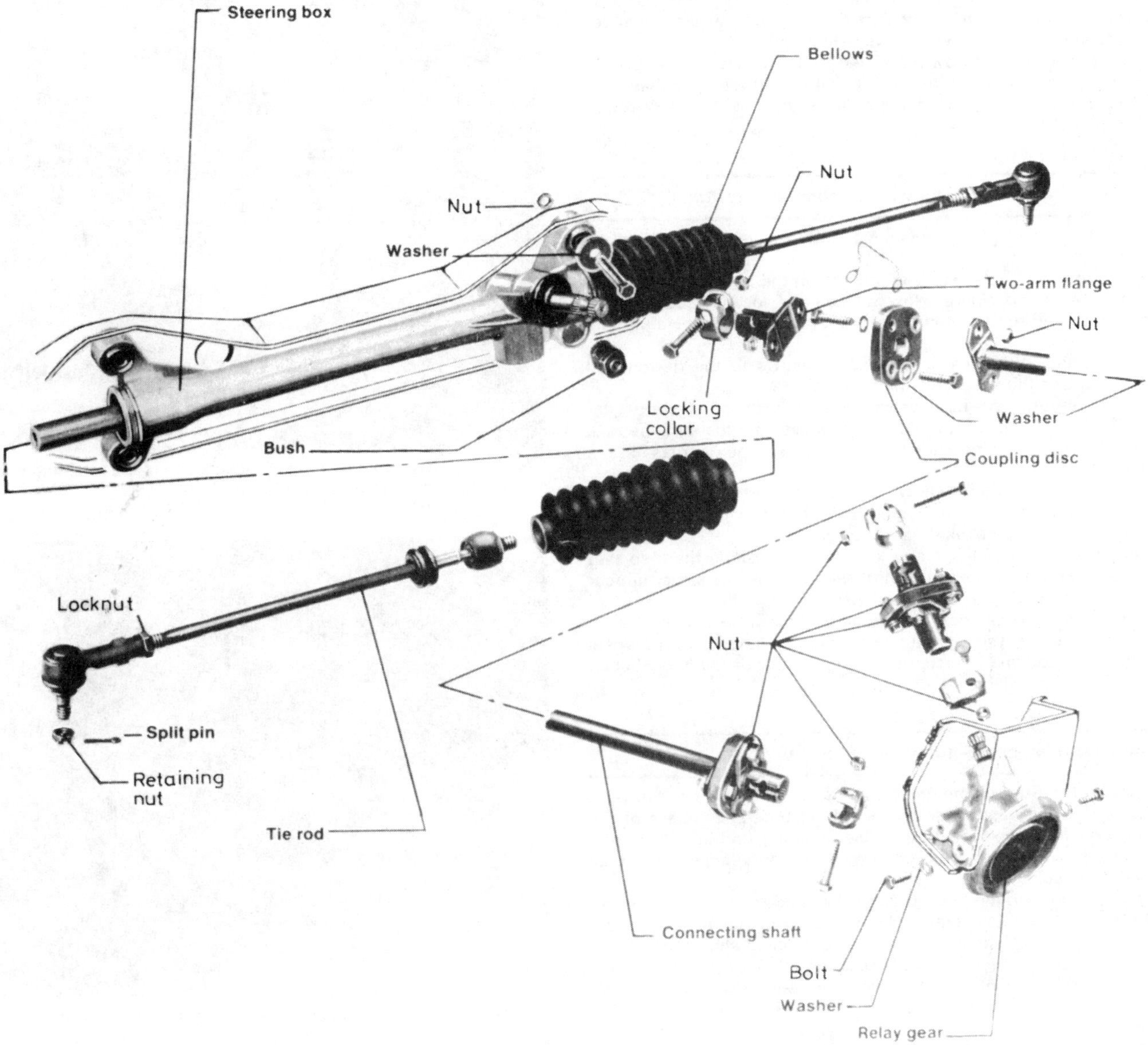

Steering box

Bellows

Nut

Nut

Washer

Two-arm flange

Nut

Washer

Bush

Coupling disc

Locking collar

Locknut

Nut

Split pin

Retaining nut

Tie rod

Connecting shaft

Bolt

Washer

Relay gear

Fig. 8.7 Exploded view of the steering gear components (Secs 14 to 18)

15 Steering tie-rod – removal and refitting

1   Begin by removing the steering box from the vehicle as described in the previous Section.

2   Count the number of exposed threads on the end of the tie-rod and make a note of this figure. Now slacken the locknut securing the balljoint to the tie-rod and unscrew the balljoint, followed by the nut.

3   Release the wire clips securing the rubber bellows to the tie-rod and steering box and then slide off the bellows.

4   Using a small punch tap back the flange of the tie-rod inner joint at the point where it is peened into the groove in the end of the rack.

5   Using a large spanner engaged with the flats on the inner joint, unscrew the joint and tie-rod assembly from the rack.

6   Before refitting, obtain a tin of steering gear grease from a VW dealer and liberally lubricate the teeth of the rack and the tie-rod inner joint. Do not use any other type of grease in the steering box.

7   Refit the tie-rod onto the end of the rack and tighten the inner joint to the specified torque. Peen the flange of the joint into the groove in the rack to lock the assembly in place.

8   Slide the rubber bellows over the tie-rod and into position over the end of the steering box. Secure the bellows with new retaining clips or alternatively use soft iron wire.

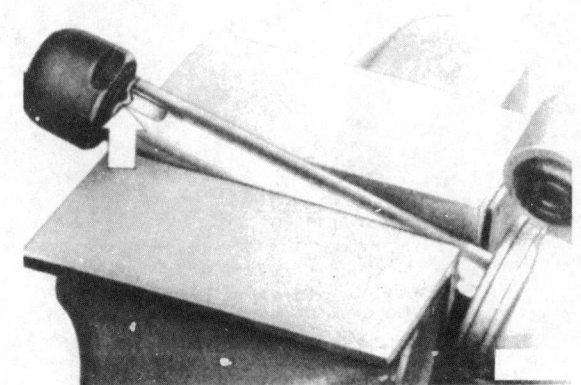

Fig. 8.8 The steering tie-rod inner joint flange is peened into a groove in the rack (Sec 15)

9   Refit the tie-rod balljoint and locknut and position them so that when the locknut is tightened against the balljoint, the same number of threads are exposed as was previously noted.

10 The steering box can now be refitted to the vehicle as described in the previous Section. After refitting it will be necessary to have the front wheel alignment checked and if necessary reset by a VW dealer (see Section 22).

16 Steering box rubber bellows – removal and refitting

1   Begin by removing the steering box from the vehicle as described in Section 14.

2   Count the number of exposed threads on the steering tie-rod and make a note of this figure. Now slacken the locknut securing the balljoint to the tie-rod and then unscrew the balljoint, followed by the nut.

3   Release the wire clips securing the bellows to the tie-rod and steering box and then slide off the bellows.

4   Before refitting the new bellows obtain a tin of steering gear grease from a VW dealer and liberally lubricate the teeth of the rack and the tie-rod inner joint. Do not use any other type of grease in the steering box.

5   Slide the new rubber bellows over the tie-rod and into position over the end of the steering box. Secure the bellows with new retaining clips or alternatively use soft iron wire.

6   Refit the tie-rod balljoint and locknut and position them so that when the locknut is tightened against the balljoint, the same number of threads are exposed as was previously noted.

7   The steering box can now be refitted to the vehicle as described in Section 14. After refitting it will be necessary to have the front wheel alignment checked and if necessary reset by a VW dealer (see Section 22).

17 Steering relay gear – removal and refitting

1   Jack up the front of the vehicle and support it on axle stands.

2   From inside the cab, slide up the rubber boot at the base of the steering column to expose the flexible coupling (photo). Undo and remove the two nuts and bolts securing the two arm flange of the relay gear to the coupling disc.

3   From underneath the front of the vehicle undo and remove the two bolts securing the relay gear lower two arm flange to the flexible coupling disc at the forward end of the connecting shaft (photo).

4   Undo and remove the four bolts securing the relay gear to its body mounting bracket (photo). Manipulate the relay gear to clear the brackets and chassis member and remove the unit from under the vehicle.

5   The relay gear cannot be dismantled for repair or overhaul but it can be lubricated using special steering gear grease, obtainable from

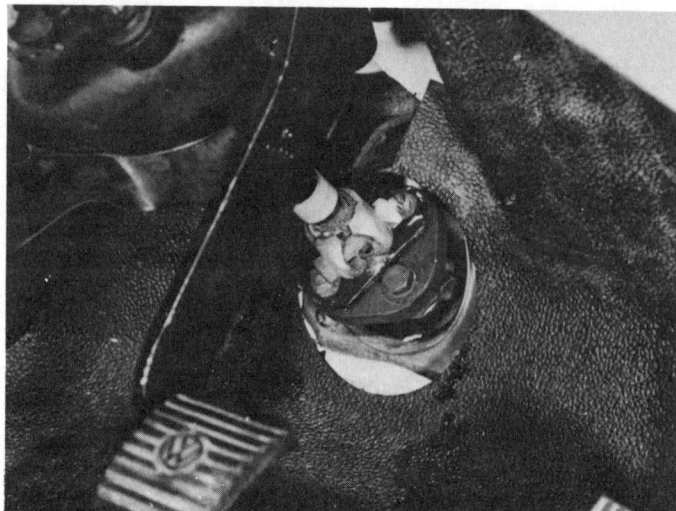

17.2 Steering column to relay gear flexible coupling

17.3 Relay gear two arm flange to flexible coupling retaining bolts (A) and left-hand side mounting bolts (B)

17.4 Relay gear right-hand side mounting bolts (arrowed)

a VW dealer. Lubrication is only necessary if the unit exhibits tight areas or becomes stiff to turn.

6   If it is necessary to remove the two arm flanges from the splined shafts, mark their positions before removal and refit them in the same place.

7   Refitting the relay gear is the reverse sequence to removal. Tighten all retaining nuts and bolts to the specified torque as shown in the Specifications.

18 Steering gear flexible couplings – removal and refitting

Three flexible couplings are used in the steering mechanism of Transporter models, two of which are located between the relay gear and steering box and one at the base of the steering column. Periodically the rubber coupling disc should be inspected for wear or deterioration of the rubber and renewed if at all suspect. The removal and refitting procedure is the same for all three couplings and is as follows.

1   Undo and remove the four nuts and bolts securing the coupling disc to each of the two armed flanges and lift out the disc with steel plate where fitted.

2   Carefully inspect the coupling disc for splits, cracks, swelling or other deformity of the rubber and renew the disc if any of these conditions are present.

3   If it is necessary to remove the two arm flanges from their splined shafts, mark their positions on the shafts accurately first, so that they may be refitted in the same place. If this is not done the actual steering of the vehicle will not be affected, but the steering wheel spokes will no longer be horizontal when the vehicle is travelling in a straight line. This will also affect the cancelling of the turn signal indicators and the operation of the steering lock.

4   Refitting the steering gear flexible couplings is the reverse sequence to removal bearing in mind the previously mentioned points. Ensure also that the retaining bolts and nuts are tightened to the correct specified torque.

19 Steering wheel – removal and refitting

1   Disconnect the battery earth terminal.
2   Carefully prise up the horn push cap from the centre of the steering wheel and disconnect the two wiring terminals (photo).
3   Using a suitable socket undo and remove the nut securing the steering wheel to the upper column.
4   Accurately mark the position of the steering wheel in relation to the upper column using a dab of quick drying paint.
5   Strike the underside of the steering wheel spokes using the palm of one hand until the wheel is released from the column. Hold the wheel with your other hand while doing this to prevent the steering wheel flying off.
6   Refitting is the reverse sequence to removal. Make sure that the previously made marks are aligned and tighten the retaining nut to the specified torque.

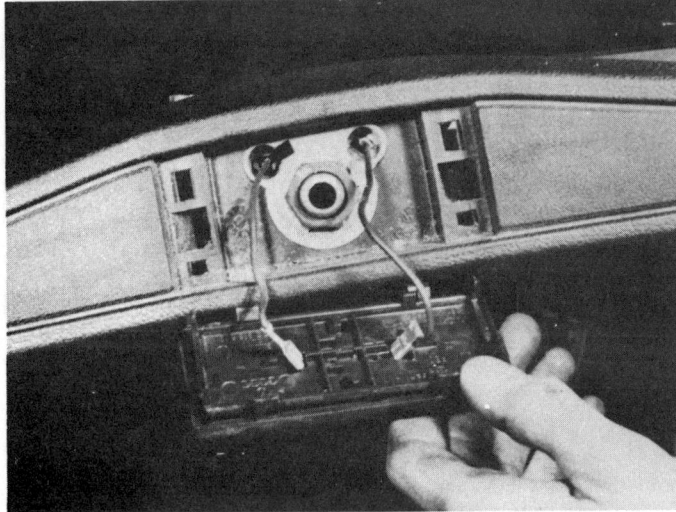

19.2 Carefully prise up the horn push and disconnect the wiring terminals to gain access to the steering wheel retaining nut

20 Steering column – removal and refitting

1   Begin by disconnecting the battery earth terminal.
2   Undo and remove the two screws securing the steering column upper and lower cowls to the column. Lift off the cowls noting that an internal retaining clip is also used to retain the lower cowl to the column (photo).
3   Disconnect the wiring harness connectors at the ignition/starter switch and multi-function switch. Place the harnesses to one side.
4   At the base of the steering column slide up the rubber boot to expose the flexible coupling. Undo and remove the locking collar clamp bolt and nut that secures the splined end of the lower column in the two arm flange of the coupling.
5   Now disconnect the earth lead that connects the two components of the safety coupling (photo).
6   Slide the lower column upwards to disengage its lower end from the flexible coupling and its upper end from the safety coupling. Place the lower column to one side.
7   Centre punch the heads of the two shear bolts that secure the

20.2 Removing the steering column cowls

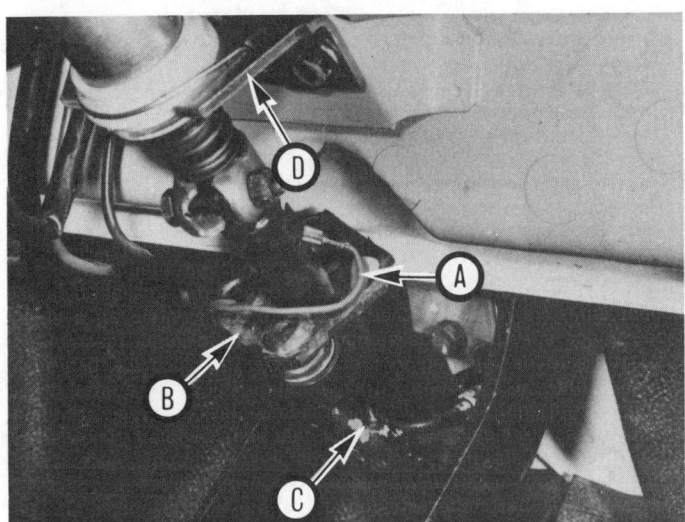

20.5 Steering column safety coupling and lower mounting

A   Earth lead
B   Safety coupling
C   Lower column
D   Column tube lower mounting
    bracket

upper column to the facia. Drill a suitable hole in the centre of each bolt and remove them using a stud extractor. Alternatively file a slot in their exposed shanks and try unscrewing them with a screwdriver. It may even be possible to free them using a pair of self-locking grips. It will of course be necessary to use new shear bolts when refitting.
8   Finally release the wire retaining clip securing the plastic ring to the lower mounting bracket and lift the column assembly away.
9   Refitting the steering column is the reverse sequence to removal bearing in mind the following points:

(a)   When refitting the lower column ensure that the roadwheels are in the straight-ahead position with the steering wheel spokes horizontal before engaging the lower column with the flexible coupling flange
(b)   Ensure that a gap of between 2 to 4 mm (0.07 to 0.15 in) exists between the steering wheel and multi-function switch before tightening the shear bolts. Ensure that the prongs of the lower column flange are fully seated in the safety coupling when taking this measurement
(c)   After setting the steering wheel clearance as described above, tighten the shear bolts until the heads break off
(d)   Tighten all remaining nuts and bolts to the specified torque where applicable

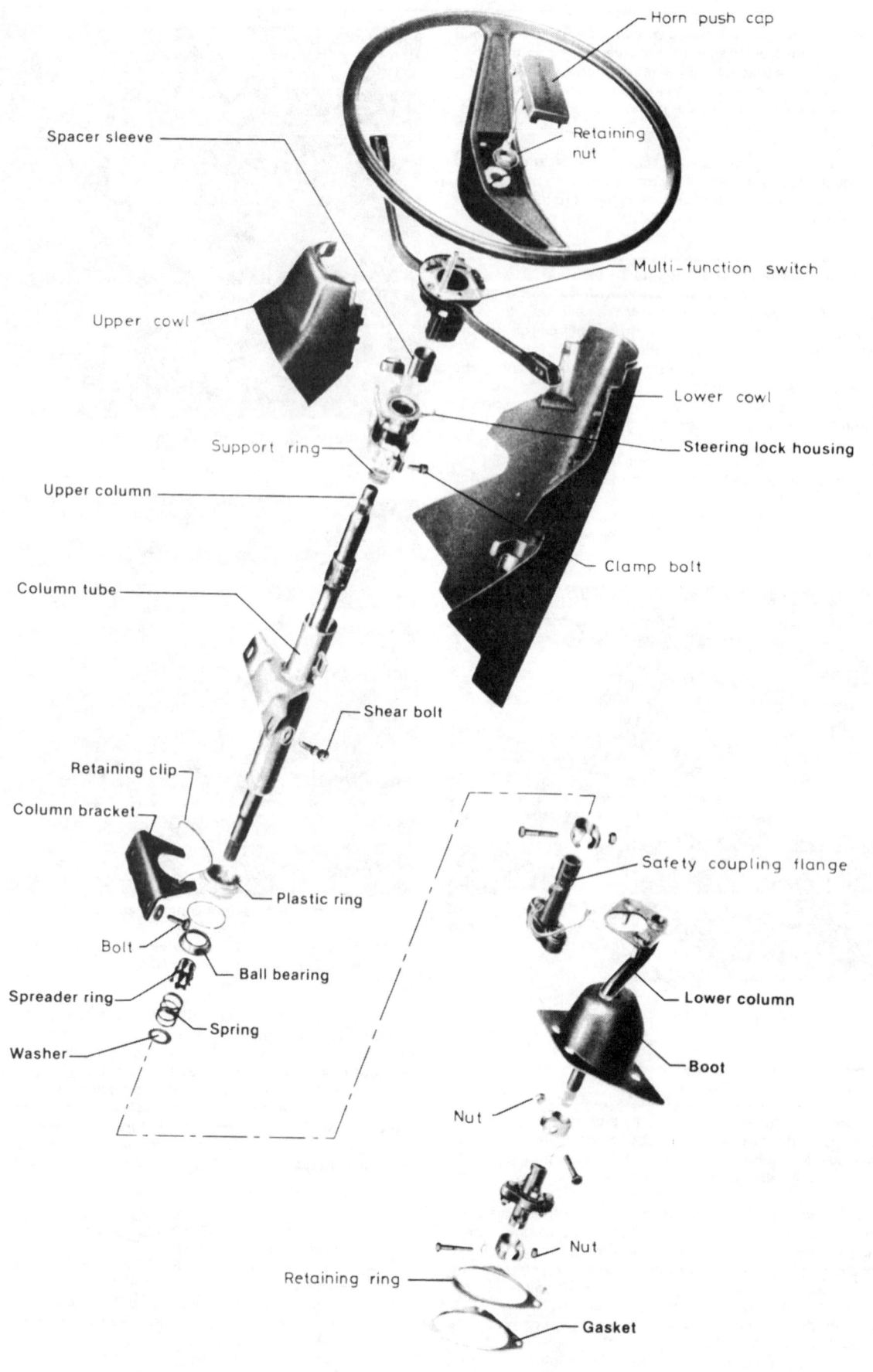

Horn push cap

Retaining nut

Spacer sleeve

Multi-function switch

Upper cowl

Lower cowl

Steering lock housing

Support ring

Upper column

Clamp bolt

Column tube

Shear bolt

Safety coupling flange

Retaining clip

Column bracket

Lower column

Plastic ring

Bolt

Ball bearing

Boot

Spreader ring

Spring

Nut

Washer

Nut

Retaining ring

Gasket

Fig. 8.9 Exploded view of the steering column assembly (Secs 20 and 21)

21 Steering column – dismantling and reassembly

1   Begin by removing the steering wheel as described in Section 19.

2   Undo and remove the two screws securing the upper and lower steering column cowls to the column. Lift off the cowls noting that an internal retaining clip is also used to secure the lower cowl to the column.

3   Disconnect the wiring harness connectors at the ignition/starter switch and multi-function switch and place the harnesses to one side.

4   Undo and remove the three screws securing the multi-function switch to the steering lock housing and lift off the switch.

5   Using a suitable key undo and remove the socket headed pinchbolt from the steering lock housing clamp.

6   With the aid of a universal balljoint separator, clamp the two parts of the steering column safety coupling together as shown in Fig. 8.10.

7   Using a conventional two legged puller draw off the steering lock housing and the upper column sleeve.

8   Remove the balljoint separator from the safety coupling.

9   Refer to Section 20 paragraphs 4 to 8 inclusive and remove the steering column assembly from the vehicle.

10 With the column assembly on the bench undo and remove the locking collar clamp bolt that secures the safety coupling two arm flange to the upper column. Mark the position of the flange on the column using a dab of quick drying paint and then slide off the flange.

11 Withdraw the washer, spring, spreader ring and bearing from the end of the upper column. Now slide the upper column out of the top of the column tube.

12 Check the upper column and column tube for straightness by rolling them along a flat surface. Also check for roughness of the support bearings in the steering lock housing and at the base of the column tube. Renew any defective components as necessary.

13 Begin reassembly by inserting the upper column into the column tube. Refit the bearing, spreader ring, spring and washer followed by the two arm flange. Ensure that the previously made marks on the flange and column are aligned and then secure the flange with the locking collar and clamp bolt.

14 Place the steering column in position in the vehicle and secure the plastic ring at the base of the column to the lower mounting using the wire retaining clip. Now attach the upper mounting to the facia using two new shear bolts. Tighten the shear bolts finger tight only at this stage.

15 Set the roadwheels to the straight-ahead position and then refit the lower column. Tighten the locking collar clamp bolt on the flexible coupling to the specified torque and then refit the rubber boot and earth lead.

16 Using the balljoint separator, clamp the two parts of the safety coupling together as was done during dismantling.

17 Slide the steering lock housing over the top of the column ensuring that the support ring is in place beneath the bearing.

18 Fit the spacer sleeve with the notched side toward the lock

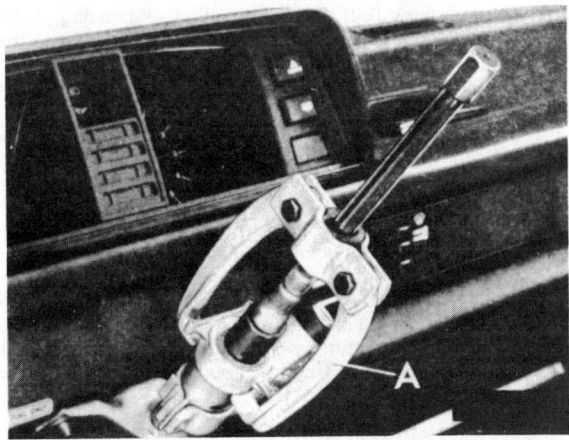

Fig. 8.11 Removing the steering lock housing and column sleeve using a two-legged puller (Sec 21)

Fig. 8.12 Correct positioning of the steering column spacer sleeve (Sec 21)

a = 51 mm (2.0 in)

Fig. 8.10 Using a universal balljoint separator to clamp the two parts of the safety coupling (Sec 21)

Fig. 8.13 Adjust gap (a), between steering wheel and multi-function switch to between 2 and 4 mm (0.07 and 0.15 in) (Sec 21)

housing and tap it on using a tube of suitable diameter. The sleeve must be positioned so that its edge is 51 mm (2.0 in) from the end of the upper column. Now refit and tighten the lock housing pinch-bolt.

19 Refit the multi-function switch assembly and secure it to the lock housing using the three screws.

20 Reconnect the wiring harness connectors to the multi-function switch and ignition switch.

21 Refit the steering wheel with the spokes horizontal and secure with the retaining nut tightened to the specified torque. Reconnect the horn push cap wires and refit the cap to the centre of the steering wheel.

22 Move the steering column tube up or down slightly, within the limits of the elongated holes in the mounting brackets, until the clearance between the steering wheel and multi-function switch is between 2 and 4 mm (0.07 and 0.15 in). When the clearance is correct tighten the two shear bolts until the heads break off.

23 Finally refit the upper and lower steering column cowls and then remove the balljoint separator from the safety coupling. Reconnect the battery earth terminal.

22 Front suspension geometry and wheel alignment

1   Accurate front wheel alignment is essential to provide positive steering and prevent excessive tyre wear. Before considering the steering/suspension geometry, check that the tyres are correctly inflated, the front wheels are not buckled, the hub bearings are not worn or incorrectly adjusted. Also check that the steering and suspension components are in good order, without slackness or wear at the joints.

2   Suspension geometry consists of four factors: *Camber* is the angle at which the front wheels are set from the vertical when viewed from the front of the vehicle. 'Positive camber' is the amount (in degrees) that the wheels are tilted outward at the top from the vertical. *Castor* is the angle between the steering axis and a vertical line when viewed from each side of the vehicle. 'Positive castor' is when the steering axis is inclined rearward. *Steering axis inclination* is the angle (when viewed from the front of the vehicle) between the vertical and an imaginary line drawn through the centres of the upper wishbone and track control arm balljoints. *Front wheel alignment (or toe setting)* is the amount by which the distance between the front inside edges of the roadwheels (measured at hub height) differs from the diametrically opposite distance measured between the rear inside edges of the front roadwheels.

3   Owing to the need for special gauges, it is not normally within the scope of the home mechanic to check and adjust any of these settings with the exception of the front wheel alignment. Where suitable equipment can be obtained, however, adjustments can be carried out in the following way, setting the tolerances to those given in the Specifications.

4   Before carrying out any measurements or adjustments, position the vehicle on level ground, tyres correctly inflated, front roadwheels set in the straight-ahead position and with it in an unladen condition. Make sure all suspension and steering components are securely attached and without wear in the moving parts.

5   *Camber adjustment:* The camber angle is adjusted by altering the position of the two eccentric washers on the upper wishbone inner mounting spindle. To do this slacken the spindle retaining nut and then turn the spindle with a spanner or socket until the correct angle is obtained. Now tighten the retaining nut.

6   *Castor adjustment:* The castor angle is adjusted by altering the length of the radius rod by means of the two nuts on the body mounting bracket. Note that the castor angle also influences the camber and front wheel alignment and these must be checked after making any alteration to the castor.

7   *Front wheel alignment:* To check the alignment a simple gauge can be made up from a length of tubing or bar and having a bolt and locknut at one end.

8   Use this gauge to measure the distance between the two inner wheel rims at hub height and at the front of the roadwheels.

9   Push or pull the vehicle forward to rotate the roadwheels by 180° (half a turn) then measure the distance between the inner wheel rims at hub height, but this time at the rear of the roadwheels. This last measurement should be greater than the first by the amount stated in the Specifications and represents the correct toe-in of the front wheels.

10 Where the toe-in is found to be incorrect proceed as follows.

11 Slacken the locknuts that secure each of the steering tie-rod balljoints to the tie-rods. Turn each tie-rod by equal amounts, not more than one quarter of a turn at a time, clockwise (viewed from the side) to decrease the toe-in and anti-clockwise to increase it. Push or pull the vehicle backwards for one complete revolution of the roadwheel and then move it forwards by the same amount. Now recheck the alignment setting as described previously and continue this procedure until the setting is correct.

12 Tighten the tie-rod balljoint locknuts and then make sure that the rubber bellows on the steering box have not become twisted due to movement of the tie-rods. If so straighten them otherwise they will be damaged in a very short time.

Fig. 8.14 Adjustment of camber is carried out by turning wishbone spindle (right arrow) after slackening retaining nut (left arrow) (Sec 22)

Fig. 8.15 Front wheel alignment is adjusted by turning both tie-rods by equal amounts in the desired direction (Sec 22)

23 Fault diagnosis – front suspension and steering

Symptom	Reason(s)
Excess free play felt at steering wheel	Worn steering flexible couplings Wear in front suspension components or balljoints Wear in steering box or relay gear internal components
Vehicle difficult to steer in a consistent straight line – wandering	As above Front hub bearings incorrectly adjusted Front wheel alignment incorrect
Steering stiff and heavy	Front wheel alignment incorrect Incorrect tyre pressures Partial seizure of one or more steering or suspension balljoints Bent or distorted steering column Lack of lubricant in steering gear due to split bellows
Wheel wobble and vibration	Roadwheels out of balance Roadwheels buckled or faulty type Wear in steering or suspension components or balljoints
Excessive pitching and rolling on corners and during braking	Weak or ineffective shock absorbers Weak front coil springs Broken or worn anti-roll bar mountings
Excessive tyre wear	Incorrect tyre pressures Incorrect front wheel alignment or suspension geometry Wear in steering or suspension components Front wheels out of balance Faulty tyre

Chapter 9 Braking system, wheels and tyres

Contents

Specifications

System type	Dual-circuit hydraulic with discs at the front and drums at the rear. Brake pressure regulator in rear hydraulic circuit. Cable operated handbrake. Servo assistance on 2.0 litre models.

Front brakes
Type	Disc with Girling or Teves twin piston fixed calipers
Disc diameter	278.0 mm (10.95 in)
Disc thickness	13.0 mm (0.512 in)
Minimum disc thickness after machining	11.0 mm (0.433 in)
Caliper piston diameter	54.0 mm (2.127 in)
Minimum brake pad lining thickness	2.0 mm (0.08 in)

Rear brakes
Type	Single leading shoe drum
Drum internal diameter	252.0 mm (9.92 in)
Maximum drum internal diameter after machining	253.5 mm (10.0 in)
Wheel cylinder piston diameter	23.81 mm (0.938 in)
Brake shoe lining thickness:	
Standard	6.0 mm (0.24 in)
Oversize	6.5 mm (0.26 in)
Minimum brake shoe lining thickness	2.5 mm (0.10 in)

Master cylinder (1.6 litre models)
Type	Teves or Schafer tandem
Bore diameter	20.64 mm (0.813 in)
Pushrod length	91.5 mm (3.605 in)

Master cylinder (2.0 litre models)
Type	Teves or Bendix tandem
Bore diameter	23.81 mm (0.938 in)

Vacuum servo unit
Type	228.6 mm (9.0 in) single diaphragm
Boost factor	2.4
Pushrod length	111.5 mm (4.393 in)

Roadwheels
Type .... Perforated steel disc
Size .... 5½J x 14

Tyres
Tyre size:
    1.6 litre models .... 7.00 14 8PR 93P, 185 SR 14 Reinforced, or 185 R14C 6PR
    2.0 litre models .... 185 SR 14 Reinforced or 185 R14C 6PR

Tyre pressures*

	Front	Rear
7.00 14 8PR 93P	2.3 bar (33 lbf/in^2)	3.3 bar (47 lbf/in^2)
185 SR 14 Reinforced	2.3 bar (33 lbf/in^2)	2.9 bar (41 lbf/in^2)
185 R14C 6PR	2.6 bar (37 lbf/in^2)	3.8 bar (54 lbf/in^2)

The pressures are also given on a sticker on the left-hand door pillar between the hinges

Torque wrench settings

	Nm	lbf ft
Brake caliper to steering knuckle	160	118
Wheel cylinder to backplate	20	15
Brake shoe lower support to backplate	65	48
Master cylinder to pedal bracket or servo	15	11
Servo to pedal bracket	15	11
Roadwheel retaining nuts and bolts	170	125

1 General description

The braking system is of the dual-circuit hydraulic type with disc brakes at the front and drum brakes at the rear. The system is servo assisted on vehicles equipped with the 2.0 litre engine. The dual-circuit layout is split on a front-to-rear basis whereby the primary hydraulic circuit operates the front brakes and the secondary circuit operates the rear brakes, from a tandem master cylinder. Under normal conditions both circuits operate in unison; however, in the event of hydraulic failure in one circuit, full braking force will still be available at two wheels. A brake pressure regulator is incorporated in the rear brake hydraulic circuit. This device regulates the pressure applied to each rear brake and reduces the possibility of the rear wheels locking under heavy braking.

The front disc brakes are operated by twin piston, fixed brake calipers.

At the rear, leading and trailing brake shoes are operated by twin piston wheel cylinders and are self-adjusted by footbrake application.

The cable operated handbrake provides an independent mechanical means of rear brake application.

2 Maintenance and inspection

1 At the intervals given in Routine Maintenance at the beginning of this manual, carry out the following service operations on the braking system.

2 Check the brake hydraulic fluid level in the master cylinder reservoir located behind the instrument panel. To gain access, remove the instrument panel cover by lifting up at the two recesses in the rear of the cover (photo). Disengage the cover at the front and lift off. Make sure that the level of fluid is maintained between the MIN and MAX marks on the side of the reservoir and if necessary top up with the specified type of brake fluid. Owing to normal brake pad and lining wear, over a period of time the level will slowly drop. However any rapid drop and the need to top up at frequent intervals will be due to a leak somewhere in the hydraulic system, which must be investigated immediately. Note that on 2.0 litre models, the upper part of the reservoir also supplies fluid to the clutch hydraulic system and a drop in the fluid level could be due to a fault in the clutch master or slave cylinder (see Chapter 4).

3 At the specified intervals check the front brake pads and rear brake shoe linings for wear as described in Sections 3 and 7. At the same time check the condition of the handbrake cables, lubricate the exposed linkages and adjust the handbrake if necessary as described in Section 19. The condition and security of the hydraulic pipes and hoses should also be inspected, further details will be found in Section 16.

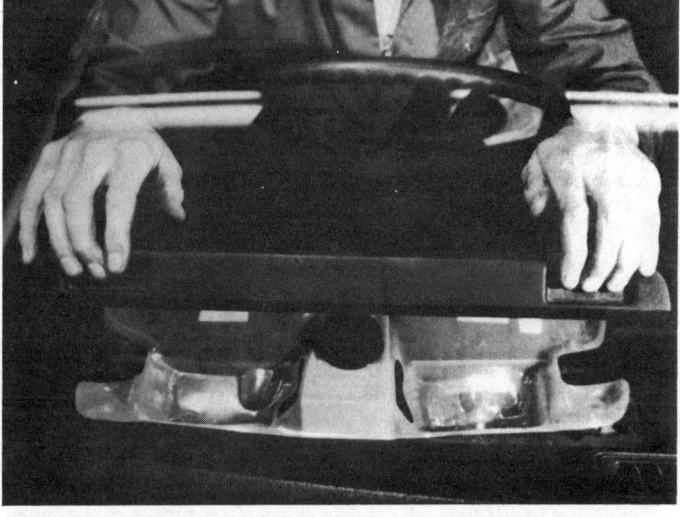

2.2 Lift up and remove the instrument panel cover to gain access to the master cylinder

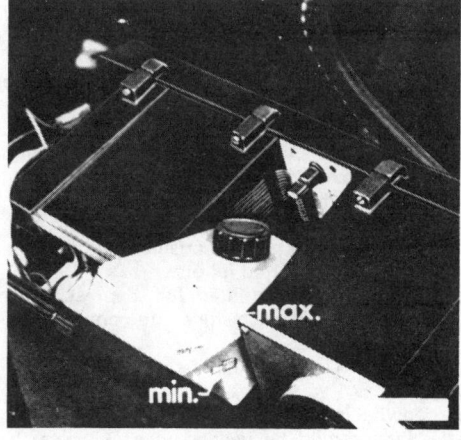

Fig. 9.1 Maximum and minimum fluid level markings on the master cylinder reservoir (Sec 2)

4   The brake hydraulic fluid should be renewed at the specified intervals by draining the system and refilling with fresh fluid as described in Section 18.

5   Check that the brake failure warning light on the instrument panel lights up with the ignition switched on and the handbrake applied, and goes out when the engine is started and the handbrake is released. If the bulb fails to illuminate, check the condition of the bulb and if satisfactory there is a fault in the switch on the handbrake or in the wiring to the bulb. If the light does not go out when the engine is started, make sure that the handbrake is fully released. If the light remains illuminated there is a fault in one of the hydraulic circuits and the vehicle should not be driven until the fault is traced and rectified.

6   On 2.0 litre models the operation of the vacuum servo unit should be checked as described in Section 27.

7   Carefully inspect each tyre, including the spare, for signs of uneven wear, lumps, bulges or damage to the sidewalls or tread face. Refer to Section 28 for further details.

8   Check the condition of the wheel rims for distortion, damage and excessive run-out. Also make sure that the balance weights are secure with no obvious signs that any are missing. Check the tightness of the wheel retaining bolts and nuts and check the tyre pressures. The spare should be maintained at the same pressure as the rear tyres.

3.8 Retract the caliper pistons using a flat bar as a lever

3   Front brake pads – inspection and renewal

1   Jack up the front of the vehicle and support it on axle stands. Remove both front road wheels.

2   Either Girling or Teves brake calipers are fitted. Both types are similar in construction, the main differences being the type of brake pad retaining pins used to secure the pads in position in the brake caliper.

3   On models fitted with Teves calipers, the retaining pins are removed by tapping them inwards towards the car, using a thin punch. To remove the retaining pins on Girling calipers, withdraw the spring clips and tap the pins outwards, away from the car, using a thin punch.

4   With the retaining pins removed, lift off the spreader spring plate and then withdraw the brake pads one at a time from the caliper. If they are initially tight, use a screwdriver inserted in the slot on the brake pad and lever against the edge of the caliper. Lift out the anti-rattle shims, if not already removed with the pads.

5   Inspect the thickness of the brake pad friction material. If the thickness of the brake pad friction material is less than specified, the pads must be renewed. The pads must also be renewed if there is any sign of oil or brake fluid contamination of the friction material, or if any heavy scoring or cracking is visible on the pad face.

6   When renewing the brake pads, they should always be renewed as a complete set (4 pads); uneven braking or pulling to one side may otherwise occur.

7   With the pads removed, carefully inspect the surface of the brake disc. Concentric scores up to 0.4 mm (0.015 in) are acceptable; however, if deeper scores are found, the brake disc must either be skimmed or preferably renewed (see Section 6).

8   To refit the pads, first ensure that the brake caliper pistons and pad seating areas are clean and free from dust and corrosion. Using a flat bar as a lever, gently push the caliper pistons back into their cylinders as far as they will go (photo). This operation will cause a quantity of brake fluid to be returned to the master cylinder via the hydraulic pipes. Place absorbent rags around the master cylinder reservoir to collect any fluid that may overflow, or preferably, drain off a small quantity of fluid from the reservoir before retracting the caliper pistons.

9   Fit the new brake pads and anti-rattle shims into their locations in the caliper. On Teves calipers the notches on the anti-rattle shims engage the recesses in the piston (photos). On Girling calipers the arrows on the anti-rattle shims point upward.

10 Place the spreader spring plate in position and refit the retaining pins, and spring clips, where fitted (photos).

11 With the brake pads correctly fitted, fully depress the brake pedal several times to bring the caliper pistons into contact with the brake pads.

12 Check the brake fluid level in the master cylinder reservoir and top up as necessary.

13 Refit the roadwheels and lower the car to the ground.

14 New brake pads should be bedded in slowly over a period of approximately 120 miles (200 km). During this time, avoid unnecessary panic stops or prolonged heavy brake applications.

3.9A Fit the brake pads ...

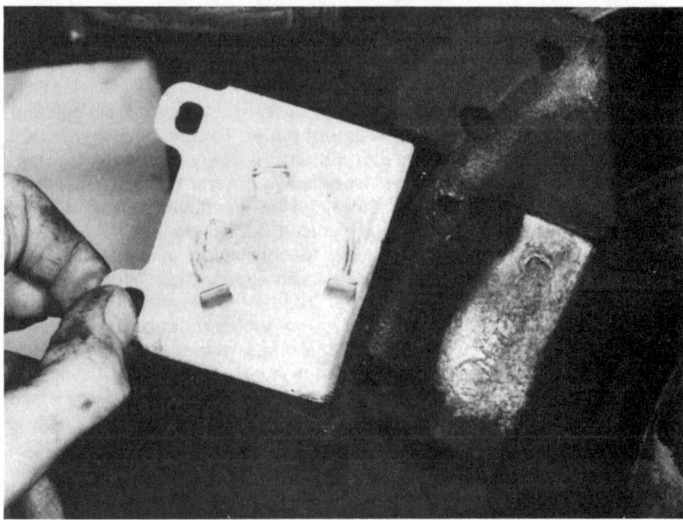

3.9B ... and anti-rattle shims

3.9C On the Teves caliper the notches in the anti-rattle shims engage with the recesses (arrowed) in the pistons

3.10A Refit the spreader spring plate ...

3.10B ... followed by the retaining pins (arrowed)

4 Front brake caliper – removal and refitting

1   Jack up the front of the vehicle and support it on axle stands. Remove the appropriate front roadwheel.

2   Remove the brake pads as described in Section 3 and mark them on their backing plates so that they can be refitted in their original positions. Store the pads face up to avoid contamination of the friction material.

3   Using a brake hose clamp or self-locking wrench with protected jaws, clamp the flexible brake hydraulic hose. This will prevent loss of brake fluid during subsequent operations.

4   Wipe clean the area around the brake pipe to caliper union nut, unscrew the nut and carefully withdraw the pipe from the caliper. Plug the pipe and caliper to prevent dirt entry.

5   Undo and remove the two bolts securing the caliper to the steering knuckle, noting that the upper bolt is a shouldered type and that on some calipers a shim is fitted between the caliper and steering knuckle at the upper bolt location.

6   With the bolts removed, withdraw the caliper from the steering knuckle and disc (photo).

4.6 Removing the brake caliper from the steering knuckle and disc

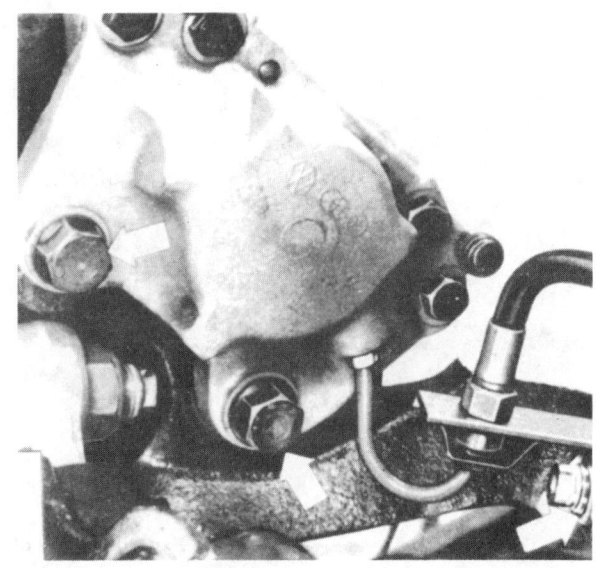

Fig. 9.2 Front brake caliper retaining bolts (arrowed) (Sec 4)

7   Refitting is the reverse sequence to removal, bearing in mind the following points:

(a) *Tighten the caliper retaining bolts to the specified torque*
(b) *Refit the brake pads as described in Section 3*
(c) *Bleed the hydraulic system as described in Section 17. If precautions described to prevent brake fluid loss were taken, it should only be necessary to bleed the caliper being worked on*

5   Front brake caliper – overhaul

1   Remove the caliper as described in the previous Section.
2   Using a screwdriver, extract the rubber dust cover around the caliper pistons. If working on the Girling caliper, first remove the dust cover retaining ring.
3   Place a thin flat block of wood over one piston and hold the block and piston in place, using a small G-clamp.

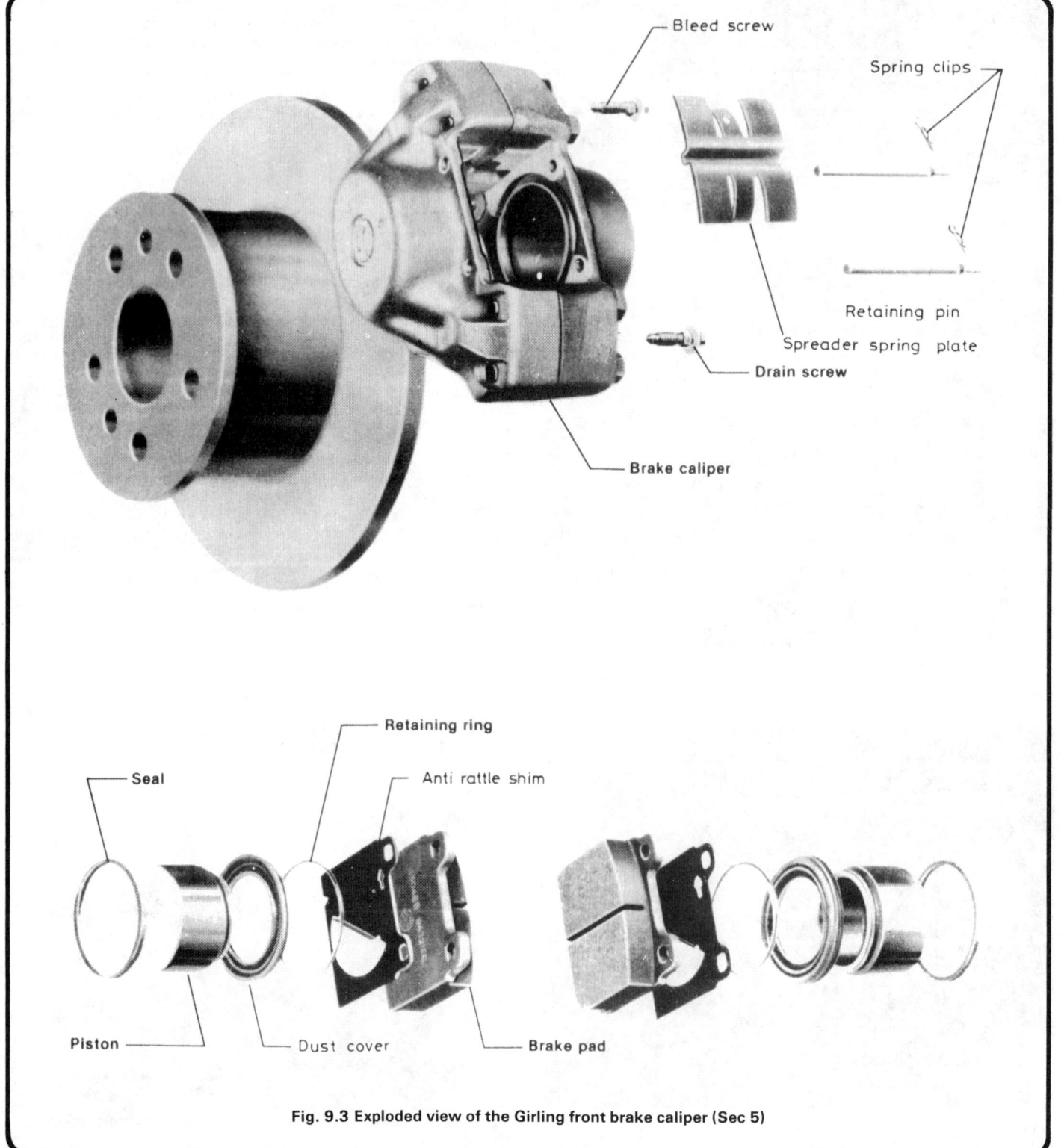

Fig. 9.3 Exploded view of the Girling front brake caliper (Sec 5)

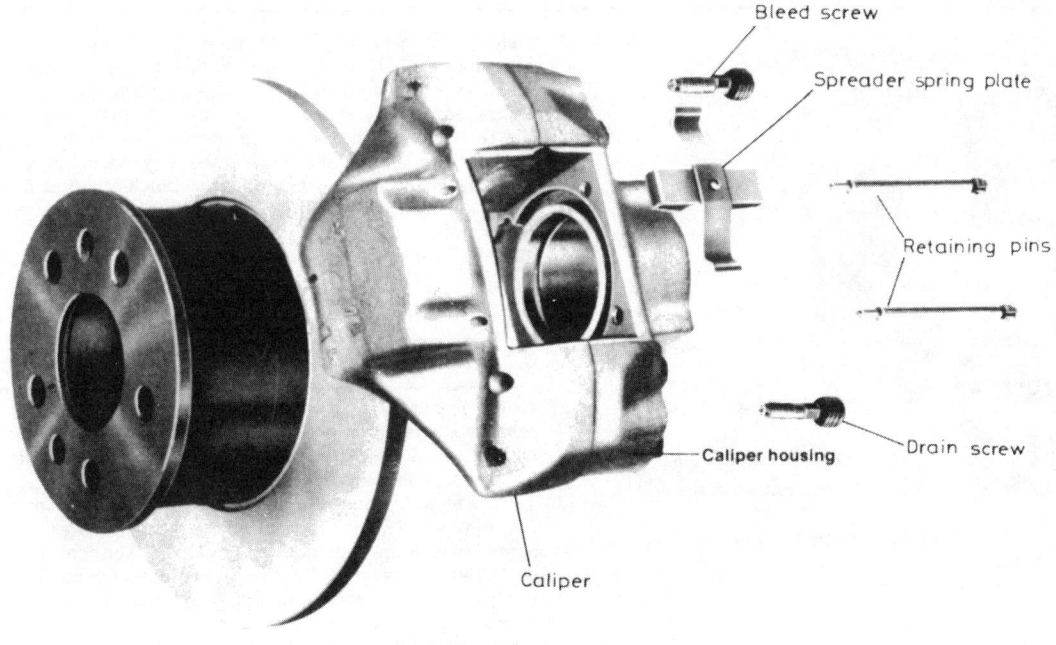

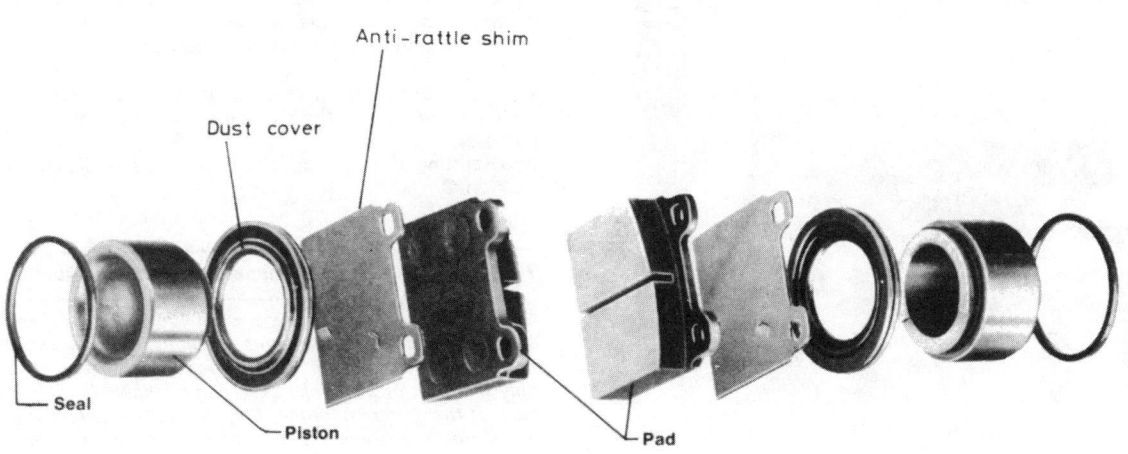

Fig. 9.4 Exploded view of the Teves front brake caliper (Sec 5)

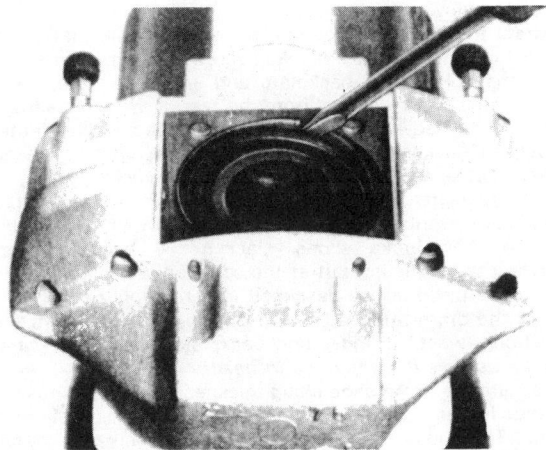

Fig. 9.5 Extract the caliper piston dust cover with a screwdriver (Sec 5)

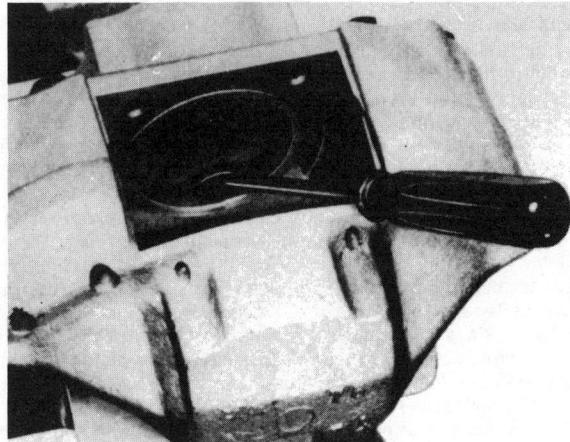

Fig. 9.6 After removing the pistons, hook out the piston seals (Sec 5)

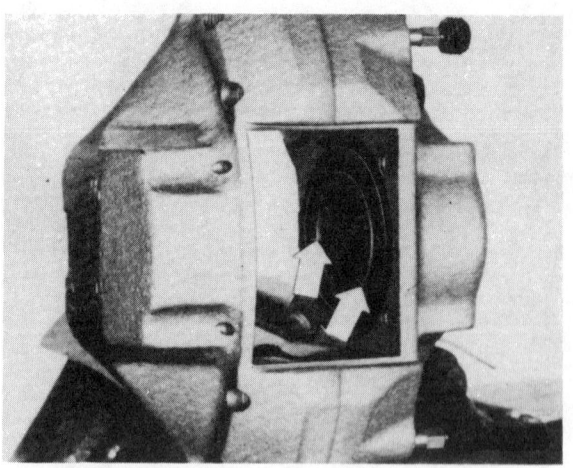

Fig. 9.7 Use the brake pad anti-rattle shims to position the piston recesses (arrowed) correctly – Teves caliper (Sec 5)

Fig. 9.8 Locate the new dust covers in the piston grooves (Sec 5)

4   The unclamped piston may now be forced out of the caliper, using a compressed air jet or the nozzle of a car foot pump held firmly against the brake pipe union.

5   With the first piston removed, use a block of wood and the G-clamp to seal off the cylinder opening on the caliper, and repeat the above procedure to remove the remaining piston.

6   Thoroughly clean the caliper and pistons, using clean brake fluid or methylated spirit. *Under no circumstances should the two halves of the caliper be separated.*

7   With all components thoroughly cleaned, the two piston seals can be removed using a thin blunt instrument such as a plastic knitting needle.

8   Inspect the dismantled components carefully for corrosion, scratches or wear. New seals are available in the form of a brake caliper repair kit, and should be renewed as a matter of course. If severe corrosion, scoring or wear is apparent on the pistons or caliper cylinders, the complete caliper will have to be renewed, as these parts are not available separately.

9   Immerse the caliper piston seals in clean brake fluid and carefully fit them to the annular groove in the cylinder, using the fingers only.

10 Liberally coat the pistons with clean brake fluid and insert them in their cylinder bores. Do not push the pistons fully home at this stage.

11 If working on the Girling caliper, locate the new dust covers in the

piston and caliper grooves then secure the dust cover with the retaining ring. The pistons should now be pushed fully into their bores.

12 If working on the Teves caliper, place the brake pad anti-rattle shims temporarily in position and turn the pistons as necessary so that the recesses engage with the notches in the anti-rattle shims. Now remove the shims and locate the new dust covers in the piston grooves. Using a G-clamp and small block of wood, press the outer lip of the dust cover into the groove in the caliper, this will also push the piston fully into its bore.

13 In all cases the caliper may now be refitted as described in Section 4.

6 Front brake disc – inspection, removal and refitting

Note: *The disc is an integral part of the front hub assembly and is removed, complete with wheel bearings as described in Chapter 8, Section 3. With the assembly removed from the stub axle a detailed inspection can be carried out as follows.*

1   Carefully inspect the surface of the disc. Concentric scores up to 0.4 mm (0.015 in) are acceptable. Also minute surface cracks and some discolouration due to localised surface heating are to be expected. However, if the disc is severely grooved, it must be skimmed until flat or preferably renewed. If the disc is to be skimmed an equal amount of metal must be removed from both sides and the disc thickness must not be reduced below the specified minimum. **Note:** *In order to maintain uniform braking, both front discs must exhibit the same surface characteristics with respect to depth of grooving and surface finish. For this reason any machining should be carried out on both discs and if renewal is necessary the discs should be renewed in pairs.*

2   If the discs are in a satisfactory condition, remove any surface corrosion by tapping the circumference of the disc lightly with a small hammer.

3   Refitting the disc and hub assembly is described in Chapter 8, Section 3.

7 Rear brake shoes – inspection and renewal

Note: *Two inspection holes are provided on each rear brake backplate and after removal of the plugs the lining thicknesses can be observed through the holes. This must be regarded purely as a quick check as only one part of the brake shoe can be viewed and it is not possible to inspect the lining condition, only its thickness. To carry out a thorough inspection the brake drum must be removed as follows.*

1   Jack up the rear of the car and support it on axle stands. Remove both rear roadwheels then release the handbrake.

2   Undo the two small bolts securing the brake drum to the rear wheel hub and withdraw the drum. Tap the circumference of the drum with a hide or plastic mallet if it is tight. If the drum cannot be removed due to it binding on the brake shoes, slacken off the brake shoe adjuster as follows.

3   Extract the plug from the rear of the brake backplate, just below the wheel cylinder. Insert a cranked screwdriver or other suitable tool through the hole in the backplate and engage it with the serrated adjuster wheel. When viewed from the rear of the vehicle the adjuster wheel on the left-hand brake assembly should be turned anti-clockwise to slacken off the brake shoes. The adjuster wheel on the right-hand brake assembly should be turned clockwise.

4   With the adjusters slackened, it should now be possible to remove the drum as described in paragraph 2. If, however, the drum is still binding on the brake shoes, slacken the handbrake cable by unscrewing the adjusting nut at the cable equalizer (see Section 19). Now remove the drum as described in paragraph 2.

5   With the drum removed, brush or wipe the dust from the drum, brake shoes, wheel cylinder and backplate. *Take great care not to inhale the dust as it is injurious to health.*

6   Measure the brake shoe lining thickness. If the thickness of any of the linings is less than the specified minimum, all four shoes must be renewed. The shoes must also be renewed if any are contaminated with brake fluid or grease, or show signs of cracking, glazing or deep scoring. If contamination is evident the cause must be traced and rectified before fitting new brake shoes.

7   Also examine the internal braking surface of the brake drum for

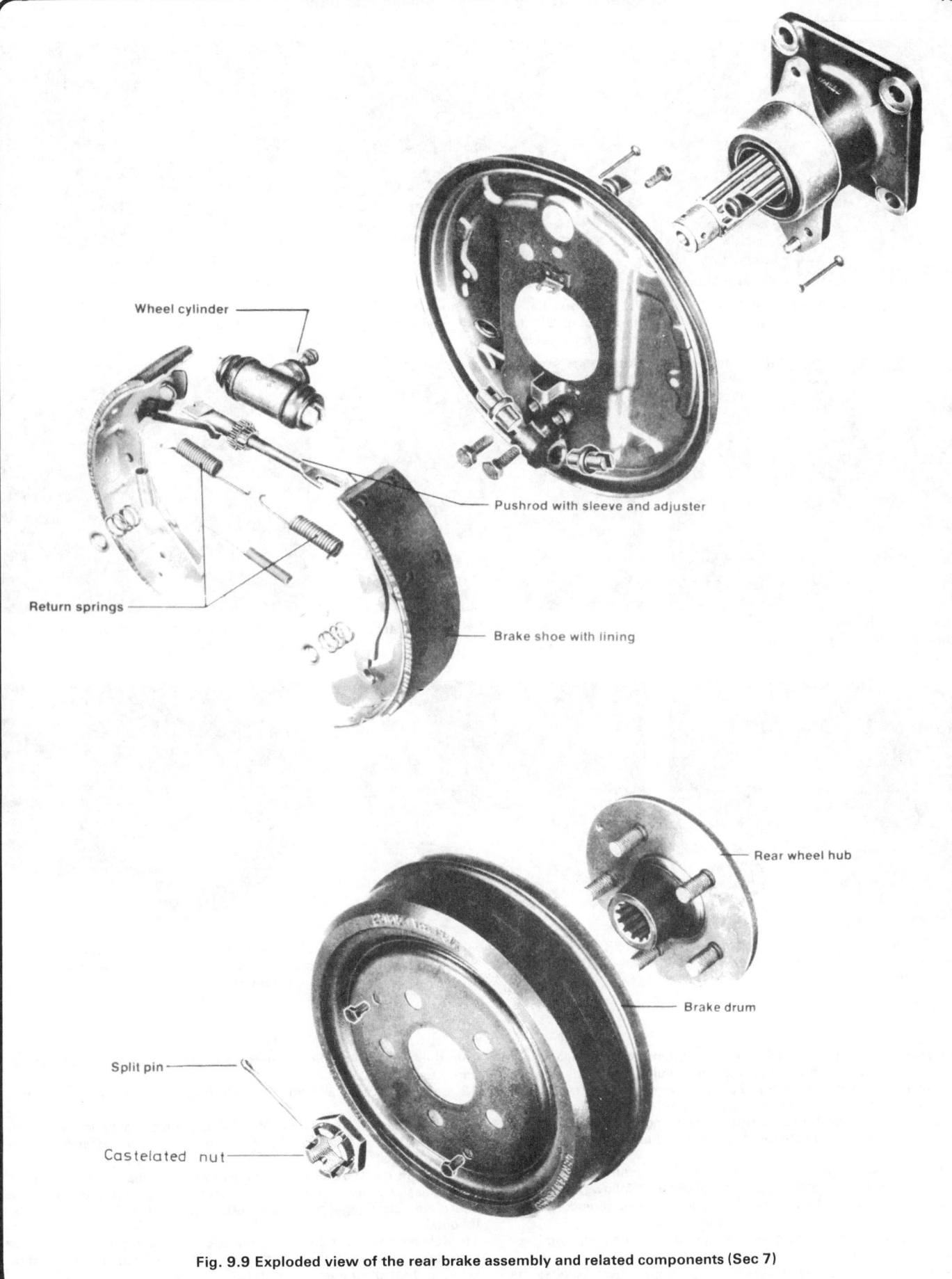

Wheel cylinder

Return springs

Pushrod with sleeve and adjuster

Brake shoe with lining

Rear wheel hub

Brake drum

Split pin

Castelated nut

Fig. 9.9 Exploded view of the rear brake assembly and related components (Sec 7)

7.10 Release the operating spring from the adjusting lever

7.11 Depress the steady spring cups and turn through 90° to remove, while holding the pin from behind

7.12 Ease the brake shoes out of their lower pivot locations

7.13A Rotate the serrated adjuster wheel so that the self-adjust mechanism is fully retracted ...

7.13B ... then withdraw the self-adjuster sleeve

7.14 Now lift out the self-adjuster pushrod and adjuster wheel

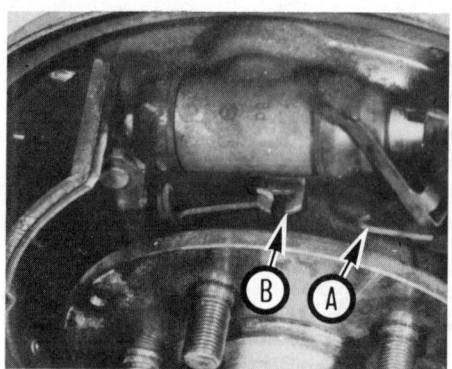

7.15A Release the leading shoe upper return spring (A) from the lug on the backplate (B)

7.15B Disengage the lower return spring and lift off the shoe

7.16 Release the trailing shoe return springs, disengage the handbrake cable and lift off the shoe

scoring or cracks. The drums may be skimmed to remove minor surface irregularities providing the maximum specified internal diameter is not exceeded. If the drum is severely scored, renewal is necessary. If the drum can be salvaged by skimming, it will be necessary to fit brake shoes with oversize linings. These are thicker than standard to compensate for the increased internal diameter of the drum.

8   If the brake shoes are in a satisfactory condition proceed to paragraph 26; if removal is necessary, proceed as follows.

9   First make a careful note of the location and fitted direction of the various springs and linkages as an aid to refitting.

10 Using pliers, release the operating spring from the adjusting lever on the leading brake shoe (photo).

11 Depress the brake shoe steady spring cups whilst holding the steady spring pins, from the rear of the backplate, with your finger. Turn the cups through 90° then remove them, followed by the springs and pins (photo).

12 Ease the leading and trailing shoes from their lower pivot locations (photo).

13 Using a screwdriver, back off fully the serrated adjuster wheel, lift the upper part of the leading shoe and withdraw the self-adjuster sleeve (photos).

14 Now lift out the self-adjuster pushrod and adjuster wheel (photo).

15 Release the leading shoe upper return spring from the lug on the backplate, disengage the lower return spring and lift off the shoe (photos).

16 Release the trailing shoe upper return spring from the lug on the backplate, disengage the handbrake cable end from the brake shoe lever, and lift off the shoe (photo).

17 Prior to installation, clean off the brake backplate with a rag, and

7.17 Apply a trace of silicone grease to the brake shoe contact areas (arrowed) before refitting the shoes

apply a trace of silicone grease to the shoe contact areas and pivots (photo), and to the threads of the self-adjuster pushrod. Ensure that the serrated wheel turns easily.

18 Engage the handbrake cable end with the lever on the trailing brake shoe and hold the shoe in position on the backplate.

19 Locate the coiled end of the upper return spring in the hole in the trailing shoe so that the spring coil is behind the brake shoe web. Using pliers, pull the straight end of the spring over the lug on the backplate.

20 Fit the lower return spring to both brake shoes ensuring that the spring is positioned behind the brake shoe webs.

21 Fit the upper return spring to the leading brake shoe using the same procedure as for the trailing shoe.

22 With the adjuster wheel wound down to the end of the thread on the adjuster pushrod, locate the forked end of the pushrod against the trailing shoe and handbrake lever. The longer projection on the fork must face the backplate.

23 Ease the leading shoe out at the top and slip the self-adjuster sleeve over the pushrod, then engage its forked end with the adjusting lever.

24 Refit the steady spring pins through the holes in the backplate and

Fig. 9.10 Set the brake shoes so that dimension 'a' equals the internal diameter of the drum less 1.5 mm (0.06 in) before refitting the drum (Sec 7)

brake shoes. Hold the pins, refit the steady springs and cups then turn the cups through 90° to lock them on the pins.

25 Refit the operating spring to the adjusting lever and leading shoe with the straight end towards the adjusting lever.

26 Before refitting the brake drum it is necessary to provide an initial, manual adjustment of the brake shoes. To do this measure the internal diameter of the brake drum and then subtract 1.5 mm (0.06 in) from this dimension. The result is the dimension to which the brake shoes must be set before refitting the drum. Centralize the shoes on the backplate then turn the serrated adjuster wheel as necessary until the correct setting is obtained (Fig. 9.10).

27 Refit the brake drum to the wheel hub and secure the drum with the two retaining bolts.

28 Depress the footbrake several times to operate the self-adjusting mechanism then refit the access plugs to the backplate.

29 If it was necessary to slacken the handbrake cable to remove the drum, adjust the cable as described in Section 19.

30 Finally, refit the roadwheel and lower the vehicle to the ground.

8   Rear wheel cylinder – removal and refitting

1   Begin by removing the appropriate rear brake drum as described in Section 7, paragraphs 1 to 4.

2   Using a brake hose clamp or self-locking wrench with protected jaws, clamp the flexible hydraulic brake hose located at the front of the rear suspension trailing arm. This will prevent loss of brake fluid during subsequent operations.

3   Wipe clean the area around the brake backplate and wheel cylinder. Unscrew the brake hydraulic pipe union at the rear of the wheel cylinder and carefully ease out the pipe. Plug or tape over the pipe end to prevent dirt entry.

4   Undo and remove the bleed screw at the rear of the wheel cylinder and the single bolt securing the cylinder to the backplate.

5   Apply the handbrake fully to move the brake shoes away from their locations in the wheel cylinder pistons. If necessary ease the shoes away further, using a screwdriver as a lever, and then withdraw the cylinder from the backplate.

6   To refit the wheel cylinder, place it in position on the backplate and engage the brake pipe and union. Screw in the union nut two or three turns to ensure the thread has started.

7   Refit the wheel cylinder retaining bolt and the bleed screw then fully tighten the bolt, bleed screw and brake pipe union nut.

8   Release the handbrake and engage the brake shoes with the wheel cylinder pistons.

9   Refit the brake drum as described in Section 7, paragraphs 26 to 27.

10 Bleed the hydraulic system as described in Section 17. If the precautions described were taken to prevent brake fluid loss, it should only be necessary to bleed the brake being worked on.

11 Refit the roadwheel and lower the vehicle to the ground.

9   Rear wheel cylinder – overhaul

1   Remove the wheel cylinder as described in the previous Section.

2   With the cylinder on the bench, withdraw the dust covers from the ends of the pistons and cylinder body.

3   Withdraw the pistons and piston spring then remove the rubber seals from the pistons.

4   Thoroughly clean all the components in methylated spirits or clean brake fluid, and dry with a lint free rag.

5   Carefully examine the surfaces of the pistons and cylinder bore for wear, score marks or corrosion and, if evident, renew the complete wheel cylinder. If the components are in a satisfactory condition, obtain a repair kit consisting of new seals and dust covers.

6   Dip the new seals and pistons in clean brake fluid and assemble the components wet, as follows.

7   Using your fingers, fit the new seals to the pistons with their sealing lips facing inwards.

8   Lubricate the cylinder bore with clean brake fluid and insert one of the pistons, followed by the spring then the second piston.

9   Place the dust covers over the pistons and cylinder edges then refit the assembled wheel cylinder to the vehicle as described in the previous Section.

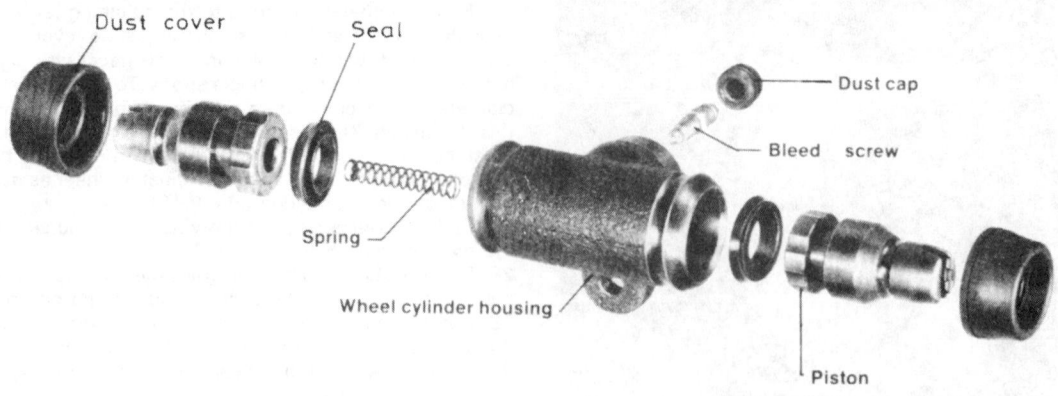

Fig. 9.11 Exploded view of the rear wheel cylinder (Sec 9)

10 Rear brake backplate – removal and refitting

1   The backplate is removed in conjunction with the rear wheel bearing housing and details of this procedure will be found in Chapter 7, Section 4.

11 Master cylinder – removal and refitting

1   To gain access to the master cylinder, refer to Chapter 10 and remove the instrument panel.
2   Remove the master cylinder filler cap and draw off as much brake fluid as possible from the reservoir using a clean syringe.
3   Place some absorbent rags beneath the master cylinder to catch any fluid that may drip out after the pipe unions are undone.
4   Unscrew the two brake pipe union nuts (photo), and carefully withdraw the pipes from the master cylinder. Immediately plug or tape over the pipe ends and cylinder orifices to prevent further loss of fluid and dirt entry.
5   Using a screwdriver if necessary, ease the clutch master cylinder fluid supply hose from its union on the side of the reservoir (where fitted). Plug or tape over the union and hose after removal.
6   Make a note of their locations. Disconnect the wires at the brake light switch and, if fitted, at the brake failure warning light switch on the master cylinder body.
7   Undo the two nuts securing the master cylinder to the pedal bracket or servo unit and withdraw the cylinder from its location. Remove the O-ring seal from the end of the cylinder (photos).

8   Refitting the master cylinder is the reverse sequence to removal, bearing in mind the following points.

   (a)   *On vehicles without a servo, measure the master cylinder pushrod length before refitting the cylinder. The distance from the centre of the clevis pin hole to the end of the pushrod should be equal to the dimension given in the Specifications. Adjust if necessary by slackening the locknut and turning the pushrod. Also ensure that there is a small amount of free play between the brake pedal and the rubber stop. Turn the rubber stop as necessary to achieve this*

   (b)   *Bleed the brake and clutch hydraulic system after fitting as described in Section 17 of this Chapter, and Chapter 4 respectively*

12 Master cylinder (1.6 litre models) – overhaul

   The master cylinder fitted to 1.6 litre models without a servo is identical in operation and very similar in construction to the unit fitted to 2.0 litre servo assisted vehicles. The only major differences between the two units are the shape of the fluid reservoir and modifications to the primary piston. The accompanying illustrations highlight these differences, but otherwise the overhaul procedure described in Section 13 is fully applicable.

13 Master cylinder (2.0 litre models) – overhaul

1   Begin by removing the master cylinder from the vehicle as described in Section 11.
2   With the cylinder on the bench undo and remove the brake light

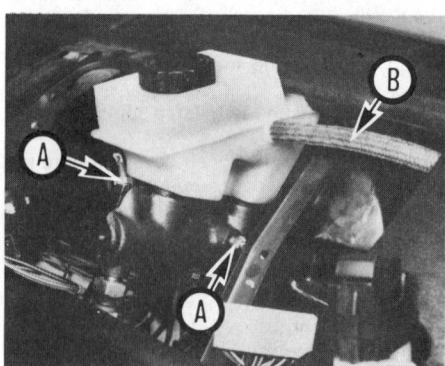

11.4 Brake pipe union nuts (A) and clutch fluid supply hose (B) on the master cylinder fitted to 2.0 litre models

11.7A Remove the master cylinder from its location ...

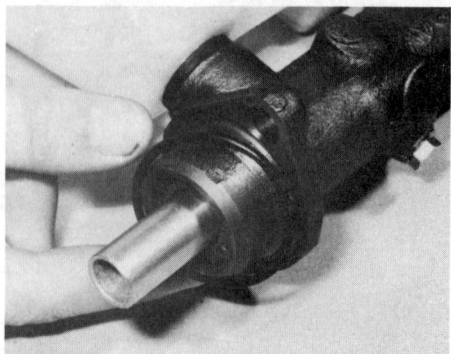

11.7B ... and recover the O-ring seal

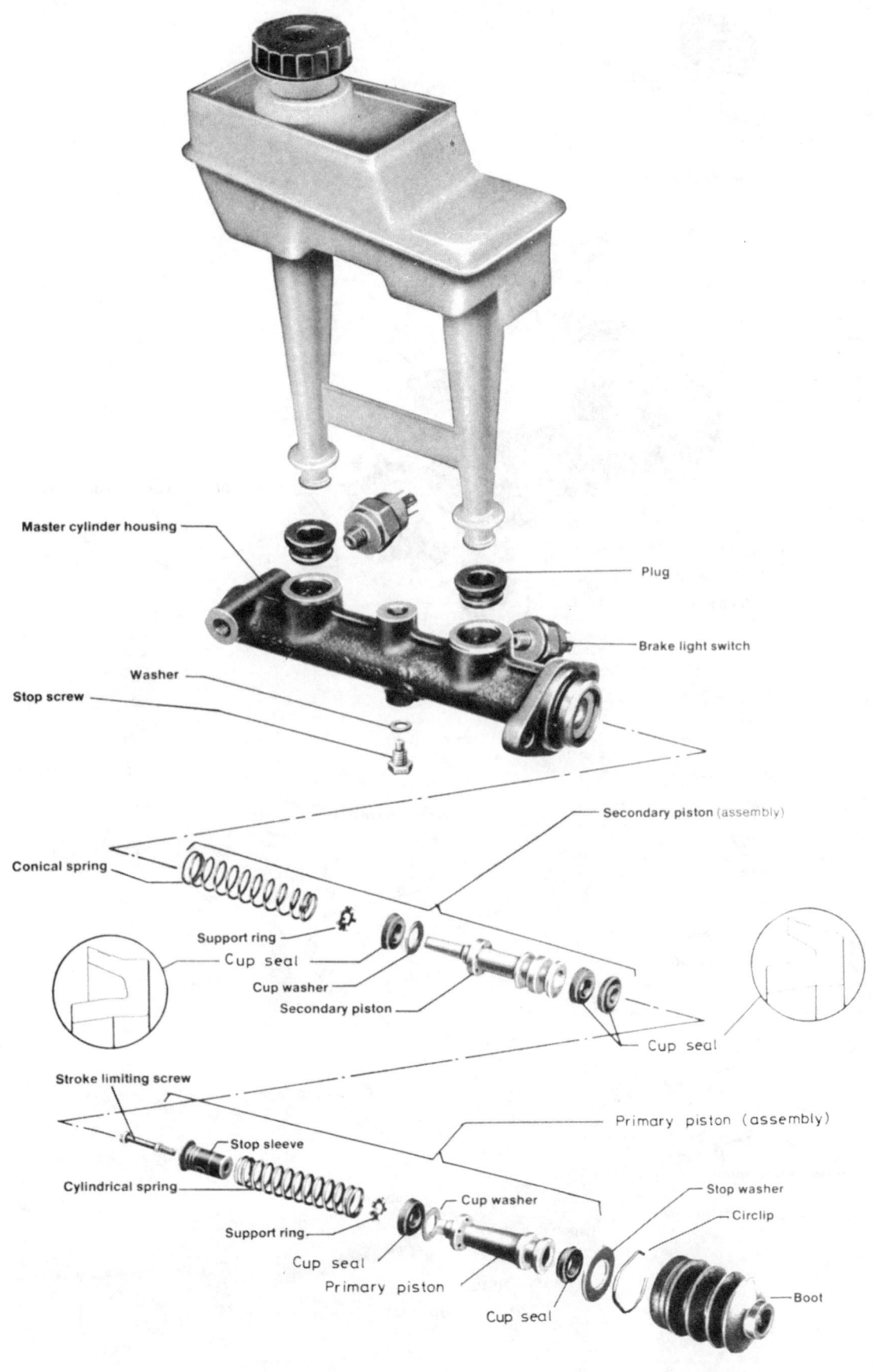

Fig. 9.12 Exploded view of the Teves master cylinder fitted to 1.6 litre models (Sec 12)

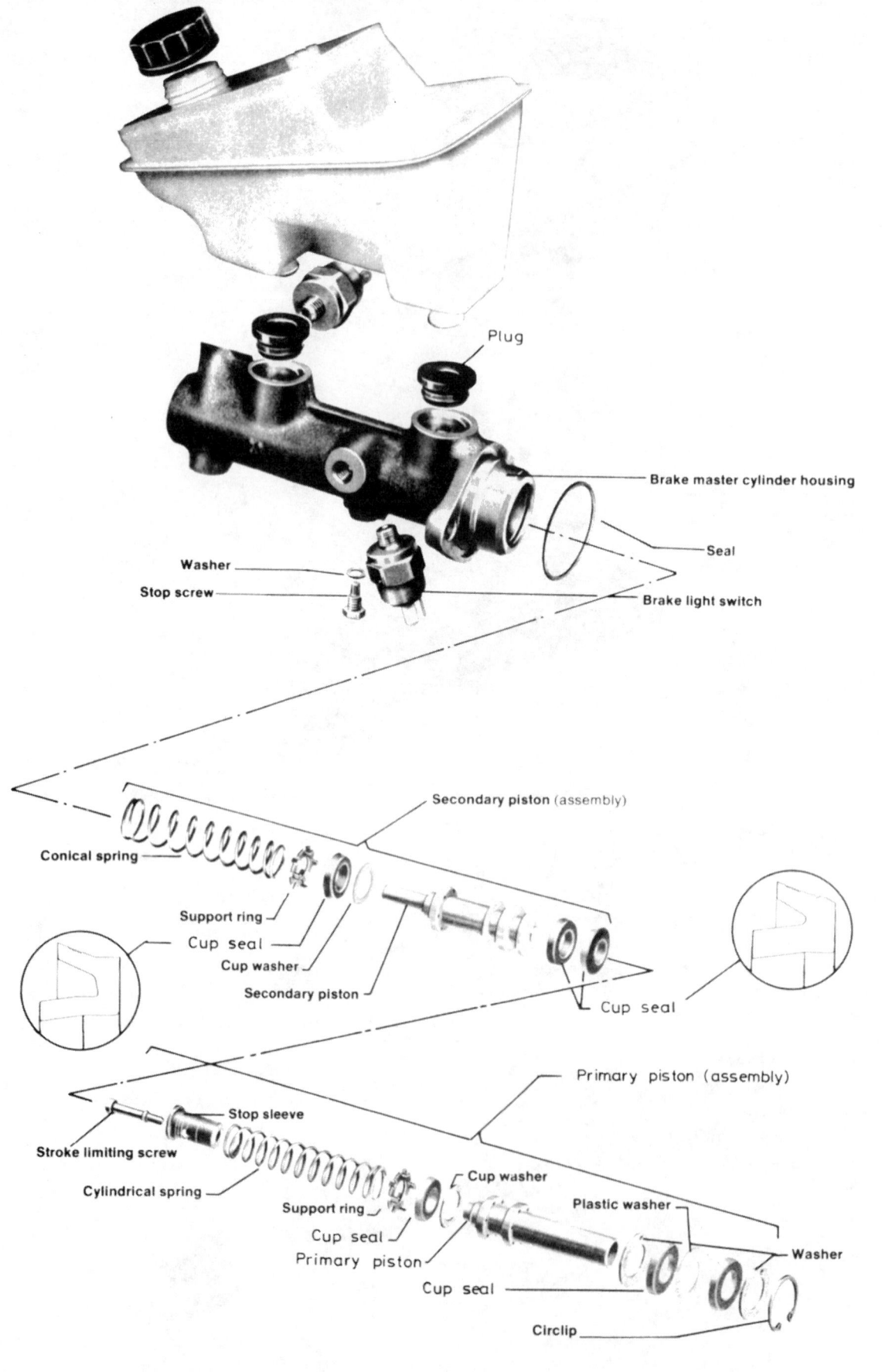

Plug

Brake master cylinder housing

Seal

Washer

Stop screw

Brake light switch

Secondary piston (assembly)

Conical spring

Support ring

Cup seal

Cup washer

Secondary piston

Cup seal

Primary piston (assembly)

Stop sleeve

Stroke limiting screw

Cylindrical spring

Support ring

Cup washer

Plastic washer

Cup seal

Primary piston

Washer

Cup seal

Circlip

Fig. 9.13 Exploded view of the Teves master cylinder fitted to 2.0 litre models (Sec 13)

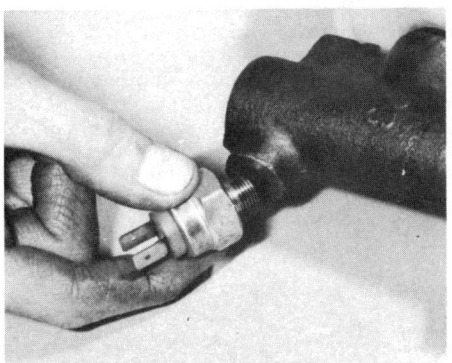

13.2 Remove the brake light switch

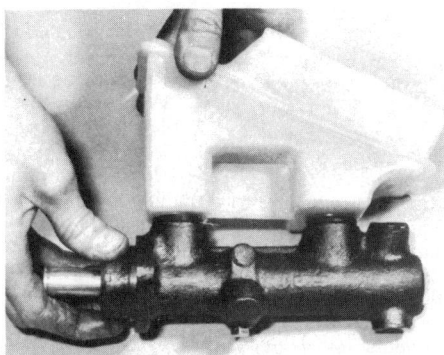

13.3A Carefully lever off the reservoir ...

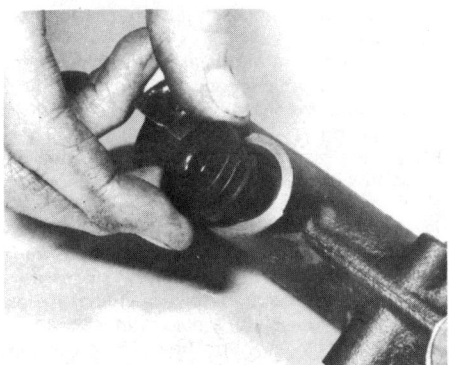

13.3B ... then remove the two rubber sealing plugs

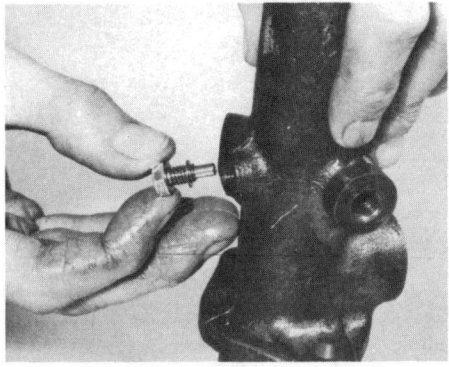

13.4 Remove the secondary piston stop screw with its washer

13.6A Slide off the cup seals, metal and plastic washers ...

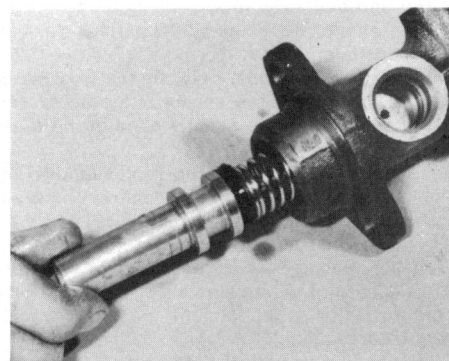

13.6B ... then withdraw the primary piston

switch and, where fitted, the brake failure warning light switch (photo).
3   Support the master cylinder body and carefully lever off the reservoir using a screwdriver. Remove the two rubber sealing plugs from the reservoir ports (photos).
4   Undo and remove the secondary piston stop screw with its washer from the base of the cylinder body (photo).
5   With the cylinder supported in a vice, push the primary piston down slightly and remove the retaining circlip from its groove in the cylinder bore.

6   Withdraw the primary piston slightly and slide off the assembly of two metal washers, two cup seals and plastic washer (photo). Now remove the primary piston from the cylinder bore (photo).
7   Tap the master cylinder on a block of wood to eject the secondary piston from the cylinder bore then withdraw the secondary piston assembly (photo).
8   Starting with the primary piston, hold the spring in compression and unscrew the stroke limiting screw. Remove the screw followed by the stop sleeve, cylindrical spring and support ring. Do not allow the

Fig. 9.14 Using circlip pliers to remove the primary piston retaining circlip (Sec 13)

13.7 Tap the cylinder on a block of wood to eject the secondary piston, then withdraw it from the cylinder bore

cylindrical spring to become interchanged with the conical spring on the secondary piston.

9   Withdraw the cup seal and washer from the primary piston.

10   Turning to the secondary piston, withdraw the conical spring and support ring, followed by the cup seal and washer from the inner end of the piston.

11   At the axle end, hook off the two cup seals using a blunt screwdriver, noting the different directions of fitting of the two seals.

12   Thoroughly clean the cylinder and the two pistons in methylated spirit or clean brake fluid then dry with a lint free cloth.

13   Carefully examine the cylinder bore and the surfaces of the two pistons for signs of scoring, wear ridges and corrosion. In order that the seals may adequately maintain hydraulic fluid pressure, the condition of the pistons and cylinder bore must be perfect. If in any doubt whatsoever about the condition of the components, renew the complete master cylinder.

14   If the cylinder and pistons are in a satisfactory condition, a new set of seals must be obtained before reassembly. These are available in the form of a master cylinder repair kit, obtainable from VW dealers or brake and clutch factors.

15   Thoroughly lubricate all the parts in clean brake fluid and assemble them wet, as follows.

16   Using your fingers only, fit the two cup seals to the secondary piston noting that the sealing edge of the innermost seal faces the piston spring and the sealing edge of the outer seal faces away from the spring.

17   Now fit the washer, cup seal, support ring and conical spring to the other end of the secondary piston. The sealing edge of the cup seal must face the spring.

18   Fit the washer and cup seal to the inner end of the primary piston, with the sealing edge of the cup seal towards the spring.

19   Slide on the support ring, cylindrical spring and stop sleeve, compress the spring and fit the stroke limiting screw. Tighten the screw securely.

20   At the other end of the primary piston, fit the assembly of metal washer, cup seal, plastic washer, cup seal and remaining metal washer. The sealing edges of both cup seals face the spring.

21   Thoroughly lubricate the cylinder bore and secondary piston assembly using clean brake fluid then carefully insert the secondary piston into the cylinder bore, spring end first. Take care not to allow the edges of the cup seals to fold over.

22   Using a thin blunt rod, push the secondary piston down to compress the spring then refit the stop screw with its washer. Tighten the screw securely.

23   Lubricate the primary piston with clean brake fluid and insert this assembly into the cylinder bore, spring end first.

24   Push the piston down and refit the retaining circlip to its groove in the cylinder bore.

25   Fit the two new rubber sealing plugs to the reservoir ports in the cylinder and push the reservoir firmly into place.

26   Refit the brake light switch and where applicable the warning light switch to the cylinder body. Tighten the switches securely.

27   The assembled master cylinder can now be refitted as described in Section 11.

14 Brake pressure regulator – description

1   A brake pressure regulator to control hydraulic fluid pressure applied to the rear brakes, is mounted on the right-hand front chassis member, just in front of the steering gear.

2   The purpose of the regulator is to prevent the rear wheels locking under heavy braking when the vehicle is lightly loaded.

3   The regulator consists of a steel ball in an inclined chamber and two spring loaded subsidiary pistons which act as pressure reducers. When braking occurs, the ball is thrown forward and depending on the rate of deceleration and the angle up which it has to roll (affected by the attitude of the vehicle), it shuts off the direct fluid flow to the rear wheel cylinders. Pressure is then directed to two intermediate pistons of different diameter which effectively reduce the output pressure to the rear brakes.

4   Testing of the valve is not possible without the use of special equipment and if the valve is suspect, testing should be left to a VW dealer.

5   In the event of the valve being proved faulty it must be renewed as a complete assembly; parts are not available separately.

15 Brake pressure regulator – removal and refitting

1   Jack up the front of the vehicle and support it on axle stands.

2   Wipe clean the area around the brake pipe unions on top of the regulator and unscrew the pipe union nuts. Carefully withdraw the pipes and then quickly plug their ends to prevent further loss of fluid.

3   Undo the two nuts and bolts securing the regulator to the chassis member, withdraw the regulator and recover the distance sleeves (photo).

15.3 Brake pressure regulator retaining nuts (arrowed)

4   Refitting is the reverse sequence to removal bearing in mind the following points:

    (a) *Ensure that the distance sleeves are fitted between the regulator and chassis member*

    (b) *Ensure that the heads of the bolts securing the two halves of the regulator body together face the front of the vehicle*

    (c) *Bleed the rear brakes as described in Section 17 after fitting the regulator*

16 Hydraulic pipes and hoses – inspection, removal and refitting

1   At the intervals given in Routine Maintenance, carefully examine all the brake pipes, hoses, hose connections and pipe unions.

2   First check for signs of leakage at the pipe unions. Then examine the flexible hoses for signs of cracking, chafing and fraying.

3   The brake pipes must be examined carefully and methodically. They must be cleaned off and checked for signs of dents, corrosion or other damage. Corrosion should be scraped off, and, if the depth of pitting is significant, the pipes renewed. This is particularly likely in those areas underneath the vehicle body where the pipes are exposed and unprotected.

4   If any section of pipe or hose is to be removed, first unscrew the master cylinder reservoir filler cap and place a piece of polythene over the filler neck. Secure the polythene with an elastic band ensuring that an airtight seal is obtained. This will minimise brake fluid loss when the pipe or hose is removed.

5   Brake pipe removal is usually quite straightforward. The union nuts at each end are undone, the pipe and union pulled out and the centre section of the pipe removed from the body clips. Where the union nuts are exposed to the full force of the weather they can sometimes be quite tight. As only an open-ended spanner can be used, burring of the flats on the nuts is not uncommon when attempting to undo them. For this reason a self-locking wrench is often the only way to separate a stubborn union.

6   To remove a flexible hose, wipe the unions and bracket free of dirt and undo the union nut from the brake pipe end(s).

7   Next extract the hose retaining clips and lift the ends of the hose out of its brackets (photo).

8   Brake pipes can be obtained individually, or in sets, from most accessory shops or garages with the end flares and union nuts in place. The pipe is then bent to shape, using the old pipe as a guide, and is ready for fitting.

9   Refitting the pipes and hoses is a reverse of the removal sequence. Make sure that the hoses are not kinked when in position and also make sure that the brake pipes are securely supported in their clips. After refitting, remove the polythene from the reservoir and bleed the brake hydraulic system, as described in Section 17.

16.7 Front brake hose pipe union nut (A) and hose retaining clip (B)

17 Hydraulic system – bleeding

1   The correct functioning of the brake hydraulic system is only possible after removal of all air from the components and circuit; this is achieved by bleeding the system. Note that only clean unused brake fluid, which has remained unshaken for at least 24 hours, must be used.

2   If there is any possibility of incorrect fluid being used in the system, the brake lines and components must be completely flushed with uncontaminated fluid and new seals fitted to the components.

3   *Never* reuse brake fluid which has been bled from the system.

4   During the procedure, do not allow the level of brake fluid to drop more than halfway down the reservoir.

5   Before starting work check that all pipes and hoses are secure, unions tight, and bleed screws closed. Take great care not to allow brake fluid to come into contact with the paintwork, otherwise the finish will be seriously damaged. Wash off any spilled fluid immediately with cold water.

6   There are a number of one man, do-it-yourself, brake bleeding kits currently available from motor accessory shops. Always follow the instructions supplied with the kit. It is recommended that one of these kits is used whenever possible, as they greatly simplify the bleeding operation, and also reduce the risk of expelled air and fluid being drawn back into the system. If one of these kits is not available, it will be necessary to gather together a clean jar and a suitable length of clear plastic tubing which is a tight fit over the bleed screw, and also to engage the help of an assistant.

7   If brake fluid has been lost from the master cylinder due to a leak in the system, ensure that the cause is traced and rectified before proceeding further.

8   If the hydraulic system has only been partially disconnected and suitable precautions were taken to prevent further loss of fluid it should only be necessary to bleed that part of the system (ie primary or secondary circuit).

9   If the complete system is to be bled then it should be done in the following sequence:

Right-hand rear then left-hand rear
Right-hand front then left-hand front

10   To bleed the system, first clean the area around the bleed screw and fit the bleed tube. Note that at the front there are two bleed screws on each brake caliper. The lower one is used for draining and the upper one is used for bleeding.

11   *If a one-man brake bleeding kit is being used,* open the bleed screw half a turn and position the unit so that it can be viewed from the cab (photo). Depress the brake pedal to the floor and slowly release it; the one-way valve in the kit will prevent expelled air from returning to the system. Repeat the procedure then top up on the brake fluid level. Continue bleeding until clean brake fluid, free from air bubbles, can be seen coming through the tube. Now tighten the bleed screw and remove the tube.

17.11 Brake bleeding kit connected to front brake caliper

12   *If a one-man brake bleeding kit is not available,* immerse the free end of the bleed tube in the jar and pour in sufficient brake fluid to keep the end of the tube submerged. Open the bleed screw half a turn and have your assistant depress the brake pedal to the floor and then slowly release it. Tighten the bleed screw at the end of each downstroke to prevent the expelled air and fluid from being drawn back into the system. Repeat the procedure, then top up the brake fluid level. Continue bleeding until clean brake fluid, free from bubbles, can be seen coming through the tube. Now tighten the bleed screw and remove the tube.

13   Repeat the procedure described in paragraphs 10 to 12 on the remaining wheels, in the correct sequence, as necessary.

14   When completed, recheck the fluid level in the reservoir, top up if required and refit the cap. Depress the brake pedal several times; it should feel firm and free from 'sponginess' which would indicate air is still present in the system.

18 Brake fluid – renewal

1   Owing to its hygroscopic nature, the brake fluid used in the hydraulic system will gradually absorb moisture from the air. This will, over a period of time, lower the boiling point of the fluid to such an extent that under conditions of prolonged heavy braking the fluid will boil. If this occurs the brakes will become virtually inoperative. Additionally the moisture in the fluid can cause corrosion of the cylinder bores and pistons in the master cylinder, calipers and wheel cylinders, leading to seal failure or seizure of the pistons. For these reasons it is important to renew the fluid in the system at the recommended service intervals using the following procedure.

2   To drain the old fluid, obtain a suitable length of plastic or rubber tubing and a large receptacle.
3   Clean the area around the bleed screws on the rear wheel cylinders and remove the dust covers over the bleed screws.
4   Connect the tube to one of the bleed screws and place its other end in the receptacle.
5   Open the bleed screw at least one full turn and pump the brake pedal until fluid ceases to flow from the tube. Close the bleed screw, transfer the tube to the other rear brake and repeat the procedure.
6   Carry out the same operations at the front, but note that there are two bleed screws on each caliper. The lower screw is used for draining and the upper screw is used for bleeding.
7   When all the old fluid has been drained, refill the master cylinder reservoir with clean fresh fluid of the specified type, up to the MAX mark.
8   Initially prime the system prior to bleeding by opening all four bleed screws. Allow the fluid to slowly trickle through the system then close each bleed screw as soon as fluid appears. Keep the reservoir topped up during this operation.
9   The system can now be bled in the normal way as described in Section 17. *Note that on 2.0 litre models with hydraulically operated clutches, it will also be necessary to bleed the clutch hydraulic system which also obtains its fluid from the brake master cylinder reservoir.*

19 Handbrake – adjustment

Note: *The handbrake will normally be kept in correct adjustment by the self-adjusting action of the rear brake shoes. If however the cable has been disconnected or renewed, or if the travel of the lever becomes excessive owing to cable stretch, the following operations should be carried out:*
1   Jack up the rear of the vehicle and support it on axle stands. Release the handbrake.
2   Apply the footbrake firmly three or four times to ensure full movement of the self-adjust mechanism on the rear brake shoes. This is particularly important if the brake drums have recently been removed.
3   Apply the handbrake sharply then release it to equalise the cable loads. Now reapply the handbrake to the second notch of the ratchet.
4   From under the vehicle, turn the adjusting nut whilst holding the primary cable (photo) until the brake shoes are just dragging on the drums.

19.4 Handbrake adjusting nut (arrowed) on the primary cable

5   Operate the handbrake and check that the rear wheels are locked between the second and fourth notches of the ratchet and are free to turn without binding when the handbrake is released.
6   When the adjustment is correct, lower the vehicle to the ground.

20 Handbrake cables – removal and refitting

1   Jack up the rear of the vehicle and support it on axle stands. Release the handbrake.

Front (primary) cable
2   From inside the cab, lift up the carpet or rubber mat then slide the handbrake lever boot up the handle.
3   Extract the circlip and withdraw the clevis pin securing the end of the cable to the handbrake lever.
4   Release the rubber boot from its location in the floor pan and push the boot and cable end through the aperture in the floor.
5   From underneath the vehicle undo the adjusting nut and withdraw the other end of the cable from the equaliser.
6   Release the cable guide from its support clip and pull the cable through the circular grommet on the underbody.
7   Slide the rubber boot off the cable then withdraw the cable from under the vehicle.
8   Refitting is the reverse sequence to removal, but adjust the handbrake as described in Section 19 after refitting.

Rear (secondary) cables
9   Slacken the adjusting nut on the primary cable then slip the secondary cable end out of the elongated slot on the cable equaliser.
10   Refer to Section 7 and remove the brake drum as described in paragraphs 2 and 3.
11   Unhook the cable end from the brake shoe lever then push the cable and guide out of the backplate.
12   Release the cable retaining clips and supports from their locations on the underbody and suspension arms then withdraw the cable from under the vehicle.
13   Refitting the cable is the reverse sequence to removal, bearing in mind the following points:

(a)   *Refit the brake drum as described in Section 7, paragraphs 26 to 30*
(b)   *After fitting the cable, adjust the handbrake as described in Section 19, before lowering the vehicle to the ground*

21 Handbrake lever – removal and refitting

1   From inside the cab, lift up the carpet or rubber mat then slide the handbrake lever boot up the handle.
2   Extract the circlip then withdraw the clevis pin securing the primary handbrake cable to the lever.
3   Where fitted, disconnect the handbrake warning light wires at the switch on the lever.
4   Undo the two bolts securing the handbrake lever to the floor (photo) and withdraw the assembly from inside the cab.
5   Refitting is the reverse sequence to removal.

22 Handbrake lever – dismantling and reassembly

1   Remove the handbrake lever from the vehicle as described in the previous Section.
2   Undo the retaining screw and lift off the warning light switch (where fitted).
3   Unscrew the push button from the end of the lever then withdraw the spring and spring seat.
4   Extract the circlip and withdraw the clevis pin securing the lever to the mounting bracket. Lift off the lever.
5   Extract the circlip and withdraw the clevis pin securing the pawl to the lever. Lift out the pawl and operating rod.
6   Examine the components for signs of wear, paying close attention to the pawl and ratchet. Also check for any elongation of the clevis pin holes. Renew any worn parts as necessary.
7   Lubricate the pawl, ratchet and clevis pins with multi-purpose grease then reassemble the handbrake using the reverse of the dismantling procedure.

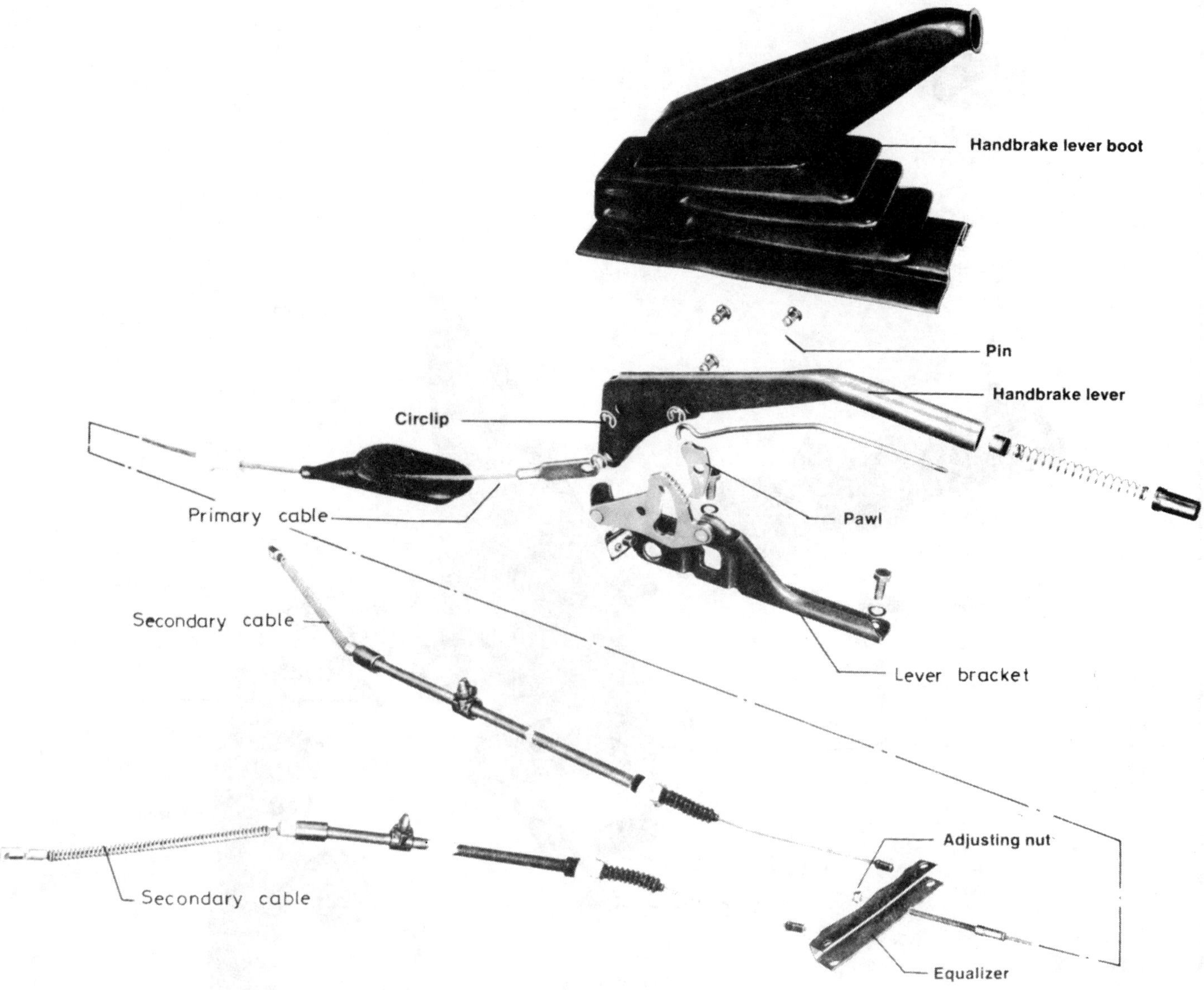

Handbrake lever boot

Pin

Handbrake lever

Circlip

Primary cable

Pawl

Secondary cable

Lever bracket

Secondary cable

Adjusting nut

Equalizer

Fig. 9.15 Exploded view of the handbrake cables and lever components (Sec 20)

21.4 Handbrake lever retaining bolts (arrowed)

23 Footbrake pedal (1.6 litre models) — removal and refitting

1   Begin by removing the instrument panel as described in Chapter 10, and the facia panel as described in Chapter 11.

2   Remove the brake master cylinder as described in Section 11 of this Chapter.

3   Jack up the rear of the vehicle and support it on axle stands.

4   Working underneath at the rear undo and remove the clutch cable adjusting wing nut at the release lever on the side of the transmission.

5   From inside the cab, slip the clutch cable out of the elongated slot on the clutch pedal clevis. Move the clutch cable clear of the pedal bracket assembly.

6   Undo and remove the four bolts securing the pedal bracket to the front bulkhead. Lift the bracket complete with pedals up, and remove the assembly from the cab.

7   Remove the clutch pedal return spring with pliers and release the brake pedal return spring using a screwdriver.

8   Extract the circlip securing the pedal pivot shaft in position then tap the shaft out of the bracket using a drift. The brake and clutch pedal can now be lifted out.

9   The bushes in the pedals can be removed by driving them out using a drift of suitable diameter. Press in new bushes using a vice. Renew the pedal pivot shaft if there are signs of scoring or wear ridges.

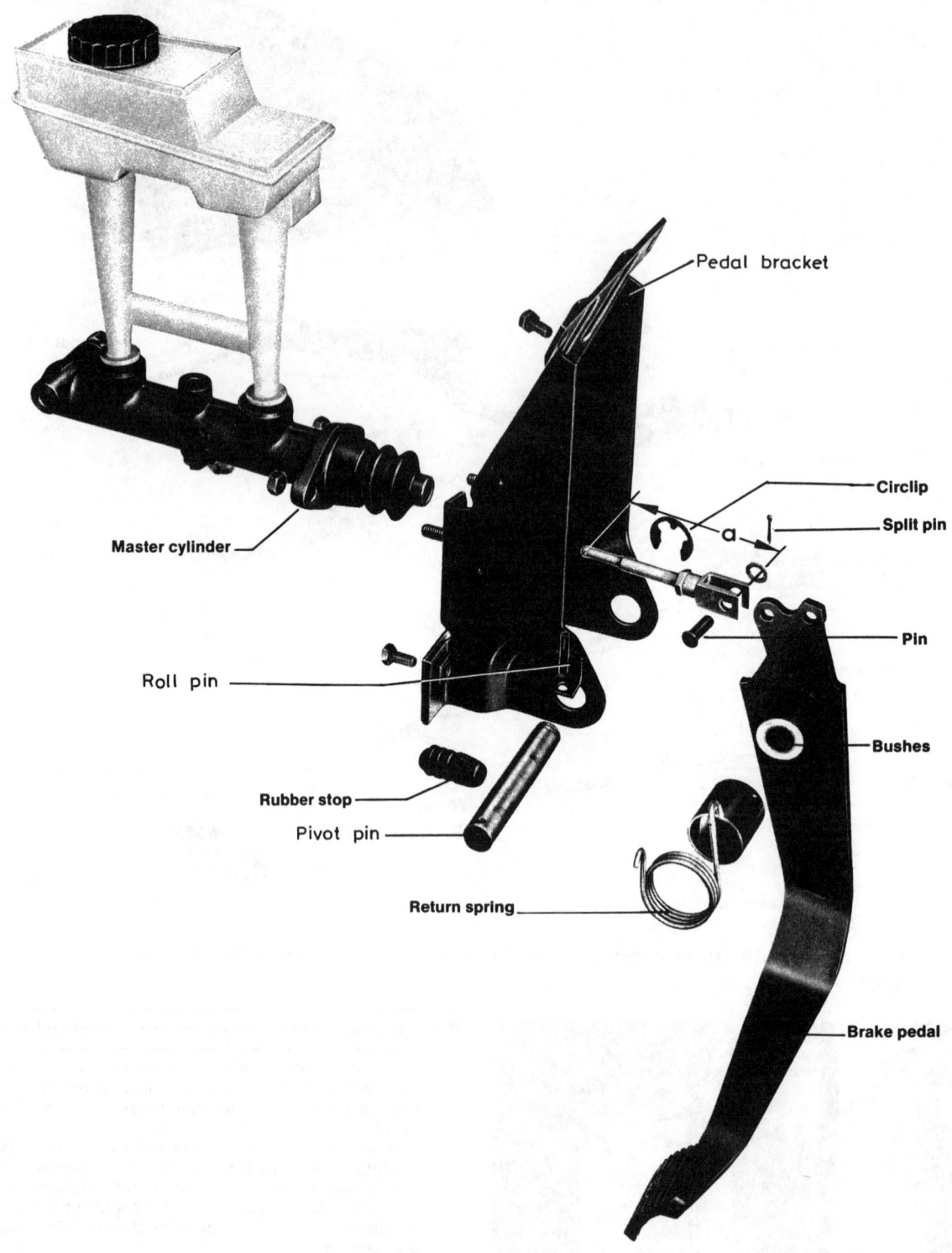

Pedal bracket

Circlip

Split pin

a

Master cylinder

Pin

Roll pin

Bushes

Rubber stop

Pivot pin

Return spring

Brake pedal

Fig. 9.16 Exploded view of the brake pedal and pedal bracket assembly – 1.6 litre models (Sec 23)

a = Specified master cylinder pushrod length

10 Lubricate the pedal bushes and pivot shaft with multi-purpose grease then place the pedals and brake pedal return spring in position.
11 Refit the pivot shaft ensuring that the roll pin in the end of the shaft locates in the groove in the pedal bracket. Secure the shaft with the retaining circlip.
12 Locate the brake pedal return spring over the pedal and refit the clutch pedal return spring.
13 Position the pedal bracket assembly in the vehicle then refit and fully tighten the four retaining bolts.
14 Slip the clutch cable into place and locate the cable end in the clevis on the pedal. Refit the adjusting wing nut to the transmission end of the cable then adjust the cable as described in Chapter 4, Section 3.

15 Refit the brake master cylinder as described in Section 11 of this Chapter.
16 Refit the facia panel as described in Chapter 11, and the instrument panel as described in Chapter 10.

24 Footbrake pedal (2.0 litre models) – removal and refitting

1 Begin by removing the instrument panel as described in Chapter 10, and the facia panel as described in Chapter 11.
2 Remove the clutch master cylinder as described in Chapter 4, and the brake master cylinder as described in Section 11 of this Chapter.

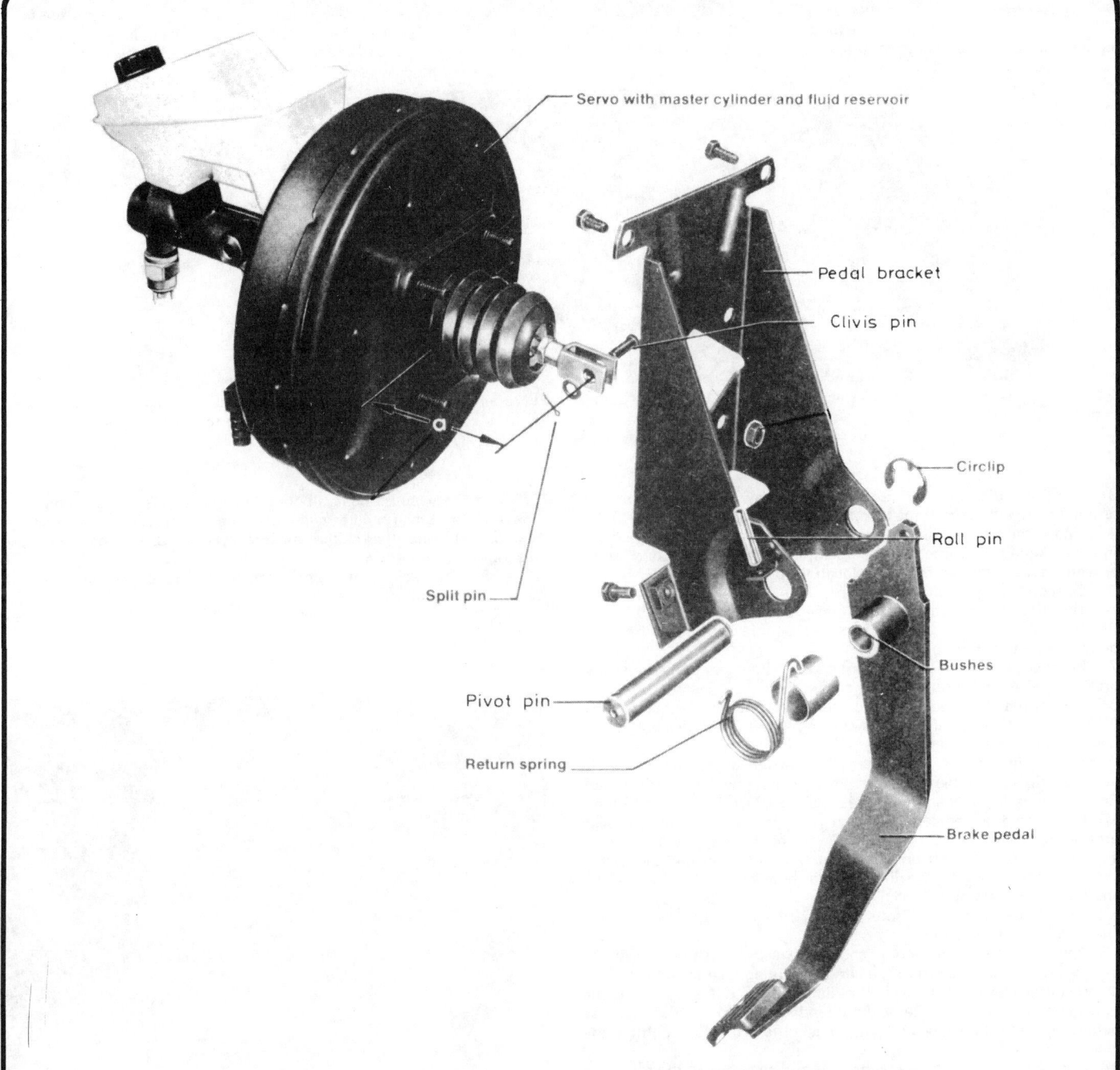

Fig. 9.17 Exploded view of the brake pedal and pedal bracket assembly – 2.0 litre models (Sec 24)

a = Specified servo unit pushrod length

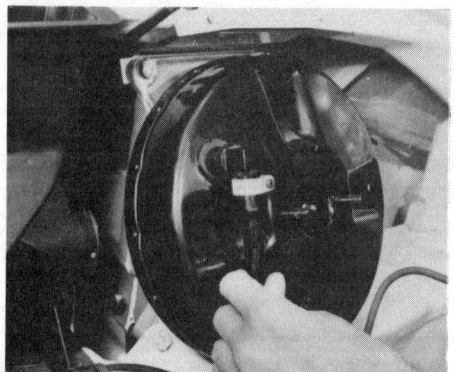

24.3 Removing the vacuum hose elbow connector from the servo grommet

24.4A Undo the four pedal bracket retaining bolts (right-hand pair arrowed) ...

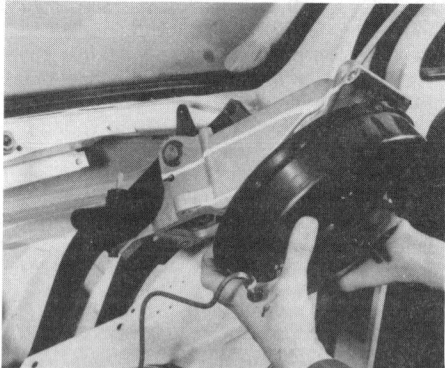

24.4B ... then lift out the bracket assembly complete with pedals and servo

24.5 Servo pushrod clevis pin, washer and retaining split pin (arrowed)

24.6 Servo to pedal bracket retaining nuts (arrowed)

24.8 Clutch pedal return spring (A) and pedal pivot shaft retaining circlip (B)

3   Carefully prise out the vacuum hose elbow connector from the grommet on the servo front face, using a screwdriver (photo).
4   Undo the four bolts securing the pedal bracket assembly to the front bulkhead. Lift the bracket complete with pedals and servo upwards and out of its bulkhead location (photos).
5   Extract the split pin and washer then withdraw the clevis pin securing the servo pushrod to the brake pedal (photo).
6   Undo the four nuts and washers and withdraw the servo from the pedal bracket (photo).
7   Remove the clutch pedal return spring with pliers and release the brake pedal return spring using a screwdriver.
8   Extract the circlip securing the pedal pivot shaft in position (photo) then tap the shaft out of the bracket using a drift. The brake and clutch pedals can now be lifted out.
9   The bushes in the pedals can be removed by driving them out using a drift of suitable diameter. Press in new bushes using a vice. Renew the pedal pivot shaft if there are signs of scoring or wear ridges.
10 Lubricate the pedal bushes and pivot shaft with multi-purpose grease then place the pedals and brake pedal return spring in position.
11 Refit the pivot shaft ensuring that the roll pin in the end of the shaft locates in the groove in the pedal bracket (photo). Secure the shaft with the retaining circlip.
12 Locate the brake pedal return spring over the pedal and refit the clutch pedal return spring.
13 Before refitting the servo, check the servo pushrod length by measuring the distance from the servo mounting face to the centre of the pushrod clevis pin hole. If the dimension is not as given in the Specifications, slacken the locknut and turn the pushrod end as necessary until the specified length is obtained. Now tighten the locknut.
14 Refit the servo to the pedal bracket and secure with the four nuts and washers.
15 Secure the pushrod to the brake pedal with the clevis pin and washer, retained with a new split pin.
16 Position the pedal bracket assembly in the vehicle then refit and fully tighten the four retaining bolts.

17 Refit the vacuum hose elbow connector to the servo grommet.
18 Refit the brake master cylinder using the procedure described in Section 11, and the clutch master cylinder using the procedure described in Chapter 4.
19 Refit the facia panel and instrument panel as described in Chapters 11 and 10 respectively.

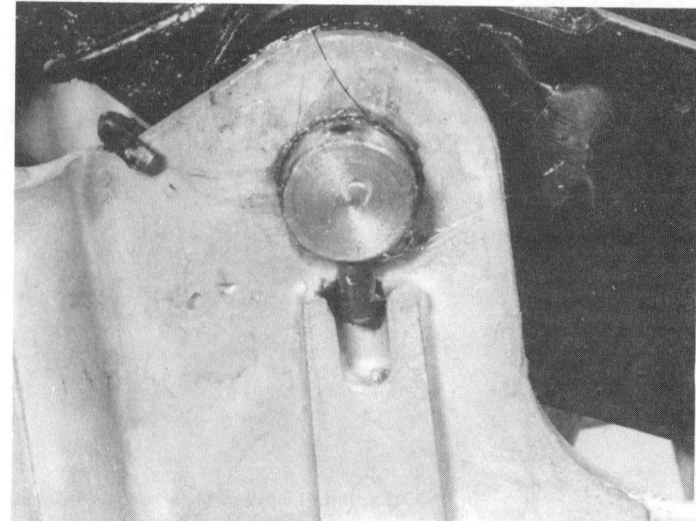

24.11 The pedal pivot shaft roll pin must engage with the bracket groove

25 Vacuum servo unit – description

On 2.0 litre models a vacuum servo unit is fitted into the brake hydraulic circuit in series with the master cylinder. The servo reduces the effort required to operate the brakes under all braking conditions.

The unit operates by vacuum obtained from the inlet manifold and consists of a booster diaphragm, control valve, and a non-return valve.

The servo unit and hydraulic master cylinder are connected together so that the servo unit piston rod acts as the master cylinder pushrod. The driver's braking effort is transmitted through another pushrod to the servo unit piston and its built-in control system. The servo unit piston does not fit tightly into the cylinder, but has a strong diaphragm to keep its edges in constant contact with the cylinder wall, so assuring an airtight seal between the two parts. The forward chamber is held under vacuum conditions created in the inlet manifold of the engine and, during periods when the brake pedal is not in use, the controls open a passage to the rear chamber so placing it under vacuum conditions as well. When the brake pedal is depressed, the vacuum passage to the rear chamber is cut off and the chamber opened to atmospheric pressure. The consequent rush of air pushes the servo piston forward in the vacuum chamber and operates the main pushrod to the master cylinder.

The controls are designed so that assistance is given under all conditions and, when the brakes are not required, vacuum in the rear chamber is established when the brake pedal is released. All air from the atmosphere entering the rear chamber is passed through a small air filter.

26 Vacuum servo unit – removal and refitting

1   The servo unit and brake master cylinder are located together behind the instrument panel. The servo is removed in conjunction with the brake and clutch pedals and pedal bracket, and full details will be found in Section 24, paragraphs 1 to 6 and 13 to 19.

27 Vacuum servo unit – testing

1   With the engine switched off depress the footbrake several times and then hold it down. Start the engine and, as this is done, there should be a noticeable 'give' in the brake pedal.

2   Allow the engine to run for at least two minutes and then switch it off. If the brake pedal is now depressed again, a slight hiss should be noticeable from the unit when the pedal is depressed. After abour four or five applications no further hissing will be heard and the pedal will feel considerably firmer.

3   If the servo does not function as described, check the vacuum hose and all unions for leaks and check the operation of the non-return valve. To do this disconnect the vacuum hose from the connector on the inlet manifold or air intake housing. Slacken the hose clamp and withdraw the non-return valve from the vacuum hose (photo). Check that it is only possible to blow through the valve in the direction of the arrow stamped on the body. Renew the valve if faulty.

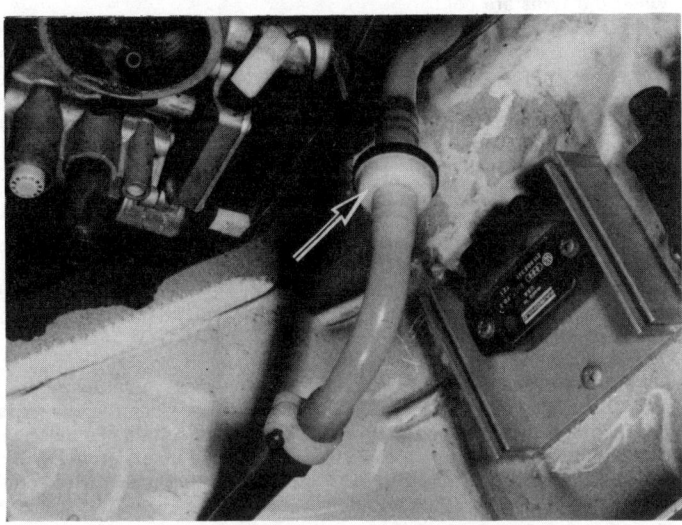

27.3 Servo vacuum hose non-return valve (arrowed)

4   If no leaks were found in the vacuum hose and the non-return valve is operating correctly, renew the servo air filter. To do this the servo must be removed as described in Section 24. Once this has been done, withdraw the rubber boot surrounding the servo pushrod, slacken the locknut and unscrew the clevis end from the pushrod.

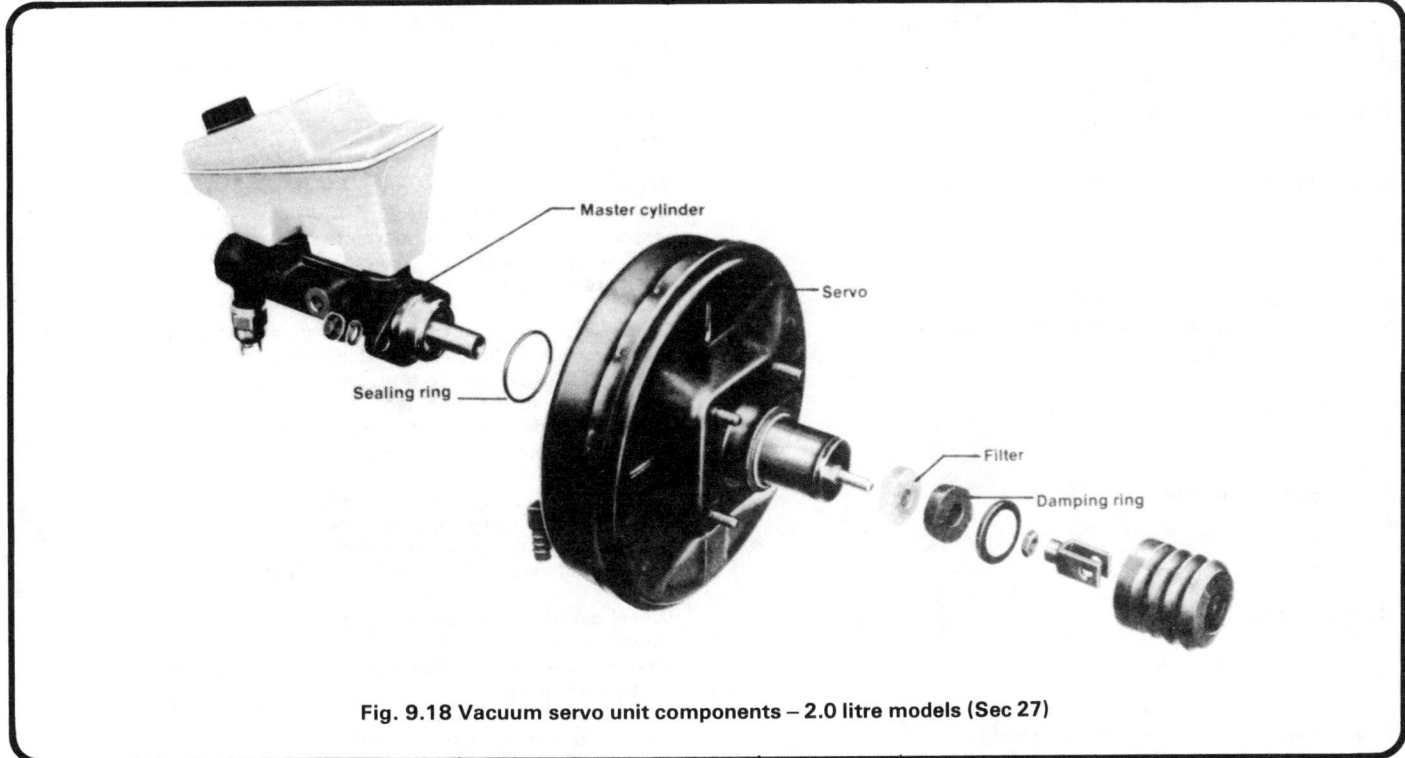

Fig. 9.18 Vacuum servo unit components – 2.0 litre models (Sec 27)

Hook out the seal, damping ring and air filter and renew these components. Reassemble, then refit the servo as described in Section 24, ensuring that the pushrod length is accurately adjusted as described.

5   If the servo is still inoperative, renewal will be necessary. It is not possible to dismantle the servo for repairs as it is a sealed unit and parts are not available separately.

28 Wheels and tyres

1   Check the tyre pressures regularly (see Routine Maintenance) when the tyres are cold.
2   Frequently inspect the tyre walls and treads for damage and pick out any stones which have become trapped in the tread pattern.
3   In the interests of extending tread life, the wheels and tyres can be moved between front and rear on the same side of the vehicle. If the tyres have been balanced on the vehicle, it may be necessary to have them rebalanced after rotation.
4   Never mix tyres of different construction, or very dissimilar tread patterns.
5   Always keep the roadwheels tightened to the specified torque, and if the wheel nut or bolt holes become elongated or flattened, renew the wheel.
6   Occasionally, clean the inner faces of the roadwheels and if there is any sign of rust or corrosion, paint them with metal preservative paint.
7   Before removing a roadwheel that has been balanced on the car, always mark one wheel stud or bolt hole and make a corresponding mark on the stud or hub flange. This will ensure that the wheel is always refitted in the same relative position to maintain the balance.
8   Should unexpected excessive wear be noticed on any of the tyres, its cause must be identified and rectified immediately. Generally speaking the wear pattern can be used as a guide to the cause. If a tyre is worn excessively in the centre of the tread face but not on the edges, over inflation is indicated. Similarly if the edges are worn, but not the centre, under inflation may be the cause. If both the front or rear tyres are wearing on their inside or outside edges, this is likely to be due to incorrect toe setting. If only one tyre is exhibiting this tendency then there may be a problem with the steering geometry, a worn steering or suspension component, or a faulty tyre. Wheel and tyre imbalance is indicated by irregular and uneven wear patches appearing periodically around the tread face.

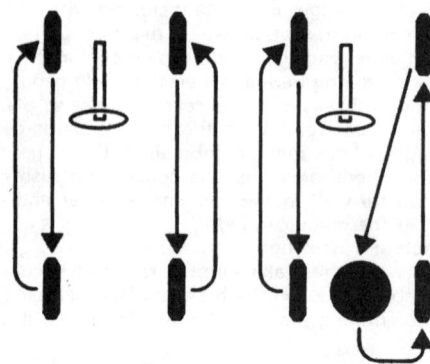

Fig. 9.19 Tyre rotational sequence (Sec 28)

Left-hand sequence – without spare
Right-hand sequence – incorporating spare

29 Fault diagnosis – braking system, wheels and tyres

Symptom	Reason(s)
Excessive pedal travel	Rear brake self-adjust mechanism inoperative Air in hydraulic system Incorrectly adjusted master cylinder or servo pushrod Faulty master cylinder Incorrectly adjusted front hub bearings – see Chapter 8
Brake pedal feels spongy	Air in hydraulic system Faulty master cylinder
Judder felt through brake pedal or steering wheel when braking	Excessive run-out or distortion of front discs or rear drums Brake pads or linings worn Insecure brake caliper or backplate Wear in suspension or steering components or mountings – see Chapters 7 and 8
Excessive pedal pressure required to stop vehicle	Faulty servo unit, non-return valve, or vacuum hose (where fitted) Wheel cylinder(s) or caliper piston seized Brake pads or linings worn or contaminated Brake shoes incorrectly fitted Incorrect grade of pads or linings fitted Primary or secondary hydraulic circuit failure
Brakes pull to one side	Brake pads or linings worn or contaminated Wheel cylinder or caliper piston seized Brake pads or linings renewed on one side only Steering or suspension defect – see Chapter 7 and 8
Brakes binding	Wheel cylinder or caliper piston seized Handbrake incorrectly adjusted Incorrectly adjusted master cylinder or servo pushrod Faulty master cylinder
Rear wheels locking under normal braking	Rear brake linings contaminated Faulty brake pressure regulator

Symptom	Reason(s)
Wheel wobble and vibration	Roadwheels out of balance Roadwheels buckled or distorted Faulty or damaged tyre Wheel nuts or wheel bolts loose Steering or suspension defect – see Chapters 7 and 8
Tyre wear uneven	Wheel alignment incorrect – see Chapters 7 and 8 Worn steering or suspension components – see Chapters 7 and 8 Roadwheels out of balance Faulty tyre Accident damage

Chapter 10 Electrical system

Contents

Specifications

System type .... 12 volt, negative earth

Battery
Type .... Low maintenance or maintenance free 'sealed for life'
Capacity .... 45 amp hr, 54 amp hr or 63 amp hr

Alternator
Type .... Bosch
Maximum output .... 45 amp or 65 amp
Brush length:
    New .... 10 mm (0.4 in)
    Minimum .... 5 mm (0.2 in)
Drivebelt deflection .... Approximately 15 mm (0.6 in) under moderate pressure midway between pulleys

Starter motor
Type .... Bosch pre-engaged
Minimum brush length .... 11.5 mm (0.45 in)

Fuses

Fuse	Circuits protected	Rating (A)
1	Left-hand tail light, parking light and side marker light	8
2	Right-hand tail light, parking light and side marker light, number plate lamps	8
3	Left-hand dipped beam	8
4	Right-hand dipped beam	8
5	Left-hand main beam, main beam warning lamp	8
6	Right-hand main beam	8
7	Not used (accessories)	
8	Interior lights, brake lights, cigarette lighter	8
9	Hazard flasher system	16
10	Windscreen wipers, windscreen washer pump, heated rear window, auxiliary heater temperature control	16
11	Direction indicators	8
12	Horn, reversing lights	8

Additional line fuses located to the right of the fuse box protect the following circuits (where fitted):
Fresh air blower 16
Foglights 16
Auxiliary heater blower 16
Auxiliary heater overheating protection 8

Relays

Relay		System (where applicable)	Nm	lbf ft
1	....	Hazard flashers	35	26
2	....	Fluorescent light (ambulance version only)	20	15
3	....	Load reduction relay	20	15
4	....	Foglamp or ignition key warning buzzer/relay	20	15
5	....	Windscreen wash/wipe delay	8	6
			5	4

Torque wrench settings

Alternator pulley nut ....
Alternator mounting bolt ....
Alternator tensioning bracket bolts ....
Alternator to heater blower housing ....
Windscreen wiper spindle retaining nuts ....
Windscreen wiper arm retaining nuts ....

1 General description

The electrical system is of the 12 volt negative earth type, and consists of a 12 volt battery, alternator, starter motor and related electrical accessories, components and wiring. The battery is of the low maintenance or maintenance free, 'sealed for life' type and is charged by an alternator which is belt-driven from the crankshaft pulley. The starter motor is of the pre-engaged type incorporating an integral solenoid. On starting, the solenoid moves the drive pinion into engagement with the flywheel ring gear before the starter motor is energised. Once the engine has started, a one-way clutch prevents the motor armature being driven by the engine until the pinion disengages from the flywheel.

Further details of the major electrical systems are given in the relevant Sections of this Chapter.

Caution: *Before carrying out any work on the vehicle electrical system, read through the precautions given in Safety First! at the beginning of this manual and in Section 2 of this Chapter.*

2 Electrical system – precautions

It is necessary to take extra care when working on the electrical system to avoid damage to semi-conductor devices (diodes and transistors), and to avoid the risk of personal injury. In addition to the precautions given in Safety First! at the beginning of this manual, observe the following items when working on the system.

1 *Always remove rings, watches, etc before working on the electrical system.* Even with the battery disconnected, capacitive discharge could occur if a component live terminal is earthed through a metal object. This could cause a shock or nasty burn.

2 *Do not reverse the battery connections.* Components such as the alternator or any other having semi-conductor circuitry could be irreparably damaged.

3 If the engine is being started using jump leads and a slave battery, connect the batteries *positive to positive* and *negative to negative.* This also applies when connecting a battery charger.

4 Never disconnect the battery terminals, or alternator wiring when the engine is running.

5 The battery leads and alternator wiring must be disconnected before carrying out any electric welding on the car.

6 Never use an ohmmeter of the type incorporating a hand cranked generator for circuit or continuity testing.

3 Maintenance and inspection

1 At the intervals given in Routine Maintenance at the beginning of this manual, carry out the following maintenance and inspection operations on the electrical system components.

2 Check the operation of all the electrical equipment, ie wipers, washers, lights, direction indicators, horn, etc. Refer to the appropriate Sections of this Chapter if any components are found to be inoperative.

3 Visually check all accessible wiring connectors, harnesses and retaining clips for security, or any signs of chafing or damage. Rectify any problems encountered.

4 Check the alternator drivebelt for cracks, fraying or damage.

Renew the belt if worn or, if satisfactory, check and adjust the belt tension. These procedures are covered in Sections 6 and 7.

5 Check the condition of the wiper blades and if they are cracked or show signs of deterioration, renew them, as described in Section 31. Check the operation of the windscreen washers and adjust the nozzles using a pin, if necessary.

6 On batteries where provision is made for topping up, check the level of electrolyte in each cell by viewing the level through the transparent casing. If the electrolyte level is below the lower level mark, add distilled or demineralized water to bring the level up to the upper mark. Do not overfill the cells or the battery may be damaged when charging.

7 Check the battery terminals, and if there is any sign of corrosion disconnect and clean them thoroughly. Smear the terminals and battery posts with petroleum jelly. If there is any corrosion on the battery tray, remove the battery, clean the deposits away and treat the affected metal with an anti-rust preparation. Repaint the tray in the original colour after treatment.

8 Top up the windscreen washer reservoir and check the security of the pump wires and water pipes.

9 It is advisable to have the headlight aim adjusted using optical beam setting equipment.

10 While carrying out a road test check the operation of all the instruments and warning lights, and the operation of the direction indicator self-cancelling mechanism.

4 Battery – removal and refitting

1 The battery is located in the driver's cab beneath the front right-hand side seat.

2 To gain access to the battery, move the seat fully forward or, if swivel seats are fitted, turn the seat through 180°.

3 Lift up the battery box lid, slacken the negative (-) terminal clamp bolt and lift the terminal off the battery post (photo).

4.3 Battery with negative terminal disconnected

4   Slacken the positive (+) terminal clamp bolt and lift the terminal off the battery post.
5   Remove the battery retaining clamp and withdraw the battery from its location.
6   Refitting the battery is the reverse sequence to removal.

5   Battery – charging

1   In winter when a heavy demand is placed on the battery, such as when starting from cold and using more electrical equipment, it may be necessary to have the battery fully charged from an external source. This can be carried out quite effectively by connecting the battery to a slow or 'trickle' charger. The charging rate should be approximately 10% of the battery capacity i.e. for a 45 amp hour battery, the charge rate should be 4.5 amps. In all cases however the charging rate should not exceed 6 amps.
2   The leads of the battery charger and the terminals of the battery must be connected positive to positive and negative to negative. Ensure that the charger is switched off before connecting or disconnecting the charger leads.
3   On batteries where provision is made for topping up, ensure that the electrolyte level is between the MIN and MAX marks on the battery case and top up with distilled water if necessary. Unscrew the vent caps before charging.
4   Rapid charging on boost charging equipment should only be carried out by a VW agent or auto electrician. It is necessary to accurately monitor the charge rate and electrolyte temperature when rapid charging, and certain maintenance free type batteries are not suited to this process. If in any doubt about the suitability of certain types of charging equipment with maintenance free batteries, consult a VW agent or automotive electrical specialist.

6   Alternator drivebelt – adjustment

1   The drivebelt should be checked and re-tensioned at regular intervals (see Routine Maintenance). It should be renewed at these service intervals if it shows any sign of fraying or deterioration.
2   The belt tension is correct when the belt will deflect under moderate finger pressure, midway along its length, by the amount given in the Specifications.
3   If adjustment is necessary slacken the alternator mounting bolt and tensioning bracket adjustment bolt (Fig. 10.2). Pivot the alternator away from the fan housing until the correct tension is obtained then tighten the two bolts.

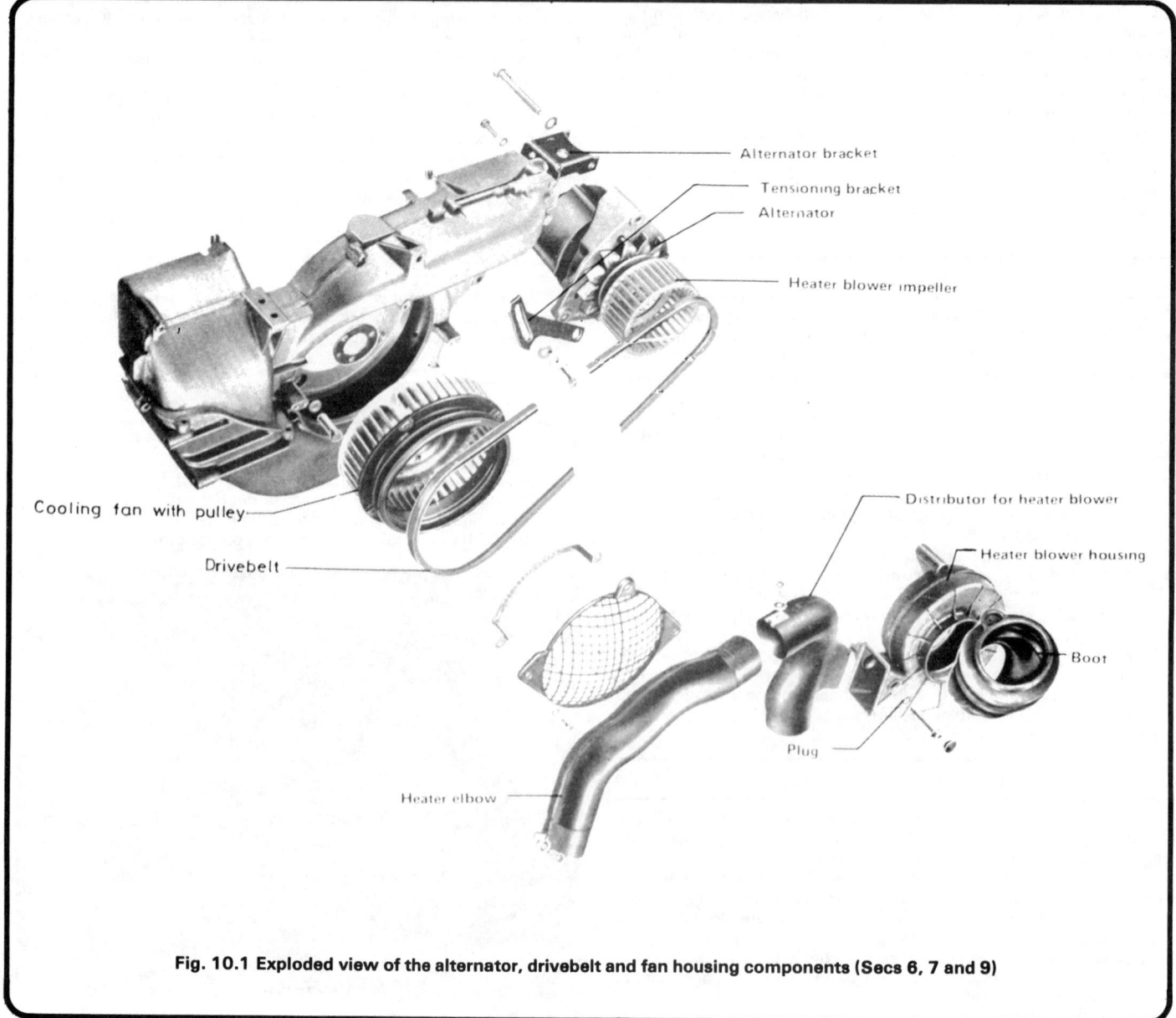

Alternator bracket

Tensioning bracket

Alternator

Heater blower impeller

Cooling fan with pulley

Drivebelt

Distributor for heater blower

Heater blower housing

Boot

Plug

Heater elbow

Fig. 10.1 Exploded view of the alternator, drivebelt and fan housing components (Secs 6, 7 and 9)

Fig. 10.2 Alternator tensioning bracket adjustment bolt (1) and mounting bolt (2) (Sec 6)

7 Alternator drivebelt – removal and refitting

1 Disconnect the battery negative terminal.
2 Withdraw the heater blower housing boot (photo).
3 Undo the retaining screws and remove the heater elbow (photo).
4 Undo the three bolts and lift off the protective grille and timing scale from the fan housing.
5 Lift out the heater blower distributor pipe (photo).
6 Slacken the alternator mounting bolt and tensioning bracket adjustment bolt, move the alternator towards the fan housing and slip the drivebelt off the fan pulley.

7 Remove the socket headed bolts and the alternator mounting bolt securing the heater blower housing to the alternator (photos).
8 Slip the drivebelt out from between the alternator pulley and heater blower housing, feed it round the housing and remove it from the engine.
9 Fit the new drivebelt then reattach the heater blower housing to the alternator.
10 With the drivebelt in place adjust the tension as described in the previous Section then refit the remaining components using the reverse of the removal sequence.

8 Alternator – general description

Vehicles covered by this manual are equipped with Bosch alternators. All are virtually identical in construction but have different outputs. The alternator generates alternating current (ac) which is rectified by diodes into direct current (dc) as this is the current needed for charging the battery.

The alternator is of the rotating field, ventilated design and consists principally of a laminated stator on which is wound the output winding, a rotor carrying the field winding, and a diode rectifier. A voltage regulator is separately mounted at the rear. The alternator generates its current in the stator windings and the rotor carries the field. The field brushes therefore are only required to carry a light current and as they run on simple slip rings they have a relatively long life. This design makes the alternator a reliable machine requiring little servicing.

The rotor is belt-driven from the crankshaft through a pulley keyed to the rotor shaft.

9 Alternator – removal and refitting

1 Refer to Section 7 and carry out the operations described in paragraphs 1 to 8.

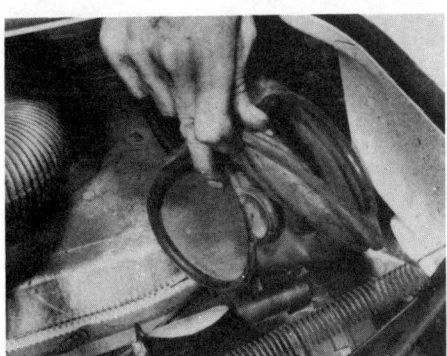

7.2 Removing the heater blower housing boot

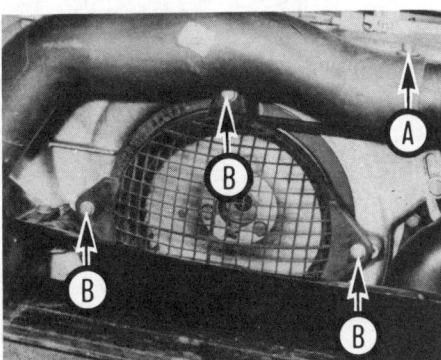

7.3 Heater elbow (A) and fan protective grille retaining bolts (B)

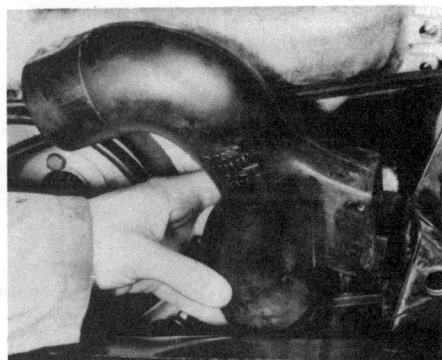

7.5 Removing the heater blower distributor pipe

7.7A Heater blower housing to alternator front retaining bolt (arrowed)

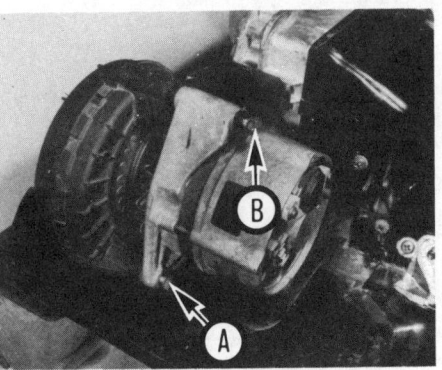

7.7B Heater blower housing rear retaining bolt (A) and alternator mounting bolt (B)

9.2 Removing the alternator and heater blower housing

Fig. 10.3 Alternator voltage regulator and brushbox assembly
(Sec 11)

2   Disconnect the wiring at the rear of the alternator then remove the
unit complete with heater blower housing from the engine (photo).
3   To refit the alternator place it in position, complete with heater
blower housing and reconnect the wiring.
4   Refit the drivebelt then secure the alternator and heater blower
housing using the reverse of the removal procedure contained in
Section 7. Adjust the drivebelt tension as described in Section 6.

10 Alternator – fault tracing and rectification

Due to the specialist knowledge and equipment required to test or
repair an alternator, it is recommended that, if the performance is
suspect, the car be taken to an automobile electrician who will have
the facilities for such work. Because of this recommendation, information is limited to the inspection and renewal of the brushes. Should
the alternator not charge, or the system be suspect, the following
points should be checked before seeking further assistance:

(a)   *Check the drivebelt condition and tension*
(b)   *Ensure that the battery is fully charged*
(c)   *Check the ignition warning light bulb, and renew it if blown*

11 Alternator brushes – inspection and renewal

1   If this operation is being carried out with the alternator in position
on the engine, first disconnect the battery negative terminal.
2   Undo and remove the two screws, spring and plain washers that
secure the brush box to the rear of the slip ring end housing. Lift away
the brush box and voltage regulator.
3   Check that the carbon brushes are able to slide smoothly in their
guides without any sign of binding.
4   Measure the length of the brushes. If they have worn below the
specified limit, they must be renewed.
5   Hold the brush wire with a pair of engineer's pliers and unsolder
it from the brush box. Lift away the two brushes.
6   Insert the new brushes and check to make sure that they are free
to move in their guides. If they bind, lightly polish with a very fine file.
7   Solder the brush wire ends to the brush box taking care that solder
is not allowed to pass to the stranded wire.
8   Whenever new brushes are fitted new springs should also be
fitted.
9   Refitting the brush box is the reverse sequence to removal.

12 Starter motor – general description

When the starter switch is operated, current flows from the
battery to the solenoid which is mounted on the starter body. The

plunger in the solenoid moves inwards, so causing a centrally pivoted
lever to push the drive pinion into mesh with the starter ring gear.
When the solenoid plunger reaches the end of its travel, it closes an
internal contact and full starting current flows to the starter field coils.
The armature is then able to rotate the crankshaft, so starting the
engine.
    A special freewheel clutch is fitted to the starter drive pinion so
that as soon as the engine fires and starts to operate on its own it does
not drive the starter motor.
    When the starter switch is released, the solenoid is de-energised
and a spring moves the plunger back to its rest position. This operates
the pivoted lever to withdraw the drive pinion from engagement with
the starter ring.

13 Starter motor – testing in the car

1   If the starter motor fails to turn the engine when the switch is
operated there are five possible causes:

(a)   *The battery is discharged*
(b)   *The electrical connections between the switch, solenoid,
        battery and starter motor are somewhere failing to pass the
        necessary current from the battery through the starter to
        earth*
(c)   *The solenoid switch is faulty*
(d)   *The starter motor is mechanically or electrically defective*
(e)   *The starter motor pinion and/or flywheel ring gear is badly
        worn and in need of replacement*

2   To check the battery, switch on the headlights. If they dim after a
few seconds the battery is in a discharged state. If the lights glow
brightly, operate the starter switch and see what happens to the lights.
If they dim then you know that power is reaching the starter motor but
failing to turn it. If the starter turns slowly when switched on, proceed
to the next check.
3   If, when the starter switch is operated the light stays bright, then
insufficient power is reaching the motor. Remove the battery connections, starter/solenoid power connections and the engine earth strap
and thoroughly clean them and refit them. Smear petroleum jelly
around the battery connections to prevent corrosion. Corroded connections are the most frequent cause of electric system malfunctions.
4   When the above checks and cleaning tasks have been carried out
but without success, you will possibly have heard a clicking noise each
time the starter switch was operated. This was the solenoid switch
operating, but it does not necessarily follow that the main contacts
were closing properly (if no clicking has been heard from the solenoid,
it is certainly defective). The solenoid contact can be checked by
putting a voltmeter or bulb across the main cable connection on the
starter side of the solenoid and earth. When the switch is operated,

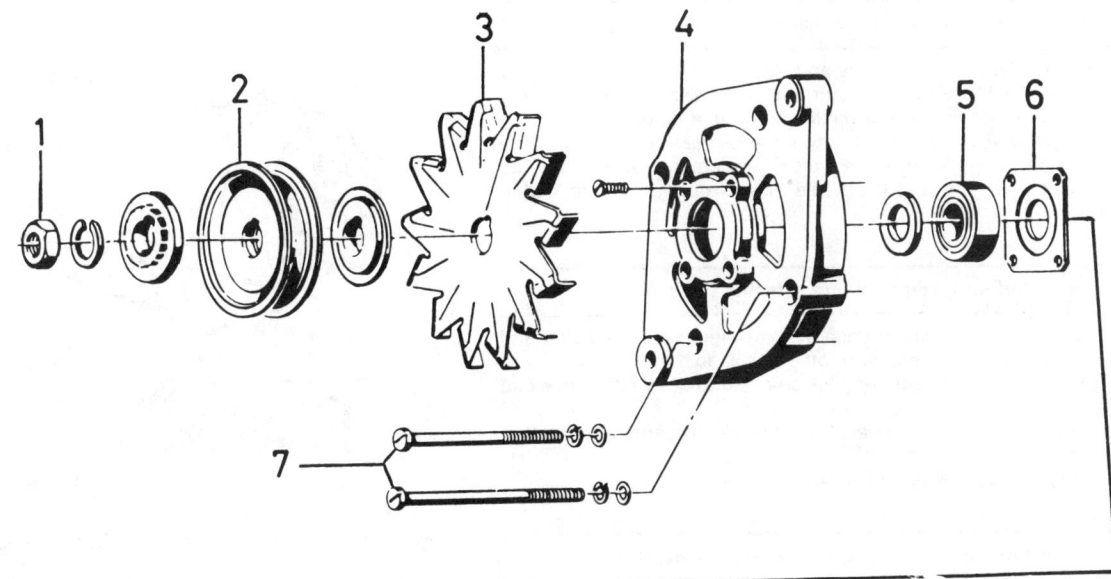

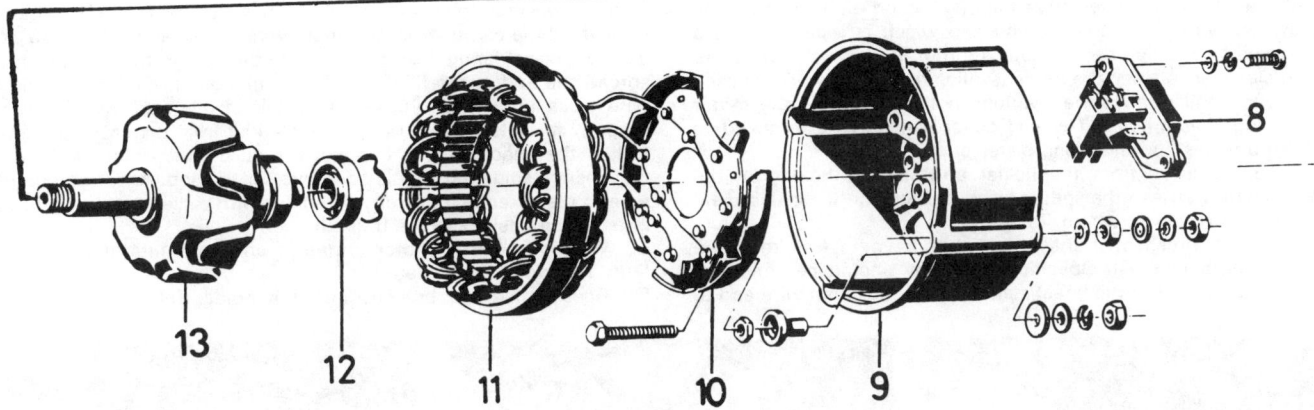

Fig. 10.4 Exploded view of the alternator – typical (Sec 11)

1 Pulley nut	5 Bearing	8 Brush holder/regulator	11 Stator
2 Pulley	6 Bearing retainer	9 Slip ring end housing	12 Bearing
3 Fan	7 Through-bolts	10 Collector ring endplate	13 Rotor
4 Drive end housing			

there should be a reading or lighted bulb. If there is no reading or lighted bulb, the solenoid unit is faulty and should be renewed.

5   If the starter motor operates but doesn't turn the engine over then it is most probable that the starter pinion and/or flywheel ring gear are badly worn, in which case the starter motor will normally be noisy in operation.

6   Finally, if it is established that the solenoid is not faulty and 12 volts are getting to the starter, then the motor is faulty and should be removed for inspection.

14 Starter motor – removal and refitting

1   Jack up the rear of the vehicle and support it on axle stands.

2   Disconnect the battery negative terminal.

3   Working under the rear right-hand side of the vehicle, make a note of the wiring connections at the solenoid and disconnect them.

4   If the wiring harness is secured to the starter motor or solenoid body with a clip or retaining band, release it and move the wiring harness aside.

5   Undo the two bolts securing the starter to the clutch housing and withdraw the starter motor from its location.

6   Refitting is the reverse sequence to removal.

Fig. 10.5 Starter motor location (Sec 14)

1   Wiring harness retaining band

15 Starter motor renovation – general

Such is the inherent reliability and strength of the starter motors fitted it is very unlikely that a motor will need dismantling until it is totally worn out and in need of replacement as a whole.

If, however, the motor is only a couple of years old or so and a pinion carriage, solenoid or brush fault is suspected then remove the motor from the engine and dismantle as described in the following Sections.

16 Starter solenoid – removal and refitting

1   At the rear of the solenoid undo the retaining nut and washer and slip the starter electrical feed wire off the solenoid stud.
2   Undo the two screws securing the solenoid to the starter drive end housing.
3   Disengage the solenoid shaft from the pinion carriage actuating arm and withdraw the solenoid.
4   Refitting is the reverse sequence to removal.

17 Starter motor brushes – inspection and renewal

1   With the starter removed from the engine and on a clean bench, begin by removing the armature end cap which is secured by two small screws on the end of the motor (photo). Remove the armature retaining clip, washers and the rubber sealing ring which were exposed (photo). Undo and remove the two long bolts which hold the motor assembly together (photo). The end cover can now be removed to reveal the brushes and mounting plate (photos).
2   Take the brushes from the holder and slip the holder off the armature shaft. Retrieve the spacer washers between the brush plate and the armature block, where fitted.
3   Inspect the brushes; if they are worn down to less than the minimum length given in Specifications, they should be renewed. Replacement brushes to the latest standard have no shunt wire and to

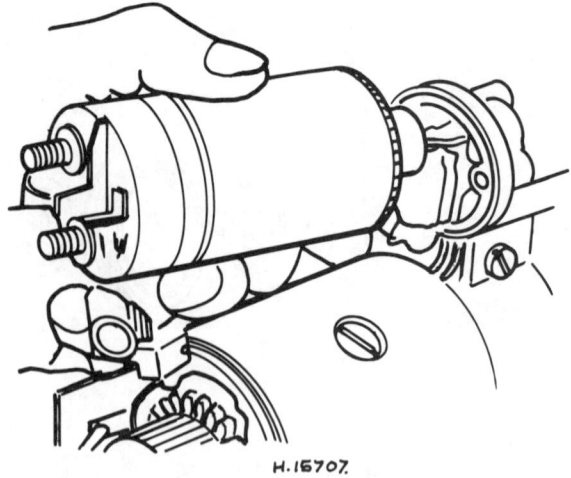

H.16707

Fig. 10.6 Releasing the solenoid from the actuating arm (Sec 16)

fit this type first crush the old brush in a vice, or with a hammer, to remove all the carbon from the shunt wire and scrape the wire to clean it ready for soldering. Insert the wire in the hole in the new brush and spread the end out to fill the countersunk hole in the brush. Hold the wire close under the brush with a pair of pliers to locate the wire properly for soldering and to prevent solder from penetrating the wire further than necessary as this would reduce its flexibility. A 12 to 15 watt pencil soldering iron is adequate for this job. After soldering the wire in place remove any excess solder with a file and check that the brush is an easy fit in the brush holder.
4   Wipe the starter motor armature and commutator with a non-fluffy rag wetted with petrol.
5   Reassemble the brushes into the holder (photo) and refit the

17.1A Remove the armature end cap ...

17.1B ... followed by the retaining clip, washers and sealing ring

17.1C Undo and remove the two long through bolts ...

17.1D ... and lift off the end cover

17.1E Commutator and field coil bushes

17.5 Brush holder with brushes ready for refitting

holder over the armature shaft, remembering to fit the two washers between the holder and armature, where fitted.

6   Refit the motor end cover and secure with two long bolts.

7   Refit the armature shaft end cap after fitting the rubber sealing ring, washer and shaft clip.

18 Starter motor – dismantling and reassembly

1   The complete overhaul of a starter motor is beyond the resources of the average home mechanic as special tools and equipment for testing are necessary, but if the appropriate spares can be obtained repairs can be made by renewing parts. With the starter on the bench proceed as follows.

2   Undo the two screws and remove the end cap from the commutator cover.

3   Prise the clip off the end of the armature and, after carefully noting the sequence of assembly, remove the washers and rubber sealing ring from the armature.

4   Mark the commutator cover relative to the starter yoke and then remove the two long bolts which hold the assembly together. Remove the commutator cover.

5   Lift the brush springs to remove the positive brushes and then remove the brushplate from the assembly. Note and remove any shims that may be fitted.

6   Disconnect the field winding lead from the solenoid terminal and then undo the two remaining screws to release the solenoid from the assembly. As the solenoid is removed unhook the end fitting from the actuating arm.

7   Unscrew and remove the actuating arm pivot and then remove the drive end housing from the yoke assembly. As this is done remove the

rubber plug and the actuating arm. Slide the armature out of the casing.

8   If it is required to remove the pinion or the clutch from the armature, press the retaining ring back on the shaft to enable the snap-ring to be removed. Then slide the components off the shaft.

9   With the starter motor dismantled the various components can be cleaned and inspected for general wear and/or signs of damage. Use a petrol/damped cloth for cleaning, but avoid wetting electrical components. Dry thoroughly with a fluff-free cloth.

10   Renew worn or damaged carbon brushes as explained in Section 17.

11   If the starter motor has shown a tendency to jam or a reluctance to disengage then the starter pinion is almost certainly the culprit. Dirt accumulation on the shaft or on the pinion could cause this. After cleaning off any such dirt, check that the pinion can move freely in a spiral movement along the shaft. If it still tends to bind or stick, or if it is defective in any way, renew the pinion.

12   A badly worn or burnt commutator will need skimming on a lathe but if it is only dirty or lightly marked, clean it up with a piece of fine grade glass paper wrapped round. If the commutator has to be skimmed have the job done by specialists. After skimming, the separators should be undercut using a piece of old hacksaw blade ground down to the same thickness as the separators. Undercut to a depth of about 0.5 to 0.8 mm (0.02 to 0.03 in) and then clean up with fine grade glass cloth. Do not use emery on the commutator as abrasive particles could get embedded in the copper and cause rapid brush wear.

13   An armature with a bent shaft or other signs of damage must be renewed. Electrical checks should be undertaken by an auto-electrician with special equipment. Although simple continuity checks are possible with a lamp and low power source, more extensive checking is needed which is beyond the scope of the home mechanic.

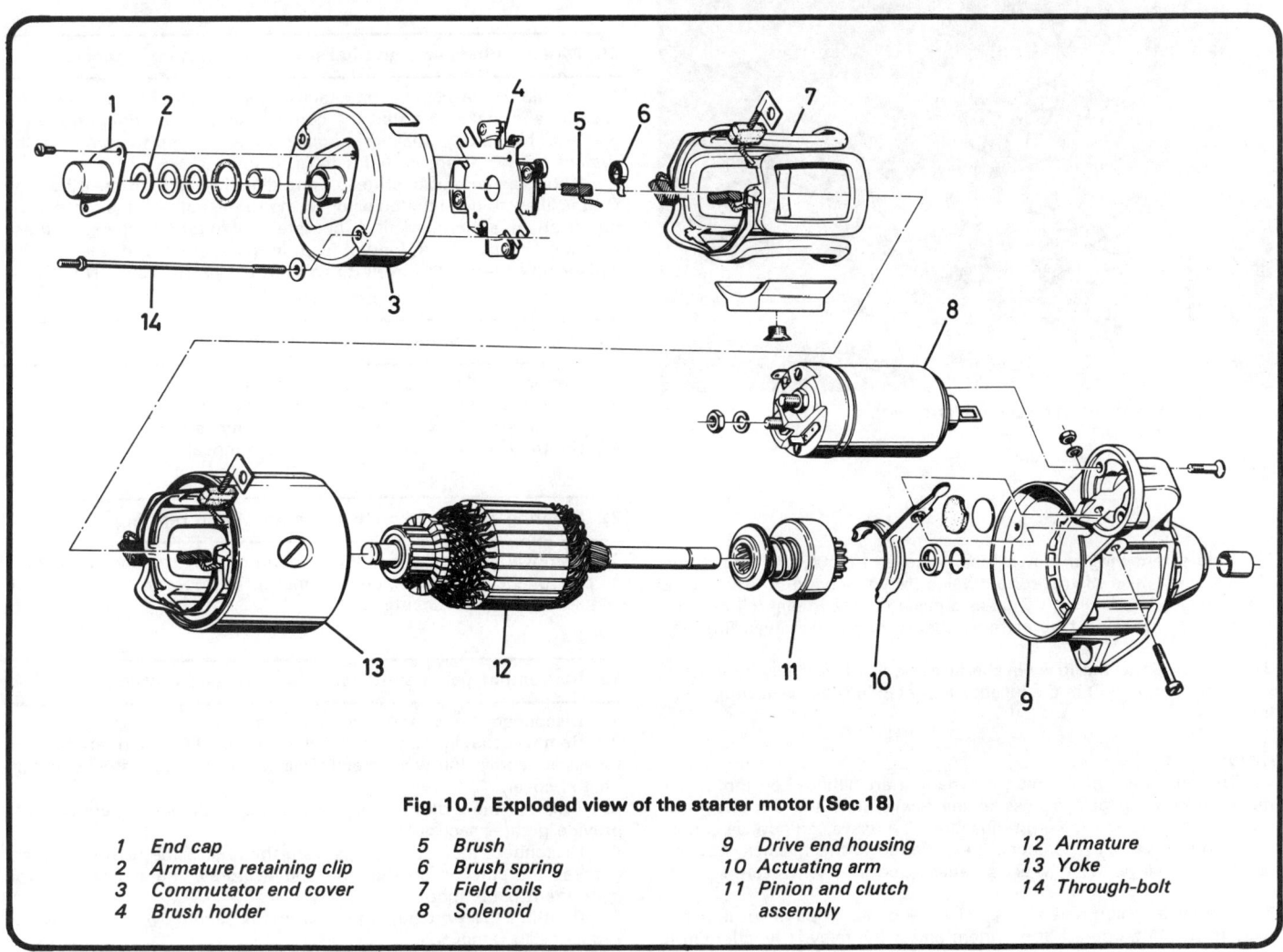

Fig. 10.7 Exploded view of the starter motor (Sec 18)

1 End cap	5 Brush	9 Drive end housing	12 Armature
2 Armature retaining clip	6 Brush spring	10 Actuating arm	13 Yoke
3 Commutator end cover	7 Field coils	11 Pinion and clutch	14 Through-bolt
4 Brush holder	8 Solenoid	assembly	

14 Reassembly of the starter motor is a straightforward reversal of the dismantling sequence, but the following points should be noted.

(a) After assembling the clutch and pinion to the armature shaft, fit the retaining ring using a new snap-ring and then reposition the retainer

(b) Make sure that all shims and washers are fitted in the correct order

(c) Align the locating key and slot when assembling the yoke to the end housing

(d) Make sure that the carbon brushes slide freely in their boxes

(e) Lightly oil all sliding parts including the armature spiral spline, the actuating arm sliding surfaces, the clutch bearing surfaces and armature bearings. Of course, no oil must contaminate the commutator or brushes

19 Fuses and relays – general

Fuses

1 The fusebox is situated below the facia on the left-hand side (photo). To gain access to the fuses simply lift off the transparent plastic cover. The fuse numbers are shown on the cover and information on the circuits they protect is given in the Specifications. Each fuse is colour coded and has its rating stamped on it. To remove a fuse, ease it carefully out of its locating contacts.

19.1 Fusebox with retaining screws (arrowed)

2 Before renewing a blown fuse, trace and rectify the cause and always use a fuse of the correct value. Never substitute a fuse of a higher rating or use such things as a piece of wire, metal foil or a pin to act as a makeshift fuse as more serious damage or even fire may result.

3 In addition to the fuses in the fusebox, line fuses may be located in holders to the right of the fusebox to protect any optional equipment fitted.

Relays

4 The relays are of the plug-in type and are situated on top of the main fusebox. To gain access to the relays undo the three fusebox retaining screws and lower the fusebox. The relays can now be simply pulled out. Five relay positions are provided in the fusebox, but the number of relays actually used varies according to vehicle specification.

5 If a system controlled by a relay becomes inoperative, and the relay is suspect, operate the system and if the relay is functioning it

should be possible to hear it click as it is energised. If this is the case the fault lies with the components of the system. If the relay is not being energized then the relay is not receiving a main supply voltage or a switching voltage, or the relay itself is faulty.

Fig. 10.8 Relay locations (1 to 5) on the fusebox (6) (Sec 19)

20 Direction indicator and hazard flasher system – general

1 Should the flashers become faulty in operation, check the bulbs for security and make sure that the contact surfaces are not corroded. If one bulb blows or is making a poor connection due to corrosion, the system will not flash on that side of the car.

2 If the flasher unit operates in one direction and not the other, the fault is likely to be in the bulbs or wiring to the bulbs. If the system will not flash in either direction, operate the hazard flashers. If these function, check for a blown fuse in position 11. If the fuse is satisfactory the fault is likely to lie with the flasher relay (No. 1).

21 Door pillar switches – removal and refitting

1 Disconnect the battery negative terminal.
2 Undo the retaining screw and withdraw the switch.
3 Disconnect the wiring terminal and remove the switch.
4 Refitting is the reverse sequence to removal.

22 Steering column switches – removal and refitting

1 Removal and refitting of the steering column switches is covered as part of the steering column dismantling procedure and reference should be made to Chapter 8.

23 Instrument panel switches – removal and refitting

1 Disconnect the battery negative terminal.
2 Remove the instrument panel cover by lifting up at the two recesses nearest the windscreen. Disengage the rear catches and lift off the cover.
3 Take out the protective plastic cover over the instrument panel to provide greater access (photo).
4 Disconnect the wiring plugs from the rear of the relevant switch, depress the catches on the side and withdraw the switch from the instrument panel (photo).
5 Refitting the switches and instrument panel cover is the reverse sequence to removal.

Fig. 10.9 Instrument panel cover recesses for removal (arrowed)
(Sec 23)

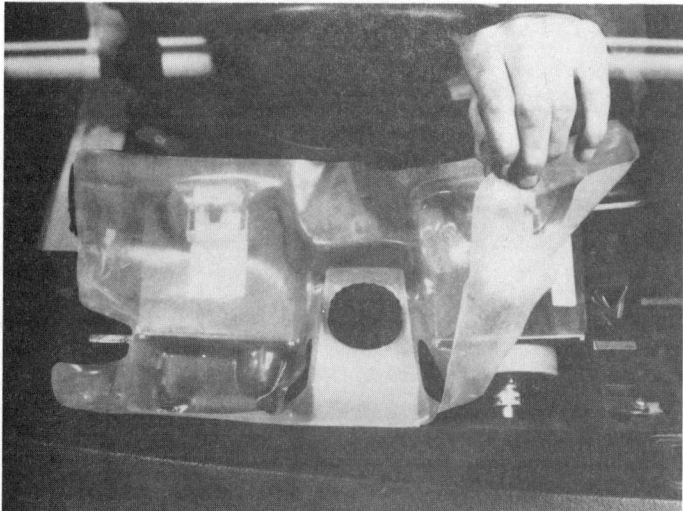

23.3 Removing the instrument panel plastic cover

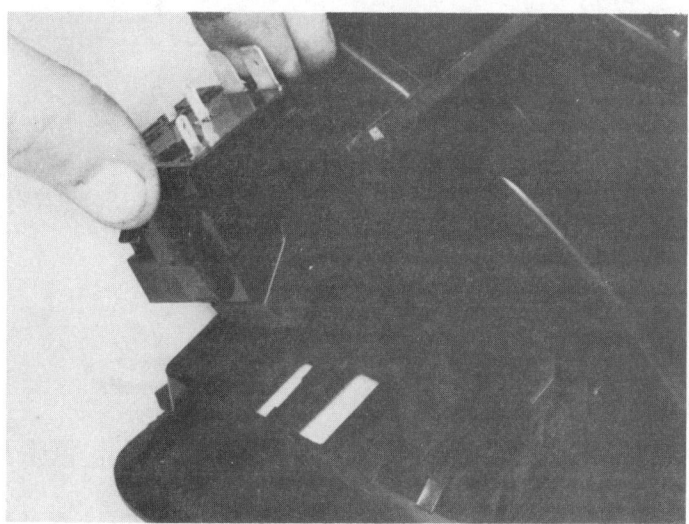

23.4 Instrument panel switch removal

24 Instrument panel illumination bulbs – renewal

1   Carry out the operations described in paragraphs 1 to 3 of the previous Section.
2   The panel illumination bulbholders can now be removed by carefully turning them 90° anti-clockwise (photos).
3   The panel illumination bulbs are a push fit in their holders.
4   Refitting is the reverse sequence to removal.

24.2A Panel illumination bulbholders (arrowed)

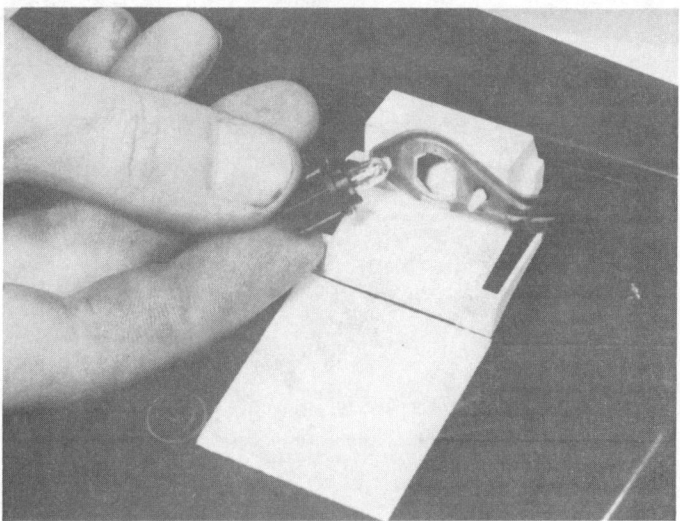

24.2B Removing a panel illumination bulbholder and bulb

25 Instrument panel – removal and refitting

1   Carry out the operations described in paragraphs 1 to 3 of Section 23.
2   Disconnect the wiring plugs from the rear of the instrument panel switches.
3   Disconnect the speedometer cable and the instrument panel wiring multi-plug connector.
4   Undo the screws securing the instrument panel to the facia then lift the panel up and out of its location.
5   Refitting is the reverse sequence to removal.

Fig. 10.10 Instrument panel retaining screws (arrowed) (Sec 25)

26 Instrument panel – dismantling and reassembly

1   Remove the instrument panel from the vehicle as described in the previous Section.

2   Undo the screws securing the warning lamp casing mounting plate and lever the plate off carefully (photo).

3   The panel warning lamp bulb or light emitting diodes (LED) can now be removed by easing back the printed circuit and withdrawing the bulb/LEDs from their terminals (photo). The bulb, where fitted, is coloured blue, all the LEDs are coloured red, yellow or green. The LEDs are polarity conscious and must be fitted into their terminals correctly. The negative terminal of the LED is slightly wider than the positive terminal (Fig. 10.13) and must engage in the corresponding negative terminal of the printed circuit (Fig. 10.14) when refitting.

4   Undo the retaining screw and slide the voltage stabilizer out of its printed circuit connections.

5   Undo the nuts, screws, terminals and tags as applicable then carefully lift off the printed circuit.

6   Undo the four screws securing the speedometer and remove the instrument from the panel.

7   Undo the four screws securing the fuel gauge baseplate and withdraw the baseplate from the panel. Remove the fuel gauge from the panel.

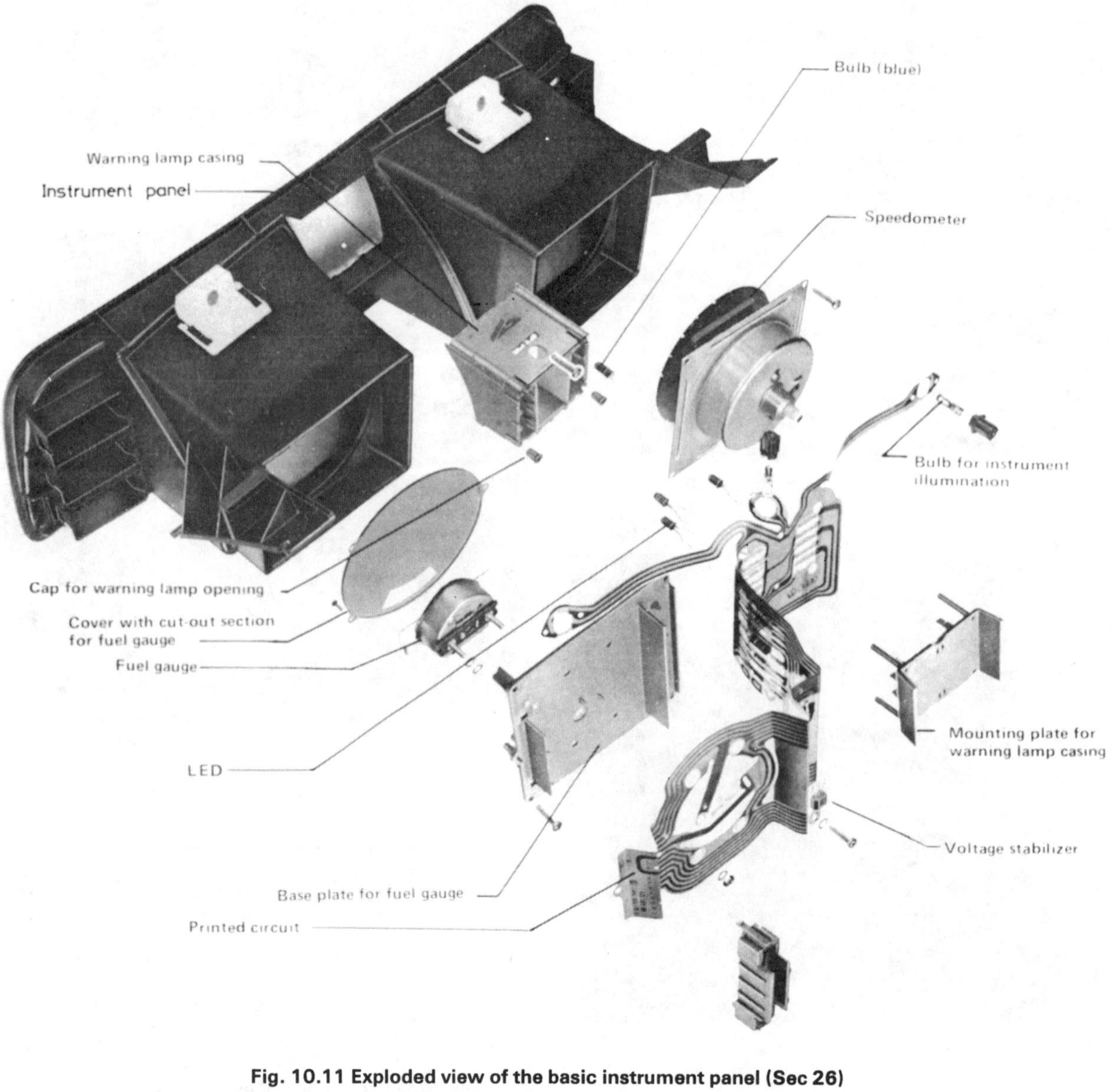

Warning lamp casing

Instrument panel

Bulb (blue)

Speedometer

Bulb for instrument illumination

Cap for warning lamp opening

Cover with cut-out section for fuel gauge

Fuel gauge

Mounting plate for warning lamp casing

LED

Voltage stabilizer

Base plate for fuel gauge

Printed circuit

Fig. 10.11 Exploded view of the basic instrument panel (Sec 26)

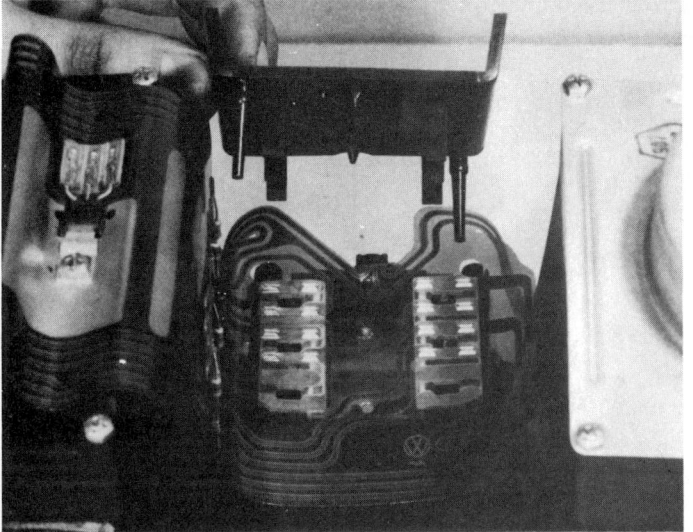

26.2 Ease off the mounting plate carefully to avoid damaging the printed circuit

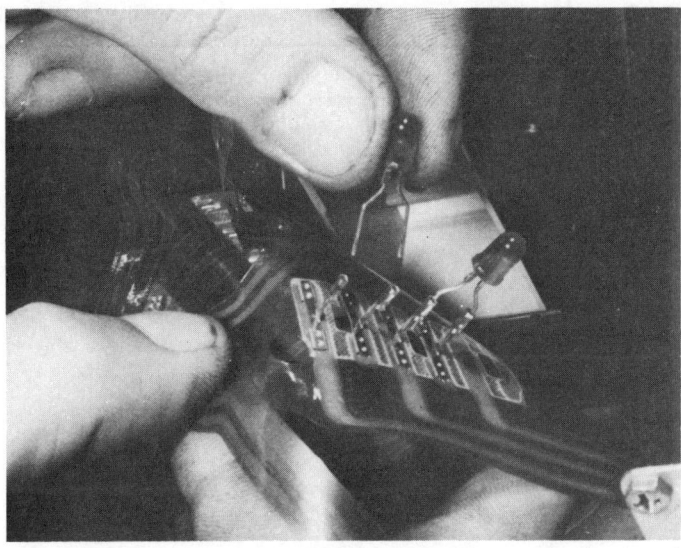

26.3 Renewing the instrument panel warning LEDs

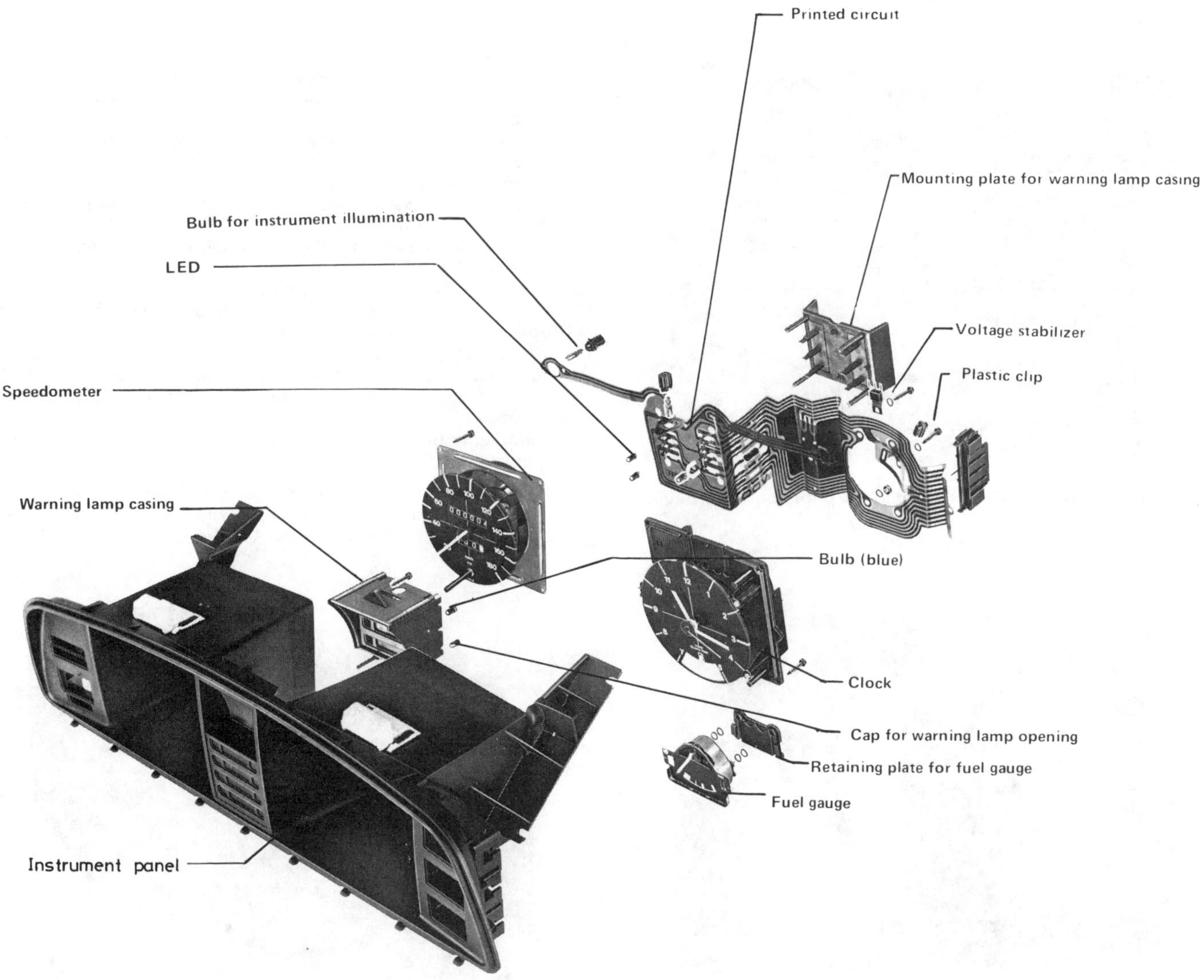

Printed circuit

Mounting plate for warning lamp casing

Bulb for instrument illumination

LED

Voltage stabilizer

Plastic clip

Speedometer

Warning lamp casing

Bulb (blue)

Clock

Cap for warning lamp opening

Retaining plate for fuel gauge

Fuel gauge

Instrument panel

Fig. 10.12 Exploded view of the comprehensive instrument panel (Sec 26)

8   If a clock is fitted undo the retaining screws and withdraw the clock then remove the retaining plate and fuel gauge from the clock face.
9   If necessary the warning lamp casing can be removed after undoing the retaining screws.
10 Reassembly of the instrument panel is the reverse sequence to dismantling.

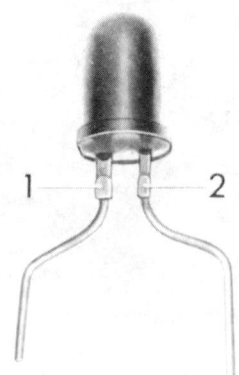

Fig. 10.13 LED negative terminal (1) and positive terminal (2) (Sec 26)

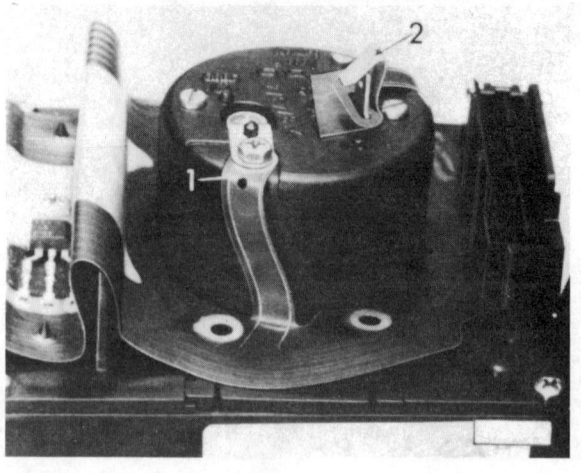

Fig. 10.16 Clock terminal mounting (Sec 26)

1   Printed circuit earth   2   Printed circuit positive

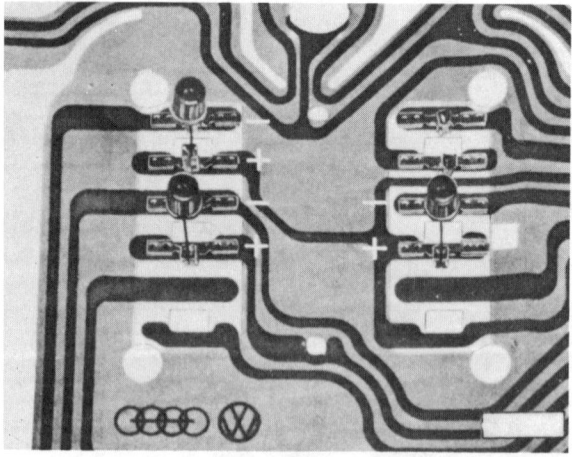

Fig. 10.14 LED terminal positioning in the printed circuit (Sec 26)

27 Speedometer cable – removal and refitting

1   Disconnect the battery negative terminal.
2   Jack up the front of the vehicle and support it on axle stands. Remove the spare wheel.
3   From inside the cab remove the instrument panel cover by lifting up at the two recesses nearest the windscreen. Disengage the rear catches and lift off the cover.
4   Unscrew the cable from the rear of the speedometer.
5   Release the cable from the retaining clips and cable ties and unscrew the cable clip retaining nut.
6   On USA vehicles unscrew the cable at its connections to the EGR/oxygen sensor mileage recorder.
7   Remove the wheel trim, extract the small circlip securing the cable to the hub cap then withdraw the cable from the steering knuckle.
8   Draw the cable down and out of the cab and remove it from under the vehicle.
9   Refitting is the reverse sequence to removal bearing in mind the following points:

(a) Renew the rubber sleeve in the steering knuckle before refitting the cable, ensuring that the sleeve is fitted flush with the edge of the hole in the knuckle

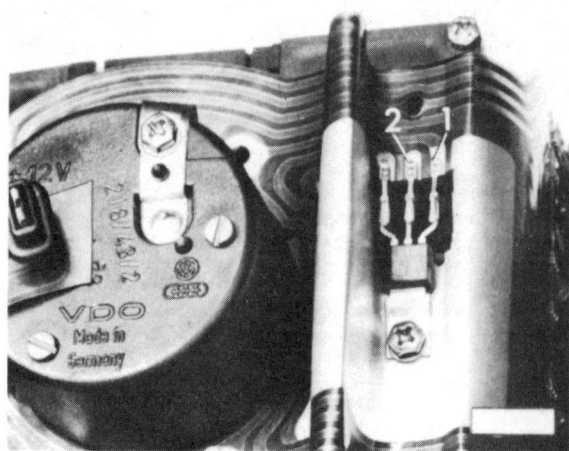

Fig. 10.15 Voltage stabilizer location on instrument panel (Sec 26)

1   Positive terminal   2   Earth terminal

Fig. 10.17 Speedometer cable retaining clip (arrowed) under vehicle (Sec 27)

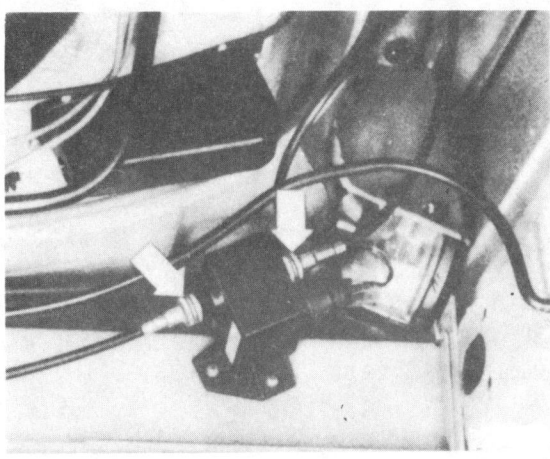

Fig. 10.18 Speedometer cable connections at EGR/oxygen sensor mileage counter (arrowed) – USA vehicles (Sec 27)

Fig. 10.19 Speedometer cable retaining circlip (arrowed) (Sec 27)

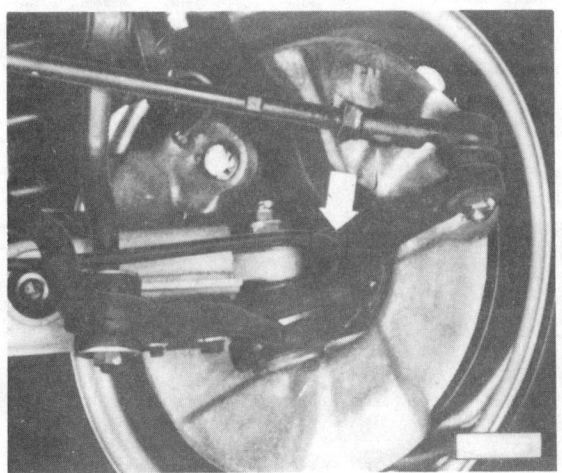

Fig. 10.20 Speedometer cable rubber sleeve location (arrow) in steering knuckle (Sec 27)

(b) *Ensure that the marks on the cable are positioned at the cable clip secured by a retaining nut and route the cable so that it is free of tension and without acute bends*

(c) *Seal the cable end at the hub cap with a rubber sealing compound to prevent water entry*

28 Horn – general

1   The horn is under the front of the vehicle bolted to the frame (photo).

28.1 Horn location under front of vehicle

2   The wires connected to it are the earth wire, which is connected, via the steering column, to the horn button and then to earth when the button is pressed, and the live feed wire which is connected directly to the fusebox.
3   If the horn refuses to function at all then check the earth circuit, testing first from the horn earth terminal, then from the flexible coupling on the steering column, and finally prise out the horn button and disconnect the wire from it and check continuity back to the horn earth terminal. The horn button contacts may be dirty or bent. Check these and clean if necessary. Check the potential at the positive terminal. It should be nearly 12 volts. If the two circuits are correct then the horn itself is at fault.
4   As a last resort the sealing compound on the back which covers the adjusting screw should be chipped away and the adjusting screw turned clockwise $\frac{1}{4}$ turn at a time. If this produces no noise then the horn should be renewed.

29 Bulbs – renewal

Headlamp
1   Either sealed beam or bulb type headlamps may be fitted. The bulb renewal procedure is the same for both types.
2   Remove the front grille panel by turning the five quick release fasteners along the top edge 90° anti-clockwise. Lift the grille up, tip it forward and remove.
3   Undo the three small securing screws around the headlamp retaining ring and lift off the ring (photo).
4   On USA vehicles, disconnect the wiring plug at the rear of the headlamp and remove the unit from the car. Refit the new headlamp unit using the reverse of the removal sequence.
5   On UK vehicles disconnect the wiring plugs from the headlamp and sidelamp bulbs (photos).

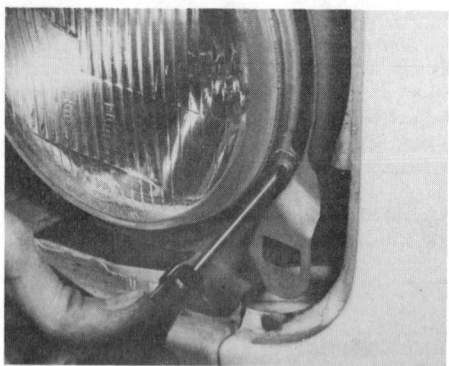

29.3 Removing the headlamp retaining ring screws

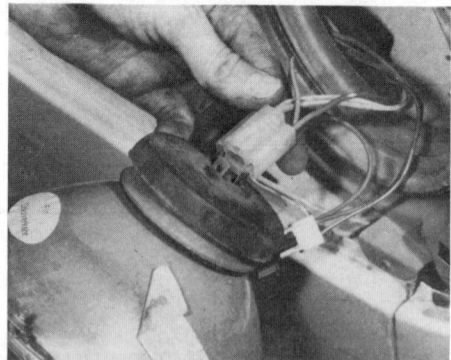

29.5A Disconnecting the wiring plugs from the headlamp ...

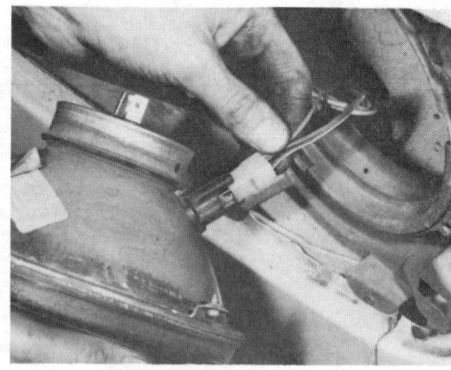

29.5B ... and sidelamp bulbs

6   Lift off the rubber cap and release the bulb by either turning the retaining ring anti-clockwise (photo) if standard bulbs are fitted, or by pivoting back the hinged retaining clip if halogen headlamps are fitted.
7   The bulb can now be lifted out of the lens unit (photo). Take care not to touch the bulb glass with your fingers; if touched, clean the bulb glass with methylated spirit.
8   Refitting the bulb is the reverse sequence to removal. Make sure that the locating tags on the bulb rim engage with the recesses in the lens unit.

Sidelamp
9   On UK vehicles, remove the headlamp assembly as described in paragraphs 2 to 5.
10   Turn the sidelamp bulbholder anti-clockwise to remove it from the headlamp, then remove the bulb by turning it anti-clockwise to remove it from the holder (photos).

11   Refitting is the reverse sequence to removal.
12   On USA vehicles the side marker lamp is incorporated in the direction indicator lens assembly and removal is described in the following sub-section.

Front direction indicators
13   Undo the retaining screws and withdraw the lens unit.
14   Lift up the rubber boot, press the spring clip inwards and remove the bulbholder (photo)
15   Turn the bulb anti-clockwise to remove it from the holder.
16   Refitting is the reverse sequence to removal.

Rear lamp cluster
17   Undo the four retaining screws and withdraw the lens unit (photo).
18   Pull back the rubber boot and disconnect the wiring connector (photo).

29.6 The standard headlamp bulb is held by a retaining ring

29.7 Headlamp bulb removal

29.10A Removing the sidelamp bulbholder from the lens unit ...

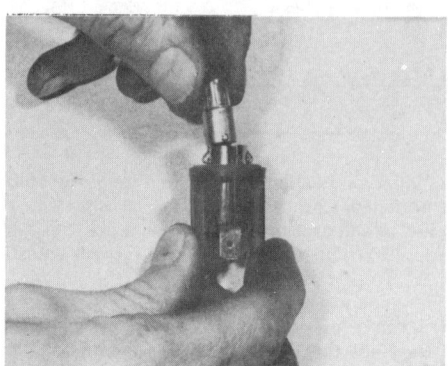

29.10B ... and the bulb from the holder

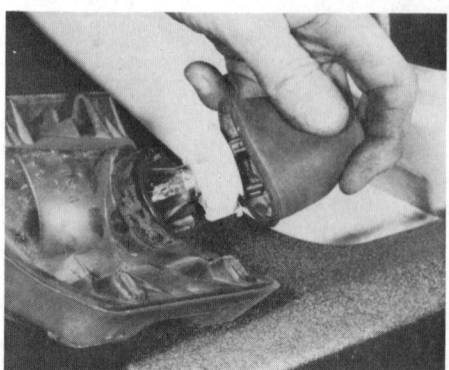

29.14 Removing the direction indicator bulbholder

29.17 The rear lamp cluster is secured by four screws

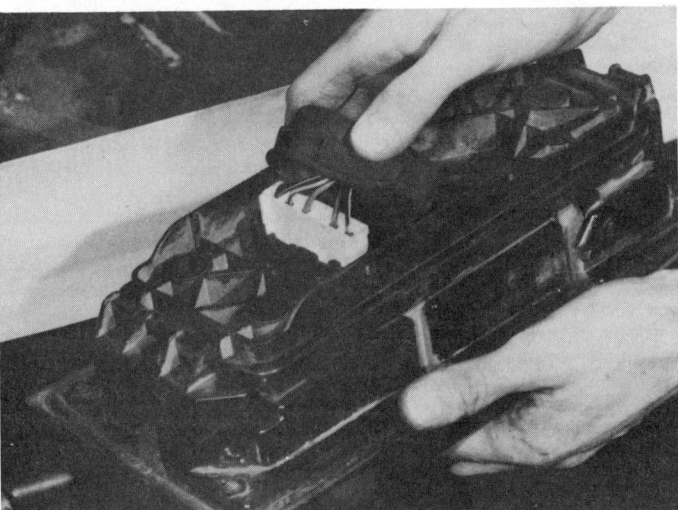

29.18 Removing the rear lamp cluster wiring connector ...

29.19 ... bulb plate ...

29.20 ... and bulb

19 Press the two side lugs together and lift out the bulb plate (photo).
20 Remove the relevant bulb by turning anti-clockwise (photo).
21 Refitting is the reverse sequence to removal.

Rear side marker lamp (USA vehicles)
22 Undo the two screws and withdraw the lens assembly.
23 Pull back the rubber boot, release the spring clip and take out the bulbholder.
24 Turn the bulb anti-clockwise to remove it from the holder.
25 Refitting is the reverse sequence to removal.

Fig. 10.21 Side marker lamp bulbholder spring clip (arrowed) – USA vehicles (Sec 29)

Number plate lamp
26 Undo the retaining screws and withdraw the lens and the bulb holder (photo).
27 Turn the bulb anti-clockwise to remove it from the holder.
28 Refitting is the reverse sequence to removal.

29.26 Number plate lens and bulbholder

Interior light
29 Depress the retaining clip on the left-hand side of the lens using a screwdriver then withdraw the lens and bulb assembly (photo).
30 Withdraw the bulb from its contacts.
31 Refitting is the reverse sequence to removal.

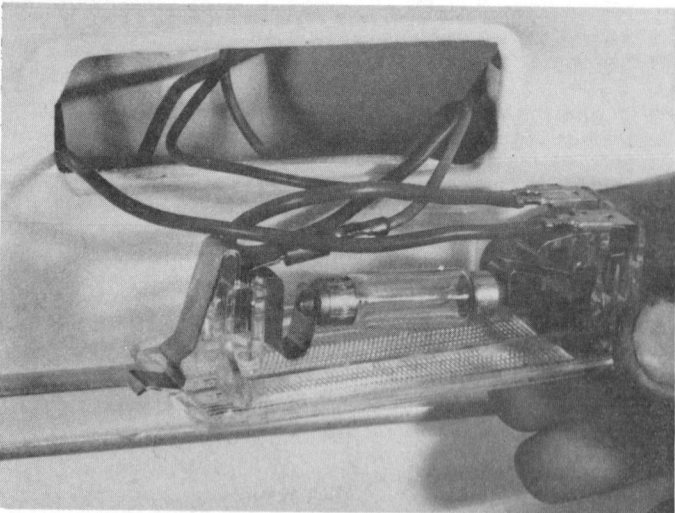

29.29 Depress the retaining clip to remove the interior light assembly

7   Switch the headlamps on to full beam and, using the adjusters, adjust each headlamp to align the beam to shine just below the corresponding cross on the wall or board.

8   Bounce the vehicle on its suspension again to check that the beams return to the correct position. At the same time check the operation of the dipswitch to confirm that the beams dip correctly. Switch off the headlamps on completion.

31 Wiper blades and arms – removal and refitting

1   Pull the wiper arm away from the glass, swivel the blade on the arm and then depress the catch on the U-shaped retainer and slide the blade from the wiper arm (photo).

2   Before removing a wiper arm make sure that it is in its parked position having been switched off by the wiper switch and not the ignition key.

3   To facilitate re-alignment of the arms on the screen, stick a length of masking tape on the glass parallel to the blade before removing the arm.

4   Lift off the plastic cover and unscrew the arm retaining nut (photo).

5   Pull the arm from the splined driving spindle.

30 Headlamp aim – adjustment

1   The headlamp beam adjustment is most important, not only for your own safety but for that of other road users as well. Accurate beam alignment can only be obtained using optical beam setting equipment and you should regard any adjustments made without such equipment as purely temporary.

2   To make a temporary adjustment, position the vehicle on level ground about 3 metres (10ft) in front of a vertical wall or a piece of board secured vertically. The wall or board should be square to the centre-line of the vehicle and the vehicle should be normally laden. Check that the tyre pressures are correct.

3   Draw a vertical line on the board or card in line with the vehicle centre-line.

4   Bounce the vehicle on its suspension several times to ensure correct levelling and then accurately measure the height between the ground and the centre of the headlamps.

5   Draw a horizontal line across the wall or board at the same height as the headlamp centres and on this line mark a cross on either side of the centre line at the same distance apart as the headlamp centres.

6   Now locate the adjusters. There are two, diagonally opposite each other on each headlamp (photo).

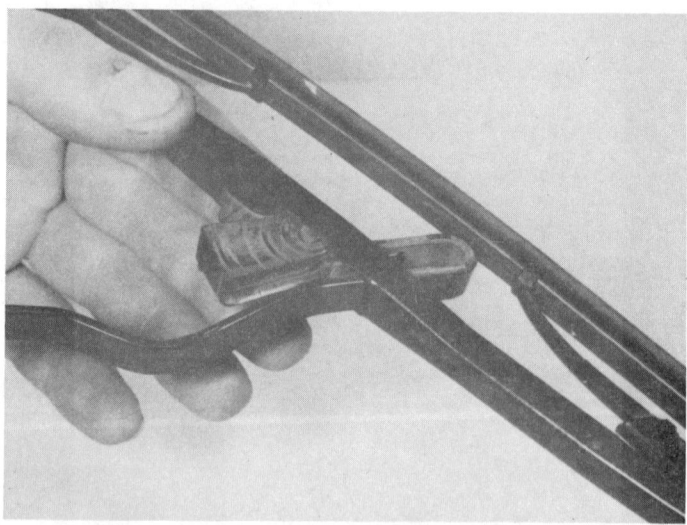

31.1 Removing the wiper blade from the arm

30.6 Headlamp aim adjusting screws (arrowed)

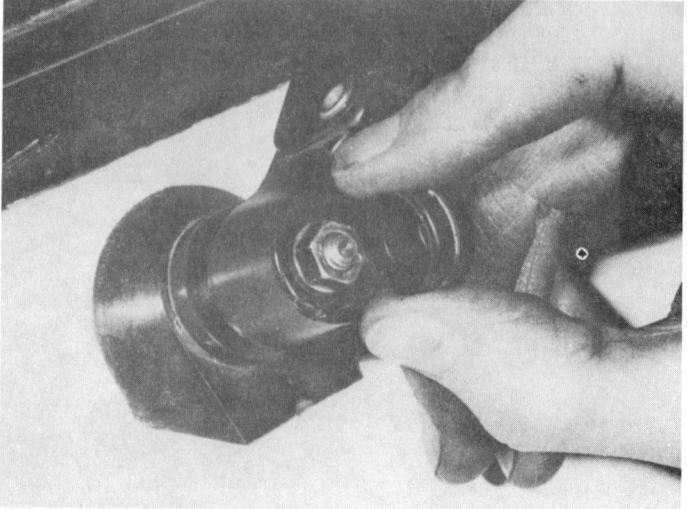

31.4 Wiper arm retaining nut

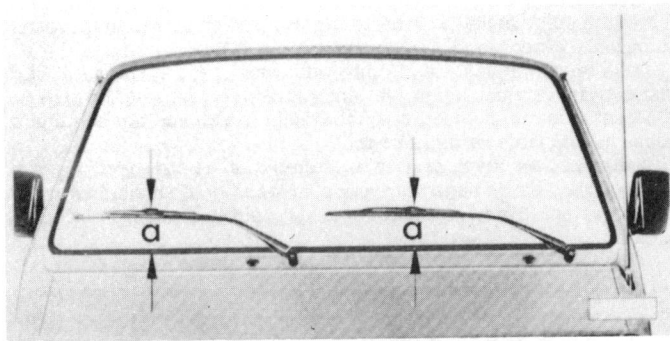

Fig. 10.22 Correct positioning of windscreen wiper arms in the parked position (Sec 31)

$a = 70 \, mm \, (2.75 \, in)$

6   Refitting is a reversal of removal, do not overtighten the nut. If tape was not applied to the glass, observe the setting dimensions in the diagram (Fig. 10.22).

32 Windscreen wiper motor and linkage – removal and refitting

1   To gain access to the wiper motor and linkage it will be necessary to remove the facia glovebox as described in Chapter 11, and the instrument panel as described in Section 25 of this Chapter.
2   Remove the wiper arms as described in Section 31.
3   Lift off the rubber covers and remove the nuts, spacers and washers from the wiper arm spindles.
4   Disconnect the wiring multi-plug from the wiper motor.

5   Undo the screws securing the wiper frame and auxiliary frame to the body and remove the frame, linkage and motor assembly from the passenger's side (Fig. 10.23) (photo).
6   With the assembly removed from the vehicle the motor may be removed as follows.
7   Mark the position of the linkage crank in relation to the motor shaft, undo the retaining nut and remove the crank from the shaft.
8   Undo the three retaining bolts and lift the motor off the frame.
9   To remove the linkage, prise the linkage arms off the spindles, extract the retaining circlips and slide the spindles out of their bushes.

32.5 Windscreen wiper motor and frame location behind facia

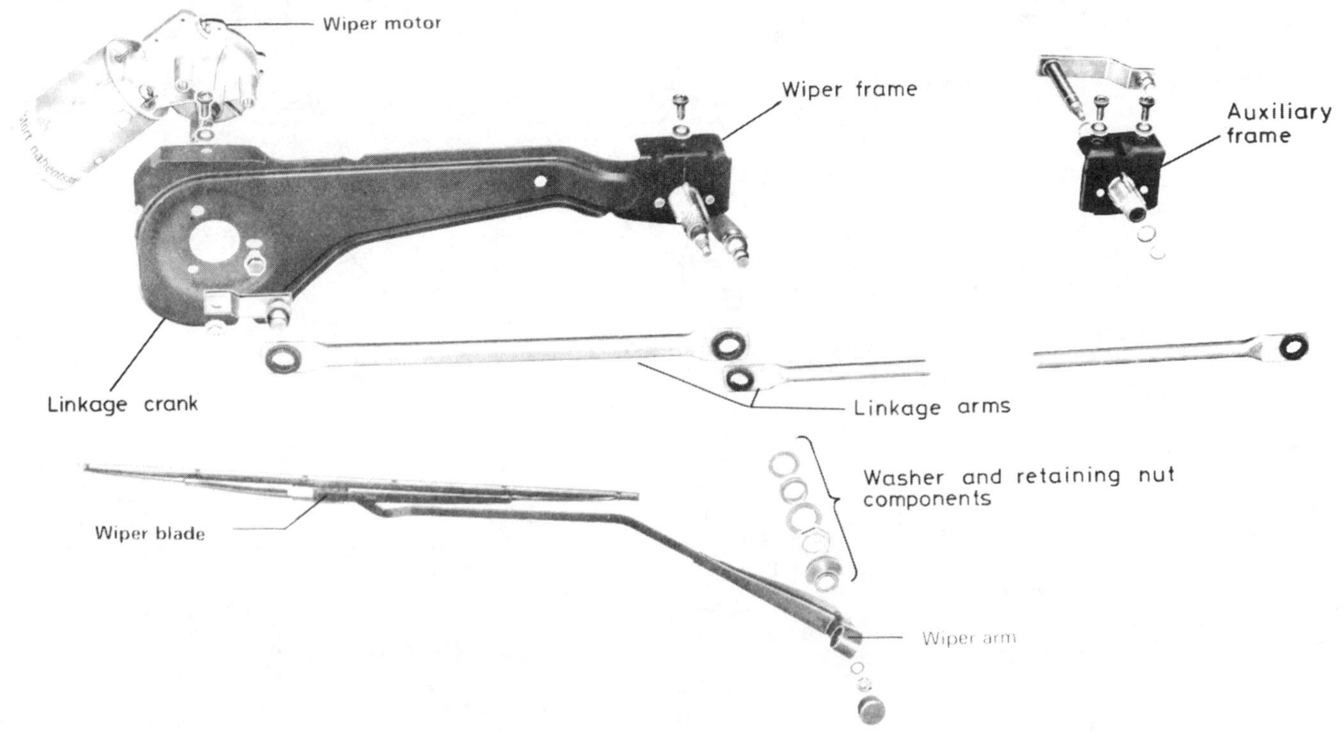

Fig. 10.23 Exploded view of the windscreen wiper motor and linkage (Sec 32)

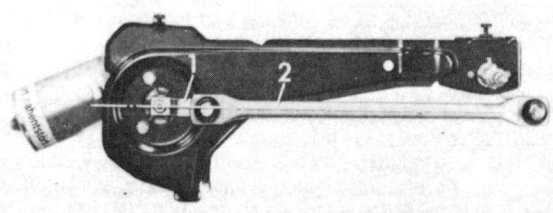

Fig. 10.24 Correct positioning of crank (1) and linkage arm (2) with wiper motor in park position (Sec 32)

10   Reassembly and refitting is the reverse of the dismantling and removal sequence. Lubricate the spindles with molybdenum disulphide grease before fitting. Ensure that the marks made on the crank and motor shaft are aligned when the crank is fitted or if no marks were made, position the crank as shown in Fig. 10.24 with the motor in the parked position.

33 Windscreen washer system – general

1   The system consists of a reservoir located under the footwell on the left-hand side of the cab, an electric pump mounted on the reservoir, two spray nozzles and related plastic tubing. The system is operated by a switch on the steering column.
2   To remove the reservoir and pump undo the three retaining bolts (photo), detach the filler pipe and washer tube, disconnect the pump wiring and remove the reservoir and pump.
3   With the reservoir removed the pump can be carefully withdrawn by prising it out of its retaining rubber grommet.
4   Refitting the reservoir and pump is the reverse sequence to removal.

5   The washer nozzles can be adjusted using a pin and should be set so that the spray of liquid lands on the windscreen in the centre of the arc of each wiper blade.
6   It is recommended that only additives specially prepared for washer systems are used in the fluid reservoir. The use of household detergent or other cleaning agents is likely to damage the pump and rubber components of the system.
7   Never use a cooling system antifreeze in a washer system or the paintwork will be damaged. In very cold weather, a small quantity of methylated spirit may be poured into the fluid to prevent freezing.

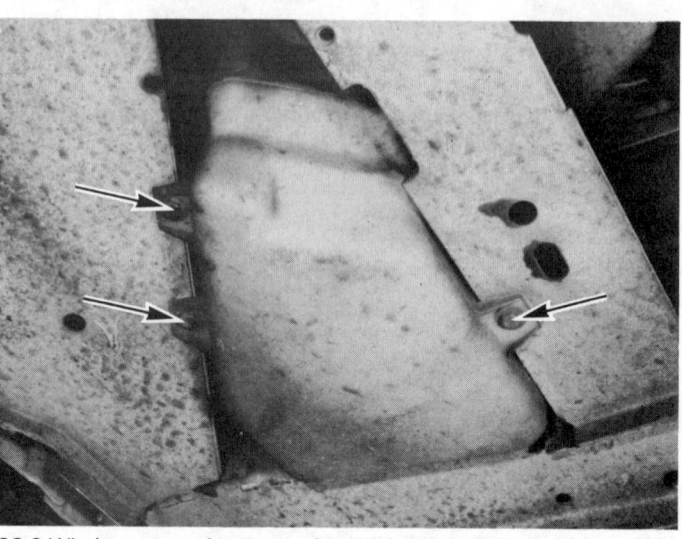

33.2 Windscreen washer reservoir retaining bolts (arrowed)

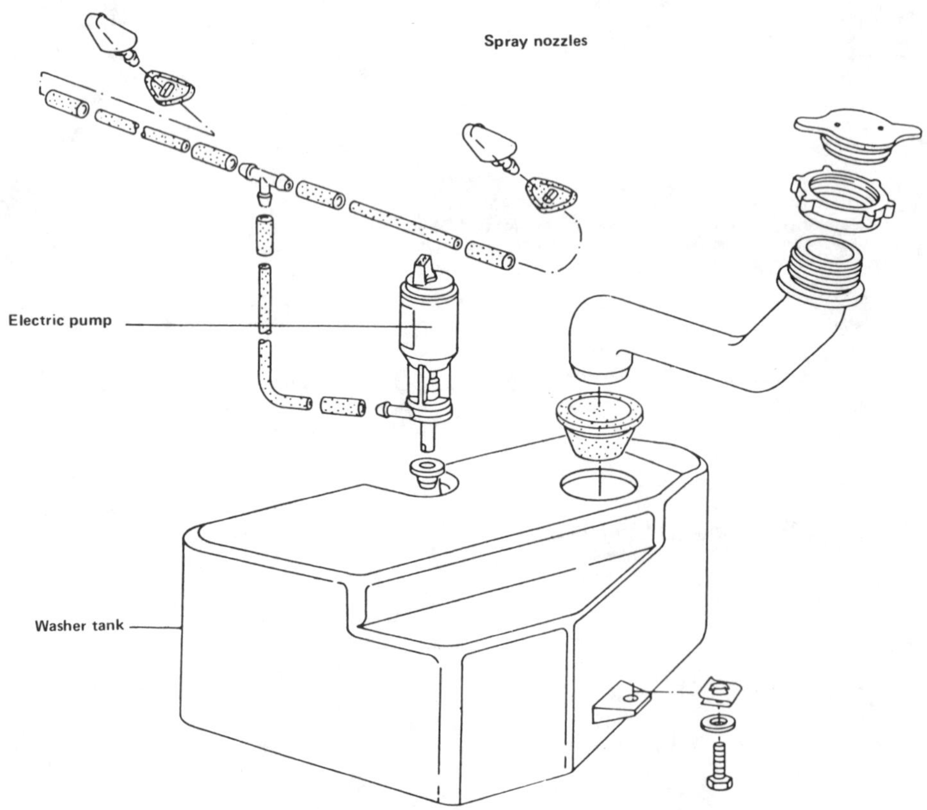

Spray nozzles

Electric pump

Washer tank

Fig. 10.25 Windscreen washer system components (Sec 33)

34 Mobile radio equipment – interference-free installation

Aerials – selection and fitting

The choice of aerials is now very wide. It should be realised that the quality has a profound effect on radio performance, and a poor, inefficient aerial can make suppression difficult.

A wing-mounted aerial is regarded as probably the most efficient for signal collection, but a roof aerial is usually better for suppression purposes because it is away from most interference fields. Stick-on wire aerials are available for attachment to the inside of the windscreen, but are not always free from the interference field of the engine and some accessories.

Motorised automatic aerials rise when the equipment is switched on and retract at switch-off. They require more fitting space and supply leads, and can be a source of trouble.

There is no merit in choosing a very long aerial as, for example, the type about three metres in length which hooks or clips on to the rear of the car, since part of this aerial will inevitably be located in an interference field. For VHF/FM radios the best length of aerial is about one metre. Active aerials have a transistor amplifier mounted at the base and this serves to boost the received signal. The aerial rod is sometimes rather shorter than normal passive types.

A large loss of signal can occur in the aerial feeder cable, especially over the Very High Frequency (VHF) bands. The design of feeder cable is invariably in the co-axial form, ie a centre conductor surrounded by a flexible copper braid forming the outer (earth) conductor. Between the inner and outer conductors is an insulator material which can be in solid or stranded form. Apart from insulation, its purpose is to maintain the correct spacing and concentricity. Loss of signal occurs in this insulator, the loss usually being greater in a poor quality cable. The quality of cable used is reflected in the price of the aerial with the attached feeder cable.

The capacitance of the feeder should be within the range 65 to 75 picofarads (pF) approximately (95 to 100 pF for Japanese and American equipment), otherwise the adjustment of the car radio aerial trimmer may not be possible. An extension cable is necessary for a long run between aerial and receiver. If this adds capacitance in excess of the above limits, a connector containing a series capacitor will be required, or an extension which is labelled as 'capacity-compensated'.

Fitting the aerial will normally involve making a $\frac{7}{8}$ in (22 mm) diameter hole in the bodywork, but read the instructions that come with the aerial kit. Once the hole position has been selected, use a centre punch to guide the drill. Use sticky masking tape around the area for this helps with marking out and drill location, and gives protection to the paintwork should the drill slip. Three methods of making the hole are in use:

(a) Use a hole saw in the electric drill. This is, in effect, a circular hacksaw blade wrapped round a former with a centre pilot drill.

(b) Use a tank cutter which also has cutting teeth, but is made to shear the metal by tightening with an Allen key.

(c) The hard way of drilling out the circle is using a small drill, say $\frac{1}{8}$ in (3 mm), so that the holes overlap. The centre metal drops out and the hole is finished with round and half-round files.

Whichever method is used, the burr is removed from the body metal and paint removed from the underside. The aerial is fitted tightly ensuring that the earth fixing, usually a serrated washer, ring or clamp, is making a solid connection. *This earth connection is important in reducing interference.* Cover any bare metal with primer paint and topcoat, and follow by underseal if desired.

Aerial feeder cable routing should avoid the engine compartment and areas where stress might occur, eg under the carpet where feet will be located. Roof aerials require that the headlining be pulled back and that a path is available down the door pillar. It is wise to check with the vehicle dealer whether roof aerial fitting is recommended.

Loudspeakers

Speakers should be matched to the output stage of the equipment, particularly as regards the recommended impedance. Power transistors used for driving speakers are sensitive to the loading placed on them.

Before choosing a mounting position for speakers, check whether the vehicle manufacturer has provided a location for them. Generally door-mounted speakers give good stereophonic reproduction, but not all doors are able to accept them. The next best position is the rear parcel shelf, and in this case speaker apertures can be cut into the shelf, or pod units may be mounted.

For door mounting, first remove the trim, which is often held on by 'poppers' or press studs, and then select a suitable gap in the inside door assembly. Check that the speaker would not obstruct glass or winder mechanism by winding the window up and down. A template is often provided for marking out the trim panel hole, and then the four fixing holes must be drilled through. Mark out with chalk and cut cleanly with a sharp knife or keyhole saw. Speaker leads are then threaded through the door and door pillar, if necessary drilling 10 mm diameter holes. Fit grommets in the holes and connect to the radio or tape unit correctly. Do not omit a waterproofing cover, usually supplied with door speakers. If the speaker has to be fixed into the metal of the door itself, use self-tapping screws, and if the fixing is to the door trim use self-tapping screws and flat spire nuts.

Rear shelf mounting is somewhat simpler but it is necessary to find gaps in the metalwork underneath the parcel shelf. However, remember that the speakers should be as far apart as possible to give a good stereo effect. Pod-mounted speakers can be screwed into position through the parcel shelf material, but it is worth testing for the best position. Sometimes good results are found by reflecting sound off the rear window.

Unit installation

Many vehicles have a dash panel aperture to take a radio/audio unit, a recognised international standard being 189.5 mm x 60 mm. Alternatively a console may be a feature of the car interior design and this, mounted below the dashboard, gives more room. If neither facility is available a unit may be mounted on the underside of the parcel shelf; these are frequently non-metallic and an earth wire from the case to a good earth point is necessary. A three-sided cover in the form of a cradle is obtainable from car radio dealers and this gives a professional appearance to the installation; in this case choose a position where the controls can be reached by a driver with his seat belt on.

Installation of the radio/audio unit is basically the same in all cases, and consists of offering it into the aperture after removal of the knobs *(not* push buttons) and the trim plate. In some cases a special mounting plate is required to which the unit is attached. It is worthwhile supporting the rear end in cases where sag or strain may occur, and it is usually possible to use a length of perforated metal strip attached between the unit and a good support point nearby. In general it is recommended that tape equipment should be installed at or nearly horizontal.

Connections to the aerial socket are simply by the standard plug terminating the aerial downlead or its extension cable. Speakers for a stereo system must be matched and correctly connected, as outlined previously.

Note: *While all work is carried out on the power side, it is wise to disconnect the battery earth lead.* Before connection is made to the vehicle electrical system, check that the polarity of the unit is correct. Most vehicles use a negative earth system, but radio/audio units often have a reversible plug to convert the set to either + or − earth. *Incorrect connection may cause serious damage.*

The power lead is often permanently connected inside the unit and terminates with one half of an in-line fuse carrier. The other half is fitted with a suitable fuse (3 or 5 amperes) and a wire which should go to a power point in the electrical system. This may be the accessory terminal on the ignition switch, giving the advantage of power feed with ignition or with the ignition key at the 'accessory' position. Power to the unit stops when the ignition key is removed. Alternatively, the lead may be taken to a live point at the fusebox with the consequence of having to remember to switch off at the unit before leaving the vehicle.

Before switching on for initial test, be sure that the speaker connections have been made, for running without load can damage the output transistors. Switch on next and tune through the bands to ensure that all sections are working, and check the tape unit if applicable. The aerial trimmer should be adjusted to give the strongest reception on a weak signal in the medium wave band, at say 200 metres.

Interference

In general, when electric current changes abruptly, unwanted electrical noise is produced. The motor vehicle is filled with electrical

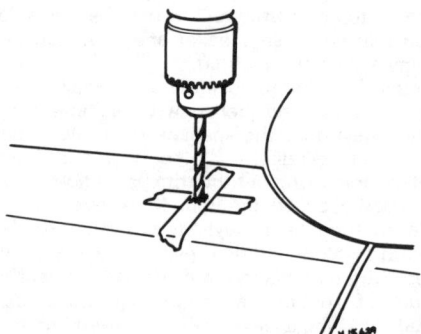

Fig. 10.26 Drilling the bodywork for aerial mounting (Sec 34)

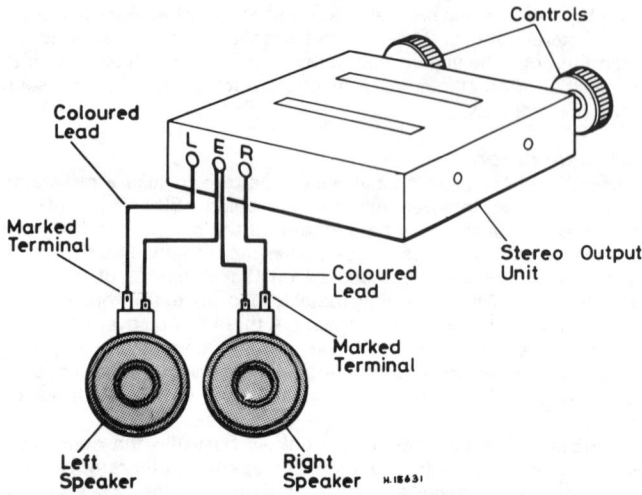

Fig. 10.28 Speaker connections must be correctly made as shown (Sec 34)

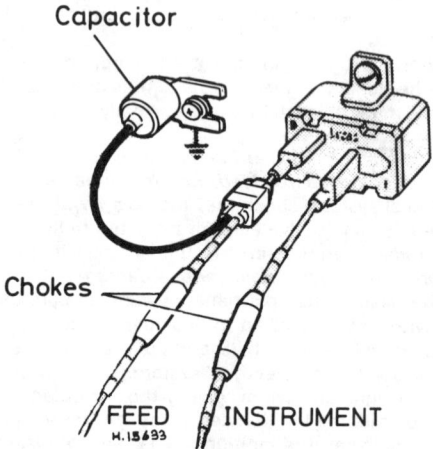

Fig. 10.30 Voltage stabilizer interference suppression (Sec 34)

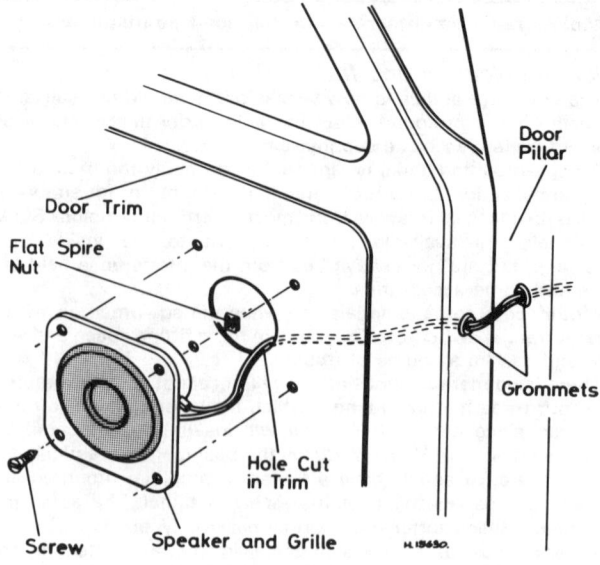

Fig. 10.27 Door-mounted speaker installation (Sec 34)

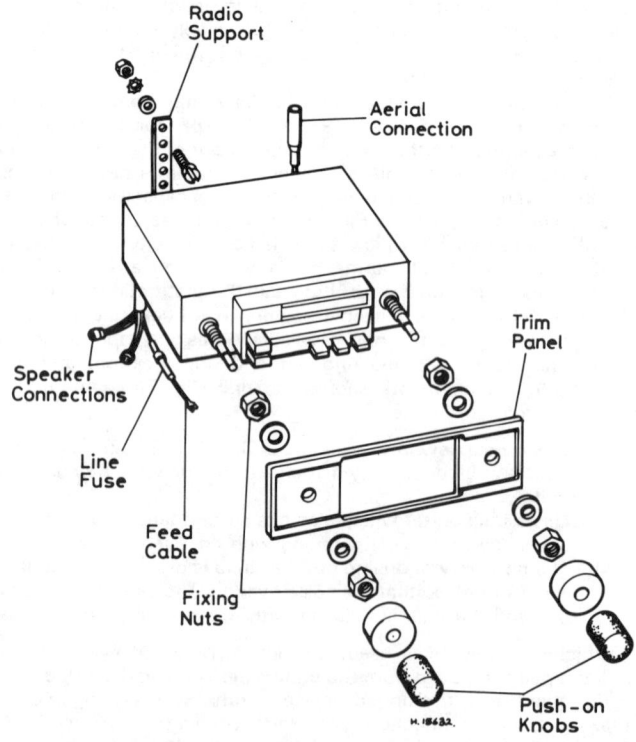

Fig. 10.29 Mounting component details for radio/cassette unit (Sec 34)

devices which change electric current rapidly, the most obvious being the contact breaker.

When the spark plugs operate, the sudden pulse of spark current causes the associated wiring to radiate. Since early radio transmitters used sparks as a basis of operation, it is not surprising that the car radio will pick up ignition spark noise unless steps are taken to reduce it to acceptable levels.

Interference reaches the car radio in two ways:

(a) by conduction through the wiring.
(b) by radiation to the receiving aerial.

Initial checks presuppose that the bonnet is down and fastened, the radio unit has a good earth connection (*not* through the aerial downlead outer), no fluorescent tubes are working near the car, the aerial trimmer has been adjusted, and the vehicle is in a position to receive radio signals, ie not in a metal-clad building.

Switch on the radio and tune it to the middle of the medium wave (MW) band off-station with the volume (gain) control set fairly high. Switch on the ignition (but do not start the engine) and wait to see if irregular clicks or hash noise occurs. Tapping the facia panel may also produce the effects. If so, this will be due to the voltage stabiliser, which is an on-off thermal switch to control instrument voltage. It is located usually on the back of the instrument panel, often attached to the speedometer. Correction is by attachment of a capacitor and, if still troublesome, chokes in the supply wires.

Switch on the engine and listen for interference on the MW band. Depending on the type of interference, the indications are as follows.

A harsh crackle that drops out abruptly at low engine speed or when the headlights are switched on is probably due to a voltage regulator.

A whine varying with engine speed is due to the dynamo or alternator. Try temporarily taking off the fan belt – if the noise goes this is confirmation.

Regular ticking or crackle that varies in rate with the engine speed is due to the ignition system. With this trouble in particular and others in general, check to see if the noise is entering the receiver from the wiring or by radiation. To do this, pull out the aerial plug, (preferably shorting out the input socket or connecting a 62 pF capacitor across it). If the noise disappears it is coming in through the aerial and is *radiation noise*. If the noise persists it is reaching the receiver through the wiring and is said to be *line-borne*.

Interference from wipers, washers, heater blowers, turn-indicators, stop lamps, etc is usually taken to the receiver by wiring, and simple treatment using capacitors and possibly chokes will solve the problem. Switch on each one in turn (wet the screen first for running wipers!) and listen for possible interference with the aerial plug in place and again when removed.

Electric petrol pumps are now finding application again and give rise to an irregular clicking, often giving a burst of clicks when the ignition is on but the engine has not yet been started. It is also possible to receive whining or crackling from the pump.

Note that if most of the vehicle accessories are found to be creating interference all together, the probability is that poor aerial earthing is to blame.

Component terminal markings

Throughout the following sub-sections reference will be found to various terminal markings. These will vary depending on the manufacturer of the relevant component. If terminal markings differ from those mentioned, reference should be made to the following table, where the most commonly encountered variations are listed.

Alternator	Alternator terminal (thick lead)	Exciting winding terminal
DIN/Bosch	B+	DF
Delco Remy	+	EXC
Ducellier	+	EXC
Ford (US)	+	DF
Lucas	+	F
Marelli	+B	F

Ignition coil	Ignition switch terminal	Contact breaker terminal
DIN/Bosch	15	1
Delco Remy	+	–
Ducellier	BAT	RUP
Ford (US)	B/+	CB/–
Lucas	SW/+	–
Marelli	BAT/+B	D

Voltage regulator	Voltage input terminal	Exciting winding terminal
DIN/Bosch	B+/D+	DF
Delco Remy	BAT/+	EXC
Ducellier	BOB/BAT	EXC
Ford (US)	BAT	DF
Lucas	+/A	F
Marelli		F

Suppression methods – ignition

Suppressed HT cables are supplied as original equipment by manufacturers and will meet regulations as far as interference to neighbouring equipment is concerned. It is illegal to remove such suppression unless an alternative is provided, and this may take the form of resistive spark plug caps in conjunction with plain copper HT cable. For VHF purposes, these and 'in-line' resistors may not be effective, and resistive HT cable is preferred. Check that suppressed cables are actually fitted by observing cable identity lettering, or

measuring with an ohmmeter – the value of each plug lead should be 5000 to 10 000 ohms.

A 1 microfarad capacitor connected from the LT supply side of the ignition coil to a good nearby earth point will complete basic ignition interference treatment. *NEVER fit a capacitor to the coil terminal to the contact breaker – the result would be burnt out points in a short time.*

If ignition noise persists despite the treatment above, the following sequence should be followed:

(a) Check the earthing of the ignition coil; remove paint from fixing clamp.

(b) If this does not work, lift the bonnet. Should there be no change in interference level, this may indicate that the bonnet is not electrically connected to the car body. Use a proprietary braided strap across a bonnet hinge ensuring a first class electrical connection. If, however, lifting the bonnet increases the interference, then fit resistive HT cables of a higher ohms-per-metre value.

(c) If all these measures fail, it is probable that re-radiation from metallic components is taking place. Using a braided strap between metallic points, go round the vehicle systematically – try the following: engine to body, exhaust system to body, front suspension to engine and to body, steering column to body (especially French and Italian cars), gear lever to engine and to body (again especially French and Italian cars), Bowden cable to body, metal parcel shelf to body. When an offending component is located it should be bonded with the strap permanently.

(d) As a next step, the fitting of distributor suppressors to each lead at the distributor end may help.

(e) Beyond this point is involved the possible screening of the distributor and fitting resistive spark plugs, but such advanced treatment is not usually required for vehicles with entertainment equipment.

Electronic ignition systems have built-in suppression components, but this does not relieve the need for using suppressed HT leads. In some cases it is permitted to connect a capacitor on the low tension supply side of the ignition coil, but not in every case. Makers' instructions should be followed carefully, otherwise damage to the ignition semiconductors may result.

Suppression methods – generators

For older vehicles with dynamos a 1 microfarad capacitor from the D (larger) terminal to earth will usually cure dynamo whine. Alternators should be fitted with a 3 microfarad capacitor from the B+ main output terminal (thick cable) to earth. Additional suppression may be obtained by the use of a filter in the supply line to the radio receiver.

It is most important that:

(a) *Capacitors are never connected to the field terminals of either a dynamo or alternator.*

(b) *Alternators must not be run without connection to the battery.*

Suppression methods – voltage regulators

Voltage regulators used with DC dynamos should be suppressed by connecting a 1 microfarad capacitor from the control box D terminal to earth.

Alternator regulators come in three types:

(a) *Vibrating contact regulators separate from the alternator. Used extensively on continental vehicles.*

(b) *Electronic regulators separate from the alternator.*

(c) *Electronic regulators built-in to the alternator.*

In case (a) interference may be generated on the AM and FM (VHF) bands. For some cars a replacement suppressed regulator is available. Filter boxes may be used with non-suppressed regulators. But if not available, then for AM equipment a 2 microfarad or 3 microfarad capacitor may be mounted at the voltage terminal marked D+ or B+ of the regulator. FM bands may be treated by a feed-through capacitor of 2 or 3 microfarad.

Electronic voltage regulators are not always troublesome, but where necessary, a 1 microfarad capacitor from the regulator + terminal will help.

Integral electronic voltage regulators do not normally generate much interference, but when encountered this is in combination with

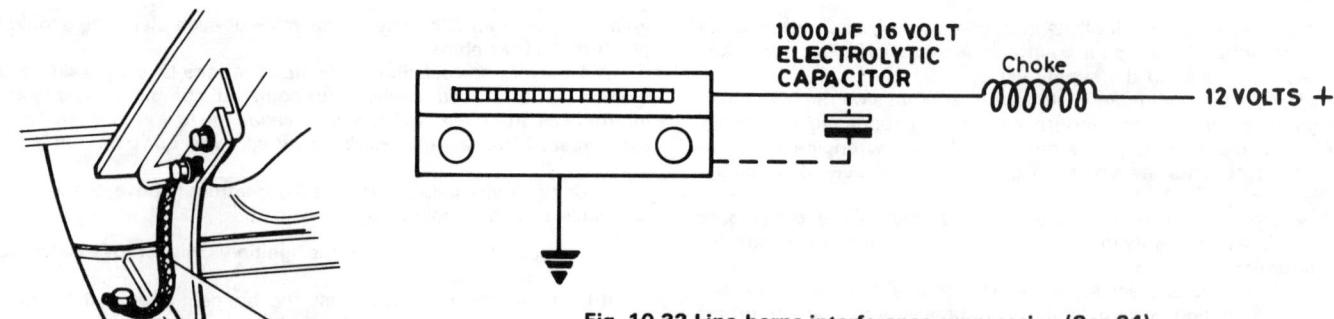

1000 µF 16 VOLT ELECTROLYTIC CAPACITOR

Choke

12 VOLTS +

Fig. 10.32 Line-borne interference suppression (Sec 34)

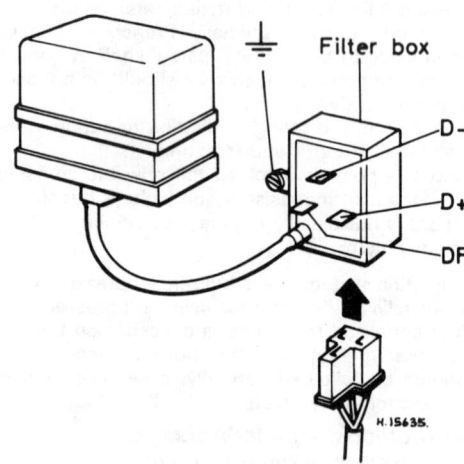

Braided Strap

Fig. 10.31 Braided earth strap between bonnet and body (Sec 34)

Filter box

D-

D+

DF

Fig. 10.33 Typical filter box for vibrating contact voltage regulator (alternator equipment) (Sec 34)

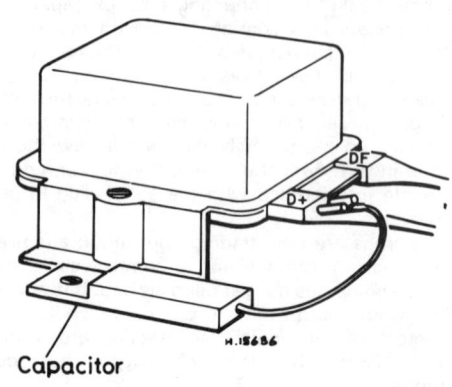

DF

D+

Capacitor

Fig. 10.34 Suppression of AM interference by vibrating contact voltage regulator (alternator equipment) (Sec 34)

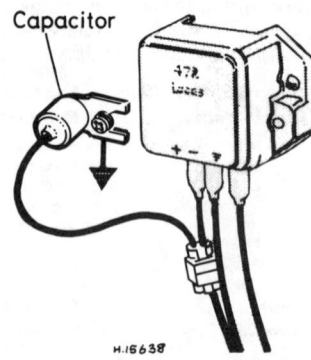

Capacitor

Fig. 10.36 Electronic voltage regulator suppression (Sec 34)

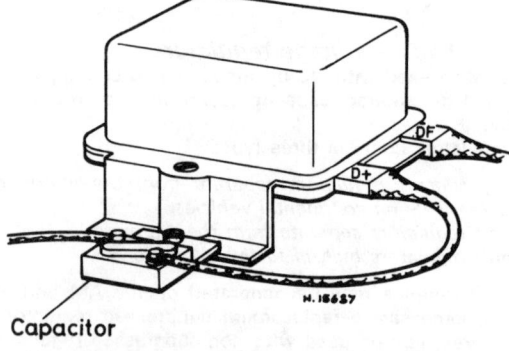

DF

D+

Capacitor

Fig. 10.35 Suppression of FM interference by vibrating contact voltage regulator (alternator equipment) (Sec 34)

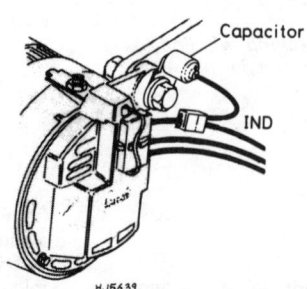

Capacitor

IND

Fig. 10.37 Suppression of interference from electronic voltage regulator when integral with alternator (Sec 34)

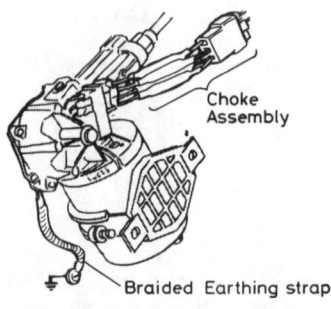

Choke Assembly

Braided Earthing strap

Fig. 10.38 Wiper motor suppression (Sec 34)

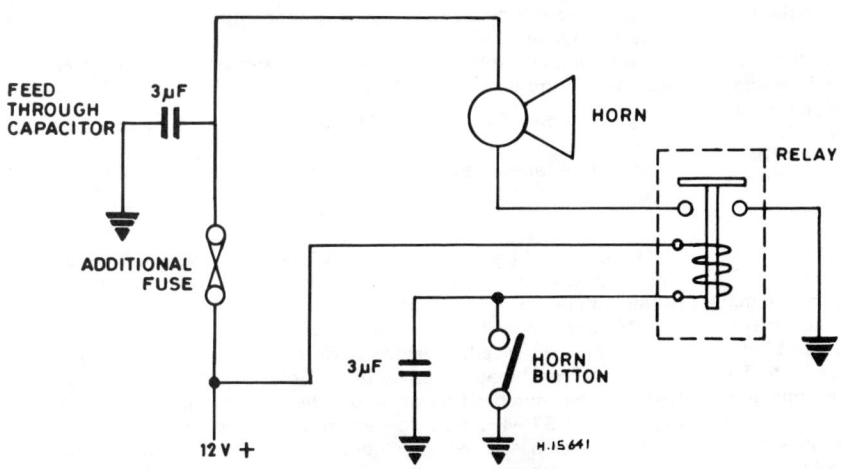

Fig. 10.39 Use of relay to reduce horn interference (Sec 34)

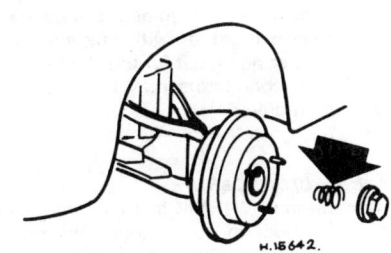

Fig. 10.40 Use of spring contacts at wheels
(Sec 34)

alternator noise. A 1 microfarad or 2 microfarad capacitor from the warning lamp (IND) terminal to earth for Lucas ACR alternators and Femsa, Delco and Bosch equivalents should cure the problem.

Suppression methods – other equipment

Wiper motors – Connect the wiper body to earth with a bonding strap. For all motors use a 7 ampere choke assembly inserted in the leads to the motor.

Heater motors – Fit 7 ampere line chokes in both leads, assisted if necessary by a 1 microfarad capacitor to earth from both leads.

Electronic tachometer – The tachometer is a possible source of ignition noise – check by disconnecting at the ignition coil CB terminal. It usually feeds from ignition coil LT pulses at the contact breaker terminal. A 3 ampere line choke should be fitted in the tachometer lead at the coil CB terminal.

Horn – A capacitor and choke combination is effective if the horn is directly connected to the 12 volt supply. The use of a relay is an alternative remedy, as this will reduce the length of the interference-carrying leads.

Electrostatic noise – Characteristics are erratic crackling at the receiver, with disappearance of symptoms in wet weather. Often shocks may be given when touching bodywork. Part of the problem is the build-up of static electricity in non-driven wheels and the acquisition of charge on the body shell. It is possible to fit spring-loaded contacts at the wheels to give good conduction between the rotary wheel parts and the vehicle frame. Changing a tyre sometimes helps – because of tyres' varying resistances. In difficult cases a trailing flex which touches the ground will cure the problem. If this is not acceptable it is worth trying conductive paint on the tyre walls.

Fuel pump – Suppression requires a 1 microfarad capacitor between the supply wire to the pump and a nearby earth point. If this is insufficient a 7 ampere line choke connected in the supply wire near the pump is required.

Fluorescent tubes – Vehicles used for camping/caravanning frequently have fluorescent tube lighting. These tubes require a relatively high voltage for operation and this is provided by an inverter (a form of oscillator) which steps up the vehicle supply voltage. This can give rise to serious interference to radio reception, and the tubes themselves can contribute to this interference by the pulsating nature of the lamp discharge. In such situations it is important to mount the aerial as far away from a fluorescent tube as possible. The interference problem may be alleviated by screening the tube with fine wire turns spaced an inch (25 mm) apart and earthed to the chassis. Suitable chokes should be fitted in both supply wires close to the inverter.

Radio/cassette case breakthrough

Magnetic radiation from dashboard wiring may be sufficiently intense to break through the metal case of the radio/cassette player. Often this is due to a particular cable routed too close and shows up as ignition interference on AM and cassette play and/or alternator whine on cassette play.

The first point to check is that the clips and/or screws are fixing all parts of the radio/cassette case together properly. Assuming good

earthing of the case, see if it is possible to re-route the offending cable – the chances of this are not good, however, in most cars.

Next release the radio/cassette player and locate it in different positions with temporary leads. If a point of low interference is found, then if possible fix the equipment in that area. This also confirms that local radiation is causing the trouble. If re-location is not feasible, fit the radio/cassette player back in the original position.

Alternator interference on cassette play is now caused by radiation from the main charging cable which goes from the battery to the output terminal of the alternator, usually via the + terminal of the starter motor relay. In some vehicles this cable is routed under the dashboard, so the solution is to provide a direct cable route. Detach the original cable from the alternator output terminal and make up a new cable of at least 6 mm^2 cross-sectional area to go from alternator to battery with the shortest possible route. *Remember – do not run the engine with the alternator disconnected from the battery.*

Ignition breakthrough on AM and/or cassette play can be a difficult problem. It is worth wrapping earthed foil round the offending cable run near the equipment, or making up a deflector plate well screwed down to a good earth. Another possibility is the use of a suitable relay to switch on the ignition coil. The relay should be mounted close to the ignition coil; with this arrangement the ignition coil primary current is not taken into the dashboard area and does not flow through the ignition switch. A suitable diode should be used since it is possible that at ignition switch-off the output from the warning lamp alternator terminal could hold the relay on.

Connectors for suppression components

Capacitors are usually supplied with tags on the end of the lead, while the capacitor body has a flange with a slot or hole to fit under a nut or screw with washer.

Connections to feed wires are best achieved by self-stripping connectors. These connectors employ a blade which, when squeezed

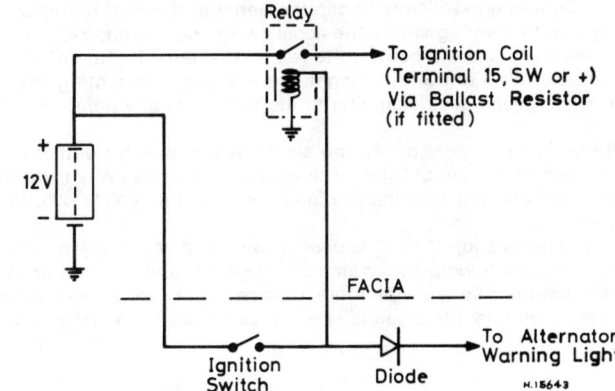

Fig. 10.41 Use of ignition coil relay to suppress case breakthrough
(Sec 34)

down by pliers, cuts through cable insulation and makes connection to the copper conductors beneath.

Chokes sometimes come with bullet snap-in connectors fitted to the wires, and also with just bare copper wire. With connectors, suitable female cable connectors may be purchased from an auto-accessory shop together with any extra connectors required for the cable ends after being cut for the choke insertion. For chokes with bare wires, similar connectors may be employed together with insulation sleeving as required.

VHF/FM broadcasts

Reception of VHF/FM in an automobile is more prone to problems than the medium and long wavebands. Medium/long wave transmitters are capable of covering considerable distances, but VHF transmitters are restricted to line of sight, meaning ranges of 10 to 50 miles, depending upon the terrain, the effects of buildings and the transmitter power.

Because of the limited range it is necessary to retune on a long journey, and it may be better for those habitually travelling long distances or living in areas of poor provision of transmitters to use an AM radio working on medium/long wavebands.

When conditions are poor, interference can arise, and some of the suppression devices described previously fall off in performance at very high frequencies unless specifically designed for the VHF band. Available suppression devices include reactive HT cable, resistive distributor caps, screened plug caps, screened leads and resistive spark plugs.

For VHF/FM receiver installation the following points should be particularly noted:

(a)   Earthing of the receiver chassis and the aerial mounting is important. Use a separate earthing wire at the radio, and scrape paint away at the aerial mounting.

(b)   If possible, use a good quality roof aerial to obtain maximum height and distance from interference generating devices on the vehicle.

(c)   Use of a high quality aerial download is important, since losses in cheap cable can be significant.

(d)   The polarisation of FM transmissions may be horizontal, vertical, circular or slanted. Because of this the optimum mounting angle is at 45° to the vehicle roof.

Citizens' Band radio (CB)

In the UK, CB transmitter/receivers work within the 27 MHz and 934 MHz bands, using the FM mode. At present interest is concentrated on 27 MHz where the design and manufacture of equipment is less difficult. Maximum transmitted power is 4 watts, and 40 channels spaced 10 kHz apart within the range 27.60125 to 27.99125 MHz are available.

Aerials are the key to effective transmission and reception. Regulations limit the aerial length to 1.65 metres including the loading coil and any associated circuitry, so tuning the aerial is necessary to obtain optimum results. The choice of a CB aerial is dependent on whether it is to be permanently installed or removable, and the performance will hinge on correct tuning and the location point on the vehicle. Common practice is to clip the aerial to the roof gutter or to employ wing mounting where the aerial can be rapidly unscrewed. An alternative is to use the boot rim to render the aerial theftproof, but a popular solution is to use the 'magmount' – a type of mounting having a strong magnetic base clamping to the vehicle at any point, usually the roof.

Aerial location determines the signal distribution for both transmission and reception, but it is wise to choose a point away from the engine compartment to minimise interference from vehicle electrical equipment.

The aerial is subject to considerable wind and acceleration forces. Cheaper units will whip backwards and forwards and in so doing will alter the relationship with the metal surface of the vehicle with which it forms a ground plane aerial system. The radiation pattern will

change correspondingly, giving rise to break-up of both incoming and outgoing signals.

Interference problems on the vehicle carrying CB equipment fall into two categories:

(a)   Interference to nearby TV and radio receivers when transmitting.

(b)   Interference to CB set reception due to electrical equipment on the vehicle.

Problems of break-through to TV and radio are not frequent, but can be difficult to solve. Mostly trouble is not detected or reported because the vehicle is moving and the symptoms rapidly disappear at the TV/radio receiver, but when the CB set is used as a base station any trouble with nearby receivers will soon result in a complaint.

It must not be assumed by the CB operator that his equipment is faultless, for much depends upon the design. Harmonics (that is, multiples) of 27 MHz may be transmitted unknowingly and these can fall into other user's bands. Where trouble of this nature occurs, low pass filters in the aerial or supply leads can help, and should be fitted in base station aerials as a matter of course. In stubborn cases it may be necessary to call for assistance from the licensing authority, or, if possible, to have the equipment checked by the manufacturers.

Interference received on the CB set from the vehicle equipment is, fortunately, not usually a severe problem. The precautions outlined previously for radio/cassette units apply, but there are some extra points worth noting.

It is common practice to use a slide-mount on CB equipment enabling the set to be easily removed for use as a base station, for example. Care must be taken that the slide mount fittings are properly earthed and that first class connection occurs between the set and slide-mount.

Vehicle manufacturers in the UK are required to provide suppression of electrical equipment to cover 40 to 250 MHz to protect TV and VHF radio bands. Such suppression appears to be adequately effective at 27 MHz, but suppression of individual items such as alternators/dynamos, clocks, stabilisers, flashers, wiper motors, etc, may still be necessary. The suppression capacitors and chokes available from auto-electrical suppliers for entertainment receivers will usually give the required results with CB equipment.

Other vehicle radio transmitters

Besides CB radio already mentioned, a considerable increase in the use of transceivers (ie combined transmitter and receiver units) has taken place in the last decade. Previously this type of equipment was fitted mainly to military, fire, ambulance and police vehicles, but a large business radio and radio telephone usage has developed.

Generally the suppression techniques described previously will suffice, with only a few difficult cases arising. Suppression is carried out to satisfy the 'receive mode', but care must be taken to use heavy duty chokes in the equipment supply cables since the loading on 'transmit' is relatively high.

Glass-fibre bodied vehicles

Such vehicles do not have the advantage of a metal box surrounding the engine as is the case, in effect, of conventional vehicles. It is usually necessary to line the bonnet, bulkhead and wing valances with metal foil, which could well be the aluminium foil available from builders merchants. Bonding of sheets one to another and the whole down to the chassis is essential.

Wiring harness may have to be wrapped in metal foil which again should be earthed to the vehicle chassis. The aerial base and radio chassis must be taken to the vehicle chassis by heavy metal braid. VHF radio suppression in glass-fibre cars may not be a feasible operation.

In addition to all the above, normal suppression components should be employed, but special attention paid to earth bonding. A screen enclosing the entire ignition system usually gives good improvement, and fabrication from fine mesh perforated metal is convenient. Good bonding of the screening boxes to several chassis points is essential.

35 Fault diagnosis – electrical system

Symptom	Reason(s)
Starter fails to turn engine	Battery discharged or defective Battery terminal and/or earth leads loose Starter motor connections loose Starter solenoid faulty Starter brushes worn or sticking Starter commutator dirty or worn Starter field coils earthed
Starter turns engine very slowly	Battery discharged Starter motor connections loose Starter brushes worn or sticking
Starter spins but does not turn engine	Pinion or flywheel ring gear teeth broken or badly worn
Starter noisy	Pinion or flywheel ring gear teeth badly worn Mounting bolts loose
Battery will not hold charge for more than a few days	Battery defective internally Battery terminals loose Alternator drivebelt slipping Alternator or regulator faulty Short circuit
Ignition light stays on	Alternator faulty Alternator drivebelt broken
Ignition light fails to come on	Warning bulb blown Indicator light open circuit Alternator faulty
Instrument readings increase with engine speed	Voltage stabilizer faulty
Fuel or temperature gauge gives no reading	Wiring open circuit Sender unit faulty
Fuel or temperature gauge give maximum reading all the time	Wiring short circuit Gauge faulty
Lights inoperative	Bulb blown Fuse blown Battery discharged Switch faulty Wiring open circuit Bad connection due to corrosion
Failure of component motor	Commutator dirty or burnt Armature faulty Brushes sticking or worn Armature bearings dry or misaligned Field coils faulty Fuse blown Wiring loose or broken
Failure of an individual component	Wiring loose or broken Fuse blown Bad circuit connection Switch faulty Component faulty

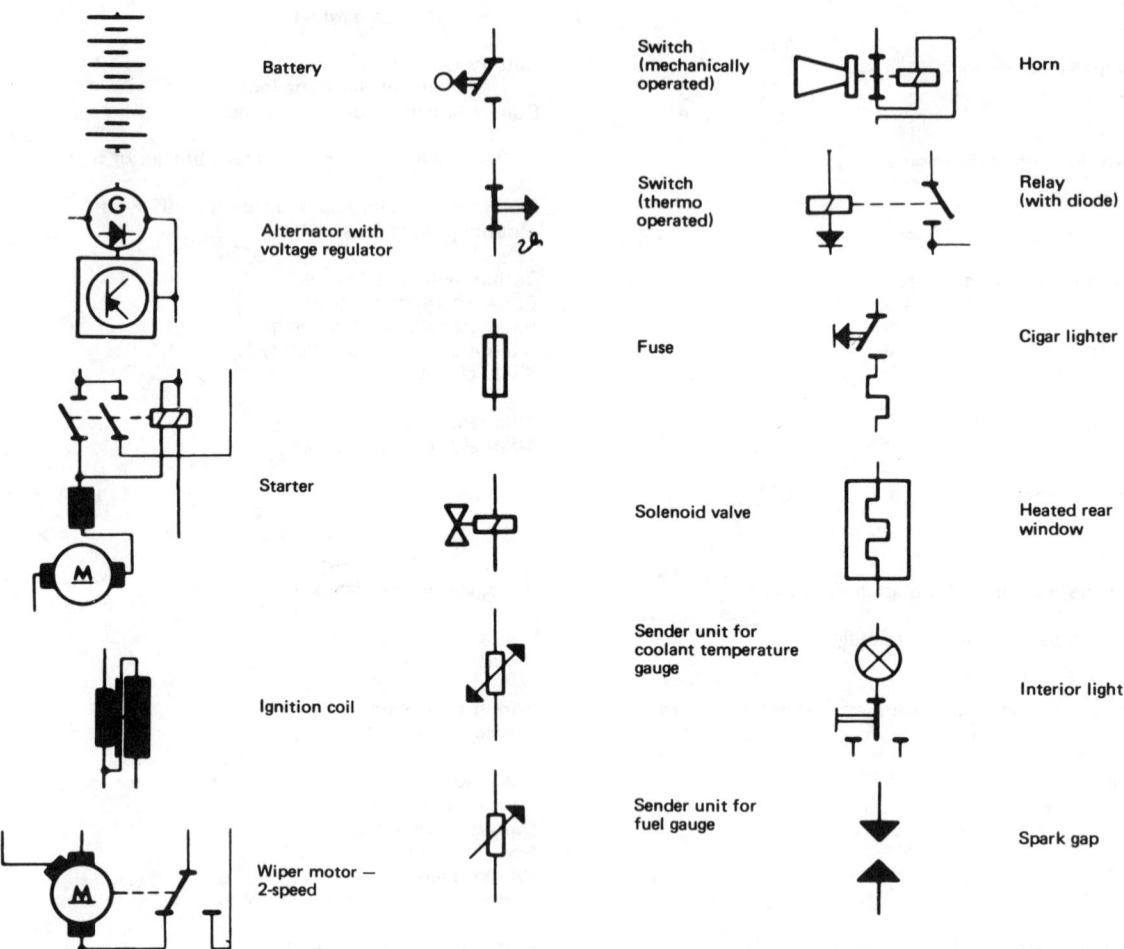

Battery

Alternator with
voltage regulator

Starter

Ignition coil

Wiper motor —
2-speed

Switch
(mechanically
operated)

Switch
(thermo
operated)

Fuse

Solenoid valve

Sender unit for
coolant temperature
gauge

Sender unit for
fuel gauge

Horn

Relay
(with diode)

Cigar lighter

Heated rear
window

Interior light

Spark gap

Fig. 10.42 Symbols used on UK wiring diagrams

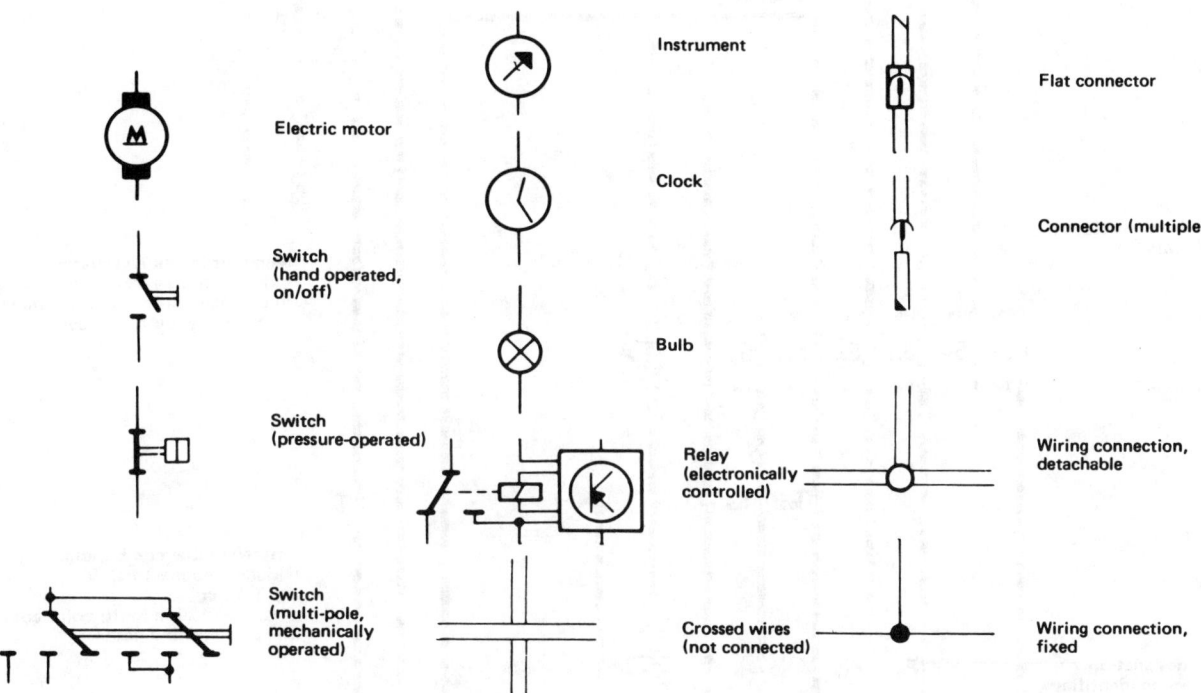

Fig. 10.42 Symbols used on UK wiring diagrams (continued)

Wiring   Color Code

BK	–	Black	R	–	Red	LT.G	–	Light Green	GY	–	Gray
BR	–	Brown	Y	–	Yellow	BL	–	Blue	W	–	White
CL	–	Clear	G	–	Green	V	–	Violet			

230

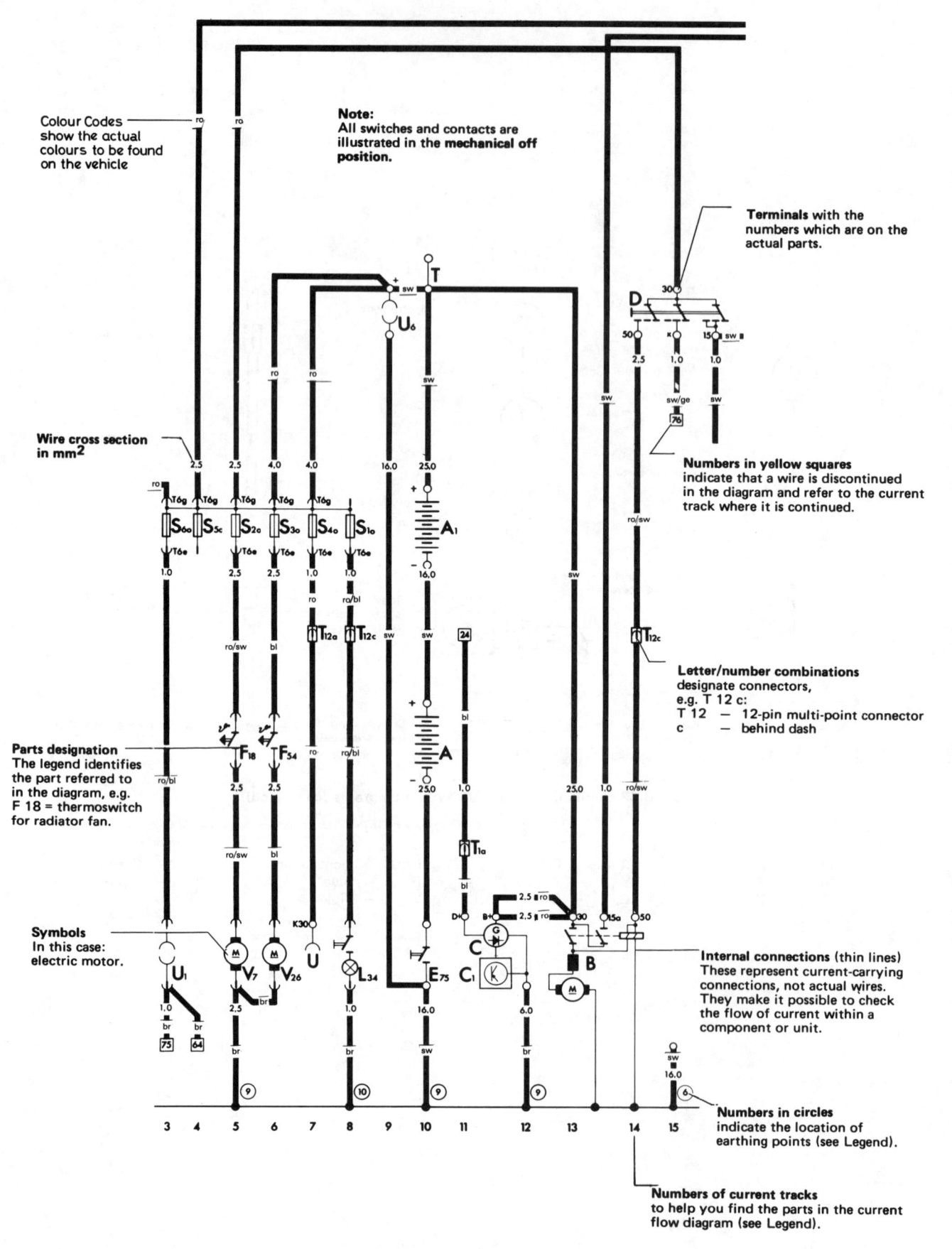

Fig. 10.43 Instructions for using UK wiring diagrams

Specimen legend

The same part designations are used in all current flow diagrams.
E.g.: A is always used for the battery

Designation			in current track
A	—	Battery	10
A 1	—	Battery	10
B	—	Starter	13, 14
C	—	Alternator	11, 12
C 1	—	Voltage regulator	11, 12
D	—	Ignition/starter switch	14—16
E 75	—	Battery master switch	10
F 18	—	Thermoswitch for radiator fan I	5
F 54	—	Thermoswitch for radiator fan II	6
L 34	—	Map reading light	8
S 1 to S 12	—	Fuses 1 to 12 in fusebox, upper	
T	—	Connector, behind dash, right	
T 1a	—	Connector, single, behind dash	
T 6e	—	Connector, white, on fusebox, upper	
T 6g	—	Connector, brown, on fusebox, upper	
T 12a	—	Connector, 12 pin, behind dash (instrument panel harness/rear harness connection)	
T 12c	—	Connector, 12 pin, behind dash (instrument panel harness/front right harness connection)	
U	—	Trailer socket	7
U 1	—	Socket — instrument panel	3
U 6	—	Socket for outside starter boost	9
V 7	—	Radiator fan I	5
V 26	—	Radiator fan II	6

⑥ — Earthing strap, body/engine

⑨ — Earthing point, engine compartment, front, left

⑰ — Earthing point behind dash, left

Explanation of where a connection is to be found on the vehicle.

Number of current track
to help you locate the part in the current flow diagram.
Current track numbers are not given for fuses, wiring connections and earthing points.

Fig. 10.43 Instructions for using UK wiring diagrams (continued)

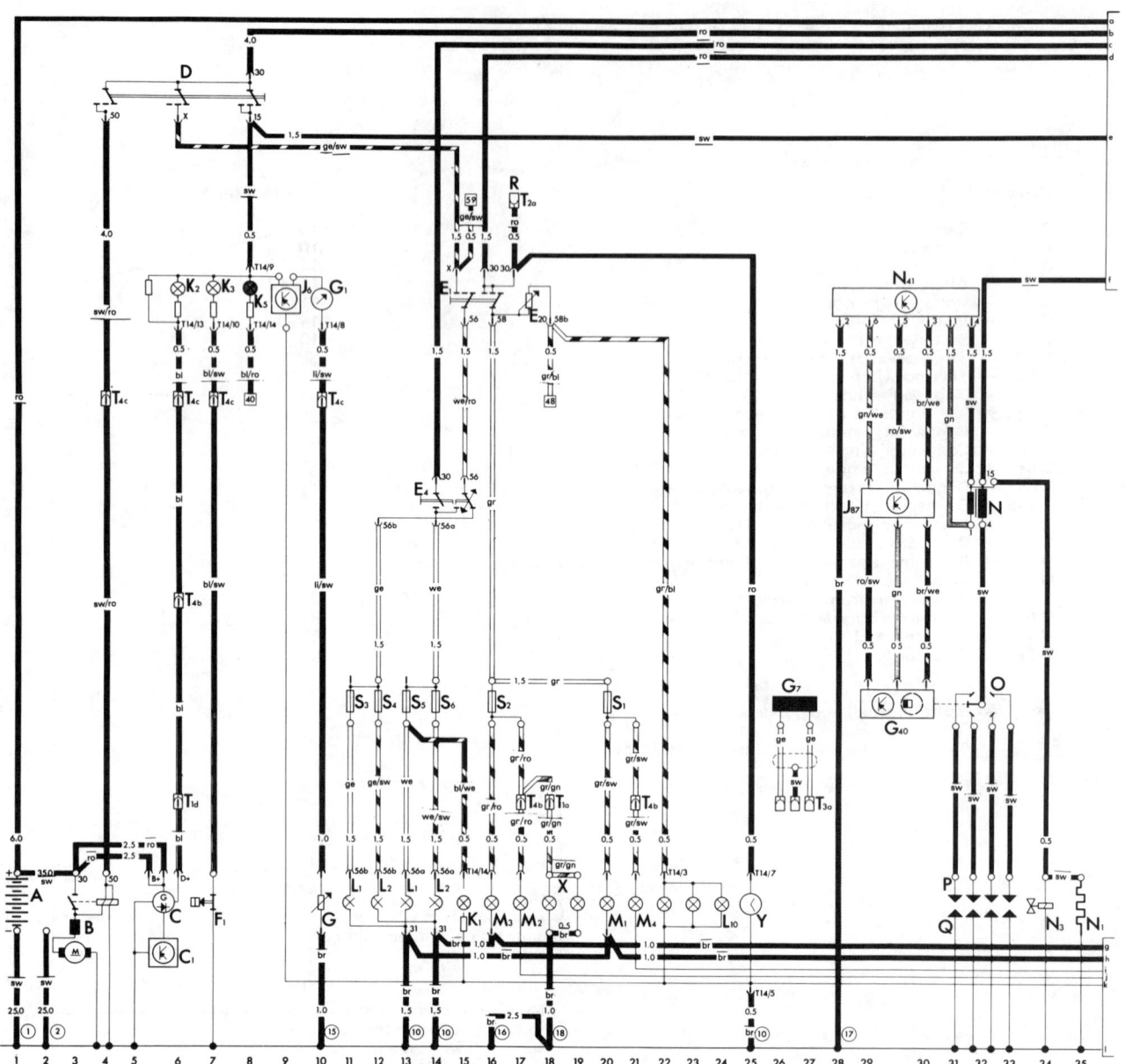

Fig. 10.44 Wiring diagram for 1.6 litre Transporter and derivatives – UK vehicles

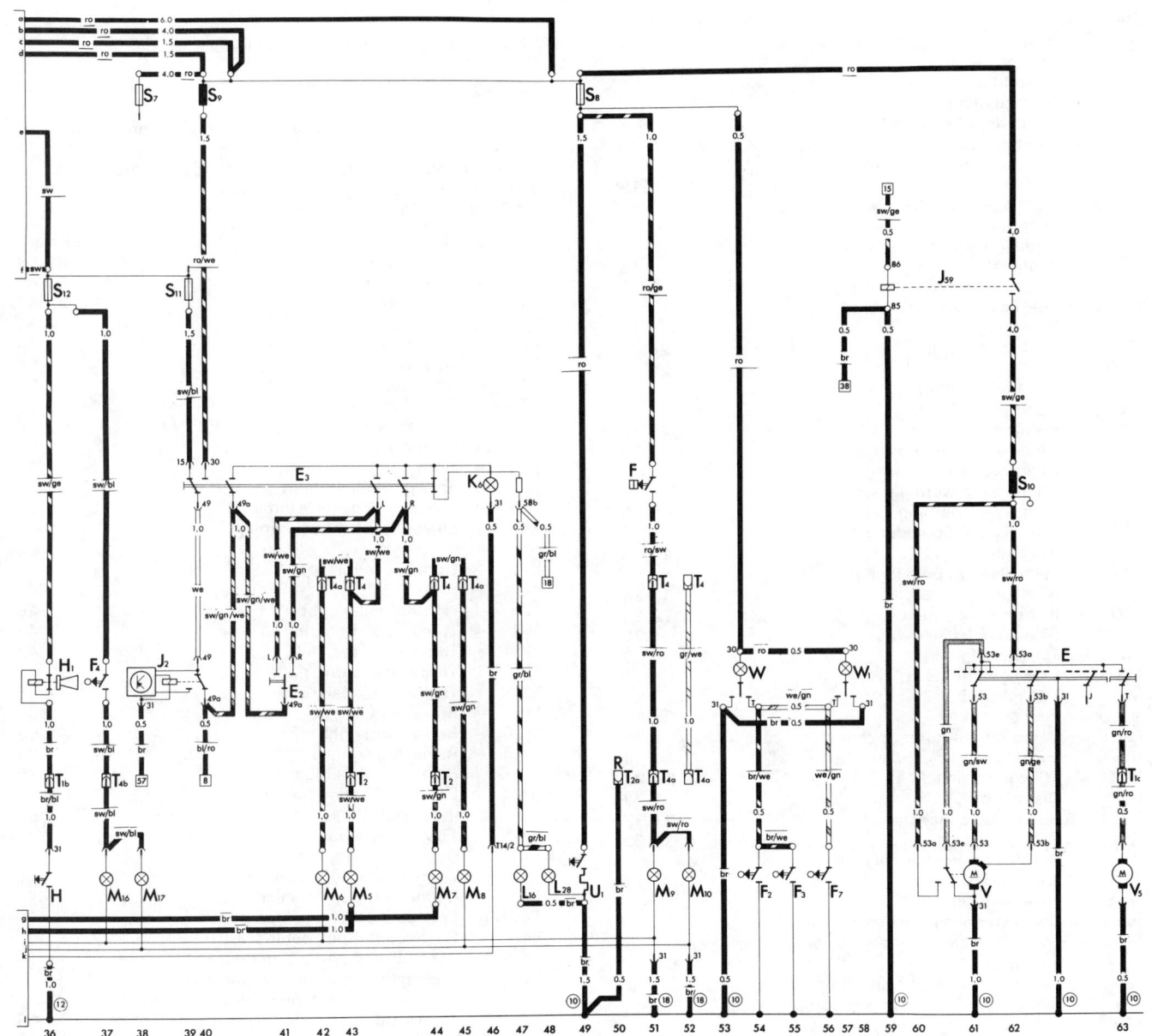

Fig. 10.44 Wiring diagram for 1.6 litre Transporter and derivatives – UK vehicles (continued)

Key to Fig. 10.44

Designation		In current track
A	– Battery	1
B	– Starter	3,4
C	– Alternator	5,6
C1	– Voltage regulator	5,6
D	– Ignition/starter switch	4-8
E1	– Light switch	15-18
E4	– Headlight dip and flasher switch	12-15
E20	– Lighting control for instruments, cigar lighter and ventilation controls	18
F1	– Oil pressure switch	7
G	– Fuel gauge sender unit	10
G1	– Fuel gauge	10
G7	– TDC sender unit	26,27
G40	– Hall sender	29,30
J6	– Voltage stabilizer	9
J87	– Control unit for idling stabilizer	29,30
K1	– High beam warning lamp	15
K2	– Alternator warning lamp	6
K3	– Oil pressure warning lamp	7
K5	– Turn signal warning lamp	8
L1	– Twin filament bulb for left headlight	11,13
L2	– Twin filament bulb for right headlight	12,14
L10	– Instrument cluster light	22-24
M1	– Side light, left	20
M2	– Tail light, right	17
M3	– Side light, right	16
M4	– Tail light, left	21
N	– Ignition coil	32
N1	– Carburettor automatic choke*	35
N3	– By-pass air cut-off valve*	34
N41	– TCI control unit	28-32
O	– Distributor	31-33
P	– Spark plug connectors	31-33
Q	– Spark plugs	31-33
R	– Positive connection for radio (behind dash)	17
S1-S6–	Fuses in fusebox	
T1a	– Connector, single, in junction box**	
T1d	– Connector, single, in engine compartment near alternator	
T2a	– Connector, 2 pin, behind dash	
T3a	– Connector, 3 pin, in engine compartment	
T4b	– Connector, 4 pin, in junction box**	
T4c	– Connector, 4 pin, behind dash	
T14/	– Connector, 14 pin, on instrument cluster	
X	– Number plate light	18,19
Y	– Clock***	25

(1) – Earthing strap, battery/body

(2) – Earthing strap, gearbox/body

(10) – Earthing point behind dash, near fusebox

(15) – Earthing point on front crossmember, left

(16) – Earthing point near junction box**

(17) – Earthing point near distributor

(18) – Connection in junction box**

*See additional current flow diagram for wiring on 2.0 litre engine.
**On vehicles without junction box, wiring goes direct from main harness to electrical components.
***On ''L'' version vehicles only.

Designation		In current track
E	– Wiper switch	61-63
E2	– Turn signal switch	41
E3	– Emergency light switch	39-47
F	– Brake light switch	51
F2	– Door contact switch, left	54
F3	– Door contact switch, right***	55
F4	– Reversing light switch***	37
F7	– Door contact switch, rear (sliding door)	56
H	– Horn control	36
H1	– Horn	36
J2	– Emergency light relay	38-40
J59	– Auxiliary relay (for contact X)	59-62
K6	– Emergency flasher warning lamp	46
L16	– Light for ventilation controls***	47
L28	– Light for cigar lighter***	48
M5	– Turn signal, front, left	43
M6	– Turn signal, rear, left	42
M7	– Turn signal, front, right	44
M8	– Turn signal, rear, right	45
M9	– Brake light, left	51
M10	– Brake light, right	52
M16	– Reversing light, left***	37
M17	– Reversing light, right***	38
R	– Earth connection for radio (behind dash)	50
S7-S12 –	Fuses in fusebox	
T1b	– Connector, single, behind dash	
T1c	– Connector, single, behind dash	
T2	– Connector, 2 pin, behind dash	
T2a	– Connector, 2 pin, behind dash	
T4	– Connector, 4 pin, behind dash	
T4a	– Connector, 4 pin, in junction box***	
T4b	– Connector, 4 pin, in junction box***	
T14/	– Connector, 14 pin, on instrument cluster	
U1	– Cigar lighter***	49
V	– Windscreen wiper motor	60-62
V5	– Windscreen washer pump	63
W	– Interior light, front	53,54
W1	– Interior light, rear	56-58

(10) – Earthing point behind dash, near fusebox

(12) – Earth lead from steering box

(18) – Connection in junction box***

**On vehicles without junction box, wiring goes direct from main harness to electrical components.
***Only on ''L'' version vehicles.

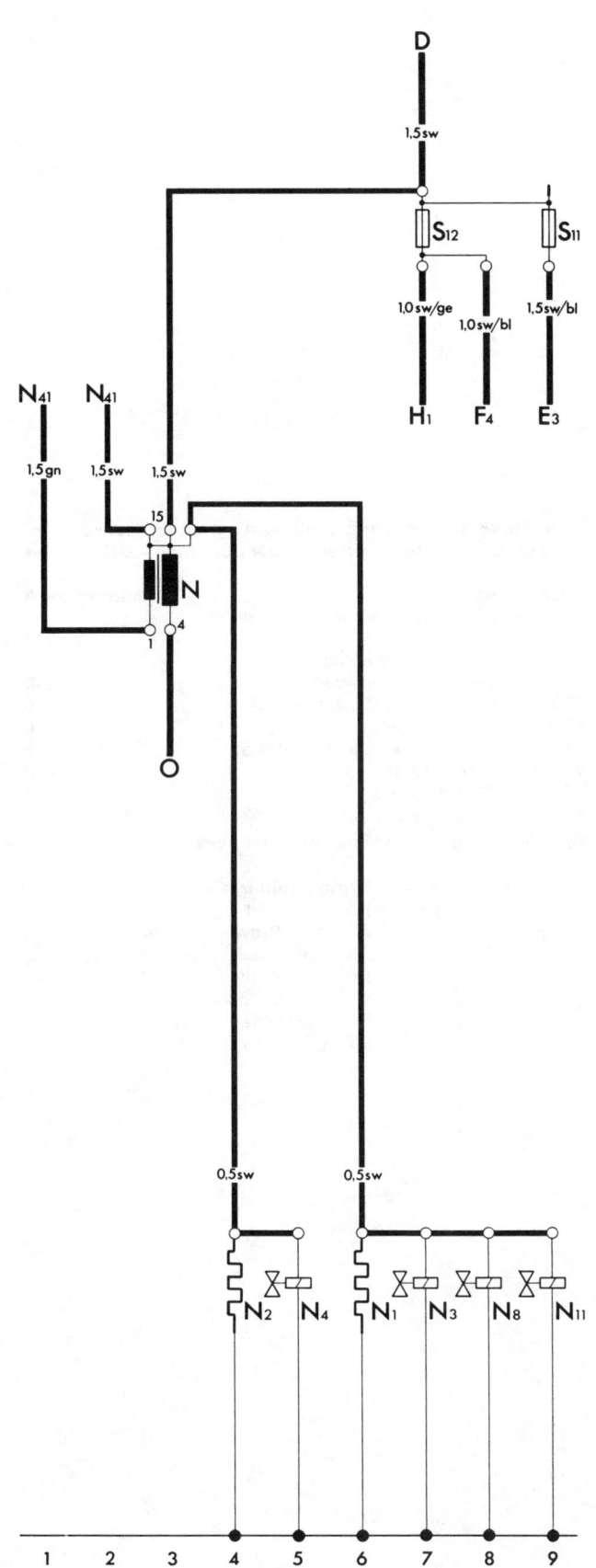

Fig. 10.45 Supplementary wiring diagram for 2.0 litre Transporter and derivatives – carburettor system – UK vehicles

Designation		In current track
D	– From ignition/starter switch, terminal 15	7
E3	– To emergency light switch, terminal 15	9
F4	– To reversing light switch	8
H1	– To horn	7
N	– Ignition coil	3
N1	– Carburettor automatic choke, left	6
N2	– Carburettor automatic choke, right	4
N3	– Idling cut-off valve, left	7
N4	– Idling cut-off valve, right	5
N8	– Bypass air cut-off valve	8
N11	– Idle enrichment valve	9
N41	– To TCI control unit	1,2
O	– To distributor	3
S11		
	– Fuses in fusebox	
S12		

Wiring colours:

sw	=	black
bl	=	blue
ge	=	yellow
gn	=	green

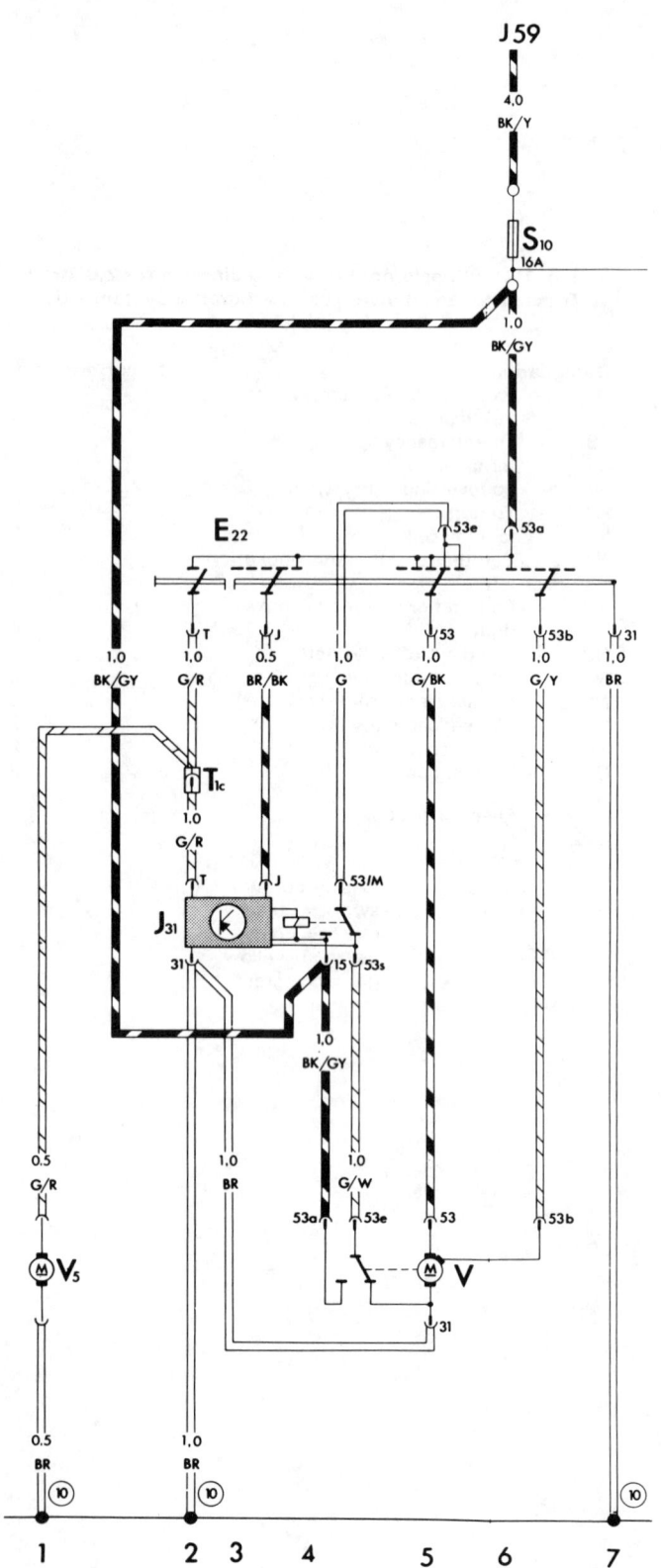

Fig. 10.46 Supplementary wiring diagram for Transporter and derivatives – intermittent wiper operation – UK vehicles

Designation		In current track
E22	– Wiper switch for intermittent operation	2-7
J31	– Relay for automatic intermittent wash/wipe	2-4
J59	– to relief relay (for X contact)	6
S10	– Fuse in fusebox	6
T1c	– Connector single, behind dash	2
V	– Wiper motor	4-6
V5	– Washer pump	1

⑩ – Earth point behind dash near fusebox

Wiring colours:

R	=	Red
BR	=	Brown
BK	=	Black
W	=	White
Y	=	Yellow
G	=	Green
GY	=	Grey

Fig. 10.47 Supplementary wiring diagram for Transporter and derivatives – rear foglamp – UK vehicles

Designation			In current track
E1	–	From lighting switch term, 56	1
E4	–	To headlight dimmer/flasher switch	1
E23	–	Rear fog light switch	1-5
K17	–	Rear fog light warning lamp (yellow)	1
L20	–	Rear fog light bulb	2
M9	–	Left hand brake light bulb	4
M10	–	To right hand brake light bulb	
S27	–	Single fuse for rear fog light (8 Amp.) fuse adaptor, 2 point, on fusebox	2
T1e	–	Connector, single, behind instrument panel	1
T4	–	Connector, 4 point, behind instrument panel	2
T4a	–	Connector, 4 point, in junction box	2

⑩ – Earthing point behind instrument panel, near fuse box

⑱ – Wiring junction in junction box

Wiring colours:

ws	=	white
sw	=	black
br	=	brown
gr	=	grey
ge	=	yellow
ro	=	red

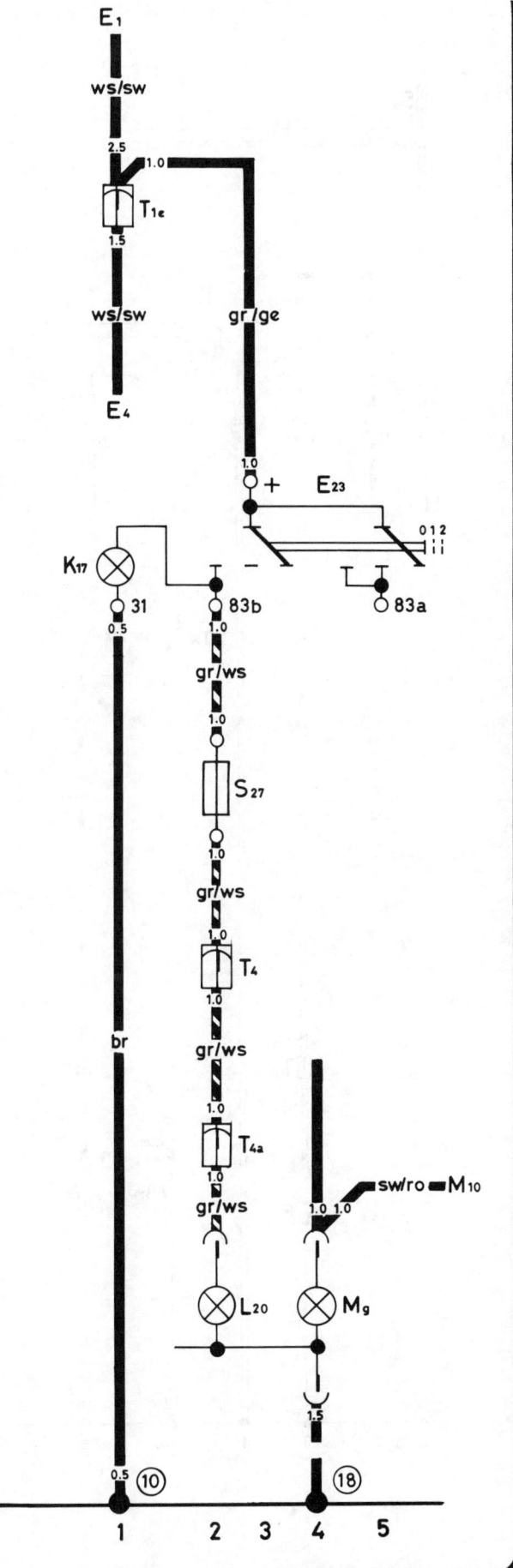

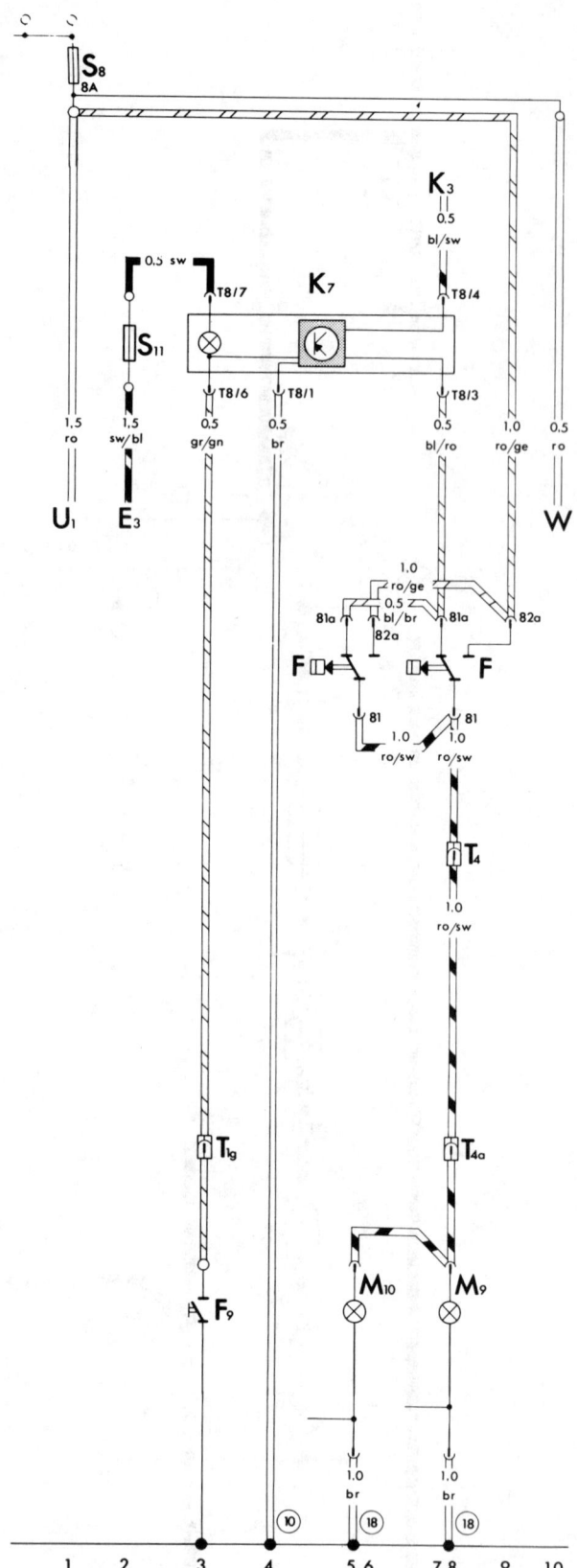

Fig. 10.48 Supplementary wiring diagram for Transporter and derivatives – dual-circuit braking system and handbrake warning light – UK vehicles

Designation		In current track
E3	– To emergency light switch, terminal 15	2
F	– Brake light switch	5-8
F9	– Handbrake switch	3
K3	– To connector T4c – connection oil pressure switch/oil pressure warning lamp	7
K7	– Dual circuit brake and handbrake warning lamp	3
M9	– Brake light, left	8
M10	– Brake light, right	5
S8, S11	– Fuses in fuse box	
T1g	– Connector, single, behind instrument panel	
T4	– Connector, four point, behind instrument panel	
T4a	– Connector, four point, in junction box	
T8	– Connector, eight point, on dual circuit brake system and handbrake insert	
U1	– To cigarette lighter	1
W	– To front interior light	10

⑩ – Earthing point behind instrument panel near fuse box

⑱ – Wiring in junction box

Wiring colours:
ro	=	red
sw	=	black
bl	=	blue
ge	=	yellow
br	=	brown
gr	=	grey
gn	=	green

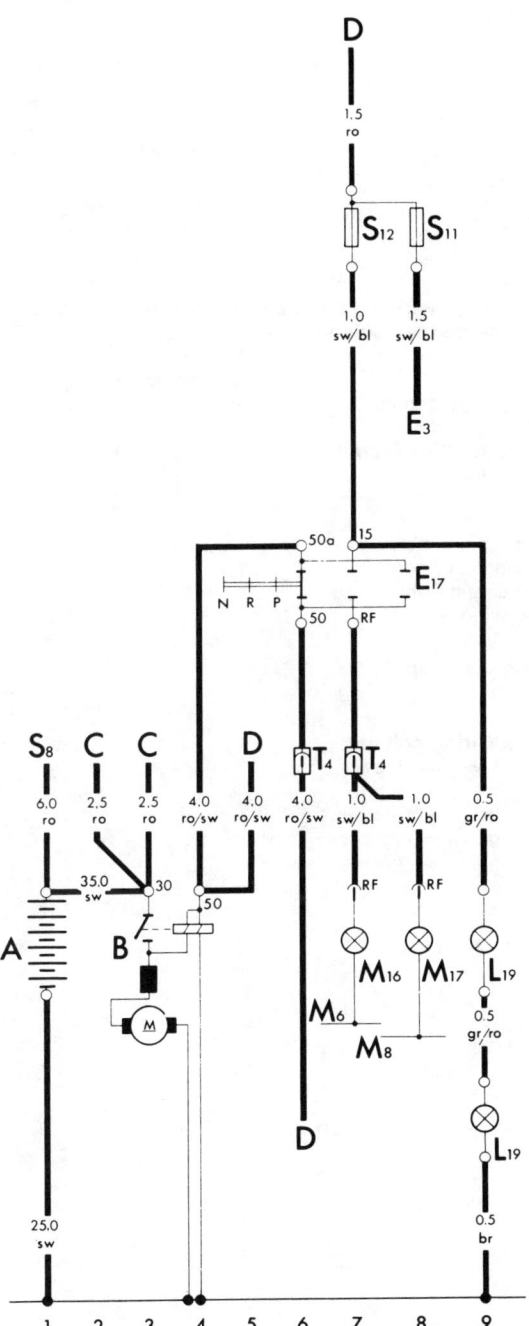

Fig. 10.49 Supplementray wiring diagram for Transporter and derivatives – automatic transmission – UK vehicles

Designation		In current track
A	– Battery	1
B	– Starter	3,4
C	– To alternator (terminal B+)	2,3
D	– To ignition/starter switch (terminal 50/15)	5,6,7
E17	– Starter inhibitor switch and switch for reversing lights	6-8
E3	– To emergency light switch (terminal 15)	8
L19	– Gear selector lever light	9
M6	– Turn signal, rear left	6
M9	– Turn signal, rear right	7
M16	– Reversing light, left	7
M17	– Reversing light, right	8
S8		
S11	– Fuses in fuse box	
S12		
T4	– Connector, four-point, in distribution box	

Wiring colours:
ro	= red
sw	= black
bl	= blue
gr	= grey
br	= brown

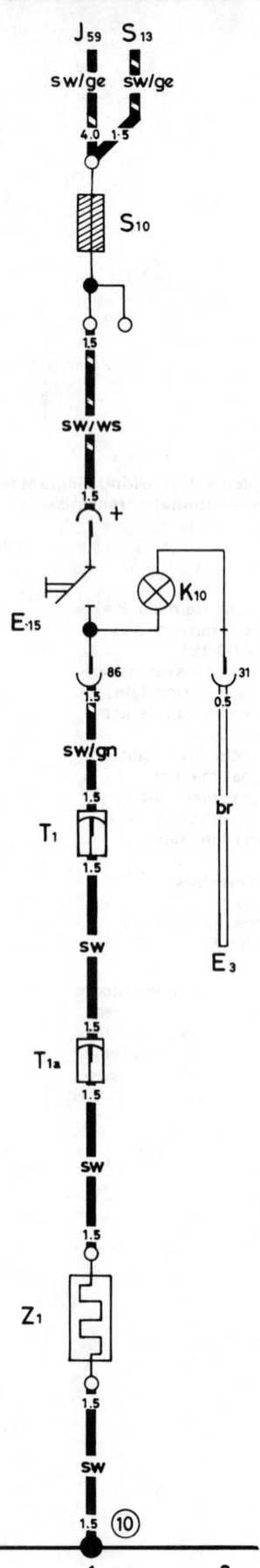

Fig. 10.50 Supplementary wiring diagram for Transporter and derivatives – heated rear window – UK vehicles

Designation			In current track
E3	–	To emergency light switch	2
E13	–	Switch for rear window	1
J59	–	To relief relay (for X contact)	1
K10	–	Warning lamp for rear	
S10		window	2
S13	–	Fuses in fuse box	
T1	–	Connector single, behind dash	
T1a	–	Connector single, on roof	
		cross member rear right	
Z1	–	Heated rear window	1
⑩	–	Earth point on rear flap	

Wiring colours:

sw	=	black
ws	=	white
br	–	brown
ge	=	yellow
gn	=	green

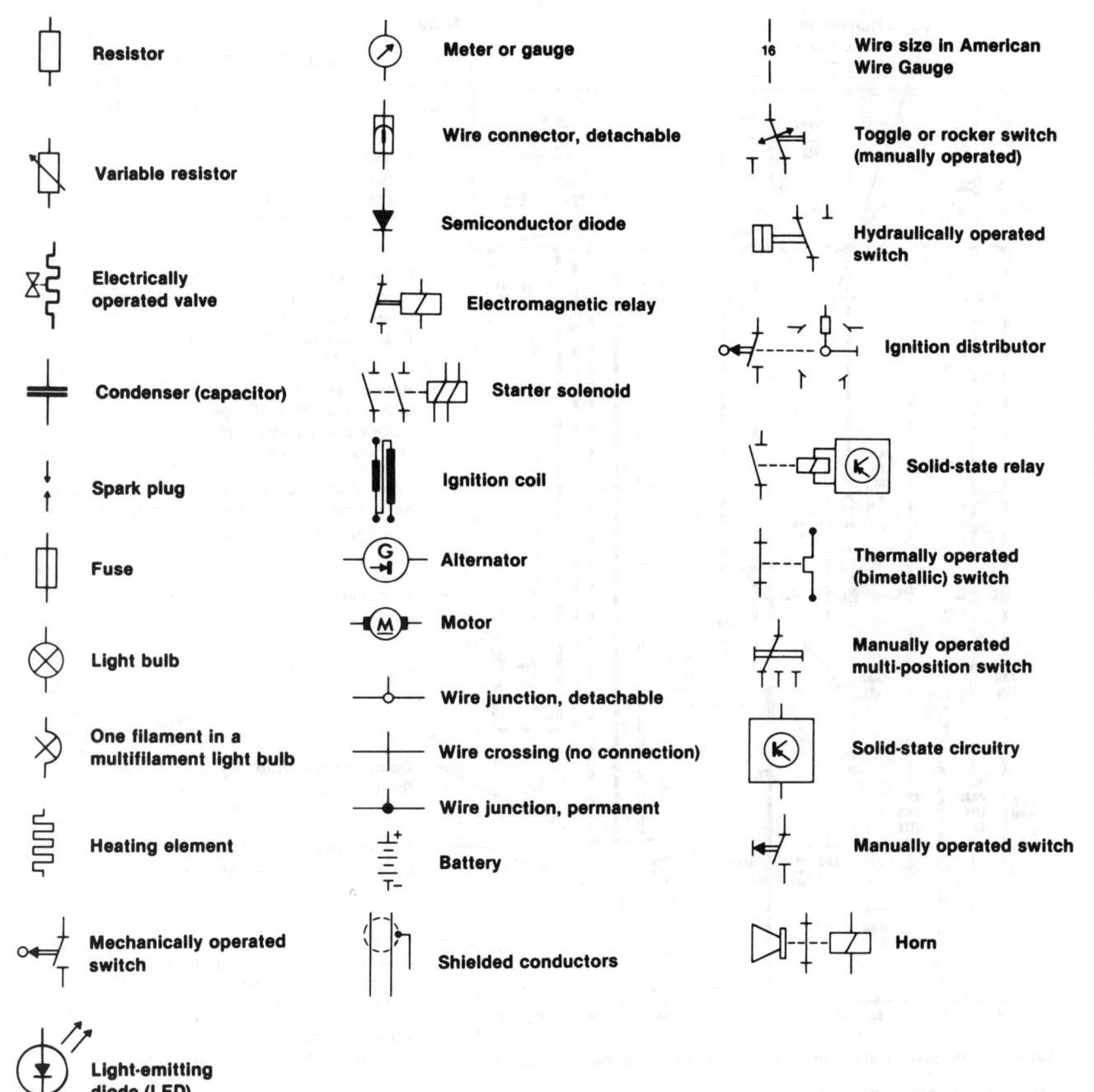

Resistor

Variable resistor

Electrically operated valve

Condenser (capacitor)

Spark plug

Fuse

Light bulb

One filament in a multifilament light bulb

Heating element

Mechanically operated switch

Light-emitting diode (LED)

Meter or gauge

Wire connector, detachable

Semiconductor diode

Electromagnetic relay

Starter solenoid

Ignition coil

Alternator

Motor

Wire junction, detachable

Wire crossing (no connection)

Wire junction, permanent

Battery

Shielded conductors

Wire size in American Wire Gauge

Toggle or rocker switch (manually operated)

Hydraulically operated switch

Ignition distributor

Solid-state relay

Thermally operated (bimetallic) switch

Manually operated multi-position switch

Solid-state circuitry

Manually operated switch

Horn

Color Code

Black	— BK	Green	— G
Brown	— BR	Light Green	— LT. G
Clear	— CL	Blue	— BL
Red	— R	Violet	— V
Yellow	— Y	Gray	— GY
		White	— W

Wire Connector Code

T1	—single	T6	—6-point
T2	—double	T8	—8-point
T3	—3-point	T12	—12-point
T4	—4-point	T14	—14-point

Fig. 10.51 Symbols used on US wiring diagrams

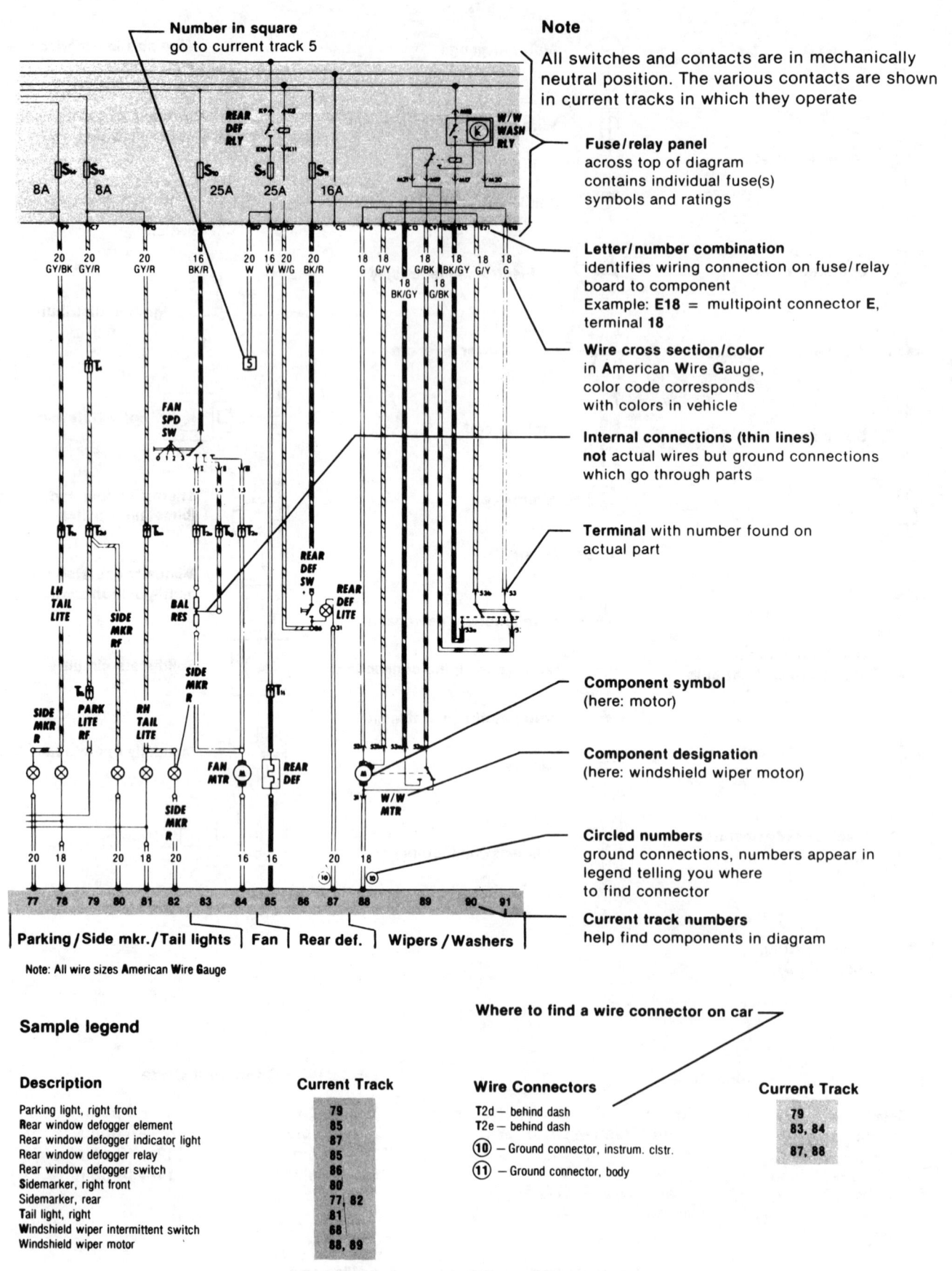

Number in square
go to current track 5

Note
All switches and contacts are in mechanically neutral position. The various contacts are shown in current tracks in which they operate

Fuse/relay panel
across top of diagram
contains individual fuse(s)
symbols and ratings

Letter/number combination
identifies wiring connection on fuse/relay board to component
Example: **E18** = multipoint connector E, terminal **18**

Wire cross section/color
in **A**merican **W**ire **G**auge, color code corresponds with colors in vehicle

Internal connections (thin lines)
not actual wires but ground connections which go through parts

Terminal with number found on actual part

Component symbol
(here: motor)

Component designation
(here: windshield wiper motor)

Circled numbers
ground connections, numbers appear in legend telling you where to find connector

Current track numbers
help find components in diagram

Note: All wire sizes American Wire Gauge

| Parking/Side mkr./Tail lights | Fan | Rear def. | Wipers/Washers |

Sample legend

Where to find a wire connector on car

Description	Current Track
Parking light, right front	79
Rear window defogger element	85
Rear window defogger indicator light	87
Rear window defogger relay	85
Rear window defogger switch	86
Sidemarker, right front	80
Sidemarker, rear	77, 82
Tail light, right	81
Windshield wiper intermittent switch	68
Windshield wiper motor	88, 89

Wire Connectors	Current Track
T2d — behind dash	79
T2e — behind dash	83, 84
⑩ — Ground connector, instrum. clstr.	87, 88
⑪ — Ground connector, body	

Fig. 10.52 Instructions for using US wiring diagrams

Key to Fig. 10.53

Description	Current Track	Description	Current Track
Alternator	31,32	Headlight dimmer switch/flasher	43,44
Alternator charging indicator light	32	Headlight, left, high	42
Auxiliary air regulator	22	Headlight, left, low	40
Back-up light, left	58	Headlight, right, high	43
Back-up light, right	59	Headlight, right low	41
Back-up light switch	58	Heater/fresh air controls light	69
Battery	26	High beam indicator light	44
Brake light, left	76	Horn	57
Brake light, right	75	Horn button	57
Brake light switch	75,76	Idle stabilizer control unit*	2-4
Brake warning light	73-76	Ignition coil	7
Cigarette lighter	71	Ignition control unit*	1-6
Cigarette lighter light	70	Ignition key warning buzzer	77,78
Clock	56	Ignition/starter switch	30-40
Cold start valve	24	Injector, cylinder 1	15
Distributor	5-8	Injector, cylinder 2	16
Door switch, left front, with buzzer		Injector, cylinder 3	17
contact	78,79	Injector, cylinder 4	14
Door switch, right front	80	Instrument light dimmer	46
Elapsed mileage switch for OXS		Instrument panel lights	53-55
indicator*	33,34	Intake air sensor	18-20
Emergency flasher indicator light	67	Interior light, front	79-81
Emergency flasher relay	59-61	Interior light, rear	82,83
Emergency flasher switch	61-69	License plate light	48,49
Fuel gauge	39	Light switch	44-47
Fuel gauge sender	39	Load reduction relay	88-93
Fuel injection control unit	10-22	Oil pressure light	36
Fuel pump	23	Oil pressure switch	36
Fuel pump relay	19-24	Oxygen sensor (OXS)*	19
Fuses S2-S12 on fuse/relay panel		Oxygen sensor (OXS) indicator light*	34
(under dash)			
Hall generator*	2-4	*California only	

Note On 49 state and Canada vehicles, a series resistance is located between fuel injection control unit and injectors. On California vehicles, series resistance is built into fuel injection control unit.

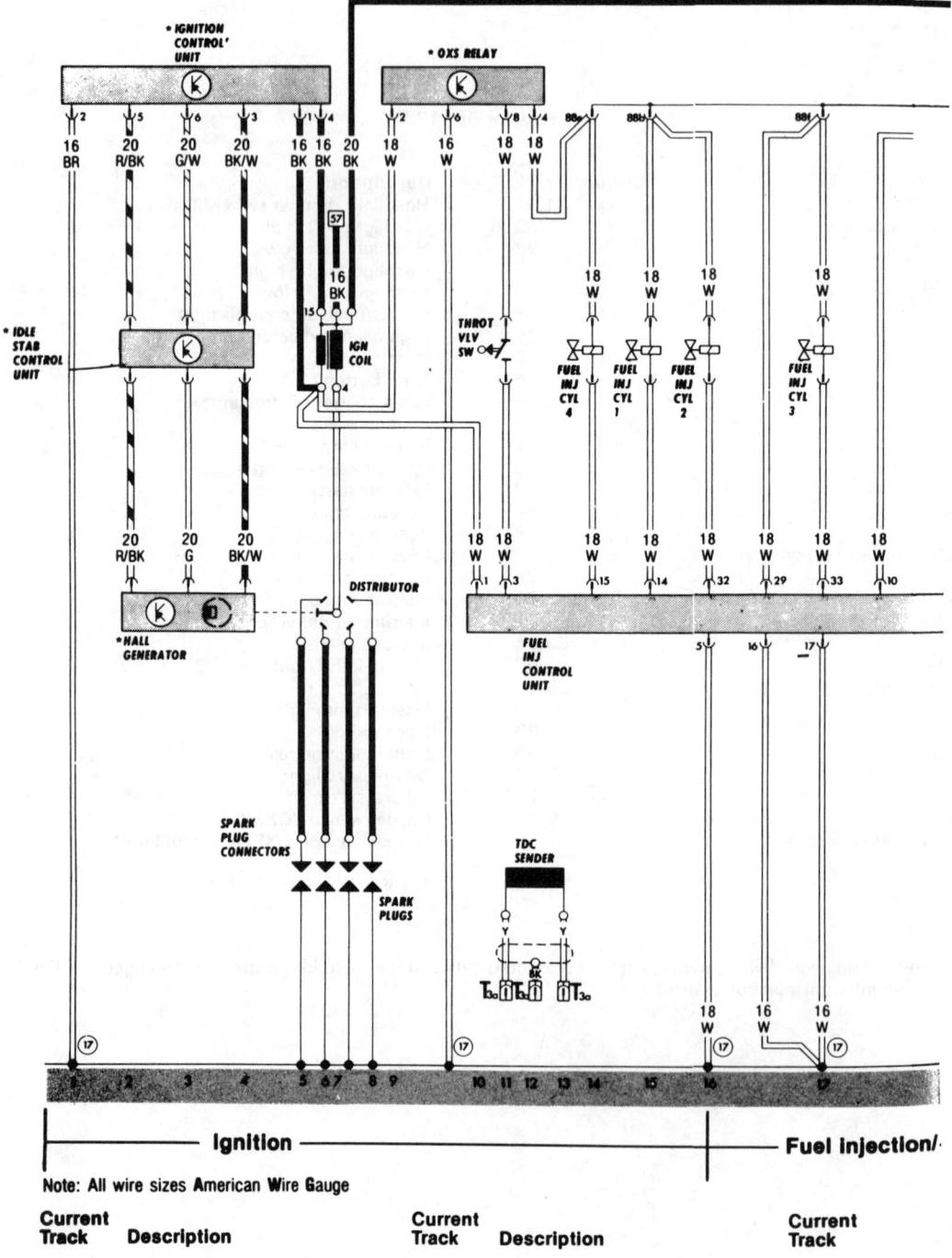

Note: All wire sizes American Wire Gauge

Fig. 10.53 Wiring diagram for Vanagon and derivatives – USA vehicles (Part 1)

Fig. 10.53 Wiring diagram for Vanagon and derivatives – USA vehicles (Part 1) (continued)

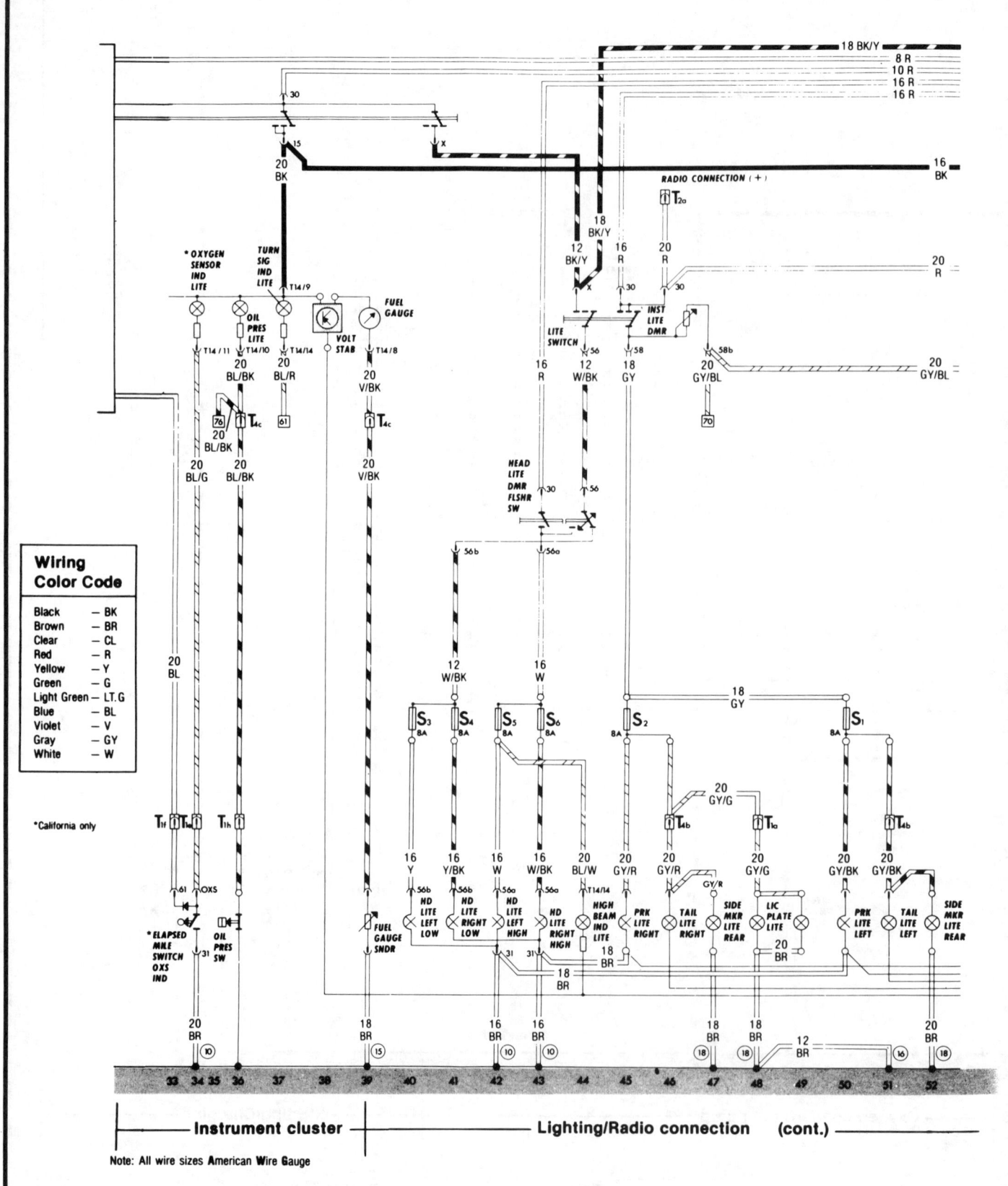

Fig. 10.54 Wiring diagram for Vanagon and derivatives – USA vehicles (Part 2)

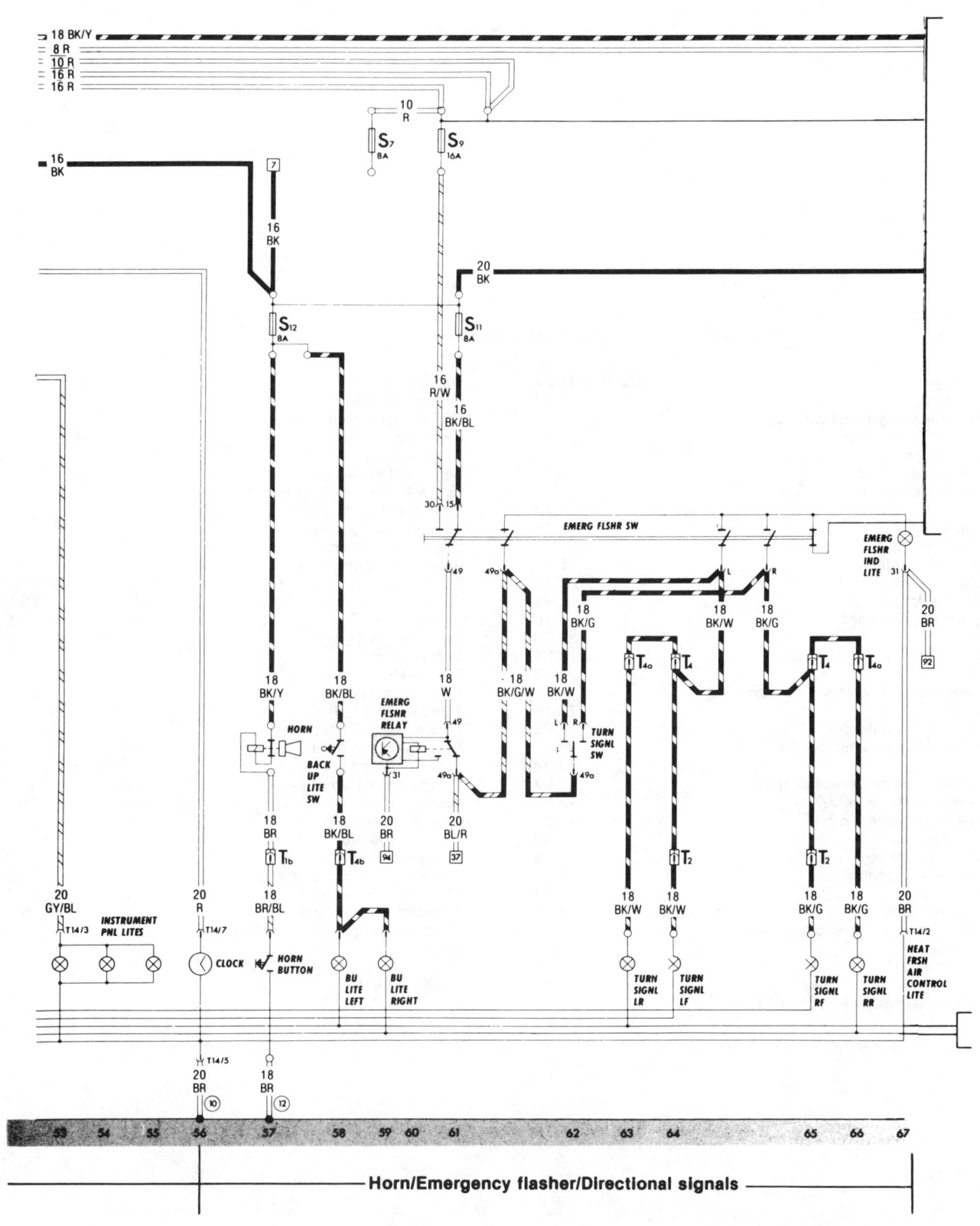

Fig. 10.54 Wiring diagram for Vanagon and derivatives – USA vehicles (Part 2) (continued)

Key to Fig. 10.54

Description	Current Track	Description	Current Track
Alternator	31,32	Parking light, left	50
Alternator charging indicator light	32	Parking light, right	45
Auxiliary air regulator	22	Radio connection (−)	72
Back-up light, left	58	Radio connection (+)	46
Back-up light, right	59	Rear window defogger	91
Back-up light switch	58	Rear window defogger switch	91,92
Battery	26	Side marker light, left	52
Brake light, left	76	Side marker light, right	47
Brake light, right	75	Sliding door switch	83
Brake light switch	75,76	Spark plug connectors	5-8
Brake warning light	73-76	Spark plugs	5-8
Cigarette lighter	71	Starter	28,29
Cigarette lighter light	70	Tail light, left	51
Clock	56	Tail light, right	46
Cold start valve	24	TDC sender	11-13
Distributor	5-8	Temperature sensor	21
Door switch, left front, with buzzer		Thermo time switch	24,25
contact	78,79	Throttle valve switch	11
Door switch, right front	80	Turn signal indicator light	37
Elapsed mileage switch for OXS		Turn signal, left front	64
indicator*	33,34	Turn signal, left rear	63
Emergency flasher indicator light	67	Turn signal, right front	65
Emergency flasher relay	59-61	Turn signal, right rear	66
Emergency flasher switch	61-69	Turn signal switch	62
Fuel gauge	39	Voltage regulator	31
Fuel gauge sender	39	Voltage stabilizer	38
Fuel injection control unit	10-22	Windshield washer pump	84
Fuel pump	23	Windshield wiper motor	86-89
Fuel pump relay	19-24	Windshield wiper switch	85-90
Fuses S2-S12 on fuse/relay panel		Windshield wiper/washer intermittent	
(under dash)		relay	85-87
Hall generator*	2-4		
Oxygen sensor (OXS) relay*	9-12	*California only	
Parking brake indicator light switch	73		

Key to Fig. 10.55

Description	Current Track	Description	Current Track
Headlight dimmer switch/flasher	43,44	Parking light, right	45
Headlight, left, high	42	Radio connection (−)	72
Headlight, left, low	40	Radio connection (+)	46
Headlight, right, high	43	Rear window defogger	91
Headlight, right low	41	Rear window defogger switch	91,92
Heater/fresh air controls light	69	Side marker light, left	52
High beam indicator light	44	Side marker light, right	47
Horn	57	Sliding door switch	83
Horn button	57	Spark plug connectors	5-8
Idle stabilizer control unit*	2-4	Spark plugs	5-8
Ignition coil	7	Starter	28,29
Ignition control unit*	1-6	Tail light, left	51
Ignition key warning buzzer	77,78	Tail light, right	46
Ignition/starter switch	30-40	TDC sender	11-13
Injector, cylinder 1	15	Temperature sensor	21
Injector, cylinder 2	16	Thermo time switch	24,25
Injector, cylinder 3	17	Throttle valve switch	11
Injector, cylinder 4	14	Turn signal indicator light	37
Instrument light dimmer	46	Turn signal, left front	64
Instrument panel lights	53-55	Turn signal, left rear	63
Intake air sensor	18-20	Turn signal, right front	65
Interior light, front	79-81	Turn signal, right rear	66
Interior light, rear	82,83	Turn signal switch	62
License plate light	48,49	Voltage regulator	31
Light switch	44-47	Voltage stabilizer	38
Load reduction relay	88-93	Windshield washer pump	84
Oil pressure light	36	Windshield wiper motor	86-89
Oil pressure switch	36	Windshield wiper switch	85-90
Oxygen sensor (OXS)*	19	Windshield wiper/washer intermittent	
Oxygen sensor (OXS) indicator light*	34	relay	85-87
Oxygen sensor (OXS) relay*	9-12		
Parking brake indicator light switch	73	*California only	
Parking light, left	50		

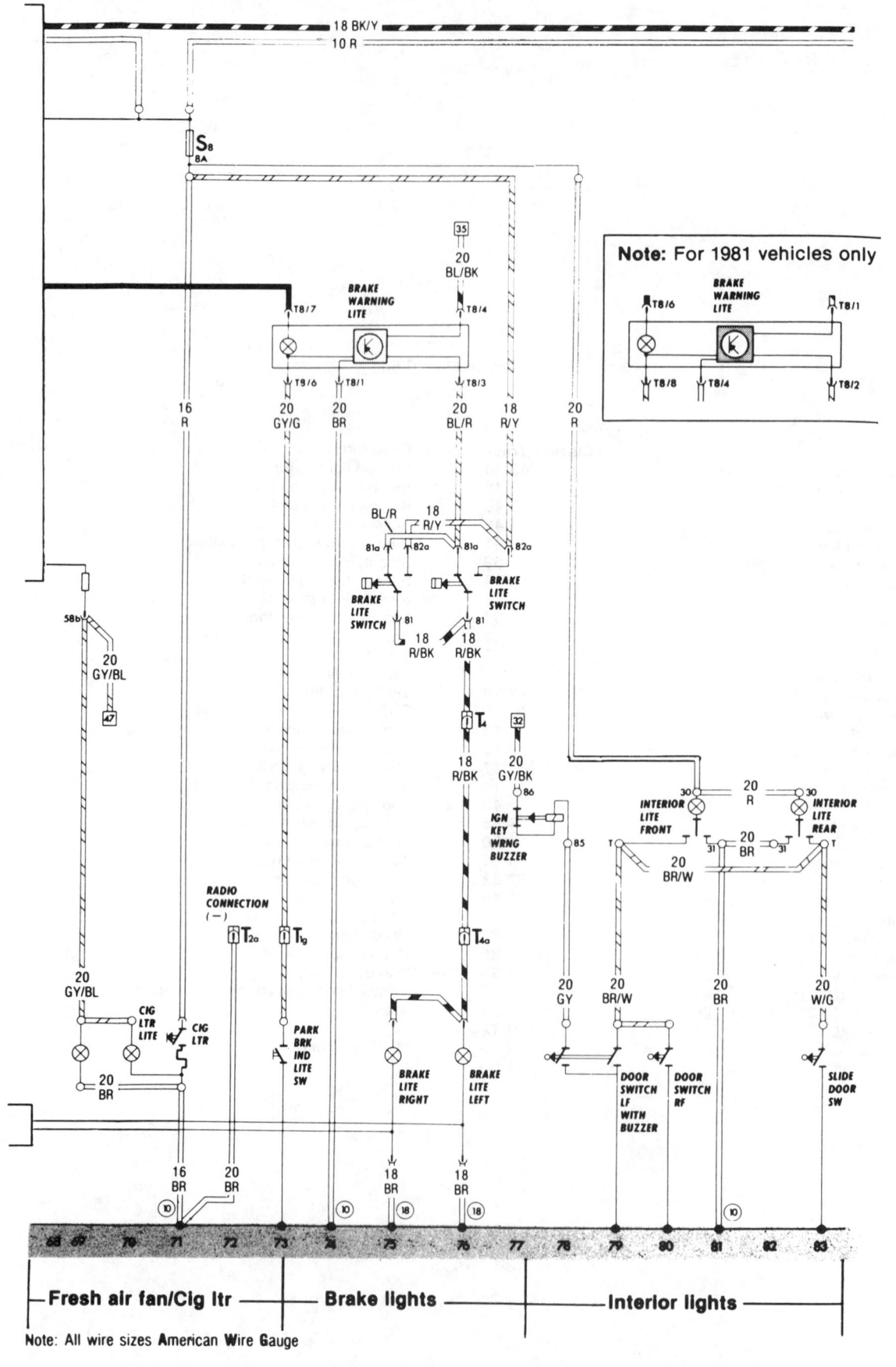

Fig. 10.55 Wiring diagram for Vanagon and derivatives – USA vehicles (Part 3)

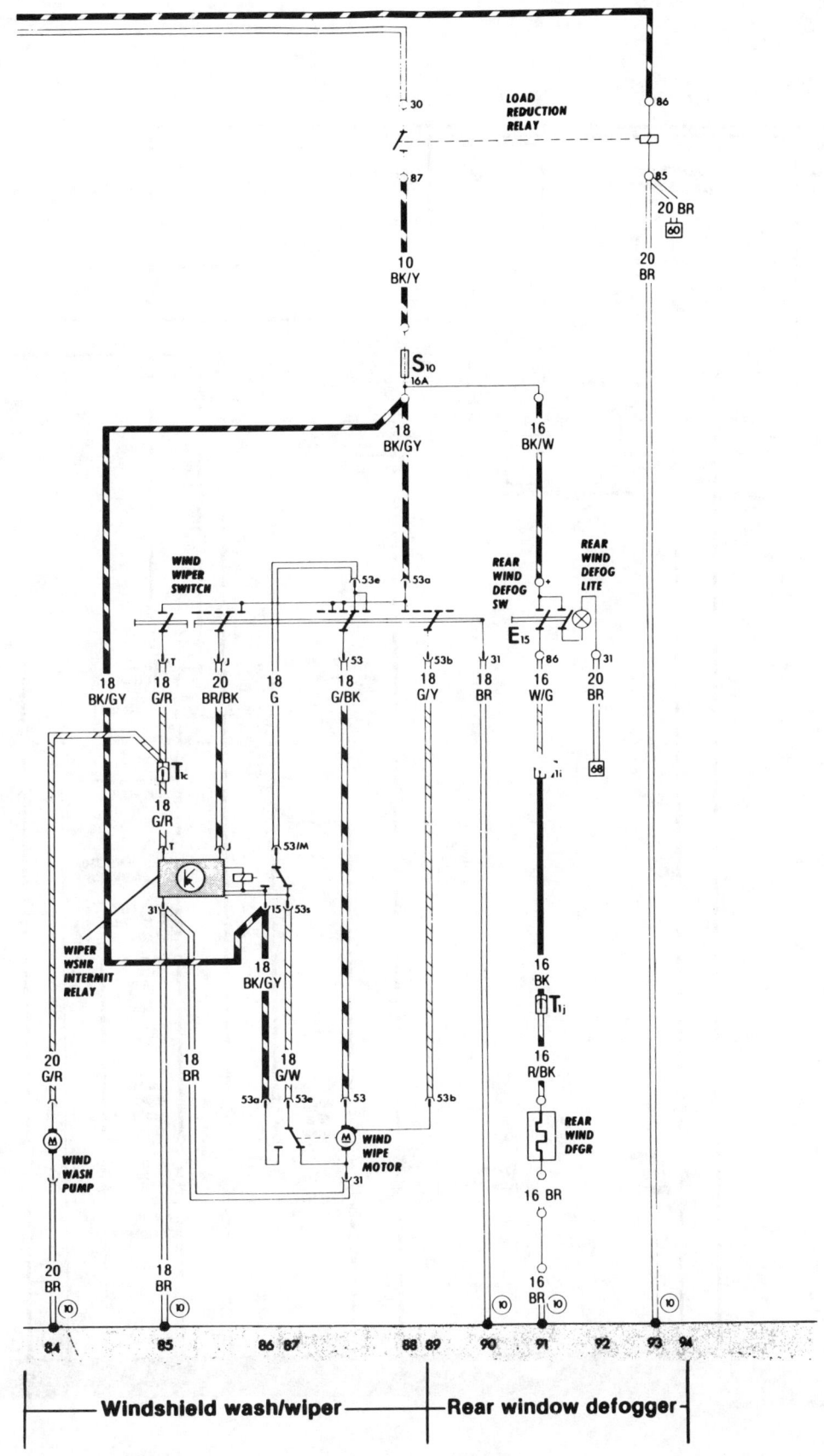

Fig. 10.55 Wiring diagram for Vanagon and derivatives – USA vehicles (Part 3) (continued)

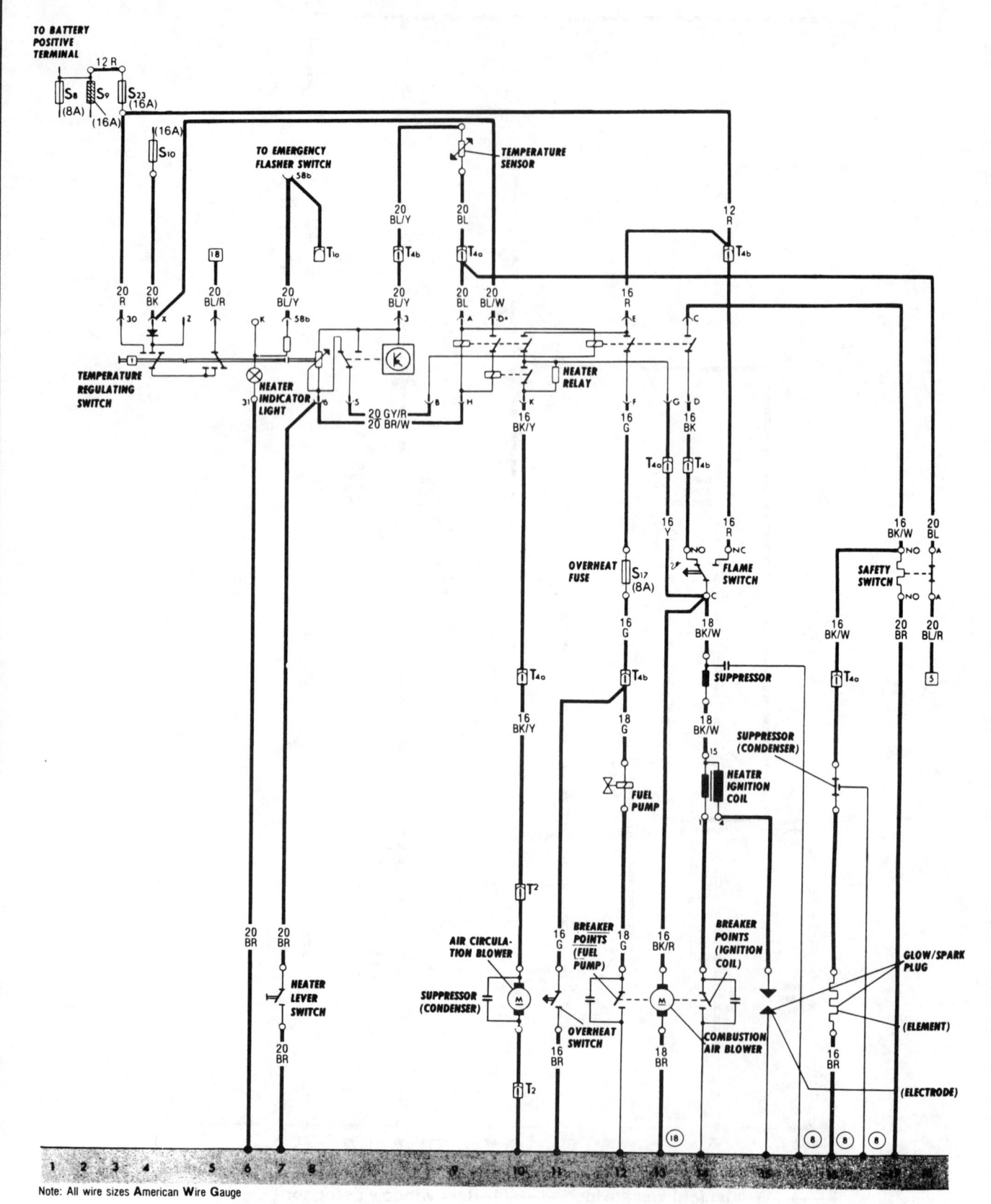

Fig. 10.56 Supplementary wiring diagram for Vanagon and derivatives – auxiliary heater – USA vehicles

Note: All wire sizes American Wire Gauge

Key to Fig. 10.56

Description	Current Track
Air circulation blower	10
Breaker points for fuel pump	12
Breaker points for ignition coil	14
Combustion air blower	13
(to) Emergency flasher switch, term. 58b	7
Flame switch	14
Fuel pump	1,3
Glow/spark plug – element	16
Glow/spark plug – electrode	15
Heater indicator light	6
Heater lever switch	7
Heater relay	9-14
Ignition coil	14
Ignition/starter switch	9
Main fuse S23	3
Overheat fuse S17	12

Description	Current track
Overheat switch	11
Safety switch	17,18
Suppressor for air circulation blower	10
Suppressor for glow/spark plug	16
Suppressor for ignition coil	14,15
Temperature regulating switch	1-8
Temperature sensor	9

Wire connectors

T1a	– at fuse holder	7
T2	– at air circulation blower	10
T4a	– at heater	9,10,13,16
T4b	– at heater	8,12,13,14

⑧ – ground connector, at heater

⑱ – ground connector, at combustion air blower

Key to Fig. 10.57

Description	Current track
Circuit breaker (15A) in cabinet front	3
Fuse S4, main, (16A) in storage compartment under driver's seat	19
Fuse S5, (3A) for water pump, on water pump	13
Fuse S6, (10A) for refrigerator 12-volt system in switch panel	19
Heater resistor for refrigerator, 12-volt, 85-watt, 1.7-ohm	18
Heater resistor for refrigerator, 115-volt, 85-watt, 150-ohm	9
Heater resistor relay for refrigerator, 12-volt system	18-20
Indicator light panel	10-15
LED – green, for battery level – above 12.5 volts	11
LED – green, for water tank level – at least 40 liters (10 1/2 gal.)	14
LED – yellow, for battery level – below 12.5 volts	11
LED – yellow, for water tank level – at least 10 liters (2 1/2 gal.)	14
LED – red, indicator light panel pilot light	10
LED – red, for battery level – above 12 volts	11
LED – red, for water tank level – at least 2 liters (1/2 gal.)	14
LED – red, for water tank level – empty (pump automatically shut off)	12
Plug, external, 115-volt, outside vehicle	2-4
Plug, interior, 115-volt, in cabinet front	2-4
Plug, refrigerator, 115-volt, in storage cabinet	2-4

Description	Current Track
Refrigerator fan, behind refrigerator	16
Refrigerator fan thermoswitch, rear of refrigerator	16
Refrigerator housing	5-9,16-20
Refrigerator switch, 12-volt, 115-volt, or gas	6,7,18,19
Refrigerator thermostat, 115-volt and gas systems	7
Safety ground wire for 115-volt plugs	1-5
Water pump, underneath cover in cabinet below sink	13
Water pump switch, in faucet	10
Water tank	15
Water tank level sender unit	14

Wire connectors

T1	– at rear of refrigerator
T2	– below sink
T2c	– next to water pump
T3a	– upper right of sink/stove cabinet
T6	– on indicator light panel
T8	– on refrigerator

Ground connectors

① – on refrigerator

② – on body, left side

③ – in 115 volt plugs

⑥ – behind sink/stove cabinet, left side

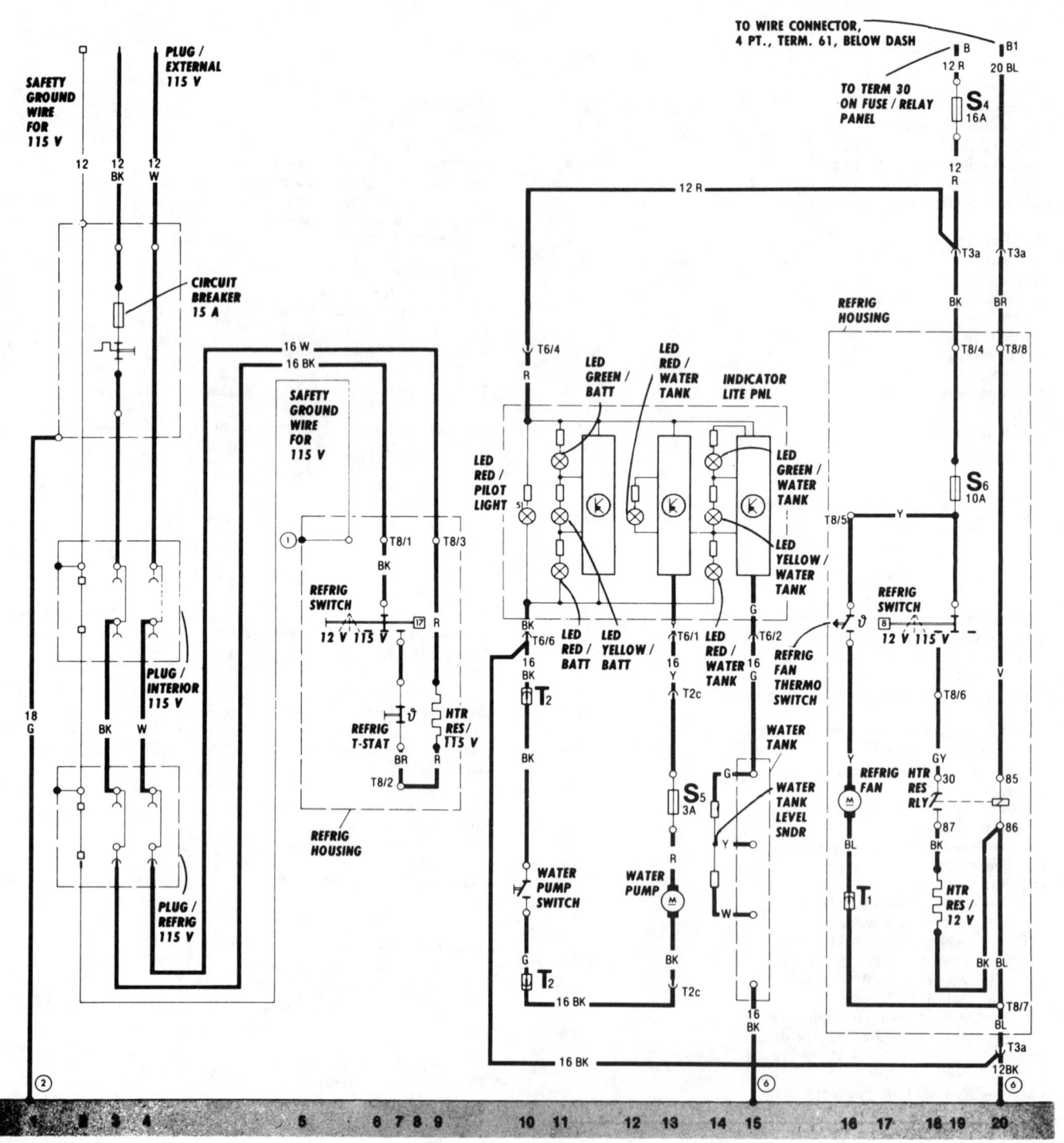

Note: All wire sizes American Wire Gauge

Fig. 10.57 Supplementary wiring diagram for Vanagon and derivatives – camper wiring – USA vehicles

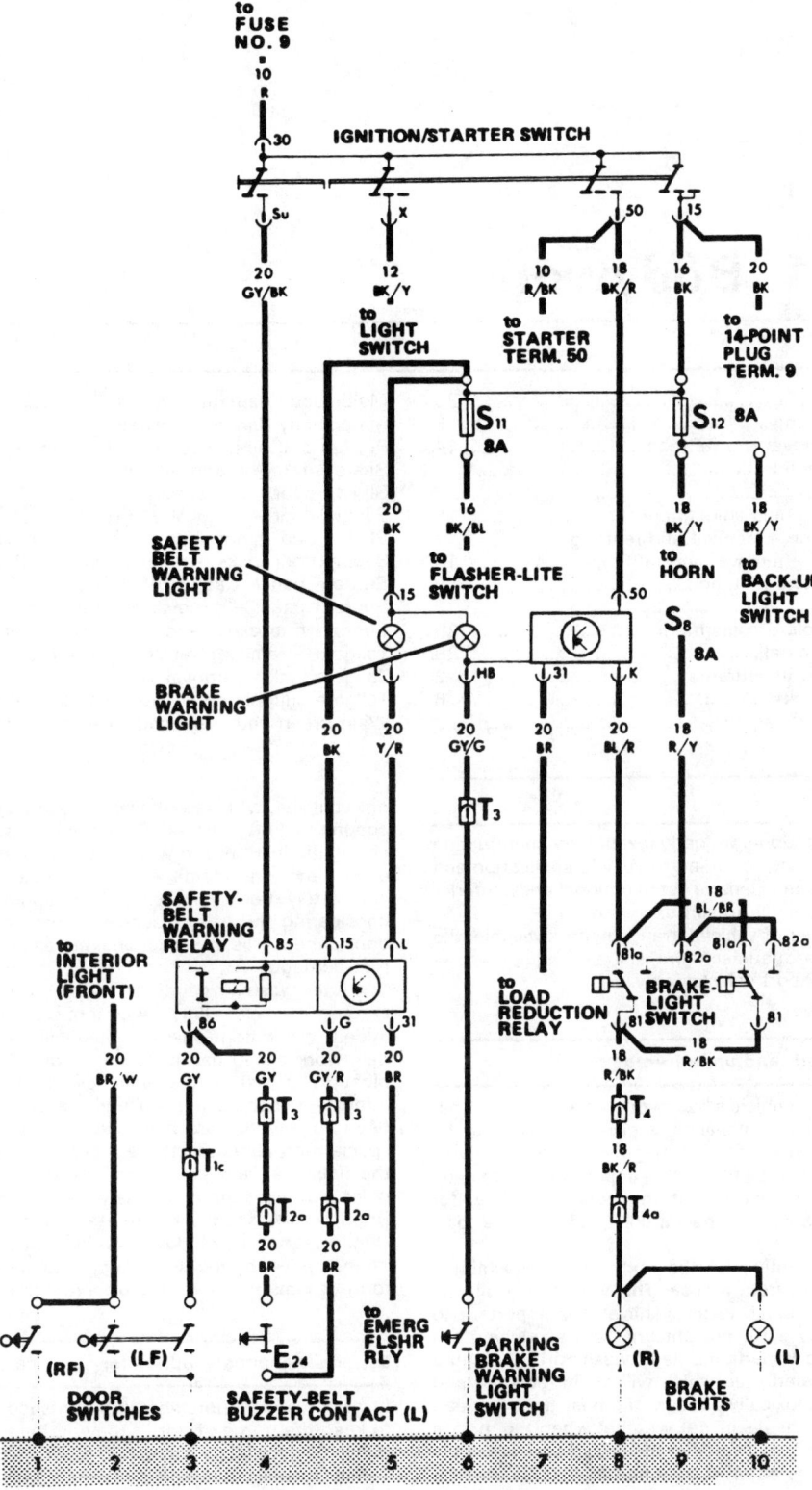

Fig. 10.58 Supplementary wiring diagram for Vanagon and derivatives — seat belt interlock system — USA vehicles

Wire connectors		Current Track	Wire connectors		Current Track
T1a	single, behind dash	3	T4	4-point, behind dash	8
T2a	double, under driver's seat	4	T4a	4-point, in engine compartment	8
T3	3-point, behind dash	4,6			

Chapter 11 Bodywork

Contents

1 General description

The bodyshell is of conventional welded steel unitary construction available in a number of versions according to vehicle application and territory of export. In addition an extensive list of optional body, interior and exterior equipment is available to suit each version.

Owing to the large number of vehicle arrangements available, the contents of this Chapter cover manufacturers' standard equipment as applicable to UK and USA export vehicles only.

2 Maintenance – bodywork and underframe

The general condition of a vehicle's bodywork is the one thing that significantly affects its value. Maintenance is easy but needs to be regular. Neglect, particularly after minor damage, can lead quickly to further deterioration and costly repair bills. It is important also to keep watch on those parts of the vehicle not immediately visible, for instance the underside, inside all the wheel arches and the lower part of the engine compartment.

The basic maintenance routine for the bodywork is washing – preferably with a lot of water, from a hose. This will remove all the loose solids which may have stuck to the vehicle. It is important to flush these off in such a way as to prevent grit from scratching the finish. The wheel arches and underframe need washing in the same way to remove any accumulated mud which will retain moisture and tend to encourage rust. Paradoxically enough, the best time to clean the underframe and wheel arches is in wet weather when the mud is thoroughly wet and soft. In very wet weather the underframe is usually cleaned of large accumulations automatically and this is a good time for inspection.

Periodically, except on vehicles with a wax-based underbody protective coat, it is a good idea to have the whole of the underframe of the vehicle steam cleaned, engine compartment included, so that a thorough inspection can be carried out to see what minor repairs and renovations are necessary. Steam cleaning is available at many garages and is necessary for removal of the accumulation of oily grime which sometimes is allowed to become thick in certain areas. If steam cleaning facilities are not available, there are one or two excellent grease solvents available which can be brush applied. The dirt can then be simply hosed off. Note that these methods should not be used on vehicles with wax-based underbody protective coating or the coating will be removed. Such vehicles should be inspected annually, preferably just prior to winter, when the underbody should be washed down and any damage to the wax coating repaired. Ideally, a completely fresh coat should be applied. It would also be worth considering the use of such wax-based protection for injection into door panels, sills, box sections, etc as an additional safeguard against rust damage.

After washing paintwork, wipe off with a chamois leather to give an unspotted clear finish. A coat of clear protective wax polish will give added protection against chemical pollutants in the air. If the paintwork sheen has dulled or oxidised, use a cleaner/polisher combination to restore the brilliance of the shine. This requires a little effort, but such dulling is usually caused because regular washing has been neglected. Care needs to be taken with metallic paintwork, as special non-abrasive cleaner/polisher is required to avoid damage to the finish. Always check that the door and ventilator opening drain holes and pipes are completely clear so that water can be drained out. Bright work should be treated in the same way as paintwork. Windscreens and windows can be kept clear of the smeary film which often appears by the use of a proprietary glass cleaner. Never use any form of wax or other body or chromium polish on glass.

3 Maintenance – upholstery and carpets

Mats and carpets should be brushed or vacuum cleaned regularly to keep them free of grit. If they are badly stained remove them from the vehicle for scrubbing or sponging and make quite sure they are dry before refitting. Seats and interior trim panels can be kept clean by wiping with a damp cloth. If they do become stained (which can be more apparent on light coloured upholstery) use a little liquid detergent and a soft nail brush to scour the grime out of the grain of the material. Do not forget to keep the headlining clean in the same way as the upholstery. When using liquid cleaners inside the vehicle do not over-wet the surfaces being cleaned. Excessive damp could get into the seams and padded interior causing stains, offensive odours or even rot. If the inside of the vehicle gets wet accidentally it is worthwhile taking some trouble to dry it out properly, particularly where carpets are involved. *Do not leave oil or electric heaters inside the vehicle for this purpose.*

4 Minor body damage – repair

The photographic sequences on pages 262 and 263 illustrate the operations detailed in the following sub-sections.

Repair of minor scratches in bodywork

If the scratch is very superficial, and does not penetrate to the metal of the bodywork, repair is very simple. Lightly rub the area of the scratch with a paintwork renovator, or a very fine cutting paste, to remove loose paint from the scratch and to clear the surrounding bodywork of wax polish. Rinse the area with clean water.

Apply touch-up paint to the scratch using a fine paint brush; continue to apply fine layers of paint until the surface of the paint in the scratch is level with the surrounding paintwork. Allow the new paint at least two weeks to harden: then blend it into the surrounding paintwork by rubbing the scratch area with a paintwork renovator or a very fine cutting paste. Finally, apply wax polish.

Where the scratch has penetrated right through to the metal of the bodywork, causing the metal to rust, a different repair technique is required. Remove any loose rust from the bottom of the scratch with a penknife, then apply rust inhibiting paint to prevent the formation of rust in the future. Using a rubber or nylon applicator fill the scratch with bodystopper paste. If required, this paste can be mixed with cellulose thinners to provide a very thin paste which is ideal for filling narrow scratches. Before the stopper-paste in the scratch hardens, wrap a piece of smooth cotton rag around the top of a finger. Dip the finger in cellulose thinners and then quickly sweep it across the surface of the stopper-paste in the scratch; this will ensure that the surface of the stopper-paste is slightly hollowed. The scratch can now be painted over as described earlier in this Section.

Repair of dents in bodywork

When deep denting of the vehicle's bodywork has taken place, the first task is to pull the dent out, until the affected bodywork almost attains its original shape. There is little point in trying to restore the original shape completely, as the metal in the damaged area will have stretched on impact and cannot be reshaped fully to its original contour. It is better to bring the level of the dent up to a point which is about $\frac{1}{8}$ in (3 mm) below the level of the surrounding bodywork. In cases where the dent is very shallow anyway, it is not worth trying to pull it out at all. If the underside of the dent is accessible, it can be hammered out gently from behind, using a mallet with a wooden or plastic head. Whilst doing this, hold a suitable block of wood firmly against the outside of the panel to absorb the impact from the hammer blows and thus prevent a large area of the bodywork from being 'belled-out'.

Should the dent be in a section of the bodywork which has a double skin or some other factor making it inaccessible from behind, a different technique is called for. Drill several small holes through the metal inside the area – particularly in the deeper section. Then screw long self-tapping screws into the holes just sufficiently for them to gain a good purchase in the metal. Now the dent can be pulled out by pulling on the protruding heads of the screws with a pair of pliers.

The next stage of the repair is the removal of the paint from the damaged area, and from an inch or so of the surrounding 'sound' bodywork. This is accomplished most easily by using a wire brush or abrasive pad on a power drill, although it can be done just as effectively by hand using sheets of abrasive paper. To complete the preparation for filling, score the surface of the bare metal with a screwdriver or the tang of a file, or alternatively, drill small holes in the affected area. This will provide a really good 'key' for the filler paste.

To complete the repair see the Section on filling and re-spraying.

Repair of rust holes or gashes in bodywork

Remove all paint from the affected area and from an inch or so of the surrounding 'sound' bodywork, using an abrasive pad or a wire brush on a power drill. If these are not available a few sheets of abrasive paper will do the job just as effectively. With the paint removed you will be able to gauge the severity of the corrosion and therefore decide whether to renew the whole panel (if this is possible) or to repair the affected area. New body panels are not as expensive as most people think and it is often quicker and more satisfactory to fit a new panel than to attempt to repair large areas of corrosion.

Remove all fittings from the affected area except those which will act as a guide to the original shape of the damaged bodywork (eg headlamp shells etc). Then, using tin snips or a hacksaw blade, remove all loose metal and any other metal badly affected by corrosion. Hammer the edges of the hole inwards in order to create a slight depression for the filler paste.

Wire brush the affected area to remove the powdery rust from the surface of the remaining metal. Paint the affected area with rust inhibiting paint; if the back of the rusted area is accessible treat this also.

Before filling can take place it will be necessary to block the hole in some way. This can be achieved by the use of aluminium or plastic mesh, or aluminium tape.

Aluminium or plastic mesh is probably the best material to use for a large hole. Cut a piece to the approximate size and shape of the hole to be filled, then position it in the hole so that its edges are below the level of the surrounding bodywork. It can be retained in position by several blobs of filler paste around its periphery.

Aluminium tape should be used for small or very narrow holes. Pull a piece off the roll and trim it to the approximate size and shape required, then pull off the backing paper (if used) and stick the tape over the hole; it can be overlapped if the thickness of one piece is insufficient. Burnish down the edges of the tape with the handle of a screwdriver or similar, to ensure that the tape is securely attached to the metal underneath.

Bodywork repairs – filling and re-spraying

Before using this Section, see the Sections on dent, deep scratch, rust holes and gash repairs.

Many types of bodyfiller are available, but generally speaking those proprietary kits which contain a tin of filler paste and a tube of resin hardener are best for this type of repair. A wide, flexible plastic or nylon applicator will be found invaluable for imparting a smooth and well contoured finish to the surface of the filler.

Mix up a little filler on a clean piece of card or board – measure the hardener carefully (follow the maker's instructions on the pack) otherwise the filler will set too rapidly or too slowly.

Using the applicator apply the filler paste to the prepared area; draw the applicator across the surface of the filler to achieve the correct contour and to level the filler surface. As soon as a contour that approximates to the correct one is achieved, stop working the paste – if you carry on too long the paste will become sticky and begin to 'pick up' on the applicator. Continue to add thin layers of filler paste at twenty-minute intervals until the level of the filler is just proud of the surrounding bodywork.

Once the filler has hardened, excess can be removed using a metal plane or file. From then on, progressively finer grades of abrasive paper should be used, starting with a 40 grade production paper and finishing with 400 grade wet-and-dry paper. Always wrap the abrasive paper around a flat rubber, cork, or wooden block – otherwise the surface of the filler will not be completely flat. During the smoothing of the filler surface the wet-and-dry paper should be periodically rinsed in water. This will ensure that a very smooth finish is imparted to the filler at the final stage.

At this stage the 'dent' should be surrounded by a ring of bare metal, which in turn should be encircled by the finely 'feathered' edge of the good paintwork. Rinse the repair area with clean water, until all of the dust produced by the rubbing-down operation has gone.

Spray the whole repair area with a light coat of primer – this will show up any imperfections in the surface of the filler. Repair these imperfections with fresh filler paste or bodystopper, and once more smooth the surface with abrasive paper. If bodystopper is used, it can be mixed with cellulose thinners to form a really thin paste which is ideal for filling small holes. Repeat this spray and repair procedure until you are satisfied that the surface of the filler, and the feathered edge of the paintwork are perfect. Clean the repair area with clean water and allow to dry fully.

The repair area is now ready for final spraying. Paint spraying must be carried out in a warm, dry, windless and dust free atmosphere. This condition can be created artificially if you have access to a large indoor working area, but if you are forced to work in the open, you will have to pick your day very carefully. If you are working indoors, dousing the floor in the work area with water will help to settle the dust which would otherwise be in the atmosphere. If the repair area is confined to one body panel, mask off the surrounding panels; this will help to minimise the effects of a slight mis-match in paint colours. Bodywork fittings (eg chrome strips, door handles etc) will also need to be masked off. Use genuine masking tape and several thicknesses of newspaper for the masking operations.

Before commencing to spray, agitate the aerosol can thoroughly, then spray a test area (an old tin, or similar) until the technique is mastered. Cover the repair area with a thick coat of primer; the thickness should be built up using several thin layers of paint rather than one thick one. Using 400 grade wet-and-dry paper, rub down the surface of the primer until it is really smooth. While doing this, the work area should be thoroughly doused with water, and the wet-and-dry paper periodically rinsed in water. Allow to dry before spraying on more paint.

Spray on the top coat, again building up the thickness by using several thin layers of paint. Start spraying in the centre of the repair area and then, using a circular motion, work outwards until the whole repair area and about 2 inches of the surrounding original paintwork is covered. Remove all masking material 10 to 15 minutes after spraying on the final coat of paint.

Allow the new paint at least two weeks to harden, then, using a paintwork renovator or a very fine cutting paste, blend the edges of the paint into the existing paintwork. Finally, apply wax polish.

5   Major body damage – repair

Where serious damage has occurred or large areas need renewal owing to neglect, it means certainly that completely new sections or panels will need welding in and this is best left to professionals. If the damage is due to impact it will also be necessary to completely check the alignment of the bodyshell structure. Due to the principle of construction the strength and shape of the whole can be affected by damage to a part. In such instances the services of a VW agent with specialist checking jigs are essential. If a frame is left misaligned it is first of all dangerous as the vehicle will not handle properly and secondly uneven stresses will be imposed on the steering, engine and transmission causing abnormal wear or complete failure. Tyre wear may be excessive.

6   Maintenance – hinges and locks

1   At regular intervals oil the hinges of the doors, tailgate and all other hinged panels as applicable with a drop or two of light oil.
2   At the same time lightly lubricate all the lock assemblies and striker plates. Do not however lubricate the steering lock.

7   Door rattles – tracing and rectification

1   Check first that the door is not loose at the hinges, and that the latch is holding the door firmly in position. Check also that the door lines up with the aperture in the body. If the door is out of alignment, adjust it, as described in the relevant Sections of this Chapter.
2   If the latch is holding the door in the correct position, but the latch still rattles, the lock mechanism is worn and should be renewed.
3   Other rattles from the door could be caused by wear in the window operating mechanism, interior lock mechanism, or loose glass channels.

8   Bumpers – removal and refitting

1   The removal and refitting procedures for both front and rear bumpers is identical and is as follows.
2   Prise out the small caps on the side of the bumper wrap around extensions (photo).
3   Undo the retaining screw securing the extensions to the body (photo).
4   Disengage the retaining catches and remove the extensions from the main bumper (photo).
5   Release the caps over the bumper retaining bolts, undo the bolts and lift off the bumper (photos).
6   Refitting is the reverse sequence to removal.

8.2 Remove the caps on the bumper extensions ...

8.3 ... to gain access to the retaining screw

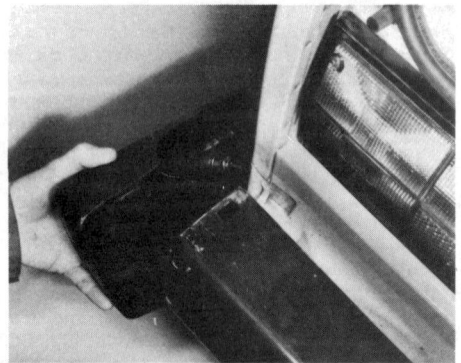

8.4 Disengage the catches and remove the extensions

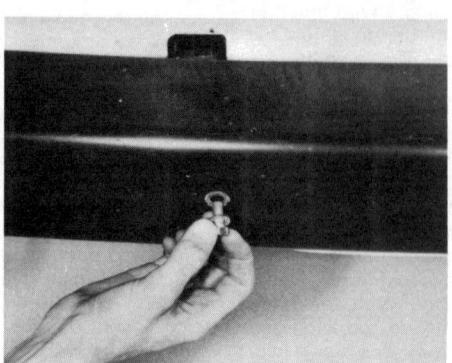

8.5A Release the caps over the bumper retaining bolts ...

8.5B ... and remove the bolts

9.1 Front grille panel quick release retainer locations (arrowed)

9 Front grille panel – removal and refitting

1 Turn the five quick release retainers along the top edge of the grille through 90° to release (photo).
2 Tip the grille out of the top then lift it up to disengage the lower locating tags.
3 Refitting is the reverse sequence to removal.

10 Tailgate – removal, refitting and adjustment

1 Disconnect the battery negative terminal.
2 Open the tailgate and disconnect the wiring to the heated rear window. Unscrew the earth lead and pull the wiring out of the tailgate.
3 Support the tailgate in the open position with the help of an assistant or with a stout length of wood.

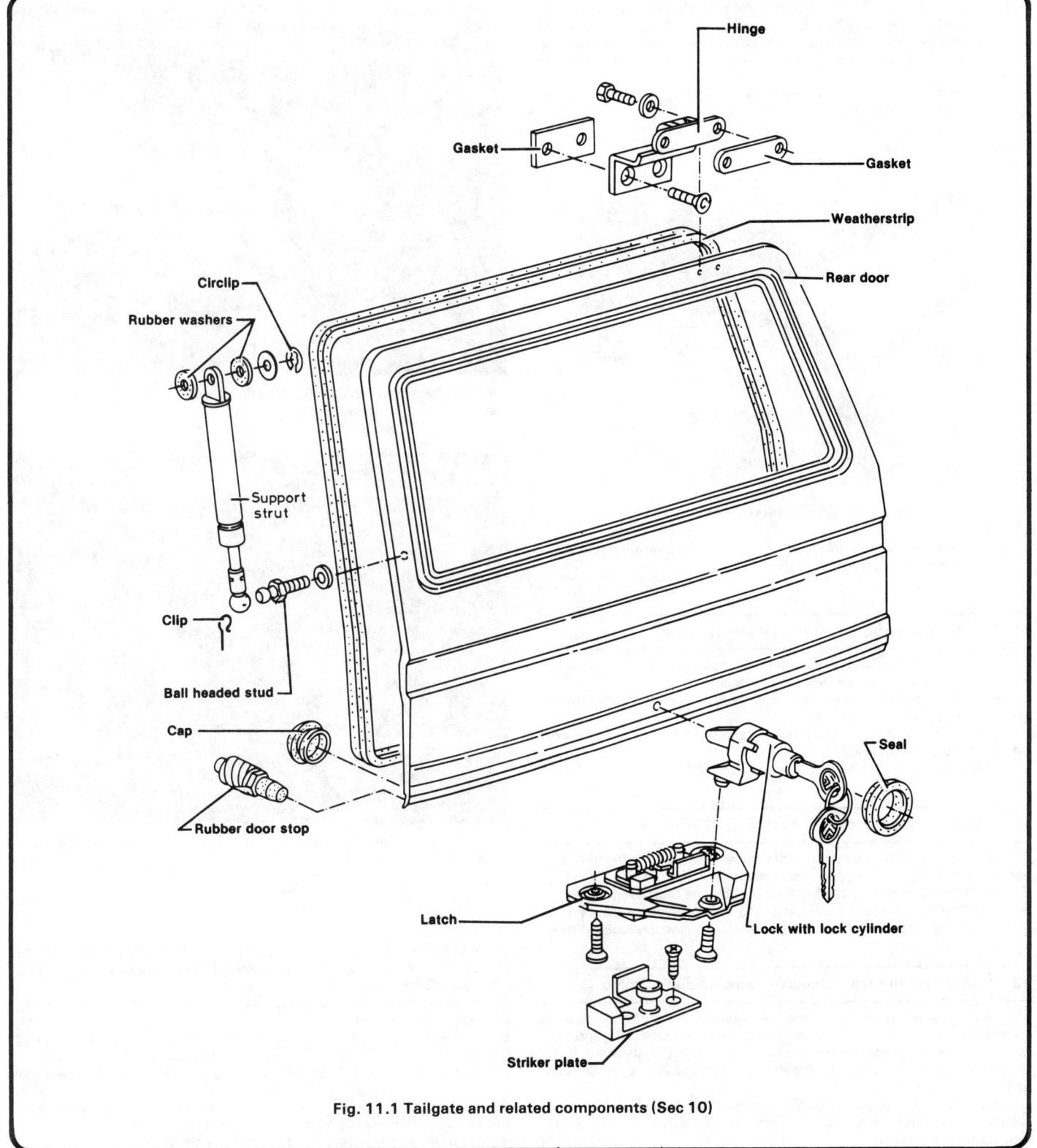

Fig. 11.1 Tailgate and related components (Sec 10)

4   Extract the circlips and washers then slip the tailgate support struts off their mounting pegs on the body.
5   Mark the outline of the hinge positions on the body with a soft pencil. Have an assistant support the tailgate then undo the four hinge retaining bolts using a suitable Allen key.
6   Carefully lift the tailgate away.
7   Refitting the tailgate is the reverse sequence to removal ensuring that the hinges are aligned with the previously made alignment marks.
8   If it is necessary, reposition the tailgate within the body aperture, this is done by moving the tailgate sideways or up and down accordingly, with the hinge retaining bolts slack. For the tailgate to open properly there must be a gap of 11 to 13 mm (0.43 to 0.51 in) between the tailgate top edge and the body. The rubber buffers should be screwed in or out as required so that the tailgate is flush with the body.
9   Adjust the position of the striker plate so that the tailgate shuts and locks without slamming.

Fig. 11.2 Tailgate removal (Sec 10)

A   Support strut mounting peg   C   Hinge retaining bolts
B   Wiring connection

11 Tailgate support strut – removal and refitting

1   Open the tailgate and support it in the open position using a stout length of wood or with the help of an assistant.
2   Extract the retaining wire clip and carefully prise the ball end of the strut piston off the tailgate peg.
3   Extract the circlip and washers then slip the other end of the strut off the body peg. Lift away the strut.
4   Refitting is the reverse sequence to removal.

12 Tailgate lock – removal and refitting

1   With the tailgate open, undo the three screws securing the lock assembly and lock cylinder to the tailgate.
2   Withdraw the lock assembly followed by the lock cylinder.
3   Refitting is the reverse sequence to removal, but apply a little thread locking compound to the screw which retains the lock cylinder.

13 Windscreen and rear window – removal and refitting

1   Removal and refitting of the windscreen and rear window is considered to be beyond the scope of the average owner. A good deal of skill and some special tools are required to install the glass and if the work is not carried out professionally, leaks or possibly even damage to the glass may occur.
2   If you are unfortunate enough to have a windscreen shatter, it is recommended that you entrust this job to a VW dealer or windscreen replacement specialist.

14 Door inner trim panels – removing and refitting

Front door

1   Lift back the trim capping, undo the retaining screw and carefully prise off the window crank handle (photo).
2   At the top and bottom of the door closing grip handle, prise out the trim caps and undo the retaining screws (photo). Lift off the handle.

14.1 Lift back the trim capping to gain access to the window crank handle retaining screw

14.2 The upper and lower door handle screws are located behind trim caps

3   Release the remote control door handle finger plate to gain access to the escutcheon retaining screw (photo). Undo the screw and lift off the escutcheon.
4   If an armrest is fitted, undo the two screws and withdraw the armrest from the door.
5   Starting at the upper rear corner, release the trim panel retaining buttons by carefully levering between the panel and door with a screwdriver or flat bar. With all the buttons released, lift off the panel (photo).
6   To gain access to the door internal components, carefully pull back the plastic condensation barrier, as necessary (photo).
7   Refitting is the reverse sequence to removal.

14.3 Release the finger plate for access to the escutcheon retaining screw

Passenger and sliding door

8   The procedure for trim panel removal on the passenger doors and sliding door (as applicable) is essentially the same as the procedure for the front doors. On certain versions additional self-tapping screws are used to retain the panel, but minor differences such as this will be obvious after a visual inspection.

15 Front door – removal, refitting and adjustment

1   Carefully mark the outline of the door hinge retaining bolt washers on the body pillar as a guide to refitting.
2   Extract the circlip then withdraw the door check strap retaining pin.
3   Support the door on blocks and have an assistant steady it, then undo the four hinge retaining bolts (photo). Carefully lift away the door.
4   Refitting is the reverse sequence to removal. Adjust the position of the door as necessary so that there is a uniform gap all round before tightening the hinge retaining bolts. Adjust the striker plate so that the door closes fully without slamming (photo). Up and down and side to side movement is possible at both hinges and at the striker plate to cater for adjustment.

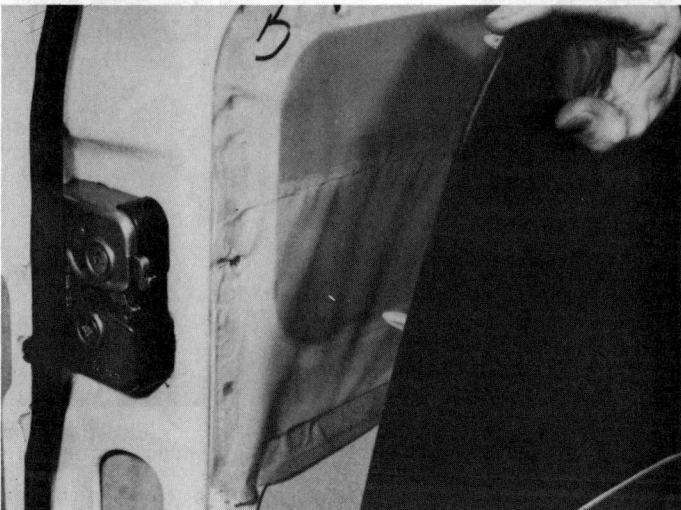

14.5 Inner trim panel removal

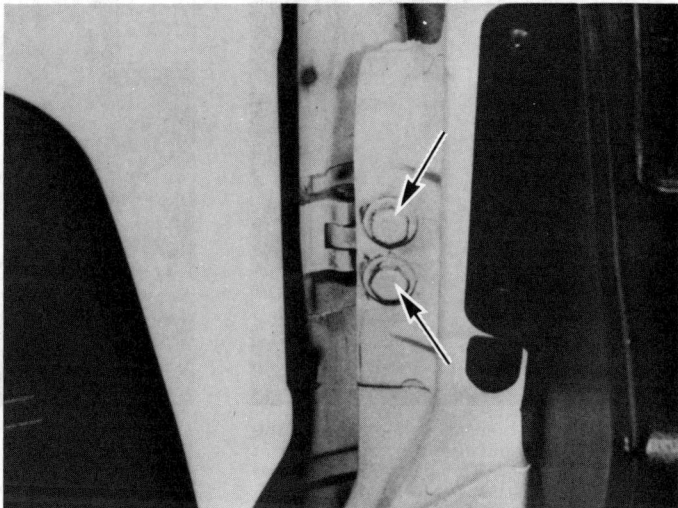

15.3 Front door hinge retaining bolts (arrowed)

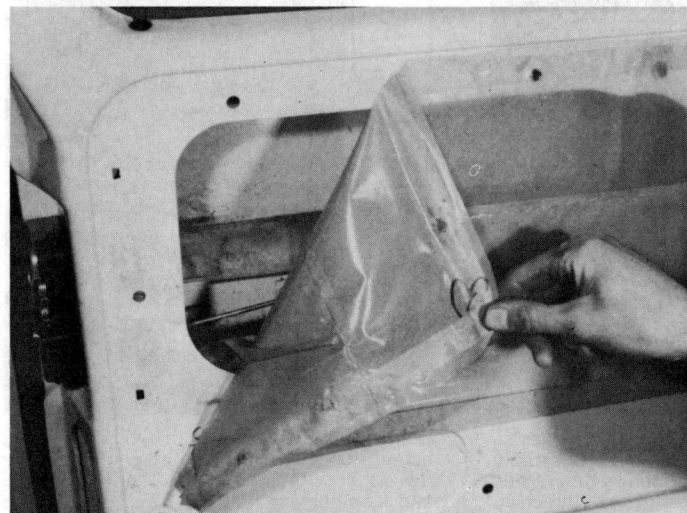

14.6 Pull back the condensation barrier to reach the door components

15.4 An Allen key is needed for the striker retaining bolts

1 This photographic sequence shows the steps taken to repair the dent and paintwork damage shown above. In general, the procedure for repairing a hole will be similar; where there are substantial differences, the procedure is clearly described and shown in a separate photograph.

2 First remove any trim around the dent, then hammer out the dent where access is possible. This will minimise filling. Here, after the large dent has been hammered out, the damaged area is being made slightly concave.

3 Next, remove all paint from the damaged area by rubbing with coarse abrasive paper or using a power drill fitted with a wire brush or abrasive pad. 'Feather' the edge of the boundary with good paintwork using a finer grade of abrasive paper.

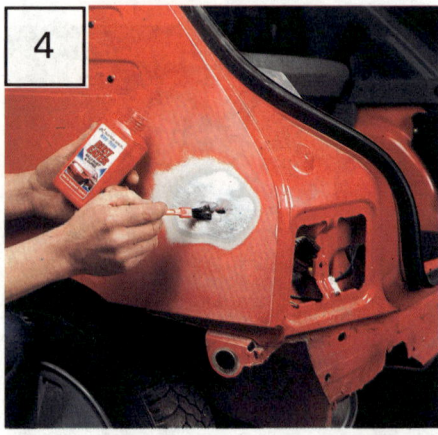

4 Where there are holes or other damage, the sheet metal should be cut away before proceeding further. The damaged area and any signs of rust should be treated with Turtle Wax Hi-Tech Rust Eater, which will also inhibit further rust formation.

5 *For a large dent or hole* mix Holts Body Plus Resin and Hardener according to the manufacturer's instructions and apply around the edge of the repair. Press Glass Fibre Matting over the repair area and leave for 20-30 minutes to harden. Then ...

5A ... brush more Holts Body Plus Resin and Hardener onto the matting and leave to harden. Repeat the sequence with two or three layers of matting, checking that the final layer is lower than the surrounding area. Apply Holts Body Plus Filler Paste as shown in Step 5B.

5B *For a medium dent*, mix Holts Body Plus Filler Paste and Hardener according to the manufacturer's instructions and apply it with a flexible applicator. Apply thin layers of filler at 20-minute intervals, until the filler surface is slightly proud of the surrounding bodywork.

5C *For small dents and scratches* use Holts No Mix Filler Paste straight from the tube. Apply it according to the instructions in thin layers, using the spatula provided. It will harden in minutes if applied outdoors and may then be used as its own knifing putty.

6 Use a plane or file for initial shaping. Then, using progressively finer grades of wet-and-dry paper, wrapped round a sanding block, and copious amounts of clean water, rub down the filler until glass smooth. 'Feather' the edges of adjoining paintwork.

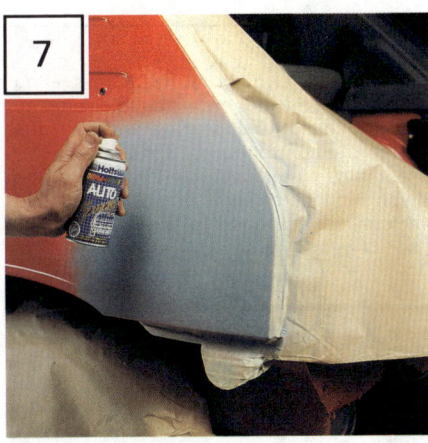

7 Protect adjoining areas before spraying the whole repair area and at least one inch of the surrounding sound paintwork with Holts Dupli-Color primer.

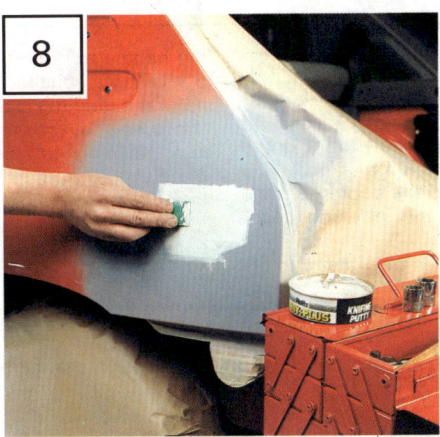

8 Fill any imperfections in the filler surface with a small amount of Holts Body Plus Knifing Putty. Using plenty of clean water, rub down the surface with a fine grade wet-and-dry paper – 400 grade is recommended – until it is really smooth.

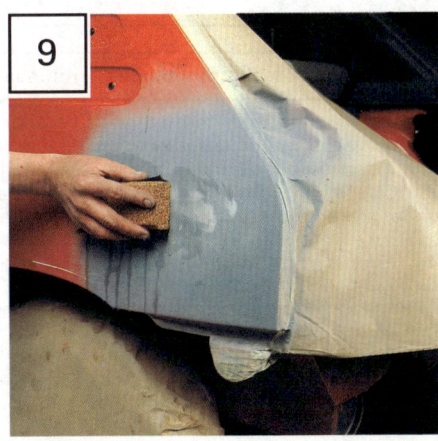

9 Carefully fill any remaining imperfections with knifing putty before applying the last coat of primer. Then rub down the surface with Holts Body Plus Rubbing Compound to ensure a really smooth surface.

10 Protect surrounding areas from overspray before applying the topcoat in several thin layers. Agitate Holts Dupli-Color aerosol thoroughly. Start at the repair centre, spraying outwards with a side-to-side motion.

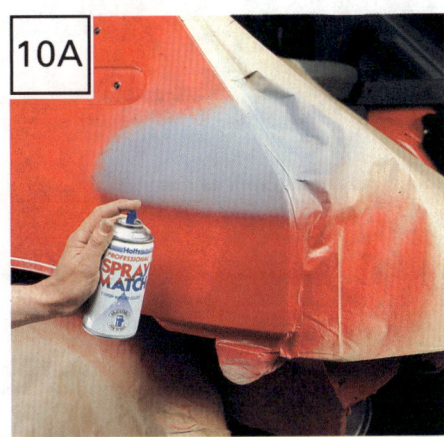

10A If the exact colour is not available off the shelf, local Holts Professional Spraymatch Centres will custom fill an aerosol to match perfectly.

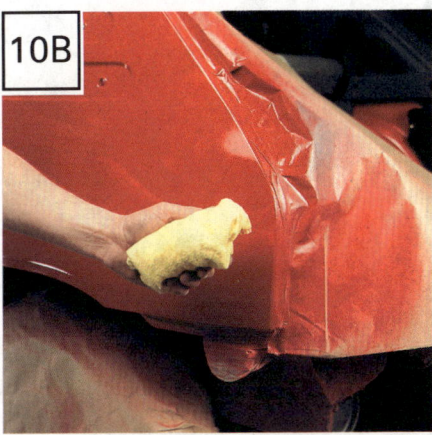

10B To identify whether a lacquer finish is required, rub a painted unrepaired part of the body with wax and a clean cloth.

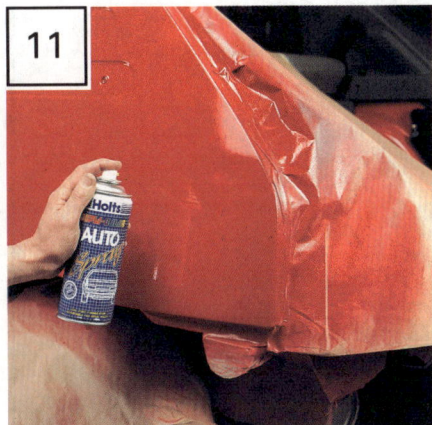

11 If *no* traces of paint appear on the cloth, spray Holts Dupli-Color clear lacquer over the repaired area to achieve the correct gloss level.

12 The paint will take about two weeks to harden fully. After this time it can be 'cut' with a mild cutting compound such as Turtle Wax Minute Cut prior to polishing with a final coating of Turtle Wax Extra.

14 When carrying out bodywork repairs, remember that the quality of the finished job is proportional to the time and effort expended.

16 Front door lock components – removal and refitting

1   Remove the inner trim panel as described in Section 14.
2   Undo the two bolts securing the remote control handle to the door and disconnect the handle from the lock pull rod (photo).
3   Carefully pull the door rubber seal away around the door lock and undo the screw securing the exterior handle to the lock and door (photo).
4   Pivot the handle outwards then release the lug at the other end of the handle from its location (photo).
5   Using a suitable Allen key undo the two socket-headed retaining bolts securing the lock to the door. Pull the lock outwards to disengage the locking lever from the sleeve on the locking rod. Now withdraw the lock assembly complete with remote control pullrod (photo).
6   Refitting is the reverse sequence to removal, but ensure that the locking rod sleeve engages with the locking lever as the lock is fitted (photo). Apply a little thread locking compound to the lock, exterior handle and remote control handle retaining screws before fitting.

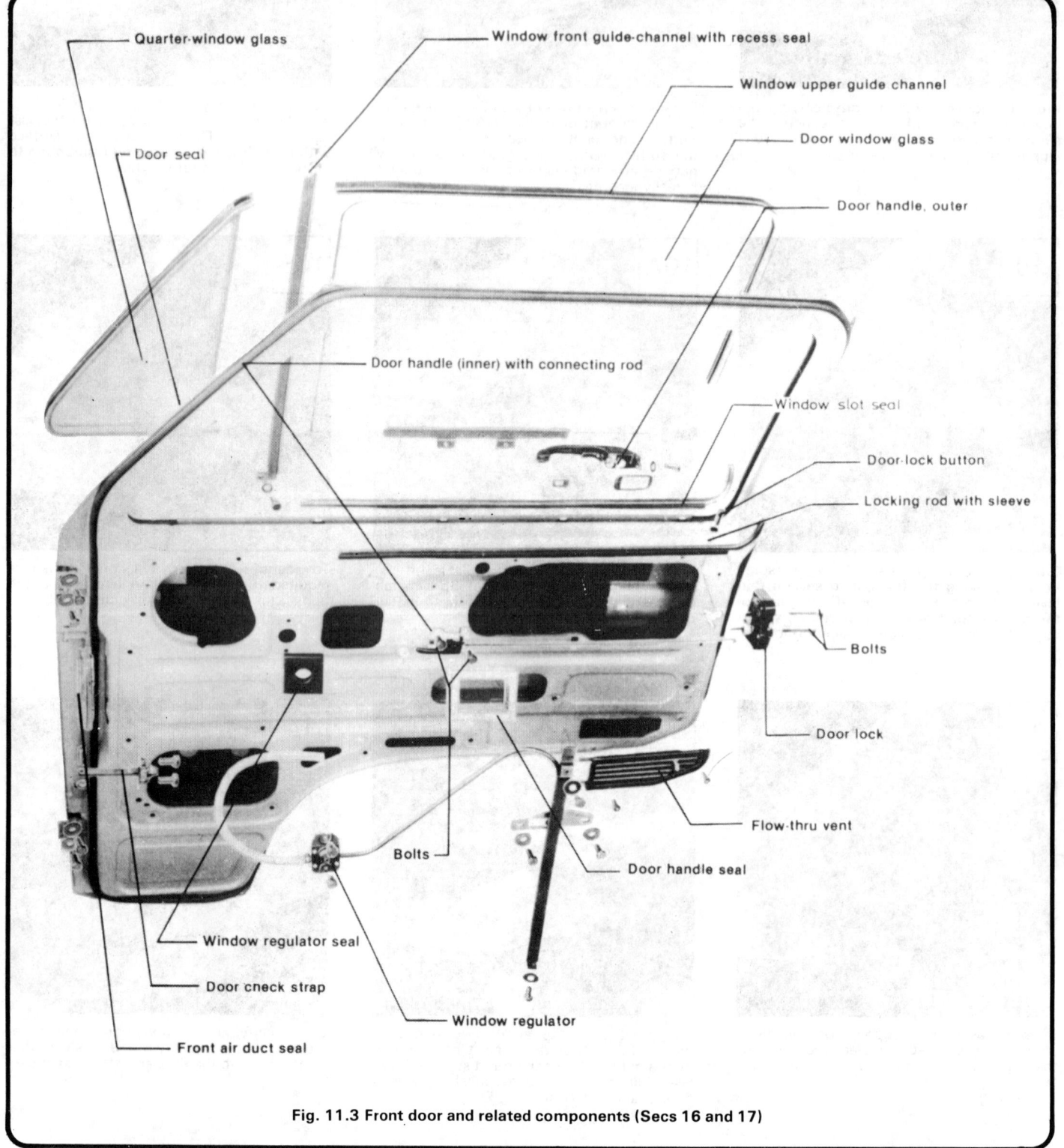

Fig. 11.3 Front door and related components (Secs 16 and 17)

16.2 Remote control handle retaining bolts (arrowed)

16.3 Outer handle retaining screw (arrowed)

16.4 Removing the outer handle from the door

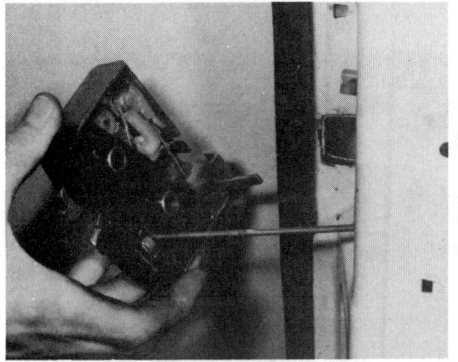

16.5 Removing the door lock

16.6 The door lock locking finger (A) must engage with the locking sleeve (B) as the lock is fitted

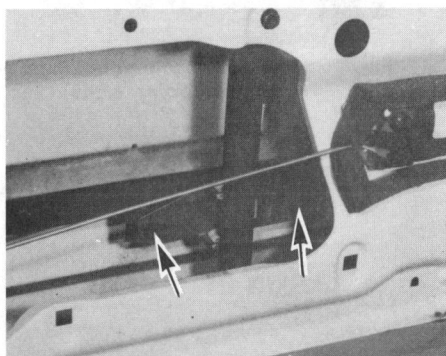

17.2 Regulator slide to window frame retaining bolts (arrowed)

17 Front door glass and regulator – removal and refitting

1   Remove the inner trim panel as described in Section 14.
2   Lower the window glass and undo the two bolts securing the regulator slide to the window frame (photo).
3   Push the window upwards and wedge it in the raised position.
4   Undo the two bolts securing the regulator slide to the door frame.
5   Lift off the foam rubber seal around the regulator crank spindle and undo the two bolts securing the regulator crank to the door.
6   Carefully bend back the metal tag supporting the regulator rack loop then manipulate the regulator assembly out of the door aperture.

Fig. 11.5 Window regulator slide lower retaining bolt (arrowed) (Sec 17)

7   Lift up the rubber seal directly above the front guide channel and undo the guide upper retaining screw.
8   Undo the front guide channel lower retaining bolt, pull the guide down and remove it from the door aperture.
9   Lower the window glass carefully to the bottom of the door.
10   Release the inner and outer window slot seals by carefully prising them free.
11   Move the corner window rearward and remove it from the door.
12   The window glass can now be carefully lifted upwards and out of the door.

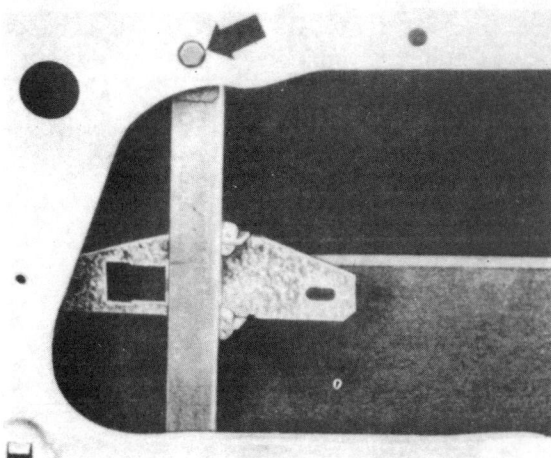

Fig. 11.4 Window regulator slide upper retaining bolt (arrowed) (Sec 17)

Fig. 11.6 Window regulator retaining bolts (arrowed) and supporting tag (5) (Sec 17)

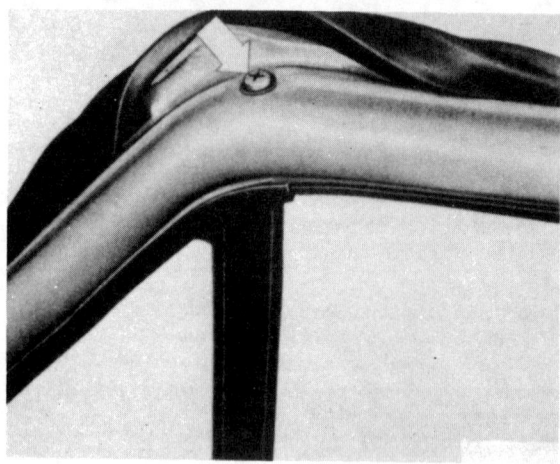

Fig. 11.7 Front guide channel upper retaining bolt (arrowed) (Sec 17)

Fig. 11.8 Front guide channel lower retaining bolt (arrowed) (Sec 17)

13   Refitting is the reverse sequence to removal. Before tightening the window frame to regulator slide retaining bolts, raise the window fully to centralise it in the channels. The glass can then be lowered slightly and the bolts tightened through the access hole.

18 Sliding door – removal and refitting

1   Undo the retaining screw securing the centre guide rail cover in position at the rear. With the door open, remove the screw securing the guide rail cover at the front. The guide rail cover must now be carefully tapped upward using a hammer and plastic drift to release it from the upper U-shaped rail into which it is passed.

2   With the guide rail cover removed and with the help of an assistant, slide the door back until the hinge guide and link can be released from the opening in the centre guide rail (Fig. 11.11).

3   Pivot the door outwards at the rear, slide it back fully and lift the door to release the upper sliding block from its guide (Fig. 11.12).

4   Pivot the door outwards as necessary and slip the lower roller out of the guide rail opening (Fig. 11.13).

5   Refitting is the reverse sequence to removal. Open and close the door several times to check its operation after refitting and check the fit of the door in the closed position. Carry out the adjustments described in Section 19 if necessary.

Fig. 11.9 Sliding door centre guide rail cover rear retaining screw (arrowed) (Sec 18)

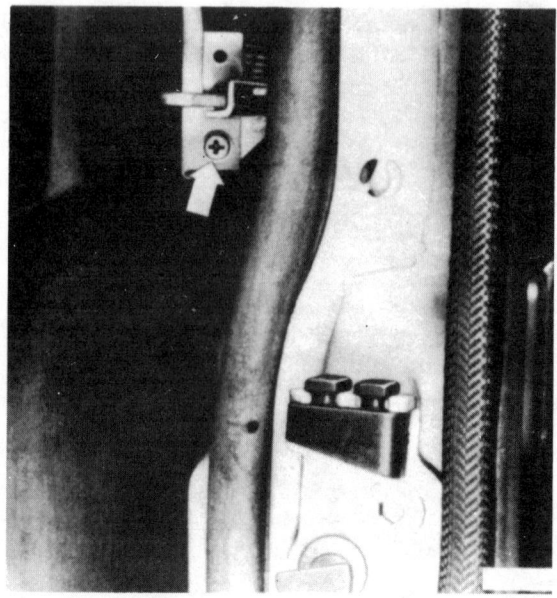

Fig. 11.10 Sliding door centre guide rail cover front retaining screw (arrowed) (Sec 18)

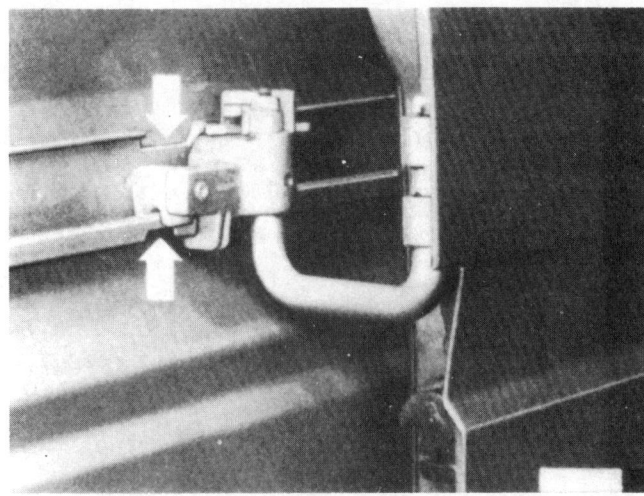

Fig. 11.11 Opening in centre guide rail (arrowed) for hinge guide and link removal (Sec 18)

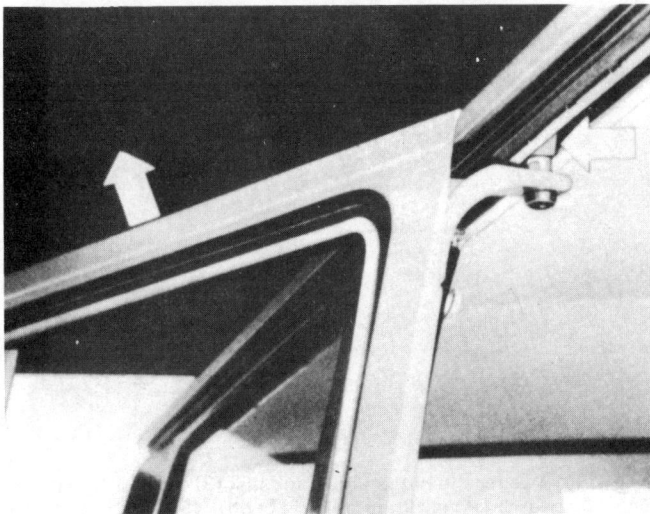

Fig. 11.12 Pivot the sliding door outwards and back to release the upper sliding block (Sec 18)

Fig. 11.13 Sliding door lower roller removal (Sec 18)

19 Sliding door – adjustment

1 The sliding door should be adjusted to give a uniform gap all round with the door closed, and a flush fit in relation to the adjacent body panels. The guides and rollers and the striker plate can be individually adjusted to achieve this after removing the centre guide rail cover as described in Section 18.

Lower roller guide

2 If the front end of the door is not in alignment slacken the bolts securing the roller arm to the door and move the door up or down as necessary. Tighten the bolts when the correct position is obtained.

3 Slacken the bolts securing the guide assembly to the roller arm and move the front of the door in or out as necessary. Tighten the bolts when the correct position is obtained.

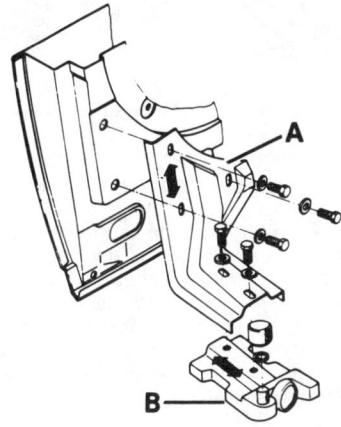

Fig. 11.14 Sliding door roller arm (A) and guide assembly (B) retaining bolt and adjustment details (Sec 19)

Upper guide block

4 If the top of the door is not aligned with the outer panel, prise off the protective cap, slacken the guide block retaining bolt and move the door in or out as required. When the correct position is achieved, tighten the bolt and refit the cap.

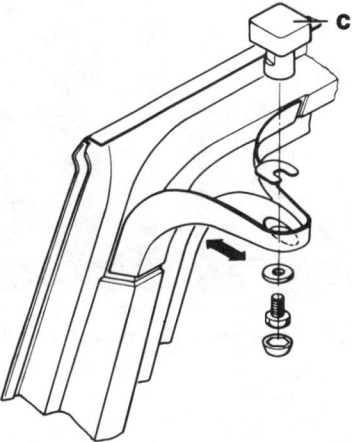

Fig. 11.15 Sliding door upper guide block (C) adjustment details (Sec 19)

Striker plate

5 To adjust the fit of the door, horizontal and vertical adjustment of the striker plate is provided. Slacken the socket headed retaining bolts using an Allen key and reposition the striker plate as necessary. Tighten the bolts fully after adjustment. If the position of the striker plate is moved appreciably the hinge link will also require adjustment.

Fig. 11.16 Sliding door striker plate adjustment details (Sec 19)

Fig. 11.18 Hinge link front (1) and rear (2) retaining bolts (Sec 19)

Remote control striker plate

6   Using a suitable Allen key slacken the two remote control striker plate retaining bolts.

7   Close the door from the inside to centralise the striker plate, hold the plate in this position and open the door again. Tighten the bolts without moving the striker plate position.

8   If, after adjustment, it is still not possible to easily lock the door from the outside using the key, and from the inside using the locking lever, then the striker plate should be moved out by placing packing pieces behind it. Up to two packing pieces may be used which are available from VW parts stockists.

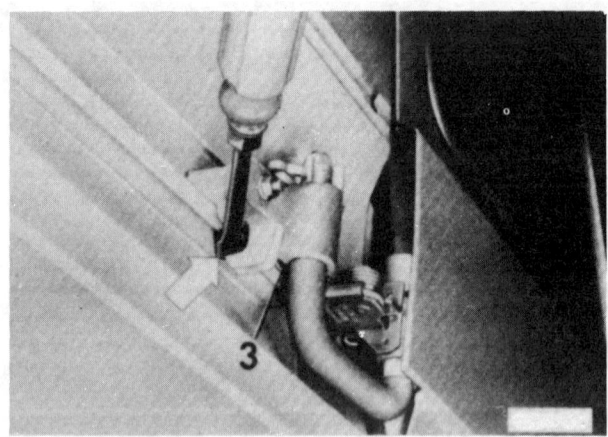

Fig. 11.19 Lever the hinge guide and link (3) down at the point arrowed until the roller is central (Sec 19)

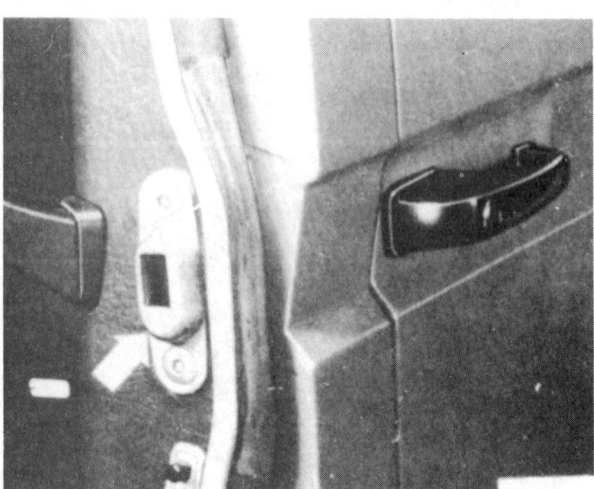

Fig. 11.17 Sliding door remote control striker plate (arrowed) (Sec 19)

Hinge link

9   Slacken the hinge link rear retaining bolts (Fig. 11.18) then close the door from the outside. Check the gap at the front and rear of the door and if necessary slacken the hinge link front retaining bolt and correct the door position. Tighten the front retaining bolt only at this stage.

10 With the door closed lever the hinge guide and link down using a screwdriver until the roller is located in the centre of the guide rail (Fig. 11.19).

11 Carefully open the sliding door while supporting it at the rear. Hold the door in this position and tighten the rear retaining bolts.

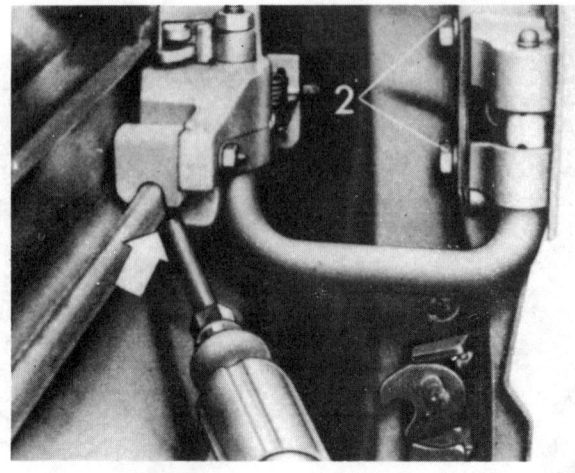

Fig. 11.20 With the sliding door open tighten the retaining bolts (2) whilst holding the roller central at the point arrowed (Sec 19)

20 Sliding door locks – removal and refitting

1   Remove the inner trim panel from the sliding door, referring to the procedure in Section 14 as a guide.

Remote control lock components

2   With the door open undo the retaining screw and pull the inner door handle off its spindle.

3   Undo the retaining screw and withdraw the outer handle with seal, escutcheon and spacer washer from the lock.

4   Extract the circlip securing the Bowden cable or pullrod to the peg on the lock lever and slip off the pullrod or cable end. Where a Bowden cable is used slacken the locknut securing the cable to the lock bracket and unscrew the cable as necessary so that it can be slipped out of the bracket.

5   Undo the three screws securing the door latch plate to the door and withdraw the latch plate.

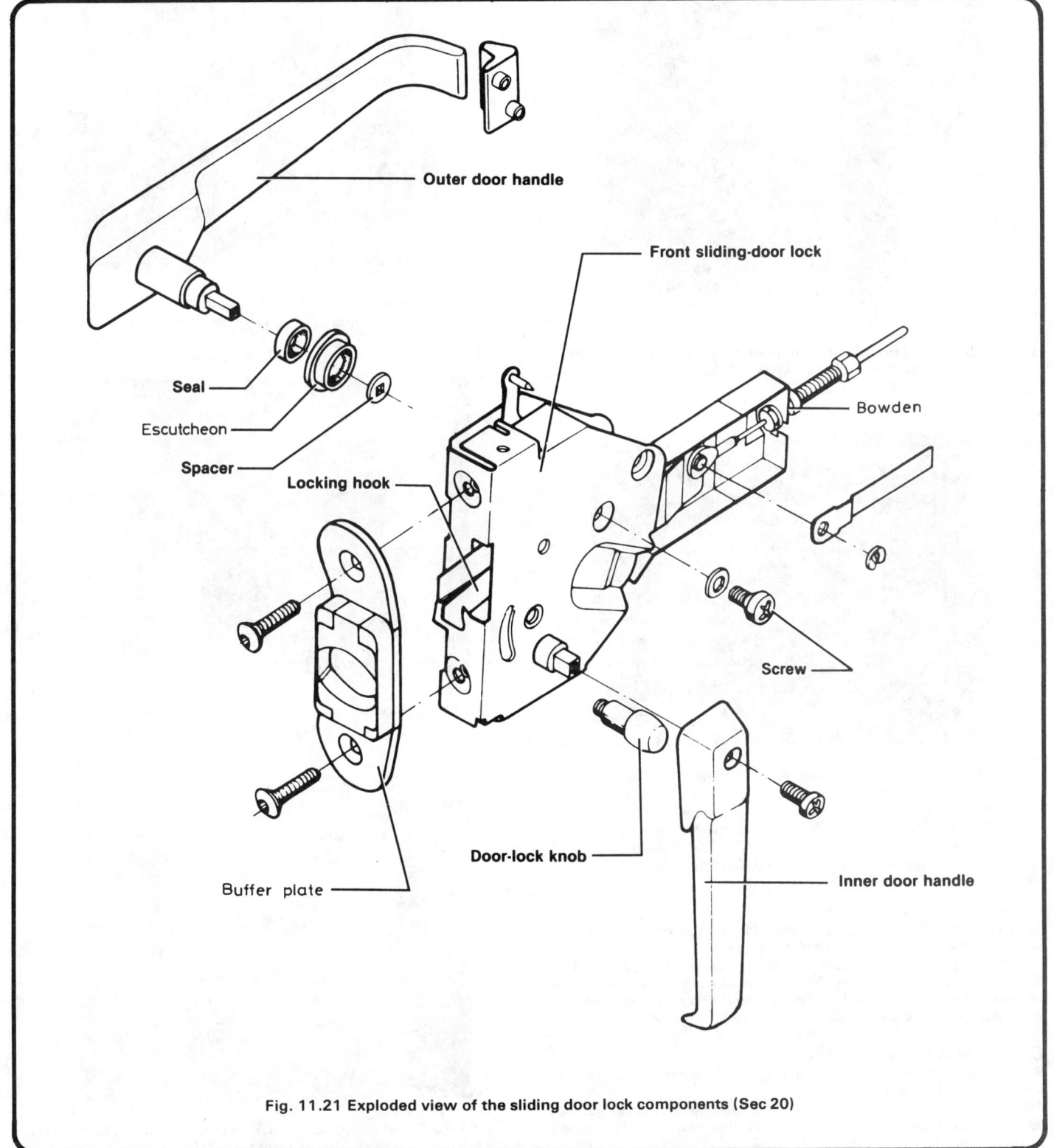

Fig. 11.21 Exploded view of the sliding door lock components (Sec 20)

Fig. 11.22 Sliding door inner handle retaining screw (1) and outer handle retaining screw (2) (Sec 20)

Fig. 11.23 Sliding door lock removal (Sec 20)

3	Circlip	7	Cable locknut
4	Lock lever peg	8	Bowden cable
5	Cable locknut	9	Door latch plate
6	Adjusting nut	10	Locking knob

6   Unscrew the locking knob.

7   Undo the three retaining screws, lift off the buffer plate then withdraw the lock assembly from inside the door.

8   Refitting the remote control lock is the reverse sequence to removal, but apply one or two drops of thread locking compound to all retaining screw threads. Adjust the operation of the lock as described in paragraph 13 before refitting the trim panel.

Central lock components

9   Pull the remote control lock inner handle to throw the central lock latch into the locked position.

10   Release the Bowden cable or pullrod from the remote control lock as described in paragraph 4 then remove the cable from its support cushions and door panel clip.

11   Undo the three screws securing the central lock to the door and remove the lock from inside the door. If necessary the Bowden cable or pullrod may be removed after extracting the retaining clip.

12   Refitting is the reverse sequence to removal, but adjust the operation of the lock as described in paragraph 13 before refitting the trim panel.

Fig. 11.24 Sliding door lock buffer plate (11), door lock (12) and retaining screws (arrowed) (Sec 20)

Fig. 11.25 Sliding door central lock (13) and retaining screws (arrowed) (Sec 20)

Fig. 11.26 Suitable M4 screw (16) in place in central lock drilling (17) prior to adjustment (Sec 20)

Fig. 11.27 Sliding door Bowden cable adjustment (Sec 20)

3	*Circlip*	7	*Cable locknut*
4	*Lock lever peg*	8	*Bowden cable*
5	*Cable locknut*	18	*Operating rod stop*
6	*Adjusting nut*		

General

13 To adjust the Bowden cable or pullrod first pull the remote control lock inner handle to throw the central lock latch into the locked position.

14 Using an M4 screw of suitable length push the screw into the drilling in the central lock and screw it into the operating lever (Fig. 11.26).

15 Slacken the Bowden cable or the threaded sleeve of the pullrod then adjust the cable or rod length so that the remote control lock operating rod just contacts its stop (Fig. 11.27). Tighten the cable or rod locknuts in this position, then remove the M4 locating screw.

16 Check the operation of the door and its fit in the body aperture and if necessary carry out the adjustments described in Section 19.

17 Refit the inner trim panel after completing the adjustments.

21 Sliding door hinge link – removal, overhaul and refitting

1   Remove the sliding door from the vehicle as described in Section 18.

2   Remove the inner trim panel, undo the three hinge link retaining bolts and withdraw the assembly from inside the door.

3   Carefully examine the hinge link assembly for wear, particularly around the roller, guide, locking lever and cam. Certain parts are available separately and if wear has taken place the assembly can be dismantled as follows for the new parts to be fitted.

4   Extract the small circlip and withdraw the housing and spring from the hinge link.

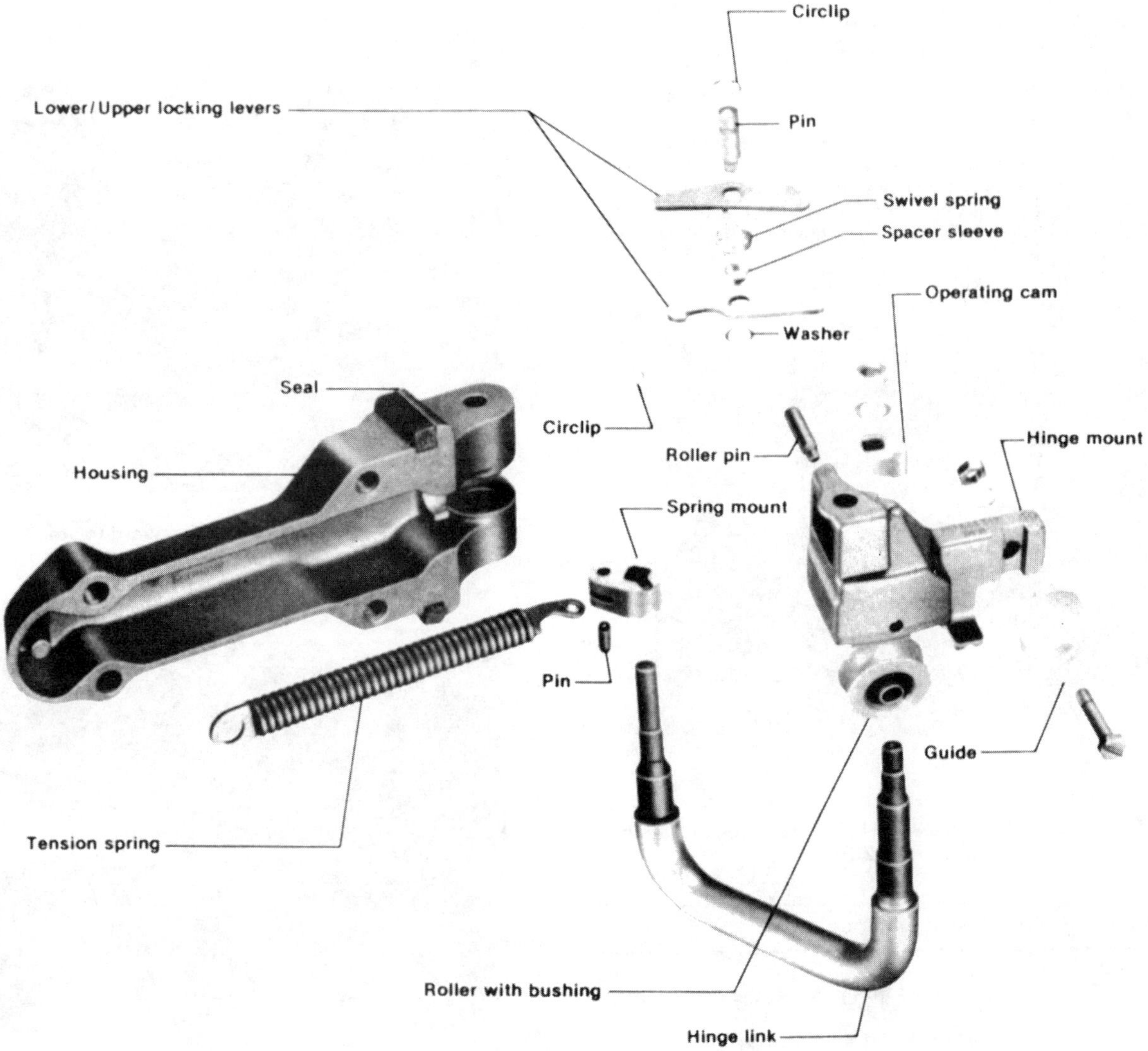

Fig. 11.28 Exploded view of the sliding door hinge link assembly (Sec 21)

5   Withdraw the spring attachment from the spring after tapping out the pin.
6   If the guide requires renewal, file or grind off the retaining rivet and remove the guide. Note that a new guide is supplied with a retaining nut, bolt and washer in place of the rivet.
7   Remove the roller from the mounting by pressing out the retaining pin.
8   Extract the locking lever pin circlip, press the pin out of the housing and recover the locking levers, springs, spacers and washers noting the fitted direction of all the parts.
9   Finally undo the nut and washer and withdraw the operating cam.
10 Renew any worn parts and then reassemble the unit using the reverse sequence to removal. Lubricate all moving parts and contact areas with a light smear of multi-purpose grease.
11 After assembly refit the hinge link to the door, tighten the single front retaining bolt in its lowest position and tighten the other two bolts finger tight only at this stage.
12 Refit the sliding door as described in Section 18, then carry out the adjustments described in Section 19.

22 Seats – removal and refitting

Front seats
1   Move the seat all the way forward on its runners.
2   Lift the small catch on the side of the seat, slide the seat off the runners and remove it through the door aperture. On vehicles equipped with a two seater front seat remove the bolts from the upper hinge on the backrest before removing the seat from the runners.
3   Refitting is the reverse sequence to removal.

Centre and rear seats
4   The centre seat is secured to the floor by four bolts. The seat can be lifted out after removal of the bolts.
5   To remove the rear seat cushion undo the bolts securing the seat to the side panels and remove it from its location.
6   The rear seat backrest is secured by two bolts on each side. Undo the bolts and lift out the backrest. Note that on some vehicles the lower bolt is also a seat belt anchorage. Note the sequence of removal of the seat belt components.
7   Refitting is the reverse sequence to removal.

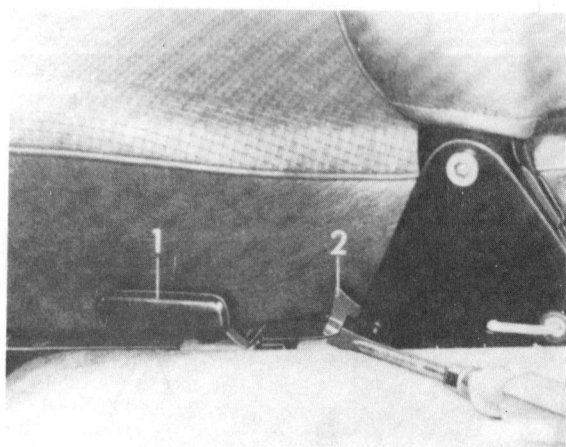

Fig. 11.29 Front seat adjusting lever (1) and seat runner retaining catch (2) (Sec 22)

23 Sunroof panel – removal and refitting

1   Open the sunroof slightly.
2   Release the five clips securing the trim panel at the front edge of the sunroof.
3   Push the trim panel to the rear as far as the stop.
4   Pull the sunroof panel forward but stop before the lifter is activated.

5   Pull the leaf spring to the centre then pull the crank out of its support.
6   Undo the two screws securing the panel to the front guide.
7   Lift the panel at the front then lift out the panel at the rear through openings in the guide rail.
8   Refitting is the reverse sequence to removal.

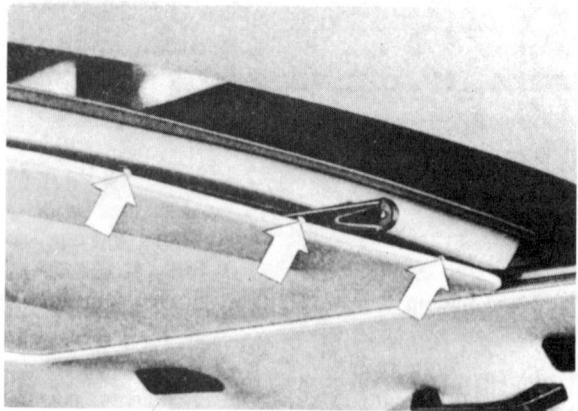

Fig. 11.30 Sunroof trim panel front edge clips (arrowed) (Sec 23)

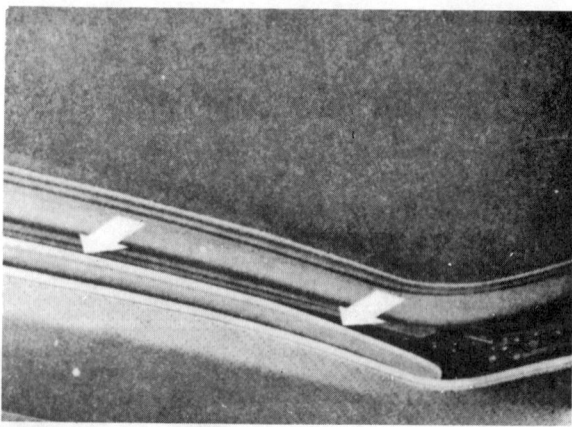

Fig. 11.31 Trim panel moved rearward to stop (Sec 23)

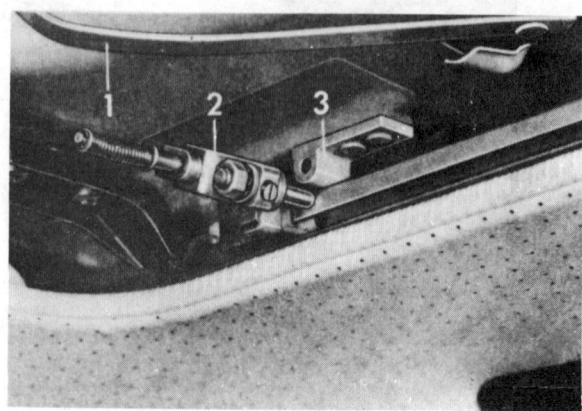

Fig. 11.32 Sunroof panel leaf spring (1) crank (2) and crank support (3) (Sec 23)

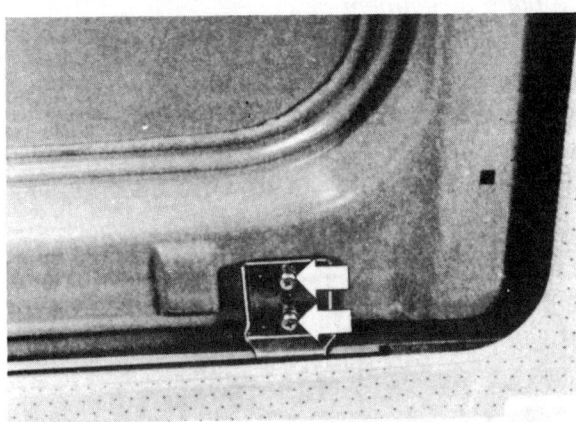

Fig. 11.33 Sunroof panel front guide retaining screws (arrowed) (Sec 23)

Fig. 11.34 Lift the sunroof panel up at the front then out through the guide rail openings at the rear (Sec 23)

24 Sunroof trim panel — removal and refitting

1 Remove the sunroof panel as described in Section 23.

2 Remove the drive handle, slacken the two handle plate retaining screws by approximately six turns then detach the cables from the drivegear.

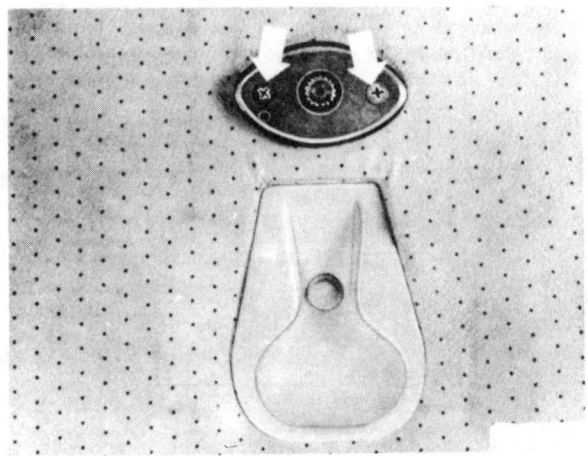

Fig. 11.35 Sunroof drive handle plate retaining screws (arrowed) (Sec 24)

3 Remove the guide block, move the guide plate forward and slide it out of the rail.

4 Move the cable guides forward and slide them out of the rail.

5 Remove all the rail securing screws on one side.

6 Push the rail to the rear and lift it together with the trim panel.

7 Push the rail to the outside slightly and remove the trim panel.

8 Refitting is the reverse sequence to removal.

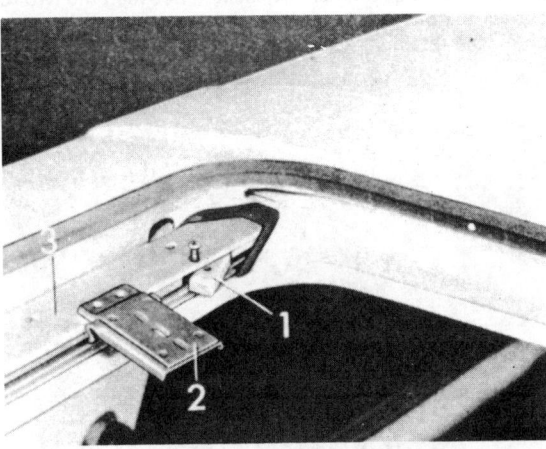

Fig. 11.36 Sunroof guide block (1) guide plate (2) and guide rail (3) (Sec 24)

Fig. 11.37 Sunroof guide rail (3) and cable guide (4) (Sec 24)

Fig. 11.38 Sunroof guide rail (3) and trim panel (5) (Sec 24)

25 Sunroof panel – adjustment

1   Refer to Section 23 and carry out the operations described in paragraphs 1 to 3.

Front height alignment

2   Slacken the two screws securing the panel to the front guide.
3   Turn the small adjusting screw, located between the two retaining screws, until the panel is in alignment.
4   Tighten the retaining screws.

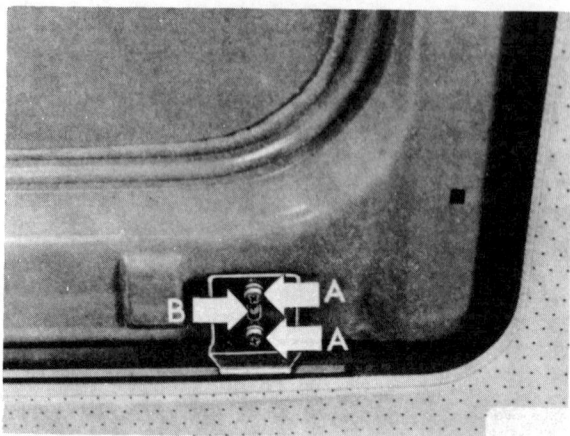

Fig. 11.39 Sunroof front guide retaining screws (A) and front height alignment adjusting screw (B) (Sec 25)

Rear height alignment

5   Lower the sunroof panel at the rear.
6   Swing the leaf spring to the centre then withdraw the crank from its support.
7   Slacken the retaining nut and the screw in the side of the crank.
8   Move the pin in the crank slot as necessary to achieve the correct alignment then tighten the screw and retaining nut.
9   Refit the crank to its support, close the sunroof and check the alignment.

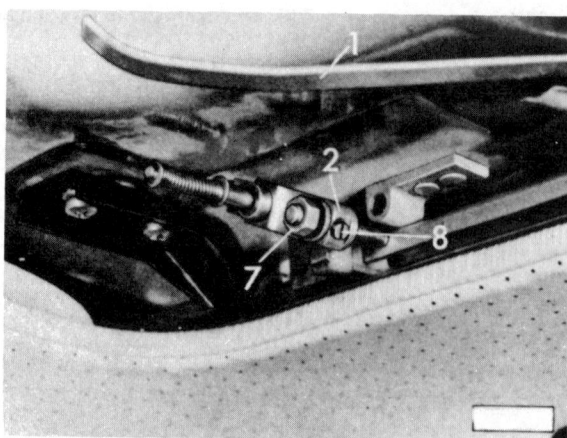

Fig. 11.40 Sunroof rear height alignment (Sec 25)

1	Leaf spring	7	Pin retaining nut
2	Crank assembly	8	Retaining screw

Guide plate adjustment

10   The guide plate should always be adjusted after adjustment of the rear height alignment and is carried out with the panel closed and the guide plates located above the slot in the rails (Fig. 11.41).
11   Lower the panel and slacken the two guide plate retaining screws.
12   Turn the adjusting screw in the guide plate until all the play between the guide plate and rail is eliminated then tighten the retaining screws.

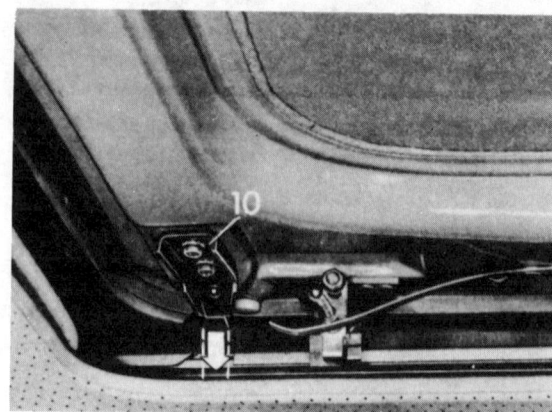

Fig. 11.41 Sunroof guide plate (10) located above guide rail slot prior to adjustment (Sec 25)

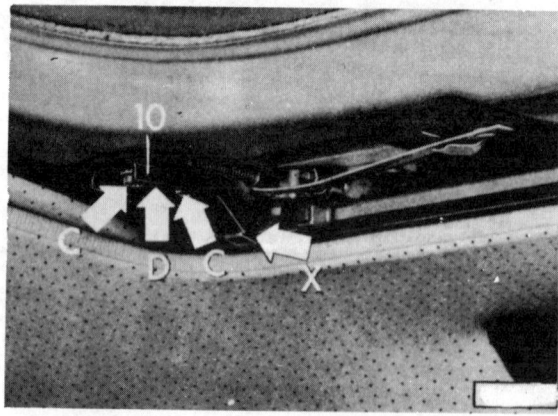

Fig. 11.42 Sunroof guide plate adjustment (Sec 25)

C	Guide plate retaining screws	X	Guide rail
D	Adjusting screw	10	Guide plate

Parallel adjustment

13   Turn the drive handle approximately two turns anti-clockwise to lower the panel at the rear.
14   Remove the drive handle and the cover plate.
15   Slacken the two handle plate retaining screws approximately six turns then detach the cables from the drivegear.
16   Move the sunroof panel back and forth several times in its guide rails by hand, then move it forward up to the stop.
17   Press the panel upward at the rear by hand then turn both the cranks to an upright position.
18   Temporarily refit the drive handle then turn the drive to the right, to its stop.
19   Lubricate the cables with multi-purpose grease and refit them to their locations.
20   Refit the cover plate and the drive handle with the handle positioned so that it rests in its recess when the panel is closed.

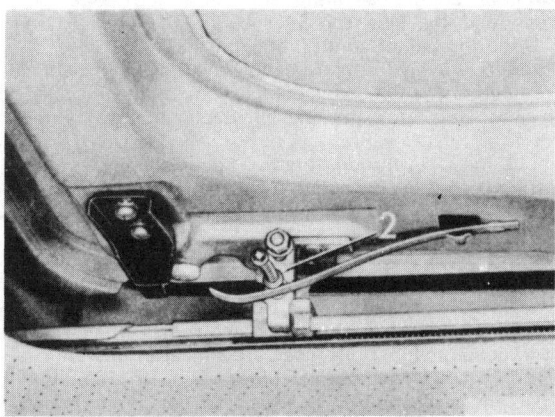

Fig. 11.43 Sunroof cranks (2) positioned vertically during panel parallel adjustment (Sec 25)

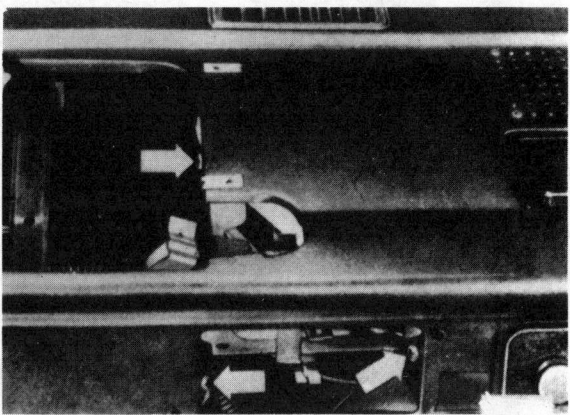

Fig. 11.44 Facia heater control and centre retaining screws (arrowed) (Sec 27)

26 Pop-up and hinged roofs – checking, maintenance and repair

1   The most important points to check on the opening type roof are the condition of the special weather seal strips and the security of the mounting bracket screws. If any sealing strip comes adrift it should be fixed before it is trapped and damaged. The main roof seal strip incorporates steel clips which may have lost some of their tension. Pull the strip clear, squeeze the clips together and then push the seal back on. See that all the pivot pins of the support brackets are lightly oiled and the slotted runners thinly greased.
2   The fabric parts should be wiped clean without the use of detergents and should never be folded and left damp. Whenever conditions require the roof to be closed whilst wet be sure to open it and dry it out at the first opportunity.
3   Removal and refitting should be left to a VW agent as a number of special tools and considerable expertise is necessary to avoid damage to the fabric parts.

27 Facia – removal and refitting

1   Remove the instrument panel as described in Chapter 10 and the steering column as described in Chapter 8.
2   Pull off the heater and ventilator operating levers then carefully prise off the heater control trim panel (photo).
3   Undo the four retaining screws and remove the glovebox.
4   From behind the facia detach the fresh air outlet hoses at the ventilators.

Fig. 11.45 Glovebox retaining screws (arrowed) (Sec 27)

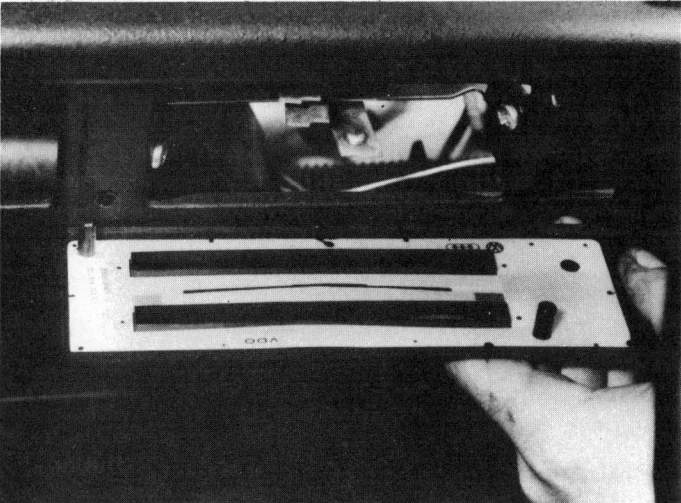

27.2 Removing the heater control trim panel

Fig. 11.46 Facia top edge retaining screw locations (Sec 27)

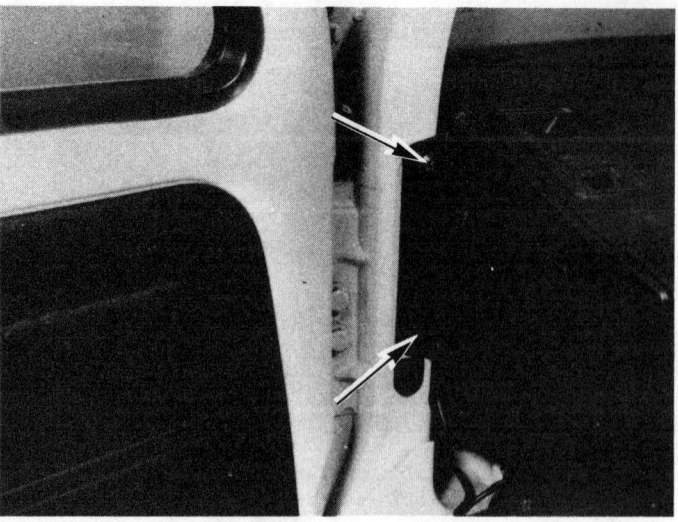

27.5 Facia to pillar retaining screws (arrowed)

5   Undo the screws securing the facia top edge below the windscreen and the side screws securing the facia to the pillars (photo). Undo the heater control retaining screws.
6   Pull the facia away from its location and when sufficient clearance exists, remove any additional optional equipment or accessories as applicable by referring to the relevant Sections and Chapters of this manual.
7   Remove the facia through the front door opening.
8   Refitting is the reverse sequence to removal.

28 Heating and ventilation – general

One of two types of heating and ventilation system may be fitted; the original system shown in Fig. 11.48 and the later modified system which incorporates a fresh air blower, shown in Fig. 11.49. Although different in construction, both types are similar in operation.
The original system consists of a warm air distributor for the driver's cab and a second unit for the passenger compartment, (where applicable), a fresh air ventilation chamber, a series of ducts and vents and the relevant control levers.
In the later system the warm air distributor and fresh air ventilation chamber are all contained in one unit which also incorporates the three speed blower.

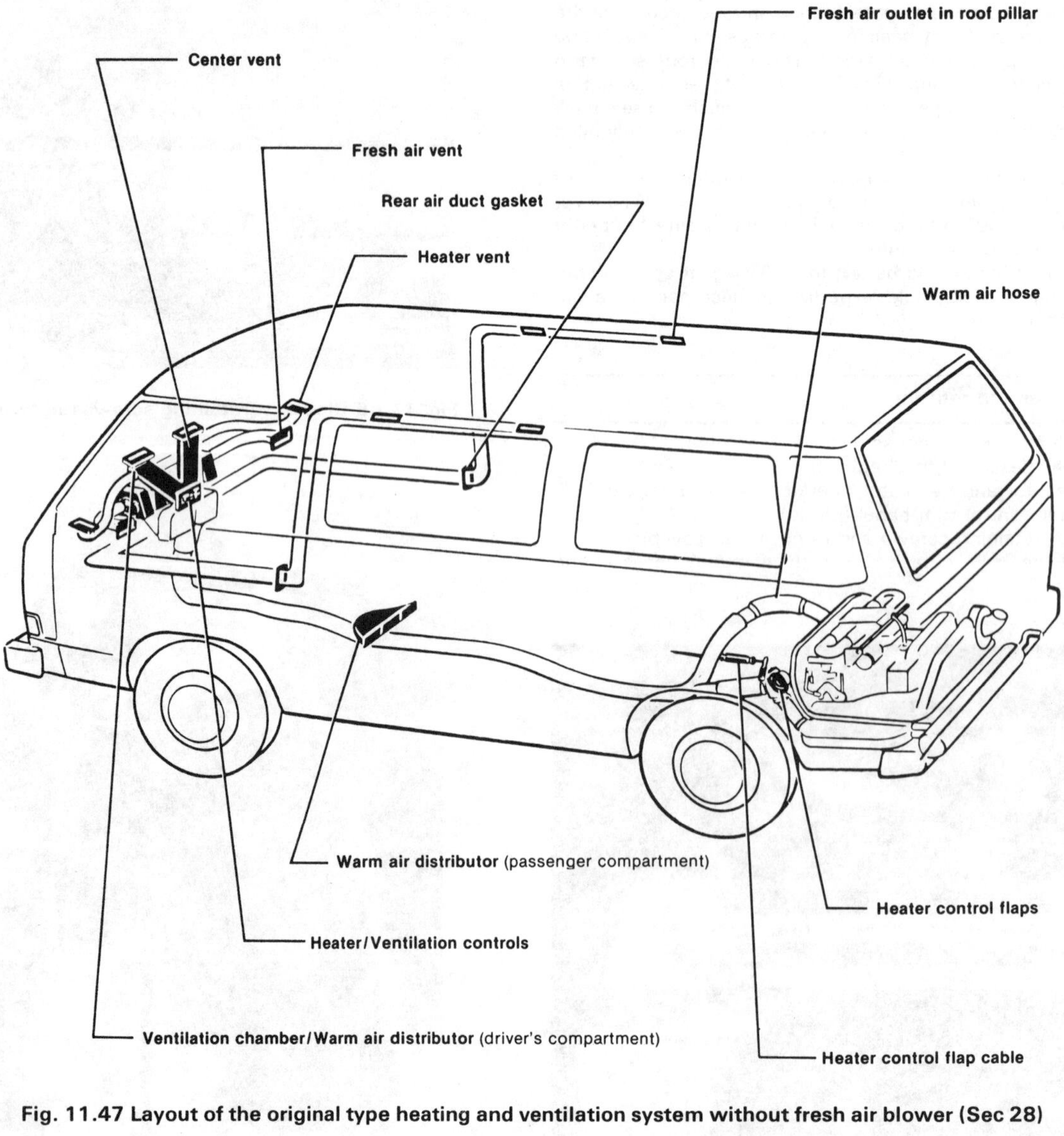

Fresh air outlet in roof pillar

Center vent

Fresh air vent

Rear air duct gasket

Heater vent

Warm air hose

Warm air distributor (passenger compartment)

Heater/Ventilation controls

Heater control flaps

Ventilation chamber/Warm air distributor (driver's compartment)

Heater control flap cable

Fig. 11.47 Layout of the original type heating and ventilation system without fresh air blower (Sec 28)

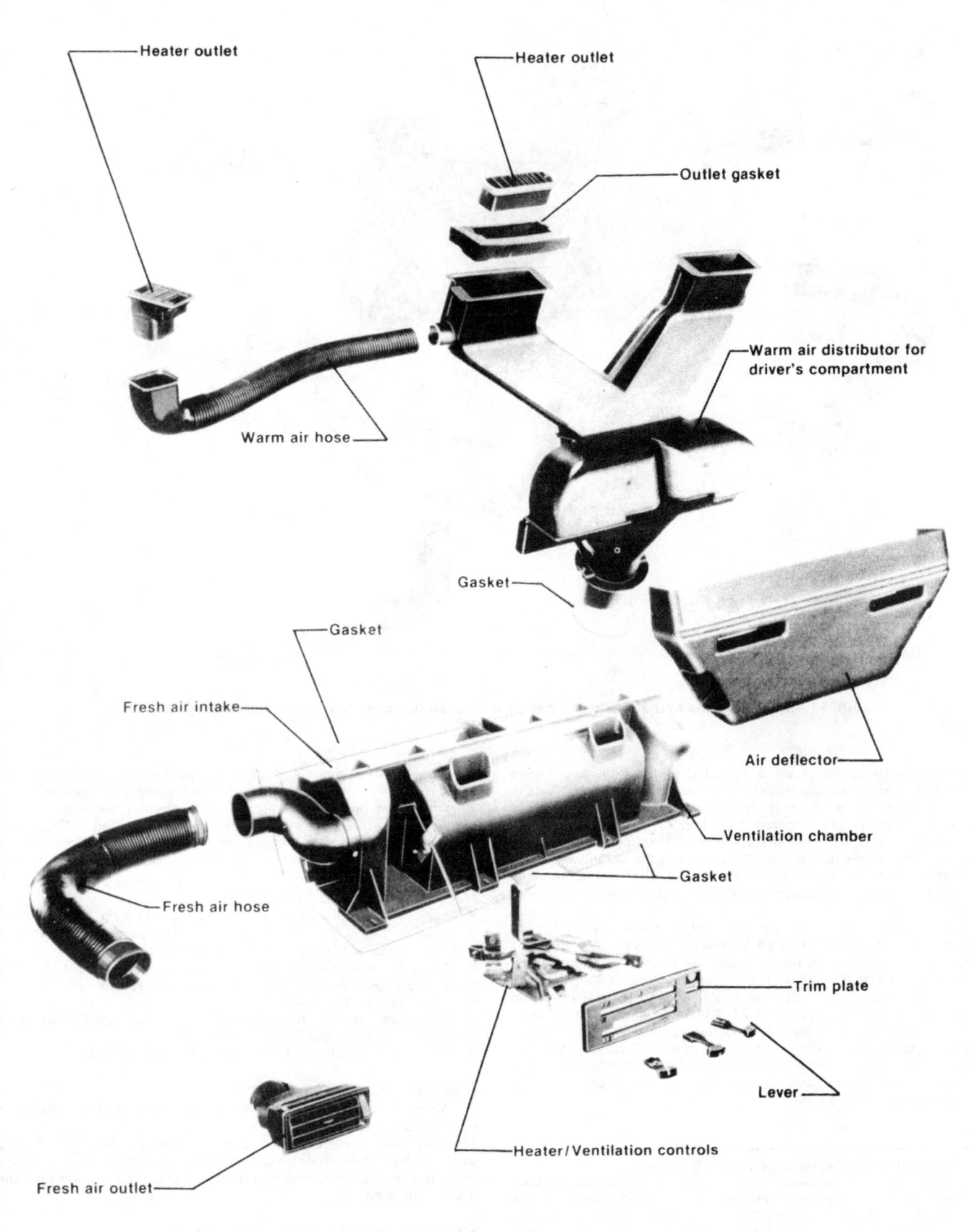

Heater outlet

Heater outlet

Outlet gasket

Warm air distributor for driver's compartment

Warm air hose

Gasket

Gasket

Fresh air intake

Air deflector

Ventilation chamber

Fresh air hose

Gasket

Trim plate

Lever

Heater/Ventilation controls

Fresh air outlet

Fig. 11.48 Heating and ventilation system components (Sec 28)

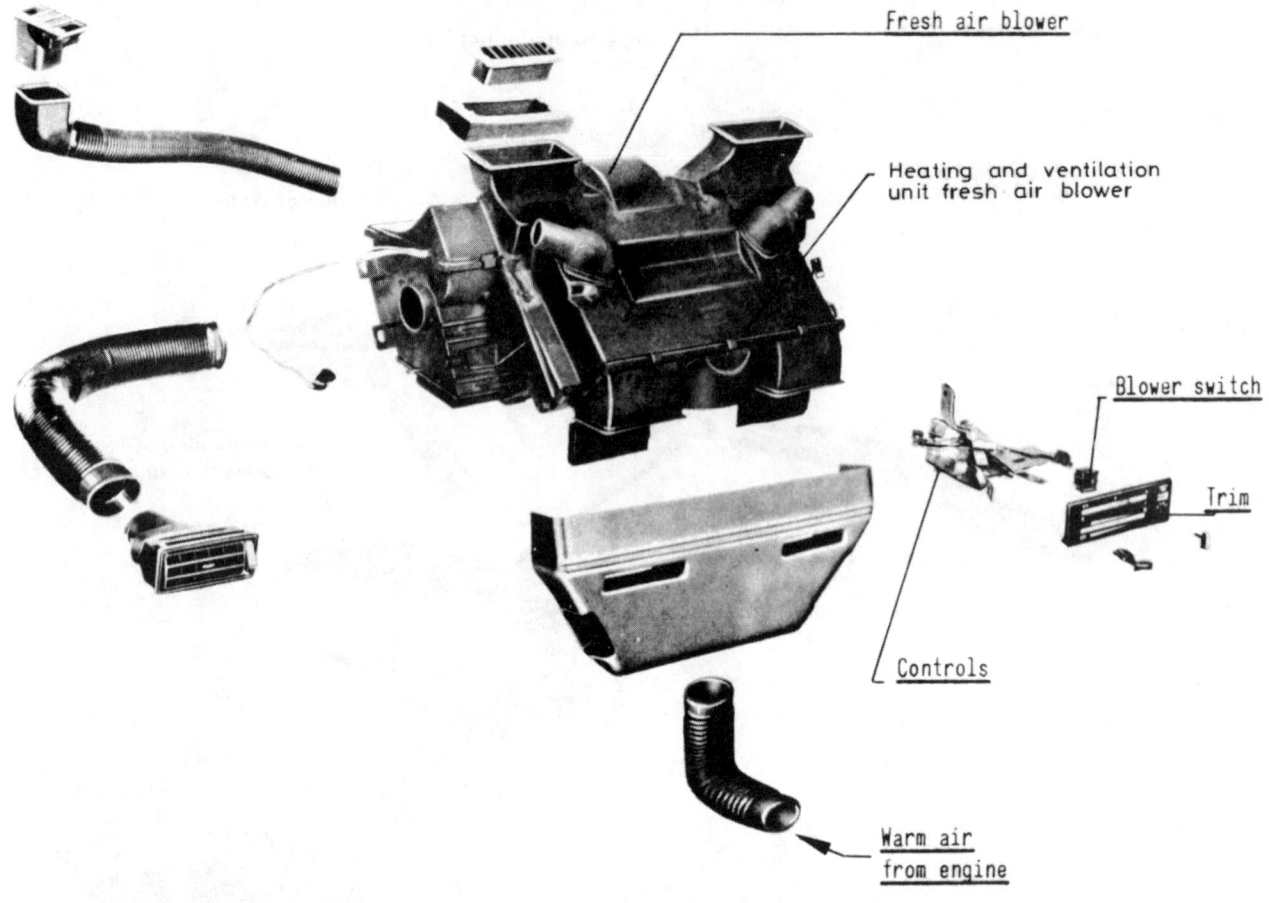

Fig. 11.49 Components of the later type heating and ventilation system with fresh air blower (Sec 28)

In both systems warm air is collected in the heat exchangers around the exhaust manifolds where it passes to the front of the vehicle through ducts. A series of flaps direct the warm air to whichever locations are selected according to the position of the heater controls and also shut the warm air off completely if desired. Fresh air may be directed around the vehicle in the same way.

Both systems are relatively simple and require no maintenance other than a periodic inspection of the ducts and control cables under the vehicle.

The control cables can be adjusted if necessary using the procedure described in Section 29. Removal of the various vent grilles is quite simple; they are carefully prised out of their locations whilst the locating lugs on the side of the unit are depressed. Access to the warm air distributor and fresh air ventilation chamber entails removal of the facia as described in Section 27. The units can then be removed after releasing the ducts and undoing the various retaining screws. Access to the passenger compartment warm air distributor entails the removal of the petrol tank as described in Chapter 2. Dismantling of the heater and ventilation unit used on later systems can be carried out with reference to Fig. 11.50.

---

29 Heater and ventilation controls – adjustment

1   The heater and ventilation control adjustment procedure varies according to the type of heater fitted. On vehicles where the heating and ventilation system incorporates a fresh air blower, adjustment consists of setting the cables as shown in the accompanying illustrations. Any small adjustments necessary to ensure full movement of the relevant flap at the heater unit can be made by slight repositioning of the cables within their clamps.

2   On vehicles without a fresh air blower the adjustment procedure is more involved and is described in the following paragraphs.
3   On both types to gain access to the heater controls it will be necessary to remove the instrument panel as described in Chapter 10, and the ashtray from its location on top of the facia. It may also be beneficial to remove the radio, if fitted, to provide additional clearance.

Heater air temperature control
4   Jack up the rear of the vehicle and support it on axle stands.
5   Slacken the clamp retaining bolts at the engine heater flaps so that the cables are free to move within their clamps.
6   Move the heater air temperature control lever as far as it will go to the left. Check that the cable ends are fitted securely over the lever pegs and held by the clamps.
7   Move the levers, at the engine heater flaps, rearward as far as they will go then tighten the clamp retaining bolts.
8   Lower the vehicle after completing the adjustment.

Fresh air distribution control
9   Move the air distribution lever on the heater control panel to the right as far as it will go.
10 Check that the lever on the ventilation chamber has moved fully as shown in Fig. 11.56. If not, slacken the clamp bolt at the control lever, move the ventilation chamber lever fully, against spring pressure, then tighten the clamp.

Heater warm air distribution control
11 Jack up the rear of the vehicle and support it on axle stands.
12 Check that both cables are securely connected to the warm air distribution control.
13 Have an assistant move the control through all its positions whilst

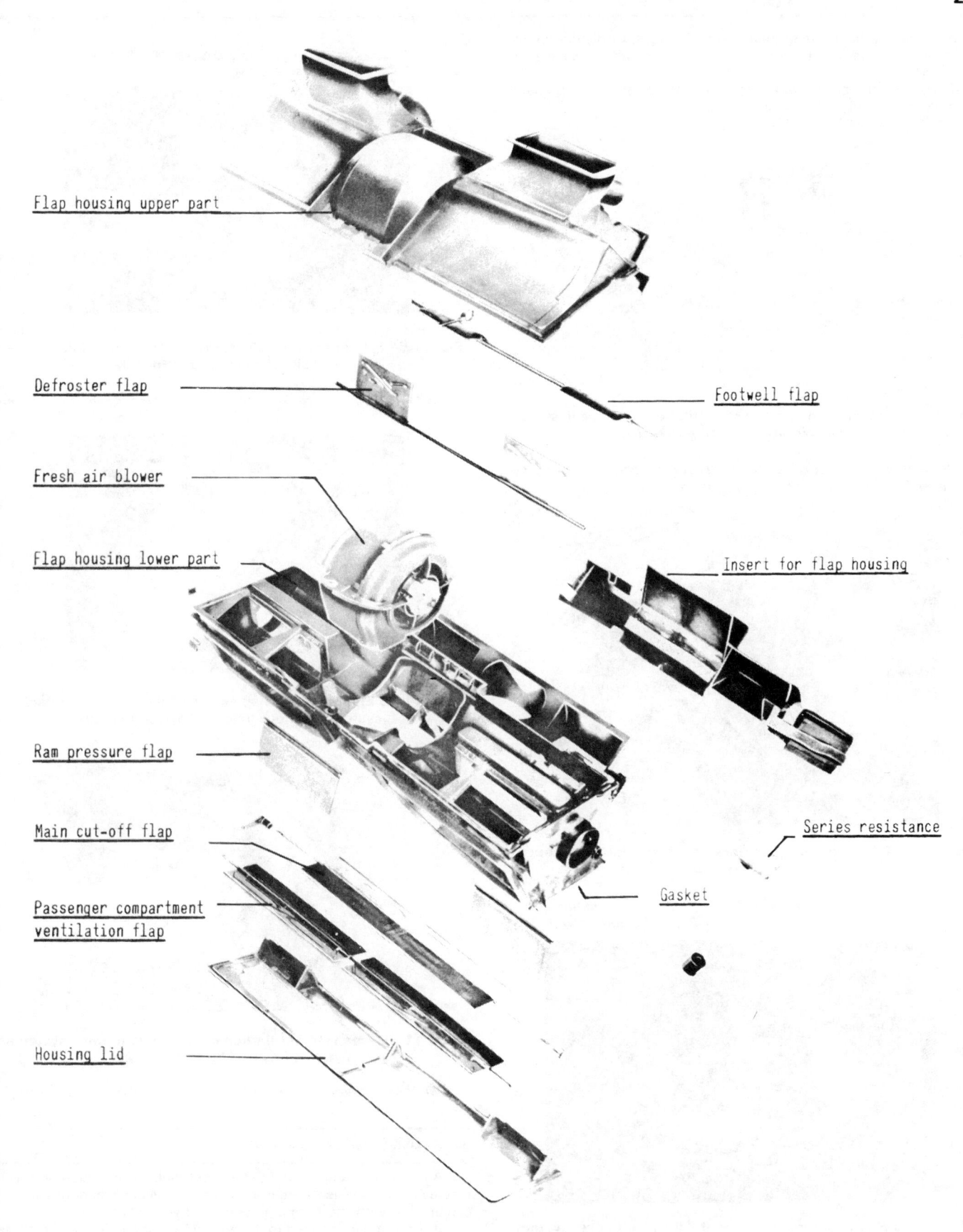

Flap housing upper part

Defroster flap

Footwell flap

Fresh air blower

Flap housing lower part

Insert for flap housing

Ram pressure flap

Main cut-off flap

Series resistance

Passenger compartment
ventilation flap

Gasket

Housing lid

Fig. 11.50 Exploded view of the heater and ventilation housing (Sec 28)

the operation of the levers at the driver's cab warm air distributor and passenger's compartment warm air distibutor (beneath the vehicle) are observed.

14 Reposition the cables within their clamps as necessary to ensure full travel of the respective levers.

15 After adjustment lower the vehicle to the ground.

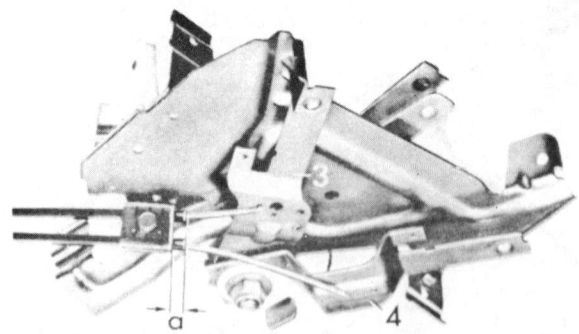

Fig. 11.51 Passenger compartment ventilation control adjustment – fresh air blower system (Sec 29)

a   3 mm (0.12 in) approximately   4   Lever for cable with two green
3   Lever for cable with yellow   marks
     mark

Fig. 11.52 Control cable positions – fresh air blower system (Sec 29)

1   Flap for passenger compartment   2   Main cut-off flap
     ventilation   3   Defroster/footwell flap

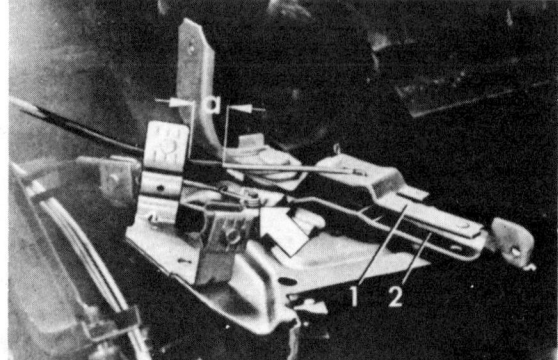

Fig. 11.53 Heater control adjustment – fresh air blower system (Sec 29)

a   38 mm (1.5 in) approximately   2   Upper lever accepts heater
1   Upper lever accepts red   flap cables (arrow)
     marked cable

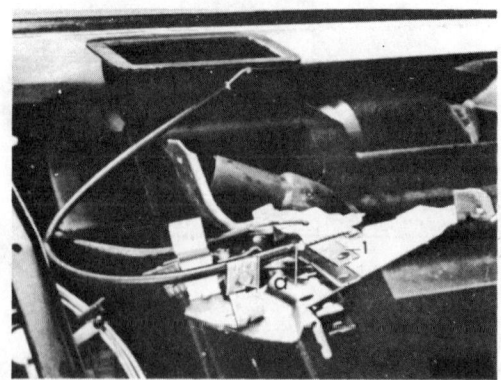

Fig. 11.54 Heater control defroster/footwell cable adjustment – fresh air blower system (Sec 29)

a   38 mm (1.5 in) approximately   1   Upper lever for red cable

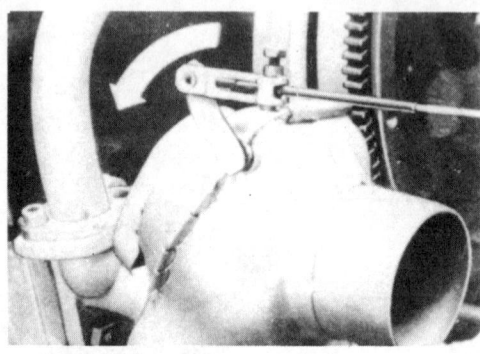

Fig. 11.55 Engine heater flap adjustment position (arrowed) – systems without fresh air blower (Sec 29)

Fig. 11.56 Fresh air distribution control adjustment – systems without fresh air blower (Sec 29)

Ventilation chamber lever must move fully in direction of arrow

30 Auxiliary heater – general

A petrol driven auxiliary heater is available as an option on certain models. The unit is located beneath the vehicle and operates in conjunction with the normal heating and ventilation system.

It is not recommended that any servicing or repair work be carried out on this unit or its related components. For the heater to function efficiently and safely any work of this nature should be left to a VW agent who will have the necessary special tools and experience to ensure correct operation of the unit. If a fault develops on the heater it should be taken to a VW agent immediately for diagnosis and repair.

Conversion factors

Length (distance)
Inches (in)	X	25.4	= Millimetres (mm)	X 0.0394	= Inches (in)
Feet (ft)	X	0.305	= Metres (m)	X 3.281	= Feet (ft)
Miles	X	1.609	= Kilometres (km)	X 0.621	= Miles

Volume (capacity)
Cubic inches (cu in; in³)	X	16.387	= Cubic centimetres (cc; cm³)	X 0.061	= Cubic inches (cu in; in³)
Imperial pints (Imp pt)	X	0.568	= Litres (l)	X 1.76	= Imperial pints (Imp pt)
Imperial quarts (Imp qt)	X	1.137	= Litres (l)	X 0.88	= Imperial quarts (Imp qt)
Imperial quarts (Imp qt)	X	1.201	= US quarts (US qt)	X 0.833	= Imperial quarts (Imp qt)
US quarts (US qt)	X	0.946	= Litres (l)	X 1.057	= US quarts (US qt)
Imperial gallons (Imp gal)	X	4.546	= Litres (l)	X 0.22	= Imperial gallons (Imp gal)
Imperial gallons (Imp gal)	X	1.201	= US gallons (US gal)	X 0.833	= Imperial gallons (Imp gal)
US gallons (US gal)	X	3.785	= Litres (l)	X 0.264	= US gallons (US gal)

Mass (weight)
Ounces (oz)	X	28.35	= Grams (g)	X 0.035	= Ounces (oz)
Pounds (lb)	X	0.454	= Kilograms (kg)	X 2.205	= Pounds (lb)

Force
Ounces-force (ozf; oz)	X	0.278	= Newtons (N)	X 3.6	= Ounces-force (ozf; oz)
Pounds-force (lbf; lb)	X	4.448	= Newtons (N)	X 0.225	= Pounds-force (lbf; lb)
Newtons (N)	X	0.1	= Kilograms-force (kgf; kg)	X 9.81	= Newtons (N)

Pressure
Pounds-force per square inch (psi; lbf/in²; lb/in²)	X	0.070	= Kilograms-force per square centimetre (kgf/cm²; kg/cm²)	X 14.223	= Pounds-force per square inch (psi; lbf/in²; lb/in²)
Pounds-force per square inch (psi; lbf/in²; lb/in²)	X	0.068	= Atmospheres (atm)	X 14.696	= Pounds-force per square inch (psi; lbf/in²; lb/in²)
Pounds-force per square inch (psi; lbf/in²; lb/in²)	X	0.069	= Bars	X 14.5	= Pounds-force per square inch (psi; lbf/in²; lb/in²)
Pounds-force per square inch (psi; lbf/in²; lb/in²)	X	6.895	= Kilopascals (kPa)	X 0.145	= Pounds-force per square inch (psi; lbf/in²; lb/in²)
Kilopascals (kPa)	X	0.01	= Kilograms-force per square centimetre (kgf/cm²; kg/cm²)	X 98.1	= Kilopascals (kPa)
Millibar (mbar)	X	100	= Pascals (Pa)	X 0.01	= Millibar (mbar)
Millibar (mbar)	X	0.0145	= Pounds-force per square inch (psi; lbf/in²; lb/in²)	X 68.947	= Millibar (mbar)
Millibar (mbar)	X	0.75	= Millimetres of mercury (mmHg)	X 1.333	= Millibar (mbar)
Millibar (mbar)	X	0.401	= Inches of water (inH₂O)	X 2.491	= Millibar (mbar)
Millimetres of mercury (mmHg)	X	0.535	= Inches of water (inH₂O)	X 1.868	= Millimetres of mercury (mmHg)
Inches of water (inH₂O)	X	0.036	= Pounds-force per square inch (psi; lbf/in²; lb/in²)	X 27.68	= Inches of water (inH₂O)

Torque (moment of force)
Pounds-force inches (lbf in; lb in)	X	1.152	= Kilograms-force centimetre (kgf cm; kg cm)	X 0.868	= Pounds-force inches (lbf in; lb in)
Pounds-force inches (lbf in; lb in)	X	0.113	= Newton metres (Nm)	X 8.85	= Pounds-force inches (lbf in; lb in)
Pounds-force inches (lbf in; lb in)	X	0.083	= Pounds-force feet (lbf ft; lb ft)	X 12	= Pounds-force inches (lbf in; lb in)
Pounds-force feet (lbf ft; lb ft)	X	0.138	= Kilograms-force metres (kgf m; kg m)	X 7.233	= Pounds-force feet (lbf ft; lb ft)
Pounds-force feet (lbf ft; lb ft)	X	1.356	= Newton metres (Nm)	X 0.738	= Pounds-force feet (lbf ft; lb ft)
Newton metres (Nm)	X	0.102	= Kilograms-force metres (kgf m; kg m)	X 9.804	= Newton metres (Nm)

Power
Horsepower (hp)	X	745.7	= Watts (W)	X 0.0013	= Horsepower (hp)

Velocity (speed)
Miles per hour (miles/hr; mph)	X	1.609	= Kilometres per hour (km/hr; kph)	X 0.621	= Miles per hour (miles/hr; mph)

Fuel consumption*
Miles per gallon, Imperial (mpg)	X	0.354	= Kilometres per litre (km/l)	X 2.825	= Miles per gallon, Imperial (mpg)
Miles per gallon, US (mpg)	X	0.425	= Kilometres per litre (km/l)	X 2.352	= Miles per gallon, US (mpg)

Temperature

Degrees Fahrenheit = $(°C \times 1.8) + 32$ Degrees Celsius (Degrees Centigrade; °C) = $(°F - 32) \times 0.56$

*It is common practice to convert from miles per gallon (mpg) to litres/100 kilometres (l/100km), where mpg (Imperial) x l/100 km = 282 and mpg (US) x l/100 km = 235

Index

Printed by
J H Haynes & Co Ltd
Sparkford Nr Yeovil
Somerset BA22 7JJ England